Feng Youlan: Selected Philosophical Writings

Feng Youlan: Selected Philosophical Writings

China Books
San Francisco

Published in the United States of America by
Sinomedia International Group
China Books
360 Swift Avenue, Suite 48
South San Francisco, CA 94080

www.chinabooks.com

A China Books Classic
ISBN 978-0-8351-0069-4

Cover design: Tiffany Cha
Text design: Rob Peters

CONTENTS

Publisher's Introduction

Feng Youlan (冯友兰, also rendered as Fung Yu-lan) was born on December 4, 1895 in Qiyi Town, Tanghe County, Henan Province. He graduated from the Department of Philosophy of Beijing University in 1918 and from the Graduate School of Columbia University in the United States, where he obtained his Ph.D. in 1923. After returning to China, he served successively as a professor at Zhongzhou University, Guangdong Sun Yat-Sen University, Yanjing University, Tsinghua University and Southwest United University. He was head of the Department of Philosophy, dean of the College of Arts and acting president of the School Synod of Tsinghua University, and president of the College of Arts of Southwest United University. He taught at Beijing University beginning in 1952.

Feng was a leading philosopher, historian of philosophy, and educator of modern China. His original works on philosophy include *A New Treatise on Neo-Confucianism, On New Affairs, Explanation of the New World, A New Treatise on the Nature of Man, The Spirit of Chinese Philosophy* and *A New Treatise on the Methodology of Metaphysics*, establishing the system of Neo-Confucianism, and making great contributions to the modernization of Chinese philosophy. As a historian of philosophy, he compiled *A History of Chinese Philosophy* (two volumes), *A Short History of Chinese Philosophy* (in English) and *A New Edition of A History of Chinese Philosophy* (seven volumes), laying the foundation for the history of Chinese philosophy. As an educator he chaired the College of Arts of Tsinghua University for 18 years, contributing to the setting up of the unique "Tsinghua School" and training a large number of qualified scholars in literature, history and philosophy. Feng authored over 30 books and more than 500 articles, with a total of 6.7 million words. These were compiled into the 14-volume *The Complete Works of the Hall of Three Pines*. His publications also include the *Selected Philosophical Writings of Fung Yu-Lan, A Taoist Classic-Chuang-Tzu*, and the collection *On the Methodology of Metaphysics: Selected Essays on East-West Philosophical Traditions*.

Feng Youlan died on November 26, 1990. His books remain in print and are available in many languages around the world.

Author's Preface to the English Edition (1987)

It is a great luxury for a scholar in his late years to be able to compare his writings in the form of a complete work and see them published. This situation depends on a combination of various factors, many of which are beyond human control. In this sense I consider myself fortunate. The People's Publishing House of Henan, my native province, is compiling my writings in a collection called *The Complete Works of the Hall of Three Pines*. The whole series being published in Henan is written in Chinese. This includes Chinese translations of work originally written in English. Concurrently, the Foreign Languages Press in Beijing is compiling an English edition, which will be a valuable complement to the work of the People's Publishing House of Henan.

The article entitled "Why China Has No Science" marked the beginning of my academic career. It was a paper read in 1922 before a biweekly conference of the Philosophy Department of Columbia University. The last article is a speech presented in 1982 at a convocation in which I was presented an honorary degree by Columbia University. This speech is a brief review of my academic career. Sixty years have passed since the beginning of that career.

The writings are many, but there is a central theme like a tapestry running through the collection. This is the strong belief that China is an ancient nation with a new mission. The new mission is modernization.

The Chinese Communist Party is leading the Chinese people in building socialism in a Chinese style: that is the meaning of the new mission as I understand it. According to my understanding, the Chinese style is not like the color pasted on a product from the outside. It is determined by the physiological factors within. The ancient Chinese culture is an inherent factor determining the Chinese style. When the modernization of China is completed, China will be both ancient and modern, both old and new. This is the fulfillment of my belief that China is an ancient nation with a new mission. This is the whole ideal that I have struggled for. The writings in this volume are part of this struggle.

冯友兰

BOOK ONE:

A COMPARATIVE STUDY OF LIFE IDEALS

INTRODUCTION

(I) Philosophy and Life

In *The Spirit of Modern Philosophy,* Josiah Royce said:

> Philosophy, in the proper sense of the term, is not a presumptuous effort to explain the mysteries of the world by means of any superhuman insight or extraordinary cunning, but has its origin and value in an attempt to give a reasonable account of our own personal attitude towards the more serious business of life. You philosophize when you reflect critically upon what you are actually doing in your world. What you are doing is of course, in the first place, living.... Such a criticism of life, made elaborate and thoroughgoing, is philosophy.[1]

No doubt this gives a fair account of the origin of philosophy, but perhaps it may not be a fair account of philosophy itself. It is true that man philosophizes only when he begins to criticize life, for otherwise he will simply make what Chuang Tzu called the "Happy Excursion" in the universe like "the fishes that forget each other in the great river and great lake," with consciousness neither of the environment nor of himself. It is only when life is not quite satisfactory that he begins to be self-conscious and to ask why; to ask why is to criticize existing conditions and thus to philosophize. He does all these because he must, not because he will.

But although this is true, there is still a question: Is philosophy criticism itself? It seems better to say that philosophy is not criticism as such, but the standard of criticism. It is obvious that the criticism of a thing presupposes a standard, ideal or actual, which the thing criticized is either different from or opposed to, otherwise the criticism would be meaningless. Lao Tzu said: "When all the world knows the beautiful is beautiful, it is already ugly; when all the world knows the good is good, it is already bad."[2] But it may be equally said that when all the world knows the ugly is ugly, it is already beautiful; when all the world knows the bad is bad, it is already good; for, as Plotinus said: "It is impossible to say, 'that is not the good,' without having some sort of knowledge of the good or acquaintance therewith."[3] So in order to criticize the ugly, we need the beautiful, ideal or real, as the standard; to criticize the bad, we need the good, ideal or real. In the same way, to criticize actual beauty we need as a standard an ideal absolute beauty; and to criticize the good, we need an ideal absolute good. Now to criticize actual life, do we not need an ideal life as a standard? Philosophy is the concrete picture of the ideal life and a philosopher is one who draws this picture. Here is the difference between literature and philosophy. Literature criticizes life by taking some standard of criticism for granted. So the contribution of literature towards life is often more negative than positive; its

---

1 Josiah Royce, *The Spirit of Modern Philosophy,* New York, 1910, pp. 1, 2.

2 Lao Tzu, *Tao Teh Ching.* Sec. 2.

3 Plotinus, *Complete Works,* tr. by K. S. Guthrie, 1918, Vol. III, p. 748.

purpose is rather to point out the wrong and the false than to tell the right and the real. But the business of philosophy is precisely to build a system of the right and the real. Plato said:

> In heaven, I replied, there is laid the pattern of such a city, and he who desires may behold this, and in beholding, govern himself accordingly. But whether there really is or ever will be such an one is of no importance to him; for he will act according to the laws of the city and of no other.[4]

Philosophy is to give the pattern not only of a city, but of life. If philosophy needs any definition, it may be defined as the ideal.

(2) The Idealization of Nature and the Idealization of Art

But the ideal is not, and cannot be, created or discovered, independent of the actual, by the philosopher in his inspired moment. As shown by Royce, philosophy is not to explain any mystery, and a philosopher is not one who has any superhuman insight and extraordinary cunning. The philosopher may build a city in Heaven, but the stones and the bricks he must draw from earth. His ideal pattern after all must be constructed with the material of actual experience. As William James said:

> We can invent no new forms of conception, applicable to the whole exclusively, and not suggested originally by facts. All philosophers, accordingly, have conceived of the whole world after the analogy of some particular feature of it, which has particularly captivated their attention.[5]

If philosophy is defined as the ideal, to philosophize may be said to idealize, that is, to idealize some feature of the world as we actually experience it, so that it may become the ideal pattern for life as a whole.

What are the more conspicuous features of the world that we actually experience? There are two features or contrasting states of experience, the distinctiveness of which is universally the most obvious. Aristotle said:

> The things we see can be divided into two classes: those which are the product of nature, and those which come from causes other than nature. Thus, it is nature that produces the animals and the varied parts of which their bodies are composed; it is also nature that produced the plants, and the simple elements such as earth, fire, and water; for we speak of these things and others like them as existing solely by the fact of nature. For all the things which we indicate present a great difference in relation to those which are not the product of nature. All the natural beings carry with themselves the principle of movement and rest. Some may be endowed with the movement of locomotion in space, others may have the internal movement of growth and decay, and finally some may have the simple movement of alteration and modification in the qualities they possess. About these motions it is not the same with those things which we call the product of art.[6]

---

4 Plato, "The Republic," 592, tr. by B. Jowett.

5 William James, *The Pluralistic Universe*, New York, 1912, p. 8.

6 Aristotle, Physics,II,I I, in from J. Barthelemy Saint-Hitaire's French translation, Paris, 1862, Vol. 1, pp. 39, 40

Huxley said:

> It may be safely assumed that, two thousand years ago, before Caesar set foot in southern Britain, the whole countryside visible from the window of the room in which I write, was in what is called "the state of nature." Except, it may be, by raising a few sepulchral mounds, such as those which still here and there, break the flowing contours of the downs, man's hands had made no mark upon it; and the thin veil of vegetation which overspread the broad-backed heights and the shelving sides of the coombs was unaffected by his industry. It is as little to be doubted, that an essentially similar state of nature prevailed, in this region, for many thousands of years before the coming of Caesar; and there is no assignable reason for denying that it might continue to exist through an equally prolonged futurity, except for the intervention of man.[7]

Three or four years have elapsed since the state of nature to which I have referred was brought to an end, so far as a small patch of the soils concerned, by the intervention of man.... In short, it was made into a garden. At the present time, this artificially treated area presents an aspect extraordinarily different from that of the land as remains in the state of nature, outside of the wall.... That the "state of art," thus created in the state of nature by man, is sustained by him, would at once become apparent, if the watchful supervision of the gardener were withdrawn, and the antagonistic influences of the general cosmic process were no longer sedulously warded off, or counteracted... It will be admitted that the garden is as much a work of art, or artifice, as anything that can be mentioned. The energy localized in certain human bodies, directed by similarly localized intellects, has produced a collocation of other material bodies which could not be brought about in the state of nature. The same proposition is true of all the works of man's hands, from a flint implement to a cathedral or a chronometer; and it is because it is true, that we call these things artificial, term them works of art, or artifice, by way of distinguishing them from the products of the cosmic process working outside man, which we call natural, or works of nature. The distinction thus drawn between the works of nature and those of man, is universally recognized; and it is, as I conceive, both useful and justified.[8]

It is easy to see that what Aristotle and Huxley called nature and art are exactly what the Chinese philosophers called the natural and the human. As Chuang Tzu said: "What is nature? What is human? That the ox and the horse have four feet is nature; to halter the head of a horse or to pierce the nose of an ox is human."[9] Thus, the ancient Oriental thinker made the same distinction between nature and art that Aristotle and Huxley did. This helps to show that it "is universally recognized." As one of the characteristics of man is to make

7 Huxley, Evolution and Ethics, and Other Essays, London and New York, 1914, pp.1, 2.

8 Huxley, Evolution and Ethics, and Other Essays, pp. 9-11.

9 *Works*, tr. by H. A. Giles, London, 1889, p. 211.

These three quotations have been given simply to show the clear contrast between the state of nature and the state of art. They have nothing to do with the evaluations of the three authors concerning the two states. Chuang Tzu's philosophy is an idealization of nature; Huxley's philosophy is an idealization of art. Aristotle's philosophy is a reconciliation of nature and art.

tools,[10] so as soon as he was introduced to this world, he began to make them. It is no wonder that the two states of the world are universally experienced, and their distinction "is universally recognized." Who has not seen the difference between the state inside the garden and that outside it? Who does not know the fact that the horse and the ox are "born free, but are everywhere in chains"? If the common people are not consciously aware of the two contrasting states in the world, it is only because they are too familiar with them.

Since philosophy is the idealization of certain features of the world as we experience them, and since the most conspicuous features of the world are the state of nature and the state of art, it is only reasonable to expect that the history of philosophy will prove that some philosophers have idealized nature and others have idealized art. The history of philosophy shows that no philosopher is so blind as to be completely unable to see the bare fact that man's present condition is a mixture of good and evil, of happiness and suffering.[11] In fact, as shown in the above quotations, men begin to philosophize only when they feel that the world is not so good as they wish. So philosophers do not differ in seeing the facts, but only in the way of criticizing them. Some attribute the present goodness of man to his original nature, and consider the present evil as due to his artificial change. According to them man is originally happy, but he suffers through his own "original sin," his own mistake. The best way to avoid evil is not to go away from nature, but to return to it. Others attribute the present badness of man to his original nature, but consider the present good as due completely to his power of control. According to them, man suffered much more in the past; and it is only through his own efforts that he has succeeded in making the bad world better. If it is still not the best and there are still evils, it is only because the artificiality is not yet complete, and either his nature has not yet been wholly adapted to the alien world, or the alien world has not yet been wholly adapted to him. How can their ways of criticizing life be so different, if it is not because their standards of criticism are different? What is the difference between their standards of criticism, if not that the one is the idealization of nature, while the other is the idealization of art?

If this is so, it is no wonder that in the history of philosophy, philosophers were often unable to understand each other. It is no wonder that Hsun Tzu accused Chuang Tzu of being one who is "blinded by nature and does not know art," while he himself was exactly blinded by art and did not know nature. It is no wonder that, as Pascal said somewhere, "one half of the philosophers ignore the greatness of man; and the other half ignore his baseness." In the history of philosophy there has been an issue as to whether human nature is good or bad; that is, whether the virtues are innate and absolute, or simply for convenience or utility. There has been an issue as to whether the universe is good or bad, that is, whether the cosmic principle is something akin to our high ideal, or nothing but a blind force. It seems that all these are but the

10 Bergson, Creative Evolution. tr. by A. Mitchell, New York, 1911, p. 137.

11 Even those who said that evils are "appearances" must see the "appearances." That there are evils is a fact; that they are "appearances" is the philosopher's interpretation of the fact.

ancient philosophical issues discussed between Plato and the Sophists as to whether the justification of virtue is nature or convention, and whether there are absolute truth, absolute beauty, and absolute good, or whether "man is the measure of all things." Why did philosophers contend so earnestly about these issues, if not because some of them idealize nature too much, while others idealize art too much?

(3) The Way of Decrease (or Retreat) and the Way of Increase (or Advance)

If there are two such diametrically opposing patterns of life, it is obvious that there must be two ways of life no less opposing for him who "may behold this, and in beholding, govern himself accordingly." According to one pattern described above, art is certainly superfluous and what Huxley called "the horticultural process" is a mistake. We are astray in establishing what is called our civilization and feeling proud of it without knowing that it is precisely this very civilization that is the cause of our present suffering. We suffer because our paradise is lost through our own mistakes. If this view is true, it is a matter of course that the right way of life is to undo the present artificial civilization and perhaps even life itself as Plotinus, quoting from Homer, advised: "Let us fly unto our dear fatherland."[12]

But according to the other pattern, although the present is far from the ideal, anyway it is much better than the past. At present we may not be able to live well, but still we are able to live. If we still suffer, it is only because, as was said above, we are not very progressive and our civilization is not yet perfect. Surely we have not yet reached our goal, but we are already on the right track. Go ahead, our happiness is in the promising future, but not in the dead past. If this view is true, it is also a matter of course that the right way of life is not negatively to undo something, but positively to do all things. We must work and struggle so that the future paradise may be built by our own hands, and the "City of God" may be turned into the "Kingdom of Man."

Lao Tzu said: "He who devotes himself to knowledge seeks from day to day to increase. He who devotes himself to *Tao* seeks from day to day to diminish."[13] Chuang Tzu said:

> There is the way of nature, and the way of art (or the way of human). Inaction and dignity are the way of nature; action and entanglement are the way of art. The way of nature may be compared to that of sovereign; the way of art to that of minister. The distance which separates them is great. We must investigate the matter earnestly.[14] Truly, between the two ways of life described above, the one is to decrease, the other to increase; the one is the way of nature, the other, the way of art. Yes, "the distance which separates them is great; we must investigate the matter earnestly."

---

12 Plotinus, *Works*, Vol. I, p. 52.

13 Lao Tzu, *Tao Tek Ching*, Sec. 48.

14 Cp. H. A. Giles' translation, p. 134

(4) The Third View

Needless to say, both these lines of thought are too one-sided and too extreme. It is natural to expect that there should be philosophers who either originally held the position of the mean state, or who, seeing the reasonableness and the extremeness of both views, and the desirability of both ways of life, try to modify them. The history of philosophy shows that there are many. Who they are and what their teachings are we need not say here. We shall examine in detail all these three lines of thought in the following chapters of our work.

Part I

THE IDEALIZATION OF NATURE AND THE WAY OF DECREASE

Let us first consider what we may call the "nature" line of thought. The common presupposition of this line of thought is that the present world, or the present state of the world, is the consequence of some original mistake, something that fundamentally ought not to be. The Christian myth that the first two ancestors of mankind were most happy in the heavenly garden which was lost afterwards through their own "sin" of eating the forbidden fruit of wisdom, is after all a statement true to this line of philosophy, if it is taken symbolically, not literally and historically. It is because of this fact that some of these philosophies are often considered as "religious." In fact, religion is itself a kind of "nature" philosophy plus dogma, convention, superstition, and myth. In the influence of every religion that has caused mankind to prefer Heaven to earth, this kind of philosophy has certainly played the most important role.

But although all of the philosophies belonging to this line of thought agree that we had a paradise but lost it, and although they agree that now we should retreat so that we may return to it, yet they are far from agreeing as to what that paradise is, and how far we should retreat. Some thought that this world was right, but that the present state of this world was wrong, so that we should retreat from civilization to primitivity; from the state of art to that of nature. Some thought that we should retreat from the nature in space and time to the realm of the supreme and the ideal. Some thought further that we should retreat from all that is thinkable to that which is unthinkable and seems, therefore, to be "nothing" to our human intellect and human will. Thus the "decrease" is complete and life is thoroughly negated. These are the three main types of what we call the "nature" line of thought. The first type we call romanticism, the second idealism, and the third, nihilism.

I ROMANTICISMS: CHUANG TZU

If our thesis that the "nature" line of thought has its origin in the idealization of the state of nature is well founded, it is natural to expect that there should be philosophies that naively consider the state of nature as such to be really good. The history of philosophy justifies this expectation. In the history of philosophy there are what is known as the romantic philosophies that consider original human nature as absolutely good, and the state of nature as the norm; philosophies that favor anarchistic individualism, and revolt against conventions and institutions; philosophies, in short, that exaggerate the self-sufficiency of the state of nature, the dexterity of savages, and the skill of animal instincts, and deny the profits produced by civilization and the expertness acquired by education and practice. To represent this type we have chosen the Chinese philosopher, Chuang Tzu, whom we consider the most consistent and the most thoroughgoing expounder of this type of thinking.

(1) His Conception of "Tao"

In order to understand Chuang Tzu's philosophy, we need first to see what he meant by the word "Tao." He said:

> Tao has its reality and evidence, but no action and form. It is transmitted in all things, but nothing can be said to have and own it. It is obtained by all things, but nothing can be said to have seen it. It exists by and through itself. It exists before Heaven and earth, and indeed for all eternity. It causes the gods to be divine and the world to be produced. It is above the zenith, but is not high. It is beneath the nadir, but is not low. It is prior to Heaven and earth, but is not ancient.
>
> It is older than the most ancient, but is not old.[15]

It sounds very much like a description of the Christian God as some of the scholastic philosophers saw Him. But one would go far astray in trying to understand this passage, if one considered *Tao* as something like the God of Christianity, who created the world with conscious design and conscious will. This is a human interpretation of the universe and an explanation of nature with the analogy of art. In fact, *Tao* did not and could not create things. As one of Chuang Tzu's best commentators, Kuo Hsian, said:

How can *Tao* cause the gods to be divine and the world to be produced? *Tao* did not cause the gods to be divine, but they are divine themselves; this means that *Tao* causes them to be divine by not causing them. *Tao* did not produce the world, but the world produced itself; this means that *Tao* produced it by not producing it.

So when we say *Tao* produces all things, we mean nothing more than the plain fact that all things produce themselves, naturally and spontaneously. *Tao* is the totality of the spontaneity of all things in the universe. "Tao" means the English

15 Cf. H. A. Giles' translation, p. 77.

word "Nature" in the sense of spontaneity, of freedom from artificiality. Since all things in nature produce themselves spontaneously and instinctively, so ought they to go on spontaneously and instinctively. This is the basis of Chuang Tzu's theory of returning to nature and of "letting alone." In fact, his conception of *Tao* is not very different from Spinoza's conception of God, nor does his conception of the genesis of the world differ greatly from Spinoza's. The difference between these two philosophers is that what Spinoza considered as necessity and mechanism, Chuang Tzu considered as spontaneity and freedom. It may be due to this difference that Chuang Tzu saw only the good aspect of human nature somewhat like Rousseau, while Spinoza saw its bad aspect somewhat like Hobbes.

(2) His Conception of Happiness

Passing from Chuang Tzu's conception of *Tao*, let us now consider his conception of happiness. The totality of the spontaneity of all things in the universe is called "Tao," or "Nature"; the totality of the spontaneity of each thing is called "The (or De)" or "Virtue." According to Chuang Tzu, each and everything is most happy, if only it lives according to its natural virtue, that is, its native disposition, or instincts. This is the only royal way to what he called the "Happy Excursion." In the chapter that bears this title, he said:

> In the Record of Marvels we read that when the great bird Rukh flies southwards, the water is smitten for a space of three thousand li around, while the bird itself mounts a typhon to a height of ninety thousand li for a flight of six months' duration.... A cicada laughed and said to a dove: "Now when I fly with my might, it is as much as I can do to get from tree to tree. And sometimes I do not reach, but fall to the ground midway. What, then, can be the use of going up ninety thousand Ii in order to start for the south?"[16]

It shows clearly that both the great Rukh and the small cicada are perfectly satisfied, each with its own excursion. As the above- mentioned commentator said:

> Everything is self-sufficient in its instinct. The great Rukh has nothing to be proud of in comparison with the small cicada; nor has the small cicada anything to be desired in the Celestial Lake [the place where the Rukh flies to]. Both of them are satisfied. Therefore, although their size is different, their happiness is the same.

If this theory is true of all things, mankind is no exception. In the state of their primitivity, humanity lived according to nothing but its own instinct and thereby enjoyed the most. Chuang Tzu said:

> The people have certain natural instincts -- to weave, and clothe themselves; to till, and feed themselves. These are common to all humanity, and all are agreed thereon. Such instincts are called "Heaven-sent." So in the days when natural instincts prevailed, men moved quietly and gazed steadily. At that time, there were no roads over mountains, nor boats, nor bridges over water. All things were produced, each for its own proper sphere. Birds and beasts

16 *Id.*, pp. 1, 2..

multiplied; trees and shrubs grew up. The latter might be led by hand; men could climb up and peep into the raven's nest, for then men dwelt with birds, and beasts, and all creation was one. There were no distinctions between good and bad men. Being all equally without knowledge, their virtue could not go astray. Being all equally without evil desires, they were in a state of natural integrity, the perfection of human existence.[17]

But when the sages came to worry them [the people] with ceremonies and music in order to rectify their bodies, and hung up, as it were, benevolence and justice for all to gaze at, in order to satisfy their mind, then the people began to develop a taste for knowledge and to struggle one with the other in their desire for gain. This was the error of the sages.[18]

This is Chuang Tzu's story of the "fall" of mankind. Mankind lost its paradise through eating the fruit of wisdom, which was presented to it, not through the deception of the serpent, but through the "error of the sages." With their power of intellect and their ingenuity of discovery and invention, the sages were chiefly responsible for bringing art into the state of nature. But what is the purpose of art? It is either to imitate nature or to modify it. If it is to imitate nature, it is simply useless. We here quote a passage from the Lieh-tzu:[19]

> There was once a man in Sung who carved a mulberry leaf out of jade for his prince. It took three years to complete it, and it imitated Nature so exquisitely in its down, its glossiness, and its general configuration from tip to stem, that, if placed in a heap of real mulberry leaves, it could not be distinguished from them. This man was subsequently pensioned by the Sung State as a reward for his skill. Lieh-tzu, hearing of it, said "If it took the creator three years to make a single leaf, there would be very few trees with leaves on them. The Sage will rely not so much on human science and skill as on the evolution of *Tao*."[20]

If it is to modify nature, it is harmful. Chuang Tzu said:

> A duck's legs, though short, cannot be lengthened without pain to the duck, and a crane's legs, though long, cannot be shortened without misery to the crane, so that which is long in nature cannot be cut off, nor that which is short lengthened.[21]

According to Chuang Tzu the purpose of art is precisely to cut the long and to lengthen the short. Thus when art is introduced into the state of nature, there is no more happiness, but suffering; nay, no more life, but death.

The following story will serve for further illustration:

> The Lord of the Southern Sea is called Change; the Lord of the Northern Sea is called Uncertainty; and the Lord of the center is called Primitivity. Change and Uncertainty often met on the territory of Primitivity, and being always well treated by him, determined to repay his kindness. They

17 *Id.*, pp. 107, 108.
18 *Id.*, p. 109.
19 For justification in quoting Lieh-tzu see Chap. VI.
20 Lionel Giles, *Taoist Teaching from the Book of Lieh Tzu*, London and New York, 1912, p. 108.
21 Cp. H. A. Giles' translation, p. 101.

said "All men have seven holes-for seeing, hearing, eating, and breathing. Primitivity alone has none. We will bore some for him." So every day they bored one hole; but on the seventh day Primitivity died.[22]

(3) Social and Political Philosophy

If the meaning of this story is clear, it is not difficult to see why Chuang Tzu went further to teach the abolition of culture and the practice of non-government. According to Chuang Tzu, primitivity and anarchism are the essentials of a Golden Age. Culture is bad, because it is intended to modify man's original nature. Chuang Tzu said:

> An old tree is cut down to make sacrificial vessels which are then decorated with beautiful colors. The stump remains in the ditch. The sacrificial vessels and the stump are very differently treated as regards honor and dishonor, but equally, as regards the destruction of their original nature. Similarly, the acts of Robber Chin [a bad man] and that of Tseng and Shih [two good men] are very different, but the loss of their original nature is in each case the same. Now the causes of the loss of man's original nature are five in number. The five colors confuse the eyes and cause them to fail to see clearly. The five sounds confuse the ears and cause them to fail to hear accurately. The fives scents confuse the nose and obstruct the sense of smell. The four tastes cloy the palate and vitiate the sense of taste. Finally, likes and dislikes disturb the mind and cause dispersion of the original nature. These are all the banes of life; yet *Yang* and Mo regarded them as the *summum bonum*. They are not what I consider the *summum bonum*, for if men who are thus fettered can be said to have *summum bonum*, the pigeons and owls in a cage may also be said to have attained the *summum bonum*![23]

Therefore, we must abolish all these things that fetter mankind. He said again:

> There was once a sea bird which alighted outside the capital of Lu. The Prince of Lu was delighted, went out to receive it, escorted it to the temple, and ordered the best meal to be served and the best music to be played for a banquet in its honor. The bird, however, was timid, sad, and dazed, and dared not eat or drink; in three days, it was dead. This was treating the bird as the Prince would treat himself, not treating the bird as a bird. Had he treated it as a bird, he would have let it roost in dense forests, wander over open land, swim in the river and lake, feed upon fishes, fly in order, and rest in peace.[24]

This story shows that the most tragic phenomenon in this world is the imposition of one's own idea of good upon others who do not consider it as good. But the chief function of government is not only to impose what it considers as good upon its subjects, but also to coerce them to behave accordingly. It is tragic; it is in tolerable. So Chuang Tzu said:

---

22 *Id.*, P. 98.

23 *Id.*, p. 155.

24 *Id.*, p. 227

> There has been such a thing as letting mankind alone; there has never been such a thing as governing mankind. Letting alone springs from the fear lest men's native dispositions be perverted and their natural virtue laid aside. But if their native dispositions be not perverted and their natural virtue be not laid aside, what room is there left for government?[25]

Clearly, according to Chuang Tzu's conception of Nature and happiness, there is certainly no more room for government than for culture.

(4) Individual Cultivation and the Ideal Man

So much for Chuang Tzu's social ethics; now let us consider his suggestions for individual cultivation, or his art of life. Just as civilized society should abolish its civilization and return to the state of primitivity, so the mature individual should eliminate his intellect and return to the state of childhood. Just like the primitive state of society, the childhood of the individual is also characterized by spontaneity and naturalness. Both belong to times when instinct was not yet disturbed by intellect, and nature was not yet confused by art. So Chuang Tzu said:

> "The method of life," said Lao Tzu, "consists in being able to preserve the unity of mind, to lose nothing, to know good and evil without conscious will, to stop, to be satisfied with what is enough, to leave others alone and to attend to one's self, to be without cares and without knowledge— to be in fact a child A child will cry all day without getting hoarse, will keep its fist tightly closed without the hand becoming cramped, and will gaze all day without the eyes becoming dulled. This is so, because the child does these things from its native disposition or natural virtue, not from conscious will. The child moves, but does not know whither; it sits, but does not know why. It is not conscious of anything but freely adapts itself to the suggestions of the environment. This is the art of life."[26]

The picture of Chuang Tzu's ideal man is as follows:

> The supreme man of the ancients slept without dreaming and awaked without anxiety. He ate without discrimination and breathed deep breaths.... He did not know how to love life or to hate death.
>
> Living, he experienced no elation; dying, he offered no resistance; unconsciously he came, unconsciously he went, that is all. He forgot the past and sought no information about the future.[27] He received anything that came to him, with delight, and left anything that he did not want, without consciousness. In short, he did not let the mind [intellect] substitute [become a substitute] for the instinct, nor [did he let] the human help nature. This is the supreme man.[28]

---

25 *Id.*, p. 119.

26 *Id.*, P. 300.

27 The text reads: "he did not forget," but the Commentary of Kuo Hsian shows that text he used reads: "he forgets."

28 H. A. Giles' translation, p. 73.

(5) The World of Pure Experience

Put in modern language, the supreme man is one who has no will, no consciousness, no knowledge. He is simply in what William James called "the world of pure experience."[29] He simply takes the pure experience, the immediate presentation, "the *that* in short (for until we have decided what it is, it must be a mere that)."[30] He simply takes "the that at its face value, neither more nor less; and taking it at its face value means, first of all, to take it just as we feel it, and not to confuse ourselves with abstract talk about it, involving words that drive us to invent secondary conceptions in order to mentalize their suggestions and make our actual experience again seem rationally possible."[31] So Chuang Tzu said:

> The knowledge of the ancients is perfect. How perfect? At first, they did not yet know that there were things. This is the most perfect knowledge; nothing can be added. Next they knew that there were things, but they did not yet make distinctions between them. Next they made distinctions between them, but they did not yet pass judgments upon them. When judgments were passed, the Whole (Tao) was destroyed. With destruction of the Whole, individual bias arose. Are there really construction and destruction? Are there really no construction and destruction? That there are construction and destruction is like the fact that one plays the lute. That there are no construction and destruction is like the fact that one does not play the lute.[32]

The above-mentioned commentator said:

> All the tunes cannot be played at once. When playing a piece of music, no matter how many hands take part in it, there must be some tunes left. To play music is to make the tunes known. But by making it known, one gets only a part; by not making it known, one gets the whole. Therefore, that there are destruction and construction is like the fact that one plays the lute; that there are no destruction and construction is like the fact that one does not play the lute.

This shows that when we give "abstract talks" about pure experience, we do not make it more, but less. According to the following quotation "construction is the same as destruction," so we must take every experience at its "face value." Chuang Tzu said:

The possible is possible, the impossible is impossible. *Tao* evolves and sequences follow. Things act and they are what they are. What are they? They are what they are. What are they not? They are not what they are not. Everything is what it is, and does what it can do. There is nothing that is not what it is, and cannot do what it can do. Therefore, a beam and pillar are identical; so are ugliness and beauty, greatness, wickedness, perverseness, and strangeness. Separation is the same as construction; construction is the same as destruction. But all things, without regard to their construction and destruction, may again be comprehended in the whole. This only

---

29 William James, *Essays in Radical Empiricism*, New York, 1910, p. 39.

30 *Id*, p. 13.

31 *Id*., pp. 48, 49.

32 Cp. H. A. Giles' translation, p. 21.

the truly intelligent can see. They, therefore, give up prejudice, arguments, words and concepts, but follow the common and the ordinary. The common and the ordinary are the natural function of all things, which expresses the common nature of the whole. Following the common nature of the whole, they are joyous. Being joyous, they are near perfection. Perfection is for them to stop. That they stop without knowing that they stop is the identification with the Whole (Tao).[33]

Thus in the world of pure experience, what is known as the union of the individual with the whole is finally reached. In this state there is an unbroken flux of experience, but the experiencer does not know it. Like the man of the ancients he does not know that there are things, to say nothing of making distinctions between them. There is no separation of things, to say nothing of the distinction between the subject and the object, between the "me" and the "non-me." So in this state of experience, there is noting but the One. This is the mental state of the primitive man of ancient times, of the child, and of the sages.

(6) The Happiness of the Union of the Individual with the Whole

In this state one would have the feeling of the union of the individual with the whole, One would have the happiness of safety, peace, evenness, and serenity. Chuang Tzu said:

> If you hide a canoe in the crevice of a mountain which is surrounded by a lake, this is safe enough. But at midnight a strong man may come and carry away the canoe on his back. The blindness of men does not see that no matter how you conceal things, small ones in large ones, there will always be a chance of losing them. But if you conceal the whole universe in the whole universe there will be no room left for it to be lost. This is an eternal tact. Men consider the attainment of human form as a source of joy. But the human form is only one of the countless forms in the universe. If one identifies one's self with the universe, one will undergo all the transitions, and attain all the forms, with only the infinite and eternity to look forward to. What incomparable bliss is that! Therefore, the supreme man makes excursion in that which can never be lost, but endure always. Those who can deal well with death, old age, beginning and end, are already considered as teachers of mankind. How much more supreme to this is he who identifies himself with that which is the supporter of all things and the condition of the whole evolution?[34]
>
> Such a man will bury gold in the hillside and cast pearls into the seas. He will not struggle for wealth, nor strive for fame. He will not rejoice at long life, nor grieve over early death. He will find no pleasure in success, nor grieve over pain in failure. He will not account a throne as his private gain, nor the empire of the world as glory personal to himself. His glory is to have the insight that all are one and that life and death are the same.[35]

---

33 *Id.*, pp. 19, 20

34 *Id.*, pp. 75, 76.

35 *Id.*, p. 137.

This is the happiness of the union of the individual with the whole.

(7) Concluding Remarks

We shall see as we go on that the union of the individual with the whole is the common aspiration and inspiration of all the systems which we include in the "nature" line of thought. The difference between Chuang Tzu and other philosophers is that Chuang Tzu did not reject this world. In fact, "Tao" is but the total spontaneity of this world. This world is after all full of harmony, beauty, and happiness, if only men can appreciate and enjoy them. His philosophy is by no means "passive" in the sense that men should sit down really "doing nothing" except contemplating the ideal and the eternal. In fact, the spontaneous flight of the Rukh and the cicada, as well as the crying and gazing of the child, is all activity and doing. They are to be preferred, because all of them are consequences of the native disposition, but not the result of the conscious will. So Chuang Tzu's antithesis is not action versus contemplation, but the action of conscious design versus that of spontaneity and instincts. His philosophy taught that we should only abolish the present state of the world that destroys natural spontaneity with human art. So, in the "nature" line of thought,

> Chuang Tzu is the philosopher who asked mankind to make the least "decrease" or retreat. His philosophy is certainly an expression of a kind of human desire and an exposition of a kind of happiness. The happiness of union of the individual with the whole will be discussed later. Here we need only to notice that when we follow our instincts and leave them in the state of nature, there is a kind of happiness unique in itself. This happiness is what William James called the "felicity of the sensorial life."[36] To quote from William James, those who fail to appreciate the philosophy of Chuang Tzu must be the boys and girls, or man or woman, who has never been touched by the spell of this mysterious sensorial life, with its irrationality, if so you like to call it, but its vigilance and its supreme felicity.[37]

It is to this mysterious sensorial life, with its irrationality, its vigilance and its supreme felicity that Chuang Tzu and all the other romantic philosophers ask us to go back.

---

36 William James, *Talks to Teachers on Psychology and Life Ideals*, New York, 1921, p. 257.

37 Id., p. 263.

II IDEALISM: PLATO

But it is not difficult to see that Chuang Tzu's philosophy presupposes too much the good nature of man and the harmony of the Universe. The state of nature is certainly good for excursion, but may not be good for residence. It certainly gives men happiness, but may also give them trouble. There is no question about the fact that the real state of nature is far from the ideal. The reason that the *Tao*ists should take so naive a view of the state of nature is that up to the time of Chuang Tzu, the general philosophic tradition in China was the belief that human nature was intrinsically good. Hsun Tzu, the Chinese philosopher who first systematically took the opposite view, and who accused Chuang Tzu of being one who was "blinded by nature but did not know art," flourished rather too late for Chuang Tzu to take into consideration his argument for the defects of the state of nature and the importance of the state of art.

(I) Plato and the Problem of His Time

But Plato, the next philosopher we are going to consider, did have the chance to hear the arguments both for nature and for art. During his time there was a great controversy known as "nature versus convention." In this controversy, the question was whether virtue was natural or conventional; that is, whether the world was originally good or bad. Most of the pre-Socratic philosophers seemed to maintain that virtue was natural and did not change with the opinions of man. Even Heraclitus and Parmenides, who were usually considered the representatives of two opposing schools, seemed to agree on this point. Heraclitus said "Even he who is esteemed knows and cherishes nothing but opinions and yet justice shall surely overcome forgers of lies and false witnesses."[38] Parmenides said: "Neither destruction doth justice permit, ne'er slackening her fetters."[39]

The Pythagoreans identified justice, soul, and reason with the eternal numbers.[40] Anaxagoras said "that reason was present—as in animals and throughout nature—as the cause of the world and of all its order."[41]

Among the Sophists themselves, who were usually considered as radicals against tradition, there were also some who held the traditional view. Prodicus, in his Education of Heracles as reported by Xenophon, represents virtue by the woman who was fair to look upon; frank and free by gift of nature, her limbs adorned with purity and her eyes with bashfulness; sobriety set the rhythm of her gait, and she was clad with white apparel.

He represented happiness or "vice and naughtiness, as it is some- times called" by the woman who was of a different type; the fleshly softness of her limbs betrayed her nurture, while the complexion of her skin was embellished that she might appear whiter and rosier than she really was, and her figure that she might

38 Bakewell, C. M. *Source Book in Ancient Philosophy*, New York, 1907, p 29.

39 *Id.*, p. 15.

40 Aristotle, *Metaphysics*, 985 b, tr. by W. D. Ross, p. 23.

41 *Id.*, 984 b, p. 15.

seem taller than nature made her; she stared with wide-open eyes, and the raiment wherewith she was clad served but to reveal the ripeness of her bloom. With frequent glances she surveyed her person, or looked to see if others noticed her; while ever and anon she fixed her gaze upon the shadow intently.[42]

The meaning of this symbolism is clear. Virtue is natural and has the excellence of simplicity, spontaneity and naturalness. Artificial pleasure is against nature and therefore is bad. There was also Hippias, who was reported by Plato as having said:

> All of you who are here present I reckon to be kinsmen and friends and fellow citizens, by nature and not by law; for by nature like is akin to like, whereas law is the tyrant of mankind, and often compels us to do many things which are against nature.[43]

The meaning here is also clear. Nature was originally good. It is law or convention that is responsible for the evils of this world.

The main body of the Sophists, however, seemed to hold the opposite view. Not nature, but man, said Protagoras, is the "measure of all things." Law, justice, and all the other virtues are but human arrangements, the productions of art, to improve the barbarian state of nature. They are all to be taught through education. He was reported by Plato to have said:

> In like manner I would have you consider that he who appears to you to be the worst of those who have been brought up in laws and humanities, would appear to be a just man and a master of justice, if he were to be compared with a man who had no education, or courts of justice, or laws, or restraints upon them which compelled them to practice virtue.[44]

Thus he was very confident of civilization and progress. Besides Protagoras, there was also Gorgias. According to Benn, Gorgias's three theses in his work *On Nature or Nothing* are to be applied to the great controversy of his time. They are simply the extreme form of the following statement:

> First, the state of nature does not exist; for such a state must be either variable or constant. If it is constant, how could civilization ever have arisen? If it is variable, what becomes the fixed standard appealed to? Second, supposing such a state ever to have existed, how could authentic information about it have come down to us through the ages of corruption which are supposed to have intervened? Third, granting that a state of nature accessible to inquiry has ever existed, how can we organize society on the basis of such discordant data as are presented to us by the physiocrats, no two of whom agree with regard to the first principle of natural order; one saying that it is equality, another aristocracy, and a third despotism?[45]

This is certainly strong dialectic artillery brought against the state of nature.[46]

---

42 Xenophon, "Memorabilia," II, I, 21, in *Works*, tr. by H. G. Dackyus, London, 1890

43 Plato, "Protagoras," 337 c.

44 *Id.*, 327 d.

45 A Benn, *The Greek Philosophers*, Vol. 1, p. 96.

46 Han Pei Tzu, a disciple of Hsun Tzu, used the same arguments against those who admired the ancients.

Besides these two great Sophists, we learn from Plat that Thrasymachus considered justice as the invention of the stronger,[47] while Callicles considered it as that of the weaker.[48] Although they did not agree as to whom in particular invented justice, they did agree that it was the invention of man. It is nothing but human convention artificially made by man for his own expedience and for his own expedience only. Whether they are right or not, these Sophists had the merit of pointing out the defects of the state of nature and the importance of the state of art. Plato, as a lover of nature, was alarmed by these radical propositions of the Sophists. He did not like them, but at the same time he was fully aware of the force of their arguments. At that time he simply could not consider the state of nature as such as our lost paradise. He was bound to put it still one step further in the past.

(2) How Plato Solved the Problem

We shall see the way in which Plato avoided trouble by analyzing two of his dialogues: the "Protagoras" and the "Meno." In the "Protagoras" we first meet the problem as to whether virtue can be taught or not. In the "Meno" the same problem appeared again, but in a different form. It was now in the following form:" Whether virtue is acquired by teaching or by practice; or if neither by teaching nor by practice, then whether it comes to man by nature, or in what other way?"[49] Or, more simply: "Whether virtue comes by instruction, or by nature, or is gained in some other way?"[50]

Here we should notice that what comes by instruction is some- thing that is alien to human nature, something that is to be acquired. So in the "Meno" Socrates spoke of the boy: "If he has acquired knowledge he could not have acquired it in this life, unless he has been taught geometry."[51] So what is acquired and what is to be taught amount to the same thing. What comes by nature needs not to be taught. At most it needs only to be brought into consciousness by the method of midwives, which Socrates exemplified in the "Meno," and of which he was always proud.

Thus the problem as to whether virtue can be taught or not was at bottom the main problem as to whether virtue is natural or conventional. In the "Protagoras" no definite solution was reached. Plato was not willing to join Protagoras in declaring that virtue is nothing but the result of human convention; but he also could not say with Hippias that it comes to us by nature as such. This can be considered as Plato's attitude towards this problem of his time before he stated what is known as his theory of ideas. But in the "Meno" he succeeded in finding one way to solve the problem. In the "Meno," to the above question he answered:

> To sum up our inquiry-the results seem to be, if we are at all right in our view, that virtue is neither natural nor acquired, but an instinct given by

47 Plato, "The Republic," 338.
48 Plato, "Gorgias," 483.
49 Plato, "Meno," 70 c.
50 *Id.*, 86 d.
51 *Id.*, 85 d.

God to the virtuous.... Then, Meno, the conclusion is that virtue comes to the virtuous by the gift of God.[52]

Thus by this "some other way" the problem was at last solved.

Under this solution, virtue still comes by nature, but not in the sense of *natura naturata*. It comes by nature in the sense of *natura naturans*. It does not come by the "nature" of modern or even of Aristotelian philosophy, but by nature conceived as some supreme and absolute reality which transcends the limit of space and time, and of which the governor is God Himself or the Good itself.

(3) The Theory of Previous Knowledge and the Theory of Ideas

The evidence of the existence of this ideal world is proved for Plato by his theory of previous knowledge. Before Plato developed his theory of ideas we know there was Socrates who, with what Aristotle called the method of "induction and universal definition," succeeded in giving a universal character and permanent basis to morality. Plato, in his early years, followed this method faithfully. In his early dialogues, he occupied himself exclusively with the definition of temperance, friendship, courage, etc. But in the "Phaedo," he began to doubt whether the universal ideas could come from mere induction. The Platonic Socrates began to point out that the same pieces of wood or stone appear at one time equal and at another time unequal, but the equals can never be unequal, nor can the idea of equality ever be unequal. How can the idea of absolute equality be gathered from the particular material things which are always "changing and hardly ever the same, either with themselves or with another?"[53] So it was concluded:

> We must have known absolute equality previous to the time when we first saw the material equals, and reflected that all these apparent equals aim at this absolute equality, but fall short of it.[54]
>
> We are not speaking only of equality absolute, but of beauty, good, justice, holiness, and all which we stamp with the name of essence in the dialectical process, when we ask and answer questions. Of all this we may certainly affirm that we acquired knowledge before birth?[55]

So in the other world there must exist, not only absolute equality, but also absolute beauty, absolute good, absolute justice, absolute holiness, and all other things to which the term "many" is applied here in this world.[56] Thus the supreme world, of which Good itself is the ruler, is in every way analogous to this world. The difference between them is that what here are many, there is one; the many are seen but not known, the one is known but not seen;[57] and the seen is the changing, and the unseen is the unchanging.[58] Thus by projecting the Socratic essence into nature Plato succeeded in rediscovering our lost paradise,

---

52 *Id*,99 c.

53 Plato, Phaedo," 78 d

54 *Id.*, 75 a.

55 *Id.*, 75 d.

56 "The Republic," 507 a.

57 *Ibid.*

58 Plato, "Phaedo.' 79 a.

our "fatherland." Of all the states of this world, even the state of physical nature, not one is as good as we wish, because this world itself is a dreaming image of the waking reality, an imitation of the real. It is only the ideal world that contains all the perfect patterns, which all things in this world aim at, but fall short of. It is thither that we should return.

(4) The Two Worlds System

Thus Plato established the sharp distinction between the two worlds, the intellectual and the visible, the eternal and the temporal. So far as the written record of Western philosophy is concerned, Plato is credited with being the first to make this distinction. In "The Republic," Plato represented the two worlds by the following diagram:

The Visible World (Opinion)		The Intellectual World (Intellect)	
Images (Knowledge of the Shadows)	**Sensible Things** (Faith or Passion)	**Scientific Notions** (Understanding)	**Absolute Ideas** (Reason)

By images in the first section he meant "in the first place, shadows, and in the second place, reflections in water or in solid, smooth and polished bodies"; by sensible things in the second section, he meant "ourselves and animals and everything in nature, and everything in art"[59] There is no question about the meaning of these passages. But we may wonder as to whether in the world there are actually people who are really interested in the mere shadows of things or the knowledge of them. If, however, we compare these passages with others in the same dialogue, we see there is reason to suppose that by the shadows of things, Plato meant something more serious. In the latter part of "The Republic," Plato considered the production of fine art as the shadow of things. He said

> Here are three beds; one is natural, which, as I think we may say, is made by God. There is another which is the work of the carpenter. And the work of the painter is the third.[60]

The bed of the painter is not the real bed, but only its appearance. The painter, therefore, "is thrice removed from the king and the truth."[61] Thus in the diagram the first section is really the place for productions of art, that is, the artificial things made by man. These passages show clearly that the productions of fine arts, literature and poetry belong to this class. As to the productions of industrial or useful art, these passages show that in the sensible world they have the same standing as the natural things. Plato now supposed that in the ideal world there are the ideas of even the table and the bed "And the maker of either of them makes a bed or he makes a table for our use in accordance with the idea."[62]

59 Plato, "The Republic," 510 a.
60 *Id*, 597 b.
61 *Id*., d.
62 *Id*., 596 b.

They have in the sensible world the same standing as the natural things, because they are all after the pattern of the eternal idea. But in another part of "The Republic," Plato did speak of "arts in general" and put them in the same category; for instance, he said:

> For the arts in general are referable to wants and opinions of men, or are cultivated for the sake of production and construction, or for the care of such productions or constructions; and as to the mathematical arts which, as we were saying, have some apprehension of true being — geometry and the like — they only dream about being, but never can they behold the waking reality so long as they leave the hypothesis they use undisturbed, and are unable to give an account of them. For when a man knows not his own first principle, and when the conclusion and the intermediate steps are also constructed out of he knows not what, how can he imagine that such an arbitrary agreement will ever become science?[63]

This shows that arts in general and what we now call the scientific notions are all human creations. They are either human constructions or arbitrary agreements. The difference between them is that the one deals with things, while the other with ideas, — that is all. For this reason, in the diagram the relation between scientific notions and absolute ideas is just the same as that between the images and sensible things. For this reason the painter is only "thrice moved from the king and the truth."

Of course, we do not claim that Plato thought of his two worlds system always in this way. Like William James of our own time, Plato was after all anything but self-consistent. Our interpretation would be justified, if only sometimes he did think in this way. But whether our interpretation is correct or not, the sharp distinction of the two worlds is clear. On the one hand, there is the world of sense, full of the sensible things, with the sun as the author of sensibility, nourishment, and growth. On the other hand, there is the world of intellect, full of ideas, essences, with the idea of Good as the author of knowledge and of the essences, although the Good itself "is not essence, but far exceeds essences in dignity and power."[64] Thus, all things in that world must be as perfect as they should be, since by definition they are the very essences. The power that governs that world can never be bad, since by definition, it is the Good. Consequently that world can never fall short of our ideal, since by definition it is the ideal. So there is not the smallest room left for any one to doubt the perfection of our lost.

(5) Soul and Body

As the macrocosm consists of these two distinct parts, in the same way the microcosm consists also of two parts: the soul and the body.

The soul is the very likeness of the divine, and immortal, and intelligible, and uniform, and indestructible and unchangeable, and the body is the very

63 *Id.*, 533 b
64 *Id*, 509 b.

likeness of the human, and mortal, and unintelligible, and uniform, and destructible and changeable.[65]

According to this passage, the relation between the soul and the body is exactly like that relationship existing between the intelligible and the sensible world. Soul is pure and divine, and is always ready to fly to its "fatherland." This is the general idea expounded in the "Phaedo." But if we compare the "Phaedo" with other dialogues, there are certain difficulties in ascertaining the exact nature of the soul. According to Archer-Hind, "the difficulties are two: (1) in the 'Phaedo' soul is simple, in the 'Phaedrus,' 'The Republic,' and 'Timaeus,' it is triform." These difficulties Archer-Hind solved in the following manner:

> (1) The apparent discrepancy between the "Phaedo" and the "Philebus" is reconciled. In the one, desires are ascribed to body, because arising from the conjunction of soul and body; in the other they are more accurately ascribed to soul, because they are affections of soul through body. (2) The argument of the "Phaedo" is entirely unaffected by the threefold division. All soul is simple, uniform, and indestructible; but in connection with body it assumes certain phases which are temporary and only exist in relation to the body. Thus though the desire and the appetite as such are not immortal, because they depend for their continuance upon body, which is mortal, yet the vital principle, which under such conditions assumes these forms, is immortal and continues to exist, though not necessary in the same mode. For the mode in which vital force acts under temporary conditions are transitory, but the acting force itself is changeless and eternal.[66]

Thus "the soul when it enters into union with matter is forced more or less to operate through matter,"[67] and the names given to this combined action of soul and matter are "desire" and "appetite."

This solution seems to be very satisfactory, but is not so in fact.

If soul is really uniform in itself, and if desires and appetites are but forms of the operation of soul through body, it follows that when death, which is "the natural separation and release of the soul from body,"[68] comes, the desire and appetite will automatically cease to be, since there is no longer body for the soul to operate through. But this is not Plato's idea. According to him, only those souls that have been purified and released from evils by philosophy[69] can "depart to the indivisible; to the divine and immortal and rational,"[70] but the impure soul that "is engrossed by the corporeal, which the association and constant care of the body have made natural to her," is different.[71] By virtue of the "heavy, earthly element of sight, such a soul is depressed and dragged down again into

65 Plato, "Phaedo," 80 b.

66 ""The Journal of Philology," Vol. X, London, 1882, pp. 130,131. The Greek words which Archer-Hind quoted in this passage are here changed into their English equivalents.

67 *Id.*, p. 127.

68 Plato, "Phaedo," 67 b.

69 *Id.*, 84 d.

70 *Id.*, 81 a

71 *Id.*, b.

the visible world, because she is afraid of the invisible and of the world below." So these souls continue" to wander until the desire which haunts them is satisfied and they are imprisoned in another body."[72] Thus, death, though it may be the natural separation of soul from body, is far from the natural release of the soul from desire. Only through philosophy, which is somewhat ascetic, can the soul be free and pure. It follows that the soul does have desires itself before it joins the body. Indeed, if she has no desires at all, there is no reason why she must join the body. According to the "Phaedrus" it is exactly through the misbehavior of the "dark horse" that the soul "drooping in her flight at last settles on the solid ground-there, finding a home, she receives an earthly frame which appears to be self-moved, but is really moved by her power, and this composition of soul and body is called living and mortal creature."[73]

That the soul has three parts before she joins the body is thus obvious. It is possible that when Plato spoke of the soul as simple, he meant the soul as a whole, just as we say a man is a man. When he spoke of the soul as consisting of three parts, he meant the fact that she has three parts, just as we say a man has one head and two arms. Here we should remember that Plato's ideal world is in every way analogous to this world. The only difference between them is that there everything is ideal; here everything falls short of the ideal. The inhabitants in this world are men; those in the ideal world are gods and the pure souls; gods and souls are ideal men, while men are short of the ideal. Now the ideal man, according to Greek ideas, is not he who has no desires, but rather he who can subordinate them under the control of reason or mind that is not only the lord of the body, but also the lord of the soul.[74] Therefore, the gods and the pure souls, besides the charioteer, do have a pair of winged horses. Only that "the winged horses and the charioteer of the gods are all of them noble, and of noble breed, while ours [the souls] are 'mixed.' "[75] But the souls that are most like the gods can keep the "self-balance,"[76] and manage to follow the gods in the great review of absolute beauty and absolute good. But those souls which fail to keep the "dark horse" in balance, thereby fall short of the ideal, and therefore "gravitate and incline and sink towards the earth, and this is the hour of great agony and extreme conflict of the soul."[77] This is the story of the "fall" of mankind. The antithesis of soul and body in the "Phaedo" is still valid, because body itself is the realization or the objectification of the soul's "dark horse." As long as the "dark horse" gains the upper hand, the soul always "is in love with and fascinated by the body, and by the desires and the pleasures of the body, until she is led to believe that the truth exists only in a bodily form, which a man may touch and see and taste and use for the purposes of his lusts."[78] In this state the bodily desires and pleasures may be said to belong both to the body and to the soul; so there is no

72 *Id.*, 81b.
73 Plato, "Phaedrus," 246 b.
74 *Id.*, 247 b.
75 *Id.*, 246 a.
76 Id.. 247 a.
77 *Ibid.*
78 Plato, "Phaedo," 81 b.

contradiction between the "Phaedo" and the "Philebus." In this state the soul is bound to be born again and again "beneath the throne of necessity."[79] "Those who have chosen the portion of injustice, and tyranny, and violence, will pass into wolves, or hawks, or kites.[80] There is no end of this evolution or revolution, until the souls receive their purification and release from philosophy and are thus enabled to return to their old place in the company of the gods. This seems to be the meaning of the myths described in the end of the "Phaedo" and "The Republic" Although the myths themselves are not exactly true, yet "something of that kind is true."[81] What is that something, if not what has been said above?

(6) Love and Philosophy

So, Plato, in the first part of "The Republic," considered the harmonization of the three parts of mind as its best state, because it is the best state of the soul when she is in company with the gods. It should be striven for, because it is the ideal. But since the body is itself the self-realization or the objectification of the "dark horse," so, as long as the soul is imprisoned in the body, the ideal harmonization of the horses and their ruler can never be fully realized. The man, as long as he is the combination of soul and body, must always strive for the ideal, but always falls short of it and does not attain it. This is the eternal law of this world.

For everything existent here in this world, even justice and virtue, is after all but the dreaming image of waking reality. Therefore, Plato, after expounding his theory of justice in the first half of "The Republic," said "There is a knowledge still higher than these, higher than justice and other virtues."[82] Thus the moral qualities as exhibited in self-cultivation or social relations in this world, no matter how perfect they are, are but the appearance or imitation of the absolute ideas just as other things in this world. But what the souls like to behold and to feed upon is "justice, temperance, and knowledge absolute, not in the form of generation or of relation, which men call existence, but knowledge absolute in existence absolute."[83] To those who have "seen the absolute justice," the human virtue and the law of the courts are but "images or shadows of images of justice."[84] Therefore those who are "intelligent" and have "the recollection of those things which our soul once saw when in company with god,"[85] can never be satisfied with the beings of this world, at which they were "looking down from above,"[86] during that time.

And therefore the mind of the philosopher alone has wings; and this is just, for he is always, according to the measure of his abilities, dinging in recollection to those things in which God abides, and in beholding which He is what He is. And he who employs aright these memories is ever being initiated into perfect mysteries and alone becomes truly perfect. But, as he forgets the earthly interests

79 Plato, "The Republic," 621 a
80 Plato, "Phaedo," 82 a.
81 *Id.*, 114 d.
82 Plato, The Republic," 504 d.
83 Plato, "Phadrus," 247 d.
84 Plato, The Republic," 517 d.
85 Plato, Phaedrus," 249 b.
86 *Ibid.*

and is rapt in the divine, the vulgar deem him mad, and rebuke him; they do not see that he is inspired.[87]

This striving for the eternal is the spirit called love. This is the spirit that "intermediates between the divine and the mortal," the "power that spans the chasm which divides them, and in this all is bound together."[88] In fact, this is that spirit that Plato devised to connect his two eternally separated worlds.

The soul, when she is "dragged by the body into the region of the changeable,"[89] is always craving for return to herself.

When returning to herself she reflects; then she passes into the realm of purity, and eternity, and immortality, and unchangeableness, which are her kindred, and with them she ever lives when she is by herself and is not let or hindered; then she ceases from her erring ways, and being in communion with the unchanging is unchanging. And this state of the soul is called wisdom.[90]

Wisdom is the best and also the original state of the soul.

Philosophy is the love of wisdom.

(7) Conversion

Wisdom and philosophy are not things; the former is a state, the latter is a process. Philosophy is "the process" which "is not the spinning round of an oyster shell, but the conversion of a soul out of darkness visible to the real ascent of the true being."[91] "The sort of knowledge that has the power of affecting this"[92] includes all the sciences that can "excite thought,"[93] and turn the soul from the sensation concrete to notions abstract. These sciences are after all but the handmaids and helpers of the soul in the work of conversion.[94] Only with the power of the dialectic, is the whole soul" turned from the world of generation into that of being, and becomes able to endure the sight of being, and of the brightest and the best of being-that is to say, of the good."[95] Then, and not until then, are the absolutes not only known, but actually "seen by the eyes of the soul.[96] "This is conversion."[97]

(8) The Difficulties of the Theory of Ideas

But exactly how the logical notion of science can be transformed into the insight or intuition of the objective ideas, Plato did not make clear. Even if scientific notions can excite thought and can thus refresh our memory and recall the ideas that we had when our souls were in company with the gods, yet the memory of a thing is still far from the actual insight or intuition of it. Having projected Socrates' definition into

87 *Id.*, 249 c.
88 Plato, "Symposium," 202 d.
89 Plato, "Phaedo," 79 c.
90 *Ibid.*
91 Plato, "The Republic," 521 c.
92 *Ibid.*
93 *Id.*, 523 b.
94 *Id.*, 533 c.
95 *Id.*, 518 c.
96 *Id.*, 517 d.
97 *Id.*, 518 c.

a world of ideal reality, Plato thought they could still be reached with the Socratic method of induction and definition, that is, the method of science, but he forgot that his ideas were no longer merely logical notions or the definitions or the general characters of things. With the method of science, the ideas may be known, but can never be seen. So he was compelled to fall back on another method which he called dialectic. But how are we able to transfer from scientific method to the dialectic method? In the "Parmenides," Parmenides said:

> And the subjective notions in our mind, which have the same name with them [ideas], are likewise only relative to one another and not to the ideas which have the same name with them, and belong to themselves and not to the ideas.[98]

This criticism seems to be fatal to the theory in "The Republic" that the study of science can lead man to conversion. But this is only one of the many difficulties that confound Plato's theory of ideas. According to the "Parmenides," the difficulties are threefold: first, in regard to the ideal world itself; second, to the relation between the ideal and the phenomenal world; third, to the possibility of knowing the ideas. Having mentioned the third difficulty above, we will now discuss the first and the second. Plato, being disappointed by the sensible world, tried to project the notions of science into heaven and thereby establish the ideal world. According to the "Phaedo" and "The Republic," in the ideal world there are ideas of all things, of which we have general notions and general names. In fact, the existence of the general name of a thing in this world is the very proof of the existence of the idea of that thing in the ideal world. But if this is so, it follows that in the ideal world there are not only absolute beauty and absolute good, but also absolute ugliness and absolute bad, since in this world we have the general notion of both of them. It follows also that the ideal world is even worse than this world, since the absolute ugliness and the absolute bad must be much more ugly and much worse than the particular things in this world, and must be eternal and unchangeable. If we say in the ideal world there is no ugliness or badness, on what ground are they denied the privilege of being there? How can we have the general notions and general names of these qualities if our souls have no previous experience of them? These are the difficulties in regard to the ideal world itself. In the "Parmenides" Socrates is represented as being sure about the existence of the ideas of the just, the beautiful, and the good, but doubtful about that of the ideas of human creatures, or of fire and water, and felt it absurd to assume an idea of hair, mud, dirt, or anything else that is foul and base.[99] Socrates said that this confusion and uncertainty always caused him to be "disturbed" and to "run away." How can the ideal world be ideal, if there are still things that are foul and base? But on what ground can we exclude them from the ideal world, since in this world we do have the general notions just as well as those of the beautiful and the good?

Granting the existence of the ideal world, we still have to ask:

"What is the relation between the ideal and this phenomenal world, or

98 Plato, "Parmenides," 133 d.

99 *Id.*, 130 b.

the relation between the one and the many?" If the many are so and so by partaking the one of so and so, then the one is subject to division and is no longer one. If the many are so and so by imitating the one of so and so, then before the many imitate the one, they must first imitate the idea of likeness. In order to imitate the idea of likeness, they must imitate another idea of likeness by virtue of which they can be like the first idea of likeness, and so on ad infinitum. Thus with the third difficulty in regard to the possibility of knowing the ideas, the theory of ideas was attacked from three sides. Whether Plato made these criticisms against himself or whether he simply mentioned the opinion of his contemporaries is a question still to be answered. Anyway, these are the difficulties of the theory of ideas.

Whether or not Plato had any "later theory of ideas" as interpreted by Jackson we need not decide here. But it is significant that Plato, in his later dialogues, became gradually silent about the theory of ideas. In the "Laws" he gave it up altogether, and fell back to find in nature the norm and guidance of human conduct and the justification of moral law. In the "Laws," he employed the phrases "according to nature" and "follow nature" more frequently than in all the other dialogues put together.[100] He spoke of the conditions of primitive men as simple, brave, temperate, and just, and represented them with a picture not much different from Chuang Tzu's. In one place he reiterated the doctrine that he fought against, the doctrine of the Sophists:

> The doctrine that all things which are, or have been, or will be, exist, some by nature, some by art, and some by chance.... In the first place, my dear friend, they would say that gods exist neither by nature nor by art, but only by the laws of states, which are different in different places, according to the agreement of those who made them; and that the honorable in one thing by nature and another thing by law, and that the principles of justice have no existence at all in nature, but that mankind are always disputing about them and altering them; and that the alterations which are made by art and by law have no basis in nature, but are of authority for the moment and at that time at which they are made: these, my friends, are the sayings of wise men, poets, and prose writers, which find a way into the minds of young men.[101]

Against this doctrine Plato took a new position. After making a statement of "the nature and power of the soul," he said:

> Then thought and care, and mind and art, and law will be prior to that which is hard and soft, and heavy and light; and the great and primitive works and actions will be works of art; they will be the first and after them will come nature and the works of nature, which, however, is a wrong word to apply to them; these will follow and be under the government of art and mind.[102]

Thus nature, art and the laws are all the manufacture of soul, mind, and reason. This position is quite near Kant's theory of the autonomy of practical

100 Benn, The *Idea* of Nature in Plato," in *Archiv fur Gesdtichte der Philosophie*, Vol. IX, 1896, p. 39.

101 Plato, "Laws," 889, 890.

102 *Id*, 892 c.

reason; and by taking this Plato was near what we call the third line of thought, which is the reconciliation of nature and art.

(9) Concluding Remarks

It must be stated again that all the philosophic systems analyzed and criticized in this work are considered, not as something unique in themselves, but rather as representative types of thought. Plato represents one type of thought to which, among others, belongs

Christianity; and Schopenhauer, the next philosopher we are going to consider, represents one type, to which belongs Buddhism.

Christianity belongs to the type of thought represented by Plato, because the God of Christianity is an idea to which many other absolute ideas are attributed. He is definitely an eternal, all-wise, all-good, and all-powerful God. Besides, the "City of God" is also sharply opposed to the city on earth. The two worlds are so sharply opposed that the chasm between them is even more impassable than that in Plato's system. Thus the difficulties that confound the Platonic system also confound the Christian system. Their ideal world is entirely in the category of reason and thus liable to fall into the antinomy of reason. In the history of Western philosophy, for instance, there is no end to the controversy about the existence and the attributes of God. There have been the arguments known as the ontological proof, the cosmological proof, and the physico-theological proof. But the ontological proof can be turned to prove that God is a mere concept; the cosmological proof that God himself must have a cause; and the physico-theological proof that God, if He exists at all, must be an artist poor and weak. After the Renaissance, Christianity gradually lost its universal influence which it had in the Middle Ages. In the eighteenth century, which is a time of rationalism, Christianity was much questioned and attacked. Finally came the skepticism of Hume, in which soul was regarded as a mere bundle of sensation and God as a mere word. At this, Kant was greatly alarmed. In the history of Western philosophy, to Kant belongs the merit of pointing out definitely and systematically that immortality, freedom, the existence of God, and the state of the highest good, which is the union of happiness and virtue, can never be proved by pure reason, but can only be indicated to us by the practical reason of morality. But having no other sources of inspiration besides that of the Western world, Kant did not change the nature of the non phenomenal world, although he had been convinced that that world could not be known by our pure reason. In the Western world it remains for Schopenhauer to introduce the Hindu wisdom and thus to teach that our lost paradise is not only beyond sense, but also beyond thought. It is not only the unseen, but also the unthinkable.

III NIHILISM: SCHOPENHAUER

Here is the difference between Buddhism and Christianity.

Christianity tries in every way to tell what God is, while Buddhism tries in every way to tell what the "Suchness" is not. The Buddhists spoke much about the phenomenal world. When they said all that could be said about the phenomenal, they told us that the "Suchness" or the non phenomenal world was not all these things. If one wants to return to the "Suchness," one must first get rid of all these things. When all these things have been got rid of, the "Suchness" will come out itself. As we shall see, this is exactly the procedure adopted by Schopenhauer.

(I) The Origin of His Philosophy

Since we have just discussed the general scheme of Plato's philosophy and the difficulties that confound it, for the sake of convenience we shall here treat Schopenhauer's philosophy as a continuation of Plato's with some improvement gained from Kant and the Hindus. Our doing so is justified by the fact that all these influences played important roles in Schopenhauer's system. He said himself that, next to the impressions of the world of perception, he owed what is best in his system to the impression made upon him by the works of Kant, by the sacred writings of the Hindus, and by Plato.[103] We shall see that with the suggestions of the Hindus, Schopenhauer succeeded in finding out the origin and the defects of the world of absolute Ideas;[104] and with the suggestions of Kant he succeeded in putting into definite terms the relation between the real and the phenomenal world. Of course I do not mean that when Schopenhauer worked on his philosophy, he must have had in mind the solution of the difficulties that confound Plato's theory of Ideas as pointed out in the "Parmenides." But it is peculiar that according to his interpretation of the Platonic theory of Ideas, all the above-mentioned difficulties disappeared immediately. This perhaps shows that the difficulties were real ones, not simply pieces of sophistry manufactured for the sake of argument. So when the theory itself improved, its difficulties vanished as a matter of course.

(2) What the Platonic Ideas Are

We have learned from the above discussions that one of the chief difficulties in maintaining the existence of the world of Ideas is that we shall be compelled to admit into that world the Idea of things that we consider as bad. Besides the absolute bad and the absolute ugliness, the Idea of "lion" must be more fierce than the particular "lion," and the idea of "serpent" must be more terrible than the particular serpent. Consequently the world above is not only not better, but is even worse than the world here below. No wonder that Socrates in the "Parmenides," in thinking of this, became "disturbed" and wanted to "run away." But according to Schopenhauer, it is true that there is

103 Schohenhauer, *The World as Will and idea*, tr. by R. B. Haldane and J. Kemp, London, 1909, Vol. 11, p. 5.

104 In this chapter the word "*Idea*" with a capital "I" indicates the Platonic "*Idea*."

the world of Ideas, but it is wrong to consider it as the ideal world. The main thesis of Schopenhauer's philosophy is well represented by the title of his chief work: The World as Will and Idea. The outside appearance of the world, the phenomenon, is the idea; the inner nature of the world, the thing-in-itself, is will. Will is the always wishing for and the striving after, the "eternal becoming and the endless flux."[105] For it, "every attained end is also the beginning of a new course, and so on ad infinitum."[106] In this endless striving the will always objectifies itself. "These grades of the objectification of Will, I say, are simply Plato's Ideas."[107]

From the lowest grades of the objectification of will such as the force of gravity[108] and other forces of nature up to the higher grades, such as plants and animals,[109] every grade is an Idea representing one species. Notwithstanding that the will itself is an endless flux, these different grades of the objectification of will remain fixed, and are subject to no change; they are always being, but never becoming. They are the unattained types or the eternal forms of the innumerable individuals that arise and pass away, always become, and never are.[110] All the individuals of one species strive for the idea, and collectively express the whole of the Idea.[111]

All their activities, events, and characteristics, except their individuality and multiplicity, which are the production of the principle of sufficient reason, are all the expression or manifestation of their fixed type, that is, the Idea. They "have significance only so far as they are letters out of which we may read the Idea, but not in and for themselves." Take the case of man, about which Schopenhauer said:

> In the manifold forms of human life and in the unceasing change of the events, he [who can distinguish between the will and the Idea and its manifestation] will regard the Idea only as the abiding and the eternal, in which the will to live has its full objectivity, and which shows its different side in the capacities, the passions, the errors, and the excellences of the human race; its self-interest, hatred, love, fear, boldness, frivolity, stupidity, shyness, wit, genius, and so forth, all of which crowding together and combining in thousands of forms (individuals), continually create the history of the great and the little world, in which it is all the same, whether they are set in motion by nuts or by crowns.[112]

Such is the Idea of man and so are the Ideas of all things. All things in this phenomenal world are full of errors and mistakes because their ideas are full of errors and mistakes. Their Ideas are full of errors and mistakes, because the will, of which the Ideas are objectifications, is in itself a great error and a fundamental mistake.

---

105 Schopenhauer, *The World as Will and Idea*, Vol. I, p. 214.
106 *Ibid.*
107 *Id*, p. 168.
108 *Id*, p. 169.
109 *Id.*, p. 170.
110 *Id.*, p. 168.
111 *Id.*, p. 172.
112 *Id.*, pp. 236, 237.

(3) The Relation Between the Idea and the Individual

Now we come to the question: What is the relation between the Idea and its expression? Or, what is the relation between the one and the many? Is it one of participation, or one of imitation, or neither of them? According to Schopenhauer, the multiplicity of the individuals is only the Idea as it appears to us. They are the phenomena, the representations, the ideas, or objects existing for the knowing subjects. Following the example of Kant, Schopenhauer supposed that there existed the a priori forms of knowledge, or what Schopenhauer called the principle of sufficient reason. The most universal forms of these are time and space. Everything to be known must be known through these mediums.

For it is only through the mediums of time and space that what is one and the same, both according to its nature and its concept, yet appears as different, as a multiplicity of coexistent and successive phenomena.[113]

Multiplicity in general is necessarily conditioned by space and time, and is only thinkable in them. In this respect they are called the *princnipium individuationis.*[114]

Thus the multiplicity of things is nothing but the manifestations through time and space of Ideas which are the objectification of the will. In the lower grades of its objectification, the will acts only as a blind, obscure, striving force. But as it attained to the higher grades, it "kindled for itself a light as a means"[115] to guide itself. This light is consciousness or knowledge. By this means, the world as idea comes into existence at a stroke, with all its forms, object and subject, time, space, multiplicity, and causality. The world now shows its second side. Till now mere will, it becomes also idea, object of the knowing subject.[116]

We may, for the sake of simplicity, regard these different Ideas [the Platonic Ideas) as in themselves individual and simple acts of the will, in which it expresses its nature more or less. Individuals, however, are again manifestations of the Ideas, thus of acts, in time, space, and multiplicity.[117]

Thus to use an expression of Plato, the multiplied individuals are "thrice removed from the king and the truth."

The question may be asked: Why must knowledge have these forms? Following the example of Kant, Schopenhauer considered them as simply a priors' and gave no clear and definite explanation. But the explanation he would give is not difficult to find. The general trend of his philosophy is to reduce everything, and ultimately the principle of sufficient reason, to will. Knowledge, in general, belongs to the objectification of will at its higher grades. Originally and according to its nature, knowledge is completely subject to will. Its function is to serve the will, not to discover truth. Consequently it knows nothing but what interests the will. As Schopenhauer said:

> Therefore, the knowledge, which is subject to the will, knows nothing further of the objects than their relations, knows the objects only in so far as they exist at

113 *Id.*, p. 146.
114 *Id.*, p. 166.
115 *Id.*, P. 196.
116 *Ibid*
117 *Id*, p. 202.

this time, in this space, under these circumstances, from these causes, and with these effects — in a word as particular things; and if all these relations were to be taken away, the objects would also have to disappear for it, because it knows nothing more about them.[118]

From this passage we can see that knowledge must be accompanied by the principle of sufficient reason, because knowledge, in order to serve the striving will, must know things, not in their pure objectivity, but only in their utility to the will on this or that occasion. The fact that they must see things as multiplied individuals is simply for the sake of convenience, and is a matter of practical, rather than logical, necessity.

(4) The Transcendental Knowledge

Anyway, by the very existence of knowledge, we are confined to the phenomenal world. The "Maya," the veil of deception, blinds the eyes of mortals,[119] and makes them behold not the Ideas, but only the ideas, their appearances in time and space. Is there some way by which we can transcend the veil? We have seen that Plato considered the practice of science as the beginning, at least, of the royal way to the world of ideas. But according to Schopenhauer science is but knowledge in its systematic form. What science considers in things is also "their relations, the connections of time and space, the causes of natural changes, the resemblance of forms, the motives of actions — thus merely relation."[120] The utility of science is to facilitate knowledge "by the comprehension of all particulars in universal, by means of subordination of concepts, and the completeness of knowledge which is thereby attained."[121] If it is precisely because of knowledge that we see the original one as the phenomenal many, how can science help us to transcend the "Maya," the deceptive veil? Science and knowledge, in general, are after all but "immanent knowledge."[122] The more complete they are, the firmer and the more permanent is the veil.

But there is one way in which "transcendental knowledge," as opposed to immanent knowledge, can be attained. As shown above, knowledge must view things through the principle of sufficient reason, because only by so doing can it serve the will. It is the will that forces the knowledge to see things through the *principium individuationis*.

If, raised by the power of mind, a man relinquishes the common way of looking at things, under the guidance of the forms of the principle of sufficient reason, their relation to each other, the final goal of which is always a relation to its own will; if he thus ceases to consider the where, the when, the why, and the whither of things, and looks simply and solely at the what; if, further, he does not allow the abstract thought, the concepts of the reason, to take possession of his consciousness, but, instead of all this, gives the whole power of his mind to

118 *Id*, p. 229.
119 *Id.*, p. 9.
120 *Id.*, p. 229.
121 *Ibid.*
122 *Id.*, p. 224.

perception, sinks himself entirely in this, and lets his whole consciousness be filled with quiet contemplation of the natural objects actually present, whether a landscape, a tree, a mountain, a building, or whatever it may be; in as much as he loses himself in the object (to use a pregnant German idiom), i.e., forgets even his individuality, his will, and only continues to exist as the pure subject, the clear mirror of the object, so that it is as if the object alone were there without any one to perceive it, and he can no longer separate the perceiver from the perception, but both have become one, because the whole consciousness is filled and occupied with one sensuous picture; if thus the object has to such an extent passed out of all relation to something outside it, and the object out of all relation to the will, then that which is so known, is no longer the particular thing as such, but is the Idea, the eternal form, the immediate objectivity of the will at this grade; and, therefore, he who is sunk in this perception is no longer individual, for in such perception the individual man has lost himself; but is pure, will-less, painless; timeless, subject of knowledge.[123]

Thus in this perception the principle of sufficient reason is at last transcended. The principle of sufficient reason is nothing but the connection of the object with its subject.[124] How can there still be that principle, when the distinction between the subject and the object no longer exists? So in this perception, there is but one—the Idea.

(5) The Works of Love

There is another way, however, through which we can transcend the forms of knowledge, the principium individuation is. It is by works of love, or in other words, by the enlargement of heart. Both love and heart belong to the category of feeling; and feeling, according to Schopenhauer, is directly opposite to rational knowledge, which is to serve the will.[125] However closely the veil of "Maya" may envelop the mind of man and thus make him regard his person as absolutely different, and separated by a wide gulf from others,[126] yet he can seldom witness the suffering of others without being moved. That all men have the feeling of sympathy is an established fact. Even the wicked man, in the inmost depths of consciousness, has also an inward horror at his own deeds, at the suffering that he himself has inflicted upon others. This is known as the feeling of remorse.[127] How can this be, if it is not due to the fact that however much time and space may separate him from other individuals and the innumerable miseries which they suffer, yet in the inmost depths of his consciousness, there is a dim foreboding that, apart from the Idea and its forms, it is the one will to live appearing in them all?[128] The bad man, the egoist, is grasped tightly enough by the principium individuationis so that he makes the sharp distinction between his own

123 *Id.*, p. 231.

124 Schopenhauer, *Fourfold Root of the Principle of Sufficient Reason*, tr. by Hillebrand, London, 1910, p. 30.

125 Schopenhauer, *The World as Will and Idea*, Vol. 1, p. 68.

126 *Id*, p. 471.

127 *Id.*, p. 474.

128 *Id.*, p. 472.

ego and that of others, and, disregarding the sting of conscience, inflicts sufferings upon others for the increase of his own happiness or pleasure. But to the man who is voluntarily just, that is, just and virtuous, not to obey law or dogma, but to follow the trend of his own inner heart, the distinction between his own ego and that of others is not so significant.

The *prinapium individuationis,* the form of the phenomenon, no longer holds him so tightly in its grasp.... He sees the distinction between himself and others, which to the bad man is so great a gulf, as only belonging to a fleeting and illusive phenomenon. He recognizes directly and without reasoning, in itself of his own manifestation is also that of others, — the will to live, which constitutes the inner nature of everything and lives in all; indeed, this applies also to the brutes and the whole of nature, and therefore he will not cause suffering even to the brutes.... For to him who does works of love, the veil of Maya is transparent, the illusion of the *prinapium individuationis* has left him.... To be cured of this illusion and the deception of Maya, and the works of love, are one and the same.... By this the heart is enlarged, as by egoism it is contracted.[129]

Thus by the enlargement of the heart, the *principium individuationis* is transcended, just as by the purification of knowledge. We may also say that the transcendental knowledge gained by the works of love is superior to that gained by the work of art. In the latter we can see only the idea, but in the former we can further realize that all ideas are after all but one and the same.

(6) Eternal Justice

As to the happiness that these two kinds of works give us, that which comes through the works of love is also superior to, and more endurable than, that which comes through the works of art.

The artist, in the contemplation of the pure object, in the representation of it into copies, surely for the time being can get rid of the tyranny of the will, and thus transcend the veil of deception. But that is only for the flashing moment. His work does not become to him a permanent "quieter of will"; it does not deliver him forever from life, but only at moments, and is therefore not for him a path out of life, but only an occasional consolation in it.[130] But he who does the works of love, will be forever free of the *principium individiationis.* Through the diminution of the interest in his own self, the anxious care for self is attacked from the very root. Hence the peace, the evenness, the serenity, the friendly and inner relation between himself and the universe, which he can never fail to possess. This is the happiness that almost all religions claim to produce. Not a few of them consider it as the supreme felicity, as the place to stop. Plato, as we have seen, thought that the ultimate reality had been reached, and the highest happiness gained, when the ascending soul saw no longer the many, but only the one; no longer, for instance, the individual men, but the Idea of Man, of which the phenomenal humanity is the dreaming image.

129 *Id*, pp. 481, 482.
130 *Id.*, p. 346.

But according to Schopenhauer, the case is quite different.

Although the permanent insight into the fact that his own nature is in all beings in this world gives the good man a certain evenness, and serenity of disposition, yet the intuitive knowledge of the common lot of mankind and of the world in general does not make this disposition a joyful one.[131] As pointed out above, the phenomenal world is full of error and mistakes not only because it is phenomenal, but also because the will, the root of the world, is itself a great error and a fundamental mistake. As Schopenhauer said:

> Accordingly with perfect right every being supports existence in general, and also the existence of its species, and its peculiar individuality, entirely as it is, and in circumstances as they are, in a world such as it is, swayed by chance and error, transient, ephemeral, and constant suffering; and in all that it experiences, or indeed can experience, it always gets its due. For the will belongs to it; as the will is, so is the world. Only the world itself can bear the responsibility of its own existence — no other; for by what means could another have assumed it? Do we desire to know what men, morally considered, are worth as a whole and in general, we have only to consider their fate as a whole and in general. This is want, wretchedness, affliction, misery, and death. Eternal justice reigns. If they were not, as a whole, worthless, then fate, as a whole, would not be so sad. In this sense we may say the world itself is the judgment of the world. If we could lay all the miseries of the world in one scale of the balance, and all the guilt of the world in the other, the needle would certainly point to the center.[132]

Those who are enveloped by the veil of "Maya" may seek comfort and consolation in the happiness and joy that chance or prudence may bring to them. But a man who recognizes in all beings his own inmost and true self, must also regard the infinite suffering of all suffering beings as his own, and take on himself the pains of the whole world. He knows the whole, comprehends its nature, and finds that it consists in constant passing away, vain striving, inward conflict, and continual suffering. He sees wherever he looks the, suffering humanity, the suffering brute creation, and the world that passes away.[133]

For the knowledge that sees through the *principium individiationis*, a happy life in time, the gift of chance or won by prudence, amid the sorrows of innumerable others, is only the dream of the beggar in which he is the king, but from which he must awake and learn from experience that only a fleeting illusion had separated him from the suffering of his life.[134]

According to Plato, when we reach the world of Ideas we shall see that suffering is relevant only to the world below, But according to Schopenhauer, the transition from the phenomenal to the ideal world only makes us realize that happiness is a real illusion and suffering is a solid reality. The essential of all

131 *Id*, P. 483
132 *Id*., pp. 453, 454.
133 *Id*., p. 489.
134 *Id*., p. 456.

life is suffering.[135] The justification of the suffering is that the will always asserts itself; and the assertion is justified and balanced by the fact that the will bears the suffering.[136] This is the eternal justice.

(7) The "Nothing"

Now what shall we do for the world? Shall we try to improve it, hoping that the supreme happiness and ultimate good may be attained in the future? But, as Schopenhauer said:

> Absolute good is a contradiction in terms; highest good, *summum bonum*, really signifies the same thing — a final satisfaction of the will... But... the will can just as little cease from willing altogether on account of some particular satisfaction as time can end and begin; for it there is no such thing as a permanent fulfillment which shall completely and forever satisfy its craving.[137]

If there is will, there is want; if there is want, there is suffering. This is the eternal justice. The best way to avoid completely the suffering of the world is the complete denial of the will.

If we compare life to a path along which we must necessarily run a path of red-hot coals, with a few cool places here and there; then he who is entangled in delusion is consoled by the cool places, on which he now stands, or which he sees near him, and sets out to run through the course. But he who sees through the *principium individuationis*, and recognizes the real nature of the thing-in-itself, and thus the whole, is no longer thus consoled; he sees himself in all places at once, and withdraws. He will turn around; he no longer asserts his own nature, which is reflected in the phenomenon, but denies it. The phenomenon by which this change is marked, is the transition from virtue to asceticism.[138]

Asceticism, which is common to almost all religions, is the intentional mortification of the will by refusal of what is agreeable, and the selection of what is disagreeable.[139] It is the quieter of the will.

What is the state after the complete denial of the will? Only he who has experience of it knows. Yet even he who has this experience cannot tell others what his experience is. So this question is unanswerable, because, as we said above, this state is not only the unseen, but also the unthinkable. So we cannot say what it is; at most we can only say what it is not. It is a state, in which there is "no will, no idea, no world."[140]

Then is it nothing, a complete void, an absolute nought? No, as distinctly pointed out later by Bergson, there is nothing which is really nothing. He said:

The representation of the void is always a representation which is full and

135 *Id.*, p. 401.
136 *Id.*, p. 427.
137 *Id.*, p. 467.
138 *Id.*, p. 490.
139 *Id.*, p. 506.
140 *Id.*, p. 531.

resolves itself on analysis into two positive elements: the idea, distinct or confused, of a constitution, and the feeling, experienced or imagined, of a desire or regret. It follows from this double analysis that the idea of the absolute nought, in the sense of annihilation of everything, is a self-destructive idea, a pseudo-idea, a mere word.[141]

When we say there is nothing, we mean there is something that is not interested by our will. In this sense, the lost paradise of Schopenhauer may be fit to be called nothing. Buddhism, however, found a better term, that is, the "Real Suchness." "Real" signifies that it is not nothing; "Suchness," that it is simply such. If one insists on asking what is that "Suchness" Buddhism can answer only negatively:

> "The nature of the Real Suchness is not being, not non-being, not not being, not not non-being, nor both being and non-being. It is not one, not many, not not one, not not many, nor both one and many.[142]

(8) Concluding Remarks

That Schopenhauer, in his chief work, devoted three volumes to the discussion of the will, the idea, and the world, but said very little about the "nothing," is therefore a very significant fact, which few in the Western world appreciate. It is significant, because in doing so he introduced not only the thought, but also the method, of the Hindus into the Western world. Whether this thought is true and whether this method is right are not our problems here. In either case Schopenhauer may be considered the forerunner of the wisdom of the Hindus in the West.

141 H. Bergson, *Creative Evolution*, p. 283.

142 Acvaghosha, *Discourse on the Awakening of Faith*, cp. Suzuki's translation, p. 59.

IV CONCLUSION OF PART I

Now is the time for us to take a general view of the "nature" line of thought. We have seen much of the difference between the three main types of thought; now we shall see what they have in common. It seems that their common points are at least three in number: (1) asceticism, (2) anti-intellectualism, and (3) mysticism.

(1) Asceticism

Professor Dewey said: " 'Give a dog a bad name and hang it'

Human nature has been the dog of the professional moralist, and consequences accord with the proverb."[143] This statement is true for all three philosophers we have just considered. But in giving the dog a bad name, they were not without reason. The reason is that they held the dog responsible for the suffering of this world.

Chuang Tzu considered the suffering of this world as due to the state of art, so he advised mankind to retain only the few instincts that are necessary to the natural man, and to give a bad name to, and to hang the other parts of, human nature, for the satisfaction of which we have civilization and progress. Plato considered this world as naturally a place of suffering, of error, and of mistake. So he advised mankind to retain only pure contemplation and pure thought, which he considered as pertaining to soul, but to give a bad name to, and to hang the other part of, human nature, the "dark horse," which he considered as chiefly related to body and as chiefly responsible for dragging the soul into its prison in this world of matter. Finally, Schopenhauer considered the suffering, the error, the mistake of this world as the necessary companion of will itself, of the soul itself. So he advised mankind to retain nothing, but to give a bad name to, and to hang everything in, human nature, both physical pleasures that pertain to the body, and mental thought that pertains to the soul. Thus, asceticism reached its climax and could go no further.

(2) Anti-Intellectualism

Next we come to anti-intellectualism. As the purest felicity cannot be attained in a sensuous way, so the highest truth cannot be attained through an intellectual procedure. We have seen that Chuang Tzu decidedly abandoned not only the conceptual world, but the perceptual world as well. Here I may remark in passing that in Chuang Tzu's time, intellectualism in Chinese philosophy was at its best. There was the school known as the "School of Logic." Hui Tzu, the leading figure of that school, was Chuang Tzu's most intimate friend. In the book of Chuang Tzu we find many of Hui Tzu's arguments with great perfection and sophistry. So, the main effort of Chuang Tzu's philosophy is to protest not only against utilitarianism of Mo Tzu and the institutionalism of Confucius, but also against the intellectualism of the "School of Logic."

143 John Dewey, *Human Nature and Conduct*, New York, 1922, P. 1.

Schopenhauer's anti-intellectualism is too obvious to need further comment. His distinction between transcendental and immanent knowledge,[144] and between intuitive and abstract knowledge, was carried through by Bergson who made the distinction between absolute and relative knowledge.[145] The central point of these arguments seems to be that the best way to get the perfect knowledge of a thing is to be one, to identify one's self with that thing. The subject, as Schopenhauer said, must pass entirely into the perceived object and thus become the object itself.[146]

Something must be said about Plato. Plato, as we have seen, was disappointed by this world, and tried to transfer the Socratic ideas which were methodological and scientific in point of view, referring to the world of discourse, to the absolute ideas, which are aesthetic, visible things and referring to the world of contemplation. Hoffding said:

> Contemplative natures are bent on gaining a conception of the whole in the light of which the relation between value and reality shall be made clear. Sometimes it is the need of the thought for comprehension, sometimes the need of the imagination for intuitive images which is the predominative factor. In Plato's doctrine of ideas he found satisfaction for both the needs; his spirit found rest in the contemplation of the eternal ideas which alone had true reality; in comparison with them the ever-changing world of science was finally regarded as mere illusion.... This type passed via Platonism into the Christian theology, where it may be recognized in Augustine.... Many of the representatives of this type believe that in this highest idea, or in the intellectual contemplation, which they regard as the highest, they have the highest science. This rests on an illusion, based on an insufficient inquiry into the conditions and limits of knowledge. When such spirits finally come to rest in philosophy, it is not philosophy as science, but as art.[147]

So Plato's dialectic, although he considered it as the true science, is in reality no longer scientific, but simply aesthetic. Whether his combination of the two methods can satisfy two kinds of human wants, or whether this very combination may not fail to satisfy either of these wants, we shall not discuss here. In any case we are justified in considering anti-intellectualism as one of the common characteristics of the "nature" line of thought.

(3) Mysticism

By mysticism we mean the experience which has been variously denoted by the names: ecstasy, rapture, illumination, revelation, and so forth. Speaking generally, this is an experience of the union of the individual with the whole. This is the experience which asceticism and anti-intellectualism lead to. We have seen that this line of thought talked much about the whole, the one, and the union of the individual with it. We naturally tend to ask: Are these statements

144 Schopenhauer, *The World as Will and Idea*, Vol. I, p. 224.

145 Bergson, H., Introduction to Metaphysics, tr. by T. E. Hulwe, New York, 1912, p.1

146 Schopenhauer, *The World as Will and Idea*, Vol. I, p. 232.

147 Hoffding, H., *Philosophy of Religion*, tr. by B. E Meyer, 2nd ed., London, 1914, pp.119, 120.

true? It seems that whether there is the whole or not, or whether, if there is a whole, the individual can internally unite with it or not, there are people who have had this kind of experience. That this experience to the experiencer is a state of insight into the depth of truth, unplumbed by the discursive intellect, and full of significance, importance, and authority,[148] is a matter of fact. Wishing to give it a bad name and hang it, people call this experience phantasy, dream, or neurological disease. But, granting that this experience is due to abnormal mental or physical condition of the subject, we still should not confuse the existential judgment with the spiritual judgment.[149] Our present position is that even if we know that this kind of experience has a low origin, we still should consider its high value; even though we do not consider it as a royal road to truth, we should still consider it as a royal road to happiness, at least to a kind of happiness.

---

148 Wm James, *The Varieties of Religious Experience*, New York, 1910, p. 380.

149 *Id.*, p. 4. <<changed author's name and title, based on Google>>

Part II

THE IDEALIZATION OF ART AND THE WAY OF INCREASE

We have seen that the characteristic of the "nature" line of thought is the common presupposition that, in the past, man had a paradise of some sort, which he lost through his own mistake. Now we are going to see that the common presupposition of the "art" line is just the opposite. Now the common presupposition is that, if there is any paradise at all, it is a paradise-to-be-gained, not a paradise lost. Fichte said:

> Even in the mere consideration of the world as it is, apart from the law (that is, the law that commands man to action), there arises within me the wish, the desire-no, not the mere desire, but the absolute demand-for a better and different world. I cast a glance on the present relation of men towards each other and towards nature; on the feebleness of their powers, the strength of their desire and passion, a voice within proclaims with irresistible conviction — it is impossible that it can remain thus; it must become different and better![150]

To gain the "different and better" is the purpose of the "art" line of thought. So far, all the philosophies belonging to this line agree. But, as to what that "different and better" is, they are far from agreeing. They do not agree as to what the paradise-to-be-gained is, although they agree that there can be and will be one. Some think that it is the state in which we can have the greatest amount of immediate pleasure, of easy-going amusement. Some think that it is a state in which we can have safety for life, wealth, and prosperity. Some think that it is a state in which we can have the most kinds of good with the least amount of sacrifice, and that this state is surely attainable if only we have enough knowledge, power, and progress. The first we call hedonism; the second, utilitarianism; the third, progressivism. In the following chapters historic systems have been chosen respectively to represent these three views.

150 Fichte, *The Vocation of Man*, Popular Works, tr. by W. Smith, 1st ed., London,1873, pp. 329,329.

V HEDONISM: YANG CHU

The representative we have chosen for hedonism is Yang Chu, whom we consider as the most persistent and thoroughgoing expounder of the supremacy of immediate pleasure. He was reported to be a disciple of Lao Tzu, and his doctrine was definitely mentioned in several works of the period of the Warring States.

His teaching has been preserved in one chapter in the work of Lieh Tzu, which bears the title of "Yang Chu." Although the genuineness of the Lieh tzu is still a matter of dispute, the said chapter is usually considered as representing hedonism in the history of ancient Chinese philosophy. In this connection, I shall have something further to say.

(I) Yang Chu's Connection with Taoism

It is an historical fact that the type of philosophy like pantheism is often liable to admit some materialistic interpretation. The similarity between Spinoza's philosophy and Taoism has already been mentioned above (pp. 14-16). Lao Tzu, the founder of Taoism, said "Nature is not benevolent."[151] Obviously, two different interpretations are possible in regard to this statement. The one is that Nature is spontaneity itself, so it has no desire or wish to be benevolent. It simply lets all things develop themselves. The other is that Nature is not benevolent, because it is a blind physical force. It produces the world not at all by design or will, but simply by necessity or chance. Obviously again, these two interpretations, if sufficiently developed, may lead to two systems of opposite character, both in theory and in practice. In the Lieh-tzu, we find both of these views. Certain chapters contain the same teaching as Chuang Tzu's, that is, the first view. In fact, many passages in these chapters are directly copied from Chuang Tzu. But other chapters take just the opposite view, the view of materialistic mechanism For instance, there is a chapter entitled "Effort and Destiny," in which one passage reads:

> Effort said to Destiny: "Your achievements are not equal to mine."
>
> "Pray, what do you achieve in the working of things," replied Destiny, "that you would compare yourself with me?"
>
> "Why," said Effort, "the length of man's life, his measure of success, his rank and his wealth, are all things which I have the power to determine."
>
> To this, Destiny made reply: "Peng Tsu's wisdom did not exceed that of Yao and Shun, yet he lived to the age of eight hundred. Yen Yuan's ability was not inferior to that of the average man, yet he died at the age of thirty-two.... If these results are compassed by your effort, how is it that you allotted long life to Peng Tsu and an untimely death to Yen Yuan; that you awarded discomfiture to the sage and success to the impious, humiliation to the wise man and high honors to the fool, poverty to the good and wealth to the wicked?"

151 Lao Tzu, *Tao Teh Ching*, Sec VI.

"If, as you say," rejoined Effort, "I have really no control over events, is it not, then, to your management that things turn out as they do?"

Destiny replied: "The very name Destiny shows that there can be no question of management in the case. When the way is straight, I push on; when it is crooked, I let be. Old age and early death, failure and success, high rank and humble station, riches and poverty — all these come naturally and of themselves. Of their ultimate causes, I am ignorant; how could it be otherwise?"[152]

Another passage in the same chapter reads:

Teng Hsi was a man who made [expounded] paradoxical doctrines and [engaged in] endless arguments. When Tzu Chan was the Premier and wrote the criminal laws in book form and enforced them in the State of Chang, Teng Hsi often argued with him about the laws and often annoyed him. Tse Chan then put Teng Hsi in prison and punished him, and later sentenced him to death. Tzu Chan wrote the laws in book form and enforced them, not because he could do it, but because he could not fail to do it. Teng Hsi annoyed Tzu Chan, not because he can do it, but because he cannot do it. Tzu Chan put Teng Hsi to death also not because he can do it, but because he cannot do it.[153]

Another passage in another chapter reads:

Mr. Tien, of the *Chi* State, was holding an ancestral banquet in his hall, to which a thousand guests were bidden. As he sat in their midst, many came up to him with presents of fish and game. Eyeing them approvingly, he exclaimed with unction: "How generous is Almighty God to man! He makes the five kinds of grain to grow, and creates the finny and the feathered tribes, especially for our benefit." All Mr. Tien's guests applauded this sentiment to the echo; but the twelve-year-old son of a Mr. Pao, regardless of seniority, came forward and said, "You are wrong, my lord. All the living creatures in the universe stand in the same category as ourselves, and one is of no greater intrinsic value than another. It is only by reason of size, strength, or cunning that some particular species gains the mastery, or that one preys upon another. None of them are produced in order to subserve the uses of others. Man catches and eats those that are fit for food; but how can it be maintained that God creates them expressly for man's use? Mosquitoes and gnats suck man's blood, and tigers and wolves devour his flesh; but we do not therefore assert that God created man expressly for mosquitoes and gnats, or to provide food for tigers and wolves."[154]

This is certainly a good illustration of the fact that "Nature is not benevolent," Mechanism reigns in the state of nature as well as in history, the realm of human activity. Free Will, design or purpose, either of God or of man, has no place at all in this view. It is thoroughly deterministic.

Whether this is Yang Chu's view or not, we shall see that his view as shown in the chapter that bears his name is somewhat like it. There is reason to

152 Lionel Giles, *Taoist Teaching from the Book of Lieh Tzu*, London, 1912, pp. 97-99

153 Lieh-tzu. This passage is omitted in Lionel Giles' translation.

154 Lionel Giles, *Taoist Teaching from the Book of Lieh Tzu*, London, 1912, pp. 119,120.

suppose that after the death of Lao Tzu, his followers, owing to the different interpretations of the meaning of "Tao," divided into two diametrically opposite schools, the one represented by Chuang Tzu, the other by Yang Chu, just as after the death of Socrates, his followers, owing to the different interpretation of the idea of good, divided into three schools, two of which were diametrically opposite: the Cynics and the Cyrenaics.

Then came a later *Tao*ist, who, seeing that both schools called themselves *Tao*ists, drew materials from both of them and composed the book, in the name of Lieh Tzu, whose existence still lacks historical proof. Without going further into the sphere of higher criticism, I think I am justified in choosing Yang Chu to represent the materialistic aspect of Taoism, which is hedonism.

(2) His View of Life

Now, let us first see what Yang Chu's view of life is. According to his view, life is short, and a great part of it is, strictly speaking, not life. He said:

> One hundred years is the limit of a long life. Not one in a thousand ever attains to it. Yet if they do, still unconscious infancy and old age take up about half this time. The time he passes unconsciously while asleep at night, and that which is wasted though awake during the day also amounts to another half of the rest. Again pain and sickness, sorrow and fear, fill up about a half, so that he really gets only ten years or so for his enjoyment. And even then there is not one hour free from some anxiety.[155]

Besides, there is absolutely no promise of an after life. He said:

> That in which all things differ is life, that in which they are all alike is death. During life there is the difference of intelligence and dullness, honor and meanness, but in death there is the equality of rottenness and putrefaction. Neither can be prevented. Although intelligence and dullness, honor and meanness exist, no human power can affect them, just as rottenness and putrefaction cannot be prevented.... Some die at the age of ten, some at one hundred. The wise and benevolent die as the cruel and imbecile. In life they are known as Yao and Shun [two sage emperors); dead, they are so many bones which cannot be distinguished. We ought, therefore, to hasten to enjoy life and pay no attention to death.[156]

This sentence is in fact *Yang* Tzu's whole philosophy. In this life nothing is real but enjoyment, which is indeed the only object and meaning of life.

We have seen that one of the chief characteristics of the "nature" line of thought is asceticism — that is, the suppression of desires.

Now we shall see that one of the chief characteristics of the "art" line of thought as here represented by Yang Chu, is just, I may say, anti-asceticism; that is, the satisfaction of desires. According to Yang Chu, we had no lost paradise in the past; we have only to look for the satisfaction of our desires in the future. The more desires are satisfied, the more is life worth living.

155 Anton Forke, *Yang Chu's Garden of Pleasure*, London, 1912, pp. 38, 39.
156 *Id.*, pp. 40, 41.

(3) Yang Chu's Art of Life

The following passage is an illustration of this point:

> Yen Ping-chung asked Kuan Yi-wu as to cherishing life. Kuan Yi-wu replied "It suffices to give it its free course, neither checking nor obstructing it." Yen Ping-chung said "And as to details?" Kuan Yi-wu replied, "Allow the ear to hear what it likes, the eye to see what it likes, the nose to smell what it likes, the mouth to say what it likes, the body to enjoy the comforts it likes to have, and the mind to do what it likes. Now what the ear likes to hear is music, and the prohibition of it is what I call obstruction to the ear. What the eye likes to look at is beauty, and it's not being permitted to regard this beauty I call obstruction of sight. What the nose likes to smell is perfume; and its not being permitted to smell I call obstruction to scent. What the mouth likes to talk about is right and wrong; and if it is not permitted to speak I call it obstruction of the understanding. The comforts the body enjoys to have are rich food and fine clothing; and if it is not permitted, then I call that obstruction of the senses of the body. What the mind likes is to be at peace; and its not being permitted rest I call obstruction of the mind's nature. All these obstructions are a source of the most painful vexation. Morbidly to cultivate this cause of vexation, unable to get rid of it, and so have a long but very sad life of a hundred, a thousand, or ten thousand years, is not what I call cherishing life. But to check this source of obstruction and with calm enjoyment to await death for a day, a month, or a year, or ten years, is what I understand by enjoying life."[157]

This is what Yang Chu considered as the royal road to happiness. In is a well-known fact that one of the chief difficulties in satisfying desires is that wherever desires are, there are also the conflicts of desires. In order to satisfy desires, the first thing for us to do is to make choice. In this passage Yang Chu seemed to have made no choice, but in fact he had already made one. He had made a choice between the desire for delicious food and the desire for permanent health. He had made a choice between the desire for free expression of passion and opinion and the desire for social approval. In each case, he preferred the desires that can be satisfied immediately to those which can be satisfied only in the long run. In each case he preferred the desires that can be easily satisfied to those which can be satisfied only with careful deliberation and troublesome preparation. In short, he wanted the pleasures that can be immediately realized, but not those that can be realized only with roundabout means. Perhaps the reason for his almost completely identifying enjoyment with physical pleasure is simply that among all kinds of pleasure, the physical one is the most easily available. His choice for the immediate pleasure is itself a means of avoiding pain.

---

157 *Id.*, pp. 43, 44.L

(4) Disregard of Social Regulations

Because of this reason Yang Chu showed great depreciation of social regulations. He thought with the Cyrenaics "that there was nothing naturally and intrinsically just, or honorable, or disgraceful, but that things were considered so because of law and fashion."[158] But law and fashion are the things, that, as Theodorus said, "Owe their existence to the consent of the fools."[159] They may have utility, but utility has meaning only in connection with the remote consequence. Disregard of remote consequence, the different kinds of law and social regulation are really the obstructions of pleasure and the sources of vexation. So, Yang Chu attacked them and taught that we should not be fooled by them.

Being warned and exhorted by punishments and rewards, urged forward and repelled by fame and laws, men are constantly rendered anxious. Striving for one glory during life and providing for splendor after death, they go their unpleasant ways, carefully considering what they should hear, should see, should do, and should think. So they lose immediate pleasure and cannot give way to their feelings. How do they differ from chained criminals?[160]

Thus:

> Po Yi was not without desire, but for wishing people to admire his purity, he was led to death by starvation. Chan *Chi* was not without sexual passion, but wishing people to admire his chastity, he remained childless. How purity and chastity lead men to miss the real good![161]

No doubt real good is the immediate pleasure.

Here we may say that the admiration of others or reputation are themselves sources of pleasure. This Yang Chu did not necessarily deny. But his point was that we should not sacrifice our immediate pleasure for fame or reputation, which could come to us only in the remote future or probably after our death. If it does come to us in the remote future time of our life, we surely have pleasure then. But how can that pleasure recompense our immediate sacrifice? If it comes to us only after our death, what would be the use of it? Yang Chu said:

> The world praises Shun, Yu, Duke Chow, and Confucius, and condemns Chieh and Chow.... All these four sages, while alive, had not one day's pleasure, and after their death [had] a reputation lasting many years. Yet reputation cannot bring back reality. You praise them, and they do not know it, and you honor them, and they are not aware of it. There is now no distinction between them and a clod of earth...These two villains [Chieh and Chow] while alive took delight in following their own inclination and desires, and after death were called fools and tyrants. Yet reality is nothing that can be given by reputation. Ignorant of censure and unconscious of praise, they differed in no respect from the stump of a tree or a clod of earth. The four sages, though objects of admiration, were troubled up to their very

158 Diogenes laertius, *The Lives and Opinions of Eminent Philosophers*, tr. by Younge, London, 1915, p. 91.

159 *Ibid.*

160 Cp. Anton Forke, *Yang Chu's Garden of Pleasure*, London, 1912, p. 39.

161 *Id.*, p. 41.

end, and were equally and alike doomed to die. The two villains, though detested and hated by many, remained in high spirits up to the very end, and they too were equally doomed to die.[162]

Therefore, why should we sacrifice immediate pleasure for unknown future fame?

(5) Disregard of Any Kind of Consequences

Thus Yang Chu's disregard of virtue and fame is simply an expression of his decisive preference for the immediate instead of the remote pleasure. His main point is that we should choose the immediate pleasure, no matter how bad the remote future consequence. Thus the following passage reads:

> Tuanmu Shu of Wei was descended from Tzu Kung. He had a patrimony of ten thousand gold pieces. Indifferent to the chances of life, he followed his own inclinations. He did all that human beings want to do. He enjoyed all that human beings desire to enjoy. With his walls and buildings, pavilions, verandas, gardens, parks, ponds and lakes, wine and food, carriages and dresses, women and attendants, he would emulate the princes of *Chi* and Chu in luxury. Whenever his passion desired something, or his ear wished to hear something, his eyes to see or his mouth to taste, he would procure it at all costs.... A hundred guests were entertained daily in his palace. In the kitchens there were always fire and smoke, and the vaults and the peristyle incessantly resounded with songs and music. The remains from his expenditure he divided first among his clansmen, then among his fellow citizens, then among the people throughout the kingdom.... Within a year he had disposed of all his fortune, and to his of spring he left nothing. When he fell ill, he had no means to buy medicines, and when he died, there was not even money for his funeral.... When Chin Ku-li[163] heard of this, he said: "Tuanmu Shu was a fool. He brought disgrace to his ancestors." When Tuan Kan-shen heard of this, he said: "Tuanmu Shu was a wise man; his excellence was much superior to his ancestors. This conduct shocked the common-sense people, but was in accord with the right reason. The gentleman of Wei only adhered to virtue and special regulation, so that they had not his insight."[164]

The worst consequence, however, that our human actions can entail, is death. The fear of death is certainly one of the chief factors that cause man to be careful in the present and to be anxious about the future. So one of the teachings of hedonism is that we should not care about death. We should escape from the fear of death with a kind of self-rationalization and pretended courage. In one of the passages quoted above, after Kuan Yi-wu told Yen Ping-chung about the art of cherishing life, he asked the latter to tell him what to do with death.

---

162 *Id.*, pp. 54-57.

163 Chin Ku-li was a famous disciple of Mo Tzu. He is also called Chin Tzu.

164 Cp. Forke, Anton "Yang Chu's Garden of Pleasure," London, 1912, pp. 49-51.From this passage we may also infer that Yang Chu, as well as some of the Cyrenaics and Epicureans, considered friendship as a source of pleasure.

Then Yen Ping-chung said, "To deal with death is very simple. What shall I say?" Kuan Yi-wu replied: "But I really wish to hear it." Yen Ping-chung answered: "What can I do when I am dead? They may burn my body or cast it into deep water, or bury it, or leave it unburied, or throw it wrapped up in a mat into some ditch, or cover it with princely apparel and embroidered garments and rest it in a stone sarcophagus. All that depends on mere chance." Kuan Yi-wu looked round at Paoshu Huang-tzu and said, "We two have made considerable progress in the doctrine of life and death."[165]

Another passage reads:

> Mengsun *Yang* asked Yang Chu: "There are men who take care of their bodies with the intention of grasping immortality. Is that possible?" Yang Chu replied: "According to the laws of nature there is no such thing as immortality." Mengsun *Yang* said, "Yet is it possible to acquire a very long life?" Yang Chu said, "According to the law of nature there is no such thing as a very long life.... All things were the same as they are now. The five passions [likes and dislikes] were of old as they are now. So also the safety and peril of the four limbs. Grief and joy for the things of this world were of old as they are now, and so are the constant changes of peace and revolution. Having seen, heard, and experienced all of these things, one would already be awearied of them at the age of one hundred. Why should he desire for more?"[166]

These passages remind us of Epicurus, who was reported to have said:

> Accustom yourself also to think death is a matter with which we are not at all concerned, since all good and all evil is sensation, and since death is only the privation of sensation. On which account, the correct knowledge of the fact that death is no concern of ours, makes the mortality of life pleasant to us, in as much as it sets forth no illimitable time, but relieves us of the longing for immortality. The most formidable of all evils, death, is nothing to us, since when we exist, death is not present to us, and when death is present, we have no existence.[167]

Thus there is nothing to be feared in death. If death is not to be feared, why should we fear any consequence of our action, that is not as bad as death?

As we should seek for immediate pleasure no matter what the bad consequences are in the future, so should we also avoid immediate pain, no matter what the good consequences are in the future?

Thus the following passage reads:

> Chin Ku-li asked Yang Chu: "If by pulling out a hair from your body, you can bring salvation to the world, would you do it?" Yang Chu answered "I surely cannot bring salvation to the whole world by simply pulling out a hair from my body. Chin Ku-li said "But suppose you can, would you do it?" Yang Chu gave no answer. Thereupon Chin Ku-Ii told Mengsun Yang,

165 *Id.*, pp. 44, 45.

166 *Id.*, pp. 51, 52.

167 Diogenes Laertius, *The Lives and Opinions of Eminent Philosophers*, tr. by Younge, London, 1915, p. 469.

who replied "I will explain to you the Master's meaning. "Supposing for tearing off a piece of your skin you were offered ten thousand gold pieces, would you do it?" Chin Ku-li said "I would" Mengsun *Yang* again asked "Supposing for cutting off one of your limbs you were to get a kingdom, would you do it?" Chin Ku-li was silent. "See now," said Mengsun Yang, "a hair is unimportant compared with skin, and the skin is also unimportant compared with a limb. However, many hairs put together form a skin, many skins form a limb. Therefore, though the skin is one of the ten thousand parts composing the body, how can it be disregarded?"[168]

Afterwards, Mencius said "The doctrine of the philosopher *Yang* was: 'each one for himself.' Though he might benefit the whole world by plucking out a single hair, he would not do it."[169] Since that time the above quotation from Yang Chu has been considered as his famous argument for egoism. The fact is that, although Yang Chu's doctrine is egoistic, this passage does not necessarily show that effect. The general trend of the argument shows that even if Chin Tzu (Chin Ku-Ii) would offer the whole world to Yang Chu himself for one of his hairs, Yang Chu still would not make the exchange. Thus this passage is simply an extreme statement of the teaching that we should not inflict any amount of pain upon ourselves, no matter how great the remote future gain is.

(6) The Salvation of the World

Of course this is an extreme theory. But in this Yang Chu saw the salvation of the world. If all people seek immediate pleasure only, then there will be no one so foolish as to struggle for wealth, power, domination and control, the pleasure of which can be gained only through troublesome preparation and tiresome means.

Then they will need nothing more than what they can possibly enjoy. As Chuang Tzu said:

> The tit, building its nest in the mighty forest, occupies but a single twig. The tapir stakes its thirst from the river but drinks enough to fill his belly.... So I have no need of the empire.[170]

And Yang Chu said:

> If the ancients by injuring a single hair could have rendered a service to the world, they would not have done it; and had the universe been offered to a single person, he would not have accepted it. As nobody would damage even a hair, and nobody would do a favor to the world, the world was in a perfect state.[171]

Of course this is too simple a way to solve the complex problems of the world. But seeing that a great part of the confusion of the world is due, not so much to the fact that there are too many people seeking immediate pleasure, as to the fact that there are too many seeking domination and control, we are inclined to think that there is a certain amount of truth and wisdom in Yang Chu's teaching.

---

168 Cp. Anton Forke, *Yang Chu's Garden of Pleasure*, London, 1912, pp. 53, 54.

169 Mencius, *Works*, Hook VII, Ch, XVI.

170 *Works*, Giles' translation, p. 6.

171 Anton Forke, *Yang Chu's Garden of Pleasure*, London, 1912, p 53.

(7) Concluding Remarks

So much for the hedonism of Yang Chu. In comparison with the philosophies of the West, Yang Chu agreed in detail with the Cyrenaics, but with the Epicureans in principle only. The Cyrenaics, as reported by Diogenes Laertius, taught that corporeal pleasures were superior to mental ones, and corporeal sufferings worse than mental ones.[172]

The banishment of pain, as it is called by Epicurus, appears to the Cyrenaics not to be pleasure; for neither is the absence of pleasure, pain; for both pleasure and pain consist in motion; and neither the absence of pleasure nor the absence of pain is motion.[173]

Thus, according to the Cyrenaics, pleasure must be something positive, something produced by human efforts to satisfy human desires. We have seen that this is exactly what Yang Chu taught.

As shown above, one of the chief difficulties in satisfying the desires is that we have to make choices. Although Yang Chu and the Cyrenaics have made a careful consideration and a reasonable choice, yet there are still difficulties. Granted that we should prefer the immediate to the 'remote pleasure,' yet even so there are still conflicts among the desires as well as among the individuals. Yang Chu supposed that if all people sought only the immediate pleasure, they would get all of the pleasures and every one would get them all, and thus the world would be in a perfect, ideal state. He seemed to overlook a most obvious fact. As Chuang Tzu's philosophy is a naive idealization of nature, so Yang Chu's is a naïve idealization of art.

We are not going to criticize the theory that we should seek only the immediate pleasure, and should absolutely pay no attention to the remote future consequences, for by principle Yang Chu preferred one day's life of pleasure to a hundred years' life of anxiety and care. We simply point out that pleasure, no matter how immediate it is, is an end. In realizing the end, one has to use some means, which may at some time be tiresome. He who wants to get some end without any sacrifice, after all but defies himself. Thus, Watson, in criticizing the Cyrenaics, said:

> The theory virtually admits that to obtain the end we must not seek it. We desire pleasure, but when we set about getting it, we are compelled to entertain unwelcome and unexpected guests. Let us "take the goods the gods provide us" and make the most of them." The longest way round is the shortest way home.'[174]

Thus, in the West, Epicurus modified the Cyrenaic doctrine and admitted that the absence of pain and the tranquility of mind are themselves pleasure. "The state of the pleased enjoyment, which may be made habitual by the man who aims at true pleasure, i.e., at that state of contentment which comes to the man who is free from an unreasoning dread of imaginary evils, and who confines

172 Diogenes laertius, *The Lives and Opinions of Eminent Philosophers*, tr by Younge, London, 1915, p. 90.

173 *Ibid.*

174 John Watson, *Hedonistic Theories*, from Aristipus to Spencer, London, 1895, p. 42.

his desires within reasonable limit"[175] is now considered as the best state that man can enjoy. Indeed, Yang Chu incidentally also held this view. Yang Chu said:

> Yuan Hsieh lived in mean circumstances in Lu, while Tzu Kung amassed wealth in Wei. Poverty galled the one, and riches caused uneasiness to the other. So poverty will not do, nor wealth either. But what, then, will do? I answer. "Enjoy life and take one's ease, for those who know how to enjoy life are not poor, and he that lives at ease requires no riches."[176]

This spirit is more Epicurean than Cyrenaic.

But if the Epicurean life were realized, men would be in a state in which they would have no faith in the past, no hope in the future, but would only await, quietly indeed, the natural dissolution of their body, which is death. This may be a good state, but it is already sad. Under the surface of melancholy pleasure, there seems to be a strong undercurrent of genuine pessimism.

175 *Id.*, p. 67.

176 Anton Forke, *Yang Chu's Garden of Pleasure*, London, 1912, p.42

VI UTILITARIANISM: MO ZTU

Thus hedonism eventually defies itself. This world is after all a very poor one, for here we must obey the injunction: "In the sweat of thy face shalt thou eat bread."[177] In order to get pleasure, or to avoid pain, in one word, to satisfy our desires, we need the means. The supposition that we can satisfy our desires without means is too optimistic a view of this world. Hedonism was closely connected with pessimism in the end, because it had been too closely connected with optimism in the beginning.

We are going to study another type of philosophy, which, in opposition to hedonism, taught that we should sacrifice any kind of immediate enjoyment for the greatest future pleasure. In opposition to hedonism, this type emphasizes the means for realizing and securing the future end. Hence it talks not so much of pleasure as of "benefit," "utility," etc. Hence it is known as utilitarianism.

(1) The Significance of Mo Tzu

To represent this type we have chosen Mo Tzu's philosophy, which we consider as the most systematic utilitarianism of ancient times. His significance in the general utilitarian philosophy is just that of Bentham as Stephen considered it. About Bentham, Stephen said:

> The writings in which Bentham deals explicitly with the general principle of ethics would hardly entitle him to a higher position than that of a disciple of Hume without Hume's subtlety; or of Paley, without Paley's singular gift of exposition. Why, then, did Bentham's message come upon his disciples with the force and freshness of new revelation? Our answer must be in general terms that Bentham founded not a doctrine, but a method; and that the doctrine, which came to him simply as a general principle, was in his hands a potent instrument applied with most fruitful results to questions of immediate interest.[178]

It was not the bare appeal to utility, but the attempt to follow the clue of utility systematically and unflinchingly into every part of the subject. This one doctrine gives the touchstone, by which every proposed measure is to be tested?[179]

It is also in this that exists Mo Tzu's excellence. As we shall see, Mo Tzu not only gave us an abstract principle of utility, by a complete structure of society, state, and religion that was built upon that principle. But I must say further that I have chosen him not only for his excellence. In his system, there is a strong element of materialism with which most of the old utilitarian systems are connected. We hope Mo Tzu may be a good illustration of both the excellence and defects of utilitarianism.

177 Gen. 3: 19.

178 Leslie Stephen, *The English Utilitarians*, London, 1900, 3 vols., Vol. 1, p. 236.

179 *Id.*, p. 268.

(2) The General Principle of Utility

Bentham said:

> Nature has placed mankind under the governance of two sovereign masters, pain and pleasure. It is for them alone to point out what we ought to do, as well as to determine what we shall do.[180]

The *principle* of utility recognizes this subjection, and assumes it for the foundation of that system, the object of which is to tear the fabric of felicity by the hands of reason and law.[181]

We shall see that this is exactly what Mo Tzu did. In his work, however, he did not speak so much of pleasure and pain as of their objective counterparts: benefit and harm. As he said "Benefit is what we are pleased to have. Harm is what we dislike to have."[182]

What Bentham called reason, Mo Tzu called intellect. Desire is always blind. To guide it in the right direction is the function of the intellect. Mo Tzu said:

> If a man desires to cut his finger, and his intellect does not foresee the harm, it is the fault of the intellect. But if the intellect makes a careful consideration and foresees all the harmful consequences, but the desire still wants to cut, then it is the desire that makes the man suffer.[183]

Thus the function of intellect is to foresee the consequences of the present action. By foreseeing the consequence, the intellect can lead us to guide and control our desires to struggle for the remote good and to avoid the remote evil. By foreseeing the consequence, the intellect can measure the incompatible benefits and harms in the immediate and remote future and thus lead the desires to an adjustment. Mo Tzu said:

> To measure the importance and unimportance of what happened to us is called measurement. Measurement is not necessarily to decide that the one is intrinsically right and the other is intrinsically wrong. Measurement is simply adjustment. To cut off the finger in order to save the arm is to take the greatest of the benefits and the smallest of the harms. To take the smallest of the harms is not to take the harm, but to take the benefit, because what we now take is not in the control of our own will. For instance, when a man meets a robber, he is compelled to cut his finger in order to save his life. The act of cutting his finger is beneficial; only the fact that he meets the robber is harmful.... In adjusting the incompatible conflicts we take the greatest of the benefits, because we will; but we take the smallest of the harms, because we must.[184]

Here we see the great difference between hedonism and utilitarianism. Now it is not the immediate, but the greatest benefit, that we should choose; not the immediate, but the greatest harm that we should avoid.

---

180 Jeremy Bentham, *An Introduction to the Principles of Morals and Legislation*, Oxford, 1907, p. 7.

181 *Id.*, pp 1, 2.

182 Mo Tzu *Works*, Chap. XL.

183 *Id.*, Chap. XLII.

184 *Id.*, Chap. XLIV.

(3) The External Standard

We have seen that, according to hedonism, the only standard for judging good and evil is subjective feeling. There is no external standard; nor is there any need of it. But according to utilitarianism, a standard of action must be an external standard; otherwise, it is not a standard at all. As Bentham said:

> What one expects to find in a principle is something that points out some external consideration, as a means of warranting and guiding the internal sentiments of approbation and disapprobation; the expectation is but ill fulfilled by a proposition, which does neither more nor lees than hold up each of those sentiments as a ground and standard for itself.[185]

And Mo Tzu said:

> For argument we must establish a standard. If we argue without a standard, it is just like calculating the time of morning and night on a constantly shifting dial. We cannot know clearly whether it is right or wrong, beneficial or harmful, for testing an argument there must be three standards. What are these three standards? They are to trace it, to examine it, and to use it. Where trace it? Trace it in the authority of the ancient philosopher kings. Where examine it? Examine it in the facts, which the common people see and hear. Where use it? Put it into practice and see whether it is useful to the benefit of the country and the people. These are the three standards for argument.[186]

These three standards are certainly external and objective enough.

The first standard seems to indicate that Mo Tzu considered authority as an important factor in determining value. The fact is that ancient authority is a factor, because it represents the experience of the past, just as the second represents the experience of the present, and the third represents the experience of the future. The following quotation may serve as an illustration:

> In an argument with Cheng Tzu, Master Mo Tzu quoted from Confucius. Cheng Tzu said "You are against Confucius. Why do you still quote from him?" Master Mo Tzu said: "This is what agrees with fact and therefore what you cannot change. When a bird feels the weather is hot, it goes upward. When the fish feels the weather is hot, it goes downward. Even Yu and Tang[187] could not advise them to do otherwise. We must admit that the bird and fish are ignorant. But Yu and Tang must follow them. Why cannot I quote from Confucius?"[188]

Thus Mo Tzu went back to authority only when the authority was in agreement with fact. He went back to the past only when it could throw light on the future, as he said: "When we cannot reach a decision in our deliberation, we examine the past in order to know the future."[189]

185 Bentham, *An Introduction to the Principles of Morals and Legislation*, p. 16.

186 Mo Tzu, *Works*, Chap. XXXV.

187 Yu and Tang were two philosopher kings.

188 Mo Tzu, *Works*, Chap. XLVIII.

189 *Id.*, Chap. X VIII.

(4) The "Pragmatic" Method

Among the three standards, however, the most important is the third. We are going to see that in the construction of his ideal society and state. Mo Tzu evaluated everything by its utility for the benefit of the country and the people. Anything that could not pass the test of this standard, he rejected without the least hesitation. Here we have cited a few quotations to illustrate the general application of what may be called his "pragmatic" method. He said: I asked the Confucians wherefore they should have music, and they answered "Music is an amusement." I said to them: "You have not answered my question. If I asked you why you should build a house and you said it was built for protection against cold in winter and heat in summer, and for the separate dwelling of persons of different sex, you would then tell me why you built the house. Now I asked you why you should have music, and you said, "Music is an amusement." That is equivalent to saying that a house is to be a house.[190]

The Duke of *Chi* asked Confucius about government. The latter answered that good government is that which draws people from afar and reforms what has become obsolete. Commenting on this conversation Mo Tzu said "The Duke did not know how to ask the question, nor did Confucius give a correct answer. Could it be that the Duke did not even know that the ideal of government was to draw people from afar and rejuvenate that which has become obsolete? He really wanted to know how to accomplish this. Wherefore Confucius told him only what he had already learned, but not that which he wanted to know."[191]

The doctrine that can be put into practice is to be honored. That which cannot be put into practice is but a group of words.[192]

Obviously Mo Tzu must have had a very pragmatic theory of the meaning of meaning. The questions, "What is music?" and "What is the use of music?" are to him really the same. When the Confucians told him that music was an amusement, he was not satisfied, because amusement is only an immediate pleasure, but has no use in regard to the future. Therefore music simply had no meaning to him. Again, if a theory or principle is to have any value, it must be practical and must be accompanied by a method of practice. Otherwise it is simply a kind of intellectual exercise, which may produce a kind of immediate pleasure, but, according to Mo Tzu, has absolutely no future utility.

(5) What Is the Greatest Benefit to the People?

Thus everything, in order to have value, must be useful to the country and the people. But what is that benefit specifically and concretely? According to Mo Tzu, it consists of two things: wealth and population. According to Mo Tzu, every measure of the government must have the increase of these two in view as its purpose. It is the increase of these two that constitutes the essence of a good government. He said:

190 *Id.*, Chap. XLVIII.

191 *Ibid.*

192 *Ibid.*

When a philosopher king governs a country, the wealth of the country can be doubled. When he governs the world, the wealth of the world can be doubled. It is doubled not at the expense of others, but by utilizing the country and by cutting off useless expenditure.... What is it that is not easy to be doubled? It is the population that is not easy to be doubled. But there is a way to double it. The philosopher king had a law saying: "When the boy is twenty years old, he must have a home; when the girl is fifteen years old, she must have her man." This is the law of the philosopher kings. When the philosopher kings disappeared from the world, the people began to act according to their own desires. Those who desire to marry early, marry when they are twenty years old. Those who desire to marry late, marry when they are forty years old. On the average, people marry ten years later than the age fixed by the philosopher kings. On the average, one couple produce one child in every three years; then three children would have to be produced within this ten years. Therefore, if we make a law that all should marry early, how can the population fail to be doubled?[193]

This passage is also a good sample of the utilitarian calculation, which hedonism never takes the pains to make. Thus, identifying the increase of wealth and population with the greatest benefit to the country and the people, Mo Tzu went on to fight against anything that had no direct utility to it. In the first place he was against any kind of luxury. He said:

The ancient philosopher kings established the law of the economy of expenditure. It says: "All the artisans in the world ... should manufacture articles according to their respective arts. These articles should not be for the purpose of luxury, but only for the use of the people. Those things that increase the expenditure, but not the benefit of the people are not to be tolerated by the philosopher kings.... The law in regard to manufacturing clothes says: "In winter people wear silk, because it is light and warm. In summer, people wear refined grass clothes, because they are light and cool. This is enough. Others that increase the expenditure, but not the benefit of the people, must not be tolerated by the philosopher kings."[194]

Mo Tzu was also against the Confucian teaching of the luxurious way of burying the dead and the three years' mourning on occasion of the death of parents. He said:

I calculate the result of the long period of mourning and therefore the long period of the interruption in the people's work is as follows: The wealth that people had in the past was buried with the dead. The wealth that they would have in the future is impossible to be got because of their inability to work. To use this for increasing wealth is just like asking one to seek a harvest and at the same time forbid him to plow.... This also interrupts very much the sexual intercourse between man and woman. To use this for increasing population is just like asking man to seek for long life

193 *Id.*, Chap. XX.

194 *Ibid.*

by committing suicide... Therefore, if those who hold the theory of the luxurious way of burying the dead and of a long period of mourning should govern the country, the country must become poor, the population must become small, and politics must become corrupted.[195]

He was also against music. He said:

People have three troubles: those who are hungry, but have no food; those who are cold, but have no clothes and those who are tired, but cannot rest. These are the three great troubles of the people. Even if you, for them, strike the great bell and beat the drum ... can they get the wealth for their food and clothes? I think not. Now the great nations attack the small ones; the great families exploit the small ones... All these confusions no one can stop. Even if you for them strike the great bell and beat the drum ... can you with this turn the turmoil of the world into peace? I think not. Therefore, music has no value in increasing the benefit, and in avoiding the harm of the world. Therefore it is wrong to have music.... If the men like music they must lose their time from planting and plowing. If the women like music, they must lose their time from spinning and sewing. If the governors like music, they must play music at the expense of the wealth, which should be used for the food and clothes of the people.... Therefore it is wrong to have music.[196]

When Mo Tzu spoke of music, he meant all that belongs to the same category. He meant to go against all of what we now call the fine arts. This step probably represents Mo Tzu's decisive attitude of opposing nature with the cold intellect. From the point of view of intellect, fine arts are really of no value at all, nay, they are simply nonsense. From the point of view of intellect, the mourning for the dead is another example of childish nonsense, as is shown by the following quotation:

Kung Mung-tzu said "The three years' mourning is an expression of our infantile feeling, which is the endless longing for the parents." Master Mo Tzu said: "The child has no other knowledge besides the longing for parents. Therefore, when its parents are absent, it continues to cry. The cause of this fact is its extreme ignorance. The Confucians are not even wiser than a child."[197]

According to Mo Tzu, the intellect should assume supreme control of our desire as well as our feeling. How different is Mo Tzu from Yang Chu who taught that we should give to our desire and feeling absolutely free expression! Here again we meet the chief difference between hedonism and utilitarianism.

(6) The Universal Love

So much for Mo Tzu's arguments against all sorts of luxury and all sorts of refinement. These, however, are not yet the greatest harms in the world. The greatest harm to the increase of wealth and population is that there is no peace.

---

195 *Id*, Chap. X X V.

196 *Id.*, Chap. XII.

197 Id., Chap. XLVIII

Mo Tzu said:

At the present time, what are to be accounted as the greatest harms of this world? They are such as the attacking of small states by the great ones; the inroads on small families by great ones; the plunder of the weak by the strong; the oppression of the few by the many.... These are the harms of the world. Again, the fact that the prince is not benevolent, that the minister is not loyal, that the father has no parental love, and that the son has no filial piety, are also the harms of the world. Again the fact that the common people rob and injure each other with the sword, poison, water, and fire is also a harm of the world. Let us ask whence all these harmful things arise. Is it from loving others and benefiting others? It must be replied: "No," and it must likewise be said: "They arise clearly from hating others and doing harm to others." Do those who hate and do harm to others hold the principle of loving all, or that of distinctions between man and man? It must be replied: "They make distinctions." So then it is the principle of making distinctions between man and man, which gives rise to all that are most harmful to the world. On this we conclude that that principle is wrong.... There is a principle of loving all, which is able to change that which makes distinctions.... If the princes were as much for other states as for their own, which one among them would raise force in his state to attack that of another? He is for that as much as for his own.... So then it is the principle of universal mutual love, which gives rise to all that is beneficial to the world. On this account we conclude that that principle is right.... Others may say: "It is good, but it is extremely hard to be put into practice." If it is really impossible to be put into practice, even I myself will consider that principle as wrong. But how can it be good, and yet incapable of being put into practice? ... I apprehend there is no one under heaven, man or woman, however stupid, though he may condemn the principle of universal love, but would at such a time [the most dangerous time] make one who holds to it the subject of his trust.

I apprehend there is no one under heaven, man or woman, however stupid, though he may condemn the principle of universal love, but would at such a time [the most dangerous time] prefer the one to be the sovereign who holds to it.[198]

Thus Mo Tzu found out the chief source of the trouble of the world and also a way to deal with it, which is his famous doctrine of universal love. This principle is not only beneficial to others, but to those as well who hold to it. In Mo Tzu's book, three chapters are devoted to describing the harm of war. War is not only harmful to the conquered, but to the conqueror as well. He said:

Though four or five nations have been benefited by war, that does not make war a practical policy. Let us take an illustration from the profession of medicine. Here is a medicine which cures four or five patients out of ten thousand to whom it has been applied. We cannot, therefore, call it a practical medicine. No dutiful son will apply it to his parents, nor [will] a faithful servant applies it to his master.[199]

---

198 *Id.*, Chap. XVI.

199 *Id.*, Chap. XVIII.

The best principle is therefore "the greatest happiness of the greatest number."

(7) Religious Sanction

Although the salvation of the world lies in the principle of universal love, Mo Tzu did not consider that men by nature love each other. In his book there is a chapter entitled "What Is Dyed," in which one passage reads:

> Master Mo Tzu saw one dyeing silk. He sighed and said "Dyed in blue, the silk becomes blue: dyed in yellow, the silk becomes yellow. What it enters changes, it changes its color accordingly. By entering five times, it turned to five colors. Therefore, it is necessary to take care of the dyeing.[200]

Following this he cited a long list of facts to show how some men become good by associating with good men, and others become bad by associating with bad men. Human nature seems to him to be a tabula rasa and its color depends entirely on how it is dyed.

People should be "dyed" with the principle of universal love and be told that this is the only road to reach the fulfillment of their own interests. But this is not enough. Men are too shortsighted to see their own interest; they cannot be convinced that loving others is beneficial to themselves and that selfishness can only do harm.

So Mo Tzu, like Bentham, emphasized the "sanctions," the "binding force,"[201] of the principle of universal love. He embodied the principle in a personified God. He said:

> Those who desire wealth and honor, must obey the will of God.
>
> Those who obey the will of God to love each other and to benefit each other, will receive the reward. Those who disobey the will of God in hating each other and doing harm to each other, will receive the punishment.[202]

It is so, because God loves the people, and it is His Will that they should love each other accordingly.

But how can we know that God loves the people? We know that because He enlightens them all. How do we know that He enlightens them all? We know that because He has them all. How do we know that He has them all? We know that because He receives sacrifices from them all. How do we know that He receives sacrifices from them all? We know that because among all within the four seas who eat human food, there is none who does not offer oxen, sheep, dogs and pigs, rice and wine, to honor God the most High and the spirits. All people are the subjects of God; why does He not love them? Besides, I said that he who kills one innocent must have bad fortune. Who kills the innocent? Man. Who imposes the bad fortune? God. If you say that God does not love the people, why in the case of homicide does God punish the unjust with bad fortune? Therefore, I know that God loves all the people of the world.[203]

This is certainly a very poor argument to prove the existence of God and His

---

200 *Id.*, Chap. IIIL.

201 Bentham, *An Introduction to the Principles of Morals and Legislation*, p. 25.

202 Mo Tzu, *Works* Chap. X X V L.

203 *Id*, Chap. XXVI.

benevolence and His power. But Mo Tzu, as the most practical philosopher of the world, had no interest at all in pure metaphysical truth. He would be quite satisfied if his religious sanction could induce the people to act in accordance with the principle of universal love.

For this purpose, however, it seemed to him that one God is not sufficient. Besides God there are the spirits who have the same function of rewarding the good and punishing the bad as God. He said:

> The philosopher kings disappeared. Now in the world, might is right. The sovereigns are not benevolent; the ministers are not loyal.
>
> The fathers have no parental love; the sons have no filial piety. The younger pay no respect to the elder; the elder take no care of the younger.... The people become adulterous and cruel. Having turned into thieves and robbers, they kill the innocent on the highways with swords, poison, fire, and water in order to steal their carts, horses, clothes, and furs for their own benefit. What is the cause of this? The cause is that people doubt the existence of ghosts and spirits, and do not know that they reward good men and punish the bad. If all people of the world believe that ghosts and spirits can reward good men and punish the bad, how can the world be in disorder?[204]

This passage is a good sample of Mo Tzu pragmatic argument for the existence of anything that he considered as useful. From this passage, however, it does not follow that people should make no effort to struggle for their own happiness, but only bribe the spirits and ask their favor. The following passage is an illustration:

> Master Mo Tzu was sick. Ti Pi came and asked, "You, Master, teach that the spirits are wise and can reward good men and punish the bad. Now, you are a sage; how can you be sick? I suppose that you have done something wrong, or that the spirits are not wise." Master Mo Tzu said "Although I am sick, it does not follow that the spirits are not wise. There are many ways through which people can be sick. Some become sick on account of the cold or hot weather; some become sick on account of overwork. The house has one hundred doors. If you shut only one of them, the thieves can still come in easily."[205]

Thus in spite of the fact that there are Gods and spirits, men still need to help themselves; and, indeed, God and the spirits help only those who help themselves.

For the same pragmatic reason, Mo Tzu also denied the theory of predestination. Reward and punishment either by God or by the state are the results of men's voluntary action. If the world is not free, men will not be responsible for their evil doing, and will not be encouraged to do well. They will think, as Mo Tzu said:

> He who is punished is predestined to be punished but not because he is bad. He who is rewarded is predestined to be rewarded, but not because he is good. Therefore, if one becomes a prince, he will not be righteous; if one becomes a minister, he will not be loyal.[206]

---

204 *Id.*, Chap. XXXI.

205 *Id*, Chap. XLVIII.

206 *Id.* Chap. XXXVI.

And Mo Tzu said elsewhere: "Teaching people to learn and preaching the doctrine of fatalism is like letting man cover his head and at the same time uncover it."[207]

(8) The Political Sanction

The whole force of religious sanction, however, is not sufficient. In order to secure peace and prosperity in the world, we need not only a God and many spirits in Heaven, but also a "Leviathan" on earth. Mo Tzu's whole political philosophy really reminds us of that of Hobbes. Mo Tzu said:

> In ancient times, when mankind had just begun to enter into the world and had no political association, every one had his own standard of right and wrong If there was one man, there was one standard; if two, two standards, if ten, ten standards; the more men, the more standards. Every one considered his own standard as right and that of others as wrong. Therefore people were against each other. There were hate and aversion, even among father and son and brothers. There were distinction and separation, but no harmony and unity. The people killed each other with water, fire, and poison. They would not help each other even when they had spare energy. They made no gifts to others, even when they had spared wealth. They would not teach each other, even when they had high wisdom. The world was in great disorder; the people were like birds and beasts. They knew that the reason of the disorder was that there was no leader. Therefore, they elected a wise and able man to be their emperor.... Then the emperor ordered the people, saying: "If you hear what is good and what is not good, tell all of it to your superior. What your superior considers as right, all of you must consider as right; what your superior considers as wrong, all of you must consider as wrong."[208]

This shows that in what Hobbes called the "natural condition of mankind,"[209] there were great confusion and great misery. Only through the "social contract" did people surrender their "natural right" to the sovereign in order to secure peace.[210] They surrendered because they had to, not because they would.

Now what is it that the emperor considers as good? Mo Tzu said:

> The emperor made a proclamation to the people of the world, saying: "If you see any one who loves and benefits the world, you must report to your superior. If you do this, that means you also love and benefit the world. The superior will reward you and the doer; the people will admire you and the doer. If you see any one who does harm to the world, you must report to your superior. If you do not do this, that means you also do harm to the world. Your superior will punish you and the doer; the people will blame you and the doer." Therefore, all the people in the world, wishing to receive the reward and the approval, and to avoid the punishment and the disapproval of the superior, report to him all the good and the bad actions.

207 *Id.*, Chap. XLVI.
208 *Id.*, Chap. XI.
209 Thomas Hobbes, *Leviathan*, Everyman's Ed., pp. 63, 64.
210 *Id.*, pp. 67, 68.

> Then the emperor is in a position to reward all good men and punish all the bad. If all the good are rewarded and all the bad punished, the world will be in perfect peace.[211]

Since the chief cause of the confusion in the natural world is the fact that there are too many standards of right and wrong, so after the establishment of the state, there should be no other standard of right and wrong except the order of the sovereign; there should be no social sanction except political sanction. The following passage may make this point clearer: Mo Tzu said:

> Now in the state why is it that the superior cannot control the inferior, and the inferior does not obey the superior, and they thus fight among themselves? The cause of this is that there is no unity in the standard of right and wrong.... If one man receives the reward from his superior, but at the same time also the disapproval of the people, then reward will not be able to encourage him to do good.... If he receives the punishment from the superior, but at the same time the approval of the people, then the punishment will not be able to discourage him from doing bad. So I calculate that the cause of the fact that the reward of the superior cannot encourage the good, and that the punishment of the superior cannot discourage the bad is that there are too many standards.[212]

This statement is the same as that of Hobbes when he described "the diseases of the Commonwealth," "that proceed from the poison of the seditious doctrines; whereof one is, that every private man is judge of good and evil actions."[213]

Mo Tzu's theory is "to agree upward, but not downward or otherwise." He proposed that first of all the members of the family must consider the head of the family as the supreme judge of right and wrong. Then the heads of the family must consider the prince of the state as the supreme judge, and unify the standards of their family to "agree upward" with the prince. Then the princes must consider the emperor as the supreme judge and in turn unify the standards of their state to "agree upward" with the emperor. Then the emperor must again consider God as the supreme judge and unify the standards of the world to "agree upward" with Him. Thus in Mo Tzu's ideal state, just as in that of Hobbes, there is uniformity but nothing else. Hsun Tzu afterwards said "Mo Tzu had vision in uniformity, but not in individuality,"[214] This criticism seems to be justified.

It is to be noticed that although Mo Tzu said that God wants people to be so and so, yet as shown above, through the hierarchy of "agreeing upward," only the emperor is in a position to "agree' with God. The net result is that the emperor governs in the name of God and the people can only obey the emperor. Thus both the social and religious sanctions are subordinated to political sanction. We know that one of the teachings of Hobbes's "Leviathan" is that the church, as a lawmaking or governing body, must be fused with the State; otherwise the sovereignty will be fatally split. He also argued that the fact that the people obey

211 Mo Tzu, *Works*, Chap. XI.

212 *Id.*, Chap. XIIL

213 Hobbes, *Leviathan*, Everyman's Ed., p. 172.

214 Hsun Tzu, *Works*, Chap. XVII.

their private inspiration or faith instead of the law is one of the causes of the dissolution of the Commonwealth.[215] In Mo Tzu the absoluteness of the Will of God and that of the will of the sovereign are combined and thus reconciled by the teaching that only the sovereign can "agree upward" with God and that God can speak only through the sovereign. Instead of an absolute monarchy, he taught an absolute theocracy. But anyway, he was in perfect accordance with Hobbes in that sovereignty must be one and the Leviathan must be all-powerful.

(9) Concluding Remarks

We have seen that one obvious fact overlooked by hedonism is the conflict between the different individuals in seeking pleasure. It thought, therefore, that we can get along without state, law, or virtue, but Mo Tzu fully recognized the weakness of man. He first set up an objective standard. But any standard, no matter how concrete and objective it is, if it is only a principle, can always be subjected to different interpretations and applications, and therefore is not objective enough. Besides, it has no force to control the uncertainty of human nature. Therefore, he devised to embody the abstract principle in a personified God in Heaven and a monarchical sovereign on earth, who, with the sanctions of pleasure and pain, that is, reward and punishment, can induce the people to take the right, way to their own greatest benefit.

Here we see the full significance of the old controversy of nature versus convention in the history of Greek philosophy. According to the convention theory, man came to the world from a low origin, and had no root of virtue in his nature. He was virtuous only when he had faced the sheer necessity that he could not be otherwise. To use the expression of deterministic Taoism, man established state, society, law, and virtue, not because he could do so but because he could not but do so. Mo Tzu, in opposition to Yang Chu, gave complete justification to social institutions, because he had a conviction of the iron necessity that drives man from behind, because he considered them as the indispensable means to secure remote future pleasure.

The teaching that we should sacrifice everything for the increase of wealth and population may seem strange at first glance. But if we reflect upon the modern theory of evolution and the recent theory of psychoanalysis, this teaching is not strange at all. What does the theory of evolution teach but that all living beings struggle for the preservation of the individual and the preservation of the race? What does the theory of psychoanalysis teach, but that the chief drives of our life are the egoistic and sexual impulse? Mo Tzu taught the simple fact that we should subordinate all to, and sacrifice all for, these two fundamental instinctive desires. He taught the simple fact that every man should have a full stomach, that he should keep the body warm, and that he should produce children in order that the human race may be preserved.

Mo Tzu devised the doctrine of universal love and many other means to enforce this great end of the human race. Of course the fundamental conception of

215 Hobbes, *Leviathan*, Everyman's Ed., p. 172.

the teaching is not only a truth, but also a truism. But that we should sacrifice every kind of immediate enjoyment for that end only is certainly too utilitarian a theory. I say it is too utilitarian, because it pays too much attention to the future. It is in this sense that Mo Tzu's philosophy is the best illustration of the defect of utilitarianism. As Yang Chu paid too little attention to future consequences, Mo Tzu had too great anxiety about it. Hsun Tzu afterwards said "Mo Tzu was blinded by utility and did not know refinement"[216] And Chuang Tzu said:

> Man will sing, but he [Mo Tzu] condemns singing; man will wail, but he condemns wailing; man will express joy, but he condemns such expression. Is this truly in accordance with man's nature? Through life toil, and at death niggardliness; causing man sorrow and melancholy and being difficult to be carried into practice; I fear it cannot be regarded as the way of the sages. Contrary to the mind of man, man will not endure it. Though Mo Tzu himself might be able to endure it, how is the aversion of the world to it to be overcome?[217]

This was Chuang Tzu's prophecy of the failure of Mohism, and this prophecy was fulfilled.

Mo Tzu, however, did not consider refinement, luxury, and the things that give man immediate pleasure, as intrinsically bad. This was to be expected from a utilitarian philosopher. A passage in a book of the second century made this point very dear. In this passage Mo Tzu is represented as holding a conversation with one of his famous disciples, Chin Ku-Ii [Chin Tzu]; the conversation reads:

> In a year of famine, one wishes to give you a pearl which cannot be sold but only kept for decoration. Another man wishes to give a bushel of grain. If you take the pearl, you cannot take the grain; if you take the grain, you cannot take the pearl. Which will you choose? Chin Tzu said "I take the wheat, because it can save me from hunger." Mo Tzu said "If so, what is the use of luxury? Those that have no utility are not considered as the most important by the sages. You seek for delicious food only when you have had enough food to fill your stomach. You seek for beautiful clothes only when you have had enough clothes to keep your body warm. You seek for amusement only when you have had a definite means of living that will guarantee your safety. This is the art of life that is practical and lasting. Therefore, the procedure of the sages is to have material goods first, then refinement."[218]

This shows that Mo Tzu considered refinement as a kind of good.

What he insisted on was simply another truism that in order to live well, we must first live. But it did seem to him that for mankind as a whole to make a living is not an easy matter. In order that every member of humanity should have enough food, clothes, and the means of rearing children, every one should work indeed so hard that one scarcely has any time and energy to seek for immediate pleasure. Mo Tzu seemed to have in his mind the Presupposition that the natural environment of man is so fixed that what man can do is after all but very little. So

216 Hsun Tzu, *Works*, Chap. XXI.

217 Chuang Tzu, *Works*, Chap. XXXIII.

218 Liu Hsian, *Stories of the Ancients*, Chap. XX.

the best policy for preserving his race is hard work and economy. Thus in spite of the difference between Mo Tzu and Yang Chu they both had the feeling that nature is very difficult to modify according to human will. In the face of iron necessity, man can only adapt himself to nature, but not nature to him.

VII PROGRESSIVISM: DESCARTES, BACON, AND FICHTE

Han Fei, a philosopher shortly after Mo Tzu, said:

> Mo Tzu made a wooden bird in three years. It flew in the air for one day, then fell down and broke to pieces. His disciple said "You are so skillful, Master, that you can make a wooden bird fly." Mo Tzu said: "I am not so skillful as those who manufacture the crossbar of the carriage. They simply make it out of a piece of wood in less than one morning. But it makes the cart able to carry a very heavy load to a distant place. It is strong and lasting. Now I made a wooden bird in three years, but it could fly only one day and finally fell and broke to pieces."[219]

If this story is true, it may indicate that Mo Tzu did make some attempt to control nature, but the failure of his experiment caused him to give up his hope. We may ask the question: Why did he not persist in that and make more experiments? A reasonable answer we can give is that he had no faith that this experiment would succeed, and that although the wooden bird might not have any practical value, yet the success of one experiment might lead man to other discoveries that might be of great utility. I venture to say that this faith has played an important role in the history of science. We certainly do not expect that men should spend wealth, time, and energy in some persistent experiment if they have not the faith that some sort of discovery or invention is possible. In other words, they would not persist in making systematic attempts to enlarge the human empire, if they did not have faith that the human empire could be greatly enlarged.

(1) The Significance of Progressivism

The essence of what I called progressivism is precisely this faith. As we shall see, all the philosophers that we are going to consider start with the presupposition that nature is intelligible and manageable, and that the human empire can be greatly enlarged by the invasion of the art of man into the mystery of nature. With this presupposition these philosophers taught modern European peoples to make persistent and systematic experiments in natural science, which is, as Fichte said, "knowledge of nature" and "power over nature."[220] They experimented so that they have succeeded.

It is not significant that they have succeeded, when they worked according to the original presupposition. But it is significant that they should have gained this presupposition at all. Of course, every group of human beings, as soon as it entered the world, produced a state of art as over, or against, the state of nature. But they usually produced the state of art in a piecemeal way to meet immediate necessity rather than by a systematic plan with the self-consciousness that they

219 Han Fei, *Works*, Chap. XXXII.

220 I. G. Fichte, *The Vocation of the Scholar*, Popular Works, tr. by W. Smith, London, 1873, p. 156.

are thereby going to become the masters of nature. In comparison with the universe, man is after all too small to have easily the persistent idea that he is to become its master. There have been the mystics, who became proud of the greatness of man by identifying all with the One. But that is quite different from the persistent idea that man, although side by side with nature, yet can control her with his mighty intellect. It does not seem strange that man should not have this persistent idea, but it does seem strange that man should have it. Thus, there is the question: Whence did the European people acquire this persistent idea? Or, what is the origin of progressivism?

(2) Its Relation to the Christian Middle Ages

The answer is that they acquired the idea from the Christian Middle Ages; the origin of modernism is medievalism. We have seen that most of the philosophies belonging to the "nature" line of thought have the conviction of the superiority of spirit over matter. But Christianity[221] especially emphasized that spirit as an individual personality standing outside the world, yet creating and controlling the world with His infinite knowledge and infinite power. We have seen that most of those philosophies teach that God and man are originally one, or even if not so, that they are originally friends or companions. But in Christianity the relation between God and man is constructed in essentially legal terms. God is creditor, judge, and king; man is debtor, culprit, and subject. God said: "I am the Lord, and there is none else.... I form the light, and create darkness: I make peace, and create evil: I the Lord do all these things."[222] As to man it is said: "And the Lord God formed man of the dust of the ground; and breathed into his nostrils the breath of life; and man became a living soul."[223] Comparing these two passages we see how Christianity elevated God at the expense of man. But this is not all. We have seen that all these philosophies belonging to the "nature" line of thought had a conviction of the existence of the "lost paradise." But in Christianity the Garden of Eden is a concrete place with concrete things for concrete individuals. In fact the Garden of Eden is in no way different from the world garden, except that the former is in Heaven, and that in the former one could eat bread without the sweat of the brow. We have seen that according to most of those philosophies belonging to the "nature" line of thought, although there is the antithesis between the world we are now in and the world we came from, yet every one of us has the free will to return to that "fatherland." But according to Christianity, after the fall of man by the condemnation of God, man can never return to the lost paradise without God's grace. Augustine held passionately that the nature of man is sinful through and through, and has lost utterly the *liberum arbitrium* to good. Salvation, therefore, comes exclusively through grace. Fearing that people may doubt why God, in view of His infinite benevolence and infinite power does not give all mankind the divine grace, Augustine said:

221 Under "Christianity" we include whatever it took over from the Jewish religion.

222 Isa. 45: 5-7.

223 Gen. 2: 7.

> Who will be so foolish and blasphemous as to say that God cannot change the evils of man, whichever, whenever, and wherever He chooses, and direct them to what is good? But when He does it, He does it of mercy; when He does it not, it is of justice that He does it not.[224] The whole human race was condemned in its rebellious head by a divine judgment so just, that if not a single member of the race had been redeemed, no one could justly question the justice of God.[225]

Thus God can redeem all, and He will purposely not redeem all.

He must redeem some to show His mercy; but at the same time He must condemn some to show His justice. The decision as to whom He will redeem and whom He will condemn is absolutely according to His own arbitrary will. Thus to his people Moses said:

> For thou art a holy people unto the Lord thy God the Lord thy God hath chosen thee to be a special people unto Himself, above all people that are upon the face of the earth. The Lord did not set His love upon you, nor choose you, because ye were more in number than any people; for ye were the fewest of all people. Speak not thou in thine heart ...saying ... for my righteousness the Lord hath brought me in to possess this land; but for the wickedness of these nations the Lord doth drive them out from before thee. Not for thy righteousness, or for the uprightness of thine heart, dost thou go to possess their land; ... for thou art a stiff-necked people.[226]

This shows how arbitrary the "election" of God is. Although there is a "City of God," man can enter it neither by his merits, nor by his virtue, but only by the free gift of God. Just as in an empire of absolute monarchy, although there is a government, the people can never take part in it unless the sovereign shows his mercy. But when the arbitrariness of the sovereign goes to the extreme, the people revolt and establish a government themselves. In the same way when the European peoples despaired of the attempt to return to the "City of God," they gave it up. They wanted no more "City of God"; they wanted a "Kingdom of Man."

Thus the European peoples got the idea of the mastery of man over nature, because they had the idea of an individual personality that stands outside the world, yet can create and control it, with his infinite knowledge and infinite power. They got the idea of the kingdom of man in which men have most of the material goods without much labor, because they had the suggestion of the Garden of Eden, in which men eat bread without the sweat of their face. They wanted to imitate God and build a Garden of Eden on earth, because the City in Heaven can be entered only by the permission of God, and God is a "jealous God."

(3) Descartes' Motivation for Knowledge

Thus Descartes said:

> I revered our theology, and aspired as much as any one to reach the heavens, but being given assuredly to understand that the way is not less open to

224 Aurelius Saint Augustine, "Enchiridion," 98.

225 *Ibid.*

226 Deut, 7:6, 7; 9: 4-6.

> the most ignorant than to the most learned, and that the revealed truths which lead to heaven are above our comprehension, I did not presume to subject them to the impotency of my reason; and I thought that in order competently to undertake their examination, there was need of some special help from heaven, and of being more than man.[227]

This passage seems to show not so much that Descartes dismissed theology with pretended courtesy as that he spoke sincerely of his despair in religion. He aspired to reach heaven, but found that the way was open only to those "elected" who had special help from God. He found one thing, however, that is very fortunate for mankind to have. In the first sentence of his Discourse of Method, he said:

> Good sense is, of all things among men, the most equally distributed; for every one thinks himself so abundantly provided with it that those even who are the most difficult to satisfy in everything else, do not usually desire a larger measure of this quality than they already possess. And in this it is not likely that all are mistaken, the conviction is rather to be held as testifying that the power of judging aright and of distinguishing truth from error, which is properly what is called good sense or reason, is by nature equal in all men.[228]

Thus, although God did not reveal to all men the "truths which lead to heaven," yet every man has his natural reason by which he can know the truth at least on earth. Why should man not stand on his own feet?

God is in truth the only being who is absolutely wise, that is, possesses a perfect knowledge of all things; but we may say that men are more or less wise as their knowledge of the most important truths is greater or less.[229]

Then why should not men try their best to struggle for the most important truths? Thus Descartes put aside theology, and, with his natural good sense, he devoted himself to the knowledge of himself and of "the great book of the world."[230]

(4) His Method

Like a boy leaving his parental roof to see the world, Descartes took every care to guard himself against its trick, its deception. He determined to accept nothing as truth, which he did not dearly know to be such.[231] He determined to reject as absolutely false all opinions in regard to which he could suppose the least ground for doubt. He doubted his sense and reasoning. He considered all thought entering his mind as having no more truth than an illusion and dream. Finally, however, he found one thing at least that he could not doubt, that is, himself. "I think, therefore I am," or, "I doubt, therefore I am."[232]

Thus everything in this world can be doubted, but the "I" cannot be doubted.

227 Rene Descartes, *Discourse on the Method*, Everyman's Ed., pp. 7, 8.

228 *Id.*, p. 1.

229 Descartes, *The Principles of Philosophy*, Everyman's Ed., p. 148.

230 Descartes, *Discourse on the Method*, Everyman's Ed., p. 8.

231 *Id.*, p. 15.

232 *Id.*, pp. 26, 27.

Everything in this world may be false, but the "I" must be real. This is self-assertion. The essence of progressivism is the "I" becoming self-conscious. The reason that the "I" becomes self-conscious is clear. According to Christianity, the individual man is only an individual. He has no internal connection with God or the universe. Therefore when he declared independence and started to establish his own empire, he could not but have the feeling that he was alone in an alien world. He dared not trust the world. He dared not trust even his sense. He thought that if anything is to be trusted, it must show its credentials. This is the reason why in the history of modern European philosophy, there was a sharp contrast between the subject and the object.[233] This is the reason why, in the history of modern European philosophy, epistemology has become a distinctive philosophical problem.

Returning to Descartes, we see that when he made a conscious assertion of what he had unconsciously presumed all along the way, he faced immediately the problem: Granted that I think, and therefore am, how can I know the outside world? This soon became one of the most important problems in modern European philosophy. Descartes started this problem; but as to its solution, he was at a loss. He was compelled to go back to God. He first restored God to the throne with his ontological argument, then he said:

But after I have discovered that God exists, seeing I also at the same time observed that all things depend on him, and that he is no deceiver, and thence inferred that all which I clearly and distinctly perceive is of necessity true: although I no longer attend to the grounds of a judgment, no opposite reason can be alleged sufficient to lead me to doubt of its truth, provided only I remember that I once possessed a clear and distinct comprehension of it. My knowledge of it thus becomes true and certain.[234]

Thus the boy, having failed to deal with the world, came back again to his father's house, and said again: "A thing is so and so, because father says so and so, and father is no deceiver!"

(5) His Aim

Whatever the result of Descartes' research might be, his spirit certainly had far-reaching consequences. His aim was to give man a new philosophy. He said:

> The word "philosophy" signifies the study of wisdom, and that by wisdom is to be understood not merely prudence in the management of affairs, but a perfect knowledge of all that man can know, as well for the conduct of his life as for the preservation of his health and the discovery of all the arts, and that knowledge to subserve these ends must necessarily be deduced from first causes; so that in order to study the acquisition of it (which is properly called philosophizing), we must commence with the investigation of those first causes which are called Principles.[235]

233 Cp. "The Logic of Hegel," tr. from *The Encyclopedia of Philosophic Science*, by W. Wallace, Oxford, 1892, p. 43.

234 Descartes, *Meditations on the First Philosophy*, Everyman's Ed., pp. 125,126.

235 Descartes, *The Principles of Philosophy*, Everyman's Ed., pp. 147, 148.

We ought to believe that it is by it [philosophy] that we are distinguished from the savages and barbarians, and that the civilization and the culture of a nation are regulated by the degree in which true philosophy flourishes in it.[236]

The supreme good, considered by natural reason without the light of faith, is nothing more than the knowledge of truth through its first cause.[237]

Thus all philosophy is like a tree, of which metaphysics is the root, physics the trunk, and all the other sciences the branches that grow out of this trunk, which are reduced to three principles, namely: medicine, mechanics, and ethics. By the science of morals I understand the highest and most perfect, which presupposing an entire knowledge of the other sciences, is the last degree of wisdom.[238]

And in another place, when he spoke of some of his generalizations respecting physics, he said:

> By them I perceived it to be possible to arrive at knowledge highly useful in life; and in room of the speculative philosophy usually taught in the schools, to discover a practical, by means of which, knowing the force and action of fire, water, air, the stars, and the heavens, and all the other bodies that surround us, as distinctly as we know the various crafts of our artisans, we might also apply them in the same way to all the uses to which they are adapted, and thus render ourselves the lords and possessors of nature. And this is a result to be desired, not only in order to the invention of infinity of arts, by which we might be enabled to enjoy without any trouble the fruits of the earth, and all of its comforts, but also and especially for the preservation of health which is without doubt, of all the blessings of this life, the first and fundamental one.[239]

Thus Descartes' aim was to give man a new philosophy, which, if completed, would contain the fundamental principles of all branches of human knowledge, and would give mankind all the satisfactions, both intellectual and practical. He thought that he had made a good start and hoped that posterity would continue his work. He said "The height of my wish is, that posterity may sometimes behold the happy issue of it, etc."[240] That "posterity may sometimes behold the happy issue" is the essential faith of progressivism.

(6) Bacon's Motivation for Power

Descartes first taught man to seek for increase of knowledge, and through it, for increase of power. There was another philosopher who taught man to seek increase of power, and for the sake of power, to seek increase of knowledge. He was Bacon.

Just as Descartes opened his Discourse on Method by appealing to man's natural good sense, Bacon opened his "Great Instauration" with the same statement. He said:

---

236 *Id.*, p. 148.

237 *Id.*, p. 149.

238 *Id.*, pp.156, 157.

239 Descartes, *Discourse on Method*, Everyman's Ed., p. 49.

240 Descartes, *The Principles of Philosophy*, Everyman's Ed., p. 161.

> Being convinced that the human intellect makes its own difficulties, and not using the true help which is at man's disposal soberly and judiciously; whence follows manifold ignorance of things, and by reason of that ignorance mischiefs innumerable; he [Bacon himself] thought all trial should be made, whether that commerce between the mind of man and the nature of things, which is more precious than anything on earth, or at least anything that is of the earth, might by any means be restored to its perfect and original condition, or if that may not be, yet reduced to a better condition than that in which it now is.[241]

It seems to me that men do not rightly understand either their store or their strength, but overrate the one and underrate the other. Hence it follows that either from an extravagant estimate of the value of the arts, which they possess, they seek no further, or else from too mean an estimate of their own powers, they spend their strength in small matters and never put it fairly to the trial in those which go to the main. These are as the pillars of fate set in the path of knowledge; for men has neither desire nor hope to encourage them to penetrate further.[242]

These statements are again to tell man that if he wants to improve the existing world, he should not underrate his own strength, and should not neglect the true help that is at his own disposal. That is to say, from now on, man should stand on his own feet and establish his own empire.

In order to establish his own empire, he must first establish his power. In order to have his own power, he must first have his own knowledge. For "human knowledge and human power, those twin objects, do really meet in one; and it is from the ignorance of cause that operation fails."[243] Bacon said:

> And therefore it is not the pleasure of curiosity, nor the quiet of resolution, nor the raising of the spirit, nor the victory of wit, nor the faculty of speech, nor lucre of profession, nor ambition of honor or fame, not enablement for business, that are the true ends of knowledge; some of these things being more worthy than others, though all inferior and degenerate: but it is a restitution and reinvesting (in great part) of man to the sovereignty and power (for when so ever he shall be able to call the creatures by their true names he shall again command them) which he had in his first state of creation.[244]

In other words the end of knowledge is to imitate God. Bacon said:

> Again discoveries are as it were new creations, and imitations of
> God's work; as well sang the poet:
> "To man's frail race great Athens long ago
> First gave the seed whence waving harvests grow,
> And recreate all our life below.[245]

From this passage we can also see how the Christian idea of creation influenced science. If God, as an individual, can create the world, why cannot man, also as

241 Francis Bacon, *Works*, Popular Edition, Vol. t, "The Great Instauration," p. 17.

242 *Id.*, p. 25.

243 *Id.*, "Novum Organum," p. 53.

244 *Id*, "Of the Interpretation of Nature," p. 34.

245 *Id.*, "Novum Organun," p. 161.

an individual, create something at least in the world? If he can create something in the world, he is God at least in the world. If he can recreate his life below, he is God at least in the life below.

(7) His Method

Having seen Bacon's motivation for power and thus for knowledge, we come to see what he considered as the right method to knowledge. One of the chief defects of Descartes' method is that he depended solely upon the subjective natural good sense. He thought that the natural good sense has "the power of judging aright and of distinguishing truth from error," if only we "rightly apply it" and "fix our attention on the same subject"[246] But, with innocent good sense, after he made the first discovery, he had no way to go from the subjective to the objective, except by what Bacon called the "anticipation of mind," that is, by forcing his old conception of God to objective reality in order to support it in short, he started with a purely subjective method and ended with it.

Bacon, however, not only emphasized the natural force of understanding, but also the "help of the aids and instruments of logic."[247] He knew the fact that "neither the naked hand nor the understanding left to itself can effect much," and that "it is by instruments and helps that the work is done."[248] He also taught that in order that man may be the master of nature, man must first be the "servant and interpreter of nature";[249] that is to say, in order to control nature, man must first obey her. Therefore, the "anticipation of the mind" must be replaced by the "interpretation of nature." The old ideas, concepts, natural bias, and conventional belief, in short, all the idols of the mind, must be cleared away, so that the entire work may start afresh. In this new start, the understanding itself must be "from the very outset not left to take its own course, but guided at every step; and the business be done as if by machinery."[250] In this new start, the understanding must first go to experience, which is the foundation of all science.[251] The understanding must first seek information, evidence, and material in natural history. Then the understanding must arrange these materials according to what Bacon called "the tables of discovery" in order to investigate their true cause, which is the end of human knowledge. To use Bacon's metaphor, the business of philosophy is like the bee that "gathers its material from the flowers of the garden and of the field, but transforms and digests it by a power of its own".[252]

But when the understanding has discovered the cause, how does it know that this is the true one? To Bacon, the true cause is distinguished from the false not by its being a clear idea, but by its being able to work. He said:

---

246 Descartes, *Discourse on Method*, Everyman's Ed., p. 3.

247 Bacon, *Works*, Popular Ed., "The Great Instauration," p. 17.

248 *Id.*, "Novum Organum," p. 67.

249 *Ibid.*

250 *Id*, pp. 60, 61.

251 *Id.*,"Novum Organum," p. 133.

252 *Id.*, p. 131.

> That which in contemplation is as the cause is in operation as the rule.[253]
> What in operation is most useful, that in knowledge is most true?[254]

Thus Bacon's method is to start from the object and to end with it. This is one point that differentiates Bacon from Descartes.

(8) His Aim

Armed with this method, Bacon thought that we can know the cause of things and thus control them with certainty and liberty —with certainty when we can control them not only sometime and somewhere, but all time and everywhere, with liberty when we can control them not only with one means, but with many means.[255] Thus the more we are advanced in knowledge, the more are we like God. Indeed, in comparison with barbarians the civilized people are already God. Bacon said:

> Again, let a man only consider what a difference there is between the life of men in the most civilized province of Europe, and the wildest and most barbarous districts of New India; he will feel it to be great enough to justify the saying that "man is a god to man," not only in regard to aid and benefit, but also by a comparison of condition. And this difference comes not from soil, not from climate, not from race, but from the art.[256]

Speaking of the three great inventions of his time, namely, printing, gunpowder, and the magnet, he said:

> These three have changed the whole face and the state of things throughout the world. It will not be amiss to distinguish the three kinds and, as it were, grades of ambition in mankind. The first is of those who desire to extend their own power in their native country; which kind is vulgar and degenerate. The second is of those who labor to extend the power of their country and its dominion among men. This certainly has more dignity, though not less covetousness. But if a man endeavors to establish and to extend the dominion of the human race itself over the universe, his ambition (if ambition it can be called) is without doubt both a more wholesome thing and more noble than the other two.[257]

Thus with the many discoveries and inventions we had already in hand, and with the increase of the higher ambition of mankind, may we not reasonably have a great hope of the most brilliant success of the future? Bacon did not think, as Descartes did, that in the future there would be one philosophy which would embody the fundamental principles of all the branches of human knowledge. He thought that there should be organization of scientists to do these works, and that it was the duty of the state to give it the highest honor. This organization is called, in his "The New Atlantis," "Solomon's House." As the Father of the House said: "The end of our foundation is the knowledge of the Causes, and

---

253 *Id*, p. 68.
254 *Id.*, p. 171.
255 *Id.*, "Of the Interpretation of Nature," p. 53. cp. "Novum Organum," p. 170.
256 *Id.*, "Novum Organum," p. 162.
257 *Ibid.*

secret motions of things; and the enlarging of the bounds of Human Empire, to the effecting of all things possible."[258]

"To the effecting of all things possible" is another essential faith of progressivism.

(9) Fichte's Interest in Moral Progress

The hope of Bacon was also the hope of Fichte. Fichte said:

> Science, first called into existence by the pressure of necessity, shall afterwards calmly and carefully investigate the unchangeable laws of nature, review its power at large and learn to calculate their possible manifestations.... Thus Nature ever becomes more and more intelligible and transparent even in her most secret depths; human power, enlightened and armed by human invention, shall rule over her without difficulty, and the conquest, once made, shall be peacefully maintained. This domination of man over Nature shall be gradually extended until, at length, no further expenditure of mechanical labor shall be necessary than what the human body requires for its development, cultivation, and health and this labor shall cease to be a burden; for a reasonable being is not destined to be a bearer of burdens.[259]

This is just the prophecy of Bacon. The industrial revolution of the modern time is the reply of this prophecy. Since the industrial revolution, it is true that human empire has been gradually enlarged through the invasion of man into the mystery of nature. But has this solved the problem of life? No, not at all. Through the application of the new science, feudalism was doomed, but capitalism took its place. Production and commerce were carried on as if the new science had no moral lesson, but only the technical lessons for the strong to oppress the weak, for the few to oppress the many. What Bacon called the two lower grades of human ambition cannot be decreased with the increase of that of the third grade. There is still the new danger, the new wave, as Plato would say, that will destroy the human empire. Fichte foresaw it. He foresaw that the crudest enemy of man is after all but man himself.

He foresaw the terrible warfare of the modern civilized nations. He said:

> Where culture has at length united these wild hordes under some social bond, they attack each other, as nations, with the power which law and function have given them. Defying toil and privation, their armies traverse peaceful plains and forests; they meet each other; and the sight of their brethren is the signal of slaughter. Equipped with the mightiest invention of human intellect, hostile fleets plow their way through the ocean; through storm and tempest man rushes to meet his fellow man upon the lonely inhospitable sea — they meet, and defy the fury of the elements that they may destroy each other with their own hands.[260]

This was Fichte's prophecy of the future evil, and this prophecy was fulfilled. But Fichte foresaw also that this state of war among the nations could not go on

---

258 *Id.*, "New Atlantis," p. 398.

259 Fichte, *The Vocation of Man, Popular Works*, pp. 331, 332.

260 *Id.*, p.332.

forever. As the savage tribes had gradually become the modern nations, so the modern nations will gradually be united into a great whole of humanity. With the improvement in moral education, man will no longer act according to what Bacon called the two lower grades of ambition, but only to the ambition of the third grade. Thus "man shall no longer be divided by selfish purposes, nor their powers exhausted in struggles towards each other." "Nothing will remain for them but to direct their united strength against the one common enemy, which still remains unsubdued-resisting uncultivated nature."[261]

Thus "will the empire of civilization, freedom, and with it universal peace, gradually embrace the whole world."[262]

In the history of philosophy it is the dream of not a few people that some time in the future there must be a time when the individuals will spontaneously strive for the "greatest happiness of the greatest number." They will do it not because of religious, social, and political sanctions, as Mo Tzu, Hobbes, and Bentham thought, but simply because of the fact that only in doing so can they find the greatest satisfaction and the true good. Thus, besides Fichte, there was Comte who believed that through his positivistic philosophy "spontaneous morality"[263] would be established. There was Spencer who believed that through the natural process of evolution human nature would be modified in such a way that "what now characterizes the exceptional high may be expected eventually to characterize all."[264] All these philosophers had faith in progress and evolution. But among them Fichte was the one who expressed most clearly the spirit of progressivism. For, referring to his exposition of the highest state of human life, he said: "Yes! It is attainable in life and through life, for reason commands me to live; -it is attainable, for I am."[265]

(10) His Assertion of Will

Why must the highest state be attainable? Simply because of the fact that it is commanded by reason and that "I am"? To answer the question we must first know what Fichte meant when he spoke of reason and "I."

We have seen that Descartes and Bacon led man to a new type of life through the general reaction of their time against Christianity. It remains to be said that although they gave man a new idea of life, they had not yet given a new metaphysical justification of it. What they taught is indeed a rebellion against Christianity, yet they still tried to justify themselves in Christianity. Descartes said:

For since God has endowed each of us with some light of reason by which to distinguish truth and error, I could not have believed that I ought for a single moment to rest satisfied with the opinions of another, unless I had resolved to exercise my own judgment in examining these whenever I should be only qualified for the task.[266]

261 *Id.*, p. 339.
262 *Id.*, p. 338.
263 Auguste Comte, *A System of Positive Polity*, London, 1875, 3 vols., Vol. 1, p. 321.
264 Herben Spencer, *Principle of Ethics*, New York, 1898, p. 257.
265 Fichte, *The Vocation of Man*, Popular Works, p. 341.
266 Descartes, *Discourse on Method*, Everyman's Ed., pp. 22, 23.

And Bacon said:

> For it was not that pure and uncorrupted natural knowledge whereby Adam gave names to the creatures according to their propriety, which gave occasion to the fall. It was the ambitious and proud desire of moral knowledge to judge of good and evil, to the end that man may revolt from God and give laws to himself, which was the form and manner of the temptation. Whereas of the sciences which regard nature, the divine philosopher declares that "it is the glory of God to conceal a thing, but it is the glory of the king to find the thing out."[267]

These passages are to be considered not so much as the pretended courtesy of the two philosophers towards Christianity as their self-rationalization for reconciling their inner conflict. This conflict was in fact the conflict of medieval and modern Europe; and this self-rationalization was no doubt made by most people at that time.

But this reconciliation was obviously not very satisfactory. It was not accepted by the Church. So this new idea of life, in order to be valid in man's thought, must have a new metaphysical justification. This justification was given, consciously or unconsciously, by Fichte.

Fichte made the starting point of his philosophy the proposition, A = A, a proposition at once recognized by us as true. In affirming this proposition we also affirm our own existence, for the affirmation itself is our mental action. This proposition, therefore, may be changed into. Ego = Ego. Thus the Ego posited itself.[268] This was the same procedure as that of Descartes. But to Descartes, thinking is the essence of the Ego; while to Fichte, "thinking is not the essence, but merely a particular determination of the Ego; and there are many other determinations of the Ego."[269] To Fichte, the essence of the Ego is activity, which is synonymous with reality.[270] To Descartes, the existence of the objective world outside the Ego is guaranteed by the old God, the God who separates from, and transcends, man and world. To Fichte, the objective world is the manifestation of the new God who is man's own will in its original whole. What he called reason is this will; what he called the "I," the finite Ego, is the will in the manifested world. So he said:

> I am a member of two orders — the one purely spiritual, in which I rule by my will alone; the other sensuous, in which I operate by my deed.... The will is the living principle of reason — is itself reason, when purely and simply apprehended.... As surely as the reason is reason, must the will operate absolutely by itself, and independently of the natural laws by which material action is determined; and hence the sensuous life of every finite being points towards something higher, into which the will, by itself alone, may open the way, and of which it may acquire possession —a possession which we must

267 Bacon, *Works*, Pop. Ed., "The Great Instauration," pp. 35, 36.

268 Fichte, *The Science of Knowledge*, tr. by Kreoger, London, 1889, pp. 67, 69.

269 *Id*, p. 73.

270 *Id.*, pp. 114,115.

indeed again sensuously conceive of as a state, and not a mere will.[271]

Thus the finite Ego should strive forward, because it is his essence to strive forward. His future success is guaranteed, because it is the Absolute Ego behind him that seeks possession. Thus the highest state must be attainable, because it is commanded by reason and because "I" am. Thus with this new metaphysics man is not only to imitate God on earth, his very subjective personality is elevated to the place of God. The Will is a God with His knowledge and his power, except that it did not create the world in six days and finish everything, but had to acquire possession now and to enjoy the fruits in the future. In this sense, it is not a God, but a would-be God.

Obviously there is a striking similarity between Fichte and Schopenhauer. Schopenhauer also considered the will as the thing-in-itself, and its manifestation as the sensuous world. He also considered the fact that the individual always strives forward to be due to the very nature of the will. The difference between these two philosophers is not in the vision of the fact, but simply in the evaluation of it. In the ever-struggling will, Schopenhauer found sorrow and despair, but Fichte found joy and hope. To Schopenhauer the will is something that leads man astray; to Fichte, it is the Father "who rulest all things for the best."[272] To Schopenhauer, as to the Buddhists, the continuous flux of life and death is the chief source of human suffering; to Fichte, "death and birth are but the struggle of life with itself to assume a more glorious and congenial form."[273] In short, what Schopenhauer considered as the blind will, Fichte considered as an enlightened reason. What Schopenhauer considered as devil, Fichte considered as God. Therefore Schopenhauer taught man the absolute denial of will, Fichte taught the absolute assertion of it; the philosophy of the former is an extreme idealization of nature, that of the latter is an extreme idealization of art.

(11) His Appeal to Faith

But what is the ground on which these philosophies passed the opposite judgments upon the will? The following quotation from Fichte will give the answer. Referring to the highest state of human life, Fichte said:

> This is not an object given to us only that we may strive after it for the mere purpose of exercising our power on something great, the real existence of which we may be compelled to doubt; it shall, it must be realized; there must be a time, in which it shall be accomplished, as surely as there is a sensible world and a race of reasonable beings existent in time with respect to which nothing earnest and rational is conceivable besides this purpose, and whose existence becomes intelligible only through this purpose. Unless all human life be metamorphosed into a mere theatrical display for the gratification of some malignant spirit, who has implanted in poor humanity this in extinguishable longing for the imperishable

271 Fichte, *The Vocation of Man*, Popular Works, pp. 350, 351.

272 *Id.*, p. 365.

273 *Id*, P. 378.

only to amuse himself with its ceaseless pursuit of that which it can never overtake —its ever-repeated efforts Ixion-like, to embrace that which still eludes its grasp — its restless hurrying onward in an ever-recurring circle — only to mock its earnest aspiration with an empty, insipid farce; unless the wise man, seeing through this mockery, and feeling an irreprehensible disgust at continuing to play his part in it, is to cast life indignantly from him and make the moment of awakening to reason also that of his physical death; unless these things are so, this purpose most assuredly must be attainable.[274]

Here Fichte argued in a circle. He insisted that if life is not to be a mere theatrical display, a mere farce, this highest purpose of human life must be attained, and that if it cannot be attained, life most be a mere theatrical display, a mere farce. He seemed to presuppose that it is intrinsically unreasonable to say that life is a mere farce. But this is exactly what Schopenhauer said. To him life is a farce, an illusion, and a dream. It is so because we can see it only as an ever-repeated game, which tends to nothing and signifies nothing, and from our past experience, we cannot see that there will be something as *summum bonum*, which can satisfy the will once and for all. Therefore, the wise man should see "through this mockery." He should feel disgust at continuing to play this meaningless game. Besides, in casting away life, he needs something more than physical death, because physical death is only the death of the sensible, but not that of the spiritual world. He needs the absolute denial of will and thus to return to the "nothing" which is his lost paradise. The reason for which Schopenhauer taught the absolute denial of will is the conviction that there cannot be a final goal for the will; while that for which Fichte taught the absolute assertion of will is the opposite conviction that there must be a final goal.

But what is Fichte's argument for his conviction? He had no argument; he appealed to faith. He appealed to faith that the will must have a "spiritual world plan';[275] that there must be a "great moral empire"[276] and "that there is one world possible—a thoroughly good world."[277] The present state of this world is "a means towards a better, and the transition point to a higher world and more perfect state."[278] He felt satisfied to be the "instrument of this progress," "the instrument for carrying out the purpose of reason."[279] He felt satisfied to have faith in a "law, a rule, absolutely without exception, according to which a will determined by duty must have consequences."[280] He felt satisfied that he knew "that they must be, although he did not know 'how they shall be.'"[281] He felt satisfied that "all that happens belongs to the plan of the eternal world, and is

274 *Id.*, pp. 340, 341.
275 *Id.*, P. 366.
276 *Id.*, P. 367.
277 *Id*, p. 366.
278 *Id.*, P. 329.
279 *Id.*, p. 373.
280 *Id.*, p. 356.
281 *Id.*, P. 357.

good in its place," although he did not know "what in this plan is pure gain, what is only a means for the removal of some existing evil."[282] In short, he felt satisfied to act according to the command of reason that sets before man the purpose, for the "infallible attainment" of which he is also the "pledge and security."[283]

(12) Concluding Remarks

We have made a brief survey of progressivism. Being different from the teaching of passive adaptation to nature as taught by hedonism and utilitarianism, progressivism teaches man to strive for a new state in which all that is bad and ugly in nature is converted into the good and the beautiful; a new state, in short, in which human art reaches its climax. In contrast with nihilism that teaches man to return to the state of "nothing," progressivism teaches man to strive for the state of the fullest and the richest of all human experience.

In his Reconstruction of Philosophy, Professor Dewey says:

> Francis Bacon of the Elizabethan age is the great forerunner of the spirit of modern life. Though slight in accomplishment, as a prophet of new tendencies, he is an outstanding figure of the world of intellectual life. Like many other prophets he suffered from confused intermingling of old and new. What is most significant in him has been rendered more or less familiar by the course of events. But page after page is filled with matter which belongs to the past from which Bacon thought he had escaped. Caught between these two sources of easy disparagement, Bacon hardly receives his due as the real founder of modern thought, while he is praised for merits which scarcely belong to him, such as the alleged authorship of the specific method of induction pursued by science. What makes Bacon memorable is that breezes blowing from a new world caught and filled his sails and stirred him to adventure in new seas. He never himself discovered the land of promise, but he proclaimed the new goal and with faith he descried its features from afar.[284]

What is true of Bacon is also true of Descartes. These two philosophers did not give man new good, but only a new idea of good. Fichte gave this new idea of good a metaphysical justification, and with this justification progressivism in Germany had its full expression, both of its excellence and of its defects. Without further remarks, I shall conclude my brief exposition of progressivism with a passage from the Lieh-tzu:

> [There are] two mountains, Tai-hsing and Wang-wu, which cover an area of seven hundred square li, and rise to an enormous altitude.... The Simpleton of the North Mountain, a man of ninety, dwelt opposite these mountains, and was vexed in spirit because their northern flanks blocked the way to travelers, who had to go all the way round. So he called all his family together and broached a plan. "Let us," he said, "put forth our utmost

282 *Id.*, p. 372.

283 *Id.*, P. 340.

284 John Dewey, *Reconstruction of Philosophy*, New York, 1920. p. 28.

> strength to clear away this obstacle, and cut right through the mountains."... So the old man, followed by his son and grandson, sallied forth with their pickaxes, and the three of them began hewing away at the rocks, and cutting up the soil, and carting it away in baskets to the promontory of Po-hai.... Engrossed in their toil, they never went home except once at the turn of the season. The Wise Old Man of the River-bend burst out laughing and urged them to stop.
>
> "Great indeed is your witlessness!" he said. "With the poor remaining strength of your declining years you will not succeed in removing a hair's breadth of the mountain, much less the whole vast mass of rock and soil." With a sigh, the Simpleton of the North Mountain replied "Surely it is you who are narrow-minded and unreasonable.... Though I myself must die, I shall leave a son behind me and through him a grandson. That grandson will beget sons in his turn, and those sons will also have sons and grandsons. With all this posterity, my line will not die out, while on the other hand the mountain will receive no increment or addition. Why then should I despair of leveling it to the ground at last?" The Wise Old Man of the River-bend had nothing to say in reply. One of the serpent-brandishing deities heard of the undertaking and, fearing that it might never be finished, went and told God Almighty, who was touched by the old man's simple faith, and commanded the two sons of Kua O to transport the mountains.... Ever since then the region lying between *Chi* in the north and Han in the south has been an unbroken plain.[285]

It is clear that Bacon and Descartes were members of the Family of Fools. Fichte, being also a member of the family and fearing that his sons and grandsons might be discouraged by the great task on their hands, made a special appeal to God Almighty, whom he called the Absolute Ego.

---

285 Lionel Giles, *Taoist Teachings form the Book of Lieh Tzu*, London, 1912, p. 86.

VIII CONCLUSION OF PART II

The types of philosophy that we have considered above seem to have three common points; namely, hedonism, intellectualism, and egoism.

(1) Hedonism

Here we use the word "hedonism" in a broader sense than above to denote all the theories that teach man to seek the satisfaction of desires. The "nature" line of thought considered desire as responsible for the "fall" of man, but the "art" line of thought that there is no other good besides the satisfaction of desires. If we are in a state in which we can satisfy all or most of our desires, that state is our paradise. We have had no other paradise in the past. This is the common presupposition of the "art" line of thought. Of course, Fichte spoke of "reason," "conscience," and "duty" as emphatically as any idealistic philosopher did. But according to him, the living principle is the Absolute Will, and the obedience of reason is our duty. But what is that Absolute Will, if not the will in Schopenhauer? Pure will without desires is meaningless. Will is after all but a metaphysical rationalization of desires. The net result of his philosophy is to us simply that we all should unite to satisfy the craving of the Absolute Will, but not that of the individual as such. To us he did not condemn desires; he simply condemned selfish desires.

(2) Intellectualism

The "nature" line of thought considered intellect as also something that is responsible for man's "fall." It is only through the denial of intellect that we can get truth and happiness. But according to the "art" line of thought, happiness and truth can be gained by us only through intellect. As to happiness, we have seen that even in hedonism (the first type of the art" line of thought), which seeks nothing but the immediate pleasure, there is a strong need of intellect to make choices and especially to get rid of superstition and thus escape from the fear of death. In utilitarianism there is the need of intellect to foresee future consequences, to make calculations and to prepare the means. In progressivism the will, to use Schopenhauer's expression, is most asserted, and therefore intellect is most needed to do its service. Besides, according to the general presupposition of the "art" line of thought, man is to know the world from outside, if he can know it at all. So in the matter of truth, man needs precision, exactness, and above all, proof. These again must be furnished by intellect. So in the extreme type of the "art" line of thought, that is, progressivism, science, the flower of intellectualism, is produced.

(3) Egoism

By egoism I mean the antithesis of what Fichte called the ego and the non-ego, or what William James called the "me," and the "non-me."[286] This is in contrast to mysticism of the "nature" line of thought in which there is the union of the

286 William James, *Psychology*, 2 vols., Vol, 1, p. 289.

individual with the whole. According to the different types of the "art" line of thought the ego has different ranges, but the opposition of the ego and the non-ego remains always the same. About Fichte, Wallace said:

> But the associations which cling to the terms Fichte used gave this thought a one-sided direction. The "I" is opposed to the "thee," and the "them" and the "it." The "thing"—or non-ego—is depreciated as compared with the thinker. It is postulated ad *majorem Dei gloriam* of the ego: in order that I may work the full fruition of my being. It is what I ought to make out of it. It is nothing but what it will be —or will be if I do what I ought to do. The identity of the two sides therefore is left as the object of an endless task, an absolute imperative. The absolute is not yet — it is only the forecast of a postulated result.[287]

The criticism is justified. But we should notice that it is not "the associations clinging to the terms" that gave Fichte's thought a one-sided direction; it is the one-sided direction of his thought that led him to use these terms. It is not simply by chance that Fichte called his would-be God the Absolute Ego.

287 W. Wallace, *The Logic of Hegel*, Prolegomena, pp. 145, 146.

Part III

THE IDEALIZATION OF THE CONTINUITY OF NATURE AND ART AND THE GOOD OF ACTIVITY

It is not difficult to see that in spite of the diametrical opposition of the two main lines of thought analyzed above, there is, at least, one point in common between them. This point is that they are both impressed by the antagonism of the different factors in the world: the antagonism of nature versus art, of human versus divine, of ideal versus real, of infinite versus finite, of society versus individual, of authority versus liberty, and so forth. We are now going to study another line of thought. The philosophies belonging to this line of thought are either originally impressed, not by the antagonism, but by the continuity of the world, or, seeing the one-sidedness of the two extreme points of view, have attempted to reconcile them. The general position of this line of thought is the mean state of the "nature" and "art" lines of thought. In this state nature and art are no longer antagonistic to each other; they are simply a continuous whole. To this line of thought the divine is more human, and the human more divine; the real is more ideal, and the ideal more real.

The "nature" line and the "art" line of thought have another point in common which may be said to be both the cause and the consequence of the first point. It is that they both try to hold something responsible for the present evil. They both try to "give a dog a bad name and hang it." The difference is only as to what should be the "dog." The line we are now considering offers another method of dealing with the evil. Hegel said:

> Our intellectual striving aims at realizing the conviction that what is intended by eternal wisdom, is actually accomplished in the domain of existent, active spirit, as well as in that of mere Nature. Our mode of treating the subject is, in this respect, a Theodicea — a justification of the ways of God — which Leibnitz attempted metaphysically, in his method, i.e., in indefinite abstract categories — so that the ill that is found in the world may be comprehended, and the thinking Spirit reconciled with the fact of the existence of evil. Indeed, nowhere is such a harmonizing view more pressingly demanded than Universal History; and it can be attained only by recognizing the positive existence, in which the negative element is a subordinate and vanquished nullity.[288]

Evil is no longer evil, if only we no longer consider it as evil. Hence, this line of thought teaches neither the way of "increase" nor that of "decrease." According to it, activity is itself a good.

For illustrations of this line of thought, I have chosen the philosophy of Confucius, that of Aristotle, Neo-Confucianism, and the philosophy of Hegel.

288 G. W. F. Hegel, *The Philosophy of History*, tr. by J. Sibree in the World's Great Classics Series, p. 15.

Each of them represents the reconciliation of one or more of the different factors analyzed in the above chapters. I do not mean that these philosophers all consciously and purposely made the reconciliation; they might, or they might not have done so. They might originally have had the impression of the unity of the world and thus worked out a system themselves, but taking these systems at what William James called their "face value," in the following discussion I shall treat the philosophy of Confucius as an attempt to reconcile the state of nature and the state of art; that of Aristotle, to reconcile the world of ideal and the world of reality; that of Neo-Confucianism, to reconcile the thing and the "nothing"; and that of Hegel, to reconcile the ego and the non-ego: In other words, I shall treat the philosophy of Confucius as an attempt to make the *Tao*istic nature more in harmony with art; that of Aristotle, to make the Platonic ideal Heaven more in harmony with the actual earth; that of Neo-Confucianism, to make nihilism more human; that of Hegel, to make progressivism more divine. In the philosophy of Confucius and Aristotle we find also substitutes for extreme hedonism and utilitarianism.

IX CONFUCIUS

Confucius said:

> "Transmitting but not inventing, believing in and loving the ancient, I venture to compare myself with Lao Peng."[289]

Lao is said to be Lao Tzu. Lao Tzu was the official historian in the court of theChow dynasty; some, if not most, of the passages in his book are said to be records of ancient sayings and proverbs. Lao Tzu was such a man as Confucius here described. According to tradition, Confucius once visited Lao Tzu and "asked him questions" about "rite."[290] But so far as we know, in Lao Tzu's book there is nothing but the exaltation of *Tao* at the expense of rite. He said:

> How all-pervading is the great *Tao*, it can be on the left and it can be on the right. All things depend upon it for their life, and it refuses them not. When its achievement is accomplished, it assumes not the name. Lovingly nourishing all things, it plays not the role of their Lord. Ever desireless it can be classed with the small. All things converge in it and it plays not the role of their Lord; it can be classed with the great.[291]
>
> Tao begets unity; unity begets duality; duality begets trinity; and trinity begets all things. All things are sustained by *Yin* and *Yang* and are living harmoniously in the harmonious atmosphere.[292]

As to culture, he said:

> Abandon your saintliness; put away your prudence: and the people will gain a hundredfold. Abandon your benevolence; put away your justice; and the people will return to filial piety and paternal love. Abandon skill; give up utility; and the thieves and robbers will no longer exist. These are the three things which show the insufficiency of culture. Therefore it is said: Hold fast that which will endure; show yourself simple, preserve the pure; lessen the self with fewer desires.[293]

His philosophy, as the forerunner of that of Chuang Tzu, is an idealization of nature and a depreciation of art. Most probably Confucius was influenced by it. But to Confucius, *Tao* is not confined in the state of nature; it also includes the state of art.

(1) The "Yi"

It has long been an established fact that the most important literature of Confucianism is the Yi Jing, or "I Ching", as it is usually called in translations, the Book of Changes. Truly following the example of Lao Peng, Confucius did not make the book himself, but transmitted it from the ancients. Before Confucius,

---

289 "The Analects of Confucius," it. by James Legge in the Four Books. Chap. VII, Sec. 1.

290 This Chinese word for "rite" is so comprehensive that it refers to all regulations that arise from the relations between man.

291 Lao Tzu, Tao Teh Cling, Sec. 34.

292 *Id*, Sec. 42.

293 *Id.*, Sec. 19.

this book was used for divination. It did not receive its meaning and significance until Confucius added to it the "Ten Wings," or the ten appendixes. The system of the book has as its basis the eight trigrams, which were supposed to be the symbolic representative of the eight fundamental elements or factors of the universe and the different abstract attributes which should be suggested and associated with them. Then the eight trigrams were added each to it and to all the others until there were sixty-four hexagrams. Each hexagram was supposed to be the symbolic representative of one or more phenomena of the universe, either natural or human. All the hexagrams put together were supposed to represent symbolically all that had happened in the universe, from heaven and earth to the complexity of human affairs. The book is indeed a remarkable treatise in the history of philosophy. Although Hegel said "that not a particle of the Notion is to be found in it,"[294] it is in fact the "Phenomenology of Mind" of Confucius. Like the "Phenomenology of Mind" it treated "tracts of experience which have each formed, from time to time the subject of separate discussion, and have engaged the undivided interest of different thinkers of Mind" "as but fragments of a single system." Like the "Phenomenology of Mind" it looked upon "movements of human history which have marked epochs in the development of the human race" "as but typical or prominent embodiments of principles at work in the spirit of man" and discussed them "in shadowy, schematic form, through which the historical reality referred to is only dimly visible."[295] Only a glance at this book, and we know that in the mind of Confucius, the universe is a united whole.

(2) Confucius's Conception of "Tao"

The word "Yi" primarily means change. In the Yi Jing, "Yi" is used interchangeably with "Tao," since "Tao" is life, spontaneity, evolution, or, in one word, change, itself. In the Analects we read:

> "As he stood by a stream, Confucius said: 'Ah! That which is passing is just like this, never ceasing day or night.'"[296]

In the Great Appendix to the Yi King Confucius said:

> The successive movement of *Yin* (the passive elements, the "matter") and *Yang* (the active element, the "form") is called *Tao.* All that follows it is good. That which ensues from it is the nature of things. When the benevolent sees it, he calls it benevolence. When the wise sees it, he calls it wisdom. The common people, acting daily according to it, are yet not conscious of it. Thus the *Tao,* as seen by the superior man, is seen by few. It is manifested in love, and is immanent in operation. It gives all things their spontaneity without being anxious about their future like the sages. How perfect is its virtue! How great is its achievement! The rich evolution is its great achievement; the daily renovation is its great virtue.

294 G.W.F.Hegle, *Lecture on the History of Philosophy,* tr. by E.S. Haldane and F. H. Simson, 3 vols., 1892-1896, Vol. 1, p. 123.

295 I. B. Bailie, Introduction to his translation of Hegel's *Phenomenology of Mind,* London, 1910, Vol. L p. 5.

296 *The Analects of Confucius,* Chap. IX, Sec. 16.

> That which gives form is called Kien (Yang that which imitates the form is called Kuen (Yin) ... That which is unfathomable in the movement is called the mystery.[297]

In another place he said:

> Yi has the Grand Terminus, which generates the Primeval Pair. The Primeval Pair produce the Four Forms, from which are derived the eight trigrams. The eight trigrams determine the good and the evil. The good and the evil produce the great achievement."[298]

Yi has no thought, no action. It is in itself still and calm. Yet in its function it embraces all phenomena and events in the universe. Is not this the great mystery?[299]

If we compare these passages with that of Lao Tzu and reflect upon what Chuang Tzu said about *Tao,* we see at once how similar is Confucius's conception of *Tao* to that of Taoism. In the Analects Confucius also said that Heaven speaks nothing, but the four seasons pursue their course and all things are being continuously produced.[300] *Tao* is a great spontaneous stream of life, "doing no- thing, but there is nothing that is not done." But according to Lao Tzu, and afterwards to Chuang Tzu, although *Tao* does all things by doing nothing, in that "all things," civilization and human art are not included. They idealized the state of nature and attributed all the evil to the state of art. According to Confucius, however, the history of the universe is a continuous whole. There is no demarcation between the state of nature and the state of art. He said:

> For the universe, the most essential is Life. For the sages, the most important is state. That which maintains the state is love. That which maintains the people is wealth. The production of wealth, the education of the people, and the prohibition of wrongdoing are called justice.[301]

Nature is Life; state, wealth, education, and prohibition, are to make life better. Art is to help nature; hence, it is in one sense natural.

(3) The Origin of Useful Art

In the Great Appendix to the Yi King, Confucius said:

> It is heaven and earth that furnish models and patterns. It is Time that changes and evolves. It is the sun and moon that are the brightest. It is wealth and nobility that are the most exalted. It is the sages that prepare things for practical use, and invent instruments for the benefit of the world.[302]
>
> They [the sages] all understand the ways of nature and know the needs of man. They thus made the skillful things for the use of the people.[303]

This shows the purpose of art. All kinds of art are for the utility of the people and the benefit of the world. They are all for the advancement of life. They are not

297 Yi King, tr. by James Legge, London, 1882, Appendix III, Sec. 1, Chap. 24.
298 *Id*, Sec. I, Chap. 70.
299 *Id*, Sec I, Chap. 62.
300 *The Analects of Confucius*, Chap. XVII, Sec. 19.
301 *Yi King*, Appendix IV, Sec II, Chap. 10.
302 *Id.*, Appendix III, Sec. I, Chap. 72.
303 *Ibid.*

produced by the artisans at random, but are devised by the sages with definite purpose and profound wisdom.

The purpose of art is the utility of man; the origin of art is the imitation of nature. According to Confucius, the Yi King is "a book of symbols" and "the origin of symbols is imitation."[304] He said:

> The sages have seen the complexity of the universe. They used the symbols to represent the different forms and to symbolize the different characteristics thereof.[305]
>
> When conceived, they are called symbols. When materially embodied, they are called "utensils." When instituted for general use, they are called laws. When wrought into the everyday life of all the people, they are called the works of the gods.[306]
>
> What manifest themselves above is called the ways of nature. What are embodied on earth below is called "utensils."... When brought to the people and practiced by them, they are called achievements.[307]

Thus the different kinds of art are the material embodiment of the symbols which the sages conceived in the complexity of nature. They are the imitation or the realization of the different symbols represented by the trigrams and hexagrams. Confucius said:

> The Book of Changes contains four ways of the sages. Its judgment serves as the models of their argument. Its change serves as the model of their activity. Its symbol serves as the model of the invention of the arts.[308]

In one chapter of the Great Appendix, Confucius tried to show that the trigrams originated in the symbolization of nature. He said. In the ancient [time] when Pao-hsi became the philosopher king, he observed the phenomena of heaven above and the forms on earth below. He noted the manners of birds and beasts and the products of the soil. Receiving suggestions both inwardly from his own self and externally from distant objects, he first invented the eight trigrams in order to penetrate the mysteries of nature and to describe the reality of all things.[309]

Following this passage Confucius went on to show that the more important inventions of the ancients all originated under the suggestion of the different symbols represented by the varied combinations of the trigrams, that is, the hexagrams. He said When Pao-hsi died, Shen-nung flourished He fashioned the wood to form shares, and bent the wood to make the plow handle. The advantage of plowing and weeding were then taught through the world. The symbol of this was taken, probably, from the hexagram "Ye."[310]

The hexagram "Ye" is formed by the combination of the trigram meaning wind, wood, and penetration, and the trigram meaning thunder, motion, and growth. Hence, the hexagram represents the symbol of penetrating of wood from above

304 *Id.*, Appendix III, Sec. II, Chap. 2.
305 *Id.*, Sec. I, Chap. 12.
306 *Id.*, Chap. II.
307 *Id.*, Chap. 12.
308 *Id.*, Chap. 10.
309 *Id.*, Appendix IV, Sec. II Chap. 11.
310 *Id.*, Chap. 13.

and the growth below. From this Shen-nung invented the art of agriculture.

He [Huang-ti] hollowed the trees to make canoes, and cut the trees to make oars. By using them man could cross what was formerly considered as impassable. By using them the most distant places were reached and the world was benefited. The symbol of this was taken probably from the hexagram "Hwan."[311]

The hexagram "Hwan" is formed by the combination of the trigram meaning wood, and the trigram meaning water. The phenomena of wood flowing on water obviously suggested the idea of constructing a boat.

He also domesticated the oxen and horses to carry cargoes to the distant places. The world was much benefited. The symbol of this was probably taken from the hexagram "Sui".[312]

The hexagram "Sui" is formed by the combination of the trigram meaning lake, pleasure, and satisfaction, and the trigram meaning motion. The combination of the symbol of satisfaction above and the movement below led Huang-ti to utilize animals to work for man. This was the origin of the useful arts. There are many other passages equally interesting; but we need not quote all of them. Art is after all not so much the conqueror of nature as her humble imitator.

(4) Rites and Music

Besides the useful arts there are other kinds of art, the main purpose of which is not to make life possible, but to make it better. These latter kinds are the fine arts and what I may call social art. Referring to the previous quotation, useful art is for "the production of wealth," fine art and social art are for "the education of the people." In "The Doctrine of the Mean and the Common" (the title of this treatise is usually translated as "The Doctrine of the Mean") it is said "What Nature confers is the nature of things; the pursuance of this nature is the way of life; the cultivation of this way is education."[313] Obviously the nature of things mentioned here is exactly what Chuang Tzu called "virtue" (cp. above, p. 16). Confucius on the one hand taught the pursuance of nature, and on the other hand emphasized the value of education. According to him, the virtuous life is the production neither of nature as such, nor of art as such. It is the proper pursuance of nature through the help of art. The above-quoted treatise, as shown by its title, is a systematic exposition of the mean and the common. The exposition of the common shows that the virtuous life is a proper pursuance of nature. The exposition of the mean shows that it is the proper pursuance of nature. In other words, it is the mean in the common. In order to secure the mean in the common, the sage devised social and fine art. They are the rites and music (including poetry).

In Confucius's system, these twin sisters are even more important than gymnastics and music in Plato's and Aristotle's systems. There is some difference between the function of rites and that of music. But the difference is not so great

311 *Id.*, Chap. 16

312 *Id.*, Chap. 17.

313 "The Doctrine of the Mean," tr. by James Legge in the *Four Books*, Chap. I, Sec. I.

and obvious as that between the function of gymnastics and that of music. Generally speaking, the function of rites is to secure the mean in desires, the most natural and common aspect of human nature. Confucius said:

> The strongest desires of man are [for] food and sex. The strongest aversion of man is [to] death and poverty. Desire and aversion are the fundamental elements of man's mind. If it be wished to give a uniform measure to these elements, there is no other way besides rite.[314]

In another place we read:

> The Master said "Sze, you live by excess, and Shang by defect!" Tzu Kung crossed the mat and asked: "May I ask by what means the mean can be secured?" The Master said: "By rite, it is rite that defines and determines the mean."[315]

The function of music is to secure the mean in sentiment and passion, another most natural and common aspect of human nature. In the "Discourse on Music," we read:

> Therefore, it is said "Music is joy." The superior man rejoices that the expression of passion is in accordance with the right way. The vulgar rejoices that there is the expression of passion. When men regulate passion in the right way, there is joy, but no disorder. When they let passion go and forget the right way, there is delusion, but no joy.[316]
>
> Music is produced by the modulation of sound, and has its source in the emotion of the mind when the mind is affected by external things. When the mind is moved to sorrow, the sound is sharp and fading away; when it is moved to joy, the sound is slow and gentle; when it is moved to pleasure, the sound is exclamatory and soon disappears; when it is moved to anger, the sound is coarse and fierce; when it is moved to reverence, the sound is straightforward and humble, when it is moved to love, the sound is fine and soft. These sentiments cannot be reproduced by mind itself, but by the affection of the external things. Therefore the ancient philosopher kings were careful about the things that might affect the mind, they instituted rite to direct man's desire, and music to harmonize man's sentiment.[317]

The purpose of both rite and music is one and the same, that is, to secure the mean in the common.

Thus the ancient kings, in their institution of rite and music, were not to give the extreme satisfaction of desires and appetites. They were to teach people to moderate their likes and dislikes and thus to return to the norm of humanity.[318]

As to society as a whole,

> Music establishes union and harmony; rite maintains difference and distinction. From union comes mutual affection; from distinction, mutual respect.[319]

---

314 *Li Chi*, Book VII, Sec. II, Chap. 20.

315 *Id*, Book XX, Sec. IV.

316 *Id*., Book VII, Sec. I, Chap. 19.

317 *Id*., Book VII, Sec. I, Chap. 2.

318 *Id*., Chap. 10.

319 *Id*., Chap. 15.

Therefore the ancient philosopher kings instituted rite and music to give measure to everybody....

> Rite is to regulate man's mind; music is to harmonize man's sentiment; government is to promote their performance; law is to guard against their violation. When rite, music, government, and law have everywhere the full course without irregularity and collision, the rule of the philosopher kings is complete.[320]

When music is perfect and attains its full result, there will be no dissatisfaction of the mind. When rite is perfect and attains its full result, there will be no quarrel among the people. Thus when we say the philosopher kings govern the world with bowing and courtesy, we mean that they govern with rite and music.[321]

This is Confucius's "Utopia"; this is the great function of rites and music. According to Confucius, these two kinds of art or institutions also originated in the imitation of nature.

Music imitates the harmony of the universe; rite imitates the order of the universe. There is heaven above and earth below, and between them there are the various things with different ranks and dignity. This gives man the pattern of rite. There is the unceasing stream of evolution, in which all things are in harmony and in accordance. This gives man the model of music. In the spring all things burst forth; in the summer all things grow. This is benevolence. In the autumn all things mature; in the winter, all things rest. This is justice. Benevolence is akin to music, justice is akin to rite.[322]

How good and beautiful is the world! The purpose of art is simply to make it better and more beautiful.

(5) The Origin of the State

Thus, according to Confucius the things most important to the community are music and rite. In comparison with them, government and law are but secondary. The main function of government and law is but to provide the conditions that make rite and music possible. But why is it that "to the sages the most important is the state"? The answer is that with the authority of the state the sage can put into practice the proper rite and proper music and lead the people to the proper way of life. He can perform the function of a teacher to full extent only by being a king. It is natural for him to govern, and it is no less natural for the people to follow. Whenever there is a sage, the people naturally follow him. With this action of the people, the state is spontaneously originated. This theory of the origin of state may be seen in the hexagram "Kien" in the Yi King. We have said that the hexagram is formed by the combination of two trigrams. Thus each hexagram has six lines. While the hexagram represents symbolically some phenomena of the universe, in the hexagram itself, each of

320 *Id.*, chap. 14.
321 *Id.*, Book VII, Sec. I, Chap. 18.
322 *Id*, Chap. 28.

the lines represents symbolically some detailed change of the phenomena. The hexagram "Kien" is the trigram "Kien" combined with itself. The trigram "Kien" "means heaven, circle, king, and father."[323] Thus the hexagram "Kien" represents heaven embracing all things in the natural world and the king ruling all people in the human world. Each line represents a specific activity of the philosopher who rises from the ranks of the common people to the position of the king. About the first line (starting below)

Confucius said:

> This is he who, with the virtue of a dragon (the symbol of the king) is yet lying hid. He does not change his conduct to conform to the ways of the vulgar. He does not care about the fame of the world. He has no regret; even if he is disconnected entirely from the world He is not sorry, even if he experiences the whole world's disapproval. What he considers as delightful to his reason, he does; what is opposite, he refuses. He is firm in his conviction and cannot be shaken. This is the dragon lying hid.[324]

About the second line Confucius said:

> This is he who, with the virtue of a dragon, yet occupies an ordinary place. He is sincere in his common sayings and earnest in his common conduct. He guards against depravity and preserves his perfection. He has already influenced the world, but he is not proud His virtue is extensively displayed and transformation and reformation ensue. This is the virtue of a king.[325]

With the ascending of every line the influence of the philosopher increases, till in the fifth line, he becomes the "flying dragon in heaven," that is, he becomes the king and rules the world. About this line Confucius said:

Musical notes of the same kind respond to each other; things of the same kind seek one another. Water flows to the damp; fire rises to the dry.... When the sage appears, all people of the world fix their eyes on him. Things that have their origin from heaven move upwards; things that have their origin on earth move downward — so everything follows its kind.[326]

When all the people follow him, he becomes the king, and the state is thus formed. It is formed not for the interest of the stronger, not for that of the weak. It is simply man's nature to go together and to obey him who is superior in virtue.

(6) The Evolution of the World

How about the sixth line of the hexagram? This line is "the dragon in extreme." About it Confucius said,

> When things have been carried to extreme, calamity ensues. The phrase "in extreme" refers to him who knows progression, but does not know that progression involves regression. He knows life; but does not know that life involves death. He knows possession, but does not know that possession involves loss. It is only the sage who knows progression and regression, life

323 *Yi King*, Appendix V, Chap. 11.

324 *Id.*, Appendix IV, Sec. 11. Chap. 4.

325 *Id.*, Chap. 5.

326 *Id.*, Chap, 8

and death, both possession and loss, and thus always maintains the mean. He only is the sage.[327]

This is the doctrine of the Yi King and is also the doctrine of Lao Tzu. He said:

Misery, alas! Rests upon happiness. Happiness, alas! Underlies misery. Who knows the end of this circle? What is ordinary becomes again extraordinary. What is good becomes again unpropitious. This bewilders people, and it has happened constantly since time immemorial. Therefore the sage is square, but not sharp, strict but not obnoxious, upright but not unrest raining, bright but not dazzling.[328]

This is not only true of human affairs, but is the very process of the evolution of the world. Lao Tzu said is not the way of Nature like stretching a bow? The high it brings down; the low it lifts up. Those who have abundance it depleteth; those who are deficient it augmenteth.[329]

In the *Yi King* this is not only made clear in the lines of the hexagram, but also in the order of the hexagrams.

The order of the hexagrams is of great significance. It is supposed to represent the natural process of the evolution of the world. In the *Yi King* one of the Confucian "Ten Wings" is "On the order of the Hexagrams." In that Appendix there are three fundamental points. In the introductory remarks of the second section of the Appendix we read:

Following the existence of heaven and earth, there is the existence of all things. Following the existence of all things, there is the distinction of sex. Following the distinction of sex, there is the relation between husband and wife. Following the relation between husband and wife, there is the relation between father and son. Following the relation between father and son there is the relation between the king and the people. Following the relation between the king and the people, there is the distinction of superiority and inferiority. Following the distinction of superiority and inferiority, there are social order and justice.[330]

The point is that all that happens in the universe, natural and human, is a continuous whole like a chain of natural sequences.

This is in fact what we have seen from the beginning of our discussion of Confucianism. This is the first point.

The second point is that in the process of evolution, every phenomenon involves its own negation. So one hexagram is usually followed by its opposite, thus:

When there is order, there is prosperity. Hence the hexagram "Li" (order) is followed by "Tai" (prosperity) But things cannot be forever in the state of prosperity. Hence "Tai" is followed by "Pi" (ill fortune).[331] When cultivation has been carried to the utmost, its progress comes to an end. Hence, "Pen"

327 *Id.*, Appendix IV, Sec. it Chaps, 35, 36.

328 Lao Tzu, *Tao Teh Ching*, Sec. 58.

329 *Id*, p. 77.

330 *Yi King*, Appendix VI, Chaps.,31, 32.

331 *Id*, Appendix VI, Chaps. 8-11.

(cultivation, decoration) is followed by the hexagram "Po" (decline) Things cannot be forever in the state of decline. When decline has reached its extreme in the one end, reintegration commences in the other. Hence, the hexagram "Po" is followed by the hexagram "Fu" (return)[332]

The hexagram "Tsen" means motion. Things cannot be forever in the state of motion. Hence, "Tsen" is followed by the hexagram "Ken" which means rest. Things cannot be forever in the state of rest. Hence "Ken" is followed by "Kiev" which means progression or advance.[333] From these passages we see how in the process of the evolution of the world, evil is a necessary counterpart of good. Confucius said:

> The "Yao" (the single line of each hexagram) is an imitation of the activity of the world. Because of activity, there is the manifestation of good and evil, of repentance and regret.[334]
>
> Good and evil are the indication of gain and loss. Repentance and regret are the indication of sorrow and fear.[335]
>
> Good and evil, repentance and fear, are produced by activity.[336]

Since good and evil are always connected with activity, and since the evolution of the world is a great activity, we cannot expect that in the universe there is absolutely no evil. "The eight trigrams determine the good and the evil; the good and the evil produce the great achievement!"[337] The great achievement must be accompanied by good and evil. This is what Schopenhauer called the eternal justice."

The third point is that there can never be a state, in which everything is absolutely completed or finished. This may be shown by quoting the first and the last sentence of this Appendix. They read:

> Following the existence of heaven and earth, there is the existence of all things. That which fills up heaven and earth is nothing but these things. Hence, the first two hexagrams "Kien" and "Kuen" (heaven and earth) are followed by the hexagram "Tun."

"Tun" means things in their first production. When so produced, they are necessarily in an undeveloped condition. Hence, the hexagram "Tun" is followed by the hexagram "Mung." "Mung" means things undeveloped.[338]

Those that are better than the existing things are certainly accomplishments; hence, the hexagram "Hsiao Kwo" (a little better) is followed by the hexagram "Chi Zi" (something accomplished). But there cannot be an end of things. Hence, the hexagram "Chi Zi" is followed by the hexagram "Wei Zi" (something not yet accomplished). With this hexagram the Book of Changes comes to a close.[339]

Obviously, all these three fundamental points are different from the "nature"

332 *Id.*, Chaps. 19-23.
333 *Id.*, Chaps. 44-48.
334 *Id.*, Appendix III, Sec. II,Chap. 2
335 *Id.*, Sec. I, Chap. 11.
336 *Id.*, Appendix III, Sec. I. Chap. I
337 *Id.*, Sec. I Chap. 70.
338 *Id.*, Appendix VI, Chaps. 1-3.
339 *Id.*, Chaps. 62-64.

line of thought on one side and from the "art" line of thought on the other. There is no end of things. There is no *summum bonum*. This is also what Schopenhauer called "the eternal justice." It is the revolt against the eternal justice that leads nihilism to abandon the "great achievement," to return to the infinite past, and progressivism to assume the endless task of working for the infinite future. The method of these two lines of thought is diametrically opposite, but their aim is fundamentally the same. They both wish to attain to a condition which is absolutely good, and in which man can stop once and for all.

(7) The Good of Activity

But according to Confucius we cannot stop, nor do we need to stop. The perfection of nature is not that it will produce a perfect end in the process of evolution, but is exactly that it produces an endless evolution. Its perfection is exactly its eternal activity. "To the most perfect there is no stop."[340] The meaning of its activity is not in the external accomplishment, but in the activity itself. *Tao*" has no thought" and "gives all things spontaneity without anxiety as the sages." She works not for something, but for nothing. She produced all things in the universe, but it is not for them that her eternal activity takes place. She is "doing by doing nothing" and is doing for nothing. These may be said to be the two characteristics of nature. As the *Tao*ists were impressed by her doing by doing nothing, Confucius was impressed by her doing for nothing. In order to be "doing" "by doing nothing," the *Tao*ists advised man to abolish all that is done by doing. They denounced civilization and intellect, and exalted primitively and instinct. But according to Confucius what is important is that *Tao* does for nothing. In doing, we must utilize our ability and consciously do something. For nothing, we must enjoy the doing itself, and disregard the external success or failure. In the Yi King it is said "The activity of nature is energetic. In accordance with this, the superior man encourages himself and never ceases to be active."[341]

In another place it is said:

> It is said in the Book of Poetry: "The ordinance of Nature, how profound and unceasing!" This shows that it is thus that Nature is Nature. "The virtue of King Wen, how illustrious and pure!" This shows that it is thus that King Wen is King Wen. He is pure and is unceasingly active.[342]

Thus the life of activity is also an imitation of nature. Confucius's own life is certainly a good example of this aspect of his teaching. Flourishing in a time of great social and political disorder, he tried his best to reform. He traveled everywhere and, like Socrates, talked with everybody. Although his efforts were in vain, he was not disappointed. He was much ridiculed by his contemporary *Tao*ists and Epicureans. For instance, in the Analects we read:

> Chang-tseu and Kee-ni were at work in the field together, when Confucius passed by and sent Tzu Lu to inquire for the ford.... Kee-ni said to him:

340 *The Doctrine of the Mean*, Chap. XXVI, Sec I.
341 *Yi King*, Appendix II, Sec. I, Chap. 1.
342 *The Doctrine of the Mean*, Chap. XXVI, Sec. X.

"Disorder, like a swelling flood, spreads over the whole world who can change it? You are following one who simply withdraws from this one man and that one man. "Would it be not better for you to follow those who withdraw from the world altogether?" Tzu Lu went and reported these remarks to the Master. The Master said with a sigh "It is impossible to associate with birds and beasts, as if they were the same with us. If I associate, not with mankind, with whom shall I associate? If right principle prevailed through the world, there would be no use for me to change its state.[343]

On another similar occasion, Tzu Lu said to an Epicurean on behalf of Confucius:

Wishing to maintain your personal purity, you neglect the great relations of mankind. The superior man tries to take part in politics, because it is his duty to do so. The fact that he is bound to fail, he knows already.[344]

Another passage reads:

Tzu Lu happened to pass the night in Shi-men. The gatekeeper said to him: "Whom do you come from?" Tzu Lu said: "From Mr. Kung." "Is it not he who knows that what he does is in vain, yet still does it?"[345] The last sentence is a concrete picture of Confucius.

(8) The Rational Happiness

The good consists in activity. The external success of activity is not in our control; it is a matter of Fate or fortune. While Confucius made the best effort to realize his ideal, at the same time he said: "If my philosophy is to prevail in the world, it is Fate. If my philosophy is to fall to the ground, it is also Fate."[346]

Generally speaking, Fate means the existent conditions of the whole universe. For the external success of our activity, the cooperation of these conditions is always needed. But this cooperation is wholly beyond our control, if we consider activity as simply a means for the result, and the meaning of it as wholly in the latter, our life will not be self-sufficient and self-independent. We have either to assume the endless task of searching for the good in the infinite future, or to remain melancholy and wait the coming of death. The "art" line of thought involves Epicureanism, which is it sown negation. According to Confucius, in order to maintain the good completely in the activity itself, we must "know Fate." He said: "Those who do not know Fate cannot be superior men."[347] "When I was fifty years old, I knew Fate."[348] To know Fate means to acknowledge the necessity of the world and thus to disregard the external success or failure. As Mencius afterwards said: "To weep for the dead is not for display". To lead the virtuous life is not for

343 *Analects of Confucius*, Book XVII, Chap. 6

344 *Id.*, Chap. 7.

345 *Id.*, Book XIV, Chap. 41.

346 *Id.*, Book XIV, Chap. 38.

347 *Id.*, Book XX, Chap. 2.

348 *Id.*, Book II, Chap. 4.

the honor of the state. To speak sincere words is not for the trust of others.[349] If we do not put our activity on a utilitarian basis, we can never fail. In other words, if we do not care for external success, we must always succeed. Thus the good of activity leads to rational happiness. In the Analects we read:

> The master said "The wise are free from superstition; the virtuous, from anxiety; the brave, from fear.[350]
>
> The Master said "The superior man is always happy; the mean man is always sad."[351]

As to himself he said:

> Living on coarse rice and water, with bent arm for pillow, I am still happy. Ill-gotten wealth and honors are to me as wandering clouds.[352] I murmur not against Nature, nor grumble against man. Learning from the lowest, I cleave to the heights.[353]

In the Yi King there is a more concrete picture of a sage. It reads: He is similar to heaven and earth and therefore there is no antagonism between him and them. His wisdom embraces all things and his doctrine gives salvation to the world, and therefore he falls into no error. He acts according to the exigencies of the circumstances without being carried away by their currents. He rejoices in Nature and knows Fate. Hence he has no sorrow.[354]

(9) The Union of the Internal and the External

Although for Nature there is no end of evolution, and for man there is no end of activity, yet for man as man there is a state something like a final completion or summum bonum. This is not a state of non activity, in which everything is negated or finished. It is a state in which, though there are still things and activities, the distinction between the internal and external no longer exists. This union of the external and internal is called "perfection." "Tao" or Nature is perfection itself, since in its very nature there is no distinction between the internal and external. Thus it is said:

> Perfection is the beginning and end of things. Without perfection there can be nothing. Therefore the superior man considers the attainment of perfection as the most excellent.[355]
>
> Perfection is the way of Nature; to become perfect is the way of human (or art).[356]
>
> From perfection to enlightenment is Nature; from enlightenment to perfection is education. When there is perfection, there is enlightenment; when, then, there is enlightenment, there is perfection.[357]

---

349 Mencius, "Works," tr. by James Legge in the *Four Books*, Book VII, Part II, Chap.

350 *Id.*, Book IX Chap. 28.

351 *Id.*, Book VII, Chap. 36.

352 *Id.*, Chap. 15.

353 *Id*, Book XIV, Chap. 37.

354 *Yi King*, Appendix III. Sec. I, Chap. 22.

355 *The Doctrine of the Mean*, Chap. 25.

356 *Id.*, Chap. 20.

357 *Id.*, Chap. 21.

He who tries to become perfect not only completes himself, but also completes others. The completion of himself is his virtue, the completion of others is his wisdom. Both of these are the attributes of human nature, and this is the way of the union of the internal and the external. Therefore this way is good at all times.[358]

The union of the internal and the external is attained with what Schopenhauer called "the works of love." Here we see the sharp contrast between nature and education. But the function of education is not to add to human nature some alien element, but simply to give the full development of "the attributes of human nature." This full development of nature is technically called in Confucianism the "exhaustion of nature." Thus it is said:

It is only he who is most perfect that can exhaust his own nature. Being able to exhaust his own nature, he can exhaust the nature of others. Being able to exhaust the nature of others, he can exhaust the nature of all things. Being able to exhaust the nature of all things, he can take part in the life and activity of heaven and earth. Being able to take part in the life and activity of heaven and earth, he can with heaven and earth form a ternion.[359]

Such a man would be the "flying dragon in heaven" and rule the world. He will discuss rites, fix the laws, and determine the measure of education.[360]

The institutions he made have their basis on his own personal experience and the attestation of the people. He examines his institutions by comparison with those of the three philosopher kings, and finds them without mistake. He sets them up before heaven and earth, and finds nothing in them contrary to them. He presents them to the gods and spirits, and no doubt about them arises. He maintains them to wait for the future sages, a hundred ages after, and they would also find in them no misgiving. He presents his institutions to the gods and the spirits, and no doubt about them arises, because he knows Nature. He maintains them to wait for the future sages, a hundred ages after, and they would also find in them no misgiving, because he knows man.[361]

In such a state and in such a world:

All things live together without injuring one another. All courses are pursued without collision with one another. The small evolves like river currents; the great manifests in mighty transformation. It is because of this that the universe is great.[362]

(10) Concluding Remarks

This is the Confucian ideal state of the world. It is not merely a state of nature nor is it merely a state of art. It is the full development of nature or of human nature at least, through the help of art. State, society, education, and virtue are all necessary parts to constitute this best and the most beautiful whole. According

358 *Id.*, Chap. 25.
359 *Id.*, Chap. 22.
360 *Id.*, Chap. 28
361 *Id.*, Chap. 29.
362 *Id*, Chap. 30.

to this view, romantic Taoism is right in conceiving the universe as a harmonious whole, but it is wrong in excluding from it the state of art.

Like hedonistic Taoism, Confucianism was in favor of the expression of passion and the satisfaction of desires. But at the same time it insisted on their mean state. Rite and music both exist for this purpose. Like hedonistic Taoism, Confucianism was in favor of enjoyment of the present and disregard of the future. But according to Confucianism, the enjoyment of the present is neither in the immediate pleasure, which, strictly speaking, is itself in the future, no matter how immediate it is, nor in the present passive or negative state, but solely in the present activity; the disregard of the future is the disregard of it as the external result, not as the meaning, of the present activity. Confucianism surrendered the future consequence of activity to Fate, but not the activity itself. According to Confucianism, in the present activity, there is already enough good for us to enjoy. In this respect Confucianism was more like Stoicism than Epicureanism. Stoicism taught man to "serve the god within" and disregard anything else. Marcus Aurelius said:

> In action, do nothing at random, or at variance with the ways of justice all outward circumstances, remember, are either chance or Providence; you cannot quarrel with chance, and you cannot arraign Providence.[363]

Stoicism also taught the good of activity. But in it there is too much tension and seriousness. It lacked the ease and naturalness which gives Confucianism the *Tao*istic atmosphere.

363 Marcus Aurelius Antoninus, *Thought*, Book XII Sec. 24.

X ARISTOTLE

(1) The Difference Between Plato and Aristotle

In his Metaphysics, Aristotle said "And all thinkers are confounded by the necessary consequence that there is something contrary to Wisdom, i.e., to the highest knowledge, but we are not."[364]

According to the Platonic two worlds system, there is not only something contrary to knowledge and Wisdom, but this world itself is that something. He established the supersensible world for those who are tired of this world to return to, but he left nothing in this world to enjoy for those who are not tired. The main attempt of Aristotle was to reconcile these two worlds in such a way that the ideal might be more real, and the real, more ideal.

Plato's weakness as well as greatness lay in his theory of the two worlds. The fundamental thought of Aristotle was that the supersensible world of ideas and the sensible world are identical.[365]

From Aristotle's dialogue "Concerning Philosophy" Cicero preserved a paragraph of some length, which reads:

> Imagine men who have always dwelt beneath the earth in good and well-illuminated habitations, habitations adorned with statues and paintings and well furnished with everything which is usually at the command of those who are deemed fortunate. Suppose these men never to have come up to the surface of the earth, but to have gathered from an obscure legend that a Deity and divine powers exist. If the earth were once to be opened for these men, so that they could ascend out of their concealed abodes to the regions inhabited by us, and they were to step forth and suddenly see before them the earth and the sea, and skies, and perceive the masses of the clouds and the violence of the winds; and if they were to look up at the sun and become cognizant of its magnitude and also of its workings, that he is the author of the day, in that he sheds his light over the entire heavens.... truly they would then believe that Gods really exist, and that these works originate with them.[366]

How similar is this passage with Plato's metaphor of the cave in "The Republic." There is, however, one difference and it is great. According to Plato, "the prison is the world of sight."[367] But according to Aristotle, the world of sight is the world of the ideal. Instead of the Platonic two worlds system, there is but one world; it is the best world. This is the fundamental difference between Plato and Aristotle.

(2) The Place of Ideas in Aristotle

The main controversy between Plato and Aristotle centered in the latter's criticism of the theory of ideas. The difference between these two philosophers, however, is

364 Aristotle, *Metaphysics*, tr. by W. D. Ross, Oxford, 1908, 1075 b, 20.

365 Windelband, W., *History of Ancient Philosophy*, tr. by H. E. Cushman, 3d ed., New York, 1910, p. 247.

366 Cicero, *De Natura Deorum*, Book II, 37, 95.

367 Plato, "The Republic," 517 b.

not so great as it appears to be. What Plato called the "ideas" Aristotle called the "essences," "substances," or "forms." In the first place, Aristotle said that essence only is nature in the strict sense.

From what has been said, then, it is plain that nature is the primacy, and in the strict sense, the essence of things which have themselves, as such, a source of movement, for the matter is called nature because it is qualified to receive this, and the processes of becoming and growing are called nature because they are movements proceeding from this. And nature in this sense is the source of movement of natural objects, being present in them somehow, either potentially or actually.[368]

In the second place he said that substances have no generation nor destruction, and that:

> Obviously then the form also, or whatever we ought to call the shape of the sensible thing, is not produced, nor does production relate to it, i.e., the essence is not produced.[369]
>
> Since substance is of two kinds, the concrete thing and the formula (I mean that one kind of substance is the formula taken with matter, while another kind is the formula in its generality), substances in the former sense are capable of destruction (for they are capable also of generation), but there is no destruction of the formula in the sense that it is ever in course of being destroyed; for there is no generation of it(the being of house is not generated, but only the being of this house),but without generation and destruction formula are and are not; for it has been shown that no one produces nor makes these.[370]

In the third place he claimed that the forms were unmovable. He said:

> But the forms and the affections and the place which are the terminals of the movement of moving things, are unmovable, e.g., knowledge or heat; it is not heat that is a movement, but heating.[371]In the fourth place, he claimed that the substance was prior to the individual things. He said "Now there are several senses in which a thing is said to be first; but substance is first in every sense—(I) in formula, (2) in order of knowledge, (3) in time."[372] Thus soul is the essence of body (see below, p. 196) but it is prior to body.

Aristotle said:

> Perfect realization is a word used in two senses: it may be understood either as an implicit state corresponding to knowledge possessed, or as an explicitly exercised process corresponding to active observation...Now in reference to the same object, it is the implicit knowledge of scientific principles which stand prior. Soul is therefore the earlier or implicit perfection of a natural body possessed potentially of life.[373]

---

368 Aristotle, *Metaphysics*, 1015 a, 10.
369 *Id*, 1033 a, 5.
370 *Id*., 1039 b, 20.
371 *Id*., 1067 b, 10.
372 *Id*., 1028 a, 30.
373 Aristotle, *Psychology*, tr. by E. Wallace, Cambridge, 1882, 412 a, 20.

In the same way, although historically household and individual are prior to State, "in the order of nature the State is prior to the household or the individual."[374] Indeed since the form is also "the end in view of which" the things more,[375] it must be prior to the things.

If the form exists implicitly prior to the individual things, it may be said to exist apart from the individual things. This is the fifth point. Aristotle said:

> There are three kinds of substance — the matter, the nature (i.e., the individual character), that it moves towards, which is a positive state; and again, thirdly, the particular substance which is composed of these two.... Now in some cases the individual character does not exist apart from the composite substance, e.g., the form of house does not exist so, unless the art of building exists apart (nor is there generation and destruction of these forms, but it is in another way that the house, apart from its matter, and health, and all ideals of art, exists and does not exist); but if the individual character exists apart from the concrete thing, it is only in the case of natural objects?[376]

Although Aristotle did not make this point very clear, he seemed to be bound to say that at least some of the forms exist apart from the individual.

If all these characteristics are granted to the forms we wonder why Aristotle persisted in his polemic against the Platonic theory of ideas. In fact he was not against the ideas as such, but only against the theory that these ideas are solely in the ideal world, while the individual things in this world are only "copies" or "imitations" of them. According to his theory, the essences of things, though indestructible, etc., are nevertheless the essences of things. So they cannot remain aloof in Heaven and have nothing to do with this world. If they are in Heaven as Plato supposed, the essence of things, "the posterior substance,"[377] or what the Platonic Parmenides called "the notions in our mind,"[378] will be "severed" from the "prior substance," or what the Platonic Parmenides called the absolute knowledge of God, that is, the absolute ideas in Heaven, Then:

> (1) there will be no knowledge of the former (the things themselves or ideas) and (2) the latter (the essence) will have no being. (By "severed" I mean, if the idea of good has not the essence of good, and the latter has not the property of being good). For (1) there is knowledge of each thing only when we know its essence. And (2) the case is the same for other things as for good; so that if the essence of good is not good, neither is the essence of reality real, nor the essence of unity one.[379]

Then this world would be a dreaming image of the waking reality. And the reality is, alas! Completely beyond our human knowledge. It was against this position that Aristotle directed his polemic. It was the Platonic depreciation of this world that Aristotle attacked. So in his own system the ideas are only the

374 Aristotle, *Politics*, tr. by J. E C. Welldon 7th ed., London, 1912, 1, III, p. 6.
375 Aristotle, *Physics*, tr. into French, 2 vols, Paris, 1862, II, VII, Vol. I p. 70.
376 Aristotle, *Metaphysics*, 1070 a, 10.
377 *Id.*, 1031 b, 5.
378 Plato "Parmenides," 133 c.
379 Aristotle, *Metaphysics*, 1031 b, 5.

"implicit perfection"; they "are and are not." They are still the ideals, but they must be in this world.

(3) Love and the Final Cause

In criticizing the Platonists, Aristotle said:

> They at the same time treat the ideas as universal substance and again as separable and individual.... The reason why those who say the ideas are universal combined these two views in one is that they did not make the ideas substances identical with the sensible things. They thought that the sensible things were in a state of flux and none of them remained, but the universal was apart from these and different.[380]

Plato considered the world as one of change and flux; he also considered it as bad. He preferred eternity to time, and the unchanging to the changing. But the more he elevated the ideas to Heaven, the more the worldly flux becomes purposeless and meaningless. According to Aristotle, the world is a flux, but not a purposeless flux. Nature is movement. Movement is "the act, realization or entelechy of the beings, which are in potentiality, with different distinctions which they can present."[381] Things do not move without a purpose. They have their end in view and strive to realize the good, good to themselves at least. The good is the idea, the formal as well as the final cause. It is compared with the "object of desires and the object of thought. They move without being moved."[382] "The final cause is (a) something for whose good the action is done, and (b) something at which the action aims...

The final cause, then, produces motion by being loved, and by that which it moves, it moves all other things."[383] This is Aristotle's theory of love. He agreed with Plato that "he who loves the good desires the possession of the good."[384] But, according to Plato, the absolute good is not in this world. It is only by return to the ideal "fatherland" that the real good and the real forms of the things can be seen and be possessed. According to Aristotle, this world is the ideal "fatherland." The eternal motion and the eternal flux, which worried Plato, are exactly the manifestation of love that links the potentiality with the actuality, the potentially good with the actually good. The final cause of things is "the reason, and the reason forms the starting point, alike in works of art and in works of nature."[385] Reason is the beginning of things as well as their end.

Ideas are not solely in the ideal world, and the individual things are not mere "copies" of them. Ideas are the very forms of things, and the very ends of their becoming and growth. Thus by projecting the forms into Heaven, Plato separated the real from the ideal; by calling them back to earth, Aristotle made the real the ideal, or the ideal the real. With the ideas, even matter itself becomes good.

Aristotle said: "And if, as we said, that matter is that which is potentially each

---

380 *Id.*, 1086 a, 35.
381 Aristotle, *Physics*, III, I.
382 Aristotle, *Metaphysics*, 1072 a, 25.
383 *Id.*, 1072 b, 1.
384 Plato, "*Symposium*," 204 c.
385 Aristotle, *De Partibus Animalium*, tr. by W. Ogle, Oxford, 1911, 639 b, 15.

thing, e.g., that of actual fire is that which is potentially fire, the bad will be just the potentially good."[386] There is nothing contrary to Wisdom. "The order of things is the best possible in nature."[387]

In his Metaphysics, Aristotle pointed out that none of his predecessors had said anything about final cause. He said:

> That which is the end for which actions and changes and movements take place, they assert it to be a cause in a way, but not in this way; i.e., not in the way in which it is its nature to be a cause. For those who speak of reason or friendship class these causes as goods; they do not speak, however, as if anything that exists either existed or came in to being for the sake of these, but as if movement started from these. In the same way those who say the One or the existent is the good, say that it is the cause of substance, but not that substance either is, or comes to be for the sake of this. Therefore, it turns out that in a sense they both say and do not say the good is a cause; for they do not call it a cause qua good, but only incidentally.[388]

They did not say final cause, because they did not attempt to justify this world.

(4) The God

Although everything in this world has its final cause, it does not follow that everything exists absolutely for its own sake, and is independent of others. On the contrary, in this world "plants are intended for the use of animals and all other animals for the service of man, domestic animals for employment and food alike, wild animals all or almost all for food and other purposes, e.g., for the supply of clothing and other instruments."[389]

"It is a constant rule equally conspicuous in the realm of Art and nature that the lower is for the sake of the higher." Obviously in the world things are not such "that one has nothing to do with another, but all are ordered together to one end."[390] This one end is the common good of things, the final case, the idea, of the world as a whole. This is God.

There is much dispute in regard to the nature of God in Aristotle and His relation to the world. But, according to Aristotle's "theology" as shown in the Metaphysics and the general spirit of his philosophy, it seems to be perfectly clear that by God he meant the formal, and hence, the final cause of the world, and His relation to the world is just like the final or formal cause of any individual thing to that individual thing. People often emphasize the fact that Aristotle considered God as the first mover of the world, but in fact He is the first mover only because He is the first final cause.

Aristotle said:

> And thought is moved by the object of thought, and one side of the list of opposites is itself the object of thought; and in this, substance is first, and in

386 Aristotle, *Metaphysics*, 1092 a, 1.
387 Aristotle, *Nichomachean Ethics*, tr. by J. E. C. Welldon, 7th ed. 1920, 1, X, p. 3.
388 Aristotle, *Metaphysics*, 988 a, 15, 988 b, 15.
389 Aristotle, *Politics*, Welldon's translation, 1, IX, p. 20.
390 Aristotle, *Metaphysics*, 1075 a, 15.

> substance, that which is simple and exists actually. (The one and the simple are not the same, for one means a measure, but simple means that a thing itself has a certain nature.) But the good, also, and those which are in themselves desirable are on this same side of the list; and the first in any class is always the best, or analogous to the best.[391]

Substance here must mean the "essence, the formula of which is a definition."[392] This passage seems to show that God is the simplest and the most actual of the substances and is the first on the side of the good. The first is always the best; He is the best of the good. All other substances are essence or form only in the relative sense. The same thing can be, in one respect, matter and potentiality, and in another, form and actuality. The animal is the former in relation to man; the latter in relation to the plant. The essence of the lower is always the matter of the higher. But there is nothing higher than the essence of the world as a whole. Hence, it is the simplest and the most actual. There is nothing for it to realize but itself. Hence, it has no object of thought, but only thinks itself. "Its thinking is thinking on thinking."[393] It has no object of thought, hence, it is not moved; it is the object of all thought, and hence, it is them over of all by its "being loved." In one sense all forms are immovable in relation to their matter. But since they are themselves relative, their immobility is also relative. But God, the form of the world, is absolutely immovable.

To call Aristotle's "theology" theistic is not correct. To him, God is simply "a principle" upon which "depend the heavens and the world of nature."[394] He is not a person. In regard to this point Aristotle clearly said:

> Our forefathers in the most remote ages have handed down to us their posterity a tradition in the form of a myth, that these substances (the heavenly substances) are gods and the divine encloses the whole of nature. The rest of the tradition has been added later in mythical form with a view to the persuasion of the multitude and its legal and utilitarian expediency; they say these gods are in the form of men, or like some of the animals.... But if we were to separate the first point from these addition... we must regard this as an inspired utterance, like relics of the ancient treasure.[395]

From this passage, may we not say that the concrete heavenly bodies are the gods, while the divine that encloses the whole of nature is God? After calling back to the earth the different ideas, Aristotle attempted to call back also the Idea of Good from the Platonic Heaven. According to Plato, this world has as its governor only the "child of the good."[396] But according to Aristotle, the good of the good is itself the final cause of the world. It is like a leader and the world is like an army. "The good or the highest good" which "the nature of the universe contains is found both in the order and the leader."[397] It is because of this

391 *Id*, 1072 a, 30.
392 *Id*., 1017 b, 23.
393 *Id*., 1074 b, 30.
394 *Id*., 1072 b, 14.
395 *Id*., 1074 b, 10.
396 Plato, "The Republic," 506 d.
397 *Id*., 1075 a, 10.

common final cause, this leader, that all things in the world are bound together and become a harmonious unity, and a connected whole.

(5) Soul and Body

God may be said to be the soul of the world, and His relation to the world is just like that of soul to the body.

Aristotle said:

> The soul must necessarily be a real substance, as the form which determines a natural body possessed potentially of life. The reality, however, of an object is contained in its perfect realization. Soul therefore will be a perfect realization of a body such as has been described.[398]

Following this he showed that the relation between soul and body is just like that between the wax and the figure impressed upon it, that between the ax and ax hood, or that between the eye and the vision. He again said:

It [the soul] is a real substance which expresses an idea. Such substance is the manifestation of the inner meaning of such and such a body.[399]

The soul, then, is the cause of the body as alive; and is so in each of the three senses in which the word "cause" is used: that is to say, it is so both as the efficient cause from which movement springs, as the end and final cause and as the real or essential substance of the animate bodies.[400]

What more do we need for the soul of the man and the soul of the world? Following this analogy we may say that God is the manifestation of the inner meaning, the expression of the idea, of the world. He may be called the world hood.

Only in this sense is everything in the world, bound up with God, through and through. He is the whole; other things are parts. The parts simply cannot separate from the whole. If the hand is separated from the body, it is no longer a hand.[401] It is also in this sense that the world is a real unity.

The analogy we made between Aristotle's theories of macrocosm and microcosm is not unjustifiable, for Aristotle made it himself. In his "Psychology" Aristotle said that reason, the highest part of the soul, "is not to be regarded as belonging to and governed by the things of sense (reason being a faculty independent of the matter of such objects), but the world of thought must be regarded as belonging to and regulated by reason."[402]

Following this he said:

> The same differences, however, as are found in nature, as a whole, must be characteristic also of the soul. Now in nature there is, on the one hand, that which acts as material substratum to each class of objects, this being that which is potentially of all of them: on the other hand, there is the element which is causal and creative in virtue of its producing all things, and which stands towards the other in the same relation as that in which art stands

398 Aristotle, *Psychology*, 412 a, 20.

399 *Id.*, 412 b, 10.

400 *Ibid.*

401 Aristotle, *Politics*, Welldon's translation, I, III, p. 6.

402 Aristotle, *Psychology*, 430 a, 5.

> towards the materials on which it operates. This reason is, on the one hand, of such a nature as to become all things; on the other hand, of such a nature as to create all things, acting then much in the same way as some positive quality, such as for instance light: for light also creates actual out of potential color. This phase of reason is separated from and uncompounded with material conditions, and, being in its essential character full and actually realized, it is not subject to impressions from without: for the creative is in every case more honorable than the passive, just as the originating principles superior to the matter which it forms.... Further, this creative reason does not at one time think, at another time not think: (it thinks eternally) and when separated from the body it remains nothing but what it essentially is; and thus it is alone immortal and eternal.[403]

From this passage we can see why Aristotle said that God is "separable from sensible things."[404]

As shown above, all forms may be said, in one sense, to be apart from the individual. Here Aristotle only laid special emphasis on the highest aspect of the world and man.

Aristotle's theory of the relation of soul and body is significant, if we compare it with that of Plato. According to Plato, the soul is completely alien to the body and is imprisoned in it in its fall. As

Aristotle said about Plato's theory:

> It is burdensome also for the soul to be united with the body without possibility of release from it: and not only so, but such union is to be, if possible, avoided, supposing it to be better for the reason to be independent of the body, as is usually said and widely believed.[405]

Aristotle's theory was apparently an attempt to overcome this dualism.

(6) The Origin of Evil

If all is good in nature, whence comes evil? In the discussion of the natural distinction of free man and slave, Aristotle said:

> But it frequently results contrary to the intention of nature that those who possess the bodies do not possess the souls of free men and vice versa.[406]
>
> It is assumed that, as the offspring of men are men, and of beasts, beasts, so the offspring of good men are good, and indeed it is Nature's object to bring about this result, although not infrequently she fails.[407]

In carrying out a plan, it often happens that the action requisite for the end in view has consequences that were not foreseen and had not entered into the consideration of the agent. This is true both in human affairs and in the operation of Nature. When these unforeseen consequences happen in human affairs we say they are by chance; when they happen in the operation of Nature

---

403 *Id.*, 10-25.

404 Aristotle, *Metaphysics*, 1073 a, 5.

405 Aristotle, *Psychology*, 407 b, I.

406 Aristotle, *Politics*, Welldon's translation, 1, VI, p. 13.

407 *Id*, Chap. VIII, pp. 15, 16.

we say they are of spontaneity. Spontaneity is "that which is produced without appreciable cause," and is the phenomenon which "takes place against the law of Nature, and which is monstrous."[408]

One can say, with no less truth, that chance is something irrational; for reason appears in the things which are eternal or, at least, the most common in such and such a manner, while chance is found only in the things that are neither eternal, nor in the majority of the cases; and as the causes of the latter kind of things are undermined, chance is as undetermined as the causes are.[409]

Both spontaneity and chance are something exceptional. But since there are these exceptions, few men in the world can be happy in all respects, although the world is essentially good.

How evident it is that all men desire to live well and to be happy! But while some have it in their power to attain these objects, there are others who from some fault of Nature or Fortune have it not.[410]

But this does not make the world less perfect. Aristotle said:

> But as chance and spontaneity are causes of phenomena which nature and intelligence could equally produce, and as chance and spontaneity can appear only in places where intelligence and nature act only accidentally and in an indirect manner, as, moreover, the accidental cannot be anterior and superior to what is in itself, it is clear also that the accidental cause cannot be superior to the essential cause. Then, spontaneity and chance come only after Intelligence and Nature. Even if one would go so far as to conceded that chance can be the cause of heaven, nevertheless Intelligence and Nature still should be the superior causes of phenomena and of the whole universe.[411]

(7) The Purpose of Art

The frequent failure of nature, however, is a matter of fact. Thus art is needed. As Aristotle said "It is the purpose of all art and culture to supply the deficiencies of Nature."[412] Man has intelligence, the mother of all arts. With intelligence, he can make up all that he has not in nature. He came to the world "barefooted, naked, and without weapon of which to avail himself." But to him:

> numerous modes of defenses are open, and these, moreover, he may change at will; as also he may adopt such weapons as he pleases, and at such time as suits him. For the hand is talon, hoof, and horn, at will. So it is spear and sword, and whatsoever other weapons or instruments you please.[413]

This is no doubt Nature's aim, and art helps to realize this aim.

Nature also aims at producing health in all the living beings. All of them have

408 Aristotle, *Physics*, II, VI.
409 *Id.*, II, V.
410 Aristotle, *Politics*, Welldon's translation, IV, XVII, p. 199.
411 Aristotle, *Physics*, II, VI.
412 Aristotle, *Politics*, Welldon's translation, IV, XVII, p. 221.
413 *De Partibus Anmalium*, 687 a, 20.

been endowed with the instinctive capacity of self-curing. But disease often defeats Nature's aim. The art of medicine again comes to help her. Thus art is far from Nature's conqueror as the "art' line of thought supposed. On the contrary, art is always Nature's best ally in the realization of the beautiful and the good. Moreover, art comes from intelligence; intelligence comes from Nature. In this sense art is simply a continuation of Nature. That men use spears and swords is just as natural as that the beasts use their hoofs and horns. That men build houses is just as natural as that the birds build their nests. All arts are simply the result of the natural development of man's nature. The power of man's intelligence is just the manifestation of Nature's wisdom.

(8) The Origin of the State

There is also nothing arbitrary in the origin of the State. "The State is a natural institution" and "man is naturally a political animal"[414] The nature of man is such that they must go together and form some union. In the first place:

> The male and female must combine for the procreation of children, nor is there anything deliberate or arbitrary in their doing so; on the contrary, the desire of leaving offspring like one's self is as natural to man as to the whole animal and vegetable world.[415]

The association of man and woman forms the household; the association of households forms the village.

Lastly [Aristotle said], the association composed of several villages in its complete form is the State, in which the goal of independence maybe said to be first attained. For as the State was formed to make life possible, so it exists to make life good. Consequently, if it be allowed that the simple associations, i.e., the household and the village have a natural existence, so has the State in all cases; for in the State they attain complete development, and Nature implies complete development, as the nature of anything, e.g., of man, a house, or a horse, may be defined to be its condition when the process of production is complete. Or the naturalness of the State may be proved in another way: the object proposed or the complete development of a thing is its highest Good; but independence, which is first attained in the State, is a complete development of the highest Good and is therefore natural.[416]

Only in the State can man have full development. In this sense he is not a man if he is not in the State. The State is the whole, and no part can exist apart from the whole.

Obviously this theory is like that of Confucius, especially that as expounded in the chapter, "On the Order of the Hexagrams." (See above, p. 173.) Like Confucius, Aristotle also taught that the State should be governed by those who are superior in virtue and wisdom, that the most essential for the State is education, rather than law and punishment, and that music is one of the most

---

414 Aristotle, *Politics*, Welldon's translation, 1, II, p. 5.

415 *Id*, p. 2.

416 *Id.*, P. 5.

efficient instruments in education, although he substituted gymnastic for rites. He also said:

> The best organized State is the one which offers the greatest happiness.[417]
> And happiness is the summum bonum; and happiness consists in a perfect activity and practice of virtue.[418]
> Virtue, then, is a state of deliberate moral purpose consisting in a mean that is relative to us, the mean being determined by reason, or as a pendent man would determine it.[419]

As to the problem whether virtue is natural or conventional, he said:

> It is neither by nature, then, nor in defiance of nature that virtues are implanted in us. Nature gives us the capacity of receiving them, and that capacity is perfected by habit.[420]

All these points are in one way or another so much in common with Confucius that we cannot discuss them without repeating what we have already said. For the purpose of the present work, however, we need not discuss them further.

(9) The Problem of Pleasure

We should not, however, omit Aristotle's discussion of pleasure.

Aristotle said "For some people say that the good is pleasure; others, on the contrary, that pleasure is utterly bad."[421] Plato has been selected to represent the second view. In criticizing him, Aristotle said:

> But it is clear that if pleasure is not the good, neither can anything else be which is made more desirable by the addition of any absolute good. What is it, then, which is incapable of such addition, but at the same time admits of our participating in it? For it is a good of this kind which is the object of our research.[422]

According to him, pleasure is good, but he insisted on the theory of the qualitative difference of pleasure. With the introduction of this theory into ethics, he refined the crude utilitarianism or hedonism of the Sophists. In this respect, Aristotle was the ancient Mill. According to the theory which Aristotle said Plato criticized, pleasure is either a process of production or a process of motion. "Pain is the destruction of that of which pleasure is the production. It is said, too, that pain is a deficiency of the natural state, and pleasure, its satisfaction."[423] Both motion and the process of production are "descriptions" which are "appropriate" only to such things "as are divisible into parts and are not wholes."[424]

But according to Aristotle, pleasure is not a satisfaction of deficiency, for "the pleasures of mathematics, for example, have no such antecedent pain, nor among the pleasures of the senses have those of smell, nor again many sounds and sights,

---

417 *Id.*, IV, XIII, p. 199.

418 *Id.*, p. 183.

419 Aristotle, *Nichomachean Ethics* Welldon's translation, II, VI, p. 47.

420 *Id.*,I,II,I, p. 35.

421 *Id.*,X,I,p.315.

422 *Id.*, X, II P. 318.

423 *Id.*, X, II, p. 320.

424 *Id.*, III, p. 325.

memories and hopes."[425] Nor is pleasure a motion. "Motions are apparently not complete in any and every period of time; on the contrary, most motions are incomplete and different in kind, in as much as the starting point and the goal constitute a difference of kind. Pleasure, on the other hand, seems to be complete or perfect of its kind, in any and every period of time."[426]

This shows that pleasure does not increase in time as motion or product increases, but "the pleasure of a moment is a whole."[427]

Aristotle said:

> It seems that the act of sight is perfect or complete at any time; it does not lack anything which will afterwards be produced, and will make it perfect of its kind. Pleasure appears to resemble sight in this respect; it is a whole, or is it possible at any time to find a pleasure which will be made perfect of its kind by increased duration.[428]

Every pleasure is unique in its kind, and is the whole at any time. So there can never be a quantitative difference of pleasure, but only a qualitative difference.

Where do we experience pleasures? "We experience them not in the process of acquiring certain powers, but in the exercise of the powers when acquired." It is wrong, therefore, to define pleasure as a "sensible process." It is better to define it as "activity of the natural state of one's being, and to call it not 'sensible' but 'unimpeded"[429] Aristotle said:

> So long as the object of thought or sensation and the critical or contemplative subjects are such as they ought to be, there will be pleasure in the exercise of the activity; for this is the natural result if the agent and patient remain in the same relation to each other.[430]

Thus "pleasure perfects activity." It therefore perfects life, which is the aim of human desire."[431] "It is not as a state or quality inherent in the subject, but as perfection superadded to it, like the bloom of youth to people in the prime of life."[432] Pleasure and life are so yoked together that we really do not know whether we desire life for pleasure or pleasure for life. "Pleasure is impossible without activity, and every activity is perfected by pleasure."[433]

As there are different kinds of activity, there are accordingly different kinds of pleasure. These pleasures are qualitatively different. The question is what kind of pleasure we should choose.

Aristotle said:

> But in all these cases it seems that the thing really is what it appears to the virtuous man to be. But if this is a true statement of the case, as it seems to be, if virtue or the good man qua good is the measure of everything, it follows

---

425 *Id.*, II, p. 321.
426 *Id.*, X, III, p. 324.
427 *Id*, p. 324.
428 *Id*, II, p. 323.
429 *Id.*, VII, XIII, p. 237.
430 *Id.*, X IV, P. 326
431 *Id.*, p. 327.
432 *Id.*, p 326.
433 *Id.*, p 327.

that it is such pleasures as appear pleasures to the good man that are really pleasures, and the things which afford him delight that are really pleasant.[434]

These are the pleasures that are "proper to man."[435]

These are the essence of happiness, the highest good.[436]

(10) The Life of Contemplation

Aristotle said:

> If happiness consists in virtuous activity, it is only reasonable to suppose that it is the activity of the highest virtue, or in other words of the best of our nature.
>
> The speculative is the highest activity, as the intuitive reason is the highest of our faculties, and the objects with which the intuitive reason is concerned are the highest of things that can be known. It is also the most continuous; for our speculation can more easily be continuous than any kind of action.... At all events it appears that philosophy possesses pleasure of wonderful purity and certainty.[437]

The life of contemplation is also the best, because in the first place it is more self-sufficient and independent than other virtues.[438] In the second place, it has its end completely in itself.[439] In the third place, it is separated from the emotions.[440] In all respects the happiness of contemplation is akin to that of the Divine. The "perfection of God or the universe is that all their actions are self-contained and there are none which have an effect external to themselves."[441] The activity of God is thinking, and is "thinking on thinking."[442] He is also free from the emotions which are "the composite or material pan of our nature."[443]

All these perfections are found in the life of contemplation. So Aristotle said:

> But such a life will be too good for man. He will enjoy such a life not in virtue of his humanity, but in virtue of some divine element within him, and the superiority of this activity to the activity of any other virtue will be proportionate to the superiority of this divine element in man to his composite or material natures.

(11) Concluding Remarks

Aristotle certainly gave us a splendid picture of the happy life. According to him:

> It is only in a secondary sense that the life which accords with others, i.e., nonspeculative virtue, can be said to be happy; for the activities of such

434 *Id.*, X, V, p. 331.
435 *Ibid.*
436 *Id.*, X, VII, p. 335.
437 *Id.*, p. 335.
438 *Id.*, p. 339.
439 *Id.*, p. 336.
440 *Id.*, p. 338.
441 Aristotle, *Politics*, Welldon's translation, IV, IV, p. 172.
442 Aristotle, *Metaphysics*, 1074 b, 30.
443 Aristotle, *Nichomachean Ethics*, Welldon's translation, X, VIII, p. 339?????.^8*Id*, p. 337.

virtue are human, they have no divine element.[444]

They have to deal with human affairs.

If this is so, there are few people who can be really happy. Few people have leisure and peace at hand; most of them must engage in business for leisure and war for peace. It seems that with the introduction of the distinction of the speculative activity, and of the superiority of the former to the latter, Aristotle led himself in ethics, at least, to his Master's two worlds system, which he fought against. He knew that in order to enjoy the good of activity, the activity must be self-dependent and self-sufficient, without ulterior ends, and without passion. But he did not see how every activity could meet these requirements. Next we shall see that in Neo-Confucianism an attempt was made to find the leisure in business, the calm in emotion, and the divine speculation in human affairs.

444 *Id*, p. 338.

XI NEO-CONFUCIANISM

Neo-Confucianism is a new name given to a most influential type of modern Chinese philosophy usually known as the "Philosophy of Sung." Most of its representatives were in their early years believers in Taoism[445] and Buddhism, and only afterwards came back to Confucius. They claimed that their teaching was the genuine Confucianism, but in fact it was Confucianism with Buddhism meaning. They also divided themselves into two rival branches; we may say, the left and the right. The left wing was nearer to the original Buddhism; the right wing, to the original Confucianism. The left accused the right of being too formal; the right accused the left of being too subjective. For our present purpose the left wing is important, because in it the influence of Buddhism is the most obvious. So in this chapter, Wang Yang-ming, the leader of the left, is our philosopher.

(1) The General System

Neo-Confucianism is in one sense the modern science of China. The similarity between it and modern European science is that besides theory it has a technical and applied side. The difference between it and modern European science is that while modern European science aims primarily to know and to control matter, the aim of Neo-Confucianism is primarily to know and to control the mind. In the following treatment of Wang Yang-ming's philosophy, I shall omit entirely the discussion of technic. The Neo-Confucian technic is hardly intelligible to the West without detailed elucidation, which is, however, far beyond the purpose and the scope of the present work.

The general system of Wang Yang-ming's philosophy is based on his interpretation of The Great Learning. The general principle of The Great Learning is shown in its opening passage: "The doctrine of The Great Learning is: to enlighten the enlightened virtue, to love others, and to stop at the supreme good."[446] Wang Yang-ming's interpretation of this passage is shown in the following dialogue:

> "Referring to The Great Learning a former scholar held that it is the learning of the Great Man. I venture to ask why the learning for the Great Man should consist in the enlightenment of the enlightened virtue."
>
> "The Great Man is an all-pervading unity, one with heaven, earth, and all things.... The small man makes a cleavage between things and distinguishes between him and others. The reason that the Great Man can be one with heaven, earth, and all things, is not that he makes himself to be, but that the nature of his mind is so. The mind of the small man is just the same, only he makes it small. The small man sees the child about to fall into the well; he certainly will experience a feeling of alarm and distress. This proves that his love is one with the child.... When he hears the pitiful cry and sees the

445 Taoism mentioned in this chapter refers to the later Taoistic religion, which is different from the earlier Taoism as a philosophy.

446 *The Great Learning*, Sec. I.

frightened appearance of the birds and the beasts that are about to be killed, he certainly will feel pain. This proves that his love is one with the birds and the beasts.... These show that the original unity is also in the small man. This nature of mind has its source in Nature and its light cannot be obscured. Therefore, it is called the enlightened virtue. But when the small man is moved by desires and obscured by selfishness, he will destroy things and do all evils ... and at last the original unity is lost. The learning of the Great Man is simply to clear away the obscuration of selfish desires and thus to enlighten the enlightened virtue so that he can restore the original unity of heaven, earth, and all other things. It is not possible to add anything to the original."

"But why does the learning of the Great Man consist in loving others?"

"To enlighten the enlightened virtue is to establish the nature of the unity of heaven, earth, and all other things; to love others is to exercise the function of that unity. Therefore, the enlightenment of the enlightened virtue consists in loving others: to love others is to enlighten the enlightened virtue. . . . For this reason, if I love my own father, the fathers of others, and the fathers of all men, my love will be truly extended with my loving all these fathers.... From all these human relations up to mountains, rivers, spirits, gods, birds, animals, and plants, all should be truly loved in order to promote my natural love. Then there is nothing left unenlightened in my enlightened virtue, then I am really one with heaven, earth, and all things..."

"But why stop at the supreme good?"

"The supreme good is the highest standard of enlightening virtue and loving others. Our original nature is purely good. White cannot be darkened if it is the supreme good, the nature of the enlightened virtue, and also intuitive knowledge. When things come to it, right is right, wrong is wrong, important is important, inferior is inferior. It responds with all things and changes always, but it eternally maintains the mean. This is the highest standard of the action of man and of things, and nothing can be added or diminished.... Among the former scholars, there were some who attempted to enlighten their enlightened virtue. But, as they did not know enough to stop at the supreme good, they used their selfish purpose to excess and lost their mind in vacuous, lifeless and lonely contemplation, and could do nothing to the world.... There were others who loved others. But their motive is selfish, base, and trifling. They simply used power, strategy, and craft, but had no real love and genuine sympathy.... All these people were wrong, because they did not know to stop at the supreme good."[447]

In the original nature, all is unity. Man lost this unity in the false distinction in what Schopenhauer called the principium individuation is. The method of the restoration of the original nature is "the works of love" or "the enlargement of heart."[448] This is the most natural way of life; this is what intuitive knowledge tells us.

447 Wang Yang-ming, *Works*, Book XXVI, "Dialogue on the Great Learning"

448 Sec above, p. 62.

(2) The Criticisms on Buddhism

But according to Schopenhauer the restoration of the original nature only assures us that in this world happiness is a real illusion and suffering is a solid reality. In the unity we really see "the eternal justice." In order to be happy we are bound to return to the original "nothing" with the complete denial of will. But as already seen in the above quotation, according to Wang Yang-ming, this is exactly selfishness. The Buddhists are equally mistaken as are the utilitarians. Their teachings are based on calculation, not on intuitive knowledge. So they both lose the mean, either by excess or by deficiency. If Buddhism tried to secure the "nothing" by means of calculation, it simply adopted a wrong method. Wang Yang-ming said:

> When the *Tao*ists speak of the "nonreal," can the Confucian philosopher add to it a hair of real? When the Buddhists speak of "nothing," can the Confucian sage add to it a hair of thing? But when the *Tao*ists speak of "nonreal," their motive is to preserve life. When the Buddhists speak of "nothing," their motive is to escape the bitterness and suffering of life and death. When they add these ideas to the original nature of mind, their original meaning of "nonreal" and "nothing" is somewhat lost and thereby the original nature of mind is not completely free from obscuration. The Confucian sage simply restores the original condition of intuitive knowledge and adds to it no idea whatsoever. Heaven, earth, and all things are all in the function and activity of our intuitive knowledge. How can anything be outside it and hinder or obstruct it?[449]

> The fact that the Buddhists pay no attention to phenomena shows that they do pay attention to them. The fact that we Confucian philosophers pay attention to phenomena shows that we do not pay attention to them The Buddhists are afraid of the trouble of the relation between father and son and hence avoid this relation. They are afraid of the trouble of the relation between sovereign and people and hence they avoid this relation. They are afraid of the relation between husband and wife and hence they avoid this relation. They must avoid these relations because they pay attention to them. But we Confucian philosophers are different. If there is the relation between father and son, we respond to it with love. If there is the relation between sovereign and the people, we respond to it with justice. If there is the relation between husband and wife, we respond to it with mutual respect. We do not pay special attention to these relations.[450]

The real way to find the "nothing" is not to make the attempt. If one makes the attempt, the attempt itself is a thing. We all have the intuitive knowledge which gives all things the natural response. If we simply let it go and follow it, we can deal with things just as though we do not deal with them. The "nothing" is to be secured within life, not without life.

449 Wang Yang-ming, *Works*, Book III.
450 *Ibid.*

(3) The Mean in Love

According to Schopenhauer, life itself is a contradiction. Our original nature makes us love others; but as a matter of fact we can maintain life only at the expense of others. At least we must eat vegetables. This means we must eat ourselves. How can we endure the eternal justice? Confucius said that the domestication of animals was good because it was useful to life, our life, certainly; but how about the life of the animal? According to the "nature" line of thought, this is something that fundamentally ought not to be.

According to the "art" line of thought this is simply a case of the fact that might is right. But to those who want to justify both nature and art, and who consider the universe as a whole is a harmony rather than an antagonism, this contradiction is certainly a very difficult problem. Aristotle gave an answer, but it is altogether too teleological for us to believe. But in the Confucian school, there was a theory of love with degrees. This theory was fully expounded by Mencius and accepted by the Neo-Confucianists.

The following quotation shows how Wang Yang-ming met this contradiction of life. It reads:

> "If the Great Man is one with all things, why did The Great Learning say that we should treat some things better than others?"

In the natural reason, there is a difference in regard to the different things. The body, for instance, is a unity. But when one uses the arms to protect the head, one does not purposely treat the arms worse than the head. According to natural reason, it is so. We love both the animals and plants. But we give plants to feed the animals, and we can tolerate it. We love both men and the animals, but we butcher the animals to feed our parents, to offer sacrifice, to entertain guests, and we can also endure it. We love both our nearest relative and the unknown people.

But suppose that there is only a little food, and that if the individual gets it he will live, otherwise he will die, and that it is absolutely impossible to save both our nearest relative and the unknown people, we most give this food to the nearest relative rather than to the unknown people, and we also tolerate it. This is in harmony with the natural reason. But among our own person and our nearest relatives, absolutely no distinction can be made; because here is the origin of our love. If we can tolerate here, there will be nothing we cannot tolerate.[451]

This theory seems to be like that of Aristotle, but is in fact different. It does not presuppose a teleological universe. It simply shows that in our intuitive knowledge there is a certain selfishness that can be justified, that is natural. The theory of love with degrees is a reconciliation of extreme altruism and extreme egoism. With this the contradiction of life is solved.

(4) Passion and the Natural Evil

Another main reason for Schopenhauer to escape from the world is that in the world there are the "infinite suffering," the natural evils, such as death, disease, etc.

451 *Id.*, Book IV.

But according to Wang Yang-ming, there are no such evils. This may be shown in the following dialogue:

When I was pulling the weeds from among the flowers, I said "In heaven and earth, how difficult it is to cultivate the good and to get rid of the evil." This is to make a distinction between good and evil from the human point of view, and this is a mistake.... The life of the universe is in the grass as well as in the flower. There is no distinction between good and evil. Because you like the flowers, you say that they are good and the grass is evil. But when you want to use the grass, you will in turn consider the grass as good. This kind of good and evil has its source in your mind, therefore I know it is a mistake."

"In that case there is neither good nor evil; is this not so?"

"In the tranquility and equilibrium of mind, there is neither good nor evil. Only with the stirring of passion, does the distinction between good and evil appear. If there are no stirrings of passion, there is neither good nor evil, and this is what is called the Supreme good."

"According to Buddhism the Supreme good is also the non- distinction between good and evil. In what way is it different from what you say?"

"The Buddhists insist on the non-distinction between good and evil and then disregard all things. For this reason they cannot enter matters of the world. The non distinction between good and evil in the case of the Confucian philosopher implies that he does neither make like nor make dislike...

"Since the grass is not bad, it should not be pulled up."

"That is the view of Buddhism. If the grass causes any hindrance, you can pluck it up."

"Then I make like and dislike?"

"To make no like and dislike does not mean that there is no like and dislike. Without these, a man would be as if devoid of consciousness. When I say do not make, I mean simply to like and dislike according to the natural reason without making any purposed effort to like and dislike. Thus one likes and dislikes as though he does not like or dislike."

"How can weedings be construed in accordance with natural reason and as making no effort?"

"If the grass causes any hindrance and you intuitively think that it should be uprooted, then uproot it. If you cannot pull it up, your mind is still not disturbed. If you make any conscious effort, the original nature of mind will be disturbed by the passion."[452]

In nature there is neither good nor evil. Natural good and natural evil are simply due to human like and dislike. Of course to abolish like and dislike is certainly one way to do away with the evil. But according to Wang Yang-ming, this is not necessary. We need only not make like or dislike, that is, not insist on like and dislike. We will not insist, if we only know that in things themselves there is no evil, and that evil is only the product of our passion. Thus we disconnect the transitory passions from their permanent cause. "If you cannot

452 *Id.*, Book I.

pull it, your mind is not disturbed," because the dislike is disconnected from the grass. In the latter part of the dialogue he concluded that one might be angry, but one should not have a thing about which one might be angry. One might like or dislike, but one should not have a thing that one likes and dislikes. This means the non-insistence. This means that one should not make like or dislike. In another place Wang Yang-ming said that there were passions, but we must not have them.[453] All these sayings mean the same thing.

(5) The Absolute Calm

A passion can no longer trouble our mind if we disconnect it from its cause. In the same way business and any kind of human activity can no longer trouble us if we disconnect them from their result. In doing a thing the mind is not so much troubled by the doing as by the calculation, the nervousness, the anxiety about the personal failure or success. All these are due to selfishness and should be avoided. If they are avoided, the mind will only enjoy the doing, but not be troubled by it. It will respond to all things, but at the same time be like "the Heavenly Prince in leisure, while the members carry out his will."[454] The popular illustration given by the Neo-Confucianist is that the mind is like the sun, the passions like the clouds; the clouds pass and vanish but the sun is not disturbed. The mind is like the mirror, human affairs are like the reflections; the reflections pass and vanish, but the mirror itself is not disturbed. But these are only popular illustrations. The mind is not outside the activity; it is the mind that is active. Only that it is still tranquil while it is active. This is the union of tranquility and activity. This is the highest state and the best state of mind.

The following is a picture of this state:

> The mind is neither tranquility as such nor activity as such. Tranquility refers to its nature; activity refers to its function. For this reason the learning of the superior man makes no distinction between tranquility and activity. When it is tranquil, it is always awakening, and therefore is different from "nothing." Therefore, it can always respond. When it is active, it is always calm and therefore it is troubled by nothing. Therefore it is always quiet.... Thus it is calm when it is tranquil; it is also calm when it is active. The mind is one and undivided. Since tranquility is its nature, he who seeks another tranquility in this tranquility destroys its very nature. Since activity is its function, he who is afraid of activity destroys its function! The very idea of seeking tranquility is itself activity. The very idea of avoiding activity is itself not tranquility, Then the mind is in disturbance both in tranquility and activity. The disturbance is endless.[455]

The last sentence shows the defect of Buddhism. Another earlier Neo-Confucianist, Cheng Ming-tao, had a treatise "On Calm," which may be quoted in part as follows:

---

453 *Id.*, Book II.

454 *Id.*, Book I.

455 *Id.*, Book V.

> What is called calm is the calm both in activity and in tranquility.
>
> In it there is no anxiety about the future, no distinction between the internal and the external. If some people consider the external things as the source of disturbance, he considers that in his nature there is a distinction between the internal and the external.... He has a conscious idea to avoid the external inducement, but he does not know that there is no distinction between the external and the internal. Keeping this dualism in mind, how can he know the real calm? The universe is unchanging, because its mind is in all things, yet of itself it has no mind. The sage is unchanging, because his feeling follows the nature of things, yet he himself has no feeling. Therefore the learning of the superior man is to keep the mind open and in response to all things.... Every man has his own one-sidedness and thus he is likely to miss the truth.
>
> The general trouble is that man is often too selfish and has too much calculation. Being too selfish, he cannot take activity as activity. Having too much calculation, he cannot take intuition as his natural guide. He has an idea of aversion towards outside things. With this mind he wants to enlighten the place of nothingness. This is just like seeking reflection in the back of a mirror. Than to disregard the outside as external and to regard only the internal, it is better to forget both the external and the internal. If both of them are forgotten, there is nothing left. If there is nothing, there is calm. If there is calm, there is light. If there is light, is there any more trouble in dealing with things?[456]

The real "nothing" is to be found, not in the negation of activity and the external, but in the union of activity and tranquility, of the external and the internal. This is what the Neo-Confucianists considered as far superior to Buddhism.

(6) Concluding Remarks

Concerning intuition or intuitive knowledge of which the Neo-Confucianists spoke, we need not take it to mean something mysterious. It means just natural feeling. We naturally have the feeling of sympathy towards others; we naturally have more sympathy towards man than towards the animals. These are our natural guides. According to the Neo-Confucianists, the first response in our mind to the external things is always the manifestation of the original good, the intuitive knowledge. The common illustration they used is that when a man sees a child about to fall into the well, his first response is to save it from falling. Other ideas, such as to show his bravery, to make friendship with the father of the child, come to the mind only afterwards. The first is the response of intuitive knowledge; the others are calculation and selfishness. Of course in a simple case like this, it is true. But it is not infrequently true that the first response is something bad or fixed simply by habit or custom.

Anyway, the Neo-Confucianists certainly gave us a concrete picture of a kind of ideal life. They also embodied the picture in their own lives and told us the method

456 Huang Tsung-hsi, *Selections front the Philosophies of Sung and Yuang*, Book XIII.

of attaining it. Whether their method is really practicable or whether their theory is sound are questions still to be answered. It is hoped that the further development of what is called "deep psychology" may not fail to throw light upon this branch of man's thought. Whether this branch of man's thought is to be verified or rejected in the future, its attempt to reconcile the "nothing" with things must remain as a great event in the history of philosophy, and its literature must remain as a body of most interesting human documents.

XII HEGEL

(1) The Criticism of Kant and Fichte

The fundamental antagonism in the modern West is that of the ego against the whole alien world. Progressivism had its origin in man's rebellion against God. Immediately after the rebellion, man was conscious of his greatness as well as his smallness. He was conscious of his greatness, because he thought that there was a great alien world for him to conquer. He was conscious of his own smallness, because he thought that the world for him to conquer was a great alien world. All the same, he was conscious of the "self" in opposition to the non-self, the whole outside world. The self may know and conquer the outside world, but it must always remain an outside world. Kant tried to establish a noumenal world for God, immortality, and freedom. But at last he succeeded in establishing only a world beyond, the existence and content of which remain matters of faith. Fichte elevated the Ego to the place of God and thus made it itself the whole. But outside the Ego there is still the non-Ego. As the Ego gains in fullness, the non-Ego moves ever before it, like a ghost that cannot be laid. The Ego must assume the infinite task of conquering the non-Ego, but the final success again remains a matter of faith. Speaking of Kant, Hegel said:

> The observations, made in the various stages of consciousness, culminate in the summary statement that the content of all we are acquainted with is only an appearance.... This stage of "appearance," however -- the phenomenal world — is not the terminus of thought: there is another and a higher region. But that region was to Kantian philosophy an inaccessible "other world"[457]

Speaking of Fichte, he said:

> Fichte, in consequence, never advanced beyond Kant's conclusion, that the finite only is knowable, while the infinite transcends the range of thought. What Kant called the-thing-by-itself, Fichte called the impulse from without-that abstraction of something else than "I," not otherwise describable or definable than as the negative or non-Ego in general.... And in this manner the "I" is but the continuous act of self-liberation from this impulse, never gaining a real freedom, because with the surcease of the impulse the "I," whose being is its action, would also cease to be.[458]

The dualism, the opposition of the self to the outside, was not conquered; the divorce of the individual from the whole was not reconciled. This is the wound that man received in his rebellion against God. Hegel attempted to heal this wound. He attempted to restore the unity of the world, and, at the same time, to justify the antagonism. He attempted to restore the dignity of the whole and at the same time to keep the dignity of the ego. This he did with his theory that the

457 *The Logic of Hegel*, Wallace's translation, London, 1892, p. 119.

458 *Id.*,p. 120.

universal Spirit must be self-conscious. The universal Spirit must scatter itself into individual selves, into diversity, and antagonism, simply because it wants to be, or needs to be self-conscious.

(2) "An Sich" and "Fur Sich"

The important idea in Hegel's philosophy is the self-consciousness. Confucius said: "There is none who does not drink and eat, but few know the taste."[459] It is the consciousness of the taste that makes eating and drinking interesting. The romantic philosopher idealized the instinctive activity of primitive people, of children, of birds and beasts. But we really wonder how these agents themselves, who act unconsciously according to the dictate of their "virtue," enjoy the highest blessing which the romantic observer attributed to them. No doubt there is happiness, but probably most of the happiness is only "known to us," to use Hegel's phrase, but not known to the agents. There is truth in the romantic philosophy that the negation of civilization and intellect and the restoration of primitivity and instinct are desirable. But they forget that it is the restoration that is significant. As Hegel said the old man may utter the same creed as the child, but for him "it is pregnant with the significance of a lifetime."[460] The romantic philosopher can enjoy the simplicity of the state of nature, simply because he has been in the entanglement of the state of art. This seems to be a matter of fact. Based upon this fact Hegel built his system. No doubt in the original state of the world Spirit, there is harmony and unity, but this primal harmony and unity are only for the observer, not for the Spirit itself.

God is God only so far as he knows himself his self-knowledge is, further, his self-consciousness in man, and man's knowledge of God, which proceeds to man's self-knowledge in God.[461]

While the embryo is certainly, in itself, implicitly a human being, it is not so explicitly, it does not take itself to be a human being (fur sich)[462] The embryo is a man an sich, the man is a man an and fur sich.

The embryo is in essence already a man, but is only a man "known to us," to the observer, but not to itself. It is not self-conscious. In order to be self-conscious, it has to pass through the whole process of development, of opposition, and struggle. The result of the whole process is nothing more than what was already in the embryo. But now it "takes itself to be a human being." It is self-conscious freedom.

This is true of everything and also of God. God, in order to be an und fur sich, must be self-conscious. In order to be self-conscious He must create the world. The Platonic ideal, in order to be conscious of it, must pass into the actual.

The Buddhistic "nothing," in order to be conscious of it, must pass over to things. There is no mistake either in God or in man in having an antagonistic world.

---

459 *The Doctrine of the Mean*, Chap. IV, Sec. II.

460 *The Logic of Hegel*, Wallace's translation, Oxford, 1892, p. 373.

461 Hegel, "Philosophy of Mind," tr. from *The Encyclopedia of Philosophic Science* by W. Wallace, Oxford, 1894, p. 299.

462 Hegel, *Phenomenology* of Mind, tr. by J. B. Bailli, London, 1910, p. 19.

(3) The Interpretation of the "Creation"

The ultimate Being, in its immediate and primal unity, is simple immediacy, the bare objective existence, but qua immediacy or existence is without Self.[463]

It has to become self-contained for itself, on its own account; it must get knowledge of spirit, and must be conscious of itself as spirit. This means, it must be presented to itself as an object.[464]

Merely eternal or abstract Spirit, then, becomes an other to itself. It enters existence, and, in the first instance, enters immediate existence. It creates a World. This "Creation" is the word which pictorial presentative thought uses to convey the absolute movement which the notion itself goes through.[465]

The world is the other of the Spirit. The Spirit must go through the other simply that it may be returned to itself. It must produce the diversity, simply because it wants to regain the unity, but when the unity is regained, it is no longer the "original primal unity as such, not an immediate unity as such."[466] It is a unity-regained; it is an unity with self-consciousness. So the Spirit must pass into the other, simply because it must transcend the other. It must transcend the other simply because it must be self-conscious. It must go over into space as Nature; it must go into Time as History. It must go through all the moments and stages. But it has only a very simple goal, "which is Absolute Knowledge or Spirit knowing itself as Spirit."[467]

(4) The Interpretation of the "Fail"

The world, however, is not merely Spirit thus thrown scattered in all its plenitude with an external order imposed on it; for since Spirit is essentially simple Self, this self is likewise present therein. It is objectively existent spirit which is individual self, that has consciousness and distinguishes itself as other, as world, from itself.[468]

At first the individual self is like a child who does not know himself. It has an innocence that is charming and attractive, but this charming and attractive innocence is again only for others, not for itself. "The harmoniousness of childhood is the gift from the hand of nature: the second harmony must spring from the labor and culture of the spirit."[469] So the self must become self-centered; it must oppose itself to nature. This is that the pictorial thought of religion represented as the "fall" of mankind. Adam and Eve fell when they ate the fruit of the tree of the knowledge of good and evil. Their first reflection after their eating the fruit was that they were naked. "The sense of shame bears the evidence to the separation of man from his natural and sensuous life."[470] And

463 Hegel, *Phenomenology of Mind*, Baillie's translation, London, 1910, p. 781.
464 *Id.*, p. 22.
465 *Id.*, p. 781.
466 *Id.*, p. 17.
467 *Id.*, p. 822.
468 *Id.*, p. 782.
469 *The Logic of Hegel*, Wallace's translation, Oxford, 1892, p. 55.
470 *Id.*, p. 56.

Hegel said:

> The hour when men leave the path of mere natural being marks the difference between him, a self-conscious agent, and the natural world. But this schism, though it forms a necessary element in the very notion of spirit, is not the final goal of man. It is to this state of inward breach that the whole finite action of thought and will belongs. In that finite sphere mats pursues ends of his own and draws from himself the material of his conduct, While he pursues these aims to the utter most, while his knowledge and his will seek himself, his own narrow self apart from the universal, he is evil; and his evil is to be subjective.[471]

Thus in the world there is tragic division and antagonism of man against man, of man against nature, of finite against the infinite, and, in short, of Spirit against Spirit. But this is not to be regretted. Man must fall in order that he may return to his former state. The original harmony must be lost in order that it may be regained.

(5) The False and the Evil

There are many other evils. The life of God and divine intelligence, can, then, if you like, be spoken of as love disporting with itself; but this idea falls into edification, and even sinks into insipidity, if it lacks the seriousness, the suffering, the patience, and the labor of the negative.[472]

In the process of the self-becoming and self-development of the Spirit, it creates its own moments in its course, and goes through them all; and the whole of this movement constitutes its positive content and its truth. This movement includes, therefore, the negative factor as well, the element which would be named falsity, if it could be considered one from which we had to abstract.[473]

All these moments together make the whole; they have meaning only with the whole. But our "thought, as Understanding, sticks to fixity of characters and their distinctness from one another."[474] It takes "such abstract forms as 'the same' and not the same,' `identity' and 'non-identity' to be something true, fixed, real," and rests on them.[475] To it good is good, evil is evil, truth is truth, and falsity is falsity. It isolates the single moment from the whole and holds it fast, without knowing that to the whole process even the negative factor has the positive significance.

Against this view it must be pointed out that truth is not like stamped coin that is issued ready from the mint and so can be taken up and used. Nor, again, is there something false, any more than there is something evil.[476]

There is not something false and evil, because in the process of the whole,

---

471 *Id.*, P. 57.
472 Hegel, *Phenomenology of Mind*, Baillie's translation, London, 1910, p. 17.
473 *Id.*, pp. 43, 44.
474 *The Logic of Hegel*, Wallace's translation, oxford, 1892, p. 143.
475 Hegel, *Phenomenology of Mind*, Baillie's translation, London, 1910, p. 790.
476 *Id.*, P. 36.

even the so-called truth and good are not to be held as something fixed and immovable. The real truth is the process as a whole. To quote from Hegel at length:

> In this way truth is the bacchanalian revel, where not a soul is sober; and because every member is no sooner detached than it *eo ipso* collapses straightway, the revel is just as much a state of transparent unbroken calm. Judged by that movement, the particular shapes which mind assumes do not indeed subsist any more than do determinate thought or ideas; but they are, all the same, as much positive and necessary moments, as negative and transitory.[477]

From the point of view of the whole, evil is inherently the same as goodness. When evil is the same as goodness, then evil is just not evil, nor goodness, good; on the contrary, both are really done away with.[478]

(6) The Purpose of Culture

The process of human culture is the process of regaining the unity which was lost, not through some mistake either of God or of man, but with the purpose that it may be regained on a higher level. Reason passes itself into space and becomes the objective world in contrast with itself, the subject. It sets up this contrast not to rest therein. It simply wants to realize "explicitly the nullity of that contrast which it sees to be implicitly null."[479]

In order to realize this purpose, Reason assumes two kinds of activity: the theoretical and the practical. In its theoretical activity, Reason "observes" the external world and translates it into its own conceptual thought. It delights itself in seeing that in the external world "what is universally normal is also universally valid: what ought to be, as a matter of fact is too; and what merely should be, and is not, has no real truth."[480] This is modern science.

In its theoretical activity, Reason only observes. In its practical activity Reason wants to realize something by itself. In its theoretical activity, Reason takes the objective world as real and true. It takes it as content with which to fill up "the abstract certitude of itself"[481] In its practical activity. Reason considers the objective world as "a mere semblance, a collection of contingencies and shapes, at bottom visionary. It modifies and informs that world by the inward nature of the subjective, which is here taken to be the genuine objective."[482] Reason now appears as will. It takes all the external and the already subsisting objectivity for the "external embodiment of the will."[483]

In the theoretical activity, Reason seeks Truth; in the practical activity, Reason seeks Good. In these activities there are many different stages and moments.

477 *Id.*, p. 44.
478 *Id*, p. 789.
479 *The Logic of Hegel*, Wallace's translation, Oxford, 1892, p. 363.
480 Hegel, *Phenomenology of Mind*, Baillie's translation, London, 1910, p. 242.
481 *The Logic of Hegel*, Wallace's translation, Oxford, 1892, p. 363.
482 *Ibid.*
483 Hegel, *The Philosophy of Mind*, Wallace's translation, Oxford, 1894, p. 240.

The length of the journey has to be borne with, for every moment is necessary. The universal mind at work in the world (Weltgeist) has had the patience to go through these forms in the long stretch of time's extent, and to take upon itself the prodigious labor of the world's history, where it bodied forth in each form the entire content of itself, which each is capable of grasping; because by nothing less could the all-pervading mind ever manage to become conscious of what itself is.[484]

(7) The Absolute Knowledge

But in all these stages, Reason is only in its finite form. It starts with the presupposition of the contrast of the subject and object.

In its theoretical activity, it presupposes "a world already in existence" and the knowing subject as a *tabula rasa.*

Reason is active here, but it is reason in the form of understanding.

The truth which such cognition can reach will therefore be only finite; the infinite truth (the notion) is isolated and made an inaccessible goal in a world of its own.[485]

In the practical activity, it tries to "mold the world it finds before it into a shape conformable to its purposed end."[486] It supposed the world to be independent of the good.[487] So the actualization of the good is again in a world beyond. It now has to assume the endless task of infinite progress for the purposed good or perfection. Fichte is an example of this type.

But when the theoretical reason and the practical reason once unite, the implicit nullity of the contrast of the subject and object is at once explicitly realized. Reason knows that the subjective purpose is no longer subjective, and that the objective world is but its own truth and substantiality.[488] It now returns to itself. It is now the Speculative or Absolute Idea.[489] Its knowledge is Absolute Knowledge. It "at once gives its complete and true content the form of the self." It now is conscious of itself as a Self. "It is Ego, which is the concrete Ego and no other, and at the same time, from its very nature, is mediated or sublated universal Ego."[490] But the Spirit does not stop here. With all its previous moments preserved in its recollection, it enters the new age of existence, a new world, and becomes a new type and new mode of Spirit. As Hegel said:

> Here it has to begin all over again at its immediacy, as freshly as before, and thence rise once more to the measure of its stature, as if, for it, all that preceded were lost, and as if it has learned nothing from the experience of the spirits that preceded. But recollection (Erinnerung) has conserved that experience, and is the inner being, and, in fact, the higher form of

484 Hegel, *Phenomenology of Mind,* Baillie's translation, London, 1910, p. 28.
485 *The Logic of Hegel,* Wallace's translation, Oxford 1892, p. 364.
486 *Id.,* p. 371.
487 *Ibid.*
488 *Id.,* p. 372.
489 *Id.,* p. 373.
490 Hegel, *Phenomenology of Mind,* Baillie's translation, London, 1910, p. 811.

the substance. While, then, this phase of Spirit begins all over again the formative development, apparently solely from itself, yet at the same time it commences at a higher level.[491]

(8) Concluding Remarks

Thus there must always be the Ego, the other, diversity, and antagonism. But with the arrangement of Hegel, all these were one, will be one, and are one. There must always be activity, struggle, and progress. But the final goal of all these were already attained, will be attained, and is attained. About this point something more will be said in the next chapter.

491 *Id.*, p. 822.

XIII CONCLUSION OF PART III

There are three points which may be said to be the common characteristics of the third line of thought.

1. There is no end of the activity of the universe. The Spirit is always self-becoming; *Tao* is everlasting activity; universe is eternal motion. This is obvious in Confucius, in Aristotle, in Wang Yang-ming, and also in Hegel, as we have just seen.

2. The activity does not take place for any ulterior end. This is also obvious in Confucius, in Aristotle, and in Wang Yang-ming.

According to Hegel, "reason is purposive activity."[492] But the purpose of reason is simply that reason may become conscious of what it already implicitly is. Hegel said:

> All work is directed at only the aim or end; and when it is attained, people are surprised to find nothing else but the very thing which they had wished for. The interest lies in the whole movement.[493]
>
> All unsatisfied endeavor ceases, when we recognize that the final purpose of the world is accomplished no less than ever accomplishing itself. Generally speaking, this is the man's way of looking; while the young imagine the world is utterly sunk in wickedness, and that the first thing needed is a thorough transformation. The religious mind, on the contrary, views the world as ruled by Divine Providence, and therefore corresponds with what ought to be. But this harmony between the "is" and the "ought to be" is not torpid and rigidly stationary. Good, the final cause of the world, has being, only when it constantly produces itself. And the world of Spirit and the world of Nature continue to have this distinction, that the latter moves only in a recurring cycle while the former certainly also makes progress.[494]

This is Hegel's criticism of both the "nature" and the "art" line of thought. To the "nature" line of thought, perfection is something already in the past. To the "art" line of thought, perfection is something to be accomplished in the future. But according to

Hegel, the final good is something that is both accomplished and is accomplishing. It is already accomplished, because it is what the Spirit already implicitly is. It is accomplishing, because only inactivity can Spirit become conscious of what itself is.

3. Although there is no cessation of activity, yet for the individual as well as for the universal Spirit, there is something like a final completion, the summum bonum. This is attained in the union of the external and the internal. Hegel said:

> The second sphere develops the relation of the different to what it primarily is,-the contradiction in its own nature. That contradiction which is seen

492 Hegel, *Plienornenclogy of Mind*, Baillie's translation, London, 1910, p. 19.

493 *The Logic of Hegel*, Wallace's translation, Oxford, 1892, p. 375.

494 *Id.*, p. 373.

in the infinite progress is resolved into the end or terminus, where the difference is explicitly stated as what it is in notion.[495]

There is a terminus when the individual is conscious of the whole, when the Spirit is conscious that all the differences are nothing but itself, that is, when the Spirit becomes self-conscious.

There are the common points with which the systems of the third line of thought reconciled the "nature" and the "art" line of thought. Both of the latter lines tried to get somewhere so that we could stop once for all. But according to the third line of thought, for the evolution of the universe there is no such thing as a final stop. Yet, besides the good of activity, there is something like the supreme good, which is the union of the individual with the whole, the union of the human with the divine.

For the three common points which characterize the "nature" line of thought in contrast with the other three common points which characterize the "art" line of thought, the third line of thought also offers compromises.

(I) Asceticism vs. Hedonism

These two extremes were reconciled by the Confucian and Aristotelian doctrine of the mean and the Aristotelian doctrine of the qualitative difference in pleasure.

(2) Anti-Intellectualism vs. Intellectualism

The compromise and reconciliation of these two extremes may be exemplified by Hegel. Hegel, on the one hand, attacked "God's beloved ones to whom He gives His wisdom in sleep.[496] On the other hand, he attacked understanding in the form of mathematical science that isolates the moving factors from the process of Spirit as a whole, and that holds them fast as the solid truth. Intuition is afraid of mediation; understanding takes the single mediation as truth. True science, Speculative Philosophy, grasps both the movement as a whole and the mediation.

(3) Mysticism vs. Egoism

The compromise of these two extremes may also be exemplified by Hegel. When the self is united with the whole, the whole becomes self-conscious. Spirit, then, "is the Ego, the concrete Ego, and no other." Besides, in its Recollection or memory, all the past experience of any individual, indeed of anything in the world, is preserved. The individual never needs to be afraid of losing itself in the whole.

495 *Id.*, P. 378.

496 Hegel, *Phenomenology of Mind*, Baillie's translation, London, 1910, p. 10.

XIV GENERAL CONCLUSION

(1) The Blindness of the Philosophers

Criticizing the different philosophic systems of his own time, Hsun Tzu said:

> Mo Tzu is blinded by utility, and does not know refinement. Sung Tzu is blinded by desire, and does not know virtue. Sheng Tzu is blinded by law, and does not know philosophy. Shen Tzu is blinded by authority, and does not know wisdom. Hui Tzu is blinded by words, and does not know facts. Chuang Tzu is blinded by nature, and does not know art. Therefore from the point of view of utility, the way of life is nothing but to seek for profit. From the point of view of desire, the way of life is nothing but to seek for satisfaction. From the point of view of law, there is nothing but regulation. From the point of view of authority, there is nothing but caprice. From the point of view of words, there is nothing but argument. From the point of view of nature, there is nothing but "laissez faire."[497]

This formula of criticism can be applied to all the philosophic systems analyzed above. As we pointed out in the introduction, philosophy is an idealization of certain features of experience in order that it may become a standard of life as a whole. No wonder that philosophers were always blinded by that which they idealized.

The philosophers belonging to what I called the third line of thought, indeed, attempted to idealize experience as a whole. With the encyclopedic knowledge of these philosophers, they worked out the "Phenomenology of Mind in which everything had its place.

But as a matter of fact, of our experience as a whole, evil is not an insignificant part. The four great evils of life: birth, old age, sickness, and death, that motivated the founder of Buddhism to build his system, are most obvious and most universal. From time immemorial, man's aspiration has always been that, as the Chinese saying goes, "May the flower be forever in bloom; may the moon be forever full; may the beloved forever live!" How can these aspirations be compatible with the "four evils"? In order to idealize experience as a whole, the first thing for these philosophers to accomplish was, as Hegel said, the "justification of the ways of God." With the Confucian and Hegelian conception of dialectic, these philosophers pointed out that death is necessarily involved in life, and that old age is necessarily involved in youth. In short, according to these philosophers, evil is necessarily involved in good. Besides, if we see things from the point of view of the whole, we know that, as Aristotle said, good is the normal, evil is the exceptional, or, as Hegel said, good is the reality, evil is an illusion. Of course this is one way to deal with evil. But in analyzing these philosophers, we cannot but think that they were blinded by the justification of the evil, and did not know that certain evils cannot be justified, that they were blinded by the idea that good

497 Hsun Tzu, *Works*, Chap. XXI

is normal, and did not know that evil is not altogether exceptional, and that they were blinded by the idea that good is the only reality, and did not know that evil is not a mere appearance. As a result these philosophers also idealized but one feature of experience. They could justify evil, but they could not idealize evil. They could only say that evil was an illusion, but they could not say that this illusion was good.

(2) The Problem of Philosophy

In no other sphere of man's life is there so many disputes as in philosophy. The reason for this is that each system of philosophy holds one feature of experience which may be a good, to be the good. As a matter of fact, few people dispute about the good. The simplicity and innocence of the state of nature are good. The richness and the splendor of the state of art are also good. About these goods as such, few people will dispute. The dispute comes in when philosophers take some of these as the good, to which all others are to be subordinated. Only in so doing does the "nature" line of thought become, to use an expression which the Neo-Confucianists used to accuse Buddhism, "too empty," and the "art" line of thought become, to use an expression with which Chuang Tzu criticized Mo Tzu, "too hard." Only in so doing, does what William James called a "certain blindness of human beings" find its full expression in philosophy.

Why did philosophers insist on the good at all? An old Chinese story says that once upon a time four persons engaged in conversation and told each other their idea of good and what they wished to be. The first person said that wealth was good and that he wished to be a millionaire. The second person said that nobility was good and that he wished to be a governor of a great city. The third person said that heavenly life was good and that he wished to be an angel. The fourth person said that all these were good and that he wished that, with one million dollars in his pocket, he might ride on a flying crane's back (a thing only the angels can do), as he proceeded to assume the office of governorship of Yang-chow (a great city). If the aspiration of this fourth person could be realized, there perhaps could never be any dispute about the good at all. But as a matter of fact, this aspiration could not, cannot, and perhaps will not, be realized. Wealth is good; nobility is good; heavenly life is good. In order to secure integration of activity, and to avoid the split of personality, man needs to have some goods as the good. The problem of philosophy is the search for the good, and its procedure is the idealization of some goods so that it may become the good.

It may be urged that we need not have the good at all. We may, as Yang Chu taught, act only for immediate goods. We may, as the philosophers of the third line of thought taught, act for the sake of activity and leave the realization of the good to chance or fate. We may not fix the good at all, since the circumstances always change. These are the better standards of action. But as a matter of fact, these standards themselves are the good. They are themselves the result of deliberate philosophic thought and the product of man's life of reason.

What is true of good is also true of evil. Every evil, taken in itself and as such, is evil. Poverty is evil; old age is evil; death is evil. People do not dispute about evils, but only about the evil. Positively the aim of philosophy is to find out the good for man to attain.

Negatively, it is to find out the evil for man to avoid. The "nature" line of thought said that the state of nature was the good, and that the state art was the evil. The "art" line of thought said that the state of art was the good, and that the state of nature was the evil. The third line of thought said that the good of activity was the good, and that the failure to enjoy this was the evil.

(3) Philosophy and Religion

With the exception of the extreme materialistic philosophy in the "art" line of thought, philosophers have been wont to hypostatize what they considered to be the good in Heaven and to call it the Absolute, the One, *Tao*, or God. Plato made it most plain that the Idea of Good is the ruler of the ideal world and that nothing can be good except by partaking of the Good. This is the procedure of religion. The philosophers like Plato are often said to be "religious." Indeed, their philosophies are religion in essence. The difference between these philosophies and religions is that in the former there are no authority, dogma, and formality, while in the latter there are all of these. Religion also gives man a definite idea of good for the standard of his action. So far it is philosophy, but with its authority, dogma, and formality, it is philosophy stereotyped.

This is the reason that although many philosophers spoke of the Good, the One, the Absolute, *Tao*, or God, yet no two of them had the same conception of these. Chuang Tzu considered *Tao* as including all things except the state of art; Confucius considered it as including both nature and art. Fichte considered the Absolute Ego as the striving force to conquer its other; Hegel considered the World Spirit as both in itself and in its other. There are also many religions, and in one religion there are many sects. Each has its own God, its own good. Perhaps there is nothing more congenial to man's aspiration than thinking that the good is the eternal and the supreme factor in the world, while the evil is nothing but its negation, its other. In the Western world, therefore, in spite of the attack of science, God still has a place in man's mind, and the reconciliation of religion and science has become a great problem in philosophy.

(4) Philosophy and Science

It is often said that the purpose of philosophy is the search for truth as such. Let us see whether this statement is true or not in the history of philosophy. In the history of Asiatic philosophy there has been no system the purpose of which was the search for truth as such. This may be taken for granted. In the history of Greek philosophy a contrast is often made between the naturalistic and humanistic movements as if there were a sharp demarcation between them. But as a matter of fact, no one can decide how far the pre-Socratic philosophers were non-humanistic. In the first place, we are not in a position to pass judgment upon any philosophy, if we know it only through the fragments of its literature and the reports of others. In the second place, even if we judge the pre-Socratic philosophers from the incomplete sources, we see that they also talked about gods and man, reason and soul. The Pythagoreans were even a school for ethical and religious reform. It seems that they were no less humanistic than the Socratic schools. Socrates' and Plato's interest in the good was obvious. Aristotle was usually considered the father of European science. But he still considered good as far more important than truth.

According to him, "the most authoritative or architectonic science" is politics, the science for the supreme good.

It is the political science or faculty which determines what science is necessary in states, and what kind of science should be learned, and how far they should be learned by particular people.[498]

It is true that he said "For it is in their wonder that men both now begin and at first began to philosophize."[499] But that men should wonder at all is only because the wise legislators of the State found out that to wonder was good. That in the Hellenistic and the Roman world, the aim of philosophy was the search for the good is also obvious. In the middle Ages it was often said that philosophy was the handmaid of religion. This simply meant that philosophy was bound to expound the good fixed by one philosophy in the form of Christian religion. Philosophy lost her liberty to search for the new good, but she still dealt with good. In the modern world, philosophy strove as usual in her search for the good or the defense of the objective existence of the good. Epistemology is a special feature of modern philosophy. Locke and Hume strove for it in order to solve some of the important human problems.

Berkeley and Kant strove for it to prove the existence of God.

Another special problem in modern philosophy is the reconciliation of religion and science. This is an attempt to defend the objective existence of the good represented by the Christian God. There have been two methods of making the reconciliation. One is that which was used by Kant and is now used by the present-day pragmatists. These philosophers said that scientific truth concerns only the phenomenal world, for practical purposes. It has no right, therefore, to say anything beyond that. The ultimate reality can be known only by moral consciousness, by intuition, or by the "will to believe." Another method is that which was used by Spinoza and is now used by the neo-realists. These philosophers admit the mechanism of science, but at the same time maintain that there are also God, or objective truth, objective beauty, and objective good.

It is science that seeks for truth as such. In the world's history every civilized nation has some germ of science. But it is the modern European people who began to make the search for truth, not for enjoyment in leisure and in peace as Aristotle did, but really as a serious business and even as a war against nature to force her to tell her secret. Their motivation for this we have seen already. We

---

498 Aristotle, *Nichomachean Ethics*, 1, I, Welldon's translation, p. 2.

499 Aristotle, *Metaphysics*, 982 b, 10.

need only reiterate here what we have said before that modern European people were interested in the increase of knowledge and in the increase of power, because they adopted a philosophy that assumes it is good to have them. Philosophy determines the idea of good; science helps to realize it.

So far as truth is also good, let science continue its work. At the same time let philosophy continue to search for the good. It maybe said that in conceiving the latter in this way we humiliate philosophy. It is often said that the proper position for philosophy in man's life of reason should be the synthesis of all sciences. But, as we have seen in the above chapters, to determine the good is not an easy matter. In doing her work, philosophy needs to take everything into consideration. She needs to make an impartial review of all sciences. But she makes it for her own purpose. It is in this that her dignity consists. Otherwise, the synthesis of all sciences may not differ very much from an "outline of science." It is better for people to get firsthand knowledge from sciences themselves than to get it through an "outline."

(5) Philosophy and History

Plato said that the highest knowledge was the search for the idea of good. Aristotle said that the good was the final cause of all activity. Hegel said that history was the embodiment of reason.

There would be no dispute about these statements; if Plato had not said that the Idea of Good was an eternal and unchanging idea in Heaven; if Aristotle had not said that good was the final cause both of the things of nature and the things of art; and if Hegel did not take reason for Reason. Whether nature is teleological or not, man is certainly teleological. In his life of reason, man has philosophy to determine the good, and science and art to realize the good. The accumulation of his activity, the embodiment of his philosophy, is his history.

(6) Philosophy and Fine Art

Plato uttered another truism, namely, that the actual always strives to attain the ideal, but always falls short of it. History, the actual realization of philosophy, cannot be as perfect as philosophy. In compensation, man tries to give Philosophy an imaginary realization, which is fine art. In its development fine art was closely connected with religion. Through fine art the ideal life of religion finds the full expression. In China, the *Tao*istic state of nature has never been, and perhaps will never be, realized in history. But it has been realized in fine art, that is, in Chinese poetry and Chinese painting.

(7) An Outlook

It may be said that philosophy is the soul of man's life of reason. Our time is the age when the different souls of the world meet in discussions. There have been some conflicts at these meetings and discussions and there will be more. "There is no end of things "and "with this hexagram the Book of Changes comes to a close.

BOOK TWO:

A SHORT HISTORY OF CHINESE PHILOSOPHY

I THE SPIRIT OF CHINESE PHILOSOPHY

The place which philosophy has occupied in Chinese civilization has been comparable to that of religion in other civilizations. In China, philosophy has been every educated person's concern. In the old days, if a man were educated at all, the first education he received was in philosophy. When children went to school, the Four Books, which consist of the Confucian Analects, the Book of Mencius, the Great Learning, and the Doctrine of the Mean, were the first ones they were taught to read. The Four Books were the most important texts of Neo-Confucianist philosophy. Sometimes when the children were just beginning to learn the characters, they were given a sort of textbook to read. This was known as the Three Characters Classics, and was so called because each sentence in the book consisted of three characters arranged so that when recited they produced a rhythmic effect, and thus helped the children to memorize them more easily. This book was in reality a primer, and the very first statement in it is that "the nature of man is originally good." This is one of the fundamental ideas of Mencius' philosophy.

Place of Philosophy in Chinese Civilization

To the Westerner, who sees that the life of the Chinese people is permeated with Confucianism, it appears that Confucianism is a religion. As a matter of fact, however, Confucianism is no more a religion than, say, Platonism or Aristotelianism. It is true that the Four Books have been the Bible of the Chinese people, but in the Four Books there is no story of creation, and no mention of a heaven or hell.

Of course, the terms philosophy and religion are both ambiguous. Philosophy and religion may have entirely different meanings for different people. When men talk about philosophy or religion, they may have quite different ideas in their minds concerning them. For my part, what I call philosophy is systematic, reflective thinking on life. Every man, who has not yet died, is in life. But there are not many who think reflectively on life, and still fewer whose reflective thinking is systematic. A philosopher must philosophize; that is to say, he must think reflectively on life, and then express his thoughts systematically.

This kind of thinking is called reflective because it takes life as its object. The theory of life, the theory of the universe, and the theory of knowledge all emerge from this type of thinking. The theory of the universe arises because the universe is the background of life — the stage on which the drama of life takes place.

The theory of knowledge emerges because thinking is itself knowledge. According to some philosophers of the West, in order to think, we must first find out what we can think; that is to say, before we start to think about life, we must first "think our thinking."

Such theories are all the products of reflective thinking. The very concept of life, the very concept of the universe, and the very concept of knowledge are also the products of reflective thinking. No matter whether we think about life or whether we talk about it, we are all in the midst of it. And no matter whether we think or speak about the universe, we are all a part of it. Now, what the philosophers call the universe is not the same as what the physicists have in mind when they refer to it. What the philosophers call the universe is the totality of all that is. It is equivalent to what the ancient Chinese philosopher, Hui Shih, called "The Great One, "which is defined as "that which has nothing beyond." So everyone and everything must be considered part of the universe. When one thinks about the universe, one is thinking reflectively.

When we think about knowledge or speak about knowledge, this thinking and speaking are themselves knowledge. To use an expression of Aristotle, it is "thinking on thinking"; and this is reflective thinking. Here is the vicious circle which those philosophers follow who insist that before we think we must first think about our thinking; just as if we had another faculty with which we could think about thinking! As a matter of fact, the faculty with which we think about thinking is the very same faculty with which we think. If we are skeptical about the capacity of our thinking in regard to life and the universe, we have the same reason to be skeptical about the capacity of our thinking in regard to thinking.

Religion also has something to do with life. In the heart of every great religion there is a philosophy. In fact, every great religion is a philosophy with a certain amount of superstructure, which consists of superstitions, dogmas, rituals, and institutions. This is what I call religion.

If one understands the term religion in this sense, which does not really differ very much from common usage, one sees that Confucianism cannot be considered a religion. People have been accustomed to say that there were three religions in China: Confucianism, Taoism, and Buddhism. But Confucianism, as we have seen, is not a religion. As to Taoism, there is a distinction between Taoism as a philosophy, which is called *Tao* chia (the *Tao*ist schools and the *Tao*ist religion (Tao chiao). Their teachings are not only different; they are even contradictory. Taoism as a philosophy teaches the doctrine of following nature, while Taoism as a religion teaches the doctrine of working against nature. For instance, according to Lao Tzu and Chuang Tzu, life followed by death is the course of nature, and man should follow this natural course calmly. But the main teaching of the *Tao*ist religion is the principle and technique of how to avoid death, which is expressly working against nature. The *Tao*ist religion has the spirit of science, which is the conquering of nature. If one is interested in the history of Chinese science, the writings of the religious *Tao*ists will supply much information.

As to Buddhism, there is also the distinction between Buddhism as a philosophy, which is called Fo hsueh (the Buddhist learning and Buddhism as a religion, which is called Fo chiao (the Buddhist religion). To the educated Chinese, Buddhist philosophy is much more interesting than the Buddhist religion. It is quite common to see both Buddhist monks and *Tao*ist monks simultaneously participating in Chinese funeral services. The Chinese people take even their religion philosophically.

At present it is known to many Westerners that the Chinese people have been less concerned with religion than other people are. For instance, in one of his articles, "Dominant Ideas in the Formation of Chinese Culture,"[500] Professor Derk Bodde says: "They [the Chinese] are not people for whom religious ideas and activities constitute an all-important and absorbing part of life.... It is ethics (especially Confucian ethics), and not religion (at least not religion of a formal, organized type), that provided the spiritual basis in Chinese civilization.... All of which, of course, marks a difference of fundamental importance between China and most other major civilizations, in which a church and a priesthood have played a dominant role."

In one sense this is quite true. But one may ask: Why is this so?

If the craving for what is beyond the present actual world is not one of the innate desires of mankind, why is it a fact that for most people religious ideas and activities constitute an all-important and absorbing part of life? If that craving is one of the fundamental desires of mankind, why should the Chinese people be an exception? When one says that it is ethics, not religion, that has provided the spiritual basis of Chinese civilization, does it imply that the Chinese are not conscious of those values which are higher than moral ones?

The values that are higher than the moral ones may be called super-moral values. The love of man is a moral value, while the love of God is a super-moral value. Some people may be inclined to call this kind of value a religious value. But in my opinion, this value is not confined to religion, unless what is meant here by religion differs from its meaning as described above. For instance, the love of God in Christianity is a religious value, while the love of God in the philosophy of Spinoza is not, because what Spinoza called God is really the universe. Strictly speaking, the love of God in Christianity is not really super-moral. This is because God, in Christianity, is a personality, and consequently the love of God by man is comparable to the love of a father by his son, which is a moral value. Therefore, the love of God in Christianity is open to question as a super-moral value. It is a quasi super-moral value, while the love of God in the philosophy of Spinoza is a real super-moral value.

To answer the above questions, I would say that the craving for something beyond the present actual world is one of the innate desires of mankind, and the Chinese people are no exception to this rule. They have not had much concern with religion because they have had so much concern with philosophy. They are not religious because they are philosophical. In philosophy they satisfy their craving for what is beyond the present actual world. In philosophy also they have the super-moral values expressed and appreciated, and in living according to philosophy these super-moral values are experienced.

According to the tradition of Chinese philosophy, its function is not the increase of positive knowledge (by positive knowledge I mean information regarding matters of fact), but the elevation of the mind — a reaching out for

500 *Journal of American Oriental Society*, Vol. 62, No. 4, pp. 293-9. Reprinted in China, pp. 18-28 (H. F. MacNair, ed., University of California Press, 1946).

what is beyond the present actual world, and for the values that are higher than the moral ones. It is said in Lao-tzu "To work on learning is to increase day by day; to work on *Tao* (the Way, the Truth) is to decrease day by day."[501] I am not concerned with the difference between increasing and decreasing, nor do I quite agree with this saying of Lao-tzu. I quote it only to show that in the tradition of Chinese philosophy there is a distinction between working on learning and working on *Tao*(the Way) The purpose of the former is what I call the increase of positive knowledge, that of the latter is the elevation of the mind. Philosophy belongs in the latter category.

The view that the function of philosophy, especially metaphysics, is not the increase of positive knowledge, is expounded by the Viennese school in contemporary Western philosophy, though from a different angle and for a different purpose. I do not agree with this school that the function of philosophy is only the clarification of ideas, and that the nature of metaphysics is only a lyric of concepts. Nevertheless, in their arguments one can see quite clearly that philosophy, especially metaphysics, would become nonsense if it did attempt to give information regarding matters of fact.

Religion does give information in regard to matters of fact. But the information given by religion is not in harmony with that given by science. So in the West there has been the conflict between religion and science. Where science advances, religion retreats; and the authority of religion recedes before the advancement of science. The traditionalists regretted this fact and pitied the people who had become irreligious, considering them as having degenerated. They ought indeed to be pitied, if, besides religion, they had no other access to the higher values. When people get rid of religion and have no substitute, they also lose the higher values. They have to confine themselves to mundane affairs and have nothing to do with the spiritual ones. Fortunately, however, besides religion there is philosophy, which provides man with an access to the higher values - an access which is more direct than that provided by religion, because in philosophy, in order to be acquainted with the higher values, man need not take the roundabout way provided by prayers and rituals. The higher values with which man has become acquainted through philosophy are even purer than those acquired through religion, because they are not mixed with imagination and superstition. In the world of the future, man will have philosophy in the place of religion. This is consistent with Chinese tradition. It is not necessary that man should be religious, but it is necessary that he should be philosophical. When he is philosophical, he has the very best of the blessings of religion.

Problem and Spirit of Chinese Philosophy

The above is a general discussion of the nature and function of philosophy. In the following remarks I shall speak more specifically about Chinese philosophy. There is a main current in the history of Chinese philosophy, which may be called the spirit of Chinese philosophy. In order to understand this spirit, we

501 *Lao-tzu*, ch. 48.

must first make clear the problem that most Chinese philosophers have tried to solve.

There are all kinds and conditions of men. With regard to any one of these kinds, there is the highest form of achievement of which any one kind of man is capable. For instance, there are the men engaged in practical politics. The highest form of achievement in that class of men is that of the great statesman. So also in the field of art, the highest form of achievement of which artists are capable is that of the great artist. Although there are these different classes of men, yet all of them are men. What is the highest form of achievement of which a man as a man is capable? According to the Chinese philosophers, it is nothing less than being a sage, and the highest achievement of a sage is the identification of the individual with the universe. The problem is, if men want to achieve this identification, do they necessarily have to abandon society or even to negate life?

According to some philosophers, this is necessary. The Buddha said that life itself is the root and fountainhead of the misery of life. Likewise, Plato said that the body is the prison of the soul. And some of the *Tao*ists said that life is an excrescence, a tumor, and death is to be taken as the breaking of the tumor. All these ideas represent a view which entails separation from what may be called the entangling net of the matter-corrupted world; and therefore, if the highest achievement of a sage is to be realized, the sage has to abandon society and even life itself. Only thus can the final liberation be attained. This kind of philosophy is what is generally known as "other-worldly philosophy."

There is another kind of philosophy which emphasizes what is in society, such as human relations and human affairs. This kind of philosophy speaks only about moral values, and is unable to, or does not wish to speak of the super-moral ones. This kind of philosophy is generally described as "this-worldly." From the point of view of a this-worldly philosophy, an other-world philosophy is too idealistic; is of no practical use and is negative. From the point of view of an other-worldly philosophy, a this-world philosophy is too realistic, too superficial. It may be positive, but it is like the quick walking of a man who has taken the wrong road the more quickly he walks the further he goes astray.

There are many people who say that Chinese philosophy is a this-world philosophy. It is difficult to state that these people are entirely right or entirely wrong. Taking a merely superficial view, people who hold this opinion cannot be said to be wrong, because according to their view, Chinese philosophy, regardless of its different schools of thought, is directly or indirectly concerned with government and ethics. On the surface, therefore, it is concerned chiefly with society, and not with the universe; with the daily functions of human relations, not hell and heaven; with man's present life, but not his life in a world to come. When he was once asked by a disciple about the meaning of death, Confucius replied: "Not yet understanding life, how can you understand death?"[502] And Mencius said "The sage is the acme of human relations,"[503] which, taken literally,

502 *Analects of Confucius*, XI, 11.

503 *Mencius*, IVa, 2.

means that the sage is the morally perfect man in society. From a surface point of view, with the ideal man being of this world, it seems that what Chinese philosophy calls a sage is a person of a very different order from the Buddha of Buddhism and the saints of the Christian religion. Superficially, this would seem to be especially true of the Confucian sage. That is why, in ancient times, Confucius and the Confucianists were so greatly ridiculed by the *Tao*ists.

This, however, is only a surface view of the matter. Chinese philosophy cannot be understood by oversimplification of this kind. So far as the main tenet of its tradition is concerned, if we understand it aright, it cannot be said to be wholly this-worldly, just as, of course, it cannot be said to be wholly other-worldly. It is both of this world and of the other world. Speaking about the Neo-Confucianism of the Sung Dynasty, one philosopher described it this way: "It is not divorced from daily ordinary activities, yet it goes straight to what antedated Heaven." This is what Chinese philosophy has striven for. Having this kind of spirit, it is at one and the same time both extremely idealistic and extremely realistic, and very practical, though not in a superficial way.

This-worldliness and other-worldliness stand in contrast to each other as do realism and idealism. The task of Chinese philosophy is to accomplish synthesis out of antithesis. That does not mean that they are to be abolished. They are still there, but they have been made into a synthetic whole. How can this be done?

This is the problem which Chinese philosophy attempts to solve. According to Chinese philosophy, the man who accomplishes this synthesis, not only in theory but also in deed, is the sage. He is both this-worldly and other-worldly. The spiritual achievement of the Chinese sage corresponds to the saint's achievement in Buddhism, and in Western religion. But the Chinese sage is not one who does not concern himself with the business of the world. His character is described as one of "sageliness within and kingliness without." That is to say, in his inner sageliness, he accomplishes spiritual cultivation; in his kingliness without, he functions in society. It is not necessary that the sage should be the actual head of the government in his society. From the standpoint of practical politics, for the most part, the sage certainly has no chance of being the head of the state. The saying "sageliness within and kingliness without" means only that he who has the noblest spirit should, theoretically, be king. As to whether he actually has or has not the chance of being king that is immaterial.

Since the character of the sage is, according to Chinese tradition, one of sageliness within and kingliness without, the task of philosophy is to enable man to develop this kind of character. Therefore, what philosophy discusses is what the Chinese philosophers describe as the *Tao* (Way, or basic principles) of sageliness within and kingliness without.

This sounds like the Platonic theory of the philosopher-king.

According to Plato, in an ideal state, the philosopher should be the king or the king should be a philosopher; and in order to become a philosopher, a man must undergo a long period of philosophical training before his mind can be "converted" from the world of changing things to the world of eternal ideas.

Thus according to Plato, as according to the Chinese philosophers, the task of philosophy is to enable man to have the character of sageliness within and kingliness without. But according to Plato, when a philosopher becomes a king, he does so against his will — in other words, it is something forced on him, and entails a great sacrifice on his part. This is what was also held by the ancient *Taoists*. There is the story of a sage who, being asked by the people of a certain state to become their king, escaped and hid himself in a mountain cave.

But the people found the cave, smoked him out and compelled him to assume the difficult task.[504] This is one similarity between Plato and the ancient *Taoists*, and it also shows the character of other-worldliness in *Taoist* philosophy. Following the main tradition of Chinese philosophy, the Neo-Taoist, Kuo Hsiang of the third century A.D., revised this point.

According to Confucianism, the daily task of dealing with social affairs in human relations is not something alien to the sage.

Carrying on this task is the very essence of the development of the perfection of his personality. He performs it not only as a citizen of society, but also as a "citizen of the universe," tien min, as Mencius called it. He must be conscious of his being a citizen of the universe, otherwise his deeds would not have super-moral value. If he had the chance to become a king he would gladly serve the people, thus performing his duty both as a citizen of society, and as a citizen of the universe.

Since what is discussed in philosophy is the *Tao* (Way) of sageliness within and kingliness without, it follows that philosophy must be inseparable from political thought. Regardless of the differences between the schools of Chinese philosophy, the philosophy of every school represents, at the same time, its political thought. This does not mean that in the various schools of philosophy there are no metaphysics, no ethics, no logic. It means only that all these factors are connected with political thought in one way or another, just as Plato's "Republic" represents his whole philosophy and at the same time is his political thought.

For instance, the School of Names was known to indulge in such arguments as "a white horse is not a horse," which seems to have very little connection with politics. Yet the leader of this school, Kungsun Lung, "wished to extend this kind of argument to rectify the relationship between names and facts in order to transform the world." We have seen in our world today how every statesman says his country wants only peace, but in fact, when he is talking about peace, he is often preparing for war. Here, then, there is a wrong relationship between names and facts. According to Kungsun Lung this kind of wrong relationship should be rectified. This is really the first step towards the transformation of the world.

Since the subject matter of philosophy is the *Tao* of sageliness within and kingliness without, the study of philosophy is not simply an attempt to acquire this kind of knowledge, but is also an attempt to develop this kind of character. Philosophy is not simply something to be known, but is also something to be experienced. It is not simply a sort of intellectual game, but something far more

504 *Lu-shih Chun-chiu* (Lu's Almanac), I, 2.

serious. As my colleague, Professor Y. L. Chin, has pointed out in an unpublished manuscript:

> Chinese philosophers were all of them different grades of Socrates. This was so because ethics, politics, reflective thinking, and knowledge were unified in the philosopher; in him, knowledge and virtue were one and inseparable. His philosophy required that he live it; he was himself its vehicle. To live in accordance with his philosophical convictions was part of his philosophy. It was his business to school himself continually and persistently to that pure experience in which selfishness and egocentricity were transcended, so that he would be one with the universe. Obviously this process of schooling could not be stopped, for stopping it would mean the emergence of his ego and the loss of his universe. Hence cognitively he was eternally groping, and conatively he was eternally behaving or trying to behave. Since these could not be separated, in him there was the synthesis of the philosopher in the original sense of that term. Like Socrates, he did not keep office hours with his philosophy. Neither was he a dusty, musty philosopher, closeted in his study, sitting in a chair on the periphery of life. With him, philosophy was hardly ever merely a pattern of ideas exhibited for human understanding, but was a system of precepts internal to the conduct of the philosopher; and in extreme cases his philosophy might even be said to be his biography.

A Western student beginning the study of Chinese philosophy is instantly confronted with two obstacles. One, of course, is the language barrier; the other is the peculiar way in which the Chinese philosophers have expressed themselves. I will speak about the latter first.

When one begins to read Chinese philosophical works, the first impression one gets is perhaps the briefness and disconnectedness of the sayings and writings of their authors. Open the Analects of Confucius and you will see that each paragraph consists of only a few words, and there is hardly any connection between one paragraph and the next. Open a book containing the philosophy of Lao Tzu, and you will find that the whole book consists of about five thousand words — no longer than a magazine article; yet in it one will find the whole of his philosophy. A student accustomed to elaborate reasoning and detailed argument would be at a loss to understand what these Chinese philosophers were saying. He would be inclined to think that there was disconnectedness in the thought itself. If this were so, there would be no Chinese philosophy. For disconnected thought is hardly worthy of the name of philosophy.

It may be said that the apparent disconnectedness of the sayings and writings of the Chinese philosophers is due to the fact that these sayings and writings are not formal philosophical works. According to Chinese tradition, the study of philosophy is not a profession. Everyone should study philosophy just as in the West everyone should go to church. The purpose of the study of philosophy is to enable a man, as a man, to be a man, not some particular kind of man. Other studies — not the study of philosophy — enable a man to be some special kind of man. So there were no professional philosophers; and non-professional philosophers did not have to produce formal philosophical writings. In China, there were far more philosophers who produced no formal philosophical writings than those who did. If one wishes to study the philosophy of these men, one has to go to the records of their sayings or the letters they wrote to disciples and friends. These letters did not belong to just one period in the life of the person who wrote them, nor were the records written only by a single person. Disconnectedness or even inconsistency between them is, therefore, to be expected.

The foregoing may explain why the writings and sayings of some philosophers are disconnected; but it does not explain why they are brief. In some philosophic writings, such as those of Mencius and Hsun Tzu, one does find systematic reasoning and arguments. But in comparison with the philosophic writings of the West, they are still not articulate enough. The fact is that Chinese philosophers were accustomed to express themselves in the form of aphorisms, apothegms, or allusions and illustrations. The whole book of Lao-tzu consists of aphorisms, and most of the chapters of the Chuangtzu are full of allusions and illustrations. This is very obvious. But even in writings such as those of Mencius and Hsun Tzu, mentioned above, when compared with the philosophical writings of the West, there are still too many aphorisms, allusions, and illustrations. Aphorisms must be very brief; allusions and illustrations must be disconnected.

Aphorisms, allusions, and illustrations are thus not articulate enough. Their insufficiency in articulateness is compensated for, however, by their suggestiveness. Articulateness and suggestiveness are, of course, incompatible. The more an expression is articulate, the less it is suggestive – just as the more an expression is prosaic, the less it is poetic. These sayings and writings of the Chinese philosophers are so inarticulate that their suggestiveness is almost boundless.

Suggestiveness, not articulateness, is the ideal of all Chinese art, whether it is poetry, painting, or anything else. In poetry, what the poet intends to communicate is often not what is directly said in the poetry, but what is not said in it. According to Chinese literary tradition, in good poetry "the number of words is limited, but the ideas it suggests are limitless." So an intelligent reader of poetry reads what is outside the poem; and a good reader of books reads "what is between the lines." Such is the ideal of Chinese art, and this ideal is reflected in the way in which Chinese philosophers have expressed themselves.

The ideal of Chinese art is not without its philosophical background. In the twenty-sixth chapter of the Chuang-tzu it is said:

> A basket-trap is for catching fish, but when one has got the fish, one need think no more about the basket. A foot-trap is for catching hares; but when one has got the hare, one need think no more about the trap. Words are for holding ideas, but when one has got the idea, one need no longer think about the words. If only I could find someone who had stopped thinking about words and could have him with me to talk to!

To talk with someone who has stopped thinking about words is not to talk with words. In the Chuang-tzu the statement is made that two sages met without speaking a single word, because "when their eyes met, the *Tao* was there." According to Taoism, the *Tao* (the Way) cannot be told, but only suggested. So when words are used, it is the suggestiveness of the words, and not their fixed denotations or connotations that reveals the *Tao*. Words are something that should be forgotten when they have achieved their purpose. Why should we trouble ourselves with them any more than is necessary? This is true of the words and rhymes in poetry, and the lines and colors in painting.

During the third and fourth centuries A.D., the most influential philosophy was the Neo-Taoist School, which was known in Chinese history as the hsuan hsueh (the dark or mystic learning). At that time there was a book entitled Shih-shoo Hsinyu (New sayings), which is a record of the clever sayings and romantic activities of the famous men of the age. Most of the sayings are very brief, some consisting of only a few words. It is stated in that book (ch. 4) that a very high official once asked a philosopher (the high official was himself a philosopher) what was the difference and similarity between Lao-Chuang (i.e., Lao Tzu and Chuang Tzu) and Confucius. The philosopher answered "Are they not the same?"

The high official was very much pleased with this answer, and instantly appointed the philosopher as his secretary. Since the answer consists of only three words in the Chinese language, this philosopher has been known as the three-word secretary. He could not say that Lao-Chuang and Confucius had nothing in common, nor could he say that they had everything in common. So, he put his answer in the form of a question, which was really a good answer.

The brief sayings in the Analects of Confucius and in the philosophy of the *Lao-tzu* are not simply conclusions from certain premises which have been lost. They are aphorisms full of suggestiveness. It is the suggestiveness that is attractive. One may gather together all the ideas one finds in the Lao-tzu and write them out in a new book consisting of fifty thousand or even five hundred thousand words. No matter how well this is done, however, it is just a new book. It may be read side by side with the original

Lao-tzu, and may help people a great deal to understand the original, but it can never be a substitute for the original.

Kuo Hsiang, to whom I have already referred, was one of the great commentators on Chuang Tzu. His commentary was itself a classic of *Tao*ist literature. He turned the allusions and metaphors of Chuang Tzu into a form of reasoning and argument, and translated his poems into prose of his own. His writing is much more articulate than that of Chuang Tzu. But, between the suggestiveness of Chuang Tzu's original and the articulateness of Kuo Hsiang's commentary, people may still ask: Which is better? A monk of the Buddhist Chan or Zen School of a later period once said "Everyone says that it was Kuo Hsiang who wrote a commentary on Chuang Tzu; I would say it was Chuang Tzu who wrote a commentary on Kuo Hsiang.

The Language Barrier

It is true of all philosophical writings that it is difficult for one to have a complete understanding and full appreciation of them if one cannot read them in the original. This is due to the language barrier. Because of the suggestive character of Chinese philosophical writings, the language barrier becomes even more formidable. The suggestiveness of the sayings and writings of the Chinese philosophers is something that can hardly be translated. When one reads them in translation, one misses the suggestiveness; and this means that one misses a great deal.

A translation, after all, is only an interpretation. When one translates a sentence from, say, the Lao-tzu, one gives one's own interpretation of its meaning. But the translation may convey only one idea, while as a matter of fact, the original may contain many other ideas besides the one given by the translator. The original is suggestive, but the translation is not, and cannot be. So it loses much of the richness inherent in the original.

There have been many translations of the Lao-tzu and the Analects of Confucius. Each translator has considered the translations of others unsatisfactory. But no matter how well a translation is done, it is bound to be poorer than the original. It needs a combination of all the translations already made and many others not yet made, to reveal the richness of the Lao-tzu and the Analects in their original form.

Kumarajiva, of the fifth century A.D., one of the greatest translators of the Buddhist texts into Chinese, said that the work of translation is just like chewing food that is to be fed to others. If one cannot chew the food oneself, one has to be given food that has already been chewed. After such an operation, however, the food is bound to be poorer in taste and flavor than the original.

II THE BACKGROUND OF CHINESE PHILOSOPHY

In the last chapter I said that philosophy is systematic reflective thinking on life. In thinking, the thinker is usually conditioned by the surroundings in which he lives. Being in certain surroundings, he feels life in a certain way, and there are therefore in his philosophy certain emphases or omissions, which constitute the characteristics of that philosophy.

This is true of an individual, as it is also true of a people. In this chapter I shall try to say something about the geographic and economic background of the Chinese people in order to show how and why Chinese civilization in general and Chinese philosophy in particular, are what they are.

Geographic Background of the Chinese People

In the Analects Confucius said "The wise man delights in water; the good man delights in mountains. The wise move; the good stay still. The wise are happy; the good endure."[505] In reading this saying, I feel there is in it something which suggests a difference between the people of ancient China and those of ancient Greece.

China is a continental country. To the ancient Chinese their land was the world. There are two expressions in the Chinese language which can both be translated as the world. One is "all beneath the sky" and the other is "all within the four seas." To the people of a maritime country such as the Greeks, it would be inconceivable that expressions such as these could be synonymous. But that is what happens in the Chinese language, and it is not without reason.

From the time of Confucius until the end of the 19th century, no Chinese thinkers had the experience of venturing out upon the high seas. Confucius and Mencius lived not far from the sea, if we think in modern terms of distance, yet in the Analects, Confucius mentions the sea only once. He is recorded as saying: "If my way is not to prevail, I shall get upon a raft and float out to the sea. He who will go with me will be [Chung] Yu."[506] Chung Yu was a disciple of Confucius known for his courage and bravery. It is said in the same work that when Chung Yu heard this statement, he was much pleased. Confucius, however, was not so pleased by Chung Yu's over-enthusiasm, and remarked: "Yu is braver than myself. I do not know what to do with him."[507]

Mencius's reference to the sea is likewise brief. "He who has seen the sea," he says, "finds it difficult to think anything about other waters; and he who has wandered to the gate of the sage, finds it difficult to think anything about the words of others."[508] Mencius is no better than Confucius, who thought only of

505 *Analects of Confucius*, VI, 21.
506 *Id.*, V, 6.
507 *Ibid.*
508 *Mencius*, VIIa, 24.

"floating out to sea." How different were Socrates, Plato, and Aristotle, who lived in a maritime country and wandered from island to island!

Economic Background of the Chinese People

The ancient Chinese and Greek philosophers not only lived under different geographic conditions, but different economic ones as well. Since China is a continental country, the Chinese people have to make their living by agriculture. In an agrarian country land is the primary basis of wealth. Hence, throughout Chinese history, social and economic thinking and policy have centered around the utilization and distribution of land.

Agriculture in such an economy is equally important not only in peacetime but in wartime as well. During the period of the Warring States (475-221 B.C.), a period in many ways similar to our own, in which China was divided into many feudal kingdoms, every state devoted its greater attention to what were then called "the arts of agriculture and war." Finally the state of Chin, one of the seven leading states of the time, gained supremacy both in agriculture and war, and as a result succeeded in conquering the other states and thus bringing unification to China for the first time in her history.

In the social and economic thinking of Chinese philosophers, there is a distinction between what they call "the root" and "the branch." "The root" refers to agriculture and "the branch" to commerce. The reason for this is that agriculture is concerned with production, while commerce is merely concerned with exchange.

One must have production before one can have exchange. In an agrarian country, agriculture is the major form of production, and therefore throughout Chinese history, social and economic theories and policies have all attempted "to emphasize the root and slight the branch."

The people who deal with the "branch," that is, the merchants, were therefore looked down upon. They were the last and lowest of the four traditional classes of society, the other three being scholars, farmers, and artisans. The scholars were usually landlords, and the farmers were the peasants who actually cultivated the land. These were the two honorable professions in China. A family having "a tradition of studying and farming" was something of which to be proud.

Although the "scholars" did not actually cultivate the land themselves, yet since they were usually landlords, their fortunes were tied up with agriculture. A good or bad harvest meant their good or bad fortune, and therefore their reaction to the universe and their outlook on life were essentially those of the farmer. In addition their education gave them the power to express what an actual farmer felt but was incapable of expressing himself. This expression took the form of Chinese philosophy, literature, and art.

Value of Agriculture

In the *Lu-shih Chun-chiu*, a compendium of various schools of philosophy written in the third century B.C., there is a chapter titled The Value of Agriculture." In this chapter a contrast is made between the mode of life of people who are engaged in the "root" occupation — the farmers, and that of those who are engaged in the "branch" occupation — the merchants. The farmers are primitive and simple and therefore always ready to accept commands. They are childlike and innocent and therefore unselfish. Their material properties are complex and difficult to move, and therefore they do not abandon their country when it is in danger. Merchants, on the other hand, are corrupt and therefore not obedient. They are treacherous and therefore selfish. They have simple properties which are easy to transport, and therefore they usually abandon their country when it is in danger. Hence this chapter asserts that not only is agriculture economically more important than commerce, but the mode of life of the farmers is also superior to that of the merchants. Herein lies "the value of agriculture."[509] The author of this chapter found that the mode of life of people is conditioned by their economic background, and his evaluation of agriculture again shows that he was himself conditioned by the economic background of his time.

In this observation of the Lu-shih Chun-chiu, we find the root and source of the two main trends of Chinese thought, Taoism and Confucianism. They are poles apart from one another, yet they are also the two poles of one and the same axis. They both express, in one way or another, the aspirations and inspirations of the farmer.

"Reversal is the Movement of the Tao"

Before considering the difference between these two schools, let us first take up a theory which both of them maintained. This is that both in the sphere of nature and in that of man, when the development of anything brings it to one extreme, a reversal to the other extreme takes place; that is, to borrow an expression from Hegel, everything involves its own negation. This is one of the main theses of Lao Tzu's philosophy and also that of the Book of Changes as interpreted by the Confucianists. It was no doubt inspired by the movements of the sun and moon and the succession of the four seasons, to which farmers must pay particular heed in order to carry on their own work. In the Appendices of the Book of Changes, it is said "When the cold goes, the warmth comes, and when the warmth comes, the cold goes."[510] And again: "When the sun has reached its meridian, it declines, and when the moon has become full, it wanes."[511] Such movements are referred to in the Appendices as "returning." Thus Appendix I says: "In returning we see the mind of Heaven and Earth." Similarly in the Lao-tzu we find the words: "Reversal is the movement of the *Tao*."[512]

This theory has had a great effect upon the Chinese people and has contributed much to their success in overcoming the many difficulties which they have encountered in their long history. Convinced of this theory, they remain cautious

509 *Cf. Lu-shih Chun-chiu*, XXVI, 3.

510 *Book of Changes*, Appendix

511 *Id.* Appendix

512 *Cf. Lao-tzu*, Ch. 40.

even in time of prosperity, and hopeful even in time of extreme danger. In the late war, the concept provided the Chinese people with a sort of psychological weapon, so that even in its darkest period, most people lived on the hope which was expressed in the phrase: "The dawn will soon come." It was this "will to believe" that helped the Chinese people to go through the war.

This theory has also provided the principal argument for the doctrine of the golden mean, favored by Confucianists and *Tao*ists alike. "Never too much" has been the maxim of both. For, according to them, it is better for one to be wrong by having too little, than to be wrong by having too much, and to be wrong by leaving things undone, than to be wrong by overdoing them. For by having too much and overdoing, one runs the risk of getting the opposite of what one wants.

Idealization of Nature

Taoism and Confucianism differ because they are the rationalization or theoretical expression of different aspects of the life of the farmers. The farmers are simple in their living and innocent in their thought. Seeing things from their point of view, the *Tao*ists idealized the simplicity of primitive society and condemned civilization. They also idealized the innocence of children and despised knowledge. In the Lao-tzu it is said:

> Let us have a small country with few inhabitants.... Let the people ere turn to the use of knotted cords [for keeping records]. Let them obtain their food sweet, their clothing beautiful, their homes comfortable, their rustic tasks pleasurable. The neighboring state might be so near at hand that one could hear the cocks crowing in it and dogs barking. But the people would grow old and die without ever having been there.[513]

Is this not an idyllic picture of a farmer's country?

The farmers are always in contact with nature, so they admire and love nature, this admiration and love were developed by the *Tao*ists to the fullest extent. They made a sharp distinction between what is of nature and what is of man, the natural and the artificial. According to them, what is of nature is the source of human happiness and what is of man is the root of all human suffering. They were, as the Confucianist Hsun Tzu puts it, "blinded by nature and had no knowledge of man."[514] As the final development of this trend of thinking, the *Tao*ists maintained that the highest achievement in the spiritual cultivation of a sage lies in the identification of himself with the whole of nature, i.e., the universe.

Family System

The farmers have to live on their land, which is immovable, and the same is true of the scholar landlords. Unless one has special talent, or is especially lucky, one has to live where one's father or grandfather lived, and where one's children will continue to live. That is to say, the family in the wider sense must live

513 *Id.*, Ch. 80.

514 *Hsun-tzu*, Ch 21.

together for economic reasons. Thus there developed the Chinese family system, which was no doubt one of the most complex and well-organized in the world. A great deal of Confucianism is the rational justification or theoretical expression of this social system.

The family system was the social system of China. Out of the five traditional social relationships, which are those between sovereign and subject, father and son, elder and younger brother, husband and wife, and friend and friend, three are family relationships. The remaining two, though not family relationships, can be conceived of in terms of the family. Thus the relationship between sovereign and subject can be conceived of in terms of that between father and son, and that between friend and friend in terms of the one between elder and younger brother. So, indeed, was the way in which they were usually conceived. But these are only the major family relationships, and there were many more. In the Erh Ya (Literary Expositor), which is the oldest dictionary of the Chinese language, dating from before the Christian era, there are more than one hundred terms for various family relationships, most of which have no equivalent in the English language.

For the same reason, ancestor worship developed. In a family living in a particular place, the ancestor worshiped was usually the first of the family who had established himself and his descendants there on the land He thus became the symbol of the unity of the family, and such a symbol was indispensable for a large and complex organization.

A great part of Confucianism is the rational justification of this social system, or its theoretical expression. Economic conditions prepared its basis, and Confucianism expressed its ethical significance. Since this social system was the outgrowth of certain economic conditions, and these conditions were again the product of their geographical surroundings, to the Chinese people both the system and its theoretical expression were very natural. Because of this, Confucianism naturally became the orthodox philosophy and remained so until the invasion of industrialization from modern Europe and America changed the economic basis of Chinese life.

This-worldliness and Other-worldliness

Confucianism is the philosophy of social organization, and so is also the philosophy of daily life. Confucianism emphasizes the social responsibilities of man, while Taoism emphasizes what is natural and spontaneous in him. In the Chuang-tzu, it is said that the Confucianists roam within the bounds of society, while the *Tao*ists roam beyond it. In the third and fourth centuries A.D., when Taoism again became influential, people used to say that Confucius valued ming chiao (the teaching of names denoting the social relationships), while Lao Tzu and Chuang Tzu valued tzu jan (spontaneity or naturalness). These two trends of Chinese philosophy correspond roughly to the traditions of classicism and romanticism in Western thought. Read the poems of Tu Fu and *Li* Po, and one sees in them the difference between Confucianism and Taoism. These two great poets lived during the same period (eighth century A.D.), and concurrently expressed in their poems the two main traditions of Chinese thought.

Because it "roams within the bounds of society," Confucianism appears more this-worldly than Taoism, and because it "roams beyond the bound of society," Taoism appears more other-worldly than Confucianism. These two trends of thought rivaled one another, but also complemented each other. They exercised a sort of balance of power. This gave to the Chinese people a better sense of balance in regard to this-worldliness and other-worldliness.

There were *Tao*ists in the third and fourth centuries who attempted to make Taoism closer to Confucianism, and there were also Confucianists in the eleventh and twelfth centuries who attempted to make Confucianism closer to Taoism. We call these *Tao*ists the Neo-Taoists and these Confucianists the Neo-Confucianists. It was these movements that made Chinese philosophy both of this world and of the other world, as I pointed out in the last chapter.

Chinese Art and Poetry

The Confucianists took art as an instrument for moral education

The *Tao*ists had no formal treatises on art, but their admiration of the free movement of the spirit and their idealization of nature gave profound inspiration to the great artists of China. This being the case, it is no wonder that most of the great artists of China took nature as their subject. Most of the masterpieces of Chinese painting are paintings of landscapes, animals and flowers, trees and bamboos. In a landscape painting, at the foot of a mountain or the bank of a stream, one always finds a man sitting, appreciating the beauty of nature and contemplating the *Tao* or Way that transcends both nature and man.

Likewise in Chinese poetry we find such poems as that by *Tao* Chien (A.D. 372-427)

I built my hut in a zone of human habitation,
Yet near me there sounds no noise of horse or coach,
Would you know how that is possible?
A heart that is distant creates a wilderness round it.
I pluck chrysanthemums under the eastern hedge,
Then gaze long at the distant summer hills.
The mountain air is fresh at the dusk of day;
The flying birds two by two return.
In these things there lies a deep meaning;
Yet when we would express it, words suddenly fail us.[515]

Here we have Taoism at its best.

The Methodology of Chinese Philosophy

In Chinese philosophy, the farmer's outlook not only conditioned its content, such as that reversal is the movement of the *Tao*, but, what is more important, it also conditioned its methodology. Professor Northrop has said that there are

515 Translated by Arthur Waley.

two major types of concepts, that achieved by intuition and that by postulation. He says:

> A concept by intuition is one which denotes, and the complete meaning of which is given by, something which is immediately apprehended. Blue in the sense of the sensed color is a concept by intuition.... A concept by postulation is one the complete meaning of which is designated by the postulates of the deductive theory in which it occurs..... Blue in the sense of the number of a wave-length in electro-magnetic theory is a concept by postulation.[516]

Northrop also says that there are three possible types of concepts by intuition: "The concept of the differentiated aesthetic continuum. The concept of the indefinite or undifferentiated aesthetic continuum. The concept of the differentiation."[517] According to him:

> Confucianism may be defined as the state of mind in which the concept of the indeterminate intuited manifold moves into the background of thought and the concrete differentiations in their relativistic, humanistic, transitory comings and goings form the content of philosophy.[518] But in Taoism, it is the concept of the indefinite or undifferentiated aesthetic continuum that forms the content of philosophy.[519]

I do not quite agree with all Northrop has said in this essay, but I think he has here grasped the fundamental difference between Chinese and Western philosophy. When a student of Chinese philosophy begins to study Western philosophy, he is glad to see that the Greek philosophers also made the distinction between Being and Non-being, the limited and the unlimited. But he feels rather surprised to find that the Greek philosophers held that Non-being and the unlimited are inferior to Being and the limited.

In Chinese philosophy the case is just the reverse. The reason for this difference is that Being and the limited are the distinct, while non-being and the unlimited are the indistinct. Those philosophers who start with concepts by postulation have a liking for the distinct, while those who start with intuition value the indistinct.

If we link what Northrop has pointed out here with what I mentioned at the beginning of this chapter, we see that the concept of the differentiated aesthetic continuum, from which come both the concept of the undifferentiated aesthetic continuum and that of differentiation,[520] is basically the concept of the farmers. What the farmers have to deal with, such as the farm and crops, are all things which they immediately apprehend. And in their primitivity and innocence, they value what they thus immediately apprehend. It is no wonder then, that their philosophers likewise take the immediate apprehension of things as the starting point of their philosophy.

---

516 Filmer S. C. Northrop, "The Complementary Emphases of Eastern Intuition Philosophy and Western Scientific Philosophy," in *Philosophy, East and West*, C. A. Moore, ed, p 187, Princeton University Press, 1946

517 *Id*, p 187.

518 *Id.*, p. 205.

519 *Ibid.*

520 *Id.*,p.187.

This also explains why epistemology has never developed in Chinese philosophy. Whether the table that I see before me is real or illusory, and whether it is only an idea in my mind or is occupying objective space, was never seriously considered by Chinese philosophers. No such epistemological problems are to be found in Chinese philosophy (save in Buddhism, which came from India), since epistemological problems arise only when a demarcation between the subject and the object is emphasized. And in the aesthetic continuum, there is no such demarcation. In it the knower and the known is one whole.

This also explains why the language used by Chinese philosophy is suggestive but not articulate. It is not articulate, because it does not represent concepts in any deductive reasoning. The philosopher only tells us what he sees. And because of this, what he tells is rich in content, though terse in words. This is the reason why his words are suggestive rather than precise.

Maritime Countries and Continental Countries

The Greeks lived in a maritime country and maintained their prosperity through commerce. They were primarily merchants.

And what merchants have to deal with first are the abstract numbers used in their commercial accounts, and only then with concrete things that may be immediately apprehended through these numbers. Such numbers are what Northrop called concepts by postulation. Hence Greek philosophers likewise took the concept by postulation as their starting point. They developed mathematics and mathematical reasoning. That is why they had epistemological problems and why their language was so articulate.

But merchants are also townsmen. Their activities demand that they live together in towns. Hence they have a form of social organization not based on the common interest of the family so much as on that of the town. This is the reason why the Greeks organized their society around the city state, in contrast with the Chinese social system, which may be called that of the family state, because under it the state is conceived of in terms of the family. In a city state the social organization is not autocratic, because among the same class of townsmen, there is no moral reason why one should be more important than, or superior to, another. But in a family state the social organization is autocratic and hierarchic, because in a family the authority of the father is naturally superior to that of the son.

The fact that the Chinese were farmers also explains why China failed to have an industrial revolution, which is instrumental for the introduction of the modern world. In the Lieh-tzu there is a story which says that the Prince of the State of Sung once asked a clever artisan to carve a piece of jade into the leaf of a tree. After three years the artisan completed it, and when the artificial leaf was put upon the tree, it was made so wonderfully that no one could distinguish it from the real leaves. Thereupon the Prince was much pleased. But when Lieh Tzu heard it, he said "If nature took three years to produce one leaf, there would be few trees with leaves on them!"[521] This is the view of one who admires the natural and condemns

521 *Lieh-tzu*, Ch. 8.

the artificial. The way of life of the farmers is to follow nature. They admire nature and condemn the artificial, and in their primitivity and innocence, they are easily made content. They desire no change, nor can they conceive of any change. In China there have been not a few notable inventions or discoveries, but we often find that these were discouraged rather than encouraged.

With the merchants of a maritime country conditions are otherwise. They have greater opportunity to see different people with different customs and different languages; they are accustomed to change and are not afraid of novelty. Nay, in order to have a good sale for their goods, they have to encourage novelty in the manufacture of what they are going to sell. It is no accident that in the West, the industrial revolution was first started in England, which is also a maritime country maintaining her prosperity through commerce.

What was quoted earlier in this chapter from the Lu-shih Chun- chiu about merchants can also be said of the people of maritime countries, provided that, instead of saying that they are corrupt and treacherous, we say that they are refined and intelligent. We can also paraphrase Confucius by saying that the people of maritime countries are the wise, while those of continental countries are the good. And so we repeat what Confucius said: "The wise delight in water; the good delight in mountains. The wise move; the good stay still. The wise are happy; the good endure."

It is beyond the scope of this chapter to enumerate evidences to prove the relationship between the geographic and economic conditions of Greece and England on the one hand, and the development of Western scientific thought and democratic institutions on the other. But the fact that the geographic and economic conditions of Greece and England are quite different from those of China suffices to constitute a negative proof for my thesis in regard to Chinese history as mentioned in this chapter.

The Permanent and the Changeable in Chinese Philosophy

The advancement of science has conquered geography, and China is no longer isolated "within the four seas." She is having her industrialization too, and though much later than the Western world, it is better late than never. It is not correct to say that the East has been invaded by the West. Rather, it is a case in which the medieval has been invaded by the modern. In order to live in a modern world, China has to be modern.

One question remains to be asked: If Chinese philosophy has been so linked with the economic conditions of the Chinese people, does what has been expressed in Chinese philosophy possess validity only for people living under those conditions?

The answer is yes and no. In the philosophy of any people or any time, there is always a part that possesses value only in relation to the economic conditions of that people or of that time, but there is always another part that is more than this. That which is not relative has lasting value. I hesitate to say that it is absolute truth, because to determine what is absolute truth is too great a task for any human being, and is reserved for God alone, if there be one.

Let us take an instance in Greek philosophy. The rational justification of the slave system by Aristotle must be considered as a theory that is relative to the economic conditions of Greek life. But to say this is not to say that there is nothing that is not relative in the social philosophy of Aristotle. The same holds true for Chinese thought. When China is industrialized, the old family system must go, and with it will go its Confucianistic rational justification. But to say this is not to say that there is nothing that is not relative in the social philosophy of Confucianism.

The reason for this is that the society of ancient Greece and ancient China, though different, both belong to the general category which we call society. Theories which are the theoretical expressions of Greek or Chinese society are thus also in part expressions of society in general. Though there is in them something that pertains only to Greek or Chinese societies *per se*, there must also be something more universal that pertains to society in general. It is this latter something that is not relative and possesses lasting value.

The same is true of Taoism. The Taoist theory is certainly wrong which says that the utopia of mankind is the primitivity of a bygone age. With the idea of progress, we moderns think that the ideal state of human existence is something to be created in the future, not something that was lost in the past. But what some moderns think of as the ideal state of human existence, such as anarchism, is not wholly dissimilar from that thought of by the Taoists.

Philosophy also gives us an ideal of life. A part of that ideal, as given by the philosophy of a certain people or a certain time, must pertain only to the kind of life resulting from the social conditions of that people or that time. But, there must also be a part that pertains to life in general, and so is not relative but has lasting value. This seems to be illustrated in the case of the Confucianist theory of an ideal life. According to this theory, the ideal life is one which, though having a very high understanding of the universe, yet remains within the bounds of the five basic human relationships. The nature of these human relationships may change according to circumstances. But the ideal itself does not change. One is wrong, then, when one insists that since some of the five human relationships have to go, therefore the Confucianist ideal of life must go as well. And one is also wrong when one insists that since this ideal of life is desirable, therefore all the five human relationships must likewise be retained. One must make a logical analysis in order to distinguish between what is permanent and what is changeable in the history of philosophy. Every philosophy has that which is permanent, and all philosophies have something in common. This is why philosophies, though different, can yet be compared with one another and translated one in terms of the other.

Will the methodology of Chinese philosophy change? That is to say, will the new Chinese philosophy cease to confine itself to "concept by intuition?" Certainly it will, and there is no reason why it should not. In fact, it is already changing. In regard to this change, I shall have more to say in the last chapter of this book.

III THE ORIGIN OF THE SCHOOLS

In the last chapter I said that Confucianism and Taoism are the two main streams of Chinese thought. They became so only after a long evolution, however, and from the fifth through the third centuries B.C. they were only two among many other rival schools of thought. During that period the number of schools was so great that the Chinese referred to them as the "hundred schools."

Ssuma Tan and the Six Schools

Later historians have attempted to make a classification of these "hundred schools." The first to do so was Ssuma Tan (died 110 B.C.), father of Ssuma Chien (145-ca. 86 B.C.) and the author with him of China's first great dynastic history, the Shih Chi, also known as *Records of the Historian*. In the last chapter of this work Ssuma Chien quotes an essay by his father, titled "On the Essential Ideas of the Six Schools." In this essay Ssuma Tan classifies the philosophers of the preceding several centuries into six major schools, as follows:

> The first is the *Yin-Yang* chia or *Yin-Yang* school, which is one of cosmologists. It derives its name from the *Yin* and *Yang* principles, which in Chinese thought are regarded as the two major principles of Chinese cosmology, *Yin* being the female principle, and *Yang* the male principle, the combination and interaction of which is believed by the Chinese to result in all universal phenomena.
>
> The second school is the Ju Chia or School of Literati. This school is known in Western literature as the Confucianist school, but the word ju literally means "literatus" or scholar. Thus the Western title is somewhat misleading, because it misses the implication that the followers of this school were scholars as well as thinkers; they, above all others, were the teachers of the ancient classics and thus the inheritors of the ancient cultural legacy. Confucius, to be sure, is the leading figure of this school and may rightly be considered as its founder. Nevertheless the term ju not only denotes "Confucian" or Confucianist," but has a wider implication as well.
>
> The third school is that of the Mo chia or Mohist school. This school had a close-knit organization and strict discipline under the leadership of Mo Tzu. Its followers actually called themselves the Mohists. Thus the title of this school is not an invention of Ssuma Tan, as were some of the other schools.
>
> The fourth school is the Ming chia, or School of Names. The followers of this school were interested in the distinction between, and relation of, what they called "names" and "actualities."
>
> The fifth school is the Fa chia or Legalist school. The Chinese word fa means law or pattern. The school derived from a group of statesmen who maintained that good government must be one based on a fixed code of law instead of on the moral institutions which the literati stressed for government.
>
> The sixth school is the *Tao-Te* chia or School of the Way and its Power. The followers of this school centered their metaphysics and social philosophy

around the concept of Non-being, which is the *Tao* or Way, and its concentration in the individual as the natural virtue of man, which is Te, translated as "virtue" but better rendered as the "power" that inheres in any individual thing. This group, called by Ssuma Tan the *Tao*-Te school, was later known simply as the *Tao* chia, and is referred to in Western literature as the *Tao*ist school. As pointed out in the first chapter, it should be kept carefully distinct from the *Tao*ist religion.

Liu Hsin and His Theory of the Beginning of the Schools

The second historian who attempted to classify the "hundred schools" was Liu Hsin (ca. 46 B.C.-A.D. 23). He was one of the greatest scholars of his day, and, with his father Liu Hsiang, made a collation of the books in the Imperial Library. The resulting descriptive catalogue of the Imperial Library, known as the "Seven Summaries," was taken by Pan Ku (A.D. 32-92) as the basis for the chapter, Yi Wen Chih or "Treatise on Literature," contained in his dynastic history, the History of the Former Han Dynasty. In this "Treatise" we see that Liu Hsin classifies the "hundred schools" into ten main groups. Out of these, six are the same as those listed by Ssuma Tan. The other four are the Tsung-Heng Chia or School of Diplomatists, Tsa chia or School of Eclectics, Nung chia or School of Agrarians, and *Hsiao*-shuo chia or School of Story Tellers. In conclusion, Liu Hsin writes: "The various philosophers consist of ten schools, but there are only nine that need be noticed." By this statement he means to say that the School of Story Tellers lacks the importance of the other schools.

In this classification itself, Liu Hsin did not go very much further than Ssuma Tan had done. What was new, however, was his attempt for the first time in Chinese history to trace systematically the historical origins of the different schools.

Liu Hsin's theory has been greatly elaborated by later scholars, especially by Chang Hsueh-cheng (1738-1801) and the late Chang Ping-lin. In essence, it maintains that in the early Chou Dynasty (1122?-255 B.C.), before the social institutions of that age disintegrated, there was "no separation between officers and teachers." In other words the officers of a certain department of the government were at the same time the transmitters of the branch of learning pertaining to that department. These officers, like the feudal lords of the day, held their posts on a hereditary basis. Hence there was then only "official learning" but no "private teaching." That is to say, nobody taught any branch of learning as a private individual. Any such teaching was carried on only by officers in their capacity as members of one or another department of the government.

According to this theory, however, when the Chou ruling house lost its power during the later centuries of the Chou Dynasty, the officers of the governmental departments lost their former positions and scattered throughout the country. They then turned to the teaching of their special branches of knowledge in a private capacity. Thus they were then no longer "officers," but only private "teachers." And it was out of this separation between teachers and officers that the different schools arose.

Liu Hsin's whole analysis reads as follows:

The members of the Ju school had their origin in the Ministry of Education.... This school delighted in the study of the Liu Yi [the Six Classics or six liberal arts] and emphasized matters concerning human-heartedness and righteousness. They regarded Yao and Shun [two ancient sage emperors supposed to have lived in the twenty-fourth and twenty-third centuries B.C.] as the ancestor of their school, and King Wen [1120?-1108? B.C. of the Chou Dynasty] and King Wu [son of King Wen] as brilliant exemplars. To give authority to their teaching, they honored Chung-ni [Confucius] as an exalted teacher. Their teaching is the highest truth. "That which is admired must be tested." The glory of Yao and Shun, the prosperity of the dynasties of *Yin* and Chou, and the achievements of Chung-ni are the results discovered by testing their reach.

Those of the *Tao*ist school had their origin in the official historians. By studying the historical examples of success and failure, preservation and destruction, and calamity and prosperity, from ancient to recent times, they learned how to hold what is essential and to grasp the fundamental. They guarded themselves with purity and emptiness, and with humbleness and meekness maintained themselves. Herein lies the strong point of this school.

Those of the *Yin-Yang* school had their origin in the official astronomers. They respectfully followed luminous heaven, and the successive symbols of the sun and moon, the stars and constellations, and the divisions of times and seasons. Herein lies the strong point of this school. Those of the Legalist school had their origin in the Ministry of Justice. They emphasized strictness in rewarding and punishing, in order to support a system of correct conduct. Herein lies the strong point of this school.

Those of the School of Names had their origin in the Ministry of Ceremonies. For the ancients, where titles and positions differed, the ceremonies accorded to them were also different. Confucius has said "If names be incorrect, speech will not follow its natural sequence. If speech does not follow its natural sequence, nothing can be established" Herein lies the strong point of this school.

Those of the Mohist School had their origin in the Guardians of the Temple. The temple was built with plain wooden rafters and thatched roofs; hence their teaching emphasized frugality. The temple was the place where the Three Elders and Five Experienced Men were honored; hence their teaching emphasized universal love. The ceremony of selecting civil officials and that of military exercises were also held in the temple; hence their teaching emphasized the preferment of virtue and ability. The temple was the place for sacrifice to ancestors and reverence to fathers; hence their teaching was to honor the spirits. They accepted the traditional teaching of following the four seasons in one's conduct; hence their teaching was against fatalism. They accepted the traditional teaching of exhibiting filial piety throughout

> the world; hence they taught the doctrine of "agreeing with the superior." Herein lies the strong point of this school.
>
> Those of the Diplomatist school had their origin in the Ministry of Embassies.... [They taught the art of] following general orders [in diplomacy], instead of following literal instructions. Herein lies the strength of their teaching.
>
> Those of the Eclectic school had their origin in the Councilors. They drew both from the Confucianists and the Mohists, and harmonized the School of Names and the Legalists. They knew that the nation had need of each of these, and saw that kingly government should not fail to unite all. Herein lies the strong point of this school.
>
> Those of the Agricultural school had their origin in the Ministry of Soil and Grain. They taught the art of sowing the various kinds of grain and urged people to plow and to cultivate the mulberry so that the clothing and food of the people would be sufficient.... Herein lies the strong point of this school.
>
> Those of the School of Story Tellers had their origin in the Petty Offices. This school was created by those who picked up the talk of streets and alleys and repeated what they heard wherever they went....Even if in their teaching but a single word can be chosen, still there is some contribution.[522]

This is what Liu Hsin says about the historical origin of the ten schools. His interpretation of the significance of the schools is inadequate, and his attribution of certain of them to certain "Ministries" is in some cases arbitrary. For instance, in describing the teaching of the Taoists, he touches only on the ideas of Lao Tzu, and omits those of Chuang Tzu altogether. Moreover, there appears to be no similarity between the teaching of the School of Names and the functions of the Ministry of Ceremonies, save that both emphasized the making of distinctions.

A Revision of Liu Hsin's Theory

Yet though the details of Liu Hsin's theory may be wrong, his attempt to trace the origin of the schools to certain political and social circumstances certainly represents a right point of view. I have quoted him at length because his description of the various schools is itself a classic in Chinese historiography.

The study of Chinese history has made great progress in China in recent times, especially during the few years just before the Japanese invasion of 1937. In the light of recent research, therefore, I have formed a theory of my own in regard to the origin of the philosophic schools. In spirit this theory agrees with that of Liu Hsin, but it must be expressed in a different way. This means that things have to be seen from a new angle.

Let us imagine what China looked like politically and socially in, say, the tenth century B.C. At the top of the political and social structure, there was the King of the Chou royal house, who was the "common lord" of all the different states. Under him were hundreds of states, each owned and governed by its Princes. Some of them were established by the founders of the Chou Dynasty,

522 Treatise on Literature, "*History of the Former Han Dynasty*".

who had allotted the newly conquered territory as feudal fiefs to their relatives. Others were ruled by the former rivals of the Chou house, who now, however, acknowledged the King of Chou as their "common lord."

Within each state, under the Prince, the land was again divided into many fiefs, each with its own feudal lord, who were relatives of the Prince. At that time, political power and economic control were one and the same. Those who had the land were the political and economic masters of it, and of the people who lived on it. They were the chun tzu, a term which literally means "sons of the Princes," but which was used as a common designation of the class of the feudal lords.

The other social class was that of the *hsiao jen*, meaning small men, or shu min, meaning common people or the mass. These were the serfs of the feudal lords, who cultivated the land for the chun tzu in time of peace, and fought for them in time of war.

The aristocrats were not only the political rulers and landlords, but also the only persons who had a chance to receive an education. Thus the houses of the feudal lords were not only centers of political and economic power, but also centers of learning. Attached to them were officers who possessed specialized knowledge along various lines. But the common people, for their part, had no chance to become educated, so that among them there were no men of learning. This is the fact behind Liu Hsin's theory that in the early Chou Dynasty there was "no separation between officers and teachers."

This feudal system was formally abolished by the First Emperor of the Chin Dynasty in 221 B.C. But hundreds of years before that, the system had already begun to disintegrate, whereas thousands of years later, economic remnants of feudalism still remained in the form of the power of the landlord class.

Historians of modern time are still not agreed as to what were the causes of the disintegration of the feudal system. Nor is it within the scope of this chapter to discuss these causes. For the present purpose, it is sufficient to say that in Chinese history the period between the seventh and third centuries B.C. was one of great social and political transformation and change.

We are not sure just when the disintegration of the feudal system began. Already as early as the seventh century there were aristocrats who through the wars of the time, or for other reasons, lost their lands and titles, and thus fell to the level of the common people. There were also common people who through skill or favoritism became high officials of the state. This illustrates the real significance of the disintegration of the Chou Dynasty. It was not only the disintegration of the political power of a particular royal house, but-and this is more important-of an entire social system.

With this disintegration, the former official representatives of the various branches of learning became scattered among the common people. They had either been actual nobles themselves, or had been specialists holding hereditary offices in the service of the aristocratic ruling families. This is the significance of a quotation made by Liu Hsin from Confucius in the course of the same "Treatise" partially quoted from above: "When ceremonies become lost [at the court], it is necessary to search for them in the countryside."

Thus when these former nobles or officials scattered throughout the country, they maintained a livelihood by carrying on, in a private capacity, their specialized abilities or skills. Those of them who expressed their ideas to other private individuals became professional "teachers," and thus there arose the separation between the teacher and the officer.

The word "school" in this chapter is a translation of the Chinese word chia, which at the same time is used to denote a family or home. Hence it suggests something personal or private. There could be no chia of thought before there were persons who taught their own ideas in a private capacity.

Likewise there were different kinds of chia because these teachers were specialists in varying branches of learning and of the arts. Thus there were some who were specialists in the teaching of the classics and the practicing of ceremonies and music. These were known as the ju or literati. There were also specialists in the art of war. These were the hsieh or knights. There were specialists in the art of speaking, who were known as the pien-che or debaters. There were specialists in magic, divination, astrology, and numerology, who were known as the fang-shih, or practitioners of occult arts. There were also the practical politicians who could act as private advisers to the feudal rulers, and who were known as fang shu chih shih or "men of methods." And finally, there were some men who possessed learning and talent, but who were so embittered by the political disorders of their time that they retired from human society into the world of nature. These were known as the *yin*-che or hermits or recluses.

According to my theory, it is from these six different kinds of people that the six schools of thought as listed by Ssuma Tan originated. Paraphrasing Liu Hsin, therefore, I would say:

Members of the Ju school had their origin in the literati.

Members of the Mohist school had their origin in the knights.

Members of the *Tao*ist school had their origin in the hermits.

Members of the School of Names had their origin in the debaters.

Members of the *Yin-Yang* school had their origin in the practitioners of occult arts.

Members of the Legalist school had their origin in the "men of methods."

The explanations of these statements will be found in the chapters that follow.

IV CONFUCIUS, THE FIRST TEACHER

Confucius is the Latinized name of the person who has been known in China as Kung Tzu or Master Kung.[523] His family name was Kung and his personal name Chiu. He was born in 551 B.C. in the state of Lu, in the southern part of the present Shandong Province in eastern China. His ancestors had been members of the ducal house of the state of Sung, which was descended from the royal house of Shang, the dynasty that had preceded the Chou.

Because of political troubles, the family before the birth of Confucius, had lost its noble position and migrated to Lu.

The most detailed account of Confucius' life is the biography which comprises the forty-seventh chapter of the Shih *Chi* or Historical Records (China's first dynastic history, completed ca. 86B.C.) From this we learn that Confucius was poor in his youth, but entered the government of Lu and by the time he was fifty had reached high official rank. As a result of political intrigue, however, he was soon forced to resign his post and go into exile. For the next thirteen years he traveled from one state to another, always hoping to find an opportunity to realize his ideal of political and social reform. Nowhere, however, did he succeed, and finally as an old man he returned to Lu, where he died three years later in 479 B.C.

Confucius and the Six Classics

In the last chapter I said that the rise of the philosophic schools began with the practice of private teaching. So far as modern scholarship can determine, Confucius was the first person in Chinese history thus to teach large numbers of students in a private capacity, by whom he was accompanied during his travels in different states. According to tradition, he had several thousand students, of whom several tens became famous thinkers and scholars. The former number is undoubtedly a gross exaggeration, but there is no question that he was a very influential teacher, and what is more important and unique, China's first private teacher. His ideas are best known through the Lun Yu or Analects of Confucius, a collection of his scattered sayings which was compiled by some of his disciples.

Confucius was the founder of the Ju school, which has been known in the West as the Confucian school. In the last chapter we saw how Liu Hsin wrote regarding this school that it "delighted in the study of the Liu Yi and emphasized matters concerning human-heartedness and righteousness." The term Liu Yi means the "six arts," i.e., the six liberal arts, but it is more commonly translated as the "Six Classics." These are the Yi or Book of Changes, the Shih or Book of Odes (or Poetry), the Shu or Book of History, the *Li* or Rituals or Rites, the Yueh or Music (no longer preserved as a separate work), and the Chun Chiu or Spring and Autumn Annals, a chronicle history of Confucius' state of Lu extending

523 The word "Tzu"or "Master" is a polite suffix added to names of most philosophers of the Chou Dynasty, such as Chuang Tzu, Hsun Tzu, etc., and meaning "Master Chuang," "Master Hsun," etc.

from 722 to 479 B.C., the year of Confucius' death. The nature of these classics is clear from their titles, with the exception of the Book of Changes. This work was in later times interpreted by the Confucianists as a treatise on metaphysics, but originally it was a book of divination.

Concerning the relation of Confucius with the Six Classics, there are two schools of traditional scholarship. One maintains that Confucius was the author of all these works, while the other maintains that Confucius was the author of the *Spring and Autumn Annals*, the commentator of the *Book of Changes*, the reformer of the *Rituals and Music*, and the editor of the *Book of History* and *Book of Odes*.

As a matter of fact, however, Confucius was neither the author, commentator, nor even editor of any of the classics. In some respects, to be sure, he was a conservative who upheld tradition. Thus in the rites and music he did try to rectify any deviations from the traditional practices or standards, and instances of so doing are reported in the Lun Yu or Analects. Judging from what is said of him in the Analects, however, Confucius never had any intention of writing anything himself for future generations. The writing of books in a private rather than official capacity was an as yet unheard-of practice which developed only after the time of Confucius. He was China's first private teacher, but not its first private writer.

The Six Classics had existed before the time of Confucius, and they constituted the cultural legacy of the past. They had been the basis of education for the aristocrats during the early centuries of feudalism of the Chou Dynasty. As feudalism began to disintegrate, however, roughly from the seventh century B.C. onward, the tutors of the aristocrats, or even some of the aristocrats themselves — men who had lost their positions and titles but were well versed in the Classics — began to scatter among the people. They made their living, as we have seen in the last chapter, by teaching the Classics or by acting as skilled "assistants," well versed in the rituals, on the occasion of funeral, sacrifice, wedding, and other ceremonies. This class of men was known as the ju or literati.

Confucius as an Educator

Confucius, however, was more than a ju in the common sense of the word. It is true that in the Analects we find him, from one point of view, being portrayed merely as an educator. He wanted his disciples to be "rounded men" who would be useful to state and society, and therefore he taught them various branches of knowledge based upon the different classics. His primary function as a teacher, he felt, was to interpret to his disciples the ancient cultural heritage. That is why, in his own words as recorded in the Analects, he was "a transmitter and not an originator."[524] But this is only one aspect of Confucius, and there is another one as well. This is that, while transmitting the traditional institutions and ideas, Confucius gave them interpretations derived from his own moral concepts. This is exemplified in his interpretation of the old custom that on the death of

524 *Analects of Confucius*, VII, 1.

a parent, a son should mourn three years. Confucius commented on this: "The child cannot leave the arms of its parents until it is three years old. This is why the three years' mourning is universally observed throughout the world."[525] In other words, the son was utterly dependent upon his parents for at least the first three years of his life; hence upon their death he should mourn them for an equal length of time in order to express his gratitude. Likewise when teaching the Classics, Confucius gave them new interpretations. Thus in speaking of the Book of Poetry, he stressed its moral value by saying: "In the Book of Poetry there are three hundred poems. But the essence of them can be covered in one sentence: 'Have no depraved thoughts.'[526] In this way Confucius was more than a mere transmitter, for in transmitting, he originated something new.

This spirit of originating through transmitting was perpetuated by the followers of Confucius, by whom, as the classical texts were handed down from generation to generation, countless commentaries and interpretations were written. A great portion of what in later times came to be known as the Thirteen Classics developed as commentaries in this way on the original texts.

This is what set Confucius apart from the ordinary literati of his time, and made him the founder of a new school. Because the followers of this school were at the same time scholars and specialists on the Six Classics, the school became known as the School of the Literati.

The Rectification of Names

Besides the new interpretations which Confucius gave to the classics, he had his own ideas about the individual and society, heaven and man.

In regard to society, he held that in order to have a well-ordered one, the most important thing is to carry out what he called the rectification of names. That is, things in actual fact should be made to accord with the implication attached to them by names. Once a disciple asked him what he would do first if he were to rule a state, whereupon Confucius replied "The one thing needed first is the rectification of names."[527] On another occasion one of the dukes of the time asked Confucius the right principle of government, to which he answered "Let the ruler be ruler, the minister minister, the father father, and the son son."[528] In other words, every name contains certain implications which constitute the essence of that class of things to which this name applies. Such things, therefore, should agree with this ideal essence. The essence of a ruler is what the ruler ideally ought to be, or what, in Chinese, is called "the way of the ruler." If a ruler acts according to this way of the ruler, he is then truly a ruler, in fact as well as in name. There is an agreement between name and actuality. But if he does not, he is no ruler, even though he may popularly be regarded as such. Every name in the social relationships implies certain responsibilities and duties. Ruler, minister, father, and son are all the names of such social relationships, and the individual

525 *Id.*, XVII, 21.
526 *Id.*, II, 2.
527 *Id*, XIII, 3.
528 *Id.*, XII,II.

bearing these names must fulfill their responsibilities and duties accordingly. Such is the implication of Confucius' theory of the rectification of names.

Human-heartedness and Righteousness

With regard to the virtues of the individual, Confucius emphasized human-heartedness and righteousness, especially the former. Righteousness (*yi*) means the "oughtness" of a situation. It is a categorical imperative. Every one in society has certain things which he ought to do, and which must be done for their own sake, because they are the morally right things to do. If, however, he does them only because of other non-moral considerations, then even though he does what he ought to do, his action is no longer a righteous one. To use a word often disparaged by Confucius and later Confucianists, he is then acting for "profit." *Yi* (righteousness) and *li* (profit) are in Confucianism diametrically opposed terms.

Confucius himself says: "The superior man comprehends yi; the small man comprehends *li*."[529] I Here in lies what the later Confucianists called the "distinction between *yi* and *li*," a distinction which they considered to be of the utmost importance in moral teaching.

The idea of *yi* is rather formal, but that of *jen* (human-heartedness) is much more concrete. The formal essence of the duties of man in society is their "oughtness," because all these duties are what he ought to do. But the material essence of these duties is "loving others," i.e., *jen* or human-heartedness. The father acts according to the way a father should act who loves his son; the son acts according to the way a son should act who loves his father. Confucius says: "Human-heartedness consists in loving others."[530] The man who really loves others is one able to perform his duties in society. Hence in the Analects we see that Confucius sometimes uses the word *jen* not only to denote a special kind of virtue, but also to denote all the virtues combined, so that the term "man of *jen*" becomes synonymous with the man of all-round virtue. In such contexts, *jen* can be translated as "perfect virtue."

Chung and Shu

In the *Analects* we find the passage: "When Chung Kung asked the meaning of *jen*, the master said: '... Do not do to others what you do not wish yourself...' "[531] Again, Confucius is reported in the *Analects* as saying:

> The man of *jen* is one who, desiring to sustain himself, sustains others, and desiring to develop himself, develops others. To be able from one's own self to draw a parallel for the treatment of others; that may be called the way to practice *jen*.[532]

Thus the practice of *jen* consists in consideration for others 'Desiring to sustain oneself, one sustains others; desiring to develop oneself, one develops others." In other words: "Do to other: what you wish yourself." This is the positive aspect

529 *Id.*, IV, 16.
530 *Id.*, XII, 22.
531 *Id*, XII, 2.
532 *Id.*, VI, 28.

of the practice which was called by Confucius Chung or "conscientiousness to others." And the negative aspect, which was called by Confucius shu or "altruism," be "Do not do to others what you do not wish yourself." The practice as a whole is called the principle of Chung and shu, which is "the way to practice *jen*."

This principle was known by some of the later Confucianists as the "principle of applying a measuring square." That is to say, it is a principle by which one uses oneself as a standard to regulate one's conduct. In the Ta Hsueh or The Great Learning, which is a chapter of the *Li Chi* (Book of Rites), a collection of treatises written by the Confucianists in the third and second centuries B.C., it is said:

> "Do not use what you dislike in your superiors in the employment of your inferiors. Do not use what you dislike in your inferiors in the service of your superiors. Do not use what you dislike in those who are before, to precede those who are behind. Do not use what you dislike in those who are behind, to follow those are before. Do not use what you dislike on the right, to display towards the left. Do not use what you dislike on the left, to display towards the right. This is called the principle of applying a measuring square.

In the *Chung Yung* or *Doctrine of the Mean*, which is another chapter of the *Li Chi*, attributed to Tzu Ssu, the grandson of Confucius, it is said:

> *Chung* and *shu* are not far from the Way. What you do not like done to yourself, do not do to others.... Serve your father as you would require your son to serve you.... Serve your ruler as you would require you subordinate to serve you... Serve your elder brother as you would require your younger brother to serve you.... Set the example in behaving to your friends as you would require them to behave to you....

The illustration given in The Great Learning emphasizes the negative aspect of the principle of Chung and shu; that in the *Doctrine of the Mean* emphasizes its positive aspect. In each case the "measuring square" for determining conduct is in one's self and not in other things.

The principle of *chung* and *shu* is at the same time the principle of *jen*, so that the practice of *chung* and shu means the practice of *jen*. And this practice leads to the carrying out of one's responsibilities and duties in society, in which is comprised the quality of yi or righteousness. Hence the principle of *chung* and shu becomes the alpha and omega of one's moral life. In the Analects we find the passage:

> The master said "Shen [the personal name of Tseng Tzu, one of his disciples,] all my teachings are linked together by one principle." "Quite so," replied Tseng Tzu. When the master had left the room, the disciples asked: "What did he mean?" Tseng Tzu replied "Our master's teaching consists of the principle of chung and shu, and that is all."[533]

Everyone has within himself the "measuring square" for conduct, and can use it at any time. So simple as this is the method of practicing *jen*, so that Confucius said "Is *jen* indeed far off? I crave for *jen*, and lo! *jen* is at hand!"[534]

---

533 *Id.*,IV , 15.

534 *Id.*, VII, 29.

Knowing Ming

From the idea of righteousness, the Confucianists derived the idea of "doing for nothing." One does what one ought to do, simply because it is morally right to do it, and not for any consideration external to this moral compulsion. In the Analects, we are told that Confucius was ridiculed by a certain recluse as "one who knows that he cannot succeed, yet keeps on trying to do it."[535] We also read that another recluse was told by a disciple of Confucius: "The reason why the superior man tries to go into politics, is because he holds this to be right, even though he is well aware that his principle cannot prevail"[536]

As we shall, see, the *Tao*ists taught the theory of "doing nothing," whereas the Confucianists taught that of "not doing nothing." A man cannot do nothing, according to Confucianism, because for every man there is something which he ought to do. Nevertheless, what he does is "for nothing," because the value of doing what he ought to do lies in the doing itself, and not in the external result.

Confucius' own life is certainly a good example of this teaching.

Living in an age of great social and political disorder, he tried his best to reform the world. He traveled everywhere and, like Socrates, talked to everybody. Although his efforts were in vain, he was never disappointed. He knew that he could not succeed, but kept on trying.

About himself Confucius said: "If my principles are to prevail in the world, it is *Ming*. If they are to fall to the ground, it is also *Ming*."[537] He tried his best, but the issue he left to *Ming*. *Ming* is often translated as Fate, Destiny or Decree. To Confucius, it meant the Decree of Heaven or Will of Heaven; in other words, it was conceived of as a purposeful force. In later Confucianism, however, *Ming* simply means the total existent conditions and forces of the whole universe. For the external success of our activity, the cooperation of these conditions is always needed. But this cooperation is wholly beyond our control, Hence the best thing for us to do is simply to try to carry out what we know we ought to carry out, without caring whether in the process we succeed or fail. To act in this way is "to know Ming." To know *Ming* is an important requirement for being a superior man in the Confucian sense of the term, so that Confucius said: "He who does not know *Ming* cannot be a superior man."[538]

Thus to know *Ming* means to acknowledge the inevitability of the world as it exists, and so to disregard one's external success or failure. If we can act in this way, we can, in a sense, never fail. For if we do our duty that duty through our very act is morally done, regardless of the external success or failure of our action.

As a result, we always shall be free from anxiety as to success or fear as to failure, and so shall be happy. This is why Confucius said: "The wise are free

535 Id., XIV, 41.

536 Analects of Confucius, XVIII, 7

537 *Id.*, XIV, 38.

538 *Id.*, XX, 2.

from doubts; the virtuous from anxiety; the brave from fear."[539] Or again: The superior man is always happy; the small man sad."[540]

Confucius' Spiritual Development

In the *Tao*ist work, the Chuang-tzu, we see that the *Tao*ists often ridiculed Confucius as one who confined himself to the morality of human-heartedness and righteousness, thus being conscious only of moral values, and not super-moral value. Superficially they were right, but actually they were wrong. Thus speaking about his own spiritual development, Confucius said:

> At fifteen I set my heart on learning. At thirty I could stand. At forty I had no doubts. At fifty I knew the Decree of Heaven. At sixty I was already obedient [to this Decree]. At seventy I could follow the desires of my mind without overstepping the boundaries [of what is right][541]

The "learning" which Confucius here refers to is not what we now would call learning. In the Analects, Confucius said: "Set your heart on the *Tao*."[542] And again: "To hear the *Tao* in the morning and then die at night that would be all right."[543] Here *Tao* means the Way or Truth. It was this *Tao* which Confucius at fifteen set his heart upon learning. What we now call learning means the increase of our knowledge, but the *Tao* is that whereby we can elevate our mind.

Confucius also said "Take your stand in the Li [rituals, ceremonies, proper conduct]."[544] Again he said: "Not to know the li is to have no means of standing."[545] Thus when Confucius says that at thirty he could "stand," he means that he then understood the li and so could practice proper conduct.

His statement that at forty he had no doubts means that he had then become a wise man. For, as quoted before, "The wise are free from doubts."

Up to this time of his life Confucius was perhaps conscious only of moral values. But at the age of fifty and sixty, he knew the Decree of Heaven and was obedient to it. In other words, he was then also conscious of super-moral values. Confucius in this respect was like Socrates. Socrates thought that he had been appointed by a divine order to awaken the Greeks, and Confucius had a similar consciousness of a divine mission. For example, when he was threatened with physical violence at a place called Kuang, he said: "If Heaven had wished to let civilization perish, later generations (like myself) would not have been permitted to participate in it. But since Heaven has not wished to let civilization perish, what can the people of Kuang do to me?"[546] One of his contemporaries also said "The world for long has been without order. But now Heaven is going to use the Master as an arousing tocsin."[547] Thus Confucius in doing what he did, was

539 *Id.*, IX, 28.
540 *Id.*, VII, 36.
541 *Id.*, II, 4.
542 *Id.*, VII, 6.
543 *Id.*, IV, 9.
544 *Id.*, VIII, S.
545 *Id.*, XX, 3.
546 *Id.*, IX 5.
547 *Id.*, III, 24.

convinced that he was following the Decree of Heaven and was supported by Heaven; he was conscious of values higher than moral ones.

The super-moral value experienced by Confucius, however, was, as we shall see, not quite the same as that experienced by the *Tao*ists. For the latter abandoned entirely the idea of an intelligent and purposeful Heaven, and sought instead for mystical union with an undifferentiated whole. The super-moral value which they knew and experienced, therefore, was freer from the ordinary concepts of the human relationships.

At seventy, as has been told above, Confucius allowed his mind to follow whatever it desired, yet everything he did was naturally right of itself. His actions no longer needed a conscious guide. He was acting without effort. This represents the last stage in the development of the sage.

Confucius is probably better known in the West than any other single Chinese. Yet in China itself, though always famous, his place in history has changed considerably from one period to another. Historically speaking he was primarily a teacher, that is, only one teacher among many. But after his death, he gradually came to be considered as the Teacher, superior to all others. And in the second century B.C. he was elevated to an even higher plane. According to many Confucianists of that time, Confucius had actually been appointed by Heaven to begin a new dynasty that would follow that of Chou. Though in actual fact without a crown or a government, he had ideally speaking become a king who ruled the whole empire. How this apparent contradiction had happened, these Confucianists said, could be found out by studying the esoteric meaning supposedly contained in the Spring and Autumn Annals. This was supposed by them not to be a chronicle of Confucius' native state (as it actually was), but an important political work written by Confucius to express his ethical and political ideas. Then in the first century B.C., Confucius came to be regarded as even more than a king. According to many people of that time, he was a living god among men — a divine being who knew that after his time there would someday come the Han Dynasty (206 B.C.-A.D. 220), and who therefore, in the Spring and Autumn Annals, set forth a political ideal which would be complete enough for the men of Han to realize. This apotheosis was the climax of Confucius' glory, and in the middle of the Han Dynasty Confucianism could properly be called a religion.

The time of glorification, however, did not last very long.

Already beginning in the first century A.D., Confucianists of a more rationalistic type began to get the upper hand. Hence in later times Confucius was no longer regarded as a divine being, though his position as that of the Teacher remained high. At the very end of the nineteenth century, to be sure, there was a brief revival of the theory that Confucius had been divinely appointed to be a king. Soon afterwards, however, with the coming of the Chinese Republic, his reputation fell until he came to be regarded as something less than the Teacher, and at present most Chinese would say that he was primarily a teacher, and certainly a great one, but far from being the only teacher.

Confucius, however, was already recognized in his own day as a man of very extensive learning. For example, one of his contemporaries said "Great indeed is the Master Kung! His learning is so extensive that he cannot be called by a single name."[548] From the quotations given earlier, we may see that he considered himself the inheritor and perpetuator of ancient civilization, and was considered by some of his contemporaries as such. By his work of originating through transmitting, he caused his school to reinterpret the civilization of the age before him. He upheld what he considered to be best in the old, and created a powerful tradition that was followed until very recent years, when, as in Confucius' own time, China again came face to face with tremendous economic and social change. In addition, he was China's first teacher. Hence, though historically speaking he was only a teacher, it is perhaps not unreasonable that in later ages he was regarded as the Teacher.

548 *Id.* IX,2

V MO TZU, THE FIRST OPPONENT OF CONFUCIUS

The next major philosopher after Confucius was Mo Tzu. His family name was Mo and his personal name was Ti. As the Shih *Chi* or Historical Records does not say where he came from, and in fact tells us almost nothing about his life, there has been a difference of opinion regarding his native state. Some scholars hold that he was a native of Sung (in what is today eastern Henan and western Shandong), and others that he came from Lu, the same state as Confucius. His exact dates are also uncertain, but probably he lived sometime within the years 479-381 B.C. The main source for the study of his thought is the book bearing his name, the Mo-tzu, which contains 53 chapters and is a collection of writings by his followers as well as by himself.

Mo Tzu was the founder of a school known after his name as the Mohist school. In ancient times his fame was as great as that of Confucius, and his teaching was no less influential. The contrast between the two men is interesting. Confucius felt a sympathetic understanding for the traditional institutions, rituals, music, and literature of the early Chou Dynasty, and tried to rationalize and justify them in ethical terms; Mo Tzu, on the contrary, questioned their validity and usefulness, and tried to replace them with something that was simpler but, in his view, more useful. In short, Confucius was the rationalizer and justifier of the ancient civilization, while Mo Tzu was its critic. Confucius was a refined gentleman, while Mo Tzu was a militant preacher. A major aim of his preaching was to oppose both the traditional institutions and practices, and the theories of Confucius and the Confucianists.

Social Background of the Mohist School

During the feudal age of the Chou Dynasty, kings, princes, and feudal lords all had their military specialists. These were the hereditary warriors who constituted the backbone of the armies of that time. With the disintegration of feudalism that took place in the latter part of the Chou Dynasty, however, these warrior specialists lost their positions and titles, scattered throughout the country, and made a living by offering their services to anyone who could afford to employ them. This class of people was known as the hsieh or *yu* hsieh, terms which can both be translated as "knights-errant." Concerning such knights-errant, the Shih *Chi* says:

> Their words were always sincere and trustworthy, and their actions always quick and decisive. They were always true to what they promised, and without regard to their own persons, they would rush into dangers threatening others.[549]

Such were their professional ethics. A large part of Mo Tzu's teaching was an extension of these ethics.

In Chinese history both the ju or literati and the hsieh or Knights-errant originated as specialists attached to the houses of the aristocrats, and were

549 *Shih Chi*, Ch. 124.

themselves members of the upper classes. In later times the ju continued to come mainly from the upper or middle classes, but the hsieh, on the contrary, more frequently were recruited from the lower classes. In ancient times, such social amenities as rituals and music were all exclusively for the aristocrats; from the point of view of the common man, therefore, they were luxuries that had no practical utility. It was from this point of view that Mo Tzu and the Mohists criticized the traditional institutions and their rationalizers, Confucius and the Confucianists. This criticism, together with the elaboration and rationalization of the professional ethics of their own social class, that of the hsieh, constituted the central core of the Mohist philosophy.

There is plenty of evidence for the inference that Mo Tzu and his followers came from the hsieh. From the Mo-tzu, as well as from other contemporary sources, we know that the Mohists constituted a strictly disciplined organization capable of military action. The leader of the Mohist organization was called the Chu Tzu, "Great Master," and had the authority of life or death over the members of the group. We are also told that Mo Tzu was the first "Great Master" of his group, and that at least once he actually led his followers to prepare for the military defense of Sung, when that state was threatened with invasion from the neighboring state of Chu.

The story of this episode is interesting. It is said in the Mo-tzu that a noted mechanical inventor, Kungshu Pan, then employed by the state of Chu, had completed the construction of a new weapon for attacking city walls. Chu was preparing to attack Sung with this new weapon. Hearing of this, Mo Tzu went to Chu to persuade its king to desist. There he and Kungshu Pan made a demonstration before the king of their weapons of attack and defense. Mo Tzu first untied his belt and laid out a city with it, using a small stick as a weapon. Kungshu Pan thereupon set up nine different miniature machines of attack, but Mo Tzu nine times repulsed him.

Finally, Kungshu Pan had used up all his machines of attack, while Mo Tzu was far from being exhausted in the defense. Then Kungshu Pan said: "I know how to defeat you, but I will not say it." To which Mo Tzu replied: "I know what it is, but I too will not say it."

On being asked by the king what was meant, Mo Tzu continued:

> "Kungshu Pan is thinking of murdering me. But my disciples Chin Ku-li and others, numbering three hundred men, are already armed with my implements of defense, waiting on the city wall of Sung for the invaders from Chu. Though I be murdered, you cannot exterminate them." To which the King exclaimed: "Very well! Let us not attack Sung."[550]

If this story is true, it would give a good example for our present world in settling disputes between two countries. A war would not need to be fought in the field. All that would be necessary would be for the scientists and engineers of the two countries to demonstrate their laboratory weapons of attacking and defense, and the war would be decided without fighting!

---

550 *Mo-tzu*.Ch. 50

Regardless of whether the story is true or not, it illustrates the nature of the Mohist organization, which is also confirmed from other sources. Thus in the Huai-nan-tzu, a work of the second century B.C., it is stated that "the disciples of Mo Tzu were one hundred and eighty in number, all of whom he could order to enter fire or tread on sword blades, and whom even death would not cause to turn on their heels."[551] And in the Motzu itself, no less than nine chapters deal with the tactics of fighting a defensive war and the techniques of building instruments for defending city walls. All of this shows that the Mohists, as originally constituted, were a group of warriors.

Mo Tzu and his followers, however, differed from the ordinary knights-errant in two respects. In the first place, the latter were men ready to engage in any fighting whatever, only provided that they were paid for their efforts or favored by the feudal lords. Mo Tzu and his followers, on the contrary, were strongly opposed to aggressive war; hence they agreed to fight only in wars that were strictly for self-defense. Secondly, the ordinary hsieh confined themselves wholly to their code of professional ethics. Mo Tzu, however, elaborated this professional ethics and gave it a rationalistic justification. Thus though Mo Tzu's background was that of a hsieh, he at the same time became the founder of a new philosophic school.

Mo Tzu's Criticism of Confucianism

According to Mo Tzu, the principles of the Confucianists ruin the whole world in four ways": (1) The Confucianists do not believe in the existence of God or of spirits, "with the result that God and the spirits are displeased." (2) The Confucianists insist on elaborate funerals and the practice of three years of mourning on the death of a parent, so that the wealth and energy of the people are thereby wasted. (3) The Confucianists lay stress on the practice of music, leading to an identical result. (4) The Confucianists believe in a predetermined fate, causing the people to be lazy and to resign themselves to this fate.[552] In another chapter entitled "Anti-Confucianism," the Mo-tzu says:

> "Even those with long life cannot exhaust the learning required for their [Confucianist] studies. Even people with the vigor of youth cannot perform all the ceremonial duties. And even those who have amassed wealth cannot afford music. They [the Confucianists] enhance the beauty of wicked arts and lead their sovereign astray. Their doctrine cannot meet the needs of the age, nor can their learning educate the people.[553]

These criticisms reveal the differing social backgrounds of the Confucianists and Mohists. Already, before Confucius, persons who were better educated and more sophisticated had been abandoning the belief in the existence of a personal God and of divine spirits. People of the lower classes, however, had, as always in such matters, lagged behind in this rise of skepticism, and Mo Tzu held the point

551 *Huai-nan-tzu*, Ch. 20.
552 Mo-tzu, Ch. 48.
553 *Id.*, Ch. 39.

of view of the lower classes. This is the significance of his first point of criticism against the Confucianists. The second and third points, too, were made from the same basis. The fourth point, however, was really irrelevant, because, though the Confucianists often spoke about Ming (fate, decreed) what they meant by it was not the predetermined fate attacked by Mo Tzu. This has been pointed out in the last chapter, where we have seen that Ming, for the Confucianists, signified something that is beyond human control. But there are other things that remain within man's power to control if he will exert himself. Only after man has done everything he can himself, therefore, should he accept with calm and resignation what comes thereafter as inevitable. Such is what the Confucianists meant when they spoke of "knowing Ming."

All-embracing Love

Mo Tzu makes no criticism of the Confucianists' central idea of *jen* (human-heartedness) and yi (righteousness) in the Mo-tzu, indeed, he speaks often of these two qualities and of the man of *jen* and man of)d. What he means by these terms, however, differs somewhat from the concept of them held by the Confucianists. For Mo Tzu, *jen* and yi signify an all-embracing love, and the man of *jen* and man of yi are persons who practice this all-embracing love. This concept is a central one in Mo Tzu's philosophy, and represents a logical extension of the professional ethics of the class of hsieh (knights-errant) from which Mo Tzu sprang. This ethic was, namely, that within their group the hsieh "enjoy equally and suffer equally." (This was a common saying of the hsieh of later times.) Taking this group concept as a basis, Mo Tzu tried to broaden it by preaching the doctrine that everyone in the world should love everyone else equally and without discrimination.

In the Mo-tzu, there are three chapters devoted to the subject of all-embracing love. In them, Mo Tzu first makes a distinction between what he calls the principles of "discrimination" and "all-embracingness." The man who holds to the principle of discrimination says: It is absurd for me to care for friends as much as I would for myself, and to look after their parents as I would my own. As a result, such a man does not do very much for his friends. But the man who holds to the principle of all-embracingness says, on the contrary: I must care for my friends as much as I do for myself, and for their parents as I would my own. As a result, he does everything he can for his friends. Having made this distinction, Mo Tzu then asks the question: Which of these two principles is the right one?

Mo Tzu thereupon uses his "tests of judgment" to determine the right and wrong of these principles. According to him, every principle must be examined by three tests, namely: "Its basis, its verifiability, and its applicability." A sound and right principle "should be based on the Will of Heaven and of the spirits and on the deeds of the ancient sage-kings." Then "it is to be verified by the senses of hearing and sight of the common people." And finally, "it is to be applied by adopting it in government and observing whether it is beneficial to the country and the people,"[554] Of these three tests, the last is the most important. "Being beneficial to the country and the people" is the standard by which Mo Tzu determines all values.

This same standard is the chief one used by Mo Tzu to prove the desirability of all-embracing love. In the third of three chapters, all of which are titled "All-embracing Love," he argues:

The task of the human-hearted man is to procure benefits for the world and to eliminate its calamities. Now among all the current calamities of the world, which are the greatest? I say that attacks on small states by large ones, disturbances of small houses by large ones, oppression of the weak by the strong, misuse of the few by the many, deception of the simple by the cunning, and disdain towards the humble by the honored these are the misfortunes of the world.... When we come to think about the causes of all these calamities, how have they arisen? Have they arisen out of love of others and benefiting others? We must reply that it is not so. Rather we should say that they have arisen out of hate of others and injuring others. If we classify those in the world who hate others and injure others, shall we call them "discriminating" or "all-embracing?" We must say that they are "discriminating." So, then, is not "mutual discrimination" the cause of the major calamities of the world? Therefore the principle of "discrimination" is wrong.

Whoever criticizes others must have something to substitute for what he criticizes. Therefore I say: "Substitute all-embracingness for discrimination." What is the reason why all-embracingness can be substituted for discrimination? The answer is that when everyone regards the states of others as he regards his own, who will attack these other states? Others will be regarded like the self. When everyone regards the cities of others as he regards his own, who will seize these other cities? Others will be regarded like the self. When everyone regards the houses of others as he regards his own, who will disturb these other houses? Others will be regarded like the self.

Now, when states and cities do not attack and seize one another, and when clans and individuals do not disturb and harm one another, is this a calamity or a benefit to the world? We must say it is a benefit. When we come to consider the origin of the various benefits, how have they arisen? Have they arisen out of hate of others and injuring others? We must say not so. We should say that they have arisen out of love of others and benefiting others. If we classify those in the world who love others and benefit others, shall we call them "discriminating" or "all-embracing"? We must say that they are "all-embracing." Then is it not the case that "mutual all embracingness" is the cause of the major benefit of the world? Therefore I say that the principle of "all-embracingness" is right.[555]

Thus, using a utilitarianistic argument, Mo Tzu proves the principle, of all-embracing love to be absolutely right. The human-hearted man whose task it is to procure benefits for the world and eliminate its calamities, must establish

554 *Id*, Ch. 35.
555 *Id*, Ch. 16.

all-embracing love as the standard of action both for himself and for all others in the world. When everyone in the world acts according to this standard, "then attentive ears and keen eyes will respond to serve one another, limbs will be strengthened to work for one another, and those who know the proper principle will untiringly instruct others. Thus the aged and widowers will have support and nourishment with which to round out their old age, and the young and weak and orphans will have a place of support in which to grow up. When all-embracing love is adopted as the standard, such are the consequent benefits."[556] This, then, is Mo Tzu's ideal world, which can be created only through the practice of all-embracing love.

The Will of God and Existence of Spirits

There remains, however, a basic question: How to persuade people thus to love one another. One may tell them, as was said above, that the practice of all-embracing love is the only way to benefit the world and that every human-hearted man is one who practices all-embracing love. Yet people may still ask: Why should I personally act to benefit the world and why should I be a human-hearted man? One may then argue further that if the world as a whole is benefited, this means benefit for every individual in the world as well. Or, as Mo Tzu says:

> He who loves others, must also be loved by others. He who benefits others, must also be benefited by others. He who hates others, must also be hated by others. He who injures others, must also be injured by others.[557]

Thus, then, the love of others is a sort of personal insurance or investment, which "pays," as Americans would say. Most people, however, are too shortsighted to see the value of a long-term investment of this sort, and there are a few instances in which such an investment does, indeed, fail to pay.

In order, therefore, to induce people to practice the principle of all-embracing love, Mo Tzu, in addition to foregoing arguments, introduces a number of religious and political sanctions. Thus in the *Mo-tzu* there are chapters on "The Will of Heaven," and also ones titled "Proof of the Existence of Spirits." In these we read that God exists; that He loves mankind; and that His Will is that all men should love one another. He constantly supervises the activities of men, especially those of the rulers of men. He punishes with calamities persons who disobey His Will, and rewards with good fortune those who obey. Besides God, there are also numerous lesser spirits who likewise reward men who practice all-embracing love, and punish those who practice "discrimination."

In this connection there is an interesting story about Mo Tzu:

> When Mo Tzu was once ill, Tieh Pi came to him and inquired "Sir, you hold that the spirits are intelligent and control calamities and blessings. They reward the good and punish the evil. Now you are a sage. How then can you be ill? Is it that your teaching is not entirely correct or that the

556 *Ibid.*
557 *Id.*, Ch. 17.

spirits are after all not intelligent?" Mo Tzu replied: "Though I am ill, why should the spirits be unintelligent? There are many ways by which a man can contract diseases. Some are contracted from cold or heat, some from fatigue. If there are a hundred doors and only one be closed, will there not be ways by which robbers can enter?"[558]

In modern logical terminology, Mo Tzu would say that punishment by the spirits is a sufficient cause for the disease of a man, but not its necessary cause.

A Seeming Inconsistency

Here it is timely to point out that both the Mohists and the Confucianists seem to be inconsistent in their attitude towards the existence of spirits and the performance of rituals connected with the spirits. Certainly it seems inconsistent for the Mohists to have believed in the existence of the spirits, yet at the same time to have opposed the elaborate rituals that were conducted on the occasion of funerals and of the making of sacrifices to the ancestors.

Likewise, it seems inconsistent that the Confucianists stressed those funeral and sacrificial rituals, yet did not believe in the existence of the spirits. The Mohists, for their part, were quite ready to point out this seeming inconsistency as regards the Confucianists. Thus we read in the Mo-tzu:

> Kungmeng Tau [a Confucianist] said "There are no spirits." Again he said "The superior man should learn the rituals of sacrifice." Mo Tzu said: "To hold that there are no spirits, and yet to learn sacrificial ceremonies, is like learning the ceremonies of hospitality when there are no guests, or throwing fish nets when there are no fish."[559]

Yet the seeming inconsistencies of the Confucianists and Mohists are both unreal. According to the former, the reason for performing the sacrificial rituals is no longer a belief that the spirits actually exist, though no doubt this was the original reason. Rather, the performance springs from the sentiment of respect towards his departed forebears held by the man who offers the sacrifice. Hence the meaning of the ceremonies is poetic, not religious. This theory was later developed by Hsun Tzu and his school of Confucianism in detail, as we shall see in Chapter XIII of this book. Hence there is no real inconsistency at all.

Likewise there is no actual inconsistency in the Mohist point of view, for Mo Tzu's proof of the existence of spirits is done primarily in order that he may introduce a religious sanction for his doctrine of all-embracing love, rather than because of any real interest in supernatural matters. Thus in his chapter on "Proof of the Existence of Spirits," he attributes the existing confusion of the world to "a doubt (among men) as to the existence of spirits and a failure to understand that they can reward the good and punish the bad." He then asks: "If now all the people of the world could be made to believe that the spirits can reward the good and punish the bad, would the world then be in chaos?"[560] Thus his doctrine of

558 *Id.*, Ch. 48.
559 *Id.*, Ch. 48
560 *Id.*, Ch. 31.

the Will of God and the existence of spirits is only to induce people to believe that they will be rewarded if they practice all-embracing love, and punished if they do not. Such a belief among the people was something useful; hence Mo Tzu wanted it. "Economy of expenditure" in the funeral and sacrificial services was also useful; hence Mo Tzu wanted it too. From his ultra-utilitarian point of view, there was no inconsistency in wanting both things, since both were useful.

Origin of the State

Besides religious sanctions, political ones are also needed if people are to practice all-embracing love. In the Mo-tzu, there are three chapters titled "Agreement with the Superior," in which Mo Tzu expounds his theory of the origin of the state. According to this theory, the authority of the ruler of a state comes from two sources: the will of the people and the Will of God. Furthermore, the main task of the ruler is to supervise the activities of the people, rewarding those who practice all-embracing love and punishing those who do not. In order to do this effectively, his authority must be absolute. At this point we may ask: Why should people voluntarily choose to have such an absolute authority over them?

The answer, for Mo Tzu, is that the people accept such an authority, not because they prefer it, but because they have no alternative. According to him, before the creation of an organized state, people lived in what Thomas Hobbes has called "the state of nature." At this early time,

> Everyone had his own standard of right and wrong. When there was one man, there was one standard. When there were two men, there were two standards. When there were ten men, there were ten standards. The more people there were, the more were there standards. Everyman considered himself as right and others as wrong.
>
> The world was in great disorder and men were like birds and beasts. They understood that all the disorders of the world were due to the fact that there was no political ruler. Therefore, they selected the most virtuous and most able man of the world, and established him as the Son of Heaven.[561]

Thus the ruler of the state was first established by the will of the people, in order to save themselves from anarchy.

In another chapter bearing the same title, Mo Tzu says:

> Of old when God and the spirits established the state and cities and installed rulers, it was not to make their rank high or their emolument substantial.... It was to procure benefits for the people and eliminate their adversities; to enrich the poor and increase the few; and to bring safety out of danger and order out of confusion.[562]

According to this statement, therefore, the state and its ruler were established through the Will of God.

No matter what was the way in which the ruler gained his power, once he was

561 *Id.*, Ch. 11.
562 *Id.*, Ch. 12.

established, he, according to Mo Tzu, issued a mandate to the people of the world, saying "Upon hearing good or evil, one shall report it to one's superior. What the superior thinks to be right, all shall think to be right. What the superior thinks to be wrong, all shall think to be wrong."[563] This leads Mo Tzu to the following dictum "Always agree with the superior; never follow the inferior."[564]

Thus, Mo Tzu argues, the state must be totalitarian and the authority of its ruler absolute. This is an inevitable conclusion to his theory of the origin of the state. For the state was created precisely in order to end the disorder which had existed owing to the confused standards of right and wrong. The state's primary function, therefore, is, quoting Mo Tzu, "to unify the standards."

Within the state only one standard can exist, and it must be one which is fixed by the state itself. No other standards can be tolerated, because if there were such, people would speedily return to "the state of nature" in which there could be nothing but disorder and chaos. In this political theory we may see Mo Tzu's development of the professional ethics of the hsieh, with its emphasis upon group obedience and discipline. No doubt it also reflects the troubled political conditions of Mo Tzu's day, which caused many people to look with favor on a centralized authority, even if it were to be an autocratic one.

So, then, there can be only one standard of right and wrong.

Right, for Mo Tzu, is the practice of "mutual all-embracingness," and wrong is the practice of "mutual discrimination." Through appeal to this political sanction, together with his religious one, Mo Tzu hoped to bring all people of the world to practice his principle of all-embracing love.

Such was Mo Tzu's teaching, and it is the unanimous report of all sources of his time that in his own activities he was a true example of it.

---

563 *Id.*, Ch. 11.

564 *Ibid.*

VI THE FIRST PHASE OF TAOISM: YANG CHU

In the *Analects of Confucius,* we are told that Confucius, while traveling from state to state, met many men whom he called *yin che,* "those who obscure themselves," and described as persons who had "escaped from the world."[565] These recluses ridiculed Confucius for what they regarded as his vain efforts to save the world. By one of them he was described as "the one who knows he cannot succeed, yet keeps on trying to do so."[566] To these attacks, Tzu Lu, a disciple of Confucius, once replied:

> It is unrighteous to refuse to serve in office. If the regulations between old and young in family life are not to be set aside, how is it then that you set aside the duty that exists between sovereign and subject? In your desire to maintain your personal purity, you subvert the great relationship of society [the relationship between sovereign and subject].[567]

The Early Taoists and the Recluses

The recluses were thus individualists who "desired to maintain their personal purity." They were also, in a sense, defeatists who thought that the world was so bad that nothing could be done for it. One of them is reported in the Analects to have said: "The world is a swelling torrent, and is there anyone to change it?"[568] It was from men of this sort, most of them living far away from other men in the world of nature, that the Taoists were probably originally drawn.

The Taoists, however, were not ordinary recluses who "escaped the world," desiring to "maintain their personal purity," and who, once in retirement, made no attempt ideologically to justify their conduct. On the contrary, they were men who, having gone into seclusion, attempted to work out a system of thought that would give meaning to their action. Among them, Yang Chu seems to have been the earliest prominent exponent.

Yang Chu's dates are not clear, but he must have lived between the time of Mo Tzu (c. 479-c. 381 B.C.) and Mencius (c. 371-c. 289B.C.). This is indicated by the fact that though unmentioned by Mo Tzu, he, by the time of Mencius, had become as influential as were the Mohists. To quote Mencius himself "The words of Yang Chu and Mo Ti fill the world."[569] In the Taoist work known as the Lieh-tzu, there is one chapter entitled "Yang Chu," which, according to the traditional view, represents Yang Chu's philosophy.[570] But the authenticity of the Lieh-tzu has been much questioned by modern scholarship, and the view expressed in most of the "Yang Chu" chapter is not consistent with Yang Chu's ideas as reported in other

565 *Analeas of Confucius*, XIV, 39.

566 *Id.*, XIV, 41.

567 *Id.*, XVIII, 7.

568 *Id.*, XVIII, 6.

569 *Menus*, IDb, 9.

570 See Anton Forke, *Yang Chu's Garden of Pleasure*, and James Legge, *The Chinese Classics*, Vol II, Prolegomena, pp. 92-9.

early reliable sources. Its tenets are those of extreme hedonism (hence Forke's title, Yang Chu's Garden of Pleasure), whereas in no other early writings do we find Yang Chu being accused as a hedonist. Yang Chu's actual ideas, unfortunately, are nowhere described very consecutively, but must be deduced from scattered references in a number of works by other writers.

Yang Chu's Fundamental Ideas

The Mencius says: "The principle of Yang Chu is: 'Each one for himself.' Though he might have profited the whole world by plucking out a single hair, he would not have done it."[571] The Lu-shih Chun-chiu (third century B.C.) says: "Yang Sheng valued self."[572] The Han fei-tzu (also third century B.C.) says:

> There is a man whose policy it is not to enter a city which is in danger, nor to remain in the army. Even for the great profit of the whole world, he would not exchange one hair of his shank.... He is one who despises things and values life.[573]

And the *Huai-nan-tzu* (second century B.C.) says: "Preserving life and maintaining what is genuine in it, not allowing things to entangle one's person: this is what Yang Chu established."[574]

In the above quotations, the *Yang* Sheng of the Lu-shih Chun-chin has been proved by recent scholars to be Yang Chu, while the man who "for the great profit of the whole world, would not exchange one hair of his shank" must also be Yang Chu or one of his followers, because no other man of that time is known to have held such a principle. Putting these sources together, we can deduce that Yang Chu's two fundamental ideas were "Each one for himself," and "the despising of things and valuing of life." Such ideas are precisely the opposite of those of Mo Tzu, who held the principle of an all-embracing love.

The statement of Han Fei Tzu that Yang Chu would not give up a hair from his shank even to gain the entire world, differs somewhat from what Mencius says, which is that Yang Chu would not sacrifice a single hair even in order to profit the whole world. Both statements, however, are consistent with Yang Chu's fundamental ideas. The latter harmonizes with his doctrine of "each one for himself"; the former with that of "despising things and valuing life." Both may be said to be but two aspects of a single theory.

Illustrations of Yang Chu's Ideas

In *Tao*ist literature, illustrations may be found for both the above-mentioned aspects of Yan Chu's ideology. In the first chapter of the Chuang-tzu, there is a story about a meeting between the legendary sage-ruler Yao and a hermit named Hsu Yu. Yao was anxious to hand over his rule of the world to Hsu Yu, but the latter rejected it, saying: "You govern the world and it is already at peace. Suppose I were to take your place, would I do it for the name?

571 *Menus*, Vila, 26.

572 *Lu-shih Chun- chiu*. XVII. 7.

573 *Han-fei-tzu*, Ch. 50

574 *Huai-nan-tzu*, Ch. 13

Name is but the shadow of real gain. Would I do it for real gain; the tit, building its nest in the mighty forest, occupies but a single twig. The tapir, slaking its thirst from the river, drinks only enough to fill its belly. You return and be quiet. I have no need of the world." Here was a hermit who would not take the world, even were it given to him for nothing. Certainly, then, he would not exchange it for even a single hair from his shank. This illustrates Han Fei Tzu's account of Yang Chu.

In the above-mentioned chapter titled "Yang Chu" in the Lieh-tzu, there is another story which reads: "Chin Tzu asked Yang Chu. 'If by plucking out a single hair of your body you could save the whole world, would you do it?' Yang Chu answered `The whole world is surely not to be saved by a single hair.' Chin Tzu said: 'But supposing it possible, would you do it?' Yang Chu made no answer. Chin Tzu then went out and told Meng sun Yang. The latter replied 'You do not understand the mind of the Master. I will explain it for you. Supposing by tearing off a piece of your skin, you were to get ten thousand pieces of gold, would you do it?' Chin Tzu said: 'I would.' Mengsun *Yang* continued: "Supposing by cutting off one of your limbs, you were to get a whole kingdom, would you do it?' For a while Chin Tzu was silent. Then Mengsun *Yang* said 'A hair is unimportant compared with the skin. A piece of skin is unimportant compared with a limb. But many hairs put together are as important as a piece of skin. Many pieces of skin put together are as important as a limb. A single hair is one of the ten thousand parts of the body. How can you disregard it?'" This is an illustration of the other aspect of Yang Chu's theory.

In the same chapter of the Lieh-tzu, Yang Chu is reported to have said "The men of antiquity, if by injuring a single hair they could have profited the world, would not have done it. Had the world been offered to them as their exclusive possession, they would not have taken it. If everybody would refuse to pluck out even a single hair, and everybody would refuse to take the world as a gain, then the world would be in perfect order." We cannot be sure that this is really a saying of Yang Chu, but it sums up very well the two aspects of his theory, and the political philosophy of the early *Tao*ists.

Yang Chu's Ideas as Expressed in the Lao-tzu and Chuang-tzu

Reflections of Yang Chu's main ideas can be found in portions of the Lao-tzu and some chapters of the Chuang-tzu and the Lu-shih Chun-chiu. In the latter work there is a chapter titled "The Importance of Self," in which it is said:

> Out life is our own possession, and its benefit to us is very great. Regarding its dignity, even the honor of being Emperor could not compare with it. Regarding its importance, even the wealth of possessing the world would not be exchanged for it. Regarding its safety, were we to lose it for one morning, we could never again bring it back. These three are points on which those who have understanding are careful.[575]

This passage explains why one should despise things and value life. Even an empire, once lost, may someday be regained, but once dead, one can never live again.

575 *Lu-shih Chun-chiu*, 1, 3.

The *Lao-tzu* contains passages expressing the same idea. For example: "He who in his conduct values his body more than he does the world, may be given the world. He who in his conduct loves himself more than he does the world, may be entrusted with the world."[576] Or. "Name or person, which is dearer? Person or fortune, which is more important?"[577] Here again appears the idea of despising things and valuing life.

In the third chapter of the Chuang-tzu, titled "Fundamentals for the Cultivation of Life," we read:

> When you do something good, beware of reputation; when you do something evil, beware of punishment. Follow the middle way and take this to be your constant principle. Then you can guard your person, nourish your parents, and complete your natural term of years.

This again follows Yang Chu's line of thought, and, according to the earlier *Tao*ists, is the best way to preserve one's life against the harms that come from the human world. If a man's conduct is so bad that society punishes him, this is obviously not the way to preserve his life. But if a man is so good in his conduct that he obtains a fine reputation, this too is not the way to preserve his life. Another chapter of the Chuang-tzu tells us:

> Mountain trees are their own enemies, and the leaping fire is the cause of its own quenching. Cinnamon is edible; therefore the cinnamon tree is cut down. *Chi* oil is useful; therefore the chi tree is gashed.[578] A man having a reputation of ability and usefulness will suffer a fate just like that of the cinnamon and chi trees.

Thus in the Chuang-tzu we find passages that admire the usefulness of the useless. In the chapter just quoted, there is the description of a sacred oak, which, because its wood was good for nothing, had been spared the ax, and which said to someone in a dream:

> "For a long time I have been learning to be useless. There were several occasions on which I was nearly destroyed, but now I have succeeded in being useless, which is of the greatest use to me. If I were useful, could I have become so great?" Again it is said that "the world knows only the usefulness of the useful, but does not know the usefulness of the useless."[579]

To be useless is the way to preserve one's life. The man who is skillful in preserving life must not do much evil, but neither must he do much good. He must live midway between good and evil. He tries to be useless, which in the end proves of greatest usefulness to him.

Development of Taoism

In this chapter we have been seeing the first phase in the development of early *Tao*ist philosophy. Altogether there have been three main phases. The ideas attributed to Yang Chu represent the first. Those expressed in the greater part

576 *Lao-tzu*, Ch. 13.

577 *Id*, Ch. 44.

578 *Chuang-tzu*, Ch. 4

579 *Ibid*.

of the Lao-tzu represent the second. And those expressed in the greater part of the Chuang-tzu represent the third and last phase. I say the greater part of the Lao-tzu and Chuang-tzu, because in the Lao-tzu there are also to be found ideas representing the first and third phases and in the Chuang-tzu ideas of the first and second phases. These two books, like many others of ancient China, are really collections of *Tao*ist writings and sayings, made by differing persons in different times, rather than the single work of any one person.

The starting point of *Tao*ist philosophy is the preservation of life and avoiding of injury. Yang Chu's method for so doing is "to escape." This is the method of the ordinary recluse who flees from society and hides himself in the mountains and forests. By doing this he thinks he can avoid the evils of the human world. Things in the human world, however, are so complicated that no matter how well one hides oneself, there are always evils that cannot be avoided. There are times, therefore, when the method of "escaping" does not work.

The ideas expressed in the greater part of the Lao-tzu represent an attempt to reveal the laws underlying the changes of things in the universe. Things change, but the laws underlying the changes remain unchanging. If one understands these laws and regulates one's actions in conformity with them, one can then turn everything to one's advantage. This is the second phase in the development of Taoism.

Even so, however, there is no absolute guarantee. In the changes of things, both in the world of nature and of man, there are always unseen elements. So despite every care, the possibility remains that one will suffer injury. This is why the Lao-tzu says with still deeper insight "The reason that I have great disaster is that I have a body. If there were no body, what disaster could there be?"[580] These words of greater understanding are developed in much of the Chuang-tzu, in which occur the concepts of the equalization of life with death, and the identity of self with others. This means to see life and death, self and others, from a higher point of view. By seeing things from this higher point of view, one can transcend the existing world. This is also a form of "escape"; not one, however, from society to mountains and forests, but rather from this world to another world. Here is the third and last phase of development in the Taoism of ancient times.

All these developments are illustrated by a story which we find in the twentieth chapter of the Chuang-tzu, titled "The Mountain Tree." The story runs:

> Chuang Tzu was traveling through the mountains, when he saw a great tree well-covered with foliage. A tree-cutter was standing beside it, but he did not cut it down. Chuang Tzu asked him the reason and he replied: "It is of no use." Chuang Tzu then said "By virtue of having no exceptional qualities, this tree succeeds in completing its natural span."
>
> When the Master (Chuang Tzu) left the mountains, he stopped at the home of a friend. The friend was glad and ordered the servant to kill a goose and cook it. The servant asked "One of the geese can cackle. The other cannot. Which shall I kill?" The Master said: "Kill the one that cannot

580 *Lao-tzu*, Ch. 13.

cackle." Next day, a disciple asked Chuang Tzu the question "Yesterday the tree in the mountains, because it had no exceptional quality, succeeded in completing its natural span. But now the goose of our host, because it had no exceptional quality, had to die. What will be your position?"

Chuang Tzu laughed and said: "My position will lie between having exceptional qualities and not having them. Yet this position only seems to be right, but really is not so. Therefore those who practice this method are not able to be completely free from troubles. If one wanders about with *Tao* and Te (the Way and its spiritual power), it will be otherwise."

Then Chuang Tzu went on to say that he who links himself with Tao and Te is with the "ancestor of things, using things as things, but not being used by things as things. When that is so, what is there that can trouble him?"

In this story, the first part illustrates the theory of preserving life as practiced by Yang Chu, while the second part gives that of Chuang Tzu. "Having exceptional quality" corresponds to the doing of good things, mentioned in the earlier quotation from the third chapter of the Chuangtzu. "Having no exceptional quality" corresponds to the doing of bad things in that same quotation. And a position between these two extremes corresponds to the middle way indicated in that quotation. Yet if a man cannot see things from a higher point of view, none of these methods can absolutely guarantee him from danger and harm. To see things from a higher point of view, however, means to abolish the self. We may say that the early *Tao*ists were selfish. Yet in their later development this selfishness became reversed and destroyed itself.

VII THE IDEALISTIC WING OF CONFUCIANISM: MENCIUS

According to the Historical Records (Ch. 74), Mencius (371?-289? B.C.) was a native of the state of Tsou, in the present southern part of Shandong Province in East China. He was linked with Confucius through his study under a disciple of Tzu-ssu, who in turn was Confucius' grandson. At that time, the Kings of Chi, a larger state also in present Shandong, were great admirers of learning. Near the west gate of their capital, a gate known as Chi, they had established a center of learning which they called Chi-hsia, that is, "below Chi." All the scholars living there "were ranked as great officers and were honored and courted by having large houses built for them on the main road. This was to show to all the pensioned guests of the feudal lords that it was the state of *Chi* that could attract the most eminent scholars in the world."

Mencius for a while was one of these eminent scholars, but he also traveled to other states, vainly trying to get a hearing for his ideas among their rulers. Finally, so the Historical Records tell us, here tired and with his disciples composed the Mencius in seven books. This work records the conversations between Mencius and the feudal lords of his time, and between him and his disciples, and in later times it was honored by being made one of the famous "Four Books," which for the past one thousand years have formed the basis of Confucian education.

Mencius represents the idealistic wing of Confucianism, and the somewhat later Hsun Tzu the realistic wing. The meaning of this will become clear as we go on.

The Goodness of Human Nature

We have seen that Confucius spoke very much about *jen* (human-heartedness), and made a sharp distinction between yi (righteousness) and li (profit) every man should, without thought of personal advantage, unconditionally do what he ought to do, and be what he ought to be. In other words, he should "extend himself so as to include others," which, in essence, is the practice of *jen*. But though Confucius held these doctrines, he failed to explain why it is that a man should act this way. Mencius, however, attempted to give an answer to this question, and in so doing developed the theory for which he is most famed that of the original goodness of human nature.

Whether human nature is good or bad — that is, what, precisely, is the nature of human nature — has been one of the most controversial problems in Chinese philosophy. According to Mencius, there were, in his time, three other theories besides his own on this subject. The first was that human nature is neither good nor bad. The second was that human nature can be either good or bad (which seems to mean that in the nature of man there are both good and bad elements and the third was that the nature of some men is good, and that of others is bad.[581] The first of these theories was held by Kao Tzu, a philosopher who was contemporary with Mencius. We know more about it than the other theories through the long discussions between him and Mencius which are preserved for us in the Mencius.

When Mencius holds that human nature is good, he does not mean that every man is born a Confucius, that is, a sage. His theory has some similarity with one side of the second theory mentioned above, that is, that in the nature of man there are good elements. He admits, to be sure, that there are also other elements, which are neither good nor bad in themselves, but which, if not duly controlled, can lead to evil. According to Mencius, however, these are elements which man shares in common with other living creatures. They represent the "animal" aspect of man's life, and therefore, strictly speaking, should not be considered as part of the "human" nature.

To support his theory, Mencius presents numerous arguments, among them the following:

> All men have a mind which cannot bear [to see the suffering of] others.... If now men suddenly see a child about to fall into a well, they will without exception experience a feeling of alarm and distress....From this case we may perceive that he who lacks the feeling of commiseration is not a man; that he who lacks a feeling of shame and dislike is not a man; that he who lacks a feeling of modesty and yielding is not a man; and that he who lacks a sense of right and wrong is not a man. The feeling of commiseration is the beginning of human-heartedness. The feeling of shame and dislike is the beginning of righteousness. The feeling of modesty and yielding is the beginning of propriety. The sense of right and wrong is the beginning of wisdom.
>
> Man has these four beginnings, just as he has four limbs.... Since all men have these four beginnings in themselves, let them know how to give them full development and completion. The result will be like fire that begins to burn, or a spring which has begun to find vent. Let them have their completed development, and they will suffice to protect all within the four seas. If they are denied that development, they will not suffice even to serve one's parents.[582]

All men in their original nature possess these "four beginnings," which, if fully developed, become the four "constant virtues," so greatly emphasized in Confucianism. These virtues, if not hindered by external conditions, develop naturally from within, just as a tree grows by itself from the seed, or a flower from the bud. This is the basis of Mencius' controversy with Kao Tzu, according to whom human nature is in itself neither good nor bad, and for whom morality is therefore something that is artificially added from without.

There remains another question, which is: Why should man allow free development to his "four beginnings," instead of to what we may call his lower instincts? Mencius answers that it is these four beginnings that differentiate man

581 Mendus,VIa, 3-6.

582 *Id*, II a,6

from the beasts. They should be developed, therefore, because it is only through their development that man is truly a "man." Mencius says: "That whereby man differs from birds and beasts is but slight. The mass of the people cast it away, whereas the superior man preserves it."[583] Thus he answers a question which had not occurred to Confucius.

Fundamental Difference between Confucianism and Mohism

Here we find the fundamental difference between Confucianism and Mohism. One of Mencius' self-appointed tasks was to "oppose Yang Chu and Mo Ti." He says:

> Yang's principle of "each one for himself' amounts to making one's sovereign of no account. Mo's principle of "all-embracing love" amounts to making one's father of no account. To have no father and no sovereign is to be like the birds and beasts.... These pernicious opinions mislead the people and block the way of human-heartedness and righteousness.[584]

It is very clear that Yang Chu's theory opposes human-heartedness and righteousness, since the essence of these two virtues is to benefit others, while Yang Chu's principle is to benefit oneself. But Mo Tzu's principle of all-embracing love also aimed to benefit others, and he was even more outspoken in this respect than the Confucianists. Why, then, does Mencius lump him together with Yang Chu in his criticism?

The traditional answer is that according to Mohist doctrine, love should have in it no gradations of greater or lesser love, whereas according to Confucianism, the reverse is true. In other words, the Mohists emphasized equality in loving others, while the Confucianists emphasized gradation. This difference is brought out in a passage in the Mo-tzu in which a certain Wu-ma Tzu is reported as saying to Mo Tzu:

> I cannot practice all-embracing love. I love the men of Tsou [a nearby state] better than I love those of Yueh [a distant state] I love the men of Lu [his own state] better than I love those of Tsou. I love the men of my own district better than I love those of Lu. I love the members of my own clan better than I love those of my district. I love my parent, better than I love the men of my clan. And I love myself better than I love my parents.[585]

Wu-ma Tzu was a Confucianist, and the representation of him as saying, "I love myself better than I love my parents," comes from a Mohist source and is probably an exaggeration. Certainly it is not consistent with the Confucianist emphasis on filial piety. With this exception, however, Wu-ma Tzu's statement is in general agreement with the Confucianist spirit. For according to the Confucianists, there should be degrees in love.

Speaking about these degrees, Mencius says:

> The superior man, in his relation to things, loves them but has no feeling of human-heartedness. In his relation to people, he has human-heartedness,

583 *Id*, IVb, 19.
584 *Id.*, IIIb, 9.
585 *Mo-tzu*, Ch. 46.

> but no deep feeling of family affection. One should have feelings of family affection for the members of one's family, but human-heartedness for people; human-heartedness for people, but love for things.[586]

In a discussion with a Mohist by the name of Yi Chih, Mencius asked him whether he really believed that men love their neighbors' children in the same way as they love their brothers' children; the love for a brother's child is naturally greater.[587] This, according to Mencius, is quite proper; what should be done is to extend such love until it includes the more distant members of society.

Treat the aged in your family as they should be treated, and extend this treatment to the aged of other people's families. Treat the young in your family as they should be treated, and extend this treatment to the young of other people's families.[588]

Such is what Mencius calls "extending one's scope of activity to include others."[589] It is an extension based on the principle of graded love.

To extend the love for one's family so as to include persons outside it as well, is to practice that "principle of *chung* [conscientiousness to others] and shu [altruism]" advocated by Confucius, which in turn is equivalent to the practice of human-heartedness. There is nothing forced in any of these practices, because the original natures of all men have in them a feeling of commiseration, which makes it impossible for them to bear to see the suffering of others. The development of this "beginning" of goodness causes men naturally to love others, but it is equally natural that they should love their parents to a greater degree than they love men in general.

Such is the Confucianist point of view. The Mohists, on the contrary, insist that the love for others should be on a par with the love for parents. Regardless of whether this means that one should love one's parents less, or love others more, the fact remains that the Confucianist type of graded love should be avoided at all costs. It is with this in mind that Mencius attacks the Mohist principle of all-embracing love as meaning that a man treats his father as of no account.

The above difference between the Confucianist and the Mohist theory of love has been pointed out very clearly by Mencius and by many others after him. Besides this, however, there is another difference of a more fundamental nature. This is, that the Confucianists considered human-heartedness as a quality that develops naturally from within the human nature, whereas the Mohists considered all-embracing love as something artificially added to man from without.

Mo Tzu may also be said to have answered a question that did not occur to Confucius, namely: Why should man practice human- heartedness and righteousness? His answer, however, is based on utilitarianism, and his emphasis on supernatural and political sanctions to compel and induce people to practice all-embracing love is not consistent with the Confucianist principle that virtue

586 *Mencius*, VIIa, 45.
587 *Id.*, IIIa, 5.
588 *Id*, Ia, 7.
589 *Ibid.*

should be done for its own sake. If we compare the Mo-tzu's chapter on "All-Embracing Love," as quoted above in the fifth chapter, with the quotations here from the Mencius on the four moral beginnings in man's nature, we see very clearly the fundamental difference between the two schools.

Political Philosophy

We have seen earlier that the Mohist theory of the origin of state is likewise a utilitarianistic one. Here again the Confucianist theory differs. Mencius says:

> If men have satisfied their hunger, have clothes to wear, and live at ease but lack good teaching, they are close to the birds and beasts. The sage [Shun, a legendary sage-ruler] was distressed about this and appointed Hsieh as an official instructor to teach men the basic relationships of life. Father and son should love each other. Ruler and subject should be just to each other. Husband and wife should distinguish their respective spheres. Elder and younger brothers should have a sense of mutual precedence. And between friends there should be good faith.[590]

The existence of the human relationships and the moral principles based on them is what differentiates man from birds and beasts

The state and society have their origin in the existence of these human relationships. Therefore, according to the Mohists, the state exists because it is useful. But according to the Confucianists, it exists because it ought to exist.

Men have their full realization and development only in human relationships. Like Aristotle, Mencius maintains that "man is a political animal" and can fully develop these relationships only within state and society. The state is a moral institution and the head of the state should be a moral leader. Therefore in Confucianist political philosophy only a sage can be a real king. Mencius pictures this ideal as having existed in an idealized past. According to him, there was a time when the sage Yao (supposed to have lived in the twenty-fourth century B.C.) was Emperor. When he was old, he selected a younger sage, Shun, whom he had taught how to be a ruler, so that at Yao's death, Shun became Emperor.

Similarly, when Shun was old, he again selected a younger sage, Yu, to be his successor. Thus the throne was handed from sage to sage, which, according to Mencius, is as it ought to be.

If a ruler lacks the ethical qualities that make a good leader, the people have the moral right of revolution. In that case, even the killing of the ruler is no longer a crime of regicide. This is because, according to Mencius, if a sovereign does not act as he ideally ought to do, he morally ceases to be a sovereign and, following Confucius' theory of the rectification of names, is a "mere fellow," as Mencius says.[591] Mencius also says: "The people are the most important element [in a state]; the spirits of the land and the grain are secondary; and the sovereign is the least."[592] These ideas of Mencius have exercised a tremendous influence

590 *Id.* IIIa, 4.

591 *Id., Mencius,* IIb, 8.

592 *Id.,* VIIb, 14.

in Chinese history, even as late as the Revolution of 1911, which led to the establishment of the Chinese Republic. It is true that modern democratic ideas from the West played their role too in this event, but the ancient native concept of the "right of revolution" had a greater influence on the mass of the people.

If a sage becomes king, his government is called one of kingly government. According to Mencius and later Confucianists, there are two kinds of government. One is that of the wang or (sage) king; the other is that of the pa or military lord. These are completely different in kind. The government of a sage-king is carried on through moral instruction and education; that of a military lord is conducted through force and compulsion. The power of the wang government is moral, that of the pa government, physical. Mencius says in this connection:

> He who uses force in the place of virtue is a pa. He who is virtuous and practices human-heartedness is a Wang. When one subdues men by force, they do not submit to him in their hearts but only outwardly, because they have insufficient strength to resist. But when one gains followers by virtue, they are pleased in their hearts and will submit of themselves as did the seventy disciples to Confucius.[593]

This distinction between *wang* and *pa* has always been maintained by later Chinese political philosophers. In terms of contemporary politics, we may say that a democratic government is a *wang* government, because it represents a free association of people, while a fascist government is that of a *pa*, because it reigns through terror and physical force.

The sage-king in his kingly government does all he can for the welfare and benefit of the people, which means that his state must be built on a sound economic basis. Since China has always been overwhelmingly agrarian, it is natural that, according to Mencius, the most important economic basis of kingly government lies in the equal distribution of land. His ideal land system is what has been known as the "well-field system." According to this system, each square li (about one third of a mile) of land is to be divided into nine squares, each consisting of one hundred mou (one mou = 1/6 acre) The central square is known as the "public field," which the eight surrounding squares are the private land of eight farmers with their families, each family having one square. These farmers cultivate the public field collectively and their own fields individually. The produce of the public field goes to the government, while each family keeps for itself what it raises from its own field. The arrangement of the nine squares # resembles in form the Chinese character for "well" #, which is why it is called the "well-field system."[594]

Describing this system further, Mencius states that each family should plant mulberry trees around its five-mou homestead in its own field so that its aged members may be clothed with silk. Each family should also raise fowls and pigs, so that its aged members may be nourished with meat. If this is done, everyone under the kingly government can "nourish the living and bury the dead without the least dissatisfaction, which marks the beginning of the kingly way."[595]

593 *Id.*, IIa, 3.

594 *Id.*, *Mencius*, IIa, 3

595 *Id.*, Ia, 3.

It marks, however, only the "beginning," because it is an exclusively economic basis for the higher culture of the people. Only when everyone has received some education and comes to an understanding of the human relationship, does the kingly way become complete.

The practice of this kingly way is not something alien to human nature, but is rather the direct outcome of the development by the sage-king of his own "feeling of commiseration." As Mencius says: "All men have a mind which cannot bear [to see the suffering of] others. The early kings, having this unbearing mind, thereby had likewise an unbearing government"[596] The "unbearing mind" and feeling of commiseration are one in Mencius' thought. As we have seen, the virtue of human-heartedness, according to the Confucianists, is nothing but the development of this feeling of commiseration; this feeling in its turn cannot be developed save through the practice of love; and the practice of love is nothing more than the "extension of one's scope of activity to include others," which is the way of *chung* and shu. The kingly way or kingly government is nothing but the result of the king's practice of love, and his practice of *chung* and shu.

According to Mencius, there is nothing esoteric or difficult in the kingly way. Mencius records that on one occasion, when an ox was being led to sacrifice, King Hsuan of *Chi* saw it and could not endure "its frightened appearance, as if it were an innocent person going to the place of death." He therefore ordered that it be replaced by a sheep. Mencius then told the King that this was an example of his "unbearing mind," and if he could only extend it to include human affairs, he could then govern in the kingly way. The King replied that he could not do this because he had the defect of loving wealth and feminine beauty. Whereupon Mencius told the King that these are things loved by all men. If the King, by understanding his own desires, would also come to understand the desires of all his people, and would take measures whereby the people might satisfy these desires, this would result in the kingly way and nothing else.

What Mencius told King Hsuan is nothing more than the "extension of one's own scope of activity to include others," which is precisely the practice of *chung* and shu. Here we see how Mencius developed the ideas of Confucius. In his exposition of this principle, Confucius had limited himself to its application to the self-cultivation of the individual, while by Mencius its application was extended to government and politics. For Confucius, it was a principle only for "sageliness within," but by Mencius it was expanded to become also a principle for "kingliness without."

Even in the former sense of "sageliness within," Mencius expresses his concept of this principle more clearly than did Confucius. He says: "He who has completely developed his mind, knows his nature. He who knows his nature, knows Heaven."[597] The mind here referred to is the "unbearing mind" or the "feeling of commiseration." It is the essence of our nature. Hence when we fully develop this mind, we know our nature. And according to Mencius, our nature

596 *Id.*, IIa, 6

597 *Id.*, Mencius, IIa, 1.

is "what Heaven has given to us."[598] Therefore, when we know our nature, we also know Heaven.

Mysticism

According to Mencius and his school of Confucianism, the universe is essentially a moral universe. The moral principles of man are also metaphysical principles of the universe, and the nature of man is an exemplification of these principles. It is this moral universe that Mencius and his school mean when they speak of Heaven, and an understanding of this moral universe is what Mencius calls "knowing Heaven." If a man knows Heaven, he is not only a citizen of society, but also a "citizen of Heaven," tien min, as Mencius says.[599] Mencius further makes a distinction between "human honors" and "heavenly honors." He says:

> There are heavenly honors and human honors. Human-heartedness, righteousness, loyalty, good faith, and the untiring practice of the good these are the honors of Heaven. Princes, ministers, and officials: these are the honors of man.[600]

In other words, heavenly honors are those to which a man can attain in the world of values, while human honors are purely material concepts in the human world. The citizen of Heaven, just because he is the citizen of Heaven, cares only for the honors of Heaven, but not those of man.

Mencius also remarks:

> All things are complete within us. There is no greater delight than to realize this through self-cultivation. And there is no better way to human-heartedness than the practice of the principle of shu.[601]

In other words, through the full development of his nature, a man can not only know Heaven, but can also become one with Heaven.

Also when a man fully develops his unbearing mind, he has within him the virtue of human-heartedness, and the best way to human- heartedness is the practice of *chung* and shu. Through this practice, one's egoism and selfishness are gradually reduced. And when they are reduced, one comes to feel that there is no longer a distinction between oneself and others, and so of distinction between the individual and the universe. That is to say, one becomes identified with the universe as a whole. This leads to a realization that "all things are complete within us." In this phrase we see the mystical element of Mencius' philosophy.

We will understand this mysticism better, if we turn to Mencius' discussion on what he calls the Hao Jan Chih Chi, a term which I translate as the "Great Morale." In this discussion Mencius describes the development of his own spiritual cultivation.

Mencius tells us that a disciple asked Mencius of what he was a specialist. Mencius replied: "I know the right and wrong in speech, and am proficient in

598 *Id.*, IIa, 15.
599 *Id.*, IIa, 19.
600 *Id.*, IIa, 16.
601 *Id.*, IIIa, 1.

cultivating my Han Jan Chih Chi." The questioner then asked what this was, and Mencius replied:

It is the *Chi*, supremely great, supremely strong. If it be directly cultivated without handicap, then it pervades all between Heaven and Earth. It is the *Chi* which is achieved by the combination of righteousness and *Tao* [the way, the truth], and without these it will be weakened.[602]

Hao Jan Chih Chi is a special term of Mencius. In later times, under his increasing influence, it came to be used not infrequently, but in ancient times it appears only in this one chapter. As to what it signifies, ever. Mencius admits that "it is hard to say."[603] The context of this discussion, however, includes a preliminary discussion about two warriors and their method of cultivating their valor. From this I infer that Mencius' *Chi* (a word which literally means vapor, gas, spiritual force) is the same chi as occurs in such terms as yung chi (courage, valor) and ship chi (morale of an army). That is why I translate Hao Jan Chih *Chi* as the "Great Morale." It is of the same nature as the morale of the warriors. The difference between the two, however, is that this *Chi* is further described as hao jan, which means "great to a supreme degree."

The morale which warriors cultivate is a matter concerning man and man, and so is a moral value only. But the Great Morale is a matter concerning man and the universe, and therefore is a super-moral value. It is the morale of the man who identifies himself with the universe, so that Mencius says of it that "it pervades all between Heaven and Earth."

The method of cultivating the Great Morale has two aspects. One may be called the "understanding of *Tao*"; that is, of the way or principle that leads to the elevation of the mind. The other aspect is what Mencius calls the "accumulation of righteousness"; that is, the constant doing of what one ought to do in the universe as a "citizen of the universe." The combination of these two aspects is called by Mencius "the combination of righteousness and *Tao*."

After one has reached an understanding of *Tao* and the long accumulation of righteousness, the Great Morale will appear naturally of itself. The least bit of forcing will lead to failure. As Mencius says:

> We should not be like the man of Sung. There was a man of Sung who was grieved that his grain did not grow fast enough. So he pulled it up. Then he returned to his home with great innocence, and said to his people: "I am tired today, for I have been helping the grain to grow." His son ran out to look at it, and found all the grain withered.[604]

When one grows something, one must on the one hand do something for it, but on the other never "help it to grow." The cultivation of the Great Morale is just like the growing of the grain. One must do something, which is the practice of virtue. Though Mencius here speaks of righteousness rather than human-heartedness, there is no practical difference, since human-heartedness is the inner content, of which righteousness is the outer expression. If one constantly

602 *Id.*, IIa, 2.
603 *Ibid.*
604 *Id.*, IIa, 2

practices righteousness, the Great Morale will naturally emerge from the very center of one's being.

Although this *Hao Jan Chih Chi* sounds rather mysterious, it can nevertheless, according to Mencius, be achieved by every man. This is because it is nothing more than the fullest development of the nature of man, and every man has fundamentally the same nature. His nature is the same, just as every man's bodily form is the same. As an example, Mencius remarks that when a shoemaker makes shoes, even though he does not know the exact length of the feet of his customers, he always makes shoes, but not baskets.[605] This is so because the similarity between the feet of all men is much greater than their difference. And likewise the sage, in his original nature, is similar to everyone else. Hence every man can become a sage, if only he gives full development to his original nature. As Mencius affirms: "All men can become Yao or Shun [the two legendary sage-rulers previously mentioned]."[606] Here is Mencius' theory of education, which has been held by all Confucianists.

605 *Id.*, IIa, 7.
606 *Id.*, IIb, 2.

VIII THE SCHOOL OF NAMES

The term *Ming Chia* has sometimes been translated as "sophists," and sometimes as "logicians" or "dialecticians." It is true that there is some similarity between the Ming chia and the sophists, logicians, and dialecticians, but it is also true that they are not quite the same. To avoid confusion, it is better to translate Ming chic literally as the School of Names. This translation also helps to bring to the attention of Westerners one of the important problems discussed by Chinese philosophy, namely that of the relation between *ming* (the name) and *shih* (the actuality).

The School of Names and the "Debaters'

Logically speaking, the contrast between ming and shih in ancient Chinese philosophy is something like that between subject and predicate in the West. For instance, when we say: "This is a table," or "Socrates is a man," "this" and "Socrates" are shih or actualities, while "table" and "man" are ming or names. This is obvious enough. Let us, however, try to analyze more exactly just what the shih or ming are, and what their relationship is. We are then apt to be led into some rather paradoxical problems, the solution of which brings us to the very heart of philosophy.

The members of the School of Names were known in ancient times as pien the (debaters, disputers, arguers). In the chapter of the Chuang-tzu titled "The Autumn Flood," Kungsun Lung, one of the leaders of the School of Names, is represented as saying:

> I have unified similarity and difference, and separated hardness and whiteness. I have proved the impossible as possible and affirmed what others deny. I have controverted the knowledge of all the philosophers, and refuted all the arguments brought against me.[607]

These words are really applicable to the School of Names as a whole. Its members were known as persons who made paradoxical statements, who were ready to dispute with others, and who purposely affirmed what others denied and denied what others affirmed. Ssuma Tan (died 110 B.C.) for example, in his essay, "On the Essential Ideas of the Six Schools," wrote: "The School of Names conducted minute examinations of trifling points in complicated and elaborate statements, which made it impossible for others to refute their ideas."[608]

Hsun Tzu, a Confucianist of the third century B.C., describes Teng Hsi (died 501 B.C.) and Hui Shih as philosophers who "liked to deal with strange theories and indulge in curious propositions."[609] Likewise, the Lu-shih Chun-chiu mentions Teng Hsi and Kungsun Lung as among those known for their paradoxical arguments.[610] And the chapter titled The World" in the Chuang-

607 *Chuang-tzu*, Ch. 17.

608 *Historical Records*, Ch. 120.

609 *Hsun-tzu*, Ch. 6.

610 *Lu-shih Chun chiu*, XVIII, 4 and 5.

tzu, after listing the paradoxical arguments famous at that time, mentions the names of Hui Shih, Huan Tuan, and Kungsun Lung. These men, therefore, would seem to have been the most important leaders of this school About Huan Tuan we know nothing further, but about Teng Hsi, we know that he was a famous lawyer of his time; his writings, however, no longer are preserved, and the book today bearing the title of Teng-hsi-tzu is not genuine. The Lu-shih Chun-chin says that when Tzu-chan, a famous statesman, was minister of the state of Cheng, Teng Hsi, who was a native of that state, was his major opponent. He used to help the people in their lawsuits, for which services he would demand a coat as a fee for a major case, and a pair of trousers for a minor one. So skilful was he that he was patronized by numerous people; as their lawyer, he succeeded in changing right into wrong and wrong into right, until no standards of right and wrong remained, so that what was regarded as possible and impossible fluctuated from day to day.[611]

Another story in the same work describes how, during a flood of the Wei River, a certain rich man of the state of Cheng was drowned. His body was picked up by a boatman, but when the family of the rich man went to ask for the body, the man who had found it demanded a huge reward. Thereupon the members of the family went to Teng Hsi for advice. He told them: "Merely wait.

There is nobody else besides yourselves who wants the body." The family took his advice and waited, until the man who had found the body became much troubled and also went to Teng Hsi. To him Teng Hsi said: "Merely wait. There is nobody else but you from whom they can get the body."[612] We are not told what was the final outcome of this episode!

It would thus seem that Teng Hsi's trick was to interpret the formal letter of the law in such a way as to give varying interpretations in different cases at will. This was how he was able to "conduct minute examinations of trifling points in complicated and elaborate statements, which made it impossible for others to refute his ideas." He thus devoted himself to interpreting and analyzing the letter of the law, while disregarding its spirit and its connection with actuality. In other words, his attention was directed to "names," instead of to "actualities." Such was the spirit of the School of Names.

From this we may see that the pien (they were originally lawyers), among whom Teng Hsi was evidently one of the first. He was, however, only a beginner in the analysis of names, and made no real contribution to philosophy as such. Hence the real founders of the School of Names were the later Hui Shih and Kungsun Lung.

Concerning these two men the Lu-shih Chun-chiu tells us: "Hui Tzu [Hui Shih] prepared the law for King Hui of Wei (370-319 B.C.).When it was completed and was made known to the people, the people considered it to be good."[613] And again:

> The states of Chao and Chin entered into an agreement which said: "From this time onward, in whatever Chin desires to do, she is to be assisted by

611 *Id.*, XII I, 4.

612 *Ibid.*

613 *Id*,VIII, 5.

Chao, and in whatever Chao desires to do, she is to be assisted by Chin." But soon afterwards Chin attacked the state of Wei, and Chao made ready to go to Wei's assistance. The King of Chin protested to Chao that this was an infringement of the pact, and the King of Chao reported this to the Lord of Ping-yuan, who again told it to Kungsun Lung. Kungsun Lung said: "We too can send an envoy to protest to the King of Chin, saying: "According to the pact, each side guarantees to help the other in whatever either desires to do. Now it is our desire to save Wei, and if you do not help us to do so, we shall charge you with infringement of the pact.[614]

Again we are told in the Han Fei Tzu: "When discussions on 'hardness and whiteness' and 'having no thickness' appear, the governmental laws lose their effect."[615] We shall see below that the doctrine of "hardness and whiteness" is one of Kungsun Lung, while that of "having no thickness" is one of Hui Shih.

From these stories we may see that Hui Shih and Kungsun Lung were, to some extent, connected with the legal activities of their time. Indeed, Kungsun Lung's interpretation of the pact between Chao and Chin are truly in the spirit of Teng Hsi. Han Fei Tzu considered the effect of the "speeches" of these two gentlemen of law to be as had as that of the practice of Teng Hsi. It may seem strange that Han Fei Tzu, himself a Legalist, should oppose, as destructive to law, the "discussions" of a school which had originated with lawyers. But, as we shall see in Chapter XIV, Han Fei Tzu and the other Legalists were really politicians, not jurists.

Hui Shih and Kungsun Lung represented two tendencies in the School of Names, the one emphasizing the relativity of actual things, and the other the absoluteness of names. This distinction becomes evident when one comes to analyze names in their relationship to actualities. Let us take the simple statement, "This is a table." Here the word "this" refers to the concrete actuality, which is impermanent and may come and go. The word "table," however, refers to an abstract category or name which is unchanging and always remains as it is. The "name" is absolute, but the "actuality" is relative. Thus "beauty" is the name of what is absolutely beautiful, but "a beautiful thing" can only be relatively so. Hui Shih emphasized the fact that actual things are changeable and relative, while Kungsun Lung emphasized the fact that names are permanent and absolute.

Hui Shih's Theory of Relativity

Hui Shih (fl. 350-260 B.C.) was a native of the state of Sung, in the present province of Henan. We know that he once became premier of King Hui of Wei, and that he was known for his great learning. His writings, unfortunately, are lost, and what we know of his ideas may be deduced only from a series of "ten points" preserved in the chapter titled "The World" in the Chuang-tzu.

The first of these points is: "The greatest has nothing beyond itself, and is called the Great One. The smallest has nothing within itself, and is called the Small

614 *Ibid.*

615 *Han-fei-tzu*, Ch. 41

One." These two statements constitute what are called analytical propositions. They make no assertions in regard to the actual; for they say nothing about what, in the actual world, is the greatest thing and the smallest thing. They only touch upon the abstract concepts or names: "greatest" and "smallest." In order to understand these two propositions fully, we should compare them with a story in the chapter titled "The Autumn Flood" in the Chuang-tzu. From this it will become apparent that in one respect Hui Shih and Chuang Tzu had very much in common.

This story describes how in autumn, when the Yellow River was in flood, the Spirit of the River, who was very proud of his greatness, moved down the river to the sea. There he met the Spirit of the Sea, and realized for the first time that his river, great as it was, was small indeed in comparison with the sea. Yet when, full of admiration, he talked with the Spirit of the Sea, the latter replied that he himself, in his relationship to Heaven and Earth, was nothing more than a single grain lying within a great warehouse.

Hence he could only be said to be "small," but not to be "great."

At this the River Spirit asked the Sea Spirit: "Are we right then in saying that Heaven and Earth are supremely great and the tip of a hair is supremely small?" The Sea Spirit answered: "What men know is less than what they do not know. The time when they are alive is less than the time when they are not alive.... How can we know that the tip of a hair is the extreme of smallness, and Heaven and Earth are the extreme of greatness?" And he then went on to define the smallest as that which has no form, and the greatest as that which cannot be enclosed (by anything else). This definition of the supremely great and supremely small is similar to that given by Hui Shih.[616]

To say that Heaven and Earth are the greatest of things and that the tip of a hair is the smallest is to make assertions about the actual, the shih. It makes no analysis of the names of the actualities, the ming. These two propositions are what are called synthetic propositions and both may be false. They have their basis in experience; therefore their truth is only contingent, but not necessary. In experience, things that are great and things that are small are all relatively so. To quote the *Chuang-tzu* again:

If we call a thing great, because it is greater than something else, then there is nothing in the world that is not great. If we call a thing small because it is smaller than something else, then there is nothing in the world that is not small.

We cannot through actual experience decide what is the greatest and what is the smallest of actual things. But we can say independently of experience that that which has nothing beyond itself is the greatest, and that which has nothing within itself is the smallest. "Greatest" and "smallest," defined in this way, are absolute and unchanging concepts. Thus by analyzing the names, "Great One" and "Small One," Hui Shih reached the concept of what is absolute and unchanging. From the point of view of this concept, he realized that the qualities and differences of actual concrete things are all relative and liable to change.

616 *Chuang-tzu*, Ch. 17.

Once we understand this position of Hui Shih, we can see that his series of "points," as reported by the *Chuang-tzu*, though usually regarded as paradoxes, are really not paradoxical at all. With the exception of the first, they are all illustrations of the relativity of things, and expressions of what may be called a theory of relativity. Let us study them one by one.

"That which has no thickness cannot be increased [in thickness], yet it is so great that it may cover one thousand miles." This states that the great and the small are so only relatively. It is impossible for that which has no thickness to be thick. In this sense it may be called small. Nevertheless, the ideal plane of geometry, though without thickness, may at the same time be very long and wide. In this sense it may be called great.

"The heavens are as low as the earth; mountains are on the same level as marshes." This, too, states that the high and the low are so only relatively. "The sun at noon is the sun declining; the creature born is the creature dying." This states that everything in the actual world is changeable and changing.

"Great similarity differs from little similarity. This is called little-similarity-and-difference. All things are in one way all similar, in another way all different. This is called great-similarity-and-difference." When we say that all men are animals, we thereby recognize that all human beings are similar in the fact that they are human beings, and are also similar in the fact that they are animals. Their similarity in being human beings, however, is greater than that in being animals, because being a human being implies being an animal, but being an animal does not necessarily imply being a human being. For there are other kinds of animals as well, which are different from human beings. It is this kind of similarity and difference, therefore, that Hui Shih calls little-similarity-and-difference. However, if we take "beings" as a universal class, we thereby recognize that all things are similar in the fact that they are beings. But if we take each thing as an individual, we thereby recognize that each individual has its own individuality and so is different from other things. This kind of similarity and difference is what Hui Shih calls great-similarity-and-difference. Thus since we can say that all things are similar to each other, and yet can also say that all things are different from each other, this shows that their similarity and difference are both relative. This argument of the School of Names was a famous one in ancient China, and was known as the "argument for the unity of similarity and difference."

"The South has no limit and yet has a limit." "The South has no limit" was a common saying of the day. At that time, the South was a little known land very much like the West of America two hundred years ago. For the early Chinese, the South was not limited by sea as was the East, nor by barren desert as were the North and West. Hence it was popularly regarded as having no limit. Hui Ship's statement may thus perhaps be merely an expression of his superior geographical knowledge, that the South is, eventually, also limited by the sea. Most probably, however, it means to say that the limited and the unlimited are both only relatively so.

"I go to the state of Yueh today and arrived there yesterday."

This states that "today" and "yesterday" are relative terms. The yesterday of today was the today of yesterday, and the today of today will be the yesterday of tomorrow. Herein lies the relativity of the present and the past.

"Connected rings can be separated" Connected rings cannot be separated unless they are destroyed. But destruction may, from another point of view, be construction. If one makes a wooden table, from the point of view of the wood, it is destruction, but from the point of view of the table, it is construction. Since destruction and construction are relative, therefore "connected rings can be separated" without destroying them.

"I know the center of the world. It is north of Yen and south of Yueh." Among the states of the time, Yen was in the extreme north and Yueh In the extreme south. The Chinese regarded China as being the world hence it was a matter of common sense that the center of the world should be south of Yen and north of Yueh.

Hui Shih's contrary assertion here is well interpreted by a commentator of the third century A.D., Ssuma Piao, who says: "The world has no limit, and therefore anywhere is the center, just as in drawing a circle, any point on the line can be the starting point." "Love all things equally; Heaven and Earth are one body." In the preceding propositions, Hui Shih argues that all things are relative and in a state of flux. There is no absolute difference, or absolute separation among them. Everything is constantly changing into something else. It is a logical conclusion, therefore, that all things are one, and hence that we should love all things equally without discrimination. In the Chuang-tzu it is also said:

> If we see things from the point of view of their difference, even my liver and gall are as far from each other as are the states of Chu and Yueh. If we see things from the point of view of their similarity, all things are one.[617]

Kungsun Lung's Theory of Universals

The other main leader of the School of Names was Kungsun Lung (fl. 284-259 B.C.), who was widely known in his day for his sophistic arguments. It is said that once when he was passing a frontier, the frontier guards said: "Horses are not allowed to pass." Kungsun Lung replied: "My horse is white, and a white horse is not a horse." And so saying, he passed with his horse.

Instead of emphasizing, as did Hui Shih, that actual things are relative and changeable, Kungsun Lung emphasized that names are absolute and permanent. In this way he arrived at the same concept of Platonic ideas or universals that has been so conspicuous in Western philosophy.

In his work titled the Kungsun Lung-tzu, there is a chapter called "Discourse on the White Horse." Its main proposition is the assertion that "a white horse is not a horse." This proposition Kungsun Lung tries to prove through three arguments. The first is: "The word 'horse' denotes a shape; the word 'white' denotes a color.

617 Chuang-tzu, Ch.5.

That which denotes color is not that which denotes shape.

Therefore I say that a white horse is not a horse." In terms of Western logic, we may say that this argument emphasizes the difference in the intension of the terms "horse," "white," and "white horse." The intension of the first term is one kind of animal, that of the second is one kind of color, and that of the third is one kind of animal plus one kind of color. Since the intension of each of the three terms is different, therefore a white horse is not a horse.

The second argument is: "When a horse is required, a yellow horse or a black one may be brought forward, but when one requires a white horse, a yellow or a black horse cannot be brought forward.... Therefore a yellow horse and a black horse are both horses. They can only respond to a call for a horse but cannot respond to a call for a white horse. It is clear that a white horse is not a horse." And again: "The term 'horse' neither excludes nor includes any color; therefore yellow and black ones may respond to it. But the term 'white horse' both excludes and includes color. Yellow and black horses are all excluded because of their color.

Therefore only a white horse can fit the requirements. That which is not excluded is not the same as that which is excluded. Therefore I say that a white horse is not a horse." In terms of Western logic, we may say that this argument emphasizes the difference in the extension of the terms "horse" and "white horse." The extension of the term "horse" includes all horses, with no discrimination as to their color. The extension of the term "white horse," however, includes only white horses, with a corresponding discrimination of color. Since the extension of the term "horse" and "white horse" is different, therefore a white horse is not a horse.

The third argument is: "Horses certainly have color. Therefore there are white horses. Suppose there is a horse without color, then there is only the horse as such. But how, then, do we get a white 'horse? Therefore a white horse is not a horse. A white horse is 'horse' together with 'white.' 'Horse' with 'white' is not horse." In this argument, Kungsun Lung seems to emphasize the distinction between the universal, "horseness," and the universal, "white-horseness." The universal, horseness, is the essential attribute of all horses. It implies no color and is just "horse as such." Such "horseness" is distinct from "white-horseness." That is to say, the horse as such is distinct from the white horse as such. Therefore a white horse is not a horse.

Besides horse as such, there is also white as such, that is, whiteness. In the same chapter it is said: "White [as such] does not specify what is white. But 'white horse' specifies what is white.

Specified white is not white." Specified white is the concrete white color which is seen in this or that particular white object. The word here translated as "specified" is ting, which also has the meaning of "determined." The white color which is seen in this or that white object is determined by this or that object. The universal, "whiteness," however, is not determined by any one particular white object. It is the whiteness unspecified.

The Kungsun Lung-tzu contains another chapter entitled "Discourse on Hardness and Whiteness." The main proposition in this chapter is that "hardness and whiteness are separate." Kungsun Lung tries to prove this in two ways. The first is expressed in the following dialogue: "[Supposing there is a hard and white stone], is it possible to say hard, white, and stone are three? No. Can they be two? Yes. How? When without hardness one finds what is white, this gives two. When without whiteness one finds what is hard, this gives two. Seeing does not give us what is hard but only what is white, and there is nothing hard in this. Touching does not give us what is white but only what is hard, and there is nothing white in this." This dialogue uses epistemological proof to show that hardness and whiteness are separated from each other. Here we have a hard and white stone. If we use our eyes to see it, we only get what is white, i.e., a white stone. But if we use our hands to touch it, we only get what is hard, i.e., a hard stone. While we are sensing that the stone is white, we cannot sense that it is hard, and while we are sensing that it is hard, we cannot sense that it is white. Epistemologically speaking, therefore, there is only a white stone or a hard stone here, but not a hard and white stone. This is the meaning of the saying "When without hardness one finds what is white, this gives two. When without whiteness one finds what is hard, this gives two."

Kungsun Lung's second argument is a metaphysical one. Its general idea is that both hardness and whiteness, as universals, are unspecified in regard to what particular object it is that is hard or that is white. They can be manifested in any or all white or hard objects. Indeed, even if in the physical world there were no hard or white objects at all, none the less, the universal, hardness, would of necessity remain hardness, and the universal, whiteness, would remain whiteness. Such hardness and whiteness are quite independent of the existence of physical stones or other objects that are hard and white. The fact that they are independent universals is shown by the fact that in the physical world there are some objects that are hard but not white, and other objects that are white but not hard. Thus it is evident that hardness and whiteness are separate from each other.

With these epistemological and metaphysical arguments Kung- sun Lung established his proposition that hardness and whiteness are separate. This was a famous proposition in ancient China, and was known as the argument for "the separateness of hardness and whiteness."

In the *Kungsun Lung-tzu* there is yet another chapter entitled "Discourse on Chih and Wu." By *wu* Kungsun Lung means concrete particular things, while by chin he means abstract universals. The literal meaning of chih is, as a noun, "finger" or "pointer," or, as a verb, "to indicate." Two explanations may be given as to why Kungsun Lung uses the word Chih to denote universals. A common term, that is, a name, to use the terminology of the School of Names, denotes a class of particular things and connotes the common attributes of that class. An abstract term, on the contrary, denotes the attribute or universal. Since the Chinese language has no inflection, there is no distinction in form between a common term and an abstract one. Thus, in Chinese, what Westerners would call a common term may also denote a universal. Likewise, the Chinese language has no articles. Hence, in Chinese, such terms as "horse," "the horse," and "a horse" are all designated by the one word ma or "horse." It would seem, therefore, that fundamentally the word ma denotes the universal concept, "horse," while the other terms, "a horse," "the horse," etc., are simply particularized applications of this universal concept. From this it may be said that, in the Chinese language, a universal is what a name points out, i.e., denotes. This is why Kungsun Lung refers to universals as chih or "pointers."

Another explanation of why Kungsun Lung uses chin to denote the universal, is that chih (finger, pointer, etc.) is a close equivalent of another word, also pronounced chih and written almost the same, which means "idea" or "concept." According to this explanation, then, when Kungsun Lung speaks of chin (pointers he really means by it "idea" or "concept." As can be seen from his arguments above, however, this "idea" is for him not the subjective idea spoken of in the philosophy of Berkeley and Hume, but rather the objective idea as found in the philosophy of Plato. It is the universal. In the final chapter of the Chuang-tzu we find a series of twenty-one arguments attributed without specification to the followers of the School of Names. Among them, however, it is evident that some are based upon the ideas of Hui Shih, and others upon those of Kungsun Lung, and they can be explained accordingly. They used to be considered as paradoxes, but they cease to be such once we understand the fundamental ideas of their authors.

Significance of the Theories of Hui Shih and Kungsun Lung

Thus by analyzing names, and their relation with, or their distinction from, actualities, the philosophers of the School of Names discovered what in Chinese philosophy is called that which lies beyond shapes and features." In Chinese philosophy a distinction is made between "being that lies within shapes and features," and "being that lies beyond shapes and features." "Being that lies within shapes and features" is the actual, the shih. For instance, the big and the small, the square and the round, the long and the short, the white and the black, are each one class of shapes and features. Anything that is the object or possible object of experience has shape and feature, and lies within the actual world. Conversely, any object in the actual world that has shape and feature is the object or possible object of experience.

When Hui Shih enunciated the first and last of his series of "points," he was talking about what lies beyond shapes and features. "The greatest," he said, "has nothing beyond itself. This is called the Great One." This defines in what manner the greatest is as it is. "Love all things equally; Heaven and Earth are one." This defines of what the greatest consists. This last statement conveys the idea that all is one and one is all. Since all is one, there can be nothing beyond the all. The all is itself the greatest one, and since there can be nothing beyond the all, the all cannot be the object of experience. This is because an object of experience always stands in apposition to the one who experiences. Hence if we say that the all can be an object of experience, we must also say that there is something that stands in apposition to the all and is its experiencer. In other words, we must say that

that which has nothing beyond itself at the same time has something beyond itself, which is a manifest contradiction.

Kungsun Lung, too, discovered what lies beyond shapes and features, because the universals he discussed can likewise not be objects of experience. One can see a white something, but one cannot see the universal whiteness as such. All universals that are indicated by names lie in a world beyond shapes and features, though not all universals in that world have names to indicate them. In that world, hardness is hardness and whiteness is whiteness, or as Kungsun Lung said: "Each is alone and true."[618]

Hui Shih spoke of "loving all things equally," and Kungsun Lung also "wished to extend his argument in order to correct the relations between names and actualities, so as thus to transform the whole world."[619] Both men thus apparently considered their philosophy as comprising the "Tao of sageliness within and kingliness without." But it was left to the *Tao*ists fully to apply the discovery made by the School of Names of what lies beyond shapes and features. The *Tao*ists were the opponents of this school, but they were also its true inheritors. This is illustrated by the fact that Hui Shih was a great friend of Chuang Tzu.

---

618 *Kungsun Lung-tzu*, Ch. 5

619 *Id.*, Ch. 1.

IX THE SECOND PHASE OF TAOISM: LAO TZU

According to tradition, Lao Tzu (a name which literally means the "Old Master) was a native of the state of Chu in the southern part of the present Henan Province, and was an older contemporary of Confucius, whom he is reputed to have instructed in ceremonies. The book bearing his name, the Lao-tzu, and in later times also known as the *Tao* Te Ching (Classic of the Way and Power), has therefore been traditionally regarded as the first philosophical work in Chinese history. Modern scholarship, however, has forced us drastically to change this view and to date it to a time considerably after Confucius.

Lao Tzu the Man and Lao-tzu the Book

Two questions arise in this connection. One is about the date of the man, Lao Tzu (whose family name is said to have been Li, and personal name, Tan), and another about the date of the book itself. There is no necessary connection between the two, for it is quite possible that there actually lived a man known as Lao Tan who was senior to Confucius, but that the book titled the Lao-tzu is a later production. This is the view I take, and it does not necessarily contradict the traditional accounts of Lao Tzu the man, because in these accounts there is no statement that the man, Lao Tzu, actually wrote the book by that name. Hence I am willing to accept the traditional stories about Lao Tzu the man, while at the same time placing the book, Lao-tzu, in a later period. In fact, I now believe the date of the book to be later than I assumed when I wrote my History of Chinese Philosophy. I now believe it was written or composed after Hui Shih and Kungsun Lung, and not before, as I there indicated. This is because the Lao-tzu contains considerable discussion about the Nameless, and in order to do this it would seem that men should first have become conscious of the existence of names themselves.

My position does not require me to insist that there is absolutely no connection between Lao Tzu the man and Lao-tzu the book, for the book may indeed contain a few sayings of the original Lao Tzu What I maintain, however, is that the system of thought in the book as a whole cannot be the product of a time either before or contemporary with that of Confucius. In the pages following however, to avoid pedantry, I shall refer to Lao Tzu as having said so and so, instead of stating that the book Lao-tzu says so and so, just as we today still speak of sunrise and sunset, even though we know very well that the sun itself actually neither rises nor sets.

Tao, the Unnamable

In the last chapter, we have seen that the philosophers of the School of Names, through the study of names, succeeded in discovering "that which lies beyond shapes and features." Most people, however, think only in terms of "what lies within shapes and features," that is, the actual world. Seeing the actual, they have no difficulty in expressing it, and though they use names for it, they are not conscious that they are names. So when the philosophers of the School of Names started to think about the names themselves, this thought represented a great advance. To think about names is to think about thinking. It is thought about thought and therefore is thought on a higher level.

All things that "lie within shapes and features" have names, or, at least, possess the possibility of having names. They are namable. But in contrast with what is namable, Lao Tzu speaks about the unnamable. Not everything that lies beyond shapes and features is unnamable. Universals, for instance, lie beyond shapes and features, yet they are not unnamable. But on the other hand, what is unnamable most certainly does lie beyond shapes and features,

The *Tao* or Way of the *Tao*ists is a concept of this sort.

In the first chapter of the Lao-tzu we find the statement:

> The *Tao* that can be comprised in words is not the eternal *Tao*, the name that can be named is not the abiding name. The Unnamable is the beginning of Heaven and Earth; the namable is the mother of all things.

And in Chapter Thirty-two: "The *Tao* is eternal, nameless, the Uncarved Block.... Once the block is carved, there are names." Orin Chapter Forty-one: "The *Tao*, lying hid, is nameless." In the Taoist system, there is a distinction between *yu* (being) and *wu* (non-being), and between *yu*-ming (having-name, namable) and *yu*-ming (having-no-name, unnamable). These two distinctions are in reality only one, for *yu* and *wu* are actually simply abbreviated terms for vu-ring and *wu*-ming. Heaven and Earth and all things are namables. Thus Heaven has the name of Heaven, Earth the name Earth, and each kind of thing has the name of that kind.

There being Heaven, Earth and all things, it follows that there are the names of Heaven, Earth, and all things. Or as Lao Tzu says:

> "Once the Block is carved, there are names." The *Tao*, however, is unnamable; at the same time it is that by which all namables come to be. This is why Lao Tzu says: "The Unnamable is the beginning of Heaven and Earth; the namable is the mother of all things."

Since the *Tao* is unnamable, it therefore cannot be comprised in words. But since we wish to speak about it, we are forced to give it some kind of designation. We therefore call it *Tao*, which is really not a name at all. That is to say, to call the *Tao Tao*, is not the same as to call a table table. When we call a table table, we mean that it has some attributes by which it can be named. But when we call the *Tao Tao*, we do not mean that it has any such namable attributes. It is simply a designation, or to use an expression common in Chinese philosophy, *Tao* is a name which is not a name. In Chapter Twenty-one of the Lao-tzu it is said "From the past to the present, its [Tao's] name has not ceased to be, and has seen the beginning [of all things]." The Tap is that by which anything and everything comes to be. Since there are always things, *Tao* never ceases to be and the name of *Tao* also never ceases to be. It is the beginning of all beginnings, and therefore it has seen the beginning of all things. A name that never ceases to be is an abiding name, and such a name is in reality not a name at all. Therefore it is said "The name that can be named is not the abiding name."

"The Unnamable is the beginning of Heaven and Earth." This proposition is only a formal and not a positive one. That is to say, it fails to give any information about matters of fact. The *Tao*ists thought that since there are things, there must be that by which all these things come to be. This "that" is designated by them as *Tao*, which, however, is really not a name. The concept of *Tao*, too, is a formal and not a positive one. That is to say, it does not describe anything about what it is through which all things come to be. All we can say is that *Tao*, since it is that through which all things come to be, is necessarily not a mere thing among these other things. For if it were such a thing, it could not at the same time be that through which all things whatsoever come to be. Every kind of thing has a name, but *Tao* is not itself a thing. Therefore it is "nameless, the Uncarved Block."

Anything that comes to be is a being, and there are many beings. The coming to be of beings implies that first of all there is Being. These words, "first of all," here do not mean first in point of time, but first in a logical sense. For instance, if we say there was first a certain kind of animal, then man, the word "first" in this case means first in point of time. But if we say that first there must be animals before there are men, the word "first" in this case means first in a logical sense. The statement about "the origin of the species" makes an assertion about matters of fact, and required many years' observation and study by Charles Darwin before it could be made. But the second of our sayings makes no assertion about matters of fact. It simply says that the existence of men logically implies the existence of animals. In the same way, the being of all things implies the being of Being. This is the meaning of Lao Tzu's saying: "All things in the world come into being from Being (Yu); and Being comes into being from Non-being (Wu)."[620]

This saying of Lao Tzu does not mean that there was a time when there was only Non-being, and that then there came a time when Being came into being from Non-being. It simply means that if we analyze the existence of things, we see there must first be Being before there can be any things. *Tao* is the unnamable, is Non-being, and is that by which all things come to be. Therefore, before the being of Being, there must be Non-being, from which Being comes into being. What is here said belongs to ontology, not to cosmology. It has nothing to do with time and actuality. For in time and actuality, there is no Being; there are only beings.

There are many beings, but there is only one Being. In the *Lao-tzu* it is said "From *Tao* there comes one. From one there comes two. From two there comes three. From three there comes all things."[621] The "one" here spoken of refers to Being. To say that "from *Tao* comes one," is the same as that from Non-being comes Being. As for "two" and "three," there are many interpretations. But this saying, that "from one there comes two. From two there comes three. From three

620 *Lao-tzu*, Ch. 40.
621 *Id.*, Ch. 42.

there comes all things," may simply be the same as saying that from Being come all things. Being is one, and two and three are the beginning of the many.

The Invariable Law of Nature

In the final chapter of the Chuang-tzu, "The World," it is said that the leading ideas of Lao Tzu are those of the Tai Yi or "Super One," and of Being, Non-being, and the invariable. The "Super One" is the *Tao*. From the *Tao* comes one, and therefore *Tao* itself is the "Super One." The "invariable" is a translation of the Chinese word chang, which may also be translated as eternal or abiding. Though things are ever changeable and changing, the laws that govern this change of things are not themselves changeable. Hence in the Lao-tzu the word change is used to show what is always so, or in other words, what can be considered as a rule. For instance, Lao Tzu tells us: "The conquest of the world comes invariably from doing nothing."[622] Or again: "The way of Heaven has no favorites, it is invariably on the side of the good man."[623]

Among the laws that govern the changes of things, the most fundamental is that "when a thing reaches one extreme, it reverts from it." These are not the actual words of Lao Tzu, but a common Chinese saying, the idea of which no doubt comes from Lao Tzu.

Lao Tzu's actual words are: "Reversing is the movement of the Tao,"[624] and: "To go further and further means to revert again."[625] The idea is that if anything develops certain extreme qualities, those qualities invariably revert to become their opposites.

This constitutes a law of nature. Therefore: "It is upon calamity that blessing leans, upon blessing that calamity rests."[626] "Those with little will acquire, those with much will be led astray."[627] "A hurricane never lasts the whole morning, nor a rainstorm the whole day."[628] "The most yielding things in the world master the most unyielding."[629] "Diminish a thing and it will increase. Increase a thing and it will diminish."[630] All these paradoxical theories are no longer paradoxical, if one understands the fundamental law of nature. But to the ordinary people who have no idea of this law, they seem paradoxical indeed. Therefore Lao Tzu says: "The gentleman of the low type, on hearing the Truth, laughs loudly at it. If he had not laughed, it would not suffice to be the Truth."[631]

It may be asked: Granted that a thing, on reaching an extreme, then reverts, what is meant by the word "extreme"? Is there any absolute limit for the development of anything, going beyond which would mean going to the extreme? In the Lao-tzu

---

622 *Id.*, Ch. 48.
623 *Id.*, Ch. 79.
624 *Id.*, Ch. 40.
625 *Id*, Ch. 25.
626 *Id.*, Ch. 58.
627 *Id*, Ch. 22.
628 *Id.*, Ch. 23.
629 *Id.*, Ch. 43.
630 *Id.*, Ch. 42.
631 *Id.*, Ch. 41.

no such question is asked and therefore no answer is given. But if there had been such a question, I think Lao Tzu would have answered that no absolute limit can be prescribed for all things under all circumstances. So far as human activities are concerned, the limit for the advancement of a man remains relative to his subjective feelings and objective circumstances, Isaac Newton, for example, felt that compared with the total universe, his knowledge of it was no more than the knowledge of the sea possessed by a boy who is playing at the seashore. With such a feeling as this, Newton, despite his already great achievements in physics, was still far from reaching the limits of advancement in his learning? If, however, a student, having just finished his textbook on physics, thinks that he then knows all there is to know about science, he certainly cannot make further advancement in his learning, and will as certainly "revert back." Lao Tzu tells us: "If people of wealth and exalted position are arrogant, they abandon themselves to unavoidable ruin."[632] Arrogance is the sign that one's advancement has reached its extreme limit. It is the first thing that one should avoid.

The limit of advancement for a given activity is also relative to objective circumstances. When a man eats too much, he suffers. In overeating, what is ordinarily good for the body becomes something harmful. One should eat only the right amount of food. But this right amount depends on one's age, health, and the quality of food one eats.

These are the laws that govern the changes of things. By Lao Tzu they are called the invariables. He says: "To know the invariables is called enlightenment."[633] Again: "He who knows the invariable is liberal. Being liberal, he is without prejudice. Being without prejudice, he is comprehensive. Being comprehensive, he is vast. Being vast, he is with the Truth. Being with the Truth, he lasts forever and will not fail throughout his lifetime."[634]

Human Conduct

Lao Tzu warns us: "Not to know the invariable and to act blindly is to go to disaster." One should know the laws of nature and conduct one's activities in accordance with them. This, by Lao Tzu, is called "practicing enlightenment." The general rule for the man "practicing enlightenment" is that if he wants to achieve anything, he starts with its opposite, and if he wants to retain anything, he admits in it something of its opposite. If one wants to be strong, one must start with a feeling that one is weak, and if one wants to preserve capitalism, one must admit in it some elements of socialism.

Therefore Lao Tzu tells us: "The sage, putting himself in the background, is always to the fore. Remaining outside, he is always there. Is it not just because he does not strive for any personal end, that all his personal ends are fulfilled?"[635] Again: "He does not show himself; therefore he is seen everywhere. He does not define himself; therefore he is distinct. He does not assert himself; therefore

632 *Id.*, Ch. 9.

633 *Id.*, Ch. 16.

634 *Ibid.*

635 *Id.*, Ch. 7.

he succeeds. He does not boast of his work; therefore he endures. He does not contend, and for that very reason no one in the world can contend with him."[636] These sayings illustrate the first point of the general rule.

In the *Lao-tzu* we also find:

> What is most perfect seems to have something missing, yet its use is unimpaired. What is most full seems empty, yet its use is inexhaustible. What is most straight seems like crookedness. The greatest skill seems like clumsiness. The greatest eloquence seems like stuttering.[637]

Again:

> Be twisted and one shall be whole. Be crooked and one shall be straight. Be hollow and one shall be filled. Be tattered and one shall be renewed. Have little and one shall obtain. But have much and one shall be perplexed.[638]

This illustrates the second point of the general rule.

Such is the way in which a prudent man can live safely in the world and achieved his aims. This is Lao Tzu's answer and solution to the original problem of the *Tao*ists, which was, how to preserve life and avoid harm and danger in the human world. (See end of Ch. 6 above.) The man who lives prudently must be meek, humble and easily content. To be meek is the way to preserve your strength and so be strong. Humility is the direct opposite of arrogance, so that if arrogance is a sign that a man's advancement has reached its extreme limit, humility is a contrary sign that that limit is far from reached. And to be content safeguards one from going too far and therefore from reaching the extreme, Lao Tzu says "To know how to be content is to avoid humiliation; to know where to stop is to avoid injury."[639] Again: "The sage, therefore, discards the excessive, the extravagant, the extreme."[640]

All these theories are deducible from the general theory that "reversing is the movement of the *Tao*." The well-known *Tao*ist theory of *wu*-uei is also deducible from this general theory. Wu-uei can be translated literally as "having-no-activity" or "nonaction." But using this translation, one should remember that the term does not actually mean complete absence of activity, or doing nothing. What it does mean is lesser activity or doing less. It also means acting without artificiality and arbitrariness.

Activities are like many other things. If one has too much of them, they become harmful rather than good. Furthermore, the purpose of doing something is to have something done. But if there is over-doing, this results in something being over-done, which may be worse than not having the thing done at all. A well-known Chinese story describes how two men were once competing in drawing a snake; the one who would finish his drawing first would win. One of them, having indeed finished his drawing, saw that the other man was still far behind, so decided to improve it by adding feet to his snake. Thereupon the other man said "You have lost the competition, for a snake has no feet." This is an illustration of over-doing

636 *Id.*, Ch. 22.
637 *Id.*, Ch. 45.
638 *Id.*, Ch. 22.
639 *Id.*, Ch. 45.
640 *Id.*, Ch. 29.

which defeats its own purpose. In the Lao-tzu we read: "Conquering the world is invariably due to doing nothing; by doing something one cannot conquer the world."[641] The term "doing nothing" here really means "not over-doing."

Artificiality and arbitrariness are the opposite of naturalness and spontaneity. According to Lao Tzu, *Tao* is that by which all things come to be. In this process of coming to be, each individual thing obtains something from the universal *Tao*, and this something is called Te. Te is a word that means "power" or "virtue," both in the moral and non-moral sense of the latter term. The Te of a thing is what it naturally is. Lao Tzu says: "All things respect *Tao* and value Te."[642] This is because *Tao* is that by which they come to be, and Te is that by which they are what they are.

According to the theory of "having-no-activity," a man should restrict his activities to what is necessary and what is natural.

"Necessary" means necessary to the achievement of a certain purpose, and never over-doing. "Natural" means following one's Te with no arbitrary effort. In doing this one should take simplicity as the guiding principle of life. Simplicity (pu) is an important idea of Lao Tzu and the *Tao*ists. *Tao* is the "Uncarved Block" (pu), which is simplicity itself. There is nothing that can be simpler than the unnamable *Tao*. Te is the next simplest, and the man who follows Te must lead as simple a life as possible.

The life that follows Te lies beyond the distinctions of good and evil. Lao Tzu tells us: "If all people of the world know that beauty is beauty, there is then already ugliness. If all people of the world know that good is good, there is then already evil."[643] Lao Tzu, therefore, despised such Confucian virtues as human-heartedness and righteousness, for according to him these virtues represent degeneration from *Tao* and Te. Therefore he says:

> When the *Tao* is lost, there is the Te. When the Te is lost, there is [the virtue of] human-heartedness. When human-heartedness is lost, there is [the virtue of] righteousness. When righteousness is lost, there are the ceremonials. Ceremonials are the degeneration of loyalty and good faith, and are the beginning of disorder in the world.[644]

Here we find the direct conflict between Taoism and Confucianism.

People have lost their original Te because they have too many desires and too much knowledge. In satisfying their desires, people are seeking happiness. But when they try to satisfy too many desires, they obtain an opposite result. Lao Tzu says: "The five colors blind the eye. The five notes dull the ear. The five tastes fatigue the mouth. Riding and hunting madden the mind. Rare treasures hinder right conduct."[645] Therefore, "there is no disaster greater than not knowing contentment with what one has; no greater sin than having desire

641 *Id.*, Ch. 48.
642 *Id.*, Ch. 51.
643 *Id.*, Ch. 2.
644 *Id.*, Ch. 38.
645 *Id.*, Ch. 5.

for acquisiting."[646] This is why Lao Tzu emphasizes that people should have few desires.

Likewise Lao Tzu emphasizes that people should have little knowledge. Knowledge is itself an object of desire. It also enables people to know more about the objects of desire and serves as a means to gain these objects. It is both the master and servant of desire. With increasing knowledge people are no longer in a position to know how to be content and where to stop. Therefore, it is said in the Lao-Tzu: "When knowledge and intelligence appeared, Gross Artifice began."[647]

Political Theory

From these theories Lao Tzu deduces his political theory. The Taoists agree with the Confucianists that the ideal state is one which has a sage as its head. It is only the sage who can and should rule. The difference between the two schools, however, is that according to the Confucianists, when a sage becomes the ruler, he should do many things for the people, whereas according to the

Taoists, the duty of the sage ruler is not to do things, but rather to undo or not to do at all. The reason for this, according to Lao Tzu, is that the troubles of the world come, not because there are many things not yet done, but because too many things are done. In the Lao-tzu we read:

> The more restriction and prohibitions there are in the world, the poorer the people will be. The more sharp weapons the people have, the more troubled will be the country. The more cunning craftsmen there are, the more pernicious contrivances will appear. The more laws are promulgated, the more thieves and bandits there will be.[648]

The first act of a sage ruler, then, is to undo all these. Lao Tzu says:

> Banish wisdom, discard knowledge, and the people will be benefited a hundredfold Banish human-heartedness, discard righteousness, and the people will be dutiful and compassionate. Banish skill, discard profit, and thieves and robbers will disappear.[649]

Again:

> Do not exalt the worthies, and the people will no longer be contentious. Do not value treasures that are hard to get, and there will be no more thieves. If the people never see such things as excite desire, their mind will not be confused. Therefore the sage rules the people by emptying their minds, filling their bellies, weakening their wills and toughening their sinews, ever making the people without knowledge and without desire.[650]

The sage ruler would undo all the causes of trouble in the world.

After that, he would govern with non-action. With non-action, he does nothing, yet everything is accomplished. The Lao-tzu says:

I act not and the people of themselves are transformed. I love quiescence and

646 *Id.*, Ch. 46.
647 *Id.*, Ch. 18.
648 *Id.*, Ch. 27.
649 *Id.*, Ch. 19
650 *Id.*, Ch. 3..

the people of themselves go straight. I concern myself with nothing, and the people of themselves are prosperous. I am without desire, and the people of themselves are simple.[651]

"Do nothing, and there is nothing that is not done." This is another of the seemingly paradoxical ideas of the *Taoists*. In the *Lao-tzu* we read: "Tao invariably does nothing and yet there is nothing that is not done."[652] *Tao* is that by which all things come to be. It is not itself a thing and therefore it cannot act as do such things. Yet all things come to be. Thus *Tao* does nothing, yet there is nothing that is not done. It allows each thing to do what it itself can do. According to the *Taoists*, the ruler of a state should model himself on *Tao*. He, too, should do nothing and should let the people do what they can do themselves. Here is another meaning of *wu-wei* (non-action), which later, with certain modifications, become one of the important theories of the Legalists (*Fa chia*).

Children have limited knowledge and few desires. They are not far away from the original Te. Their simplicity and innocence are characteristics that every man should if possible retain. Lao Tzu says "Not to part from the invariable Te is to return to the state of infancy."[653] Again: "He who holds the Te in all its solidity may be likened to an infant."[654] Since the life of the child is nearer to the ideal life, the sage ruler would like all of his people to be like small children. Lao Tzu says "The sage treats all as children."[655] He "does not make them enlightened, but keeps them ignorant."[656]

"Ignorant" here is a translation of the Chinese *yu*, which means ignorance in the sense of simplicity and innocence. The sage not only wants his people to be *yu*, but wants himself to be so too. LaoTzu says: "Mine is the mind of the very ignorant."[657] In Taoism *yu* is not a vice, but a great virtue.

But is the *yu* of the sage really the same as the *yu* of the child and the common people? Certainly not. The *yu* of the sage is the result of a conscious process of cultivation. It is something higher than knowledge, something more, not less. There is a common

Chinese saying: "Great wisdom is like ignorance." The *yu* of the sage is great wisdom, and not the *yu* of the child or of ordinary people. The latter kind of *yu* is a gift of nature, while that of the sage is an achievement of the spirit. There is a great difference between the two. But in many cases the *Taoists* seemed to have confused them. We shall see this point more clearly when we discuss the philosophy of Chuang Tzu.

651 *Id.*, Ch. 57.
652 *Id.*, Ch. 37.
653 *Id.*, Ch. 28.
654 *Id.*, Ch. 55.
655 *Id.*, Ch. 49.
656 *Id.*, Ch. 65.
657 *Id.*, Ch. 20.

X THE THIRD PHASE OF TAOISM: CHUANG TZU

Chuang Chou, better known as Chuang Tzu (c. 369-c. 286 B.C.), is perhaps the greatest of the early *Tao*ists. We know little of his life save that he was a native of the little state of Meng on the border between the present Shandong and Henan provinces, where he lived a hermit's life, but was nevertheless famous for his ideas and writings. It is said that King Wei of Chu, having heard his name, once sent messengers with gifts to invite him to his state, promising to make him chief minister. Chuang Tzu, however, merely laughed and said to them: "... Go away, do not defile me....I prefer the enjoyment of my own free will."[658]

Chuang Tzu the Man and Chuang-tzu the Book

Though Chuang Tzu was a contemporary of Mencius and a friend of Hui Shih, the book titled the Chuang-tzu, as we know it today, was probably compiled by Kuo Hsiang, Chuang-tzu the book's great commentator of the third century A.D. We are thus not sure which of the chapters of Chuang-tzu the book were really written by Chuang Tzu himself. It is, in fact, a collection of various *Tao*ist writings, some of which represent Taoism in its first phase of development, some in its second, and some in its third. It is only those chapters representing the thought of this third climactic phase that can properly be called Chuang Tzu's own philosophy, yet even they may not all have been written by Chuang Tzu himself. For though the name of Chuang Tzu can be taken as representative of the last phase of early Taoism, it is probable that his system of thought was brought to full completion only by his followers. Certain chapters of the Chuang-tzu, for example, contain statements about Kungsun Lung who certainly lived later than Chuang Tzu.

Way of Achieving Relative Happiness

The first chapter of the Chuang-tzu, titled "The Happy Excursion," is a simple text, full of amusing stories. Their underlying idea is that there are varying degrees in the achievement of happiness. A free development of our natures may lead us to a relative kind of happiness; absolute happiness is achieved through higher understanding of the nature of things.

To carry out the first of these requirements, the free development of our nature, we should have a full and free exercise of our natural ability. That ability is our Te, which comes directly from the *Tao*. Regarding the *Tao* and Te, Chuang Tzu has the same idea as Lao Tzu. For example, he says:

> At the great beginning there was Non-being. It had neither being nor name and was that from which came the One. When the One came into existence, there was the One but still no form. When things obtained that by which

658 *Historian Records*, Ch. 63

they came into existence, it was called the Te.[659] Thus our Te is what makes us what we are. We are happy when this Te or natural ability of ours is fully and freely exercised, that is, when our nature is fully and freely developed.

In connection with this idea of free development, Chuang Tzu makes a contrast between what is of nature and what is of man.

He says:

> What is of nature is internal. What is of man is external.... That oxen and horses should have four feet is what is of nature. That a halter should be put on a horse's head, or a string through an ox's nose, is what is of man.[660]

Following what is of nature, he maintains, is the source of all happiness and goodness, while following what is of man is the source of all pain and evil.

Things are different in their nature and their natural ability is also not the same. What they share in common, however, is that they are all equally happy when they have a full and free exercise of their natural ability. In "The Happy Excursion" a story is told of a very large and a small bird. The abilities of the two are entirely different. The one can fly thousands of miles, while the other can hardly reach from one tree to the next. Yet they are both happy when they each do what they are able and like to do. Thus there is no absolute uniformity in the natures of things, nor is there any need for such uniformity. Another chapter of the Chuang-tzu tells us:

> The duck's legs are short, but if we try to lengthen them, the duck will feel pain. The crane's legs are long, but if we try to shorten them, the crane will feel grief. Therefore we are not to amputate what is by nature long, nor to lengthen what is by nature short.[661]

Political and Social Philosophy

Such, however, is just what artificiality tries to do, The purpose of all laws, morals, institutions, and governments, is to establish uniformity and suppress difference. The motivation of the people who try to enforce this uniformity may be wholly admirable.

When they find something that is good for them, they may be anxious to see that others have it also. This good intention of theirs, however, only makes the situation more tragic. In the *Chuang-tzu* there is a story which says:

> Of old, when a seabird alighted outside the capital of Lu, the Marquis went out to receive it, gave it wine in the temple, and had the Chiu-shat music played to amuse it, and a bullock slaughtered to feed it. But the bird was dazed and too timid to eat or drink anything. In three days it was dead. This was treating the bird as one would treat oneself, not the bird as a bird.... Water is life to fish but is death to man. Being differently constituted, their likes and dislikes must necessarily differ. Therefore the early sages did not make abilities and occupations uniform.[662]

---

659 *Chuang-tzu*, Ch. 12.

660 *Id*. Ch. 17.

661 *Id*. Ch. 8.

662 *Id*., Ch. 18.

When the Marquis treated the bird in a way which he considered the most honorable, he certainly had good intentions. Yet the result was just opposite to what he expected. This is what happens when uniform codes of laws and morals are enforced by government and society upon the individual.

This is why Chuang Tzu violently opposes the idea of governing through the formal machinery of government, and maintains instead that the best way of governing is through non-government.

He says:

> I have heard of letting mankind alone, but not of governing man- kind. Letting alone springs from the fear that people will pollute their innate nature and set aside their Te. When people do not pollute their innate nature and set aside their Te, then is there need for the government of mankind?[663]

If one fails to leave people alone, and tries instead to rule them with laws and institutions, the process is like putting a halter around a horse's neck or a string through an ox's nose. It is also like lengthening the legs of the duck or shortening those of the crane. What is natural and spontaneous is changed into something artificial, which is called by Chuang Tzu "overcoming what is of nature by what is of man."[664] Its result can only be misery and unhappiness.

Thus Chuang Tzu and Lao Tzu both advocate government through non-government, but for somewhat different reasons. Lao Tzu emphasizes his general principle that "reversing is the movement of the *Tao*." The more one governs, he argues, the less one achieves the desired result. And Chuang Tzu emphasizes the distinction between what is of nature and what is of man. The more the former is overcome by the latter, the more there will be misery and unhappiness.

Thus far we have only seen Chuang Tzu's way of achieving relative happiness. Such relative happiness is achieved when one simply follows what is natural in oneself. This every man can do.

The political and social philosophy of Chuang Tzu aims at achieving precisely such relative happiness for every man. This and nothing more is the most that any political and social philosophy can hope to do.

Emotion and Reason

Relative happiness is relative because it has to depend upon something. It is true that one is happy when one has a full and free exercise of one's natural ability. But there are many ways in which this exercise is obstructed. For instance, there is death which is the end of all human activities. There are diseases which handicap human activities. There is old age which gives man the same trouble. So it is not without reason that the Buddhists consider these as three of the four human miseries, the fourth, according to them, being life itself. Hence, happiness which depends upon the full and free exercise of one's natural ability is a limited and therefore relative happiness.

In the *Chuang-tzu* there are many discussions about the greatest of all disasters

663 *Id.*, Ch. 11.
664 *Id.*, Ch. 17.

that can befall man, death. Fear of death and anxiety about its coming are among the principal sources of human unhappiness. Such fear and anxiety, however, may be diminished if we have a proper understanding of the nature of things. In the Chuang-tzu there is a story about the death of Lao Tzu. When Lao Tzu died, his friend Chin Shih, who had come after the death, criticized the violent lamentations of the other mourners, saying:

> This is to violate the principle of nature and to increase the emotion of man, forgetting what we have received [from nature]. These were called by the ancients the penalty of violating the principle of nature. When the Master came, it was because he had the occasion to be born. When he went, he simply followed the natural course. Those who are quiet at the proper occasion and follow the natural course cannot be affected by sorrow or joy. They were considered by the ancients as the men of the gods, who were released from bondage.[665]

To the extent that the other mourners felt sorrow, to that extent they suffered. Their suffering was the "penalty of violating the principle of nature." The mental torture inflicted upon man by his emotions is sometimes just as severe as any physical punishment.

But by the use of understanding, man can reduce his emotions. For example, a man of understanding will not be angry when rain prevents him from going out, but a child often will. The reason is that the man possesses greater understanding, with the result that he suffers less disappointment or exasperation than the child who does get angry. As Spinoza has said "In so far as the mind understands all things are necessary, so far has it greater power over the effects, or suffers less from them."[666] Such, in the words of the *Tao*ists, is "to disperse emotion with reason."

A story about Chuang Tzu himself well illustrates this point. It is said that when Chuang Tzu's wife died, his friend Hui Shih went to condole. To his amazement he found Chuang Tzu sitting on the ground, singing, and on asking him how he could be so unkind to his wife, was told by Chuang Tzu:

> When she had just died, I could not help being affected. Soon, however, I examined the matter from the very beginning. At the very beginning, she was not living, having no form, nor even substance. But somehow or other there was then her substance, then her form, and then her life. Now by a further change, she has died. The whole process is like the sequence of the four seasons, spring, summer, autumn, and winter. While she is thus lying in the great mansion of the universe, for me to go about weeping and wailing would be to proclaim myself ignorant of the natural laws. Therefore I stop.[667]

On this passage the great commentator Kuo Hsiang comments:

"When ignorant, he felt sorry. When he understood, he was no longer affected. This teaches man to disperse emotion with reason." Emotion

665 *Id.*, Ch. 3.
666 *Ethics*, Pt 5, Prop. VI.
667 *Chuang-tzu*, Ch. 18.

can be counteracted with reason and understanding. Such was the view of Spinoza and also of the *Tao*ists.

The *Tao*ists maintained that the sage who has a complete understanding of the nature of things, thereby has no emotions.

This, however, does not mean that he lacks sensibility. Rather it means that he is not disturbed by the emotions, and enjoys what may be called "the peace of the soul." As Spinoza says:

> The ignorant man is not only agitated by external causes in many ways, and never enjoys true peace in the soul, but lives also ignorant as it were, both of God and of things, and as soon as he ceases to suffer ceases also to be. On the other hand, the wise man, in so far as he is considered as such, is scarcely moved in his mind, but being conscious by a certain eternal necessity of himself, of God, and things, never ceases to be, and always enjoys the peace of the soul.[668]

Thus by his understanding of the nature of things, the sage is no longer affected by the changes of the world. In this way he is not dependent upon external things, and hence his happiness is not limited by them. He may be said to have achieved absolute happiness. Such is one line of *Tao*ist thought, in which there is not a little atmosphere of pessimism and resignation. It is a line which emphasizes the inevitability of natural processes and the fatalistic acquiescence in them by man.

Way of Achieving Absolute Happiness

There is another line of *Tao*ist thought, however, which emphasizes the relativity of the nature of things and the identification of man with the universe. To achieve this identification, man needs knowledge and understanding of still a higher level, and the happiness resulting from this identification is really absolute happiness, as expounded in Chuang Tzu's chapter on "The Happy Excursion."

In this chapter, after describing the happiness of large and small birds, Chuang Tzu adds that among human beings there was a man named Lich Tzu who could even ride on the wind. "Among those who have attained happiness," he says, "such a man is rare. Yet although he was able to dispense with walking, he still had to depend upon something." This something was the wind, and since he had to depend upon the wind, his happiness was to that extent relative. Then Chuang Tzu asks:

> But suppose there is one who chariots on the normality of the universe, rides on the transformation of the six elements, and thus makes excursion into the infinite, what has he to depend upon? Therefore it is said that the perfect man has no self; the spiritual man has no achievement; and the true sage has no name.[669]

What is here said by Chuang Tzu describes the man who has achieved absolute happiness. He is the perfect man, the spiritual man, and the true sage. He is

668 *Ethics*, Pt, 5, Prop. XLII.

669 *Chuang-tzu*, Ch. 1.

absolutely happy, because he transcends the ordinary distinctions of things. He also transcends the distinction between the self and the world, the "me" and the "non-me." Therefore he has no self. He is one with the *Tao*. The

Tao does nothing and yet there is nothing that is not done. The

Tao does nothing, and therefore has no achievements. The sage is one with the *Tao* and therefore also has no achievements. He may rule the whole world, but his rule consists of just leaving mankind alone, and letting everyone exercise his own natural ability fully, freely. The *Tao* is nameless and so the sage who is one with the Tao is also nameless.

The Finite Point of View

The question that remains is this: How can a person become such a perfect man? To answer it, we must make an analysis of the second chapter of the Chuang-tzu, the "Chi Wu Lon," or "The Equality of Things and Opinions." In "The Happy Excursion"

Chuang Tzu discusses two levels of happiness, and in "The Equality of Things and Opinions" he discusses two levels of knowledge. Let us start our analysis with the first or lower level. In our chapter on the School of Names, we have said that there is some similarity between Hui Shih and Chuang Tzu. Thus in the "Chi Wu Lun,"

Chuang Tzu discusses knowledge of a lower level which is similar to that found in Hui Shih's ten so-called paradoxes.

The chapter "Chi Wu Lun" begins with a description of the wind. When the wind blows, there are different kinds of sounds, each with its own peculiarity. This chapter calls "the sounds of earth." But in addition there are other sounds that are known as "the sounds of man." The sounds of earth and the sounds of man together constitute the sounds of Heaven."

The sounds of man consist of the words (yen) that are spoken in the human world. They differ from such "sounds of earth" as those caused by the wind, inasmuch as when words are said, they represent human ideas. They represent affirmations and denials, and the opinions that are made by each individual from his own particular finite point of view. Being thus finite, these opinions are necessarily one-sided. Yet most men, not knowing that their opinions are based on finite points of view, invariably consider their own opinions as right and those of others are wrong. "The result," as the "Chi Wu Lun" says, "is the affirmations and denials of the Confucianists and Mohists, the one regarding as right what the other regards as wrong, and regarding as wrong what the other regards as right."

When people thus argue each according to his own one-sided view, there is no way either to reach a, final conclusion, or to determine which side is really right or really wrong. The "Chi Wu Lun" says: "Suppose that you argue with me. If you beat me, instead of my beating you, are you necessarily right and am I necessarily wrong? Or, if I beat you, and not you me, am I necessarily right and are you necessarily wrong? Is the one of us right and the other wrong? Or are both of us right or both of us wrong? Neither you nor I can know, and others are all the more in the dark. Whom shall we ask to produce the right decision? We may ask someone who agrees with you; but since he agrees with you, how can he make the decision? We may ask someone who agrees with me; but since he agrees with me, how can he make the decision? We may ask someone who agrees with both you and me; but since he agrees with both you and me, how can he make the decision? We may ask some one who differs from both you and me; but since he differs from both you and me, how can he make the decision?" This passage is reminiscent of the manner of argument followed by the School of Names. But whereas the members of that school argue thus in order to contradict the common sense of ordinary people, the purpose of the "Chi Wu Lun" is to contradict the followers of the School of Names. For this school did actually believe that argument could decide what is really right and really wrong.

Chuang Tzu, on the other hand, maintains that concepts of right and wrong are built up by each man on the basis of his own finite point of view. All these views are relative. As the "Chi Wu Lun" says: "When there is life, there is death; and when there is death, there is life. When there is possibility, there is impossibility, and when there is impossibility, there is possibility. Because there is right, there is wrong. Because there is wrong, there is right." Things are ever subject to change and have many aspects. Therefore many views can be held about one and the same things. Once we say this, we assume that a higher standpoint exists. If we accept this assumption, there is no need to make a decision ourselves about what is right and what is wrong. The argument explains itself.

The Higher Point of View

To accept this premise is to see things from a higher point of view, or, as the "Chi Wu Lun" calls it, to see things "in the light of Heaven." "To see things in the light of Heaven" means to see things from the point of view of that which transcends the finite, which is the *Tao*. It is said in the Chi Wu Lun:

> The "this" is also "that" The "that" is also "this." The "that" has a system of right and wrong. The "this" also has a system of right and wrong. Is there really a distinction between "that" and "this"? Or is there really no distinction between "that" and "this"? That the "that" and the "this" cease to be opposites is the very essence of *Tao*. Only the essence, an axis as it were, is the center of the circle responding to the endless changes. The right is an endless change. The wrong is also an endless change. Therefore it is said that there is nothing better than to use the "light."

In other words, the "that" and the "this," in their mutual opposition of right and wrong, are like an endlessly revolving circle. But the man who sees things from the point of view of the *Tao* stands, as it were, at the center of the circle. He understands all that is going on in the movements of the circle, but does not himself take part in these movements. This is not owing to his inactivity or resignation, but because he has transcended the finite and sees things from a higher point of view. In the Chuang-tzu, the finite point of view is compared with the view of the well-frog. The frog in the well can see only a little sky, and so thinks that the sky is only so big.

From the point of view of the *Tao*, everything is just what it is.

It is said in the Chi Wu Lun:

> The possible is possible. The impossible is impossible. The *Tao* makes things and they are what they are. What are they? They are what they are. What are they not? They are not what they are not. Everything is something and is good for something. There is nothing which is not something or is not good for something. Thus it is that there are roof-slats and pillars, ugliness and beauty, the peculiar and the extraordinary. All these by means of the *Tao* are united and become one.

Although all things differ, they are alike in that they all constitute something and are good for something. They all equally come from the *Tao*. Therefore from the viewpoint of the *Tao*, things, though different, yet are united and become one.

The Chi Wu Lun says again:

> To make a distinction is to make some construction. But construction is the same as destruction. For things as a whole there is neither construction nor destruction, but they turn to unity and become one. For example, when a table is made out of wood, from the viewpoint of that table, this is an act of construction. But from the viewpoint of the wood or the tree, it is one of destruction. Such construction or destruction are so, however, only from a finite point of view. From the viewpoint of the *Tao*, there is neither construction nor destruction. These distinctions are all relative. The distinction between the "me" and the "non-me" is also relative. From the viewpoint of the *Tao*, the "me" and the "non-me" are also united and become one.

The Chi Wu Lun says:

> There is nothing larger in the world than the point of a hair, yet Mount Tai is small. There is nothing older than a dead child, yet Peng Tsu [a legendary Chinese Methuselah] had an untimely death, Heaven and Earth and I came into existence together, and all things with me are one.

Here we again have Hui Shih's dictum "Love all things equally, Heaven and Earth are one body."

Knowledge of the Higher Level

This passage in the Chi Wu Lun, however, is immediately followed by another statement:

> Since all things are one, what room is there for speech? But since I have already spoken of the one, is this not already speech? One plus speech make two. Two plus one make three. Going on from this, even the most skillful reckoner will not be able to reach the end, and how much less able to do so are ordinary people! If proceeding from nothing to something we can reach three, how much further shall we reach, if we proceed from something to something! Let us not proceed. Let us stop here.

It is in this statement that the Chi Wu Lun goes a step further than Hui Shih, and begins to discuss a higher kind of knowledge. This higher knowledge is "knowledge which is not knowledge."

What is really "one" can neither be discussed nor even conceived. For as soon as it is thought of and discussed, it becomes something that exists externally to the person who is doing the thinking and speaking. So since its all-embracing unity is thus lost, it is actually not the real "one" at all. Hui Shih said: The greatest has nothing beyond itself and is called the Great One." By these words he described the Great One very well indeed, yet he remained unaware of the fact that since the Great One has nothing beyond itself, it is impossible either to think or speak of it. For anything that can be thought or spoken of has something beyond itself, namely, the thought and the speaking. The *Tao*ists, on the contrary, realized that the "one" is unthinkable and in expressible. Thereby, they had a true understanding of the "one" and advanced a step further than did the School of Names.

In the Chi Wu Lun it is also said:

> Referring to the right and the wrong, the "being so" and "not being so": if the right is really right, we need not dispute about how it is different from the wrong; if the "being so" is really being so, we need not dispute about how it is different from "not being so." ... Let us forget life. Let us forget the distinction between right and wrong. Let us take our joy in the realm of the infinite and remain there.

The realm of the infinite is the realm wherein lives the man who has attained to the *Tao*. Such a man not only has knowledge of the "one," but also has actually experienced it. This experience is the experience of living in the realm of the infinite. He has forgotten all the distinctions of things, even those involved in his own life. In his experience there remains only the undifferentiable one, in the midst of which he lives.

Described in poetical language, such a man is he "who chariots on the normality of the universe, rides on the transformations of the six elements, and thus makes excursion into the infinite." He is really the independent man, so his happiness is absolute.

Here we see how Chuang Tzu reached a final resolution of the original problem of the early *Tao*ists. That problem is how to preserve life and avoid harm and danger. But, to the real sage, it ceases to be a problem. As is said in the Chuang-tzu:

> The universe is the unity of all things. If we attain this unity and identify ourselves with it, then the members of our body are but so much dust and dirt, while life and death, end and beginning, are but as the succession of day and night, which cannot disturb our inner peace. How much less shall we be troubled by worldly gain and loss, good-luck and bad-luck![670]

Thus Chuang Tzu solved the original problem of the early *Tao*ists simply by abolishing it. This is really the philosophical way of solving problems. Philosophy

670 *Id.*, Ch. 20

gives no information about matters of fact, and so cannot solve any problem in a concrete and physical way. It cannot, for example, help man either to gain longevity or defy death, nor can it help him to gain riches and avoid poverty. What it can do, however, is to give man a point of view, from which he can see that life is no more than death and loss is equal to gain. From the "practical" point of view, philosophy is useless, yet it can give us a point of view which is very useful. To use an expression of the Chuang-tzu, this is the "usefulness of the useless."[671]

Spinoza has said that in a certain sense, the wise man "never ceases to be." This is also what Chuang Tzu means. The sage or perfect man is one with the Great One, that is, the universe. Since the universe never ceases to be, therefore the sage also never ceases to be. In the sixth chapter of the Chuang-tzu, we read: "A boat may be stored in a creek; a net may be stored in a lake; these may be said to be safe enough. But at midnight a strong man may come and carry them away on his back. The ignorant do not see that no matter how well you store things, smaller ones in larger ones, there will always be a chance for them to be lost. But if you store the universe in the universe, there will be no room left for it to be lost. This is the great truth of things. Therefore the sage makes excursions into that which cannot be lost, and together with it he remains." It is this sense that the sage never ceases to be.

Methodology of Mysticism

In order to be one with the Great One, the sage has to transcend and forget the distinctions between things. The way to do this is to discard knowledge, and is the method used by the Taoists for achieving "sageliness within." The task of knowledge in the ordinary sense is to make distinctions; to know a thing is to know the difference between it and other things. Therefore to discard knowledge means to forget these distinctions. Once all distinctions are forgotten, there remains only the undifferentiable one, which is the great whole. By achieving this condition, the sage may be said to have knowledge of another and higher level, which is called by the *Tao*ists "knowledge which is not knowledge."

In the *Chuang-tzu* there are many passages about the method of for getting distinctions. In the sixth chapter, for example, a report is given of an imaginary conversation between Confucius and his favorite disciple, Yen Hui. The story reads: "Yen Hui said: 'I have made some progress,' 'What do you mean?' asked Confucius.' I have forgotten human-heartedness and righteousness,' replied Yen Hui. 'Very well, but that is not enough,' said Confucius. Another day Yen Hui again saw Confucius and said: 'I have made some progress. "What do you mean?' asked Confucius. 'I have forgotten rituals and music,' replied Yen Hui. 'Very well, but that is not enough,' said Confucius. Another day Yen Hui again saw Confucius said: 'I have made some progress.' What do you mean?' asked Confucius. 'I sit in forgetfulness,' replied Yen Hui.

"At this Confucius changed countenance and asked 'What do you mean by

671 *Id.*, Ch. 4.

sitting in forgetfulness?" To which Yen Hui replied 'My limbs are nerveless and my intelligence is dimmed. I have abandoned my body and discarded my knowledge. Thus I become one with the Infinite. This is what I mean by sitting in forgetfulness." Then Confucius said 'If you have become one with the Infinite, you have no personal likes and dislikes. If you have become one with the Great Evolution [of the universe], you are one who merely follow its changes. If you really have achieved this, I should like to follow your steps.' "

Thus Yen Hui achieved "sageliness within" by discarding knowledge. The result of discarding knowledge is to have no knowledge. But there is a difference between "having-no knowledge" and "having no-knowledge." The state of "having-no knowledge" is one of original ignorance, whereas that of "having no-knowledge" comes only after one has passed through a prior stage of having knowledge. The former is a gift of nature, while the latter is an achievement of the spirit.

Some of the *Tao*ists saw this distinction very clearly. It is significant that they used the word "forget" to express the essential idea of their method. Sages are not persons who remain in a state of original ignorance. They at one time possessed ordinary know-ledge and made the usual distinctions, but they since forgot them. The difference between them and the man of original ignorance is as great as that between the courageous man and the man who does not fear simply because he is insensible to fear.

But there were also *Tao*ists, such as the authors of some chapters of the Chuang-tzu, who failed to see this difference. They admired the primitive state of society and mind, and compared sages with children and the ignorant. Children and the ignorant have no knowledge and do not make distinctions, so that they both seem to belong to the undifferentiable one. Their belonging to it, however, is entirely unconscious. They remain in the undifferentiable one, but they are not conscious of the fact. They are ones who have-no knowledge, but not who have no-knowledge. It is the latter acquired state of no-knowledge that the *Tao*ists call that of the "knowledge which is not knowledge."

XI THE LATER MOHISTS

In the *Mo-tzu,* there are six chapters (Chs. 40-45) which differ in character from the other chapters and possess a special logical interest. Of these, chapters forty to forty-one are titled "Canons" and consist of definitions of logical, moral, mathematical, and scientific ideas. Chapters forty-two to forty-three are titled "Expositions of the Canons," and consist of explanations of the definitions contained in the preceding two chapters. And chapters forty-four and forty-five are titled "Major Illustrations" and "Minor Illustrations" respectively. In them, several topics of logical interest are discussed. The general purpose of all six chapters is to uphold the Mohist point of view and refute, in a logical way, the arguments of the School of Names. The chapters as a whole are usually known as the "Mohist Canons."

In the last chapter we have seen that in the Chi Wu Lun, Chuang Tzu discussed two levels of knowledge. On the first level, he proved the relativity of things and reached the same conclusion as that of Hui Shih. But on the second level, he went beyond him. On the first level, he agreed with the School of Names and criticized common sense from a higher point of view. On the second level, however, he in turn criticized the School of Names from a still higher point of view. Thus the *Tao*ists refuted the arguments of the School of Names as well, but the arguments they used are, logically speaking, on a higher level than those of the School of Names. Both their arguments and those of the School of Names require an effort of reflective thinking to be understood. Both run counter to the ordinary canons of common sense.

The Mohists as well as some of the Confucianists, on the other hand, were philosophers of common sense. Though the two groups differed in many ways, they agreed with one another in being practical. In opposition to the arguments of the School of Names, they developed, almost along similar lines of thought, epistemological and logical theories to defend common sense.

These theories appear in the "Mohist Canons" and in the chapter titled "On the Rectification of Names" in the Hsun-tzu, the author of which, as we shall see in Chapter Thirteen, was one of the greatest Confucianists of the early period.

Discussions on Knowledge and Names

The epistemological theory set forth in the "Mohist Canons" is a kind of naive realism. There is, it maintains, a knowledge faculty which "is that by means of which one knows, but which itself does not necessarily know."[672] The reason for this is that, in order to have knowledge, the knowing faculty must be confronted with an object of knowledge. "Knowledge is that in which the knowing [faculty] meets the object and is able to apprehend its form and shape."[673] Besides the sensory organs for knowing, such as those of seeing and hearing, there also

672 *Mo-tzu,* Ch. 42.
673 *Id.,* Ch. 42.

exists the mind, which is "that by means of which one understands the object of knowledge."[674] In other words, the mind interprets the impressions of external objects which are brought to it by the senses.

The "Mohist Canons" also provide various logical classifications of knowledge. From the point of view of its source, knowledge is to be classified into three types that derived through the personal experience of the knower; that transmitted to him by authority (i.e., obtained by him either through hearsay or written records); and knowledge by inference (i.e., obtained through making deductions on the basis of what is known about what is unknown). Also from the point of view of the various objects of knowledge, it is to be classified into four kinds: knowledge of names, that of actualities, that of correspondence, and that of action.[675]

It will be remembered that names, actualities, and their relationships to one another, were the particular interest of the School of Names. According to the "Mohist Canons," "a name is that with which one speaks about a thing," while "an actuality is that about which one speaks."[676] When one says: "This is a table," "table" is a name, and is that with which one speaks about "this," while "this" is the actuality about which one is speaking. Expressed in terms of Western logic, a name is the predicate of a proposition, and an actuality is the subject of it.

In the "Mohist Canons," names are classified into three kinds: general, classifying, and private.

"Thing" is a general name. All actualities must bear this name.

"Horse" is a classifying name. All actualities of that sort must have that name. "Tsang" [the name of a person] is a private name. This name is restricted to this actuality.[677]

The knowledge of correspondence is that which knows which name corresponds to which actuality. Such kind of knowledge is required for the statement of such a proposition as: "This is a table."When one has this kind of knowledge, one knows that "names and actualities pair with each other."[678]

The knowledge of action is the knowledge of how to do a certain thing. This is what Americans call "know-how."

Discussions on Dialectic

Of the chapter titled "Minor illustrations," a large part is devoted to the discussions of dialectic. This chapter says:

> Dialectic serves to make clear the distinction between right and wrong, to discriminate between order and disorder, to make evident points of similarity and difference, to examine the principles of names and actualities, to differentiate what is beneficial and what is harmful, and to remove doubts

---

674 *Ibid.*
675 *Id.*, Ch. 40.
676 *Id.*, Ch. 42.
677 *Id.*, Ch. 42.
678 *Ibid.*

and uncertainties. It observes the happenings of all things, and investigates the order and relation between the various judgments. It uses names to designate actualities, propositions to express ideas, statements to set forth causes, and taking and giving according to classes.[679]

The first part of this passage deals with the purpose and function of dialectic the second part with its methodology. In another part of the same chapter, it is said that there are seven methods of dialectic:

A particular judgment indicates what is not all so. A hypothetical judgment indicates what is at present not so. Imitation consists in taking a model. What is imitated is what is taken as a model. If the cause is in agreement with the imitation, it is correct. If it is not in agreement with the imitation, it is not correct. This is the method of imitation. The method of comparison consists in using one thing to explain another. The method of parallel consists in comparing two series of propositions consistently throughout. The method of analogy says: "You are so. Why should I alone not be so?" The method of extension consists in attributing the same to what is not known as to what is known. When the other is said to be the same [as this], how can I say that it is different?"[680]

The method of imitation in this passage is the same as that of "using statements to set forth causes" of the preceding quotation.

And the method of extension is the same as the "taking and giving according to classes" of the preceding passage. These are the two most important of the methods, and correspond roughly to the deductive and inductive methods of Western logic.

Before giving further explanation of these two methods, something may be said regarding what in the "Mohist Canons" Is called a cause. A cause is defined as "that with which something becomes," and is also classified into two kinds, the major and minor.[681] "A minor cause is one with which something may not necessarily be so, but without which it will never be so." "A major cause is one with which something will necessarily be so, and without which it will never be so."[682] It is evident that what the "Mohist Canons" call a minor cause is what in modern logic would be called a necessary cause, while what the "Mohist Canons" call a major cause is what modern logic would describe as a necessary and sufficient cause. In modern logic there is the distinction of yet another kind of cause, the sufficient cause, which is one with which something will necessarily be so, but without which it may or may not be so. This distinction the Mohists failed to make.

In modern logical reasoning, if we want to know whether a general proposition is true or not, we verify it with facts or experiment. If, for example, we want to make sure that certain bacteria are the cause of a certain disease, the way to verify the matter is to take as a formula the general proposition that the bacteria A are the cause of the disease B, and then make an experiment to see whether the supposed cause really produces the expected result or not. If it does, it really is the cause; if

679 *Id*, Ch. 45.
680 *Id*., Ch. 45.
681 *Id*., Ch. 40.
682 *Id*., Ch. 42.

not, it is not. This is deductive reasoning and is also what the "Mohist Canons" call the method of imitation. For to take a general proposition as a formula is to take it as a model, and to make an experiment with it is to make an imitation of it. That the supposed cause produces the expected result, means that "the cause is in agreement with the imitation." And that it does not, means that "the cause is not in agreement with the imitation." It is in this way that we can distinguish a true from a false cause, and determine whether a cause is a major or minor one.

As regards the other form of reasoning through extension, it may be illustrated through the dictum that all men are mortal. We are able to make this dictum, because we know that all men of the past were mortal, and that men of today and of the future are the same in kind as those of the past. Hence we draw the general conclusion that all men are mortal. In this inductive reasoning, we use "the method of extension." That men of the past were mortal is what is known. And that men of today and of the future are and will be mortal is what is not known. To say that all men are mortal, therefore, is "to attribute the same to what is not known as to what is known." We can do this because "the other is said to be the same [as this]." We are "taking and giving according to class."

Clarification of All-embracing Love

Versed in the method of dialectic, the later Mohists did much in clarifying and defending the philosophical position of their school.

Following the tradition of Mo Tzu's utilitarianistic philosophy the later Mohists maintain that all human activities aim at obtaining benefit and avoiding harm. Thus in the "Major Illustrations" we are told:

> When one cuts a finger in order to preserve a hand, this is to choose the greater benefit and the lesser harm. To choose the lesser harm is not to choose harm, but to choose benefit.... If on meeting a robber one loses a finger so as to save one's life, this is benefit. The meeting with the robber is harm. Choice of the greater benefit is not a thing done under compulsion. Choice of the lesser harm is a thing done under compulsion. The former means choosing from what has not yet been obtained. The latter means discarding from what one has already been burdened with.[683]

Thus for all human activities the rule is: "Of the benefits, choose the greatest; of the harms, choose the slightest."[684]

Both Mo Tzu and the later Mohists identified the good with the beneficial. Beneficialness is the essence of the good. But what is the essence of beneficialness? Mo Tzu did not raise this question, but the later Mohists did and gave an answer. In the first "Canon," it is said "The beneficial is that with the obtaining of which one is pleased. The harmful is that with the obtaining of which one is displeased."[685] Thus the later Mohists provided a hedonistic justification for the utillitarianistic philosophy of the Mohist school.

683 *Id.*, Ch. 44.
684 *Ibid.*
685 *Id.*, Ch. 40.

This position reminds us of the "principle of utility" of Jeremy Bentham. In his *Introduction to the Principles of Morals and Legislation*, Bentham says:

> Nature has placed mankind under the governance of two sovereign masters, pain and pleasure. It is for them alone to point out what we ought to do.... The principle of utility recognizes this subjection, and assumes it for the foundation of that system, the object of which is to rear the fabric of felicity by the hands of reason and law.[686]

Thus Bentham reduces good and bad to a question of pleasure and pain. According to him the aim of morality is "the greatest happiness of the greatest number."[687]

This is also what the later Mohists do. Having defined "the beneficial," they go on to define the virtues in the light of this concept. Thus in the first "Canon" we find "Righteousness consists in doing the beneficial." "Loyalty consists in benefiting one's ruler." "Filial piety consists in benefiting one's parents." "Meritorious accomplishment consists in benefiting the people."[688] "Benefiting the people" means "the greatest happiness of the greatest number."

Regarding the theory of all-embracing love, the later Mohists maintain that its major attribute is its all-embracing character. In the "Minor illustrations" we read:

> In loving men one needs to love all men before one can regard oneself as loving men. In not loving men one does not need not to love any man [before one can regard oneself as not loving men]. Not to have all-embracing love is not to love men. When riding horses, one need not ride all horses in order to regard oneself as riding a horse. For if one rides only a few horses, one is still riding horses. But when not riding horses, one must ride no horse at all in order to regard oneself as not riding horses. This is the difference between all-inclusiveness [in the case of loving men] and the absence of all-inclusiveness [in the case of riding horses].[689]

Every man, as a matter of fact, has someone whom he loves.

Every man, for example, loves his own children. Hence the mere fact that a man loves someone does not mean that he loves men in general. But on the negative side, the fact that he does wrong to someone, even his own children, does mean that he does not love men. Such is the reasoning of the Mohists.

Defense of All-embracing Love

Against this view of the later Mohists, there were at that time two main objections. The first was that the number of men in the world is infinite; how, then, is it possible for one to love them all? This objection was referred to under the title: "Infinity is incompatible with all-embracing love." And the second objection was that if failure to love a single man means failure to love men in general, there should then be no such punishment as "killing a robber." This objection was known under the title: "To kill a robber is to kill a man." The later Mohists used their dialectic to try to refute these objections.

686 Jeremy Bentham, *Introduction to the Principles of Morals and Legislation*, P. 1.

687 *Ibid.*

688 *Mo-tzu*, Ch.40.

689 *Id*, Ch. 44.

In the second "Canon" there is the statement: "Infinity is not incompatible with all-embracingness. The reason is given under 'full or not.'"[690] The second "Exposition of the Canons" develops this statement as follows:

> Infinity: (Objection:) "If the South has a limit, it can be included in toto. [There was a common belief in ancient China that the South had no limit.] If it has no limit, it cannot be included in toto. It is impossible to know whether it has a limit or not and hence it is impossible to know whether it can all be included or not. It is impossible to know whether people fill this [space] or not, and hence it is impossible to know whether they can be included in toto or not. This being so, it is perverse to hold that all people can be included in our love." (Answer:)"If people do not fill what is unlimited, then [the number of] people has a limit, and there is no difficulty in including anything that is limited [in number]. But if people do fill what is unlimited, then what is [supposed to be] unlimited is limited, and then there is no difficulty in including what is limited."[691]

"To kill a robber is to kill a man" is the other major objection to the Mohists, because killing a man is not consistent with loving all men equally and universally. To this objection the "Minor Illustrations" answers as follows:

> A white horse is a horse. To ride a white horse is to ride a horse. A black horse is a horse. To ride a black horse is to ride a horse. Huo [name of a person] is a man. To love Huo is to love a man. Tsang [name of a person] is a man. To love Tsang is to love a man. This is to affirm what is right.

But Huo's parents are men. Yet when Huo serves his parents, he is not serving men. His younger brother is a handsome man. Yet when he loves his younger brother, he is not loving handsome men. A cart is wood, but to ride a cart is not to ride wood. A boat is wood, but to ride a boat is not to ride wood. A robber is a man, but that there are many robbers does not mean that there are many men; and that there are no robbers does not mean that there are no men.

How is this explained? To hate the existence of many robbers is not to hate the existence of many men. To wish that there were no robbers is not to wish that there were no men. The world generally agrees on this. And this being the case, although a robber-man is a man, yet to love robbers is not to love men, and not to love robbers is not to love men. Likewise to kill a robber-man is not to kill a man. There is no difficulty in this proposition.[692]

With such dialectic as this the later Mohists refuted the objection that the killing of a robber is inconsistent with their principle of all-embracing love.

Criticism of Other Schools

Using their dialectic, the later Mohists not only refute the objections of other schools against them, but also make criticisms of their own against these schools. For example, the "Mohist Canons" contain a number of objections against the

690 *Id.*, Ch. 40.
691 *Id.*, Ch. 43.
692 *Id.*, Ch. 45.

arguments of the School of Names. Hui Shih, it will be remembered, had argued for the "unity of similarity and difference." In his ten paradoxes he passed from the premise that "all things are similar to each other, "to the conclusion: "Love all things equally. Heaven and Earth are one body." This, for the later Mohists, is a fallacy arising from the ambiguity of the Chinese word *tung*. Tung may be variously used to mean "identity," "agreement," or "similarity." In the first "Canon" there is a statement which reads: "Tung: There is that of identity, that of part-and-whole relationship, that of coexistence, and that of generic relation."[693] And the "Exposition" explains further: "Tung: That there are two names for one actuality is identity. Inclusion in one whole is part-and-whole relationship. Both being in the same room is coexistence. Having some points of similarity is generic relation."[694] The same "Canon" and "Exposition" also have a discussion on "difference," which is just the reverse of *tung*.

The "Mohist Canons" fail actually to mention Hui Shih by name. As a matter of fact, no name is ever mentioned in these chapters.

But from this analysis of the word tung, Hui Shih's fallacy becomes clear. That all things are similar to each other means that they have generic relationship that they are of the same class, the class of "things." But that Heaven and Earth are one body means that they have a part-and-whole relationship. The truth of the one proposition as applied to a particular situation cannot be inferred from the truth of the other, even though the same word, tung, is used in both cases.

As regards Kungsun Lung's argument for "the separation of hardness and whiteness," the later Mohists thought only in terms of concrete hard and white stones as they actually exist in the physical universe. Hence they maintained that the qualities of hardness and whiteness both simultaneously inhere in the stone. As a result, they "are not mutually exclusive," but "must pervade each other."[695]

The later Mohists also criticized the *Tao*ists. In the second "Canon" we read "Learning is useful. The reason is given by those who oppose it."[696] The second "Exposition" comments on this:

> "Learning: By maintaining that people do not know that learning is useless, one is thereby informing them of this fact. This informing that learning is useless, is itself a teaching. Thus by holding that learning is useless, one teaches. This is perverse."[697]

This is a criticism of a statement in the Lao-tzu: "Banish learning and there will be no grieving."[698] According to the later Mohists, learning and teaching are related terms. If learning is to be banished, so is teaching. For once there is teaching, there is also learning, and if teaching is useful, learning cannot be useless. The very teaching that learning is useless proves in itself that it is useful.

693 *Id.*, Ch. 40.
694 *Id.*, Ch. 42.
695 *Id.*, Chs. 40, 42.
696 *Id.*, Ch. 41.
697 *Id.*, Ch. 43.
698 *Id.*, Ch. 20.

In the second "Canon" we read: "To say that in argument there is no winner is necessarily incorrect. The reason is given under 'argument'." The second "Exposition" comments on this:

> In speaking, what people say either agrees or disagrees? There is agreement when one person says something is a puppy, and another says it is a dog. There is disagreement when one says it is an ox, and another says it is a horse. [That is to say, when there is disagreement, there is argument.] When neither of them wins, there is no argument. Argument is that in which one person says the thing is so, and another says it is not so. The one who is right will win.[699]

In the second "Canon" we also read: "To hold that all speech is perverse is perverse. The reason is given under 'speech.'"[700] The second "Exposition" comments on this:

[To hold that all speech] is perverse, is not permissible. If the speech of this man [who holds this doctrine] is permissible, then at least this speech is not perverse, and there is some speech that is permissible. If the speech of this man is not permissible, then it is wrong to take it as being correct.[701]

The second "Canon" also says: "That knowing it and not knowing it are the same, is perverse. The reason is given under 'no means.'"[702] And the second "Exposition" comments: "When there is knowledge, there is discussion about it. Unless there is knowledge, there is no means [of discussion]."[703]

Yet again the second "Canon" states: "To condemn criticism is perverse. The reason is given under 'not to condemn.'"[704] On which the second "Exposition" comments: "To condemn criticism is to condemn one's own condemnation. If one does not condemn it, there is nothing to be condemned. When one cannot condemn it, this means not to condemn criticism."[705]

These are all criticisms against Chuang Tzu. Chuang Tzu maintained that nothing can be decided in argument. Even if someone wins, he said, the winner is not necessarily right or the loser necessarily wrong. But according to the later Mohists, Chuang Tzu, by expressing this very doctrine, showed himself in disagreement with others and was himself arguing. If he won the argument, did not this very fact prove him to be wrong? Chuang Tzu also said:"Great argument does not require words." And again: "Speech that argues falls short of its aim."[706] Hence "all speech is perverse." Furthermore, he held that everything is right in its own way and in its own opinion, and one should not criticize the other.[707] But according to the later Mohists, what Chuang Tzu said itself consists of speech and itself constitutes a criticism against others. So if all speech is perverse, is not

699 *Mo-tzu*, Ch. 42
700 *Id.*, Ch. 41.
701 *Id.*, Ch. 43.
702 *Id.*, Ch. 41.
703 *Id.*, Ch. 43.
704 *Id.*, Ch. 41.
705 *Id.*, Ch. 43.
706 Chuang-tzu, Ch. 2
707 *Ibid.*

this saying of Chuang Tzu also perverse? And if all criticism against others is to be condemned, then Chuang Tzu's criticism should be condemned first of all. Chuang Tzu also talked much about the importance of having no knowledge. But such discussion is itself a form of knowledge. When there is no knowledge, there can be no discussion about it.

In criticizing the *Tao*ists, the later Mohists pointed out certain logical paradoxes that have also appeared in Western philosophy. It is only with the development of a new logic in recent times that these paradoxes have been solved. Thus in contemporary logic, the criticisms made by the later Mohists are no longer valid. Yet it is interesting to note that the later Mohists were so logically minded. More than any other school of ancient China, they attempted to create a pure system of epistemology and logic.

XII THE YIN-YANG SCHOOL AND EARLY CHINESE COSMOGONY

In the second chapter of this book I said that the *Yin-Yang* School had its origin in the occultists. These occultists were anciently known as the *fang shih*, that is, practitioner of occult arts. In the "Treatise on Literature" (Ch. 30) in the *History of the Former Han Dynasty*, which is based on the *Seven Summaries* by Liu Hsin, these occult arts are grouped into six classes.

The Six Classes of Occult Arts

The first is astrology. "Astrology," says this chapter in the *Han History*, "serves to arrange in order the twenty-eight constellations, and note the progressions of the five planets and of the sun and the moon, so as to record thereby the manifestations of fortune and misfortune"

The second deals with almanacs. "Almanacs," says the same treatise, "serve to arrange the four seasons in proper order, to adjust the times of the equinoxes and solstices, and to note the concordance of the periods of the sun, moon, and five planets, so as thereby to examine into the actualities of cold and heat, life and death....Through this art, the miseries of calamities and the happiness of prosperity all appear manifest."

The third is connected with the Five Elements. "This art," says the "Treatise on Literature," "arises from the revolutions of the Five Powers [Five Elements], and if it is extended to its farthest limits, there is nothing to which it will not reach."

The fourth is divination by means of the stalks of the milfoil plant and that done with the tortoise shell or shoulder bones of the ox. These were the two main methods of divination in ancient China. In the latter method, the diviner bored a hole in a tortoise shell or a flat piece of bone, and then applied heat to it by a metal rod in such a way as to cause cracks to radiate from the hole. These cracks were interpreted by the diviner according to their configuration as an answer to the question asked. In the former method the diviner manipulated the stalks of the milfoil in such a way as to produce certain numerical combinations which could be interpreted by means of the Book of Changes. Such interpretation was the primary purpose of the original corpus of this work.

The fifth group is that of miscellaneous divinations and the sixth is the system of forms. The latter included physiognomy together with what in later times has been known as feng-shui, literally, "wind and water." Feng-shui is based on the concept that man is the product of the universe. Hence his house or burial place must be so arranged as to be in harmony with the natural forces, i.e., with "wind and water."

In the days when feudalism was in its prime during the early centuries of the Chou Dynasty, every aristocratic house had attached to it hereditary experts in these various occult arts, who had to be consulted when any act of importance was contemplated. But with the gradual disintegration of feudalism, many of these experts lost their hereditary positions and scattered throughout the country, where they continued to practice their arts among the people. They then came to be known as the fang shih or practitioners of occult arts.

Occultism or magic is itself, of course, based on superstition, but it has often been the origin of science. The occult arts share with science the desire to interpret nature in a positive manner, and to acquire the services of nature through its conquest by man. Occultism becomes science when it gives up its belief in supernatural forces, and tries to interpret the universe solely in terms of forces that are natural. The concepts of what these natural forces are may in themselves initially look rather simple and crude, yet in them we find the beginnings of science.

Such has been the contribution of the *Yin-Yang* school to Chinese thought. This school represents a scientific tendency in the sense that it tried to give a positive interpretation to natural events in terms solely of natural forces. By the word positive I mean that which has to do with matters of fact.

In ancient China there were two lines of thought that thus tried to interpret the structure and origin of the universe. One is found in the writings of the *Yin-Yang* school, while the other is found in some of the "Appendices" added by anonymous Confucianists to the original text of the Book of Changes. These two lines of thought seem to have developed independently. In the "Grand Norm" and "Monthly Commands," which we will examine below, there is stress on the Five Elements but no mention of the *Yin* and Yang; in the "Appendices" of the Book of Changes, on the contrary, much is said about the *Yin* and Yang, but nothing about the Five Elements. Later, however, these two lines of thought became intermingled. This was already the case by the time of Ssuma Tan (died 110 B.C.) so that in the Historical Records he lumps them together as the *Yin-Yang* school.

The Five Elements as Described in the "Grand Norm"

The term *Wu Hsing* is usually translated as the Five Elements. We should not think of them as static, however, but rather as five dynamic and interacting forces. The Chinese word hsing means "to act" or "to do," so that the term *Wu Hsing*, literally translated, would mean the Five Activities, or Five Agents. They are also known as the *Wu Te*, which means Five Powers.

The term *Wu Hsing* appears in a text traditionally said to antedate the 20th century B.C. (See the *Book of History*, Part III. Book II, Ch. I, 3.) The authenticity of this text cannot be proved, however, and even if it were proved, we cannot be sure whether the term *Wu Hsing* means the same thing in it as it does in other texts whose date is better fixed. The first really authentic account of the *Wu Hsing*, therefore, is to be found in another section of the *Book of History* (Pan V, Book 4), known as the *Hung Fan* or "Great Plan" or "Grand Norm." Traditionally, the "Grand Norm" is said to be the record of a speech delivered to King Wu of the Chou Dynasty by the Viscount of Chi, a prince of the Shang Dynasty which King Wu conquered at the end of the 12th century B.C. In this speech, the Viscount of *Chi* in turn attributes his ideas to Yu, traditional founder of the Hsia Dynasty who is said to have lived in the 22nd century B.C. These traditions are mentioned as examples of the way the writer of this treatise tried to give importance to the Wu Hsing theory. As to the actual date of the "Grand Norm," modern scholarship inclines to place it within the 4th or 3rd centuries B.C.

In the "Grand Norm" we are given a list of "Nine Categories."

"First [among the categories]," we read, "is that of the Wu Hsing. The first [of these] is named Water; the second, Fire; the third, Wood; the fourth, Metal; the fifth, Soil. [The nature of] Water is to moisten and descend; of Fire, to flame and ascend; of Wood, to be crooked and straighten; of Metal, to yield and to be modified; of Soil, to provide for sowing and reaping."

Next comes the category of the Five Functions. "Second," we read, "is that of the Five Functions. The first [of these] is personal appearance; the second, speech; the third, vision; the fourth, hearing; the fifth, thought. Personal appearance should be decorous; speech should follow order; vision should be clear; hearing, distinct; thought, profound. Decorum produces solemnity; following order, regularity; clearness, intelligence; distinctness, deliberation; profundity, wisdom."

Skipping now to the eighth of the Nine Categories, we come to what the "Grand Norm" calls the various indications: "The eighth is that of various indications. These are rain, sunshine, heat, cold, wind, and seasonableness. When these five come fully and in their regular order, the various plants will be rich and luxuriant. If there is extreme excess in any of them, disaster follows. The following are the favorable indications: the solemnity of the sovereign will be followed by seasonable rain; his regularity, by seasonable sun-shine; his intelligence, by seasonable heat; his deliberation, by seasonable cold; his wisdom, by seasonable wind. The following are the unfavorable indications: the madness of the sovereign will be followed by steady rain; his insolence, by steady sunshine; his idleness, by steady heat; his haste, by steady cold; his ignorance, by steady wind."

In the "Grand Norm" we find that the idea of the Wu Hsing is still crude. In speaking of them, its author is still thinking in terms of the actual substances, water, fire, etc., instead of abstract forces bearing these names, as the Wu Hsing came to be regarded later on. The author also tells us that the human and natural worlds are interlinked; bad conduct on the part of the sovereign results in the appearance of abnormal phenomena in the world of nature. This theory, which was greatly developed by the *Yin-Yang* school in later times, is known as that of "the mutual influence between nature and man."

Two theories have been advanced to explain the reasons for this interaction. One is teleological. It maintains that wrong conduct on the part of the sovereign causes Heaven to become angry. That anger results in abnormal natural phenomena, which represent warnings given by Heaven to the sovereign. The other theory is mechanistic. It maintains that the sovereign's bad conduct automatically results in a disturbance of nature and thus mechanically produces abnormal phenomena. The whole universe is a mechanism. When one part of it becomes out of order, the other part must be mechanically affected. This theory represents the scientific spirit of the *Yin-Yang* school, while the other reflects its occult origin.

The "Monthly Commands"

The next important document of the *Yin-Yang* school is the *Yueh Ling* or "Monthly Commands," which is first found in the *Lu-shih Chun-chiu*, a work of the late 3rd century B.C., and later was also embodied in the *Li Chi* (*Book of Rites*). The "Monthly Commands" gains its name from the fact that it is a small almanac which tells the ruler and men generally what they should do month by month in order to retain harmony with the forces of nature. In it, the structure of the universe is described in terms of the *Yin-Yang* school. This structure is spacio-temporal, that is, it relates both to space and to time. The ancient Chinese, being situated in the northern hemisphere, quite naturally regarded the south as the direction of heat and the north as that of cold. Hence the *Yin-Yang* school correlated the four seasons with the four compass points. Summer was correlated with the south; winter with the north; spring with the east, because it is the direction to sunrise, and autumn with the west, because this is the direction of sunset. The school also regarded the changes of day and night as representing, on a miniature scale, the changes of the four seasons of the year. Thus morning is a miniature representation of spring; noon, of summer; evening, of autumn; and night, of winter.

South and summer are hot, because south is the direction and summer the time in which the Power or Element of Fire is dominant. North and winter are cold, because north is the direction and winter the time in which the Power of Water is dominant, and water is associated with ice and snow, which are cold. Likewise, the Power of Wood is dominant in the east and in spring, because spring is the time when plants (symbolized by "wood") begin to grow and the east is correlated with spring. The Power of Metal is dominant in the west and in autumn, because metal was regarded as something hard and harsh, and autumn is the bleak time when growing plants reach their end, while the west is correlated with autumn. Thus four of the five Powers are accounted for, leaving only the Power of Soil without a fixed place and season. According to the "Monthly Commands," however, Soil is the central of the Five Powers, and so occupies a place at the center of the four compass points. Its time of domination is said to be a brief interim period coming between summer and autumn.

With such a cosmological theory, the *Yin-Yang* school tried to explain natural phenomena both in terms of time and space, and furthermore maintained that these phenomena are closely interrelated with human conduct. Hence, as stated above, the "Monthly Commands" sets forth regulations as to what the sovereign should do month by month, which is the reason for its name.

Thus we are told "In the first month of spring the east wind resolves the cold. Creatures that have been torpid during the winter begin to move.... It is in this month that the vapors of heaven descend and those of earth ascend. Heaven and earth are in harmonious cooperation. All plants bud and grow."[708]

Because man's conduct should be in harmony with the way of nature, we are told that in this month, "He the sovereign] charges his assistants to disseminate [lessons of] virtue and harmonize governmental orders, so as to give effect to the expressions of his satisfaction and to bestow his favors to the millions of the people.... Prohibitions are issued against cutting down trees. Nests should not be thrown down.... In this month no warlike operations should be undertaken; the undertaking of such is sure to be followed by calamities from Heaven. This avoidance of warlike operations means that they are not to be commenced on our side."

If, in each month, the sovereign fails to act in the manner befitting that month, but instead follows the conduct appropriate to another month, abnormal natural phenomena will result. "If in the first month of spring, the governmental proceedings proper to summer are carried out, rain will fall unseasonably, plants and trees will decay prematurely, and the state will be kept in continual fear. If the proceedings proper to autumn are carried out, there will be great pestilence among the people, boisterous winds will work their violence, and rain will descend in torrents.... If the proceedings proper to winter are carried out, pools of water will produce destructive effects, and snow and frost will prove very injurious..."

Tsou Yen

A major figure of the *Yin-Yang* school in the 3rd century B.C. was Tsou Yen. According to Ssuma Chien's Shih *Chi* or Historical Records, Tsou Yen was a native of the State of *Chi* in the central part of present Shandong Province, and lived shortly after Mencius. He "wrote essays totaling more than a hundred thousand words," but all have since been lost. In the Historical Records itself, however, Ssuma Chien gives a fairly detailed account of Tsou Yen's theories. According to this work (Ch. 74), Tsou Yen's method was "first to examine small objects, and to extend this to large ones until he reached what was without limit." His interests seem to have been centered on geography and history.

As regards geography, Ssuma Chien writes:

> He began by classifying China's notable mountains, great rivers and connecting valleys; its birds and beasts; the productions of its waters and soils, and its rare products; and from this he extended his survey to what is beyond the seas, and which men are unable to see.... He maintained that what scholars call the Middle Kingdom (i.e., China) holds a place in the whole world of but one part in eighty-one. He named China the Spiritual Continent of the Red Region.... Besides China [there are other continents] similar to the Spiritual Continent of the Red Region, making (with China] a total of nine continents.... Around each of these is a small

708 *Book of Rites*, Ch. 4.

encircling sea, so that men and beasts cannot pass from one to another. These [nine continents] form one division. There are nine divisions like this. Around their outer edge is a vast ocean which encompasses them at the point where heaven and earth meet.

As regards Tsou Yen's historical concepts, Ssuma Chien writes:

He first spoke about modern times, and from this went back to the time of Huang Ti [the legendary Yellow Emperor], all of which has been recorded by scholars. Moreover, he followed the great events in the rise and fall of ages, recorded their omens and institutions, and extended his survey backward to the time when heaven and earth had not yet been born, to what was profound and abstruse and not to be examined.... Starting from the time of the separation of heaven and earth and coming down, he made citations of the revolutions and transformations of the Five Powers, and the [different ways of] government and different omens appropriate to each of the Powers.

A Philosophy of History

The last few lines of the quotation show that Tsou Yen developed a new philosophy of history, according to which historical changes are interpreted in accordance with the revolutions and transformations of the Five Powers. The details of this theory are not reported by Ssuma Chien, but it is treated in one section of the Lu-shih Chun-ii, even though in this section Tsou Yen's name is not explicitly mentioned. Thus this work states (XIII, 2):

Whenever an emperor or king is about to arise, Heaven must first manifest some favorable omen to the common people. In the time of the Yellow Emperor, Heaven first made huge earthworms and mole crickets appear. The Yellow Emperor said: "The force of Soil is in ascendancy." Therefore he assumed yellow as his color, and took Soil as the pattern for his affairs.

In the time of Yu [founder of the Hsia Dynasty] Heaven first made grass and trees appear which did not die in the autumn and winter. Yu said "The force of Wood is in ascendancy." Therefore he assumed green as his color and took Wood as the pattern for his affairs.

In the time of Tang [founder of the Shang Dynasty] Heaven made some knife blades appear in the water. Tang said: "The force of Metal is in ascendancy." He therefore assumed white as his color and took Metal as the pattern for his affairs.

In the time of King Wen [founder of the Chou Dynasty] Heaven made a flame appear, while a red bird, holding a red book in its mouth, alighted on the altar of soil of the House of Chou. King Wen said: "The force of Fire is in ascendancy." Therefore he assumed red as his color, and took Fire as the pattern of his affairs.

Water will inevitably be the next force that will succeed Fire. Heaven will first make the ascendancy of Water manifest. The force of Water being in ascendancy, black will be assumed as its color, and Water will be taken as the pattern for affairs.... When the cycle is complete, the operation will revert once more to Soil.

The *Yin-Yang* school maintained that the Five Elements produce one another and also overcome one another in a fixed sequence.

It also maintained that the sequence of the four seasons accords with this process of the mutual production of the Elements. Thus Wood, which dominates spring, produces Fire, which dominates summer. Fire in its turn produces Soil, which dominates the "center"; Soil again produces Metal, which dominates autumn; Metal produces Water, which dominates winter; and Water again produces Wood, which dominates spring.

According to the above quotation, the succession of dynasties likewise accords with the natural succession of the Elements. Thus Earth, under whose Power the Yellow Emperor ruled, was overcome by the Wood of the Hsia Dynasty. The Wood of this dynasty was overcome by the Metal of the Shang Dynasty, Metal was overcome by the Fire of the Chou Dynasty, and Fire would in its turn be overcome by the Water of whatever dynasty was to follow the Chou. The Water of this dynasty would then again be overcome by the Soil of the dynasty following, thus completing the cycle.

As described in the Lu-shih Chun-chiu, this is but a theory, but soon afterwards it had its effect in practical politics. Thus in the year 221 B.C., the First Emperor of the Chin Dynasty, known as Chin Shih Huang-Ti (246-210 B.C.) conquered all the rival feudal states and thus created a unified Chinese empire under the Chin.

As the successor to the Chou Dynasty, he actually believed that the force of Water is in ascendancy," and so, according to Ssuma Chien's Historical Records "assumed black as his color" and "took Water as the pattern for affairs."

The name of the Yellow River was changed to that of Power Water, because it was supposed to mark the beginning of the Power of Water. With harshness and violence, and an extreme severity, everything was decided by the law. For by punishing and oppressing, by having neither human-heartedness nor kindness, but only conforming to strict justice, there would come an accord with [the transformations of] the Five Powers.[709]

Because of its very harshness, the Chin Dynasty did not last long, and was soon succeeded by that of Han (206 B.C.-A.D. 220) The Han emperors also believed that they had become emperors "by virtue of one of the Five Powers, but there was considerable dispute as to which of the Powers it was. This was because some people maintained that the Han was the successor of the Chin, and therefore ruled through Soil, whereas others maintained that the Chin had been too harsh and short to be counted as a legitimate dynasty, so that the Han Dynasty was actually the successor of the Chou. Support for both sides was found from many omens which were subject to varying interpretations. Finally, in 104 B.C., the emperor Wu decided and formally announced that Soil was the Power for the Han. Even afterwards, however, there were still differences of opinion.

Following the Han Dynasty, people no longer paid very much attention to this question. Yet as late as 1911, when the last dynasty was brought to an end

709 *Historical Records*, Ch. 6.

by the Republic of China, the official title of the Emperor was still "Emperor through [the Mandate of] Heaven and in accordance with the Movements [of the Five Powers]."

The Yin and Yang Principles as Described in the "Appendices" of the Book of Changes

The theory of the Five Elements interpreted the structure of the universe, but did not explain the origin of the world. This was provided by the theory of the *Yin* and Yang.

The word *yang* originally meant sunshine, or what pertains to sunshine and light; that of *yin* meant the absence of sunshine, i.e., shadow or darkness. In later development, the *Yang* and *Yin* came to be regarded as two cosmic principles or forces, respectively representing masculinity, activity, heat, brightness, dryness, hardness, etc., for the Yang, and femininity, passivity, cold, darkness, wetness, softness, etc., for the *Yin*. Through the interaction of these two primary principles, all phenomena of the universe are produced. This concept has remained dominant in Chinese cosmological speculation down to recent times. An early reference to it appears already in the Kuo Yu or Discussions of the States (which was itself compiled, however, probably only in the 4th or 3rd century B.C.) This historical work records that when an earthquake occurred in the year 780 B.C., a savant of the time explained: "When the *Yang* is concealed and cannot come forth, and when the *Yin* is repressed and cannot issue forth, then there are earthquakes." (Chou Yu, I, 10.)

Later, the theory of the *Yin* and *Yang* came to be connected primarily with the Book of Changes. The original corpus of this book consists of what are known as the eight trigrams, each made up of combinations of three divided or undivided lines, as follows: ☰, ☱, ☲, ☳, ☴, ☵ ☶. By combining any two of these trigrams with one another into diagrams of six lines each, ䷀, ䷁, ䷂, etc., a total of sixty-four combinations is obtained which are known as the sixty-four hexagrams. The original text of the Book of Changes consists of these hexagrams, and of descriptions of their supposed symbolic meaning.

According to tradition, the eight trigrams were invented by Fu Hsi, China's first legendary ruler, antedating even the Yellow Emperor. According to some scholars, Fu Hsi himself combined the eight trigrams so as to obtain the sixty-four hexagrams; according to others, this was done by King Wen of the 20th century B.C. The textual comments on the hexagrams as a whole and on their *hsiao* (the individual lines in each hexagram) were, according to some scholars, written by King Wen; according to others, the comments on the hexagrams were written by King Wen, while those on the *hsiao* were by the Duke of Chou, the illustrious son of King Wen. Whether right or wrong, these attributions attest the importance which the Chinese attached to the eight trigrams and sixty-four hexagrams.

Modern scholarship has advanced the theory that the trigrams and hexagrams were invented early in the Chou Dynasty as imitations of the cracks formed on a piece of tortoise shell or bone through the method of divination that was practiced under the Shang Dynasty (1766?-1123? B.C.), the dynasty that preceded the Chou. This method has already been mentioned at the beginning of this chapter. It consisted of applying heat to a shell or bone, and then, according to the cracks that resulted, determining the answer to the subject of divination. Such cracks, however, might assume an indefinite number of varying configurations, and so it was difficult to interpret them according to any fixed formula. Hence during the early part of the Chou Dynasty this kind of divination seems to have been supplemented by another method, in which the stalks of a certain plant, known as the milfoil, were shuffled together so as to get varying combinations yielding odd and even numbers. These combinations were limited in number and so could be interpreted according to fixed formulas. It is now believed that the undivided and divided (i.e., odd and even) lines of the trigrams and hexagrams were graphic representations of these combinations. Thus the diviners, by shuffling the stalks of the milfoil, could obtain a given line or set of lines, and then, by reading the comments on it contained in the Book of Changes, could give an answer to the question on which divination was made.

This, then, was the probable origin of the Book of Changes, and explains its title, which refers to the changing combinations of lines. Later, however, many supplementary interpretations were added to the Book of Changes, some moral, some metaphysical, and some cosmological These were not composed until the latter part of the Chou Dynasty, or even the earlier portion of the following Han Dynasty, and are contained in a series of appendices known as the "Ten Wings." In this chapter we shall discuss only the cosmological interpretations, leaving the remainder for Chapter XV.

Besides the concept of *Yin* and Yang, another important idea in the "Appendices" is that of number. Since divination was usually regarded by the ancients as a method for revealing the mystery of the universe, and since divination through the use of stalks of the milfoil plant was based on the combination of varying numbers, it is not surprising that the anonymous writers of the "Appendices" tended to believe that the mystery of the universe is to be found in numbers. According to them, therefore, the numbers of the *Yang* are always odd, and those of the *Yin* are always even. Thus in "Appendix III" we read:

> The number for Heaven [i.e., Yang) is one, that for Earth [i.e. *Yin*] is two; that for Heaven is three; that for Earth is four; that for Heaven is five; that for Earth is six that for Heaven is seven; that for Earth is eight; that for Heaven is nine; that for Earth is ten. The numbers for Heaven and the numbers for Earth correspond with and complement one another. The numbers of Heaven [put together] are twenty-five; the numbers of Earth [put together] are thirty; the numbers of both Heaven and Earth [put together] are fifty-five. It is by these numbers that the evolutions and mystery of the universe are performed.

Later the *Yin-Yang* school tried to connect the Five Elements with the *Yin* and *Yang* by means of numbers. Thus it maintained that one, the number for

Heaven, produces Water, and six, the number for Earth, completes it. Two, the number for Earth, produces Fire, and seven, the number for Heaven, completes it. Three, the number for Heaven, produces Wood, and eight, the number for Earth, completes it. Four, the number for Earth, produces Metal, and nine, the number for Heaven, completes it. Five, the number for Heaven, produces Soil, and ten, the number for Earth, completes it. Thus one, two, three, four and five are the numbers that produce the Five Elements; six, seven, eight, nine and ten are the numbers that complete them.[710] This is the theory, therefore, that was used to explain the statement just quoted above: "The numbers for Heaven and the numbers for Earth correspond with and complement one another." It is remarkably similar to the theory of the Pythagoreans in ancient Greece, as reported by Diogenes Laertius, according to which the four elements of Greek philosophy, namely Fire, Water, Earth and Air, are derived, though indirectly, from numbers.[711]

This, however, is in China a comparatively late theory, and in the "Appendices" themselves there is no mention of the Five Elements. In these "Appendices" each of the eight trigrams is regarded as symbolizing certain things in the universe. Thus we read in "Appendix V":

> (The trigram) Chien ☰ is Heaven, round, and is the father....
> (The trigram) Kun ☷ is Earth and is the mother.... (The trigram) Chen ☳ is thunder.... (The trigram) Sun ☴ is wood and wind.... (The trigram) Kan ☵ is water... and is the moon.... (The trigram) Li ☲ is fire and the sun.... (The trigram) Ken ☶ is mountain.... (The trigram) Tui ☱ is marsh.

In the trigrams, the undivided lines symbolize the *Yang* principle, and the divided lines the *Yin* principle. The trigrams Chien and Kun, being made up entirely of undivided and divided lines respectively, are the symbols par excellence of the *Yang* and *Yin*, while the remaining six trigrams are supposedly produced through the intercourse of these primary two. Thus Chien and Kun are father and mother, while the other trigrams are usually spoken of in the "Appendices" as their "sons and daughters."

Thus the first line (from the bottom) of Chien ☰, combined with the second and third lines of Kun ☷, results in Chen ☳, which is called the eldest son. The first line of Kun, similarly combined with Chien, results in Sun ☴, which is called the eldest daughter. The second line of Chien, combined with the first and third lines of Kun, results in Kan ☵, which is called the second son. The second line of Kun, similarly combined with Chien, results in Li ☲, which is called the second daughter. The third line of Chien, combined with the first and second lines of Kun, results in Ken ☶, which is called the youngest son. And the third line of Kun, similarly combined with Chien, results in Tui ☱, which is called the youngest daughter.

This process of combination or intercourse between Chien and Kun, which results in the production of the remaining six trigrams, is a graphic symbolization

710 See Cheng Hsuan's (A.D. 127-200) commentary to the "Monthly Commands" in the *Book of Rites*; Ch. 4.

711 See *Lives and Opinions of Eminent Philosophers*, Book VIII, Ch. 19.

of the process of intercourse between the *Yin* and the Yang, whereby all things in the world are produced. That the world of things is produced through such intercourse of the *Yin* and Yang, is similar to the fact that living beings are produced through the intercourse of the male and female. It will be remembered that the *Yang* is the male principle, and the *Yin*, the female principle.

There is an intermingling of the genial influences of heaven and earth, and the transformation of all things proceeds abundantly. There is a communication of seed between male and female, and all things are produced.

Heaven and earth are the physical representations of the *Yin* and Yang, while Chien and Kun are their symbolic representations. The *Yang* is the principle that "gives beginning" to things; the *Yin* is that which "completes" them. Thus the process of the production of things by the *Yang* and *Yin* is completely analogous to that of the production of living beings by the male and female.

In the religion of the primitive Chinese, it was possible to conceive of a father god and mother goddess who actually gave birth to the world of things. In the *Yin-Yang* philosophy, however, such anthropomorphic concepts were replaced by, or interpreted in terms of, the *Yin* and *Yang* principles, which, though analogous to the female and male of living beings, were nevertheless conceived of as completely impersonal natural forces.

XIII THE REALISTIC WING OF CONFUCIANISM: HSUN TZU

The three greatest figures of the School of Literati in the Chou Dynasty were Confucius (551-479 B.C.), Mencius (371?-289? B.C.) and Hsun Tzu. The latter's dates are not definitely known, but probably lay within the years 298 and 238 B.C.

Hsun Tzu's personal name is Kuang, but he was also known under the alternative name of Hsun Ching. He was a native of the state of Chao in the southern part of the present Hopei and Shansi provinces. The *Shih Chi or Historical Records* says in its biography of him (Ch. 74) that when he was fifty he went to the state of Chi, where he was probably the last great thinker of the academy of Chi-hsia, the great center of learning of that time. The book bearing his name contains thirty-two chapters, many of them detailed and logically developed essays which probably come directly from his pen.

Among the literati, Hsun Tzu's thought is the antithesis of that of Mencius. Some people say that Mencius represents the left wing of the school, while Hsun Tzu represents its right wing. This saying, while suggestive, is too much of a simplified generalization. Mencius was left in that he emphasized individual freedom, but he was right in that he valued super-moral values and therefore was nearer to religion. Hsun Tzu was right in that he emphasized social control, but left in that he expounded naturalism and therefore was in direct opposition to any religious ideas.

Position of Man

Hsun Tzu is best known because of his theory that human nature is originally evil. This is directly opposed to that of Mencius, according to which human nature is originally good. Superficially it may seem that Hsun Tzu had a very low opinion of man, yet the truth is quite the contrary. Hsun Tzu's philosophy may be called a philosophy of culture. His general thesis is that everything that is good and valuable is the product of human effort. Value comes from culture and culture is the achievement of man. It is in this that man has the same importance in the universe as Heaven and Earth. As Hsun Tzu says: "Heaven has its seasons, Earth has its resources, man has his culture. This is what is meant [when it is said that man] is able to form a trinity [with Heaven and Earth]."[712]

Mencius said that by developing one's mind to the utmost, one knows one's nature, and by knowing one's nature, one knows Heaven.[713] Thus, according to Mencius, a sage, in order to become a sage, must "know Heaven." But Hsun Tzu maintains, on the contrary: "It is only the sage who does not seek to know Heaven."[714]

712 *Hsun-tzu*, Ch. 17.

713 *Mencius*, VIIa, 1.

714 HSVn-tm, Ch. 17.

According to Hsun Tzu, the three powers of the universe, Heaven, Earth and man, each has its own particular vocation: "The stars make their rounds; the sun and moon alternately shine; the four seasons succeed one another; the *Yin* and *Yang* go through their great mutations; wind and rain are widely distributed; all things acquire their harmony and have their lives."[715] Such is the vocation of Heaven and Earth. But the vocation of man is to utilize what is offered by Heaven and Earth and thus create his own culture. Hsun Tzu asks: "Is it not much better to heap up wealth and use it advantageously than to exalt Heaven and think about it?"[716] And then he continues: "If we neglect what man can do and think about Heaven, we fail to understand the nature of things."[717] For in so doing, according to Hsun Tzu, man forgets his own vocation; by daring to "think" about Heaven, he arrogates the vocation of Heaven. This is "to give up that wherewith man can form a trinity with Heaven and Earth, and yet still desire such a trinity. This is a great illusion."[718]

Theory of Human Nature

Human nature, too, should be cultured, for, from Hsun Tzu's view, the very fact that it is uncultured means that it cannot be good. Hsun Tzu's thesis is that "the nature of man is evil; his goodness is acquired training."[719] According to him,

> Nature is the unwrought material of the original; what are acquired are the accomplishments and refinements brought about by culture. Without nature there would be nothing upon which to add the acquired. Without the acquired, nature could not become beautiful of itself."[720]

Although Hsun Tzu's view of human nature is the exact opposite of that of Mencius, he agrees with him that it is possible for every man to become a sage, if he chooses. Mencius had said that any man can become a Yao or Shun (two traditional sages). And HsunTzu says likewise that "any man in the street can become a Yu [another traditional sage]."[721] This agreement has led some people to say that there is no real difference between the two Confucianists after all. Yet as a matter of fact, despite this seeming agreement, the difference is very real.

According to Mencius, man is born with the "four beginnings" of the four constant virtues. By fully developing these beginnings, he becomes a sage. But according to Hsun Tzu, man is not only born without any beginnings of goodness, but, on the contrary, has actual "beginnings" of evilness. In the chapter titled "On the Evilness of Human Nature," Hsun Tzu tries to prove that man is born with inherent desire for profit and sensual pleasure. But, despite these beginnings of evilness, he asserts that man at the same time possesses intelligence, and that this intelligence makes it possible for him to become good.

---

715 *Ibid.*
716 *Ibid.*
717 *Ibid.*
718 *Ibid.*
719 *Id.*, Ch. 23.
720 *Ibid.*
721 *Ibid.*

In his own words:

> Every man on the street has the capacity of knowing human-heartedness, righteousness, obedience to law and uprightness, and the means to carry out these principles. Thus it is evident that he can become a Yu.[722]

Thus whereas Mencius says that any man can become a Yao or Shun, because he is originally good, Hsun Tzu argues that any man can become a Yu, because he is originally intelligent.

Origin of Morality

This leads to the question: How, then, can man become morally good? For if every man is born evil, what is the origin of good? To answer this question, Hsun Tzu offers two lines of argument.

In the first place, Hsun Tzu maintains that men cannot live without some kind of a social organization. The reason for this is that, in order to enjoy better living, men have need of cooperation and mutual support. Hsun Tzu says:

> A single individual needs the support of the accomplishments of hundreds of workmen. Yet an able man cannot be skilled in more than one line, and one man cannot hold two offices simultaneously. If people all live alone and do not serve one another, there will be poverty.[723]

Likewise, men need to be united in order to conquer other creatures:

> Man's strength is not equal to that of the ox; his running is not equal to that of the horse; and yet ox and horse are used by him. How is this? I say that it is because men are able to form social organizations, whereas the others are unable.... When united, men have greater strength; having greater strength, they become powerful; being powerful, they can overcome other creatures.[724]

For these two reasons, men must have a social organization. And in order to have a social organization, they need rules of conduct. These are the *li* (rites, ceremonies, customary rules of living), which hold an important place in Confucianism generally, and are especially emphasized by Hsun Tzu. Speaking about the origin of the *li*, he says:

> Whence do the *li* arise? The answer is that man is born with desires. When these desires are not satisfied, he cannot remain without seeking their satisfaction. When this seeking for satisfaction is without measure or limit, there can only be contention. When there is contention, there will be disorder. When there is disorder, everything will be finished. The early kings hated this disorder, and so they established the *li* [rules of conduct] and yi [righteousness, morality], to set an end to this confusion.[725]

In another chapter, Hsun Tzu writes: "People desire and hate the same things. Their desires are many, but things are few. Since they are few there will inevitably

722 *Ibid.*
723 *Id.*, Ch. 10.
724 *Ibid.*
725 *Id.*, Ch. 19.

be strife."[726] Hsun Tzu here points to one of the fundamental troubles in human life. If people did not all desire and hate the same things — for instance, if one liked to conquer and the other enjoyed being conquered — there would be no trouble between them and they would live together quite harmoniously. Or, if all the things that everyone desired were very plentiful, like the free air, then too there would be no trouble. Or yet again if people could live quite apart from one another, the problem would be much simpler. But the world is not so ideal.

People must live together, and in order to do so without contention, a limit must be imposed on everyone in the satisfaction of his desires. The function of the *li* is to set this limit. When there are the *li*, there is morality. He who acts according to the *li* acts morally. He who acts against them acts immorally.

This is one line of Hsun Tzu's argument to explain the origin of moral goodness. It is quite utilitarianistic, and resembles that of *Mo Tzu*.

Hsun Tzu also employs another line of argument. He writes:

> Man is not truly man in the fact that he, uniquely, has two feet and no hair [over his body], but rather in the fact that he makes social distinctions. Birds and beasts have fathers and offspring, but not the affection between father and son. They are male and female, but do not have the proper separation between males and females. Hence in the Way of Humanity there must be distinctions. No distinctions are greater than those of society. No social distinctions are greater than the *li*.[727]

Here Hsun Tzu points out the difference between what is of nature and what is of culture, or, as Chuang Tzu puts it, what is of nature and what is of man. The fact that birds and beasts have fathers and offspring and that they are either male or female, is a fact of nature. The social relationships between father and son, husband and wife, on the contrary, are products of culture and civilization. They are not gifts of nature, but achievements of spirit. Man should have social relations and the li, because it is these that distinguish him from birds and beasts. According to this line of argument, man must have morality, not because he cannot help it, but because he ought to have it. This line of argument is more akin to that of Mencius.

In Confucianism, *li* is a very comprehensive idea. It can be translated as ceremonies, rituals, or rules of social conduct. It is all these, but in the above arguments, it is taken more or less in the third sense. In this sense, the function of the li is to regulate. The li provide regulation for the satisfaction of man's desires. But in the sense of ceremonies and rituals, the li have another function, that of refining. In this sense, the li give refinement and purification to man's emotions. In this latter interpretation, Hsun Tzu also made a great contribution.

Theory of Rites and Music

For the Confucianists, the most important of the ceremonies are those of mourning and sacrifice (especially to the ancestors). These ceremonies were

726 *Id.*. Ch. 10.

727 *Hsun-tzu*. Ch. 5.

universal at that time, and as popularly practiced they contained not a little of superstition and mythology. In justifying them, however, the Confucianists gave them new interpretations and read into them new ideas. These we find in the*Hsun-tzu* and the *Li Chi* or *Book of Rites*.

Among the Confucian classics, there are two devoted to the rites.

One is the *Yi Li* or *Book of Etiquette and Ceremonial*, which is a factual record of the procedures of ceremonies as practiced at that time. The other is the *Li Chi*, which consists of the interpretations on the ceremonies given by the Confucianists. I believe that most of the chapters of the *Li Chi* were written by the followers of Hsun Tzu.

Our mind has two aspects, the intellectual and the emotional.

When our loved ones die, we know, through our intellect, that the dead are dead and that there is no rational ground for believing in the immortality of the soul. If we were to act solely under the direction of our intellect, therefore, we would need no mourning rites. But since our mind also has its emotional aspect, this causes us, when our loved ones die, to hope that the dead may live again and that there may be a soul that will continue existing in the otherworld. When we thus give way to our fancy, we take superstition as truth, and deny the judgment of our intellect.

Thus there is a difference between what we know and what we hope. Knowledge is important, but we cannot live with knowledge only. We need emotional satisfaction as well. In determining our attitude towards the dead, we have to take both aspects into consideration. As interpreted by the Confucianists, the mourning and sacrificial rites did precisely this. I have said that these rites were originally not without superstition and mythology. But with the interpretations of the Confucianists, these aspects were purged. The religious elements in them were transformed into poetry, so that they were no longer religious, but simply poetic.

Religion and poetry are both expressions of the fancy of man.

They both mingle imagination with reality. The difference between them is that religion takes what it itself says as true, while poetry takes what it itself says as false. What poetry presents is not reality, and it knows that it is not. Therefore it deceives itself, yet it is a conscious self-deception. It is very unscientific, yet it does not contradict science. In poetry we obtain emotional satisfaction without obstructing the progress of the intellect.

According to the Confucianist, when we perform the mourning and sacrificial rites, we are deceiving ourselves without being really deceived. In the *Li* Chi, Confucius is reported to have said:

In dealing with the dead, if we treat them as if they were really dead, that would mean a want of affection, and should not be done. If we treat them as if they were really alive, that would mean a want of wisdom, and should not be done.[728]

That is to say, we cannot treat the dead simply as we know, or hope, them to be. The middle way is to treat them both as we know and as we hope them to be. This way consists in treating the dead as if they were living.

728 *Li Chi*, Ch. 2.

In his "Treatise on Rites," Hsun Tzu says:

> The rites are careful about the treatment of man's life and death. Life is the beginning of man, death is his end. If the beginning and end of man are both well treated, the Way of Humanity is complete.... If we render adequate service to our parents when they are living but not when they are dead, that means that we respect our parents when they have knowledge, but neglect them when they do not. One's death means that one is gone forever. That is the last chance for a subject to serve his sovereign, and a son his parents.... The mourning rites serve to decorate the dead by the living, to send off the dead as if they were still living, and to render the same service to the dead as that to the living, a service uniform from the beginning to the end.... Therefore the function of the mourning rites is to make clear the meaning of life and death, to send off the dead with sorrow and respect, and thus to complete the end of man.[729]

In the same chapter, Hsun Tzu says:

> The sacrificial rites are the expression of man's affectionate longing. They represent the height of piety and faithfulness, of love and respect. They represent also the completion of propriety and refinement. Their meaning cannot be fully understood except by the sages. The sages understand their meaning. Superior men enjoy their practice. They become the routine of the officer. They become the custom of the people. Superior men consider them to be the activity of man, while ordinary people consider them as something that has to do with spirits and ghosts.... They exist to render the same service to the dead as to the living, to render the same service to the lost as to the existing. What they serve has neither shape nor even a shadow, yet they are the completion of culture and refinement.[730]

With this interpretation, the meaning of the mourning and sacrificial rites becomes completely poetic, not religious.

There are other kinds of sacrifice besides those offered to ancestors. These Hsun Tzu interprets from the same point of view.

In his chapter titled "Treatise on Nature," one passage reads:

> Why is it that it rains after people have offered sacrifice for rain? Hsun Tzu said "There is no reason for that. It is the same as if there had been rain without praying for it. When there is an eclipse of the sun and the moon, we make demonstrations to save them. When rain is deficient, we pray for it. And when there are important affairs, we divine before we reach any decision. We do these things not because we can thereby get what we want. They are simply a sort of decorum. The superior man considers them as a sort of decorum, while ordinary people consider them as having supernatural force. One will be happy if one considers them as a sort of decorum; one will not, if one considers them as having supernatural force."[731]

729 *Hsun-tzu*, Ch. 19.
730 *Ibid.*
731 *Id.*, Ch. 17.

We pray for rain, and divine before we make any important decision, because we want to express our anxiety. That is all. If we were to take prayer as really being able to move the gods, or divination as really being able to make predictions about the future, this would result in superstition with all its consequences.

Hsun Tzu is also the author of a "Treatise on Music," in which he writes:

> Man cannot be without joy, and when there is joy, it must have a physical embodiment. When this embodiment does not conform to the right principle, there will be disorder. The early kings hated this disorder, and so they established the music of the *Ya* and *Sung* [two of the divisions of the *Book of Odes*] to guide it. They caused its music to be joyful and not degenerate, and its beauty to be distinct and not limited They cause it in its indirect and direct appeals, its complexity and simplicity, its frugality and richness, its rests and notes, to stir up the goodness in men's minds and to prevent evil feelings from gaining any foothold. This is the manner in which the early kings established music.[732]

Thus music, for Hsun Tzu, functions as an instrument for moral education. This has been the prevailing Confucianist view of music.

Logical Theories

In the *Hsun-tzu* there is a chapter titled "On the Rectification of Names." This subject is an old one in Confucianism. The term itself was originated by Confucius, as we have seen in Chapter IV. He said: "Let the ruler be ruler, the subject be subject; let the father be father and the son be son."[733] Likewise Mencius said: "To be without the relationship of ruler and of father is to be like the beasts."[734] Because the interests of these two thinkers were purely ethical, their application of the rectification of names was likewise confined primarily to the sphere of ethics. Hsun Tzu, however, lived in an age when the School of Names was flourishing. Hence his theory of the rectification of names possesses logical as well as ethical interest.

In his chapter, "On the Rectification of Names," Hsun Tzu first describes his epistemological theory, which is similar to that of the later Mohists. He writes: "That in man by which he knows is [called the faculty of] knowing. That in [the faculty of] knowing which corresponds [to external things] is called knowledge."[735] The faculty of knowing consists of two parts. One is what he calls "the natural senses," such as those of the ears and eyes. The other is the mind itself. The natural senses receive impressions, and the mind interprets and gives meaning to them. Hsun Tzu writes:

> The mind gives meaning to impressions. It gives meaning to impressions, and only then, by means of the ear, can sound be known; by means of the eye, can forms be known.... When the five senses note something but cannot

732 *Id.*, Ch. 20.
733 *Andean*, XII, 11.
734 *Mendus*, IVb, 9.
735 *Hsun-tzu*, Ch. 22.

classify it, and the mind tries to identify it but fails to give it meaning then one can only say that there is no knowledge.[736]

As to the origin and use of names, Hsun Tzu says:

> Names were made in order to denote actualities, on the one hand so as to make evident the distinctions between superior and inferior [in society], and on the other hand to distinguish similarities and differences.[737]

That is to say, names were originated partly for ethical and partly for logical reasons.

As to the logical use of names, he says:

> Names are given to things. When things are alike, they are named alike; when different, they are named differently.... The one who knows that different actualities have different names, and who therefore never refers to different actualities otherwise than by different names, will not experience any confusion. Likewise he who refers to the same actualities should never use any other but the same names.[738]

Regarding the logical classification of names, he writes further:

> Although things are innumerable, there are times when we wish to speak of them all in general, so we call them "things." "Things" is the most general term. We press on and generalize; we generalize and generalize still more, until there is nothing more general. Then only we stop. There are times when we wish to speak of one aspect, so we say "birds and beasts." "Birds and beasts" is the great classifying term. We press on and classify: We classify and classify still more, until there is no more classification to be made, and then we stop.[739]

Thus Hsun Tzu distinguishes two kinds of names, the general and the classifying. The general name is the product of the synthetic process of our reasoning, while the classifying name is that of its analytic process.

All names are man-made. When they were in the process of invention, there was no reason why an actuality should be designated by one particular name rather than another. The animal that came to be known as "dog," for example, might equally well have been called "cat" instead. Once, however, certain names came through convention to be applied to certain actualities, they could be attached to these and none other. As Hsun Tzu explains: "There are no names necessarily appropriate themselves. Names were named by convention. But when the convention having been established, it has become customary, this is called an appropriate name."[740]

He also writes "Should a true king arise, he must certainly follow the ancient terms and make the new ones."[741] Thus the invention of new names and determination of their meanings is a function of the ruler and his government.

---

736 *Ibid.*
737 *Ibid.*
738 *Ibid.*
739 *Ibid.*
740 *Ibid.*
741 *Ibid.*

Hsun Tzu says:

> When the kings had regulated names, the names were fixed and actualities distinguished. Their principles were thus able to be carried out, and their will could be known. They thus carefully led the people to unity. Therefore, the making of unauthorized distinctions between words, and the making of new words, so as thus to confuse the correct nomenclature, cause the people to be in doubt, and bring much litigation, was called great wickedness. It was a crime like that of using false credentials or false measures.[742]

Fallacies of Other Schools

Hsun Tzu considered most of the arguments of the School of Names and the later Mohists to be based upon logical sophistries and therefore fallacious. He grouped them into three classes of fallacies. The first is what he calls "the fallacy of corrupting names with names."[743] In this class, he includes the Mohist argument that "to kill a robber is not to kill a man." This is because, according to Hsun Tzu, the very fact of being a robber implies being a man, since by extension the category which bears the name "man" includes the category which has the name "robber." When one speaks of a robber, therefore, one means by this a being who is at the same time a man.

The second class Hsun Tzu calls "the fallacy of corrupting names with actualities."[744] In this group he includes the argument that "mountains and abysses are on the same level," which is a rephrasing by Hsun Tzu of Hui Shih's argument that "mountains and marshes are on the same level." Actualities, being concrete, are individual cases, while names, being abstract, represent general individual cases, while names, being abstract, represent general categories or rules. When one tries to disprove general rules by individual exceptions, the result is a corruption of the name by the actuality. Thus a particular abyss that happens to be located on a high mountain may indeed be on the same level as a particular mountain that happens to be on low land. But one cannot infer from this exceptional instance that all abysses are on the same level with all mountains.

The third class is what Hsun Tzu calls "the fallacy of corrupting actualities with names."[745] Here he includes the Mohist argument that "ox-and-horse are not horse," an argument which is the same in kind as *Kungsun Lung's* statement that "a white horse is not a horse." If one examines the name of ox-and-horse, one sees that it is indeed not equivalent to that of the name horse. Yet as a matter of fact some of the creatures belonging to the group known as "ox-and-horse" are, as actualities, indeed horses.

Hsun Tzu then concludes that the rise of all these fallacies is due to the fact that no sage-king exists. Were there to be such a sage-king, he would use his political authority to unify the minds of the people, and lead them to the true way of life in which there is no place or need for disputation and argument.

742 *Ibid.*
743 *Ibid.*
744 *Ibid.*
745 *Ibid.*

Hsun Tzu here reflects the spirit of the troubled age of his time. It was an age in which men longed desperately for a political unification, which would bring these troubles to an end. Such a unification, though in actual fact one of China only, was regarded, by these people, as equivalent to a unification of the whole world. Among Hsun Tzu's disciples, the two most famous were *Li* Ssu and *Han Fei Tzu,* both of whom were to have a great influence on Chinese history. *Li* Ssu later became Prime Minister of the First Emperor of the Chin Dynasty, the man who finally forcibly unified China in 221 B.C. Together with his master, he labored not only for a political but an ideological unification as well, a movement which culminated in the Burning of the Books in 213 B.C. The other disciple, Han Fei Tzu, became a leading figure in the Legalist school which supplied the theoretical justification for this political and ideological unification. The ideas of this school will be described in the next chapter.

XIV HAN FEI TZU AND THE LEGALIST SCHOOL

The feudalistic society of the early Chou Dynasty operated according to two principles: one was that of the *li* (rituals, ceremonies rules of conduct, mores) the other was that of the *hsing* (penalties, punishments). The *li* formed the unwritten code of honor governing the conduct of the aristocrats, who were known as *chun tzu* (a term literally meaning son of a prince, princely man, or gentleman) the *hsing*, on the contrary, applied only to the people of ordinary birth who were known as *shu jen* (common men) or *hsiao jen* (small men) This is the meaning of the saying in the *Li Chi* (*Book of Rites*) "The *li* do not go down to the common people; the *hsing* do not go up to the ministers."[746]

Social Background of the Legalists

This was possible because the structure of Chinese feudalistic society was comparatively simple. Kings, princes, and feudal lords were all related to each other either by blood or by marriage. In theory the princes of each state were subordinate to the king, and the feudal lords within these states were in turn subordinate to their prince. But in actual fact, these nobles, having long inherited their rights from their ancestors, came in the course of time to regard these rights as existing independently of their theoretical allegiance to their superiors. Thus the many states that belonged to the hegemony theoretically controlled by the central Chou King were in actual fact semi-independent, and within each of these states there were likewise many semi-independent "houses" of lesser nobles. Being relatives, these various feudatories maintained social and diplomatic contacts, and transacted business, if any, according to their unwritten code of "gentleman's agreements."

That is to say, their conduct was governed by *li*.

The kings and princes at the top had no direct dealings with the common people. They left such matters to the lesser feudal lords, each of whom ruled the common people living within his own fief. Since such fiefs were usually not large, their populations were limited. Hence the nobles were able in considerable measure to rule the people under them on a personal basis. Punishments were applied to keep their subjects obedient. Thus we find that in early Chinese feudalistic society, relationships, both high and low, were maintained on a basis of personal influence and personal contact.

The disintegration of this type of society in the later centuries of the Chou Dynasty brought with it far-reaching social and political changes. The social distinctions between the class of princely men on the one hand and small men on the other were no longer so absolutely demarcated. Already in the time of Confucius, we see how aristocrats sometimes lost their land and titles, and how members of the common people, either by talent or good luck, succeeded in becoming socially and politically prominent.

746 *Book of Rites*, Ch. 10

The old fixity of social classes was breaking down. Likewise, as time wore on, the territories of the larger states became ever larger through aggression and conquest. In order to carry on warfare or prepare for war, these states needed a strong government, that is, a government with a high concentration of power. As a consequence, the structure as well as the functions of government became ever more complex than formerly.

New situations brought with them new problems. Such were the conditions faced by all the rulers of the feudal states of the time, and it was the common endeavor of all the schools of thought since Confucius to solve these problems. Most of their proposed solutions, however, were not realistic enough to be practical. What the rulers needed were not idealistic programs for doing well to their people, but realistic methods for dealing with the new situations faced by their government.

There were certain men who had a keen understanding of real and practical politics. The rulers of the time used to seek the advice of these men, and if their suggestions proved effective, they often became trusted advisers of the rulers, and in some cases became prime ministers. Such advisers were known as *fang shu chih shih* or "men of method."

They were so called because they developed methods for governing large areas; methods which left a high concentration of power in the person of the ruler, and which they boasted were foolproof. According to them, it was quite unnecessary that a ruler be a sage or superman. By faithfully applying their methods, a person of even merely average intelligence could govern, and govern well. There were also some "men of method" who went further and supplied a rational justification or theoretical expression for their techniques. It was this that constituted the thought of the Legalist school.

Thus it is wrong to associate the thought of the Legalist school with jurisprudence. In modern terms, what this school taught was the theory and method of organization and leadership. If one wants to organize people and be their leader, one will find that the Legalist theory and practice are still instructive and useful, but only if one is willing to follow totalitarian lines.

Han Fei Tzu, the Synthesizer of the Legalist School

In this chapter, I take Han Fei Tzu as the culminating representative of the Legalist school. He was a descendant of the royal house of the state of Han, in present western Henan Province. The *Shih Chi* or *Historical Records* says of him: "Together with *Li* Ssu, he studied under Hsun Tzu. *Li* Ssu considered himself not equal to Han Fei."[747] He was an able writer and composed a lengthy work bearing his name in fifty-five chapters. Ironically enough, it was in Chin, the state which more than any other applied his principles and thus conquered the other states that he died in prison in 233 B.C. The cause was a political intrigue on the part of his former fellow student, *Li* Ssu, who was an official in Chin, and who may have been jealous of the growing favor accorded to Han Fei Tzu.

747 *Historical Records*, Ch. 63.

Before Han Fei Tzu, who was the last and greatest theorizer of the Legalist school, there had been three groups, each with its own line of thought. One was headed by Shen *Tao*, a contemporary of Mencius, who held that *shih* was the most important factor in politics and government. Another was headed by Shen Pu-hai (died 337 B.C.), who stressed that *shu* was the most important factor. Still another was headed by Shang Yang, also known as Lord Shang (died 338 B.C.), who, for his part, emphasized *fa*. *Shih* means power or authority; *fa* means law or regulation; *shu* means the method or art of conducting affairs and handling men, i.e., "state-craft."

Han Fei Tzu considered all three alike as indispensable. He said:

> The intelligent ruler carries out his regulations as would Heaven, and handles men as if he were a divine being. Being like Heaven, he commits no wrong, and being like a divine being, he falls into no difficulties. His shih [power] enforces his strict orders, and nothing that he encounters resists him.... Only when this is so can his laws [*fa*] be carried out in concert.[748]

The intelligent ruler is like Heaven because he acts in accordance with law fairly and impartially. This is the function of fa. He is like a divine being, because he has the art of handling men, so that men are handled without knowing how they are handled. This is the function of the *shu*. And he has the authority or power to enforce his orders. This is the function of *shih*. These three together are the implements of emperors and kings,"[749] no one of which can be neglected.

Legalist Philosophy of History

Perhaps the Chinese traditional respect for past experience stems from the ways of thought of their overwhelmingly agrarian population. Farmers are rooted to the soil and travel but rarely.

They cultivate their land in accordance with seasonal changes, which repeat themselves year after year. Past experience is a sufficient guide for their work, so that whenever they want to try something new, they first look back to past experience for precedent.

This mentality has influenced Chinese philosophy a great deal, so that since the time of Confucius, most philosophers have appealed to ancient authority as justification for their own teaching. Thus Confucius' ancient authorities were King Wen and the Duke of Chou, of the beginning of the Chou Dynasty. In order to improve upon Confucius, Mo Tzu appealed to the authority of the legendary Yu, who supposedly lived a thousand years earlier than King Wen and the Duke of Chou. Mencius, to get the better of the Mohists, went still further back to Yao and Shun, who were supposed to have antedated Yu. And finally the *Tao*ists, in order to gain a hearing for their ideas against those of both the Confucianists and Mohists, appealed to the authority of Fu Hsi and Shen Nung, who were reputed to have lived several centuries earlier than either Yao or Shun.

---

748 *Han-fei-tzu*, Ch. 48.
749 *Id.*, Ch. 43.

By thus looking to the past, these philosophers created a regressive view of history. Although belonging to different schools, they all agreed that the golden age of man lies in the past rather than the future, the movement of history since then has been one of progressive degeneration. Hence man's salvation consists not in the creation of something new, but in a return to what has already existed.

To this view of history the Legalists, the last major school of the Chou period, took sharp exception. They fully understood the changing needs of the time and viewed them realistically. Although admitting that the people of ancient times were more innocent and in this sense perhaps more virtuous, they maintained that this was due to material circumstances rather than to any inherent superior goodness. Thus according to Han Fei Tzu in ancient times:

> There were few people but plenty of supplies, and therefore the people did not quarrel. But nowadays people do not consider a family of five children as large, and each child having again five children before the death of the grandfather there may be twenty-five grand-children. The result is that there are many people but few supplies, and that one has to work hard for a meager return. So the people fall to quarreling.[750]

Because of these completely new circumstances, according to Han Fei Tzu, new problems can only be solved by new measures.

Only a fool can fail to realize this obvious fact. Han Fei Tzu illustrates this kind of folly with a story:

> There was once a man of Sung who tilled his field. In the midst of the field stood a stem of a tree, and one day a hare in full course rushed against that stem, broke its neck, and died. Thereupon the man left his plough and stood waiting at that tree in the hope that he would catch another hare. But he never caught another hare and was ridiculed by the people of Sung. If, however, you wish to rule the people of today by the methods of government of the early kings, you do exactly the same thing as the man who waited by the tree.... Therefore affairs go according to their time, and preparations are made in accordance with affairs.[751]

Before Han Fei Tzu, Lord Shang already said similarly: "When the guiding principles of the people become unsuited to the circumstances, their standards of value must change. As conditions in the world change, different principles are practiced."[752]

This conception of history as a process of change is a common- place to our modern mind, but it was revolutionary viewed against the prevailing theories of the other schools of ancient China.

Way of Government

To meet new political circumstances, the Legalists proposed new ways of government, which, as stated above, they claimed to be infallible. The first

750 *Id.*, Ch. 49.
751 *Ibid.*
752 *Book of Lord Shang*, II, 7.

necessary step, according to them, was to set up laws. Han Fei Tzu writes: "A law is that which is recorded on the registers, set up in the government offices, and promulgated among the people."[753] Through these laws the people are told what they should and should not do. Once the laws are promulgated, the ruler must keep a sharp watch on the conduct of the people. Because he possesses shih or authority, he can punish those who violate his laws, and reward those who obey them. By so doing he can successfully rule the people, no matter how numerous they may be.

Han Fei Tzu writes on this point:

> In his rule of a state, the sage does not depend upon men doing good themselves, but brings it about that they can do no wrong. Within the frontiers of a state, there are no more than ten people who will do good of themselves; nevertheless, if one brings it about that the people can do no wrong, the entire state can be kept peaceful. He who rules a country makes use of the majority and neglects the few, and so does not concern himself with virtue but with law.[754]

Thus with law and authority, the ruler rules his people. He need have no special ability or high virtue, nor need he, as the Confucianists maintained, set a personal example of good conduct, or rule through personal influence.

It may be argued that this procedure is not really foolproof, because the ruler needs ability and knowledge to make laws and keep a watch on the conduct of the people, who may be large in number. The Legalists answer this objection by saying that the ruler need not do all these things himself. If he merely possesses shu, the art of handling men, he can then get the right men to do everything for him.

The concept of *shu* is of philosophical interest. It is also one aspect of the old doctrine of the rectification of names. The term used by the Legalists for this doctrine is "holding the actualities responsible for their names."[755]

By "actualities," the Legalists mean the individuals who hold government office, while by "names," they mean the titles of the offices thus held. These titles are indicative of what the individuals who hold the office in question should ideally accomplish. Hence "holding the actualities responsible for their names," means holding the individuals who occupy certain offices responsible for carrying out what should be ideally accomplished in these offices. The ruler's duty is to attach a particular name to a particular individual, that is to say, confer a given office upon a given person. The functions pertaining to this office have already been defined by law and are indicated by the name given to it. Hence the ruler need not, and should not, bother about the methods used to carry out his work, so long as the work itself is done and well done. If it is well done, the ruler rewards him; if not, he punishes him. That is all.

It may yet be asked how the ruler is to know which man is the best for a certain office. The Legalists answer that this too can be known by the same *shu* or method of statecraft. Han Fei Tzu says:

753 *Han-fei-tzu*, Ch. 38.
754 *Id.*, Ch. 50.
755 *Id.*, Ch. 43.

> When a minister makes claims, the ruler gives him work according to what he has claimed, but holds him wholly responsible for accomplishment corresponding to this work. When the accomplishment corresponds to this work, and the work corresponds to what the man has claimed he could do, he is rewarded. If the accomplishment does not correspond to the work, nor the work correspond to what the man has claimed for himself, he is punished.[756]

After this procedure has been followed in several instances, if the ruler is strict in his rewards and punishments, incompetent people will no longer dare to take office even if it is offered to them. Thus all incompetents are eliminated, leaving government positions only to those who can successfully fill them.

Yet the problem still remains: How is the ruler to know whether an "actuality" does in fact correspond to its "name"? The Legalist reply is that it is up to the ruler himself, if he is uncertain, to test the result. If he is not sure that his cook is really a good cook, he can settle the matter simply by tasting his cooking. He need not always judge results for himself, however. He can appoint others to judge for him, and these judges will then, in their turn, be held strictly responsible for their names.

Thus, according to the Legalists, their way of government is really foolproof. The ruler need only retain the authority of rewards and punishments in his own hands. He will then rule by "doing nothing, yet there is nothing that is not done."

Such rewards and punishments are what Han Fei Tzu calls "the two handles of the ruler."[757] Their effectiveness derives from the fact that it is the nature of man to seek profit and to avoid harm. Han Fei Tzu says:

> In ruling the world, one must act in accordance with human nature. In human nature there are the feelings of liking and disliking, and hence rewards and punishments are effective. When rewards and punishments are effective, interdicts and commands can be established, and the way of government is complete.[758]

Han Fei Tzu, as a student of Hsun Tzu, was convinced that human nature is evil. But he differed from Hsun Tzu in that he was not interested in the latter's stress on culture as a means of changing human nature so as to make it something good. According to him and the other Legalists, it is precisely because human nature is what it is, that the Legalist way of government is practical. The Legalists proposed this way of government on the assumption that man is what he is, i.e., naturally evil, and not on the assumption that he is to be converted into what he ought to be.

Legalism and Taoism

"Doing nothing, yet there is nothing that is not done." This is the *Tao*ist idea of *wu wei*, having-no-activity or non-action, but it is also a Legalist idea. According to Han Fei Tzu and the Legalists, the one great virtue required of a ruler is that

756 *Id*, Ch. 7.
757 *Id*, Ch. 7.
758 *Id*., Ch. 48.

he follows the course of non-action. He should do nothing himself but should merely let others do everything for him. Han Fei Tzu says:

> Just as the sun and moon shine forth, the four seasons progress, the clouds spread, and the wind blows, so does the ruler not encumber his mind with knowledge, or himself with selfishness. He relies for good government or disorder upon laws and methods [*shu*]; leaves right and wrong to be dealt with through rewards and punishments; and refers lightness and heaviness to the balance of the scale.[759]

In other words, the ruler possesses the implements and mechanism through which government is conducted, and having these, does nothing, yet there is nothing that is not done.

Taoism and Legalism represent the two extremes of Chinese thought. The *Tao*ists maintained that man originally is completely innocent; the Legalists, on the other hand, that he is completely evil. The *Tao*ists stood for absolute individual freedom; the Legalists for absolute social control. Yet in the idea of non action, the two extremes meet. That is to say, they had here some common ground.

Under somewhat different wording, the Legalist way of government was also maintained by the later *Tao*ists. In the *Chuang-tzu* we find a passage that speaks about "the way of employing human society." In this passage distinctions are made between having-activity and having-no-activity, and between "being employed by the world" and "employing the world." Having-no-activity is the way of employing the world; having-activity is the way of being employed by the world. The ruler's reason for existence is to rule the whole world. Hence his function and duty is not to do things himself, but to tell others to do them for him. In other words, his method of rule is to employ the world by having-no-activity. The duty and function of subordinates, on the other hand, is to take orders and do things accordingly. In other words, the function of the subordinate is to be employed be the world by having activity. The same passage says: "The superior must have no activity, so as thus to employ the world; but the subordinates must have activity, so as thus to be employed by the world. This is the invariable way."[760]

The Chuang-tzu continues:

> Therefore, the rulers of old, although their knowledge spread throughout the whole universe, did not themselves think. Although their eloquence beautified all things; they did not themselves speak. Although their abilities exhausted all things within the four seas, they did not themselves act.[761]

A ruler should be so, because if he once thinks about something, this means that there is something else about which he does not think; yet his whole duty and function is to think about all things under his rule. The solution, therefore, is for him not to try to think, speak, and act himself, but merely to tell others to think, speak, and act in his place. In this way he does nothing, and yet there is nothing that is not done.

759 *Id*, Ch. 29.

760 *Chuang-tzu*, Ch. 13.

761 *Ibid*.

As to the detailed procedure by which the ruler is thus to "employ the world," the same passage says:

> Those of old who made manifest the great *Tao*, first made manifest Heaven, and *Tao* and *Te* came next. *Tao* and *Te* being manifested, the virtues of human-heartedness and righteousness came next. These being manifested, the division of offices came next. These being manifested, actualities and names came next. These being manifested, employment without interference came next. This being manifested, examinations and discriminations came next. These being manifested, judgment of right and wrong came next. This being manifested, rewards and punishments came next. With the manifestation of rewards and punishments, the foolish and the wise assumed their proper positions, the noble and the humble occupied their proper places, and the virtuous and the worthless were employed according to their nature.... This is perfect peace, the acme of good government.[762]

It is clear that the latter part of this program is the same as that of the Legalists. Yet the passage goes on by saying:

> Those of antiquity who spoke about the great *Tao*, mentioned actualities and names only at the fifth step, and rewards and punishments only at the ninth step. He who speaks immediately about actualities and names, does not know the fundamentals [that underlie them]. He who speaks immediately about rewards and punishments, does not know their beginning.... Such a one knows the implements of government, but not its principles. He can be employed by the world, but is not sufficient to employ the world. He is a one-sided man and only knows how to talk.[763]

Here we have the criticism of the *Tao*ists against the Legalists. The Legalist way of government requires unselfishness and impartiality on the part of the ruler. He must punish those who ought to be punished, even though they be his friends and relatives, and he must reward those who ought to be rewarded, even though they be his enemies. If he fails only a few times to do this, the whole mechanism breaks down. Such requirements are too much for a man of only average intelligence. He who can really fulfill them is nothing less than a sage.

Legalism and Confucianism

The Confucianists maintained that the people should be governed by *li* and morality, not by law and punishment. They upheld the traditional way of government, but did not realize that the circumstances that had once rendered this way practical had already changed. In this respect, they were conservative. In another respect, however, they were at the same time revolutionary, and reflected in their ideas the changes of the time. Thus they no longer upheld the traditional class distinctions that were based merely on the accident of birth of fortune. Confucius and Mencius, to be sure, continued to speak about the difference between the princely man and the small man. Yet for them, this distinction

762 *Ibid.*
763 *Ibid.*

depended upon the moral worth of the individual, and was not necessarily based upon inherited class differences.

I pointed out at the beginning of this chapter that in early Chinese feudalistic society, the nobles were governed according to the li, but the common people only according to the punishments. Hence the Confucian insistence that not only the nobles, but the mass of the people as well, should be governed by li rather than by punishment was in fact a demand for a higher standard of conduct to be applied to the people. In this sense the Confucianists were revolutionary. In Legalist thought, too, there were no class distinctions. Everyone was equal before law and the ruler. Instead of elevating the common people to a higher standard of conduct, however, the Legalists lowered the nobles to a lower standard by discarding li and putting sole reliance on rewards and punishments for all alike.

The Confucianist ideas are idealistic, while those of the Legalists are realistic. That is the reason why, in Chinese history, the Confucianists have always accused the Legalists of being mean and vulgar, while the Legalists have accused the Confucianists of being bookish and impractical.

XV CONFUCIANIST METAPHYSICS

In Chapter XII we have seen that the *Yi Ching* or *Book of Changes* (also known simply as the Yi) was originally a book of divination. Later the Confucianists gave it cosmological, metaphysical, and ethical interpretations, which constitute the "Appendices" now found in the *Book of Changes*.

The cosmological theory contained in the "Appendices" has already been considered in Chapter XII, and we shall revert to it again in Chapter XXIII. In the present chapter we shall confine ourselves to the metaphysical and ethical theories found in the "Appendices" and in the *Chung Yung*.

The *Chung Yung* or *Doctrine of the Mean* is one of the chapters in the *Li Chi* (*Book of Rites*). According to tradition, it was written by Tzu Ssu, the grandson of Confucius, but in actual fact a large part of it seems to have been written at a somewhat later date. The "Appendices" and the *Chung Yung* represent the last phase in the metaphysical development of ancient Confucianism. So great is their metaphysical interest, indeed, that the Neo-Taoists of the 3rd and 4th centuries A.D. considered the Yi as one of the three major classics of speculative philosophy, the others being the *Lao-tzu* and *Chuang-tzu*. Similarly, Emperor Wu (502-549) of the Liang Dynasty, himself a Buddhist, wrote commentaries on the *Chung Yung*, and in the 10th and 11th centuries, monks of the Chan sect of Buddhism also wrote such commentaries, which marked the beginning of Neo-Confucianism.

The Principles of Things

The most important metaphysical idea in the "Appendices," as in Taoism, is that of *Tao*. Yet it is quite different from the concept of *Tao* of the *Tao*ists. For the latter, *Tao* is nameless, unnamable. But for the authors of the "Appendices," not only is *Tao* nameable, but, strictly speaking, it is *Tao* and *Tao* only that is thus nameable. We may distinguish between the two concepts by referring to the *Tao* of Taoism as the *Tao*, and to that of the "Appendices" as tao. The *Tao* of Taoism is the unitary "that" from which springs the production and change of all things in the universe. The tao of the "Appendices," on the contrary, are multiple, and are the principles which govern each separate category of things in the universe. As such, they are somewhat analogous to the concept of the "universal" in Western philosophy. Kungsun Lung, as we have seen, regarded hardness as a universal of this kind, since it is this hardness that enables concrete objects in our physical universe to be hard. Likewise, in the terminology of the "Appendices," that by which hard things are hard would be called the tao of hardness.

This tao of hardness is separable from the hardness of individual physical objects, and constitutes a namable metaphysical principle. There are many such tao, such as the tao of sovereignship and of ministership, or of fatherhood and sonhood. They are what a sovereign, a minister, a father, and a son ought to be. Each of them is represented by a name, and an individual should ideally act according to these various names. Here we find the old theory of the rectification of names of Confucius. In him, however, this was only an ethical theory, whereas in the "Appendices" it becomes metaphysical as well.

The Yi, as we have seen, was originally a book of divination. By the manipulation of the stalks of the milfoil plant, one is led to a certain line of a certain hexagram, the comments on which in the Yi are supposed to provide the information one is seeking. Hence these comments are to be applied to the various specific cases in actual life. This procedure led the authors of the "Appendices" to the concept of the formula Seeing the Yi from this point of view, they considered the comments on the hexagrams and the individual lines of these hexagrams as formulas, each representing one or more tao or universal principles. The comments on the entire sixty-four hexagrams and their 384 individual lines are thus supposed to represent all the tao in the universe.

The hexagrams and their individual lines are looked upon as graphic symbols of these universal tao. "Appendix III" says "The Yi consists of symbols." Such symbols are similar to what in symbolic logic are called variables. A variable functions as a substitute for a class or a number of classes of concrete objects. An object belonging to a certain class and satisfying certain conditions can fit into a certain formula with a certain variable; that is, it can fit into the comment made on a certain hexagram or a certain line within a hexagram, these hexagrams or lines being taken as symbols. This formula represents the tao which the objects of this class ought to obey. From the point of view of divination, if they obey it, they will enjoy good luck, but if not, they will suffer bad fortune. From the point of view of moral teaching, if they obey it, they are right, but if not, they are wrong.

The first of the sixty-four hexagrams, Chien, for example, is supposed to be the symbol of virility, while the second hexagram, Kun, is that of docility. Everything that satisfies the condition of being virile can fit into a formula in which the symbol of Chien occurs, and everything that satisfies the condition of being docile can fit into one in which the symbol of Kun occurs. Hence the comments on the hexagram Chien acid its individual lines are supposed to represent the tao for all things in the universe that are virile; those on the hexagram Kun and its individual lines represent the tao for all things that are docile.

Thus in "Appendix I," the section dealing with the hexagram Kun says: "If it takes the initiative, it will become confused and lose the way. If it follows, it will docilely gain the regular [way]." And in "Appendix IV":

> Although the *Yin* has its beauties, it keeps them under restraint in its service of the king, and does not dare to claim success for itself. This is the tao of Earth, of a wife, of a subject. The tao of Earth is, not to claim the merit of achievement, but on another's behalf to bring things to their proper issue.

Quite the opposite is the hexagram of Chien, the symbol of Heaven, of a husband, of a sovereign. The judgments made on this hexagram and its individual lines represent the tao of Heaven, of a husband, of a sovereign.

Hence if one wants to know how to be a ruler or a husband, one should look up what is said in the Yi under the hexagram Chien, but if one wants to know how to be a subject or a wife, one should look under the hexagram Kun. Thus in "Appendix III" it is said "With the expansion of the use of the hexagrams, and the application of them to new classes, everything that man can do in the world is there." Again:

> What does the Yi accomplish? The Yi opens the door to the myriad things in nature and brings man's task to completion. It embraces all the governing principles of the world. This, and no more or less, is what the Yi accomplishes.

It is said that the name of the Yi has three meanings: (1) easiness and simpleness, (2) transformation and change, and (3) invariability.[764] Transformation and change refers to the individual things of the universe. Simpleness and invariability refer to their tao or underlying principles. Things ever change, but tao are invariable. Things are complex, but tao are easy and simple.

The Tao of the Production of Things

Besides the tao of every class of things, there is another *Tao* for all things as a whole. In other words, besides the specific multiple tao, there is a general unitary *Tao* which governs the production and transformation of all things. "Appendix III" says: "One *Yang* and one *Yin*: this is called the *Tao*. That which ensues from this is goodness, and that which is completed thereby is the nature [of man and things]" This is the *Tao* of the production of things, and such production is the major achievement of the universe. In "Appendix III" it is said: "The supreme virtue of Heaven is to produce."

When a thing is produced, there must be that which is able to produce it, and there must also be that which constitutes the material from which this production is made. The former is the active element and the latter the passive one. The active element is virile and is the Yang; the passive element is docile and is the *Yin*. The production of things needs the cooperation of these two elements. Hence the words: "One *Yang* and one *Yin*: this is the *Tao*."

Everything can in one sense by *Yang* and in another sense *Yin*, according to its relation with other things. For instance, a man is *Yang* in relation to his wife, but *Yin* in relation to his father. The metaphysical *Yang* which produces all things, however, can only be Yang, and the metaphysically *Yin* out of which everything is produced can only be *Yin*. Hence in the metaphysical statement:

"One *Yang* and one *Yin*: this is called the *Tao*," the *Yin* and *Yang* thus spoken of are *Yin* and *Yang* in the absolute sense.

It is to be noticed that two kinds of statement occur in the "Appendices." The first consists of statements about the universe and the concrete things in it; the other consists of statements about the system of abstract symbols of the Yi itself. In "Appendix III" it is said: "In the Yi there is the Supreme Ultimate which produces the Two Forms. The Two Forms produce the Four Emblems, and these Four Emblems produce the eight trigrams." Although this saying later became the foundation of the metaphysics and cosmology

764 See Cheng .sun (A.D. 127-200), *Discussion of the Yi*, quoted by Kung Ying-ta (574648), in the Preface to his sub-commentary on Wang Pi's (226-49) *Commentary on the Yi*.

of the Neo-Confucianists, it does not refer to the actual universe, but rather to the system of symbols in the Yi. According to the "Appendices," however, these symbols and formulas have their exact counterparts in the universe itself. Hence the two kinds of statement are really interchangeable. Thus the saying, "One Yang and one *Yin*: this is called the *Tao*," is a statement about the universe. Yet it is interchangeable with the other saying that "in the Yi there is the Supreme Ultimate which produces the Two Forms." The *Tao* is equivalent to the Supreme Ultimate, while the *Yin* and *Yang* correspond to the Two Forms.

"Appendix III" also states: "The supreme virtue of Heaven is to produce." Again: "To produce and to reproduce is the function of the Yi." Here again are two kinds of statement. The former relates to the universe, and the latter to the Yi. Yet they are at the same time interchangeable.

The Tao of the Transformation of Things

One meaning of the name Yi, as we have seen, is transformation and change. The "Appendices" emphasize that all things in the universe are ever in a process of change. The comment on the third line of the eleventh hexagram states. "There is no level place without a bank, and no departure without a return." This saying is considered by the "Appendices" as the formula according to which things undergo change. This is the *Tao* of the transformation of all things.

If a thing is to reach its completion and the state of completion is to be maintained, its operation must occur at the right place, in the right way, and at the right time. In the comment of the Yi, this rightness is usually indicated by the words cheng (correct, proper) and Chung (the mean, center, middle) As to cheng, "Appendix I" states:

> The woman has her correct place within, and the man has his correct place without. The correctness of position of man and woman is the great principle of Heaven and Earth.... When the father is father, and the son son; when the elder brother is elder brother, and the younger brother younger brother; when husband is husband, and wife wife: then the way of the family is correct. When it is correct, all under Heaven will be established.

Chung means neither too much nor too little. The natural inclination of man is to take too much. Hence both the "Appendices" and the Lao-tzu consider excess a great evil. The Lao-tzu speaks about fan (reversal, Ch. 40) and *fu* (returning, Ch. 16), and the "Appendices" also speak about *fu*. Among the hexagrams, indeed, there is one titled *Fu* (the 24th hexagram). "Appendix I" says about this hexagram: "In *Fu* we see the mind of Heaven and Earth."

Using this concept of *fu*, "Appendix VI" interprets the order of arrangement of the sixty-four hexagrams. The Yi was originally divided into two books. This "Appendix" considers the first of these as dealing with the world of nature, and the second as dealing with that of man. Concerning the first book, it says:

> Following the existence of Heaven and Earth, there is the production of all things. The space between Heaven and Earth is full of all these things.

Hence [true hexagram] Chien [Heaven] and [the hexagram] Kun [Earth] are followed by the hexagram Tun, which means fullness.

Then the "Appendix" tries to show how each hexagram is usually followed by another which is opposite in character.

About the second book, this same "Appendix" says:

Following the existence of Heaven and Earth, there is the existence of all things. Following the existence of all things, there is the distinction of male and female. Following this distinction, there is the distinction between husband and wife. Following this distinction, there is the distinction between father and son. Following this distinction, there is the distinction between sovereign and subject. Following this distinction, there is the distinction between superiority and inferiority. Following this distinction, there are social order and justice.

Then, as in the case of the first part of the Yi, the "Appendix" tries to show how one hexagram is usually followed by another which is opposite in character.

The sixty-third hexagram is Chi-chi, which means something accomplished. At this point this "Appendix" says: "But there can never be an end of things. Hence Chi-chi is followed by Wei-chi [the sixty-fourth hexagram, meaning something not yet accomplished]. With this hexagram, [the Yi] comes to a close."

According to this interpretation, the arrangement of the hexagrams implies at least three ideas: (1) that all that happens in the universe, natural and human alike, forms a continuous chain of natural sequence; (2) that in the process of evolution, everything involves its own negation; and (3) that in the process of evolution, "there can never be an end of things."

The "Appendices" agree with the Lao-tzu that in order to do something with success, one must be careful not to be too successful; and that in order to avoid losing something, one must complement it with something of its opposite. Thus "Appendix III" says:

The man who keeps danger in mind is one who retains his position. The man who keeps ruin in mind is one who survives. The man who has disorder in mind is one who has peace. Therefore, the superior man, when all is peaceful, does not forget danger. When he is acting, he does not forget about ruin. When he has society under control, he does not forget disorder. Hence it is possible, with his own person secure, for him to protect the state.

The "Appendices" also agree with the Lao-tzu that modesty and humbleness are the great virtues. "Appendix I" remarks:

It is the way of Heaven to diminish the swollen and augment the modest. It is the way of Earth to subvert the swollen and give free course to the modest.... It is the way of man to hate the swollen and love the modest. Modesty, in a high position, sheds lustre on it; in a low position it cannot be passed by unobserved. This is the final goal of the superior man.

The Mean and Harmony

The idea of *chung* is fully developed in the *Chung Yung* or *Doctrine of the Mean*. *Chung* is like the Aristotelian idea of the "golden mean." Some would understand it as simply doing things no more than halfway, but this is quite wrong. The real meaning of *chung* is neither too much nor too little, that is, just right.

Suppose that one is going from Washington to New York. It will then be just right to stop at New York, but to go right through to Boston, will be to do too much, and to stop at Philadelphia, will be to do too little. In a prose poem by Sung Yu of the 3rd century

B.C., he describes a beautiful girl with the words: "If she were one inch taller, she would be too tall. If she were one inch shorter, she would be too short. If she used powder, her face would be too white. If she used rouge, her face would be too red."[765] The description means that her figure and complexion were just right. "Just right" is what the Confucianists call *chung*.

Time is an important factor in the idea of being just right. It is just right to wear a fur coat in winter, but it is not just right to wear it in summer. Hence the Confucianists often use the words shih (time or timely) in conjunction with the word *chung*, as in the term shih *chung* or "timely mean." Mencius, for example, says of Confucius:

> When it was proper to go into office, then to go into it; when it was proper to remain out of office, then to remain out of it; when it was proper to continue in it long, then to continue in it long; when it was proper to withdraw from it quickly, then to withdraw from it quickly: such was Confucius.[766]

Hence "among the sages, Confucius was the timely one."[767]

The *Chung Yung* says:

> To have no emotions of pleasure or anger, sorrow or joy, welling up: this is to be described as the state of *chung*. To have these emotions swelling up but in due proportion: this is to be described as the state of ho [harmony]. Chung is the chief foundation of the world. Ho is the great highway for the world. Once *chung* and ho are established, Heaven and Earth maintain their proper position, and all creatures are nourished.[768]

When the emotions do not come forth at all, the mind neither goes too far nor falls short. It is just right. This is an illustration of the state of *chung*. And when the emotions do come forth, but in due proportion, this is also the state of *chung*, for harmony results from *chung*, and *chung* serves to harmonize what might otherwise be discordant.

What is said about the emotions also applies to the desires. In personal conduct as well as in social relations, there are medium points which serve as right limits for the satisfaction of the desires and the expression of the emotions. When all desires and emotions of a person are satisfied and expressed to the right degree,

765 *Wen Hsuan, chuan* 19.

766 *Mencius*, IIa, 22.

767 *Id*, Vb, 1.

768 *Chung Yung*, Ch. 1.

the person achieves a harmony within his person which results in good mental health. Likewise, when all the desires and feelings of the various types of people who comprise a society are satisfied and expressed to the right degree, the society achieves harmony within itself which results in peace and order.

Harmony is the reconciling of differences into a harmonious unity. The Tso Chuan reports a speech by the statesman Yen Tzu (died 493 B.C.), in which he makes a distinction between harmony and uniformity or identity. Harmony, he says, may be illustrated by cooking. Water, vinegar, pickles, salt, and plums are used to cook fish. From these ingredients there results a new taste which is neither that of the vinegar nor of the pickles. Uniformity or identity, on the other hand, may be likened to the attempt to flavor water with water, or to confine a piece of music to one note. In both cases there is nothing new,[769] Herein lies the distinction between the Chinese words rung and ho. Tung means uniformity or identity, which is incompatible with difference. Ho means harmony, which is not incompatible with difference; on the contrary, it results when differences are brought together to form a unity. But in order to achieve harmony, the differences must each be present in precisely their proper proportion, which is *chung*. Thus the function of *chung* is to achieve harmony.

A well-organized society is a harmonious unity in which people of differing talents and professions occupy their proper places, perform their proper functions, and are all equally satisfied and not in conflict with one another. An ideal world is also a harmonious unity. The Chung Yung says: "All things are nurtured together without injuring one another. All courses are pursued without collision. This is what makes Heaven and Earth great."[770]

Harmony of this sort, which includes not only human society, but permeates the entire universe, is called the Supreme Harmony. In "Appendix I", of the Yi, it is said "How vast is the originating power of [the hexagram] *Chien*.... Unitedly to protect the Supreme Harmony: this is indeed profitable and auspicious."

The Common and the Ordinary

The *Chung Yung* says:

> What Heaven confers is called the nature. The following of this nature is called the Way [*Tao*]. The cultivation of this Way is called spiritual culture. The Way is that which no man for a moment can do without. What a man can do without is not the Way.[771]

Here we touch upon the idea of the importance of the common and the ordinary, which is another important concept in the *Chung Yung*. This concept is expressed by the word *yung*, in the title of this work, which means common or ordinary.

Everyone finds it necessary to eat and drink every day. Hence eating and drinking are the common and ordinary activities of mankind. They are common and ordinary just because they are so important that no man can possibly do

769 See the *Tso Chuan*, twentieth year of Duke Chao, 522 B.C.

770 *Chung Yung*, Ch. 30.

771 *Id.*, Ch. 1.

without them. The same is true of human relations and moral virtues. They appear to some people as so common and ordinary as to be of little value. Yet they are so simply because they are so important that no man can do without them. To eat and drink, and to maintain human relations and moral virtues, is to follow the nature of man. It is nothing else but the Way or *Tao*. What is called spiritual culture or moral instruction is nothing more than the cultivation of this Way.

Since the Way is that which no man in actual fact can do without, what is the need of spiritual culture? The answer is that although all men are, to some extent, really following the Way, not all men are sufficiently enlightened to be conscious of this fact. The Chung Yung says: "Amongst men there are none who do not eat and drink, but there are few who really appreciate the taste."[772] The function of spiritual culture is to give people an understanding that they are all, more or less, actually following the Way, so as to cause them to be conscious of what they are doing.

Furthermore, although all men are, as a matter of necessity, compelled to follow the Way to some extent, not all can follow it to perfection. Thus no one can live in a society utterly devoid of human relationships; at the same time there are few who can meet with perfection all the requirements made by these human relationships. The function of spiritual culture is to perfect what man is, as a matter of fact, already doing to a greater or lesser degree. Thus the *Chung Yung* says:

> The Way of the superior man is obvious and yet obscure. The ordinary man and ordinary woman in all their ignorance can yet have knowledge of it, yet in its perfection even a sage finds in it something which he does not know. The ordinary man and ordinary woman with all their stupidity can yet practice it, yet in its perfection even a sage finds in it something which he cannot practice.... Thus the Way of the superior man begins with the relationship between husband and wife, but in its fullest extent reaches to all that is in Heaven and Earth.[773] Thus though all men, even in their ignorance and stupidity, are following the Way to some extent, spiritual cultivation is nevertheless required to bring them to enlightenment and perfection.

Enlightenment and Perfection

In the *Chung Yung*, this perfection is described as *cheng* (sincerity, realness) and goes together with enlightenment. The *Chung Yung* says:

> Progress from perfection to enlightenment is called the nature. From enlightenment to perfection it is called spiritual culture. When there is perfection, there is enlightenment. When there is enlightenment, there is perfection.[774]

That is to say, once one understands all the significance of the ordinary and common acts of daily life, such as eating, drinking, and the human relationships, one is already a sage. The same is true when one practices to perfection what one understands. One cannot fully understand the significance of these things

772 *Id.*, Ch. 4.
773 *Id.*, Ch. 12.
774 *Id.*, Ch. 21.

unless one practices them. Nor can one practice them to perfection, unless one fully understands their significance.

The *Chung Yung* says again:

> The quality of *cheng* does not simply consist in perfecting oneself. It is that whereby one perfects all other things. The perfection of the self lies in the quality of *jen* [human-heartedness]. The perfection of other things lies in wisdom. In this is the virtue of the nature, It is the way through which comes the union between inner and outer.[775]

The meaning of this passage seems clear, yet I wonder whether the words, human-heartedness and wisdom, should not be interchanged.

The *Chung Yung* says also:

> It is only he who has the most cheng who can develop his nature to the utmost. Able to do this, he is able to do the same to the nature of other men. Able to do this, he is able to do the same to the nature of things. Able to do this, he can assist the transforming and nourishing operations of Heaven and Earth. Being able to do this, he can form a trinity with Heaven and Earth.[776]

While perfecting oneself, one must also see that others are likewise perfected. One cannot perfect oneself while disregarding the perfection of others. The reason is that one can develop one's nature to the utmost only through the human relationships, that is, within the sphere of society. This goes back to the tradition of Confucius and Mencius, that for self-perfection one must practice *Chung, shu,* and human-heartedness; that is, it consists in helping others. To perfect oneself is to develop to the utmost what one has received from Heaven. And to help others is to assist the transforming and nourishing operations of Heaven and Earth. By fully understanding the significance of these things, one is enabled to form a trinity with Heaven and Earth. Such understanding is what the Chung Yung calls enlightenment, and forming a trinity in this way is what it calls perfection.

Is anything extraordinary needed in order to achieve this trinity? No, nothing more is needed than to do the common and ordinary things and to do them "just right," with understanding of their full significance. By so doing, one can gain the union of inner and outer, which is not only a trinity of Heaven, Earth, and man, but means a unity of man with Heaven and Earth. In this way one can achieve other-worldliness, yet at the same time not lose this-worldliness. It is with the development of this idea that the later Neo-Confucianists attacked the other-worldly philosophy of Buddhism.

Such is the Confucianist way of elevating the mind to a state in which the individual becomes one with the universe. It differs from the *Tao*ist method, which is, through the negation of knowledge, to elevate the mind above the mundane distinctions between the "this" and the "other." The Confucianist method, on the other hand, is, through the extension of love, to elevate the mind above the usual distinctions between the self and other things.

---

775 *Id.*, Ch. 25.

776 *Id.*, Ch. 22.

XVI WORLD POLITICS AND WORLD PHILOSOPHY

It is said that "history never repeats itself," yet also that "there is nothing new under the sun." Perhaps the whole truth lies in a combination of these two sayings. From a Chinese point of view, so far as international politics is concerned, the history of our world in the present and immediately preceding centuries looks like a repetition of the Chinese history of the Chun Chiu and Chan Kuo periods.

Political Conditions Preceding the Unification by Chin

The Chun Chiu period (722-481 B.C.) is so named because it is the period covered by the *Chun Chiu or Spring and Autumn Annals.* And the Chan Kuo period (480-222 B.C.) derives its name, which means Warring States, from the fact that it was a period of intensified warfare between the feudal states. As we have seen, men's conduct during the feudal age was governed by li (ceremonies, rituals, rules of proper conduct). Not only were there li governing the conduct of the individual, but also those for the state as well. Some of these were to be practiced in time of peace, but others, were designed for use in war. These peacetime and wartime li, as observed by one state in its relations to another, were equivalent to what we now would call international law.

We see that in recent times international law has become more and more ineffective. In late years there have been many instances in which one nation has attacked another without first sending an ultimatum and declaring war, or the airplanes of one nation have bombed the hospitals of another, while pretending that they did not see the Red Cross. And in the periods of Chinese history mentioned above, we see a similar decline in the effectiveness of the li.

In the Chun Chin period, there were still people who respected the international li. The Tso Chuan reports a famous battle of Hung that took place in 638 B.C. between the states of Chu and Sung. The old-fashioned Duke Hsiang of Sung personally directed the Sung forces. At a certain moment, the Chu army was crossing a river to form its lines, whereupon the commander under Duke Hsiang immediately asked for permission to attack the army during its crossing. To this the Duke replied, however, that he would not attack an army before it had formed its lines. The result was a disastrous defeat of the Sung army, in which the Duke himself was wounded. In spite of this, however, he defended his original decision, saying: "A superior man does not inflict a second wound on one who has already been wounded, nor does he take prisoner any one who has gray hair." This infuriated one of his commanders, who told the Duke: "If it is good to refrain from inflicting a second wound, why not refrain from inflicting any wound at all? If it is good to refrain from taking prisoner any one who has gray hair, why not surrender to your enemy?" (Tso Chuan, twenty-second year of Duke Hsi). What the Duke said accorded with the traditional li, which represented the chivalrous spirit of the feudal knights. What the commander said represented the practice of a changing age.

It is interesting though discouraging to note that all the known methods which statesmen of today use in an effort to keep peace among nations are much the same as those which the statesmen of these early periods of Chinese history attempted without success. For example, a conference for the limitation of armaments was held in 551. B.C. (Tso Chuan, twenty-seventh year of Duke Hsiang.) Some time later a proposal was made to divide the "world" of that time into two "spheres of influence"; one in the east, to be controlled by the King of *Chi* with the title of Eastern Emperor; the other in the west, to be controlled by the King of Chin with the title of Western Emperor.[777] There were also various alliances of states with one another. During the Chan Kuo period these fell into two general patterns: the "vertical," which ran from north to south, and the "horizontal," which ran from west to east. At that time there were seven major states, of which Chin was the most aggressive. The vertical type of alliance was one directed against Chin by the other six states, and was so called because Chin lay in the extreme west, while the other six states were scattered to the east of it, ranging from north to south. The horizontal type of alliance, on the other hand, was one in which Chin combined with one or more of the other six states in order to attack the remainder, and therefore was extended from the west towards the east.

Chin's policy was "to make alliance with distant states, but attack the ones that were near." In this way it always eventually succeeded in breaking up the vertical alliances that opposed it. By its superiority in "agriculture and war" and extensive use of "fifth column" techniques among the other states, Chin, after a series of bloody campaigns, succeeded in conquering the other six states one by one, and finally unified the whole of China in 221 B.C.

Thereupon the King of Chin gave to himself the grandiose title of First Emperor of Chin (Chin Shih Huang Ti) by which he is known to history. At the same time he abolished feudalism and thus for the first time in history created a centralized Chinese empire under the Chin Dynasty.

The Unification of China

Though the First Emperor was thus the first to achieve actual unity, the desire for such unity had been cherished by all people for a long time previous. In the *Mencius* we are told that King Hui of Liang asked "How may the world be at peace?" To which Mencius replied "When there is unity, there will be peace." "But who can unify the world?" asked the King. "He who does not delight in killing men can unify it," answered Mencius.[778] This statement clearly expresses the aspiration of the time.

The word "world" used here is a translation of the Chinese term *tien-hsia*, which literally means "all beneath the sky." Some translators render it as "empire,"

777 *Historical Records*, Ch. 46.

778 *Mencius*, Ia, 6.

because, so they maintain, what the Chinese in ancient times called the *tien-hsia* was confined to the limits of the Chinese feudal states. This is quite true. But we should not confuse the intention of a term with its extension as it was understood by the people of a particular time. The latter usage is limited by the knowledge of facts possessed by these people, but the former is a matter of definition. For instance, we cannot say that the word *jen* (persons) should be translated as "Chinese," simply because in ancient times what the Chinese meant by the word was confined to people of Chinese blood. When the ancient Chinese spoke about *jen*, what they meant was really human beings, even though at that time their knowledge of human beings was limited to those of China. In the same way, when they spoke about the *tien-hsia*, they meant the world, even though in early times their knowledge of the world did not extend beyond the Chinese states.

From the age of Confucius onward, the Chinese people in general and their political thinkers in particular began to think about political matters in terms of the world. Hence the unification of China by Chin seemed, to the people of that time, very much as the unification of the whole world would seem to us today. Since the unification of 221. B.C., for more than two thousand years, with the exception of certain periods which the Chinese have considered as abnormal, they have lived under one government in one world. They have thus been accustomed to a centralized organization that would operate for world peace. But in recent times they have been plunged into a world with international political conditions similar to those of the remote periods of the Chun Chiu and Chan Kuo. In the process they have been compelled to change their habits of thinking and acting. In this respect, in the eyes of the Chinese, there has been a repetition of history, which has contributed much to their present suffering. (See note at the end of the chapter.)

The Great Learning

To illustrate the internationalistic character of Chinese philosophy, let us turn now to some of the ideas of the *Ta Hsueh*, or Great Learning. The *Ta Hsueh*, like the *Chung Yung*, is a chapter in the *Li Chi* (*Book of Rites*), and like the *Chung Yung*, it was, during the Sung Dynasty (960-1279), grouped by the Neo-Confucianists with the *Analects of Confucius* and the *Mencius*, to form the "Four Books" which comprised the primary texts for Neo-Confucian philosophy.

The *Great Learning* was attributed by the Neo-Confucianists, though with no real proof, to Tseng Tzu, one of the chief disciples of Confucius. It was considered by them to be an important manual for the learning of *Tao*. Its opening section reads:

> The teaching of the *Great Learning* is to manifest one's illustrious virtue, love the people, and rest in the highest good.... The ancients, who wished to manifest illustrious virtue throughout the world, first ordered well their own states. Wishing to order well their own states, they first regulated their own families. Wishing to regulate their own families, they first cultivated their own selves. Wishing to cultivate their own selves, they first rectified their own minds. Wishing to rectify their own minds, they first sought for

absolute sincerity in their thoughts. Wishing for absolute sincerity in their thoughts, they first extended their knowledge. This extension of knowledge consists in the investigation of things.

Things being investigated, only then did their knowledge become extended. Their knowledge being extended, only then did their thought become sincere. Their thought being sincere, only then did their mind become rectified. Their mind being rectified, only then did their selves become cultivated. Their selves being cultivated, only then did their families become regulated. Their families being regulated, only then did their states become rightly governed. Their states being rightly governed, only then could the world be at peace.

These statements have been known as the three "main cords" and eight "minor wires" of the *Ta Hsueh*. According to later Confucianists, the three cords really comprise only one cord, which is "to manifest one's illustrious virtue." To love the people" is the way "to manifest one's illustrious virtue," while "to rest in the highest good" is "to manifest one's illustrious virtue" in the highest perfection.

The "eight wires" are likewise really only one wire, which is the cultivation of one's own self. In the above quotation, the steps preceding the cultivation of the self such as the investigation of things, extension of knowledge, etc., are the ways and means for cultivating the self. And the steps following the cultivation of the self, such as the regulation of the family, etc., are the ways and means for cultivating the self to its highest perfection, or as the text says, for "resting in the highest good." Man cannot develop his nature to perfection unless he tries his best to do his duties in society. He cannot perfect himself without at the same time perfecting others.

"To manifest one's illustrious virtue" is the same as "to cultivate one's self." The former is merely the content of the latter. Thus several ideas are reduced to a single idea, which is central in Confucianism.

It is unnecessary that one should be head of a state or of some world organization, before one can do something to bring good order to the state and peace to the world. One should merely do one's best to do good for the state as a member of the state, and do good for the world as a member of the world. One is then doing one's full share of bringing good order to the state and peace to the world. By thus sincerely trying to do one's best, one is resting in the highest good.

For the purpose of the present chapter, it is enough to point out that the author of the *Ta Hsueh* was thinking in terms of world politics and world peace. He was not the first to think in this way, but it is significant that he did it so systematically. For him, the good order of one's own state is neither the final goal in terms of politics nor in terms of the spiritual cultivation of the self. Here we need not discuss the problem of how the investigation of things can be the ways and means for the spiritual cultivation of the self. This problem will return to us when we take up Neo-Confucianism later.

Eclectic Tendency in the Hsun-tzu

In the world of Chinese philosophy, the latter part of the third century B.C saw a strong tendency towards syncretism and eclecticism. The major work of the School of Eclectics, the *Lu-shih Chun-chiu*, was composed at that time. But, although this work devoted chapters to most of the schools of its time, it failed to give a theoretical justification for the idea of eclecticism as such. Both Confucianist and *Tao*ist writers, however, did present such a theory, which shows how, despite their other differences, they both reflected the eclectic spirit of the time.

These writers agreed that there is a single absolute Truth which they called the *Tao*. Most of the different schools have seen some one particular aspect of the *Tao*, and in this sense have made some contribution to its manifestation. The Confucianist writers, however, maintained that it was Confucius who had seen the whole Truth, and so the other schools were subordinate to the Confucian school, though in a sense complementary to it. The *Tao*ist writers, on the contrary, maintained that it was Lao Tzu and Chuang Tzu who had seen the whole Truth, and therefore that Taoism was superior to all other schools.

In the *Hsun-tzu* there is a chapter titled "On Freedom from Blindness," in which we read:

> In the past, the traveling scholars were blinded, so they had different schools of thought. Mo Tzu was blinded by utility and did not know the value of culture. Sung Tzu [a contemporary of Mencius, who maintained that the desires of men are really very few] was blinded by desire, but did not know [that men seek for] gain. Shen Tzu [Shen *Tao*,a member of the Legalist school] was blinded by law but did not know [the value of] talent. Shen Tzu [Shen Puhai, another member of the Legalist school] was blinded by authority but did not know wisdom. His Tzu [Hiu Shih of the School of Names] was blinded by words but did not know facts. Chuang Tzu was blinded by what is of nature but did not know what is of man.
>
> From the point of view of utility, the *Tao* is nothing more than seeking for profit. From the point of view of [fewness of] desires, the *Tao* is nothing more than satisfaction. From the point of view of law, the *Tao* is nothing more than regulations. From the point of view of authority, the *Tao* is nothing more than caprice. From the point of view of what is of nature, the *Tao* is nothing more than *laissez-faire*. From the point of view of words, the *Tao* is nothing more than argumentation.
>
> These different views are single aspects of the *Tao*. The essence of the *Tao* is constant and includes all changes. It cannot be grasped by a single corner. Those with perverted knowledge who see only a single aspect of the *Tao* will not be able to comprehend its totality.... Confucius was human-hearted and wise and was not blinded. Therefore he comprehended the *Tao* and was sufficient to be ranked with the early rulers.[779]

In another chapter *Hsun Tzu* says:

> Lao Tzu had vision regarding acquiescence, but did not see exertion. Mo Tzu had vision regarding uniformity, but did not see individuality. Sung

779 *Hsu-tzu*, Ch. 21.

> Tzu had vision regarding [the fact that the desires of some men are] few, but did not see [the fact that those of other men are] many.[780]

According to *Hsun Tzu,* the vision and blindness of a philosopher go together. He has vision, yet usually at the same time is blinded by his vision. Hence the excellence of his philosophy is at the same time its shortcoming.

Eclectic Tendency in the Chuang-tzu

The author of the last chapter of the *Chuang-tzu, Tien Hsia* or "The World," gives the *Tao*ist view of syncretism. This chapter is really a summarized account of ancient Chinese philosophy. We are not sure who the author was, but he was certainly one of the best historians and critics of early Chinese philosophy.

This chapter first makes a distinction between the whole Truth and partial truth. The whole Truth is the *Tao* of "sageliness within and kingliness without," the study of which is called "the *Tao* method." Partial truth is a particular aspect of the whole Truth, the study of which is called "the art method." This chapter says: "In the world there are many who use the art method. Each one considers his own [thought] as perfect without need of any addition. Where is there then what the ancients called the *Tao* method?... There is that by which the sage flourishes; there is that through which the king completes his achievement. Both originate in the One."

The One is the "Tao of sageliness within and kingliness without" The chapter goes on to make a distinction between the fundamental and the branch, the fine and the coarse, in the *Tao*. It says:

> How perfect were the men of old.... They understood the fundamental principles and connected them with minute regulations reaching to all points of the compass, embracing the great and the small, the fine and the course; their influence was everywhere.

Some of their teachings which were correctly embodied in measures and institutions are still preserved in ancient laws and the records of historians. Those teachings that were recorded in the books of *Poetry, History, Rites,* and *Music* were known to most of the gentlemen and teachers of [the states of] Tsou and Lu [i.e., the Confucianists]. The *Book of Poetry* describes aims; the *Book of History* describes events; the *Rites* directs conduct; *Music* secures harmony. The *Yi* [Book of Changes] shows the principles of the *Yin* and *Yang.* The *Chun Chiu* [*Spring and Autumn Annals*] shows names and duties.

Thus the *Tien Hsia* chapter maintains that the Confucianists had some connection with the *Tao.* But what they knew is confined to "measures and institutions." They knew nothing about the underlying principle. That is to say, they knew only the coarser aspects and lesser branches of the *Tao,* but not what is fine and fundamental in it.

The *Tien Hsia* chapter continues by saying:

> Now the world is in great disorder. The virtuous and the sage are obscured. *Tao* and virtue lose their unity and many in the world get hold of some one

780 *Id.*, Ch 17.

aspect of the whole to enjoy for themselves. The case is like the senses of hearing, sight, smell, and taste, which have specific functions, but cannot be interchanged. Or like the skill of the various artisans, which are each excellent in its kind and useful in its turn, yet are not comprehensive. Each is a student of some one aspect.... Thus the *Tao* of sageliness within and kingliness without becomes obscured and loses its clearness; it becomes repressed and loses its development.

Then the same treatise makes a classification of the different schools, granting to each that it has "heard" of some one aspect of the *Tao,* but at the same time making sharp criticisms of the school's shortcomings. Lao Tzu and Chuang Tzu are greatly admired. Yet, remarkably enough, these two leaders of Taoism, like the other schools, are by implication criticized by the remark that they, too, have merely "heard some one aspect of the *Tao.*"

It thus seems to be the implication of the *Tien Hsia* chapter that the Confucianists knew the concrete "measures and institutions" but not their underlying principle, whereas the *Tao*ists knew the principle but not the measures and institutions. In other words, the Confucianists knew the "branches" of the *Tao,* but not its fundamental aspect, while the *Tao*ists knew its fundamental aspect, but not its branches. Only a combination of the two constitutes the whole Truth.

Eclecticism of Ssuma Tan and Liu Hsin

This eclectic tendency was continued in the Han Dynasty. The *Huai-nan-tzu* or *Book of the Prince* of *Huai-nan* is a book of the same nature as the *Lu-shih Chun-chiu,* though with a stronger tendency towards Taoism. In addition to this book, the two historians, Ssuma Tan (died 110 B.C.) and Liu Hsin (ca. 46 B.C.-A.D. 23), who have been quoted in Chapter III, also display eclectic tendencies. Of them, Ssuma Tan was a *Tao*ist. In the essay quoted in Chapter III, "On the Essential Ideas of the Six Schools," he says:

In the "Great Appendix" ["Appendix III"] of the Yi, there is the statement "In the world there is one purpose, but there are a hundred ideas about it; there is single goal, but the paths towards it differ." This is just the case with the different schools of thought,... all of which seek social order but follow widely different paths in their words of explanation, some of which are clear and others not.[781]

He then goes on to mention the excellencies and shortcomings of the six philosophic schools, but concludes by considering Taoism as combining all the best points of the other schools, and therefore as being superior to all.

Liu Hsin, on the other hand, was a Confucianist. In his *Seven Summaries,* as quoted in the chapter on literature contained in the *History of the Former Han Dynasty,* he lists ten schools of thought, and quotes the same passage from "Appendix III" of the *Book of Changes* as does Ssuma Tan. Then he concludes:

Each of the schools developed its strong points; and each developed knowledge and investigation to the utmost in order to set forth clearly

781 Historical Records Ch. 130.

its main purposes. Although they had prejudices and shortcomings, still a summary of their teachings shows that they were branches and descendants of the *Liu Yi* (Six Classics)... If one were able to cultivate the *Liu Yi* and observe the sayings of the nine schools [omitting that of the Story Tellers as of no philosophical importance], discarding their errors and gathering their good points, it would be possible to master the manifold aspects of thought.[782]

All these statements reflect the strong desire for unity that existed even in the world of thought. The people of the third century B.C., discouraged by centuries of inter-state warfare, longed for a political unification; their philosophers, consequently, also tried to bring about unification in thought. Eclecticism was the first attempt. Eclecticism in itself, however, cannot build a unified system. The eclectics believed in the whole Truth, and hoped by selecting from the various schools their "strong points," to attain to this Truth or *Tao*. What they called the *Tao*, however, was, it is to be feared, simply a patch-work of many disparate elements, unconnected by any underlying organic principle, and hence unworthy of the high title they attached to it.

Note on the Chinese concept of Nationalism (see p. 181).

Dr. Derk Bodde writes "I would question this statement. The Six Dynasties (third through sixth century) Yuan (1280-1367) and Ching (1644-1911) periods, for example, were in actual fact of so long duration as to accustom the Chinese to the idea of disunity or foreign domination, even though such a situation was in theory regarded as 'abnormal.' Moreover, even in the 'normal' periods of unity, there was often extensive political maneuvering and military action against a succession of outside peoples, such as the Hsiung-nu, as well as against occasional rebels within the empire. I would hardly regard the present conditions as presenting an unfamiliar situation to the Chinese, therefore, even though their effects are accentuated by the fact that they operate on a truly worldwide scale."

The historical facts which Dr. Bodde mention are no doubt correct, but what concerns me in this paragraph is not these historical facts themselves, but what the Chinese people up to the end of the last century, or even the beginning of this century, have felt about them. The emphasis upon the foreign domination of the Yuan and Ching dynasties is one made from the point of view of modern nationalism It is true that from early times the Chinese have made a sharp distinction between *Chung Kuo* or *hua hsia* (Chinese) and *yi ti* (barbarian) but the emphasis of this distinction is more cultural than racial. The Chinese have traditionally considered that there are three kinds of living beings: Chinese, barbarians, and beasts. Of these, the Chinese are most cultured, the barbarians come next, and the beasts are completely uncultured.

When the Mongols and Manchus conquered China, they had already to a considerable extent adopted the culture of the Chinese. They dominated the

782 *History of the Former Han Dynasty*, Ch. 30.

Chinese politically, but the Chinese dominated them culturally. They therefore did not create a marked break or change in the continuity and unity of Chinese culture and civilization, with which the Chinese were most concerned. Hence traditionally the Chinese have considered the Yuan and Ching as simply two of the many dynasties that have followed each other in Chinese history. This can be seen from the official arrangement of the dynastic histories. The Ming Dynasty, for instance, in one sense represented a nationalistic revolution against the Yuan; nevertheless, the official *History of the Yuan Dynasty*, compiled under the Ming, treated the Yuan as the normal successor of the purely Chinese Sung Dynasty. Likewise Huang Tsung-hsi (1610-1695), one of the nationalistic scholars who opposed the Manchus, in his *Sung Yuan Hssaeh-an* or *Biographical History of Confucianist Philosophers of the Sung and Yuan Dynasties*, found no moral fault in such scholars as Hsu Heng (1209-1281) and Wu Cheng (1249-1333), who though Chinese had served under the Yuan with high official rank.

The Chinese Republic has similarly compiled an official *History of the Ching Dynasty*, in which this dynasty is treated as the normal successor of the Ming. This history was later banned by the present government, because the treatment of certain events connected with the revolution of 1911 was regarded as unsatisfactory. Hence it is possible that the new official *History of the Ching Dynasty* will eventually be written in a quite different way. What I am here concerned with, however, is the traditional view. So far as tradition is concerned, the Yuan and Ching were just as "normal" as other dynasties. One may say that the Chinese lack nationalism, but that is precisely my point. They lack nationalism because they have been accustomed to think in terms of *tien hsia*, the world.

As to the fact that the Chinese have had to fight such non-Chinese groups as the Hsiung-nu, etc., traditionally what the Chinese have felt is that sometimes it was necessary for them to fight the barbarians, just as sometimes it was necessary to fight the beasts. They did not feel that such people as the Hsiung-nu were in a position to divide the world with China, just as the American people do not feel that the American Indians are in a position to divide America with them.

Because the Chinese did not greatly emphasize racial distinctions, it resulted that during the third and fourth centuries A.D. various non-Chinese peoples were allowed to move freely into China. This movement constituted what is called the "inner colonization," and was a primary cause for the political troubles of the Six Dynasties period. Such "inner colonization" is precisely what Hitler, in his *Mein Kampf*, criticized from a super-nationalistic point of view.

The introduction of Buddhism seems to have given many Chinese the realization that civilized people other than the Chinese existed, but traditionally there have been two kinds of opinion regarding India. Those Chinese who opposed Buddhism believed that the Indians were simply another tribe of barbarians. Those who believed in Buddhism, on the other hand, regarded India as the "pure land of the West" Their praise of India were that of a realm transcending this world. Hence even the introduction of Buddhism, despite its enormous effect upon Chinese life, did not change the belief of the Chinese that they were the only civilized people in the *human* world.

As a result of these concepts, when the Chinese first came in contact with Europeans in the sixteenth and seventeenth centuries, they thought that they were simply barbarians like preceding barbarians, and so they spoke of them as barbarians. As a consequence they did not feel greatly disturbed, even though they suffered many defeats in fighting with them. They began to be disturbed, however, when they found that the Europeans possessed a civilization equal to, though different from, that of the Chinese. What was novel in the situation was not that peoples other than the Chinese existed, but that their civilization was one of equal power and importance. In Chinese history one can find a parallel for such a situation only in the Chun Chin and Chan Kuo periods, when different but equally civilized states existed that fought with one another. That is why the Chinese now feel that there is a repetition in history.

If one reads the writings of the great statesmen of the last century, such as Tseng Kuo-fan (1811-1872) and *Li* Hung-chang (1823-1901), there is much evidence that they felt about the impact of the West precisely in this way. This note attempts to, describe the reasons for their feeling.

XVII THEORIZER OF THE HAN EMPIRE: TUNG CHUNG-SHU

Mencius once said that those who do not delight in killing men would unify the world.[783] It would seem that he was wrong, because, some hundred years later, it was the state of Chin that unified the whole of China. Chin was superior to the other states in the arts of both "agriculture and war," that is, it was superior both economically and militarily. It was known at the time as "the state of tigers and wolves." By sheer force of arms, coupled with the ruthless ideology of the Legalists, it succeeded in conquering all its rivals.

The Amalgamation of the Yin-Yang and Confucianist Schools

Yet Mencius was not wholly wrong, for the Chin Dynasty, which was established after the unification of 221 B.C., lasted only about fifteen years. Soon after the death of the First Emperor his empire disintegrated in a series of rebellions against the harsh Chin rule, and was succeeded by the Han Dynasty (206 B.C.-A.D. 220).

The Han inherited the concept of political unity of the Chin, and continued its unfinished work, that is, the building up of a new political and social order.

Tung Chung-shu (c. 179-c. 104 B.C.) was the great theorizer in such an attempt. A native of the southern part of the present Hopei Province, he was largely instrumental in making Confucianism the orthodox belief of the Han Dynasty, at the expense of the other schools of thought. He was also prominent in the creation of the institutional basis for this Confucian orthodoxy: the famed Chinese examination system, which began to take form during his time. Under this system, entry into the ranks of the government officials who ruled the country was not dependent upon noble birth or wealth, but rather upon success in a series of periodic examinations which were conducted by the government simultaneously throughout the country, and were open to all members of society with but trifling exceptions. These examinations, to be sure, were still embryonic in the Han Dynasty and did not become really universal until several centuries later. It is to Tung Chung-shu's credit, however, that he was one of the first to propose them, and it is also significant that in so doing he insisted upon the Confucian classics as the ideological basis for their operation.

It is said of Tung Chung-shu that he was so devoted to his literary studies that once for three years he did not even look out into his garden. As a result, he wrote a lengthy work known as the *Chun-chiu Fan-lu*, or *Luxuriant Dew from the Spring and Autumn Annals*. It is also said that he used to expound his teachings from behind a curtain, and that these were transmitted by his disciples, one to another, to a remote distance, so that there were some who never had the privilege of seeing his countenance (See his biography in the *History of the Former Han Dynasty*, Ch. 56.).

783 *Mencius*, Ia, 6.

What Tung Chung-shu tried to do was to give a sort of theoretical justification to the new political and social order of his time. According to him, since man is a part of Heaven, the justification of the behavior of the former must be found in the behavior of the latter. He thought with the *Yin-Yang* school that a close Inter connection exists between Heaven and man. Starting with this premise, he combined a metaphysical justification, which derives chiefly from the *Yin-Yang* school, with a political and social philosophy which is chiefly Confucianist.

The word Heaven is a translation of the Chinese word Tien, which is sometimes rendered as "Heaven" and sometimes as "nature." Neither translation is quite adequate, however, especially in Tung Chung-shu's philosophy. My colleague Professor Y. L. Chin has said "Perhaps if we mean by *Tien* both nature and the divinity which presides over nature, with emphasis sometimes on the one and sometimes on the other, we have something approaching the Chinese term." (Unpublished manuscript.) This statement is not true in certain cases, for instance, in those of Lao Tzu and Chuang Tzu, but it is certainly so in the case of Tung Chung-shu. In this chapter, when the word Heaven occurs, I ask the reader to recall this statement of Professor Chin as the definition of the word Tien in Tung Chung-shu's philosophy.

In Chapter XII it was pointed out that there were two distinct lines of thought in ancient China, those of the *Yin* and *Yang* and of the Five Elements, each of which provided a positive interpretation for the structure and origin of the universe. Later, however, these two lines became amalgamated, and in Tung Chung-shu this amalgamation is particularly conspicuous. Thus in his philosophy we find both the theory of the *Yin* and *Yang* and that of the Five Elements.

Cosmological Theory

According to Tung Chung-shu, the universe has ten constituents: Heaven, Earth, the *Yin* and *Yang*, the Five Elements of Wood, Fire, Soil, Metal, and Water, and finally man.[784] His idea of the *Yin* and *Yang* is very concrete. He says:

> Within the universe there exist the ethers of the *Yin* and Yang. Men are constantly immersed in them, just as fish are constantly immersed in water. The difference between the *Yin* and *Yang* ethers and water is that water is visible, whereas the ethers are invisible.[785]

The order of the Five Elements given by Tung Chung-shu differs from that given by the "Grand Norm." (See Ch. XII of this book.) According to him, the first is Wood, the second, Fire, the third Soil, the fourth Metal, and the fifth Water. These Five Elements "each in turn produces the next and is overcome by the next but one in turn"[786] Thus Wood produces Fire, Fire produces Soil, Soil produces Metal, Metal produces Water, and Water produces Wood. This is the process of their mutual production. But Wood overcomes Soil, Soil overcomes

784 *Chun-chiu Fan-lu*, Ch. 81.

785 *Id.*, Ch. 81.

786 *Id.*, Ch. 42.

Water, Water overcomes Fire, Fire overcomes Metal, and Metal overcomes Wood. This is the process of their mutual overcoming.

For Tung Chung-shu, as for the *Yin-Yang* school, Wood, Fire, Metal, and Water each presides over one of the four seasons as well as one of the four directions of the compass. Wood presides over the east and spring, Fire over the south and summer, Metal over the west and autumn, and Water over the north and winter. Soil presides over the center and gives assistance to all the other elements. The alternation of the four seasons is explained by the operations of the *Yin* and *Yang*.[787]

The *Yin* and *Yang* wax and wane and follow fixed circuits which take them through all the four directions. When the *Yang* first waxes, it moves to assist Wood in the east, and then there comes spring. As it grows in strength, it moves to the south where it assists Fire, and then there comes summer. But according to the universal law of "reversal" as maintained by the Lao tzu and the Yi "Appendices," growth must be followed by decay. Hence the Yang, having reached its extreme height, begins to wane, while at the same time the *Yin* begins to wax in turn. The *Yin*, as it does this, moves east to assist Metal,[788] and then there comes autumn. As it gains more strength, it moves north to assist Water, and then there comes winter. But having there reached its climax, it begins to wane, while at the same time the *Yang* starts a new cycle of growth.

Thus the changes of the four seasons result from the waxing and waning movements of the *Yin* and *Yang*, and their succession is really a succession of the *Yin* and *Yang*. Tung Chung-shu says:

> The constant principle of the universe is the succession of the *Yin* and Yang. The *Yang* is Heaven's beneficent force, while the *Yin* is its chastising force.... In the course of Heaven, there are three seasons [spring, summer, and autumns of formation and growth, and one season [winter] of mourning and death.[789]

This shows, according to Tung, that "Heaven has trust in the *Yang* but not in the *Yin*; it likes beneficence but not chastisement."[790] It also shows that "Heaven has its own feelings of joy and anger, and a mind which experiences sadness and pleasure, analogous to those of man. Thus if a grouping is made according to kind, Heaven and man are one."[791]

Man, therefore, both in his physiological and mental aspects, is a replica or duplicate of Heaven.[792] As such, he is far superior to all other things of the world. Man, Heaven, and Earth are "the origins of all things." "Heaven gives them birth, Earth gives them nourishment, and man gives them perfection."[793] As to how man accomplishes this perfection, Tung says that it is done through *li* (ritual) and *yueh*

787 *Id.*, Ch. 42.

788 Not west, though west is the direction for autumn. The reason for this is, according to Tung, is that "Heaven has trust in the *Yang*, but not in the Yin"

789 Chun-chiu Fan-lu, Ch. 49.

790 *Id.*, Ch. 47.

791 *Id.*, Ch. 49.

792 *Id.*, Ch. 41.

793 *Id.*, Ch. 19.

(music), that is to say, through civilization and culture. If there were no civilization and culture, the world would be like an unfinished work, and the universe itself would suffer imperfection. Thus of Heaven, Earth, and man, he says: "These three are related to each other like the hands and feet; united they give the finished physical form, so that no one of them may be dispensed with."[794]

Theory of Human Nature

Since Heaven has its *Yin* and Yang, and man is a replica of Heaven, the human mind consequently also contains two elements:

> *hsing* (man's nature) and *ching* (the emotions or feelings). The word *hsing* is used by Tung Chung-shu sometimes in a broader and sometimes a narrower sense. In the narrow sense, it is something that exists separate from and in opposition to *ching*, whereas in the broader sense it embraces *ching*. In this latter meaning, Tung sometimes refers to *hsing* as the "basic stuff."[795] This basic stuff of man, therefore, consists both of *hsing* (used in the narrow sense) and *ching*. From *hsing* comes the virtue of human-heartedness, whereas from *ching* comes the vice of covetousness. This *hsing*, in the narrow sense, is equivalent to Heaven's *Yang*, and *ching* to its *Yin*.[796]

In this connection Tung Chung-shu takes up the old controversy as to whether human nature, that is, the basic stuff of man, is good or bad. He cannot agree with Mencius that the nature is good, for he says:

> Goodness is like a kernel of grain, and the nature is like the growing plant of the grain. Though the plant produces the kernel, it cannot itself be called a kernel. [Similarly] though the *hsing* [here used in its broader sense, i.e., the basic stuff] produces goodness, it cannot itself be called goodness. The kernel and goodness are both brought to completion through man's continuation of Heaven's work, and are external to the latter]. They do not lie within [the scope of] what Heaven itself does. What Heaven does extends to a certain point and then stops. What lies within this stopping point pertains to Heaven. What lies outside of it pertains to the *chiao* [teaching, culture] of the [sage-] kings. The *chiao* of the [sage-] kings lies outside the *hsing* [basic stuff], yet without it the *hsing* cannot be fully developed.[797]

Thus Tung Chung-shu emphasizes the value of culture, which is indeed that which makes man equal to Heaven and Earth. In this respect he approaches Hsun Tzu. He differs from him, however, in that he does not consider the basic stuff of man to be actually evil.

Goodness is a continuation of nature, not a reversal of it.

Inasmuch as culture, for Tung, is a continuation of nature, he also approaches Mencius. Thus he writes:

> It is said by some that since the nature [of man] contains the beginning of goodness and the mind contains the basic stuff of goodness, how, then,

794 *Ibid.*

795 *Id.*, Ch. 35.

796 *Ibid.*

797 *Id.*, Cl. 36.

can it be that [the nature itself] is not good? But I reply that this is not so. For the silk cocoon contains silk fibers and yet is not itself silk, and the egg contains the chicken, yet is not itself a chicken. If we follow these analogies, what doubt can there be?[798]

The question raised here represents the view of Mencius. In answering it, Tung Chung-shu makes clear the difference between Mencius and himself.

But the difference between these two philosophers is really not much more than verbal. Tung Chung-shu himself says:

> Mencius evaluates [the basic stuff of man] in comparison with the doings of the birds and beasts below, and therefore says that human nature is itself already good. I evaluate it in comparison with the sages above, and therefore say that human nature is not yet good.[799]

Thus the difference between Mencius and Tung Chung-shu is reduced to that between two phrases: "already good" and "not yet good."

Social Ethics

According to Tung Chung-shu, the theory of the *Yin* and *Yang* is also a metaphysical justification of the social order. He writes:

> In all things there must be correlates. Thus if there is the upper, there must be the lower. If there is the left, there must be the right.... If there is cold, there must be heat. If there is day, there must be night. These are all correlates. The *Yin* is the correlate of the Yang, the wife of the husband, the subject of the sovereign. There is nothing that does not have a correlate, and in each correlation there is the *Yin* and Yang. Thus the relationship between sovereign and subject, father and son, and husband and wife, are all derived from the principles of the *Yin* and Yang. The sovereign is Yang, the subject is *Yin*; the father is Yang, the son is *Yin*; the husband is Yang, the wife is *Yin*.... The three cords [*kang*] of the Way of the [true] King may be sought in Heaven.[800]

According to the Confucianists before this period, there are in society five major human relationships, namely, those between sovereign and subject, father and son, husband and wife, elder and younger brother, and friend and friend. Out of these, Tung selects three and calls them the three *kang*. The literal meaning of *kang* is a major cord in a net, to which all the other strings are attached. Thus the sovereign is the *kang* of his subjects, that is, he is their master. Likewise the husband is the *kang* of the wife, and the father is the *kang* of the son.

Besides the three *kang* there exist the five Chang, which were upheld by all Confucianists. *Chang* means a norm or constant, and the five *Chang* are the five constant virtues of Confucianism, namely, *jen* (human-heartedness), *yi* (righteousness), *li* (propriety, rituals, rules of proper conduct), *chih* (wisdom) and *hsin* (good faith) Although Tung Chung-shu did not especially emphasize

---

798 *Id.*, Ch. 5.

799 *Id.*, Ch. 25.

800 *Id.*, Ch. 53.

this point himself, it was commonly held by all the Han scholars that the five virtues have their correlations in the Five Elements. Thus human-heartedness is correlated with Wood in the east; righteousness with Metal in the west; propriety with Fire in the south; wisdom with Water in the north; and good faith with Soil in the center.[801]

The five *chang* are the virtues of an individual, and the three *kang* are the ethics of society. The compound word *kang-chang* meant, in olden times, morality or moral laws in general. Man must develop his nature in the direction of the moral laws, which are the essentials of culture and civilization.

Political Philosophy

Not all men, however, can do this by themselves. Hence it is the function of government to help them in their development. Tung Chung-shu writes:

> Heaven has produced men with natures that contain the "basic stuff" of goodness but are not able to be good in themselves. Therefore Heaven has established for them the institution of the king to make them good. This is the purpose of Heaven.[802]

The king governs with beneficence, rewards, punishments, and executions. These "four ways of government" are modeled on the four seasons. Tung says:

> Beneficence, rewards, punishments, and executions, match spring, summer, autumn, and winter respectively, like the fitting together of the two parts of] a tally. Therefore I say that the king is co-equal with Heaven, meaning that Heaven has four seasons, while the king has four ways of government. Such are what Heaven and man share in common.[803]

The organization of government is also modeled on the pattern of the four seasons. According to Tung, the fact that government officials are graded into four ranks is modeled on the fact that a year has four seasons. Likewise, the fact that each official in each rank has three assistants under him, is modeled on the fact that each season has three months. The officials are thus graded, because men naturally fall into four grades in regard to their ability and virtue. Hence the government selects all men who deserve to be selected, and employs them according to these natural grades of virtue and ability.

Thus Heaven selects the four seasons, and brings them to completion with the twelve [months]; in this way the transformations of Heaven are completely expressed. And it is only the sage who can similarly give complete expression to the changes of man and harmonize them with those of Heaven.[804]

Since the relation between Heaven and man is so close and intimate, hence, Tung maintains, all wrongdoings in human government must result in the manifestation of abnormal phenomena in the world of nature. As had

---

801 See *the Pai Hu Tung Yi or Central Principles from the White Tiger* [Lodge] , a work compiled in A.D. 79, Chaan 8.

802 *Chun-chiu Fan-lu*, Ch. 35.

803 *Id.*, Ch. 55.

804 *Id.*, Ch 24.

already been done by the *Yin-Yang* school, he supplies both a teleological and a mechanistic explanation for this theory.

Teleologically speaking, when there is something wrong in human government, this necessarily causes displeasure and anger on the part of Heaven. Such displeasure or anger is expressed through natural visitations or prodigies, such as earthquakes, eclipses of the sun or moon, droughts or floods. These are Heaven's way of warning the ruler to correct his mistakes.

Mechanistically speaking, however, according to Tung Chung-shu, "all things avoid that from which they differ and cleave to that to which they are similar," and "things definitely call to themselves their own kind." Hence abnormalities on the part of man necessarily call forth abnormalities on the part of nature. Tung Chung-shu, contradicting his teleological theory expressed elsewhere, maintains that this is the law of nature and that in it, there is nothing supernatural.[805]

Philosophy of History

In Chapter XII we saw how Tsou Yen maintained the theory that the changes of dynasties in history are influenced by the movements of the Five Powers. A certain dynasty, because it is associated with a certain Power, must conduct its government in a manner appropriate to that Power. Tung Chung-shu modifies this theory by maintaining that the succession of dynasties does not accord with the movement of the Five Powers, but with a sequence of what he calls the "Three Reigns." These are the Black, White, and Red Reigns. Each has its own system of government and each dynasty represents one Reign.[806]

In actual history, according to Tung, the Hsia Dynasty (traditionally 2205-1766 B.C.) represented the Black Reign; the Shang Dynasty (1766-1122? B.C.) the White Reign; and the Chou Dynasty (1122?-255 B.C.) the Red Reign. This constituted one cycle in the evolution of history. After the Chou Dynasty, the new dynasty would again represent the Black Reign, and the same sequence would recur.

It is interesting to note that in modern times, colors have also been used to denote varying systems of social organization, and that they are the same three as those of Tung Chung-shu. Thus, following his theory, we might say that Fascism represents the Black Reign, Capitalism the White Reign, and Communism the Red Reign. Of course, this is only coincidence. According to Tung Chung-shu, the three Reigns do not differ fundamentally. He maintains that when a new king founds a dynasty, he does so because he has received a special Mandate from Heaven. Hence he must effect certain external changes to make apparent that he has received the new Mandate. These include the shifting of his capital to a new place, assumption of a new title, changing the beginning of the year, and altering the color of clothing worn on official occasions.

As to the great bonds of human relationships and as to morality, government, moral instruction, customs and the meaning of words, these remain wholly as they were before. For why, indeed, should they be changed? Therefore, the king

805 *Id.*, Ch. 57.
806 *Id.*, Ch. 23.

of a new dynasty has the reputation of changing his institutions, but does not as a matter of fact alter the basic principles.[807]

These basic principles are what Tung calls the *Tao*. His biography in the *History of the Former Han Dynasty* (Ch. 56) quotes him as saying: "The great source of *Tao* derives from Heaven; Heaven does not change, nor does the *Tao*."

The theory that the ruler rules through the Mandate of Heaven is not a new one. In the *Book of History* we find sayings implying this theory, and Mencius made it already sufficiently clear. But Tung Chung-shu made it the more articulate by incorporating it into his whole philosophy of nature and man.

In the feudal age, all rulers inherited their authority from their ancestors. Even the First Emperor of the Chin Dynasty was no exception. But the founder of the Han Dynasty was different.

Rising from the common people, he succeeded in becoming Emperor of the (to the Chinese) entire civilized world. This needed some justification, and Tung Chung-shu provided that justification.

His theory that a ruler rules through the Mandate of Heaven justified the exercise of imperial authority and at the same time set certain limits on it. The emperor had to be watchful for manifestations of Heaven's pleasure or displeasure, and to act accordingly. It was the practice of the Han emperors, and to a greater or lesser extent, of the emperors of later dynasties, to examine themselves and the policies of their government, and to try to reform them when abnormal natural phenomena gave them cause to be uneasy.

Tung's theory of the succession of the Reigns also set a certain limit to the tenure of a given dynasty. No matter how good an imperial house may be, the length of its rule is limited. When the end comes, it must give way to another dynasty, the founder of which has received a new Mandate. Such are the measures through which the Confucianists tried to lay restraints upon the power of an absolute monarchy.

Interpretation of the Chun Chiu

According to Tung Chung-shu, neither the Chin nor the Han was the direct successor of the Chou Dynasty. In actual fact, he asserted, it was Confucius who received the Mandate of Heaven to succeed the Chou and to represent the Black Reign. He was not a king *de facto*, but one *de jure*.

This is a strange theory, but it was actually maintained and believed by Tung Chung-shu and his school. The *Chun Chiu*, or *Spring and Autumn Annals*, which was originally a chronicle of Confucius' native state of Lu, was supposed by them (incorrectly) to be a very important political work of Confucius in which he exercised his right as the new king. He represented the Black Reign and instituted all the changes that go with this Reign. Tung Chung-shu was famous for his interpretation of the Chun Chiu, and could justify all aspects of his philosophy by quotations from it. As a matter of fact, he commonly quoted the *Chun Chiu* as the main source of his authority. That is why his work is titled the *Chun-chiu Fan-lu* or *Luxuriant Dew from the Chun Chiu*.

807 *Id.*, Ch. 1.

Tung divides the centuries covered by the Chun Chiu (722-481 B.C.) into three periods, which he calls the "three ages." These are: (1) the age that was personally witnessed by Confucius; (2) that which he heard of through the oral testimony of elder living contemporaries; (3) that which he heard of through transmitted records. According to Tung Chung-shu, Confucius, when writing the Chun Chiu, used differing words or phrases to record the events occurring in these three periods. It is by studying the way in which these words or phrases are used that one may discover the esoteric meaning of the Chun Chiu.

These Stages of Social Progress

There have been three important commentaries written on the *Chun Chiu*, and since the Han Dynasty these have become classics themselves. They are the Tso Commentary, known as the *Tso Chuan* (which probably was originally not written *in toto* as a commentary on the *Chun Chiu*, but was later attached to that work), and the Kung *Yang* and Ku Liang Commentaries. All three are supposedly named after the authors who composed them.

Among the three, the Kung *Yang* Commentary, in particular, interprets the Chun Chiu in agreement with the theories of Tung Chung-shu. Thus in this Commentary we find the same theory of the "three ages." During the latter part of the Han Dynasty, Ho Hsiu (129-182) wrote a commentary on the Kung *Yang* Commentary, in which he still further elaborated this theory.

According to Ho Hsiu, the *Chun Chiu* is a record of the process through which Confucius ideally transformed the age of decay and disorder into that of "approaching peace," and finally into that of "universal peace." He identifies the earliest of the three ages, "the age of which Confucius heard through transmitted records," as one of "decay and disorder." In this period Confucius devoted his whole attention to his own state of Lu, and took Lu as the center of his reforms. The next period, "the age of which Confucius heard through oral testimony," is identified by Ho Hsiu as that of "approaching peace." It was an age in which Confucius, having given good government to his own state, next brought peace and order to all the other Chinese states lying within the "Middle Kingdom." Finally, the last of the three periods, "the age which Confucius personally witnessed," is identified by Ho Hsiu as that of "universal peace." It was an age in which Confucius, having brought all the Chinese states to peace and order, also civilized all the surrounding barbarian tribes. In this period, Ho Hsiu said: "The whole world, far and near, great and small, was like one."[808] Of course Ho Hsiu did not mean that these things were actually accomplished by Confucius. He meant that they were what Confucius would have accomplished if he had actually had the power and authority. Even so, however, the theory remains fantastic, since Confucius himself was alive only during the latter part of the three supposed ages of the *Chun Chiu*.

Ho Hsiu's account of the way in which Confucius, working out from his own state, ideally brought the entire world to peace and order, is similar to the stages in

---

808 See Ho Hsiu's *Commentary on the Kung Yang Commentary to the Chun Chiu*, 1st year of Duke Yin, 722 B.C.

acquiring world peace that are expounded in the *Great Learning*. In this respect, therefore, the *Chun Chiu* becomes an exemplification of the *Great Learning*.

This theory of the three stages of social progress is also found in the *Li Yun* or "Evolution of Rites," one of the chapters in the *Li Chi*. According to this treatise, the first stage was a world of disorder, the second was that of "small tranquility," and the third that of "great unity." The *Li Yun* describes this final age as follows:

> When the great *Tao* was in practice, the world was common to all; men of talents, virtue and ability were selected; sincerity was emphasized and friendship was cultivated. Therefore, men did not love only their own parents, nor did they treat as children only their own sons. A competent provision was secured for the aged till their death, employment was given to the able-bodied, and a means was provided for the upbringing of the young. Kindness and compassion were shown to widows, orphans, childless men, and those who were disabled by disease, so that they all had the wherewithal for support. Men had their proper work and women had their homes. They hated to see the wealth of natural resources undeveloped, [so they developed it, but this development] was not for their own use. They hated not to exert themselves, [so they worked, but their work] was not for their own profit... This was called the great unity.[809]

Though the author of the *Li Yun* put this great unity into a golden age of the past, it certainly represented a current dream of the Han people, who would surely have liked to see something more than simply the political unity of the empire.

809 *Li Chi*, Ch. 7.

XVIII THE ASCENDANCY OF CONFUCIANISM AND REVIVAL OF TAOISM

The Han Dynasty was not only the chronological successor of the Chin, but in many ways was its continuator as well. It stabilized the unification which the Chin had first achieved.

The Unification of Thought

Among the many policies adopted by Chin for this purpose, one of the most important had been that for the unification of thought. After it had conquered all the rival states, *Li* Ssu, its Prime Minister, submitted a memorial to the Chin First Emperor (Chin Shi-huang-ti) which said:

> Of old, the world was scattered and in confusion.... Men valued what they had themselves privately studied, thus casting into disrepute what their superiors had established. At present, Your Majesty has united the world.... Yet there are those who with their private teachings mutually abet each other, and discredit the institutions of laws and instructions....If such conditions are not prohibited, the imperial power will decline above and partisanships will form below.[810]

Then he made a most drastic recommendation: All historical records, save those of Chin, all writings of the "hundred schools" of thought, and all other literature, save that kept in custody of the official Erudites, and save works on medicine, pharmacy, divination, agriculture, and arboriculture, should be delivered to the government and burned. As for any individuals who might want to study, they should "take the official as their teachers."[811]

The First Emperor approved this recommendation and ordered it carried out in 213 B.C. Actually, sweeping though it was, it was nothing more than the logical application of an idea that had long existed in Legalist circles. Thus Han Fei Tzu had already said: "In the state of the intelligent ruler, there is no literature of books and records, but the laws serve as teachings. There are no sayings of the former kings, but the officials act as teachers."[812]

The purpose of *Li* Ssu's recommendation is apparent. He wanted to be sure that there should be but one world, one government, one history, and one way of thought. Books on medicine and other practical subjects were therefore exempted from the general destruction because, as we should say now, they were technical works and so had nothing to do with "ideology."

The very violence of the Chin Dynasty, however, led to its speedy downfall, and following the rise of the Han Dynasty, a good deal of the ancient literature and the writings of the "hundred schools" came to light again. Yet though they disapproved of the extreme measures of their predecessors, the Han rulers came to feel that a second attempt along different lines should be made to unify the

810 *Historical Records*, Ch. 87.

811 *Id.*, Ch. 6.

812 *Han-fei-tzu*, Ch. 49.

thought of the empire, if political unity were to be long maintained. This new attempt was made by Emperor Wu (140-87 B.C.), who in so doing was following a recommendation made by Tung Chung-shu.

In a memorial presented to the Emperor around the year 136 B.C., Tung wrote:

> The principle of Great Unification in the Chun Chin is a permanent warp passing through the universe, and an expression of what is proper extending from the past to the present. But the teachers of today have diverse Ways, men have diverse doctrines, and each of the philosophic schools has its own particular position and differs in the ideas which it teaches. Hence it is that the rulers possess nothing whereby they may effect general unification.

And he concluded his memorial by recommending: "All not within the field of the Liu Yi [Six Classics] should be cut short and not allowed to progress further."[813]

Emperor Wu approved this recommendation and formally announced that Confucianism, in which these Six Classics held a dominant place, was to be the official state teaching. A considerable time was needed, to be sure, before the Confucianists consolidated their newly gained position, and in the process they adopted many ideas from the other rival schools, thus making of Confucianism something very different from the early Confucianism of the Chou Dynasty. We have seen in the last chapter how this process of eclectic amalgamation operated. Nevertheless, from the time of Emperor Wu onward, the Confucianists were given a better chance by the government to expound their teachings than were the other schools.

The principle of Great Unification referred to by Tung Chung-shu is also discussed in the *Kung Yang Commentary* on the *Chun Chiu*. Thus the opening sentence of the Chun Chiu is: "First year [of Duke *Yin*], spring, the King's first month." And on this the *Commentary* remarks: "Why does [the *Chun Chiu*] speak of 'the King's first month'? It has reference to the Great Unification." According to Tung Chung-shu and the Kung *Yang* school, this Great Unification was one of the programs that Confucius set up for his ideally established new dynasty when he wrote the *Chun Chiu*.

The measure carried out by Emperor Wu at Tung Chung-shu's recommendation was more positive and yet more moderate than that suggested by *Li* Ssu to the First Emperor of Chin, even though both equally aimed at an intellectual unification of the entire empire. Instead of rejecting all schools of philosophy indiscriminately, as did the Chin measure, thus leaving a vacuum in the world of thought, the Han measure selected one of them, Confucianism, from among the "hundred schools," and gave it preeminence as the state teaching. Another difference is that the Han measure decreed no punishment for the private teaching of the ideas of the other schools. It only provided that persons who wished to be candidates for official positions should study the Six Classics and Confucianism. By thus making Confucianism the basis of government education, it laid the foundation

813 *History of the Former Han Dynasty*, Ch. 56.

for China's famed examination system used to recruit government officials. In this way the Han measure was in fact a compromise between the Chin measure and the previous practice of private teaching, which had become general after the time of Confucius. It is interesting to see that China's first private teacher now became her first state teacher.

The Position of Confucius in Han Thought

As a result, the position of Confucius became very high by the middle of the first century B.C. About this time, a new type of literature came into existence known as the *wei shu* or apocrypha. *Shu* means book or writing, and wei literally means the woof of a fabric, and is used in apposition to *ching*, a word which is usually translated as classic, but literally means warp. It was believed by many people of the Han period that Confucius, after writing the Six Classics, that is, the six warps of his teaching, had still left something unexpressed. Hence, they thought, he then wrote the six woofs, corresponding to the six warps, by way of supplement. Thus the combination of the six warps and six woofs would constitute the entire teaching of Confucius. Actually, of course, the apocrypha are Han forgeries.

In the apocrypha the position of Confucius reached the highest level it has ever had in China. In one of them, for example, the *Chun Chiu Wei: Han Han Tzu, or Apocryphal Treatise on the Spring and Autumn Annals Guarded Shoots of the Han Dynasty*, it is written: "Confucius said: 'I have examined the historical records, drawn upon ancient charts, and investigated and collected cases of anomalies, so as to institute laws for the emperors of the Han Dynasty.'" And another apocryphal treatise on the *Spring and Autumn Annals*, known as the *Expository Charts on Confucius*, states that Confucius was actually the son of a god, the Black Emperor, and recounts many supposed miracles in his life. Thus in these apocrypha we find Confucius being regarded as a super-human being, a god among men who could foretell the future. If these views had prevailed, Confucius would have held in China a position similar to that of Jesus Christ, and Confucianism would have become a religion in the proper sense of the term.

Soon afterwards, however, Confucianists of a more realistic or rationalistic way of thinking protested against these "extraordinary and strange views" about Confucius and Confucianism. According to them, Confucius was neither a god nor a king, but simply a sage. He neither foresaw the coming of the Han Dynasty, nor did he institute laws for any dynasty. He simply inherited the cultural legacy of the great tradition of the past, to which he gave a new spirit and transmitted for all ages.

The Controversy of the Old and New Text Schools

These Confucianists formed a group known as the Old Text School. This school was so called because it claimed to possess texts of the Classics which went back before the "fires of Chin," that is, the burning of the books of 213 B.C., and hence were written in a form of script that had already become archaic by the time of their recovery. In opposition to this group, Tung Chung-shu and others belonged to the New Text School, so called because its versions of the Classics were written in the form of script that was generally current during the Han Dynasty.

The controversy between these two schools has been one of the greatest in the history of Chinese scholarship. It is not necessary here to go into its details. All that need be said is that the Old Text School arose as a reaction or revolution against the New Text School. At the end of the Former Han Dynasty, it received backing from Liu Hsin (ca. 46 B.C.-A.D. 23), one of the greatest scholars of the time. Indeed, so great was his enthusiasm that at a much later time he was accused, quite falsely, by followers of the New Text school, of having singlehandedly forged all the classics written in the old script.

In recent years it has occurred to me that the origin of these two schools may perhaps go back to the two "wings" of Confucianism that existed before the Chin Dynasty. The New Text School would thus be a continuation of the idealistic wing in early Confucianism, and the Old Text of the realistic wing. In other words, the one would derive from the group headed by Mencius and the other from that headed by Hsun Tzu.

In the *Hsun-tzu*, there is a chapter titled "Against the Twelve Philosophers," one passage of which says:

> There were some who in a general way followed the former kings but did not know their fundamentals.... Basing themselves on ancient traditions, they developed theories which were called those of the Five Elements. Their views were peculiar, contradictory, and without standards; dark and without illustrations; confined and without explanations. Tzu-ssu [grandson of Confucius] began these and Meng Ko [Mencius] followed.[814]

This passage has long puzzled modern scholars, because both in the *Chung Yung*, supposedly the work of Tzu-ssu, and in the *Mencius*, there is no mention of the Five Elements. Nevertheless, we do find in the *Chung Yung* one passage which reads: "When a nation is about to flourish, there are sure to be happy omens; when it is about to perish, there are sure to be unlucky omens." Likewise the *Mencius* states at one point: "In the course of five hundred years, it is inevitable that a [true] king will arise."[815] These passages would seem to indicate that both *Mencius* and the author of the *Chung Yung* (who, if not Tzu-ssu himself, must have been one of his followers) did believe to some extent that an interaction exists between Heaven and man and that history operates in cycles.

These doctrines, it will be remembered, were prominent in the *Yin-Yang* or Five Elements school.

If, then, we consider Tung Chung-shu as being in some way connected with Mencius' wing of Confucianism, Hsun Tzu's accusations against this wing assume added significance. For if Tung Chung-shu's views actually go back in

814 *Hsun-tzu*, Ch. 4.
815 *Mencius*, VIIb, 13.

embryonic form to those of the followers of Mencius, then the latter, judging from their later development by Tung Chung-shu, could indeed be characterized as "peculiar" and "dark."

This hypothesis is further strengthened by the fact that Mencius, like Tung Chung-shu, attached particular value to the Chun Chiu as the work of Confucius. Thus he said:

> Confucius was alarmed [by the disorder of the world] and made the *Chun Chiu*. The *Chun Chiu* should be the work of the Son of Heaven. Therefore Confucius said "Those who understand me, will do so because of the *Chun Chiu*, and those who blame me, will do so also because of the *Chun Chiu*."[816]

Mencius' theory that Confucius, in composing the Chun Chiu, was doing work that pertains to the Son of Heaven, could, if further developed, easily lead to Tung Chung-shu's theory that Confucius had actually received a Mandate from Heaven to become the Son of Heaven.

Tung Chung-shu, furthermore, in expounding his theory of human nature, explicitly compared it with that of Mencius. As we have seen in the last chapter, the differences between the two theories are actually only nominal.

If we accept the hypothesis that the New Text school is the continuation of the idealistic wing of Confucianism headed by Mencius, it is only reasonable to suppose that the Old Text school likewise stems from the realistic wing of Hsun Tzu. Thus it is noticeable that the thinkers of the first century A.D., who were followers of the Old Text school, all took a naturalistic view of the universe similar to that of Hsun Tzu and the *Tao*ists. (Hsun Tzu himself, as we have seen earlier, was influenced by the *Tao*ists In this respect.)

Yang Hsiung and Wang Chung

An example of this point of view is provided by *Yang* Hsiung (53 B.C.-A.D. 18), one of the members of the Old Text school. His *Tai Hsuan* or *Supreme Mystery* is to a considerable extent permeated with the concept that "reversal is the movement of the *Tao*" -- a concept basic both in the *Lao-tzu* and *Book of Changes*.

He also wrote a treatise known as the *Fa Yen* or *Model Speeches*, in which he attacked the *Yin-Yang* school. In this same work, to be sure, he expresses praise for Mencius. This in itself, however, does not invalidate my theory, because even though Mencius may have had some inclination towards the *Yin-Yang* school, he certainly never reached the extremes that characterized the New Text school in the Han Dynasty.

The greatest thinker of the Old Text school is undoubtedly Wang Chung (A.D. 27-ca. 100), an iconoclast with a remarkable spirit of scientific skepticism, whose chief work is the *Lun Heng* or *Critical Essays*. Writing of the spirit which characterizes this work, he says:

> Though the *Shih* [*Book of Odes*] numbered three hundred, one phrase can cover them all, namely, "With undepraved thoughts" [a saying of Confucius in the *Analects*]. And though the chapters of my *Lun Heng* may be numbered

816 *Mencius*, IIIb, 9.

in the tens, one phrase covers them all, namely, "Hatred of fictions and falsehoods."[817]

Again he says: "In things there is nothing more manifest than having results, and in argument there is nothing more decisive than having evidence."[818]

Using this spirit, he vigorously attacks the theories of the *Yin- Yang* school, and especially its doctrine that an interaction exists between Heaven and man, either teleologically or mechanistically.

As to its teleological aspect, he writes:

> The Way of Heaven is that of spontaneity, which consists of non- activity. But if Heaven were to reprimand men, that would constitute action and would not be spontaneous. The school of Huang [the legendary Yellow Emperor] and Lao [Lao Tzu], in its discussion on the Way of Heaven, has found the truth.[819]

As to the mechanistic aspect of the theory, Wang Chung says:

> Man holds a place in the universe like that of a flea or louse under a jacket or robe.... Can the flea or louse, by conducting themselves either properly or improperly, affect the changes or movements in the ether under the jacket?... They are not capable of this, and to suppose that man alone is thus capable is to misconceive of the principle of things and of the ether.[820]

Taoism and Buddhism

Thus Wang Chung prepared the way for the revival of Taoism that came one century later. In speaking about Taoism, I must emphasize again the distinction between *Tao chia* and *Tao chiao*, that is, between Taoism as a philosophy and Taoism as a religion. By the revival of Taoism, I here mean that of *Tao*ist philosophy. This revived *Tao*ist philosophy I will call Neo-Taoism.

It is interesting to note that Taoism as a religion also had its beginnings towards the end of the Han Dynasty, and there are some who refer to this popular form of Taoism as new Taoism.

The Old Text school purged Confucianism of its *Yin-Yang* elements, and the latter later mingled with Taoism to form a new kind of eclecticism known as the *Tao*ist religion. In this way, while the position of Confucius was being reduced from that of a divinity to one of a teacher, Lao Tzu was becoming the founder of a religion which ultimately, in imitation of Buddhism, developed temples, a priesthood, and a liturgy. In this way it became an organized religion almost totally unrecognizable to early *Tao*ist philosophy, which is why it is known as the *Tao*ist religion.

In the first century A.D., already before this was happening, Buddhism was introduced into China from India via Central Asia. In the case of Buddhism as of Taoism, I must emphasize the distinction between *Fo chiao* and *Fo hsueh*, that is, between Buddhism as a religion and Buddhism as a philosophy. As just

817 *Lun Heng*, Ch. 61.
818 *Id.*, Ch. 67.
819 *Id.*, Ch 42.
820 *Id.*, Ch. 43.

stated, Buddhism as a religion did much to inspire the institutional organization of religious Taoism. The latter, as an indigenous faith, was greatly stimulated in its development by the nationalistic sentiments of people who watched with resentment the successful invasion of China by the foreign religion of Buddhism. By some, indeed, Buddhism was considered as a religion of the barbarians. Religious Taoism, to some extent, thus grew as an indigenous substitute for Buddhism, and in the process it borrowed a great deal, including institutions, rituals, and even the form of much of its scriptures, from its foreign rival.

But besides Buddhism as an institutionalized religion, there also existed Buddhism as a philosophy. And whereas the *Tao*ist religion was almost invariably opposed to the Buddhist religion, *Tao*ist philosophy took Buddhist philosophy as its ally. Taoism, to be sure, is less other-worldly than Buddhism. Nevertheless, some similarity exists between their forms of mysticism. Thus the *Tao* of the Taoists is described as unnamable, and the "real suchness" or ultimate reality of the Buddhists is also described as something that cannot be spoken of. It is neither one, nor is it many; it is neither not-one, nor is it not not-many. Such terminology represents what is called in Chinese "thinking into the not-not."

In the third and fourth centuries A.D., famous scholars, who were usually *Tao*ists, were often intimate friends of famous Buddhist monks. The scholars were usually well-versed in Buddhist *sutras*, and the monks in *Tao*ist texts, especially the *Chuang-tzu*. When they met together, they talked in what was known at that time as *Ching tan*, or "pure conversation." When they reached the subject of the not-not, they stopped talking and just silently understood each other with a smile.

In this kind of situation, one finds the spirit of Chan (commonly known in the West under its Japanese name of Zen). The Chan school is a branch of Chinese Buddhism which is really a combination of the most subtle and delicate aspects of both the Buddhist and *Tao*ist philosophies. It exercised a great influence later on in Chinese philosophy, poetry and painting, as we shall see in chapter twenty-two, where it will be discussed in detail.

Political and Social Background

For the moment, let us turn back to the political and social background that lay behind the ascendancy of Confucianism in the Han Dynasty and the subsequent revival of Taoism. The triumph of the formers was not due to mere good luck or the fancy of certain people of the time. There were certain circumstances which made it almost inevitable.

The Chin conquered the other states by a spirit of severity and ruthlessness which was shown both in its domestic control and foreign relations, and was based on the Legalist philosophy. After the fall of Chin, therefore, everyone blamed the Legalist school for its harshness and complete disregard of the Confucian virtues of human-heartedness and righteousness. It is significant that Emperor Wu, besides issuing his decree making Confucianism the state teaching, also decreed in 141 B.C. that all persons who had become experts in the philosophies of Shen Pu-hai, Shang *Yang* and Han Fei (leaders of the Legalist school), as well as Su Chin and Chang Yi (leaders of the Diplomatist school), should be rejected from government posts.[821]

Thus the Legalist school became the scapegoat for all the blunders of the Chin rulers. And among the various schools, those farthest removed from the Legalist were the Confucianist and *Tao*ist. Hence it is natural that there should be a reaction in their favor. During the early part of the Han Dynasty, in fact, Taoism, then known as the "learning of Huang [the Yellow Emperor] and Lao [Lao Tzu]," became quite influential for some time. This can be illustrated by the fact that Emperor Wen (179-157 B.C., grandfather of Emperor Wu) was a great admirer of the "Huang-Lao school"; also that, as pointed out in the last chapter, the historian Ssuma Tan, in his "Essay On the Essential Ideas of the Six Schools," gave highest rank to the Taoist school.

According to the political philosophy of Taoism, a good government is not one that does many things, but on the contrary that does as little as possible. Therefore if a sage-king rules, he should try to undo the bad effects caused by the over-government of his predecessor. This was precisely what the people of the early part of the Han Dynasty needed, for one of the troubles with the Chin had been that it had had too much government. Hence when the founder of the Han Dynasty, Emperor Kao-tsu, led his victorious revolutionary army towards Chang-an, the Chin capital in present Shaanxi Province, he announced to the people his "three-item contract": Persons committing homicide were to receive capital punishment; those injuring or stealing were to be punished accordingly; but aside from these simple provisions, all other laws and regulations of the Chin government were to be abolished.[822] In this way the founder of the Han Dynasty was practicing the "learning of Huang and Lao," even though, no doubt, he was quite unconscious of the fact.

Thus the *Tao*ist philosophy accorded well with the needs of the rulers of the earlier part of the Han Dynasty, whose policy it was to undo what the Chin government had done, and to give the country a chance to recuperate from its long and exhausting wars. When this end had been accomplished, however, the *Tao*ist philosophy became no longer practical, and a more constructive program was called for. This the rulers found in Confucianism.

The social and political philosophy of Confucianism is both conservative yet at the same time revolutionary. It is conservative in that it is essentially a philosophy of aristocracy, yet it is revolutionary in that it gave a new interpretation of this aristocracy. It maintained the distinction between superior man and small man, which had been generally accepted in the feudal China of Confucius' time. But at the same time it insisted that this distinction should not be based, as originally, upon birth, but rather upon individual talent and virtue. Therefore, it considered it quite right that the virtuous and talented among the people should be the ones to occupy noble and high positions in society.

---

821 See the *History of the Former Han Dynasty*, Ch. 6.

822 See *Historical Records*, Ch. 8.

It has been pointed out in Chapter II that Confucianism gave a theoretical justification for the family system which has been the backbone of Chinese society. With the disintegration of the feudal system, the common people gained emancipation from their feudal lords, but the old family system remained. Hence Confucianism likewise remained the underlying philosophy of the existing social system.

The main result of the abolition of the feudal system was the formal separation of political power from economic power. It is true that the new landlords retained great influence, even politically, in their local communities. At least, however, they were no longer the actual political rulers of these communities, even though through their wealth and prestige they could often influence the government-appointed officials. This represented a step forward.

The new aristocrats, such as officials and landlords, though many of them were far from being the virtuous and talented persons demanded by Confucianism, nevertheless all had need for something that Confucianism was particularly qualified to supply. This was a knowledge of the complicated ceremonies and rituals needed to maintain the social distinctions. Thus one of the early acts of the founder of the Han Dynasty, having conquered all his rivals, was to order Shusun Tung, a Confucianist, together with his followers, to draw up a court ceremonial. After the first audience was held at court with the new ceremonies, the founder of the dynasty exclaimed with satisfaction: "Now I realize the nobility of being the Son of Heaven!"[823]

Shusun Tung's action was disapproved of by some of his fellow Confucianists, but its success suggests one reason why the new aristocrats liked Confucianism, even though they might be opposed to or be ignorant of its true spirit.

Most important of all, however, is the fact pointed out by me in Chapter III, that what is known in the West as the Confucianist school is really the School of Literati. The Literati were not only thinkers but also scholars versed in the ancient cultural legacy, and this was a combination that the other schools failed to offer. They taught the literature of the past and carried on the great cultural traditions, giving them the best interpretation they could find. In an agrarian country in which people were unusually respectful of the past, these Literati could not fail to become the most influential group.

As for the Legalist school, though it became the scapegoat for the blunders of the Chin rulers, it was never wholly discarded. In Chapter XIII, I have pointed out that the Legalists were realistic politicians. They were the ones who could present new methods of government to meet new political conditions. Hence, as the Chinese empire expanded, its rulers could not but rely on the principles and techniques of the Legalists. Consequently, ever since the Han Dynasty, orthodox Confucianists have commonly accused the rulers of dynasties of being "Confucianists in appearance but Legalists in reality." As a matter of fact, both Confucianism and Legalism have had their proper sphere of application. The proper sphere for Confucianism is that of social organization, spiritual and

823 *Historical Records*, Ch. 8.

moral culture, and learned scholarship. And the proper sphere for Legalism is that of the principles and techniques of practical government.

Taoism, too, has had its opportunities. In Chinese history there have been many periods of political and social confusion and disorder, when people have had little time or interest for classical scholarship, and have been inclined to criticize the existing political and social system. At such times, therefore, Confucianism has naturally tended to weaken and Taoism to become strong. Taoism has then supplied a sharp criticism against the existing political and social system, as well as an escapist system of thought for avoiding harm and danger. These are exactly what meet the desires of a people living in an age of disorder and confusion.

The collapse of the Han Dynasty in A.D. 220 was followed by a prolonged period of disunity and confusion which was brought to a close only when the country was finally reunited under the Sui Dynasty in A.D. 589. These four centuries were marked by frequent warfare and political cleavage between a series of dynasties that ruled in Central and South China, and another series that had control in the North. It was also marked by the rise to prominence of various nomadic non-Chinese groups, some of whom forcibly broke their way through the Great Wall and settled in North China, and others of whom entered through peaceful colonization. A number of the dynasties of the north were ruled by these alien groups, who, however, failed to extend their power as far south as the Yangtze River. Because of these political characteristics, this period of four centuries from the Han to the Sui Dynasties is commonly known as that of the Six Dynasties, or again, as that of the Northern and Southern Dynasties.

This, then, was politically and socially a dark age, in which pessimism was rife. In some respects it somewhat resembled the roughly contemporary period of the Middle Ages in Europe, and just as in Europe Christianity was the dominant force, so in China the new religion of Buddhism made great strides. It is quite wrong to say, however, as some people do, that it was an age of inferior culture. On the contrary, if we take the word culture in a narrower sense, we may say that it was an age in which, in several respects, we reach one of the peaks of Chinese culture. Painting, calligraphy, poetry, and philosophy were at this time all at their best.

In the next two chapters I shall present the leading indigenous philosophy of the age, a philosophy which I call Neo-Taoism.

XIX NEO-TAOISM: THE RATIONALISTS

Neo-Taoism is a new term for the thought which in the third and fourth centuries. A.D. was known as the *hsuan hsueh*, or literally, "dark learning." The word *hsuan*, meaning dark, abstruse, or mysterious, occurs in the first chapter of the *Lao tzu*, for example, in which the *Tao* is described as "*hsuan* of the *hsuan*," i.e., "mystery of mysteries." Hence the term *hsuan hsueh* indicates that this school is a continuation of Taoism.

The Revival of Interest in the School of Names

In Chapters VIII, IX, and X, we have seen how the School of Names contributed to Taoism the idea of "transcending shapes and features." In the third and the fourth centuries, with the *Tao*ist revival, there came a revival of interest in the School of Names. The Neo-Taoists studied Hui Shih and Kungsun Lung, and linked their *hsuan hsueh* with what they called *ming-li*, i.e., the "distinguishing of terms [*ming*] and analysis of principles [li] ." (This phrase is used by Kuo Hsiang in his commentary to the last chapter of the *Chuang-tzu*). As we have seen in Chapter VIII, this is what Kungsun Lung also did.

In the *Shih-shuo Hsin-yu*, a book about which we shall read more in the next chapter, it is said:

> A visitor asked Yueh Kuang for the meaning of the statement "A chih does not reach," Yueh Kuang made no comment on the statement, but immediately touched the table with the handle of a fly whisk, saying: "Does it reach or does it not?" The visitor answered "It does," Yueh then lifted the fly whisk and asked "If it reaches, how can it be taken away?"[824]

This statement that a chih does not reach is one of the arguments used by the followers of Kung-sun Lung, as reported in the last chapter of the *Chuang-tzu*. The word *chih* literally means a finger, but in Chapter VIII I translated it as "universal." Here, however, Yueh Kuang evidently takes it in its literal sense as finger. The flywhisk cannot reach the table, just as the finger cannot reach the table.

To touch a table with a finger or something else is ordinarily considered as reaching the table. According to Yueh Kuang, however, if the reaching is really reaching, then it cannot be taken away. Since the handle of the fly whisk could be taken away, its apparent reaching was not a real reaching. Thus by examining the term "reaching," Yueh Kuang analyzed the principle of reaching.

This is an illustration of what was known at that time as "conversation on the *ming-li*."

A Reinterpretation of Confucius

It is to be noticed that the Neo-Taoists, or at least a large part of them, still considered Confucius to be the greatest sage. This was partly because the place of

824 *Shin-shuo Hsin-yu*, Ch. 4.

Confucius as the state teacher was by now firmly established, and partly because some of the important Confucian Classics were accepted by the Neo-Taoists, though in the process they were reinterpreted according to the spirit of Lao Tzu and Chuang Tzu.

For instance, the *Analects* contains a saying of Confucius: "YenHui was nearly perfect, yet he was often empty."[825] By this Confucius probably meant that although Yen Hui, his favorite disciple, was very poor, i.e., "empty," that is, devoid of worldly goods, he was nevertheless very happy, which showed that his virtue was nearly perfect. In the *Chuang-tzu*, however, as we have seen in Chapter X, there is an apocryphal story about Yen Hui's "sitting in forgetfulness," i.e., engaging in mystic meditation, Hence with this story in mind one commentator on the Analects, *Taishih Shuming* (474-546), said:

> Yen Hui disregarded human-heartedness and righteousness, and forgot ceremonies and music. He gave up his body and discarded his knowledge. He forgot everything and became one with the infinite. This is the principle of forgetting things. When all things were forgot-ten, he was thus empty. And yet, compared with the sages, he was still not perfect. The sages forget that they forget, whereas even the great worthies cannot forget that they forget. If Yen Hui could not forget that he forgot, it would seem that something still remained in his mind. That is why he is said to have been often empty.[826]

Another commentator, Ku Huan (died 453), commenting on the same passage, remarks:

> The difference between the sages and the worthies is that the latter retain a desire to be without desire, while the former do not have that desire for no desire. Therefore the mind of the sages is perfectly empty, while that of the worthies is only partially so. From the point of view of the world, the worthies lack any desire. But from the point of view of what is not of this world, the worthies do desire to be without desire. The emptiness of Yen Hui's mind was not yet complete. That is why he is said to have been often empty.[827]

The Neo-Taoists, despite their Taoism, considered Confucius to be even greater than Lao Tzu and Chuang Tzu. Confucius, they maintained, did not speak about forgetfulness, because he had already forgotten that he had learned to forget. Nor did he speak about absence of desire, because he had already reached the stage of lacking any desire to be without desire. Thus the Shih-shuo Hsin-*yu* records a "pure conversation" between Pei Hui and Wang Pi. The latter was one of the great figures of the school of "dark learning," whose Commentaries on the Lao-Tzu and Book of Changes have become classics in themselves. The conversation reads:

> Wang Pi [226-249] when young, once went to see Pei Hui. [Pei] Hui asked him why, since *Wu* [Non-being] is fundamental for all things, Confucius

825 *Analects of Confucius*, XI, 18.

826 Quoted by Huang Kan (488-545), in his *Sub-Commentary on the Analects*," *Chuan* 6

827 *Ibid.*

did not speak about it, whereas Lao Tzu expounded this idea without stopping. To this Wang Pi answered:

"The sage [Confucius] identified himself with Wu [Non-being] and realized that it could not be made the subject of instruction, with the result that he felt compelled to deal only with *Yu* [Being]. But Lao Tzu and Chuang Tzu had not yet completely left the sphere of *Yu* [Being], with the result that they constantly spoke of their own deficiencies."[828]

This explanation reflects the idea expressed by Lao Tzu that "he who knows does not speak; he who speaks does not know."[829]

Hsiang Hsiu and Kuo Hsiang

One of the greatest, if not the greatest, philosophical works of this period is the *Commentary* on the *Chuang-tzu* by Kuo Hsiang (died ca. 312) There had been a historical problem as to whether this work was really his, for he was accused of being a plagiarist by his contemporaries, who asserted that his *Commentary* was really the work of another slightly earlier scholar, Hsiang Hsiu (ca.221-ca. 300). It would seem that both men wrote *Commentaries* on the *Chuang-tzu*, and that their ideas were very much the same, so that in the course of time their *Commentaries* probably became combined to form single work. The *Shih-shuo Hsin-yu* (Ch. 4), for example, speaks of a Hsiang-Kuo interpretation (i.e., an interpretation by Hsiang Hsiu and Kuo Hsiang) made on the "Happy Excursion" (the first chapter of the *Chuang-tzu*), as existing in apposition to one by Chih-tun (314-366), a famous Buddhist monk of the time. Hence the present *Commentary* on the *Chuang-tzu*, though it bears the name of Kuo Hsiang, seems to represent the joint Hsiang-Kuo interpretation of the *Chuang-tzu*, and probably was the work of both men. The *Chin Shu* or *History of the Chin Dynasty* is probably right, therefore, when in its biography of Hsiang Hsiu it says that he wrote a *Commentary on the Chuang-tzu*, and that then Kuo Hsiang "extended it."[830]

According to this same *History of the Chin Dynasty*, both Hsiang Hsiu and Kuo Hsiang were natives of the present Henan Province, and were great figures in the school of "dark learning," as well as being "fine or pure conversationalists." In this chapter I shall take these two philosophers as representative of the exponents of the rationalistic group in Neo-Taoism, and refer to their *Commentary on the Chuang-tzu* as the Hsiang-Kuo interpretation, following the usage of the *Shih-shuo Hsinyu*.

The Tao is "Nothing"

The Hsiang-Kuo interpretation made several most important revisions in the original Taoism of Lao Tzu and Chuang Tzu. The first is that the *Tao* is really *wu*, i.e., "nothing" or "nothingness." Lao Tzu and Chuang Tzu also had maintained that the *Tao* is Wu, but by Wu they meant having no name. That is, according to them, the Tao is not a thing; hence it is unnamable. But according

828 *Shih-shuo Hsin-yu*, Ch. 4.

829 *Lao-tzu*, Ch. 56.

830 *History of the Chin Dynasty*, Ch. 49.

to the Hsiang-Kuo interpretation, the *Tao* is really literally nothing. "The *Tao* is everywhere, but everywhere it is nothing."[831]

The same text says:

> In existence, what is prior to things? We say that the *Yin* and *Yang* are prior to things. But the *Yin* and *Yang* are themselves things; what then, is prior to the *Yin* and *Yang*? We may say that Tzu Jan [nature or naturalness is prior to things. But Tzu Jan is simply the naturalness of things. Or we may say that the *Tao* is prior to things. But the *Tao* is nothing. Since it is nothing, how can it be prior to things? We do not know what is prior to things, yet things are continuously produced. This shows that things are spontaneously what they are; there is no Creator of things.[832]

In another passage, it is also stated:

> Some people say that the penumbra is produced by the shadow, the shadow by the bodily form, and the bodily form by the Creator. I would like to ask whether the Creator is or is not. If He is not, how can He create things? But if He is, He is simply one of these things, and how can one thing produce another? ... Therefore there is no Creator, and everything produces itself. Everything produces itself and is not produced by others. This is the normal way of the universe.[833]

Lao Tzu and Chuang Tzu denied the existence of a personal Creator by substituting in His place an impersonal *Tao*, which is that by which all things come to be. Hsiang-Kuo went a step further by insisting that the *Tao* is really *nothing*. According to them, the statement of the earlier *Tao*ists that all things come into being from the *Tao* simply means that all things come to be by themselves. Hence they write: "The *Tao* is capable of nothing. To say that anything is derived from the *Tao* means that it comes of itself."[834]

Likewise, the statement of the earlier *Tao*ists that all things come into being from Being, and Being comes into being from Non-being, simply means that Being comes into being by itself. In one passage of the *Commentary* it is said:

> Not only is it the case that Non-being cannot become Being, but Being also cannot become Non-being. Though Being may change in thousands of ways, it cannot change itself into Non-being. Therefore there is no time when there is no Being. Being eternally exists.[835]

The "Self-transformation" of Things

That everything spontaneously produces itself is what Hsiang- Kuo call the theory of tu hua or self-transformation. According to this theory, things are not created by any Creator, but these things are nevertheless not lacking in relations, one with another. Relations exist and these relations are necessary. Thus the *Commentary* states:

831 *Commentary on the "Chuang-tzu"*, Ch. 6.
832 *Id.*, Ch. 22.
833 *Id*, Ch. 2.
834 *Id.*, Ch. 6.
835 *Id.*, Ch. 22.

When a man is born, insignificant though he be, he has the properties that he necessarily has. However trivial his life may be, he needs the whole universe as a condition for his existence. All things in the universe, all that exist, cannot cease to exist without some effect on him. If one factor is lacking, he might not exist. If one principle is violated, he might not be living.[836]

Everything needs every other thing, but everything nevertheless exists for its own sake and not for the sake of any other thing. The *Commentary* says:

In the world, everything considers itself as "this" and other things as "other." The "this" and the "other" each works for itself. They seem to be far away from each other like] the mutual opposition of east and west. Yet the "this" and the "other" have a relation to each other like that between the lips and the teeth. The lips do not exist for the teeth, but when the lips are lost, the teeth feel cold. Therefore the work of the "other" for itself has contributed a great deal to help the "this."[837]

According to Hsiang-Kuo, the interrelationship of things is like that between the armies of two allied forces. Each army fights for its own country, but each at the same time helps the other, and the defeat or victory of the one cannot but have an effect on the other.

Everything that exists in the universe needs the universe as a whole as a necessary condition for its existence, yet its existence is not directly produced by any other particular thing. When certain conditions or circumstances are present, certain things are necessarily produced. But this does not mean that they are produced by any single Creator or by any individual. In other words, things are produced by conditions in general and not by any other specific thing in particular. Socialism, for instance, is a product of certain general economic conditions, and was not manufactured by Marx or Engels, still less by the former's Communist Manifesto.

In this sense, we can say that everything produces itself and is not produced by others.

Hence everything cannot but be what it is. The *Commentary* states:

It is not by accident that we have our life. It is not by chance that our life is what it is. The universe is very extended; things are very numerous. Yet, in it and among them, we are just what we are.... What we are not, we cannot be. What we are, we cannot but be. What we do not do, we cannot do. What we can do, we cannot but do. Let everything be what it is, then there will be peace.[838]

This is also true of social phenomena. The *Commentary* says again: "There is nothing which is not natural.... Peace or disorder, success or failures ... are all the product of nature, not of man."[839] By "the product of nature," Hsiang-Kuo mean that they are the necessary result of certain conditions or circumstances. In Chapter 14 of the *Chuang-tzu*, the text states that sages disturb the peace of the world; to which the *Commentary* says:

836 *Id.*, Ch. 6.
837 *Id.*, Ch. 17.
838 *Id*, Ch. 5.
839 *Id*, Ch. 7.

> The current of history, combined with present circumstances, is responsible for the present crisis. It is not due to any certain individuals. It is due to the world at large. The activity of the sages does not disturb the world, but the world itself becomes disorderly.

Institutions and Morals

Hsiang-Kuo considers the universe as being in a continuous state of flux. They write in their *Commentary:*

> Change is a force, unobservable yet most strong. It transports heaven and earth towards the new, and carries mountains and hills away from the old. The old does not stop for a moment, but immediately becomes the new. All things ever change.... All that we meet secretly passes away. We ourselves in the past are not we ourselves now. We still have to go forward with the present. We cannot keep ourselves still.[840]

Society, too, is always in a state of flux. Human needs are constantly changing. Institutions and morals that are good for one time may not be good for another. The *Commentary* says: "The institutions of the former kings served to meet the needs of their own time. But if they continue to exist when time has changed, they become a bogey to the people, and begin to be artificial."[841]

Again:

> Those who imitate the sages imitate what they have done. But what they have done has already passed away, and therefore it cannot meet the present situation. It is worthless and should not be imitated. The past is dead while the present is living. If one attempts to handle the living with the dead, one will certainly fail.[842]

Society changes with circumstances. When the circumstances change, institution and morals should change with them. If they do not, they become artificial and are "a bogey to the people." It is natural that new institutions and new morals should spontaneously produce themselves. The new and the old differ from each other because their times are different. Both of them serve to meet the needs of their time, so neither is superior nor inferior to the other. Hsiang-Kuo do not oppose institutions and morals as such, as did Lao Tzu and Chuang Tzu. They simply oppose those institutions and morals that are out-of-date and therefore unnatural for the present world.

Yu-wei and Wu-wei

Thus Hsiang-Kuo gave a new interpretation to the earlier *Tao*ist ideas about the natural and the artificial and about *yu-wei* or having activity, and *wu-wei* or having no activity (also translated as non-action). When there is a change of social circumstances, new institutions and morals spontaneously produce themselves. To let them go means to follow the natural and be *wu-wei,* i.e., without action.

840 *Id,* Ch. 6.
841 *Id,* Ch. 14
842 *Id.,* Ch. 9.

To oppose them and to keep the old ones those are already out-of-date is to be artificial and *yu*-wei, i.e., with action. In one passage of the *Commentary* it is said:

> When water runs down from a high to a low place, the current is irresistible. When small things group with what is small, and large things with what is large, their tendency cannot be opposed. When a man is empty and without bias, everyone will contribute his wisdom to him. What does he do, who is the leader of men, when facing these currents and tendencies? He simply trusts the wisdom of the time, relies on the necessity of circumstances, and lets the world take care of itself. That is all.[843]

If an individual, in his activities, allows his natural abilities to exercise themselves fully and freely, he is *wu-wei*. Otherwise he is *yu-wei*. In one passage of the Commentary it is said:

> A good driver must let his horse exercise itself to the full of its ability. The way to do so is to give it freedom.... If he allows his horses to do what they can do, compelling neither the slow ones to run fast nor the fast ones to walk slowly, though he may travel through the whole world with them, they rather enjoy it. Hearing that horses should be set free, some people think that they should be left wild. Hearing the theory of non-action, some people think that lying down is better than walking. These people are far wrong in understanding the ideas of Chuang Tzu.[844]

Despite this criticism, it would seem that in their understanding of Chuang Tzu such people were not far wrong. Yet Hsiang-Kuo, in their own interpretation of him, were certainly highly original.

Hsiang-Kuo also give a new interpretation to the ideas of simplicity and primitivity of the earlier *Tao*ists. In their *Commentary* they write:

> If by primitivity we mean the undistorted, the man whose character is not distorted is the most primitive, though he may be capable of doing many things. If by simplicity we mean the unmixed, the form of the dragon and the features of the phoenix are the most simple, though their beauty is all surpassing. On the other hand, even the skin of a dog or a goat cannot be primitive and simple, if its natural qualities are distorted by, or mixed with, foreign elements.[845]

Knowledge and Imitation

Lao Tzu and Chuang Tzu both opposed sages of the sort ordinarily regarded as such by the world. In the earlier *Tao*ist literature, the word "sage" has two meanings. By it, the *Tao*ists either mean the perfect man (in the *Tao*ist sense) or the man with all sorts of knowledge. Lao Tzu and Chuang Tzu attacked knowledge, and hence the sage of the latter kind, the man who has knowledge. But from the preceding pages we can see that Hsiang-Kuo had no objection to some men's being sages. What they did object to is the attempt of some people to

843 *Id.*, Ch. 6.

844 *Id.*, Ch. 9.

845 Id., Ch. 15.

imitate the sages. Plato was born a Plato, and Chuang Tzu a Chuang Tzu. Their genius was as natural as the form of a dragon or the features of a phoenix. They were as "simple" and "primitive" as anything can be. They were not wrong in writing their Republic and "Happy Excursion," for in so doing they were merely following their own natures.

This view is exemplified in the following passage from the *Commentary*:

> By knowledge we mean [the activity that attempts] what is beyond [one's natural ability]. That which is within the proper sphere [of one's natural ability] is not called knowledge. By being within the proper sphere we mean acting according to one's natural ability, attempting nothing that is beyond. If carrying ten thousand *chun* [thirty carries] is in accordance with one's ability, one will not feel the burden as weighty. If discharging ten thousand functions [is in accordance with one's ability], one will not feel the task as taxing.[846]

Thus if we understand knowledge in this sense, neither Plato nor Chuang Tzu should be considered as having any knowledge.

It is only the imitators that have knowledge. Hsiang-Kuo seems to have regarded imitation as wrong for three reasons. First, it is useless. They write in the *Commentary*:

> Events in ancient times have ceased to exist. Though they may be recorded, it is not possible for them to happen again in the present. The ancient is not the present, and the present is even now changing. Therefore we should give up imitation, act according to our nature, and change with the times. This is the way to perfection.[847]

Everything is in flux. Every day we have new problems, new needs, and meet new situations. We should have new methods to deal with these new situations, problems, and needs. Even at a single given moment, the situations, problems, and needs of different individuals differ from one another. So must their methods. What, then, is the use of imitation?

Second, imitation is fruitless. One passage of the Commentary tells us:

> With conscious effort, some people have tried to be a *Li* Chu [a great artisan] or a Shih Kuang [a great musician], but have not succeeded. Yet without knowing how, *Li* Chu and Shih Kuang were especially talented in their eye and ear. With conscious effort, some people have tried to be sages, but have not succeeded. Yet without knowing how, the sages became sages. Not only is it the sages and *Li* Chu and Shih Kuang who are difficult to imitate. We cannot even be fools, or dogs, by simply wishing or trying to be so.[848]

Everything must be what it is. One thing simply cannot be the other.

Third, imitation is harmful. The Commentary states again:

> There are some people who are not satisfied with their own nature and always attempt what is beyond it. This is to attempt what is impossible, and is like a circle imitating a square, or a fish imitating a bird.... They go ever

846 *Id.*, Ch. 3.

847 *Id.*, Ch. 13.

848 *Id.*, Ch. 5.

further, the more remote their goal seems to be. The more knowledge they gain, the more nature they lose.[849]

Again:

> The nature of everything has its limit. If one is led on by what is beyond it, one's nature will be lost. One should disregard the inducement, and live according to oneself, not according to others. In this way the integrity of one's nature will be preserved.[850]

Not only is there no possibility for one to succeed by imitating others, but by that very act, there is a great probability that one will lose one's self. This is the harm of imitation.

Thus imitation is useless, fruitless, and harmful. The only sensible mode of life is "to live according to oneself," which is also to practice the theory of non-action.

The Equality of Things

But if one can really live according to oneself, disregarding the inducements offered by others, that means that one is already able to get rid of what Hsiang-Kuo call the "trouble of preferring one thing to another."[851] In other words, one is already able to understand the principle of the equality of things and to see things from a higher point of view. One is already on the royal road to the state of non-distinction of the undifferentiable whole.

In the second chapter of the *Chuang-tzu,* Chuang Tzu emphasized the theory of non-distinction, especially the non-distinction of right and wrong. In their *Commentary,* Hsiang-Kuo expound this theory with more eloquence. Thus to the saying of Chuang Tzu that "the universe is a finger, all things are a horse," the *Commentary* observes:

> In order to show that there is no distinction between right and wrong, there is nothing better than illustrating one thing with another. In so doing we see that all things agree in that they all consider themselves to be right and others to be wrong. Since they all agree that all others are wrong, hence in the world there can be no right; and since they all agree that they themselves are right, hence in the world there can be no wrong.

How can it be shown that this is so? If the right is really absolutely right, in the world there should be none that considers it to be wrong. If the wrong is really absolutely wrong, in the world there should be none that considers it to be right. The fact that there are uncertainty between right and wrong, and confusion in distinctions, shows that the distinctions between right and wrong are due to a partiality of view, and that all things are really in agreement. In our observation, we see this truth everywhere. Therefore, the perfect man, knowing that the universe is a finger and all things are a horse, thus rests in great peace. All things function according to their nature, and enjoy themselves. [Between them] there is no distinction between right and wrong.[852]

---

849 *Id.*, Ch. 2.
850 *Id.*, Ch. 10.
851 *Id.*, Ch. 2.
852 *Ibid*

Absolute Freedom and Absolute Happiness

If one can transcend the distinctions between things, one can enjoy the absolute freedom and have the absolute happiness that are described in the first chapter of the Chuang-tzu. In the many stories contained in this chapter, Chuang Tzu mentions the great roc bird, the small bird, the cicada, the "small knowledge" of the morning mushroom, whose life extends only to the same evening, the "great knowledge" of the old trees whose experience covers thousands of years, small officers of limited talents, and the philosopher Lieh Tzu who could ride on the wind. Regarding these stories, the Hsiang-Kuo Commentary says:

> If there is satisfaction for their natures, the roc has nothing to be proud of in comparison with the small bird, and the small bird has no desire for the Celestial Lake [the dwelling place of the roc]. Therefore, though there is a difference between the great and the small, their happiness is the same.[853]

Their happiness, however, is only relative happiness. If things only enjoy themselves in their finite spheres, their enjoyment must also be finite. Thus in his first chapter, Chuang Tzu concludes his stories with one about the really independent man who transcends the finite and becomes one with the infinite, so that he enjoys infinite and absolute happiness. Because he transcends the finite and identifies himself with the infinite, he has "no self." Because he follows the nature of things and lets everything enjoy itself, he has "no achievement." And because he is one with the *Tao*, which is unnamable, he has "no name."

This idea is developed by the Hsiang-Kuo Commentary with charity and eloquence:

> Everything has its proper nature, and that nature has its proper limitation. The differences between things are like those between small and great knowledge, short and long life.... All believe in their own sphere and none is intrinsically superior to others.

After giving different illustrations, Chuang Tzu concludes with the independent man who forgets his own self and its opposite, and who ignores all the differences.

All things enjoy themselves in their own sphere, but the independent man has neither achievement nor name. Therefore, he who unites the great and the small is one who ignores the distinction between the great and the small. If one insists on the distinctions, the roc, the cicada, the small officer, and Lieh Tzu riding on the wind, are all troublesome things. He who equalizes life and death is one who ignores the distinction of life and death. If one insists on the distinction, the <??ta chun> [an old tree] and the chrysalis, Peng Tsu [a Chinese Methuselah] and the morning mushroom, all suffer early death. Therefore, he who makes excursion into the realm of non-distinction between great and small has no limitation. He who ignores the distinction of life and death has no terminal. But those whose happiness lies within the finite sphere will certainly suffer limitation. Though they are allowed to make excursions, they are not able to be independent.[854]

---

853 *Id.*, Ch. 1.

854 *Chuang-tzu*, Ch. 1.

In the first chapter, Chuang Tzu describes the independent man as "one who chariots on the normality of the universe, rides upon the transformation of the six elements, and makes excursion into the infinite." On this the Hsiang-Kuo *Commentary* remarks:

> The universe is the general name of all things. The universe has all things as its contents, and all things must take Tzu Jan [the natural] as their norm. What is spontaneously so, and not made to be so, is the natural. The roc can fly in high places, the quail in low ones. The ta chun tree can live for a long time, the mushroom for a short one. All these capacities are natural, and are not caused or learned. They are not caused to be so, but are naturally so; that is the reason why they are normal. Therefore to chariot on the normality of the universe is to follow the nature of things. To ride upon the transformation of the six elements is to make excursion along the road of change and evolution. If one proceeds in this way, where can one reach the end? If one chariots on whatever one meets, what will one be required to depend upon? This is the happiness and freedom of the perfect man who unites his own self with its opposite.
>
> If one has to depend upon something, one cannot be happy, unless one gets hold of the thing upon which one depends. Although Lieh Tzu could pursue his way in such a fine manner, he still had to depend upon the wind, and the roc was even more dependent. Only he who makes no distinction between himself and other things and follows the great evolution, can really be independent and always free. He not only sets himself free, but also follows the nature of those who have to depend upon something, allowing them to have that something upon which they depend. When they have that upon which they depend, they all enjoy the Great Freedom.[855]

In the Hsiang-Kuo system, the *Tao* is really nothing. In this system, *Tien* or *Tien Ti* (literally "Heaven" or "Heaven and Earth," but here translated as the universe) becomes the most important idea. *Tien* is the general name of things, and is thus the totality of all that is. To see things from the point of view of *Tien* and to identify oneself with *Tien*, is to transcend things and their differences, or, as the Neo-Taoists said, "to transcend shapes and features."

Thus the Hsiang-Kuo Commentary, besides making important revisions in original Taoism, also expressed more articulately what in the Chuang-tzu is only suggestive. Those, however, who prefer suggestiveness to articulateness, would no doubt agree with a certain Chan monk who remarked "People say that it was Kuo Hsiang who wrote a commentary on Chuang Tzu. I would say that it was Chuang Tzu who wrote a commentary on Kuo Hsiang." (See Chapter I).

855 *Commentary* on the "Chuang-tzu," Ch. 1.

XX NEO-TAOISM: THE SENTIMENTALISTS

In their *Commentary on the "Chuang-tzu,"* Hsiang Hsiu and Kuo Hsiang gave a theoretical exposition of the man who has a mind or spirit transcending the distinctions of things and who lives "according to himself but not according to others." This quality of such a man is the essence of what the Chinese call *feng liu*.

Feng Liu and the Romantic Spirit

In order to understand *feng liu*, we must turn to the *Shih-shuo Hsin yu* or *Contemporary Records of New Discourses* (abbreviated as *Shih-shuo*), a work by Liu Yi-ching (403-444 supplemented by a commentary by Liu Hsun (463-521). The Neo-Taoists and their Buddhist friends of the Chin Dynasty were famous for what was known at the time as *ching tan*, that is, pure or fine conversation. The art of such conversation consisted in expressing the best thought, which was usually *Tao*istic, in the best language and tersest phraseology. Because of its rather precious nature, it could be held only between friends of a comparable and rather high intellectual level, and hence it was regarded as one of the most refined of intellectual activities. The *Shih-shuo* is a record of many such "pure conversations" and their famous participants. Through them, it gives a vivid picture of those people of the third and fourth centuries who were followers of the *feng liu* ideas. Ever since its compilation, therefore, it has been a major source for studying the *feng liu* tradition.

What, then, is the meaning of *feng liu*? It is one of those elusive terms which to the initiated conveys a wealth of ideas, but is most difficult to translate exactly. Literally, the two words that form it mean "wind and stream," which does not seem to help us very much. Nevertheless, they do, perhaps, suggest something of the freedom and ease which are some of the characteristics of the quality of *feng liu*.

I confess that I have not yet understood the full significance of the words romanticism or romantic in English, but I suspect that they are a fairly rough equivalent of *feng liu*. *Feng liu* is chiefly connected with Taoism. This is one of the reasons why I have said in Chapter II that the Confucianist and *Tao*ist traditions in Chinese history are in some degree equivalent to the classical and romantic traditions in the West.

The Han (206 B.C.-A.D. 220) and Tsin (265-420) are not only the names of two different dynasties in Chinese history, but also, because of their very different social, political, and cultural characteristics, are designations of two different styles of literature and art, and of two different manners of living. The Han style and manner are ones of dignity and grandeur; those of the Tsin are ones of elegance and freedom. Elegance is also one of the characteristics of *feng liu*.

"Yang Chu's Garden of Pleasure"

Something must first be said here about the seventh chapter in the *Tao*ist work known as the Lieh-tzu, a chapter titled "Yang Chu"(translated by Anton Forke as Yang Chu's Garden of Pleasure). As we have already seen in our Chapter VI, what is said in this "Yang Chu" chapter cannot represent the view of the genuine Yang Chu of ancient times. The Lieh-tzu itself, indeed, is now considered by Chinese scholars as a work of the third century A.D. Hence its "Yang Chu" chapter must also be a production of this period. It accords well with the general trend of thought of that time, and is in fact an expression of one aspect of *feng liu*.

In the "Yang Chu" chapter, a distinction is made between the external and the internal. Thus the spurious "Yang Chu" is reported as saying "There are four things which do not allow people to have peace. The first is long life, the second is reputation, the third is rank, and the fourth is riches. Those who have these things fear ghosts, fear men, fear power, and fear punishment. They are called fugitives.... Their lives are controlled by externals. But those who follow their destiny do not desire long life. Those who are not fond of honor do not desire reputation. Those who do not want power desire no rank. And those who are not avaricious have no desire for riches. Of this sort of men it may be said that they live in accordance with their nature.... They regulate their lives by internal things."

In another passage an imaginary conversation is recorded between Tzu-chan, a famous statesman of the state of Cheng who lived in the sixth century B.C., and his two brothers. Tzu-chan governed the state for three years and governed well. But his two brothers were out of his control; one of them was fond of feasting and the other of gallantry.

One day, Tzu-chan spoke to his brothers, saying: "Those things in which man is superior to beasts and birds are his mental faculties. Through them he gets righteousness and propriety, and so glory and rank fall to his share. You are only moved by what excites your sense, and indulge only in licentious desires, endangering your lives and natures...."

To this the brothers answered: "If one tries to set external things in order, these external things do not necessarily become well-ordered, and one's person is already given toil and trouble. But if one tries to set the internal in order, the external things do not necessarily fall into disorder, and one's nature becomes free and at ease. Your system of regulating external things will do temporarily and for a single kingdom, but it is not in harmony with the human heart. Our method of regulating what is internal, on the contrary, can be extended to the whole world, and [when it is extended] there is no need for princes and ministers."

What this chapter calls regulating the internal corresponds to what Hsiang-Kuo call living according to oneself; what it calls regulating external things corresponds to what Hsiang-Kuo call living according to others. One should live according to oneself, and not according to others. That is to say, one should live in accord with one's own reason or impulse, and not according to the customs and morals of the time. To use a common expression of the third and fourth centuries, one should live according to *tzu-jan* (the spontaneous, the natural), and not according to *ming-chiao* (institutions and morals). All the Neo-Taoists agree on this. But there is still a difference among them between the rationalists and sentimentalists. The former, as represented by Hsiang-Kuo, emphasize living according to reason, while the latter, as represented by the men who will be mentioned below, emphasize living according to impulse.

The ideas of living according to impulse is expressed in extreme form in the "Yang Chu" chapter. In one passage we read that Yen Ping-chung asked Kuan Yi-wu (both famous statesmen of the state of *Chi* in ancient times, though historically they were not contemporaries) about cultivating life. "Kuan Yi-wu replied: 'The only way is to give it its free course, neither checking nor obstructing it.' Yen Ping-chung asked: 'And as to details?'

"Kuan Yi-wu replied: 'Allow the ear to hear anything that it likes to hear. Allow the eye to see whatever it likes to see. Allow the nose to smell whatever it likes to smell. Allow the mouth to say whatever it likes to say. Allow the body to enjoy whatever it likes to enjoy. Allow the mind to do whatever it likes to do.

"What the ear likes to hear is music, and prohibition of the hearing of music is called obstruction to the ear. What the eye likes to see is beauty, and prohibition of the seeing of beauty is called obstruction to sight. What the nose likes to smell is perfume, and prohibition of the smelling of perfume is called obstruction to smell. What the mouth likes to talk about is right and wrong, and prohibition of the talking about right and wrong is called obstruction to understanding. What the body likes to enjoy is rich food and fine clothing, and prohibition of the enjoying of these is called obstruction to the sensations of the body. What the mind likes is to be free, and prohibition of this freedom is called obstruction to the nature.

"'All these obstructions are the main causes of the vexations of life. To get rid of these causes and enjoy oneself until death, for a day, a month, a year, or ten years -- this is what I call cultivating life. To cling to these causes and be unable to rid oneself of them, so as thus to have a long but sad life, extending a hundred, a thousand, or even ten thousand years -- this is not what I call cultivating life.[856]

"Kuan Yi-wu then went on: 'Now that I have told you about cultivating life, what about the way of taking care of the dead?' Yen Ping-chung replied: 'Taking care of the dead is a very simple matter.... For once I am dead, what does it matter to me? They may burn my body, or cast it into deep water, or inter it, or leave it uninterred, or throw it wrapped up in a mat into some ditch, or cover it with princely apparel and embroidered garments and rest it in a stone sarcophagus. All depends on chance.'

"Turning to Pao-shu Huang-tzu, Kuan Yi-wu then said to him:

We two have by this made some progress in the way of life and death.'"

Living According to Impulse

What the "Yang Chu" chapter here describes represents the spirit of the age of Tsin, but not the whole or best of that spirit. For in this chapter, as exemplified by the above, what "Yang Chu" seems to be interested in is mostly the search for pleasure of a rather coarse sort. To be sure, the pursuit of such pleasure is not, according to Neo-Taoism, necessarily to be despised. Nevertheless, if this is

856 *Shih-s1wo Hsin-yu*, CS. 23.

made our sole aim, without any understanding of what "transcends shapes and features," to use the Neo-Taoist expression, this can hardly be called *feng liu* in the best sense of the term.

In the Shih-shuo we have a story about Liu Ling (c. 221-c. 300), one of the Seven Worthies of the Bamboo Grove (seven "famous scholars" who gathered for frequent convivial conversations in a certain bamboo grove). This story tells us that Liu evoked criticism through his habit of remaining completely naked when in his room. To his critics he rejoined "I take the whole universe as my house and my own room as my clothing. Why, then, do you enter here into my trousers?"' Thus Liu Ling, though he sought for pleasure, had a feeling of what lies beyond the world, i.e., the universe. This feeling is essential for the quality of *feng liu.*

Those who have this feeling and who cultivate their mind in Taoism, must have a more subtle sensitivity for pleasure and more refined needs than sheerly sensual ones. The *Shih-shuo* records many unconventional activities among the "famous scholars" of the time. They acted according to pure impulse, but not with any thought of sensuous pleasure. Thus one of the stories in the *Shih-shuo* says: "Wang Hui-chih [died c. 388, son of China's greatest calligrapher, Wang Hsi-chih] was living at Shan-yin [near present Hangzhou]. One night he was awakened by a heavy snowfall. Opening the window, he saw a gleaming whiteness all about him....Suddenly he thought of his friend Tai Kuei. Immediately he took a boat and went to see Tai. It required the whole night for him to reach Tai's house, but when he was just about to knock at the door, he stopped and returned home. When asked the reason for this act, he replied: 'I came on the impulse of my pleasure, and now it is ended, so I go back. Why should I see Tai?'"[857]

The *Shih-shuo* records another story which says that Chung Hui (225-264, a statesman, general, and writer) regretted that he had not yet enjoyed the opportunity of meeting Chi Kang (223-262, a philosopher and writer). Therefore, he one day went with several other notables to visit him. Chi Kang's hobby was that of forging metal, and when Chung Hui arrived there, he found Chi Kang at his forge under a great tree. Hsiang Hsiu (author of the *Commentary on the "Chuang-tzu"* described in the last chapter) was assisting Chi Kang to blow the fire with a bellows, and Chi Kang himself continued his hammering just as if no one else were there. For a while the host and guests did not exchange a single word. But when Chung Hui started to go, Chi Kang asked him: "What did you hear that caused you to come, and what have you seen that causes you to go?" To this Chung Hui answered: "I heard what I heard, so I came, and I have seen what I have seen, so I go."[858] The men of the Tsin Dynasty greatly admired the physical and spiritual beauty of a great personality. Chi Kang was famous for his personality, which was compared by some people to a jade mountain and by others to a pine tree.[859] Perhaps it was these things that Chung heard of and saw.

Another story in the *Shih-shuo* tells us:

When Wang Hui-chih was traveling by boat, he met Huan Yi traveling by

857 *Ibid.*

858 *Id.*, Ch. 24.

859 *Id.*, Ch. 14.

> land along the bank. Wang Hui-chih had heard of Huan Yi's fame as a flute player but he was not acquainted with him. When someone told him that the man traveling on the bank was Huan Yi, he sent a messenger to ask him to play the flute. Huan Yi had also heard of the fame of Wang Hui-chih, so he descended from his chariot, sat on a chair, and played the flute three times. After that, he ascended his chariot and went away. The two men did not exchange even a single word.[860]

They did not do this because what they wished to enjoy was only the pure beauty of the music. Wang Hui-chih asked Huan Yi to play the flute for him, because he knew he could play it well, and Huan Yi played for him, because he knew Wang could appreciate his playing. When this had been done, what else was there to talk about?

The *Shih-shuo* contains another story which says that Chih-tun (314-366, famous Buddhist monk) was fond of cranes. Once a friend gave him two young ones. When they grew up, Chih-tun was forced to clip their wings so that they would not fly away.

When this was done, the cranes looked despondent, and Chih-tun too was depressed, and said: "Since they have wings that can reach the sky, how can they be content to be a pet of man?" Hence when their feathers had grown again, he let the cranes fly away.[861]

Another story tells us about Juan *Chi* (210-263, a philosopher and poet), and his nephew Juan Hsien, who were two of the Seven Worthies of the Bamboo Grove. All members of the Juan family were great drinkers, and when they met, they did not bother to drink out of cups, but simply sat around a large wine jar and drank from that. Sometimes the pigs also came, wanting a drink, and then the Juans drank together with the pigs.[862]

The sympathy of Chih-tun for the cranes and the indiscriminate generosity of the Juans to the pigs show that they had a feeling of equality and non-differentiation between themselves and other things of nature. This feeling is essential in order to have the quality of *feng liu* and to be artistic. For a true artist must be able to project his own sentiment to the object he depicts, and then express it through his medium. Chih-tun himself would not have liked to be a pet of man, and he projected this sentiment to the cranes. Though he is not known to have been an artist, he was, in this sense, a very real one.

The Emotional Factor

As we have seen in Chapter X, the sage, according to Chuang Tzu, has no emotions. He has a high understanding of the nature of things, and so is not affected by their changes and transformations. He "disperses emotion with reason." The *Shih-shuo* records many people who had no emotions. The most famous case is that of Hsieh An (320-385). When he was Prime Minister at

860 *Id.*, Ch 23.
861 *Id.*, Ch. 2.
862 *Id*, Ch. 23.

the Tsin court, the northern state of Chin started a large-scale offensive against Tsin. Its army was led by the Chin Emperor in person, and so great was it that the Emperor boasted that his soldiers, by throwing their whips into the Yangtze River, could block its course. The people of Tsin were greatly alarmed, but Hsieh An calmly and quietly appointed one of his nephews, Hsieh Hsun, to lead an army against the invaders. At a battle famous in history as the Battle of the Fei River, in the year 383, Hsieh Hsun won a decisive victory and the men of Chin were driven back. When the news of the final victory reached Hsieh An, he was playing chess with a friend. He opened the letter, read it, and then put it aside and continued to play as before. When the friend asked what was the news from the front, Hsieh An, as calmly as ever, replied "Our boys have decisively defeated the enemy."[863]

The *San Kuo Chih* or *History of the Three Kingdoms,* however, records a discussion between Ho Yen (died 249) and Wang Pi (226-249, greatest commentator on the Lao-tzu) on the subject of the emotions. Ho Yen, following the original theory of Chuang Tzu, maintained that "the sage has neither pleasure nor anger, sorrow nor gladness." In this he was seconded by Chung Hui (the man who went to visit Chi Kang in the story given above). Wang Pi, however, held a different opinion. According to him, "that in which the sage is superior to ordinary people is the spirit. But what the sage has in common with ordinary people are the emotions.

The sage has a superior spirit, and therefore is able to be in harmony with the universe and to hold communion with Wu [i.e., the *Tao*]. But the sage has ordinary emotions, and therefore cannot respond to things without joy or sorrow. He responds to things, yet is not ensnared by them. It is wrong to say that because the sage has no ensnarement, he therefore has no emotions." (Ch. 28, *Commentary*).

The theory of Wang Pi can be summarized by the statement that the sage "has emotions but no ensnarement" What this statement exactly means, Wang Pi does not make clear. Its implications were developed much later by Neo-Confucianism, and we shall have a chance to analyze them in Chapter XXIV. At present we need merely point out that though many of the Neo-Taoists were very rational, there were also many who were very sentimental.

As stated earlier, the Neo-Taoists stressed subtle sensitivity. Having this sensitivity, coupled with the aforementioned theory of self-expression, it is not surprising that many of them gave free vent to their emotions anywhere and at any time these emotions arose.

An example is the *Shihshuo*'s story about Wang Jung (234-305), one of the Seven Worthies of the Bamboo Grove. When Wang lost a child, his friend Shan Chien went to console him. Wang could not restrain himself from weeping, whereupon Shan said to him:

> "It was only a baby, so why do you behave like this?" Wang Jung replied "The sage forgets emotions, and lowly people [who are insensitive] do not

863 *Id*, Ch. 6.

reach emotions. It is people like us who have the most emotions." To this Shan Chien agreed and wept also.[864]

This saying of Wang Jung explains very well why many of the Neo-Taoists were sentimentalists. In most cases, however, they were sentimental, not about some personal loss or gain, but about some general aspect of life or of the universe. The *Shih-shuo* says that Wei Chieh (286-312, known as the most beautiful personality of his time), when about to cross the Yangtze River, felt much depressed, and said "When I see this vast river, I cannot help but feel that all kinds of sentiments are gathering in my mind. Being not without feeling, how can one endure these emotions?"[865]

The *Shih-shuo* says also that every time Huan Yi, the flute player mentioned earlier, heard people singing, he would exclaim: "What can I do!" Hsieh An heard of this and remarked: "Huan Yi can indeed be said to have deep feelings."[866]

Because of this subtle sensitivity, these men of *feng liu* spirit were often impressed by things that would not ordinarily impress others. They had sentiments about life and the universe as a whole, and also about their own sensitivity and sentiments. The *Shih-shuo* tells us that when Wang Chin ascended the Mao Mountain (in present Shandong Province), he wept and said: "Wang Po-*yu* of Lang-ya [i.e., myself] must at last die for his emotions."[867]

The Factor of Sex

In the West, romanticism often has in it an element of sex. The Chinese term *feng liu* also has that implication, especially in its later usage. The attitude of the Tsin Neo-Taoists towards sex, however, seems to be purely aesthetic rather than sensuous. As illustration, the *Shih-shuo* tells us that the neighbor of Juan *Chi* had a beautiful wife. The neighbor was a wine merchant, and Juan *Chi* used to go to his house to drink with the merchant's wife. When Juan became drunk, he would sleep beside her. The husband at first was naturally suspicious, but after paying careful attention, he found that Juan *Chi* did nothing more than sleep there.[868]

The *Shih-shuo* says again that Shan *Tao* (205-283, statesman and general), Chi Kang, and Juan *Chi* were great friends. Shan *Tao*'s wife, Han, noticed the close friendship of the three and asked her husband about it. Shan *Tao* said, "At present they are the only men who can be my friends." It was the custom in China then that a lady was not allowed to be introduced to the friends of her husband. Hence, Han told her husband that, when next his two friends came, she would like to have a secret peep at them. So on the next visit, she asked her husband to have them stay overnight. She prepared a feast for them, and, during the night, peeped in at the guests through a hole in the wall. So absorbed was she in looking at them that she stood there the whole night. In the morning the husband came to her room and asked: "What do you think of them?" She replied "In talent you are not equal to

---

864 *Id.*, Ch. 17.
865 *Id.*, Ch. 2.
866 *Id.*, Ch. 23.
867 *Ibid.*
868 *Ibid.*

them, but with your knowledge, you can make friends with them." To this Shan *Tao* said "They, also, consider my knowledge to be superior."[869]

Thus both Juan *Chi* and the Lady Han seemed to enjoy the beauty of the opposite sex without any sensuous inclinations. Or, it may be said, they enjoyed the beauty, forgetting the sex element. Such are the characteristics of the *feng liu* spirit of the Tsin Neo-Taoists. According to them, *feng liu* derives from *tzu-jan* (spontaneity, naturalness), and *tzu-jan* stands in opposition to *ming chiao* (morals and institutions which form the classical tradition of Confucianism. Even in. this period, however, when Confucianism was in eclipse, one famous scholar and writer named Yueh Kuang (died 304) said "In the *ming-chiao*, too, there is fundamentally room for happiness."[870] As we shall see in Chapter XXIV, Neo-Confucianism was an attempt to find such happiness in *ming-chiao*.

869 *Id.*, Ch. 19.
870 *Id.*, Ch. 1.

XXI THE FOUNDATION OF CHINESE BUDDHISM

The introduction of Buddhism into China has been one of the greatest events in Chinese history, and since its coming, it has been a major factor in Chinese civilization, exercising particular influence on religion, philosophy, art, and literature.

Introduction and Development of Buddhism in China

The exact date of the introduction of Buddhism is a disputed question not yet settled by historians, but it took place probably in the first half of the first century A.D. Traditionally, it is said to have entered during the reign of Emperor Ming (58-75), but there is now evidence that it had already been heard of in China before this time. Its subsequent spread was a long and gradual process. From Chinese literary sources we know that in the first and second centuries A.D., Buddhism was considered as a religion of the occult arts, not greatly differing from the occultism of the *Yin-Yang* school or of the later *Tao*ist religion.

In the second century the theory was actually developed in certain circles that Buddha had been nothing more than a disciple of Lao Tzu. This theory gained its inspiration from a statement in the biography of Lao Tzu in the *Shih Chi* or *Historical Records* (Ch.63), where it is said that Lao Tzu, late in life, disappeared and nobody knew where he went. Elaborating this statement, ardent *Tao*ists created the story that when Lao Tzu went to the West, he finally reached India, where he taught the Buddha and other

Indians, and had a total of twenty-nine disciples. The implication was that the teaching of the Buddhist *Sutras* (sacred texts) was simply a foreign variant of that of the *Tao Te Ching*, that is, of the *Lao-tzu*.

In the third and fourth centuries an increasing number of Buddhist texts of a more metaphysical nature were translated, so that Buddhism became better understood. At this time Buddhism was regarded as similar to philosophical Taoism, especially the philosophy of Chuang Tzu, rather than to Taoism as a religion.

Often the Buddhist writings were interpreted with ideas taken from philosophical Taoism. This method was called that of ko yi, that is, interpretation by analogy.

Such a method naturally led to inaccuracy and distortion. Hence in the fifth century, by which time the flood of translations was rapidly increasing, the use of analogy was definitely abandoned. Yet the fact remains that the great Buddhist writers of the fifth century, even including the Indian teacher, Kumarajiva, continued to use *Tao*ist terminology, such as *Yu* (Being, existent), *Wu* (Non-being, non-existent), *yu-wei* (action) and *wu-wei* (non-action), to express Buddhist ideas. The difference between this practice and the method of analogy, however, is that in the latter one sees only the superficial similarity of words, while in the former one sees the inner connections of the ideas expressed by them. Hence, judging from the nature of the works of these writers, this practice, as we shall see later, did not indicate any misunderstanding or distortion of Buddhism, but rather a synthesis of Indian Buddhism with Taoism, leading to the foundation of a Chinese form of Buddhism. Here it should be pointed out that the terms, "Chinese Buddhism" and "Buddhism in China," are not necessarily synonymous.

Thus there were certain schools of Buddhism which confined themselves to the religious and philosophical tradition of India, and made no contact with those of China. An example is the school known by the Chinese as the *Hsiang tsung* or *Wei-shih tsung* (School of Subjective Idealism), which was introduced by the famous Chinese pilgrim to India, Hsuan-tsang (596-664). Schools like this may be called "Buddhism in China." Their influence was confined to restricted groups of people and limited periods. They did not and could not reach the thought of every intellectual, and therefore played little or no part in the development of what may be called the Chinese mind.

On the other hand, "Chinese Buddhism" is the form of Buddhism that has made contact with Chinese thought and thus has developed in conjunction with Chinese philosophical tradition. In later pages we will see that the Middle Path school of Buddhism bears some similarity to philosophical Taoism. Its interaction with the latter resulted in the Chan or Zen school, which though Buddhist, is at the same time Chinese. Although a school of Buddhism, its influence on Chinese philosophy, literature, and art has been far reaching.

General Concepts of Buddhism

Following the introduction of Buddhism into China, tremendous efforts were made to translate the Buddhist texts into Chinese. Texts of both the Hinayana (Small Vehicle) and Mahayana (Great Vehicle) divisions of Buddhism were translated, but only the latter gained a permanent place in Chinese Buddhism.

On the whole, the way in which Mahayana Buddhism most influenced the Chinese has been in its concept of the Universal Mind, and in what may be called its negative method of metaphysics. Before going into a discussion of these, we must first survey some of the general concepts of Buddhism.

Although there are many schools of Buddhism, each with something different to offer, all generally agree in their belief in the theory of *Karma* (translated in Chinese as *Yeh*). *Karma* or *Yeh* is usually rendered in English as deed or action, but its actual meaning is much wider than that, for, what it covers is not merely confined to overt action, but also includes what an individual sentient being speaks and thinks. According to Buddhism, all the phenomena of the universe, or, to be more exact, of the universe of an individual sentient being, are the manifestations of his mind. Whenever he acts, speaks, or even thinks, his mind is doing something, and that something must produce its results, no matter how far in the future. This result is the retribution of the *Karma*. The *Karma* is the cause and its retribution is the effect. The being of an individual is made up of a chain of causes and effects.

The present life of a sentient being is only one aspect in this whole process. Death is not the end of his being, but is only another aspect of the process. What an individual is in this life comes as a result of what he did in the past, and what he does in the present will determine what he will be in the future. Hence what he does now will bear its fruits in a future life, and what he will do then will again bear its fruits in yet another future life, and so on *ad infinitum*. This chain of causation is what is called *Samsara*, the Wheel of Birth and Death. It is the main source from which come the sufferings of individual sentient beings.

According to Buddhism, all these sufferings arise from the individual's fundamental ignorance of the nature of things. All things in the universe are the manifestations of the mind and therefore are illusory and impermanent, yet the individual ignorantly craves for and cleaves to them. This fundamental ignorance is called *Avidya*, which in Chinese is translated as *Wu-ming*, non-enlightenment. From ignorance comes the craving for and cleaving to life, because of which the individual is bound to the eternal Wheel of Birth and Death, from which he can never escape.

The only hope for escape lies in replacing ignorance with enlightenment, which in Sanskrit is called *Bodhi*. All the teachings and practices of the various Buddhist schools are attempts to contribute something to the *Bodhi*. From them the individual, in the course of many rebirths, may accumulate *Karma* which does not crave for and cleave to things, but avoids craving and cleaving. The result is an emancipation of the individual possessing this *Karma* from the Wheel of Birth and Death. And this emancipation is called *Nirvana*.

What, exactly, does the state of *Nirvana* signify? It may be said to be the identification of the individual with the Universal Mind, or with what is called the Buddha-nature; or it is the realization or self-consciousness of the individual's original identification with the Universal Mind. He is the Universal Mind, but formerly he did not realize it, or was not self-conscious of it. The school of Mahayana Buddhism known by the Chinese as the *Hsing tsung* or School of Universal Mind expounded this theory. (For this school, *hsing* or nature and *hsing* or mind are the same). In expounding it, the school introduced the idea of Universal Mind into Chinese thought.

There were other schools of Mahayana Buddhism, however such as that known by the Chinese as the *Kung tsung* or School of Emptiness, also known as the School of the Middle Path, which would not describe *Nirvana* in this way. Their method of approach is what I call the negative method.

The Theory of Double Truth

This School of the Middle Path proposed what it called the theory of double truth: truth in the common sense and truth in the higher sense. Furthermore, it maintained, not only are there these two kinds of truth, but they both exist on varying levels. Thus, what on the lower level is truth, in the higher sense becomes on the higher level merely truth in the common sense. One of the great Chinese Masters of this school, Chi-tsang (549-623), describes this theory as including the three following levels of double truth:

(1) The common people take all things as really *yu* (having being, existent) and know nothing about *wu* (having no being, non-existent). Therefore the Buddhas have told them that actually all things are *wu* and empty. On this level, to say that all things are *yu* is the common sense truth, and to say that all things are *wu* is the higher sense truth.

(2) To say that all things are *yu* is one-sided, but to say that all things are *wu* is also one-sided. They are both one sided, because they give people the wrong impression that *wu* or non-existence only results from the absence or removal of *yu* or existence. Yet in actual fact, what is *yu* is simultaneously what is *wu*. For instance, the table standing before us need not be destroyed in order to show that it is ceasing to exist. In actual fact it is ceasing to exist all the time. The reason for this is that when one starts to destroy the table, the table which one thus intends to destroy has already ceased to exist. The table of this actual moment is no longer the table of the preceding moment. It only looks like that of the preceding moment. Therefore on the second level of double truth, to say that all things are *yu* and to say that all things are *wu* are both equally common sense truth. What one ought to say is that the "not-one-sided middle path" consists in understanding that things are neither *yu* nor *wu*. This is the higher sense truth.

(3) But to say that the middle truth consists of what is not one-sided (i.e., what is neither *yu* nor *wu*), means to make distinctions. And all distinctions are themselves one-sided. Therefore on the third level, to say that things are neither *yu* nor *wu*, and that herein lies the not-one-sided middle path, is merely common sense truth. The higher truth consists in saying that things are neither *yu* nor *wu*, neither not-*yu* nor not-*wu*, and that the middle path is neither one-sided nor not-one-sided.[871]

In this passage I have retained the Chinese words *yu* and *wu*, because in their use the Chinese thinkers of the time saw or felt a similarity between the central problem discussed by Buddhism and that discussed by Taoism, in which the same words are prominent. Though deeper analysis shows that the similarity is in some respects superficial, nevertheless, when the *Tao*ists spoke of *Wu* as transcending shapes and features, and the Buddhists spoke of *Wu* as "not-not," there is a real similarity.

Still another real similarity between the Buddhists of this particular school and the *Tao*ists is their method of approach and the final results achieved by this method. The method is to make use of different levels of discourse. What is said on one level is to be immediately denied by a saying on a higher level. As we have seen in Chapter X, this is also the method 'used in the Chi Wu Lun or "Equality of Things" in the *Chuang-tzu*, and it is the method that has just been discussed above.

When all is denied, including the denial of the denial of all, one arrives at the same situation as found in the philosophy of Chuang Tzu, in which all is forgotten, including the fact that one has forgotten all. This state is described

871 *Erh-ti Chang or Chapter on the Double Truth*, Sec. 1.

by Chuang Tzu as "sitting in forgetfulness," and by the Buddhists as *Nirvana*. One cannot ask this school of Buddhism what, exactly, the state of *Nirvana* is, because, according to it, when one reaches the third level of truth, one cannot affirm anything.

Philosophy of Seng-chao

One of the great teachers of this same school in China in the fifth century was Kumarajiva, who was an Indian but was born in a state in the present Chinese Turkistan. He came to Chang-an (the present Xian in Shaanxi Province) in 401, and lived there until his death in 413. During these thirteen years, he translated many Buddhist texts into Chinese and taught many disciples, among them some who became very famous and influential. In this chapter I shall mention two of them, Seng-chao and *Tao*-sheng.

Seng-chao (384-414) came from the vicinity of the above- mentioned city of Chang-an. He first studied Lao Tzu and Chuang Tzu, but later became a disciple of Kumarajiva. He wrote several essays which have been collected as the *Chao Lun* or *Essays of Seng-chao*. One of them, titled "There Is No Real Unreality," says:

> All things have that in them which makes them not be *yu* [having being, existent] and also have that in them which makes them not be *wu* [having no being, non-existent]. Because of the former, they are *yu* and yet not *yu*. Because of the latter, they are *wu* and yet not *wu*.... Why is this so? Suppose the *yu* is really *yu*, then it should be *yu* for all time and should not owe its *yu* to the convergence of causes. [According to Buddhism, the existence of anything is due to the convergence of a number of causes.] Suppose the ten is really *wu*, then it should be *wu* for all time and should not owe its *wu* to the dissolution of causes. If the *yu* owes its *yu* to causation, then the *yu* is not really *yu*.... But if all things are *wu*, then nothing would come about. If something comes about, it cannot be altogether nothing.... If we want to affirm that things are *yu*, yet there is no real existence of this *yu*. If we want to affirm that they are *wu*, yet they have their shapes and features. To have shapes and features is not the same as *wu*, and to be not really *yu* is not the same as *yu*. This being so, the principle of "no real unreality" is clear.[872]

In another essay, titled "On the Immutability of Things," Seng-chao says:

> Most men's idea of mutability is that things in the past do not come down to the present. They therefore say that there is mutability and no immutability. My idea of immutability is also that things of the past do not come down to the present. Therefore I on the contrary say that there is immutability and no mutability. That there is mutability and no immutability is because things of the past do not come down to the present. That there is immutability and no mutability is because things of the past do not vanish away with the past [i.e., though they do not exist today, they did exist in the past].... If we search for past things in

872 *Chao Lun*, Ch. 2.

the past, they were not *wu* in the past. If we search for these past things in the present, they are not *yu* in the present.... That is to say, past things are in the past, and are not things that have receded from the present. Likewise present things are in the present, and are not something that have come down from the past.... The effect is not the cause, but because of the cause there is the effect. That the effect is not the cause shows that the cause does not come down to the present. And that, there being the cause, there is therefore the effect, shows that cause do not vanish in the past. The cause has neither come down nor has it vanished. Thus the theory of immutability is dear.[873]

The idea here is that things undergo constant change at every moment. Anything existing at any given moment is actually a new thing of that moment and not the same as the thing that has existed in the past. In the same essay Seng-chao says:

[There was a man by the name off Fan-chih who, having become a monk in his early years, returned home when his hair was white. On seeing him the neighbors exclaimed at seeing a man of the past who was still alive. Fan-chih said "I look like the man of the past, but I am not he."

At every moment there has been a Fan-chih. The Fan-chih of this moment is not a Fan-chih who has come down from the past, and the Fan-chih of the past was not a Fan-chih of the present who receded into the past. Judging from the fact that everything changes at every moment, we say that there is change but no permanence. And judging from the fact that everything at every moment remains with that moment, we say that there is permanence but no change.

This is Seng-chao's theory to substantiate the double truth on the second level. On this level, to say that things are *yu* and permanent, and to say that things are *wu* and mutable, are both common sense truth. To say that things are neither *yu* nor *wu*, neither permanent nor mutable, is the higher sense truth.

Seng-chao also gives arguments to substantiate the double truth on the third or highest level. This he does in an essay titled "On *Prajna* [i.e., Wisdom of the Buddha] Not Being Knowledge." *Prajna* is described by Seng-chao as Sage-knowledge, but, he says, this:

Sage-knowledge is really not knowledge. For knowledge of a thing consists in selecting a quality of that thing and taking that quality as the object of knowledge. But Sage-knowledge consists in knowing about what is called Wu (Non-being), and this Wu "transcends shapes and features" and has no qualities; hence it can never be the object of knowledge. To have knowledge of Wu is to be one with it. This state of identification with Wu is called *Nirvana*. *Nirvana* and *Prajna* are two aspects of one and the same state of affairs. As Nirvana is not something to be known, so *Prajna* is knowledge which is not knowledge.[874] (*Chao Lun*, Ch. 3.) Hence, on the third level of truth, nothing can be said and one must remain silent.

---

873 *Id.*, Ch. 1.

874 *Id.*, Ch. 3.

Philosophy of Tao-sheng

Seng-chao died when only thirty years old, so that his influence was less than it might otherwise have been. *Tao*-sheng (died 434), who was a fellow student with Seng-chao under Kumarajiva, was born at Peng cheng in the northern part of the present Jiangsu Province. He became a monk of wide learning, great brilliance, and eloquence, of whom it is said that when he spoke even the stones beside him nodded their heads in assent. In his later years he taught at Lushan in the present Jiangxi Province, which was the center of Buddhist learning at that time, and the place where such great monks as *Tao*-an (died 385) and Hui-yuan (died 416) had lectured. *Tao*-sheng advanced many theories so new and revolutionary that once he was publicly banished from Nanking by the conservative monks.

Among these is the doctrine that "a good deed entails no retribution." His essay on this subject is now lost. But in the Hung Ming *Chi* or Collected Essays on Buddhism, a work compiled by Seng-yu (died 518), there is a treatise by Hui-yuan titled "On the Explanation of Retribution." This essay may represent some aspects of *Tao*-sheng's concept, though we cannot be sure. Its general idea is to apply the *Tao*ist ideas of *wu-wei* and wu-hsin to metaphysics. As we have seen, *wu-wei* literally means non-action, but this non action does not really signify no action; rather it signifies action that takes place without effort. When one acts spontaneously, without any deliberate discrimination, choice, or effort, one is practicing non-action. Wu-hsin also literally means no mind. When one practices *wu-wei* in the manner described above, one is also practicing *wu-hsin*. If, argues Hui-yuan, one follows the principles of *wu-wei* and *wu-hsin*, one then has no craving for or cleaving to things, even though one may pursue various activities. And since the effect or retribution of one's Karma is due to one's craving and cleaving or attachment, one's Karma under these circumstances will not entail any retribution.[875] This theory of Hui-yuan, regardless of whether it is the same as *Tao*-sheng's original idea or not, is an interesting extension to Buddhist metaphysics of a *Tao*ist theory which originally possessed purely social and ethical significance. As such, it is certainly an important development in Chinese Buddhism, and one that was to be followed later by the Chan school.

Another theory of *Tao*-sheng is that Buddhahood is to be achieved by Sudden Enlightenment. His essay on this subject is also lost, but the theory is preserved in Hsieh Ling-gun's (died 433) *Pien Tsung Lun* or "Discussion of Essentials." It was developed in opposition to another theory, that of gradual attainment, according to which Buddhahood is to be achieved only through the gradual accumulation of learning and practice. *Tao*-sheng and Hsieh Ling-yun did not deny the importance of such learning and practice, but they maintained that its accumulation, no matter how great, is only a sort of preparatory work, which in itself is insufficient for one ever to achieve Buddhahood. Such achievement is an instantaneous act, like the leaping over of a deep chasm. Either one makes the leap successfully, in which case one reaches the other side and thus achieves

875 *Hung Ming Chi*, Chuan 5.

Buddhahood in its entirety in a flash, or one fails in one's leap, in which case one remains as one was. There are no intermediate steps between.

The reason advanced for this theory is that to achieve Buddhahood means to be one with *Wu* (Non-being) or, as one might say, with the Universal Mind. The *Wu*, since it transcends shapes and features, is not a "thing" in itself, and so is not something that can be divided into parts. Therefore one cannot gain oneness with a part of it today and oneness with another part of it tomorrow. Oneness means oneness with the whole of it. Anything less than this is no longer oneness.

The *Pien Tsung Lun* records many arguments on this subject between Hsieh Ling-yun and others. One monk named Seng-wei argued that if the student is one with *Wu*, he will no longer speak about it, but if he is to learn about *Wu* in order to get rid of *Yu* (Being), this learning represents a process of gradual enlightenment. To this Hsieh Ling-yun answered that when a student is still in the realm of *Yu*, whatever he does is learning, but not Enlightenment. Enlightenment itself is something beyond *Yu*, though a student must devote himself first to learning, in order to attain Enlightenment.

Seng-wei again asked: If a student devotes himself to learning and hopes thereby for identification with *Wu*, does he in this way make some advancement? If he does not, why does he pursue learning? But if he does, is this not gradual enlightenment? To this Hsieh Ling-yun answered that devotion to learning can have the positive achievement of suppressing the impure element of the mind. Though such suppression seems to be its extinction, in actual fact it is still not without impure attachment. It is only with Sudden Enlightenment that all attachments are gone.

Again Seng-wei asked: If a student devotes himself to learning and practice, can he achieve a temporary identification with *Wu*?

If he can, this temporary identification is better than no identification at all, and is it not gradual enlightenment? To this Hsieh Ling-yun answered that such temporary identification is a false one. A real identification is by its nature everlasting. Though the temporary identification seems to be a real identification, it is so only in the same sense that the suppression of the impure element of the mind seems to be its extinction.

All these arguments are endorsed by *Tao*-sheng in a letter also included in the *Pien Tsung Lun*. The latter is now to be found in the *Kuang Hung Ming Chi* or *Further Collections of Essays on Buddhism* (*Chuan* 18) a work compiled by *Tao*-hsuan (596-667).

Another of *Tao*-sheng's theories is that every sentient being possesses the Buddha-nature or Universal Mind. His essay on this subject is also lost, but its ideas can be gathered from his commentaries on several Buddhist Sutras. According to these, every sentient being has the Buddha-nature; only he does not realize that he has it. This Ignorance (*Avidya*) is what binds him to the Wheel of Birth and Death. The necessity, therefore, is for him first to realize that he has the Buddha-nature originally within him, and then, by learning and practice, to "see" his own Buddha-nature. This "seeing" comes as a Sudden Enlightenment, because the Buddha-nature cannot be divided; therefore he either sees it as a whole or does not see it at all. Such "seeing" also means to be one with the Buddha-nature, because the Buddha-nature is not something that can be seen from outside. This is the meaning of *Tao*-sheng's statement. "By gaining freedom from illusion, one returns to the Ultimate, and by returning to the Ultimate, one attains the Original."[876] The state of attainment of the Original is the state of *Nirvana*.

But *Nirvana* is not something external to and altogether different from the Wheel of Birth and Death, nor is the reality of the Buddha-nature external to and altogether different from the phenomenal world. Once one gains Sudden Enlightenment, the latter is at once the former. Thus *Tao*-sheng says: "The Enlightenment of Mahayana Buddhism is not to be sought outside the Wheel of Birth and Death. Within it one is enlightened by the affairs of birth and death."[877] The Buddhists use the metaphor of "reaching the other shore" to express the idea of achieving *Nirvana*. *Tao*-sheng says:

As to reaching the other shore, if one reaches it, one is not reaching the other shore. Both not-reaching and not-not-reaching are really reaching. This shore here means birth and death; the other shore means *Nirvana*.[878]

Again he says: "If one sees Buddha, one is not seeing Buddha. When one sees there is no Buddha, one is really seeing Buddha."[879]

This is perhaps also the meaning of another theory of *Tao*-sheng, that for Buddha there is no "Pure Land" or other world. The world of Buddha is simply here in this present world.

In an essay titled "The Treasure House," which has been traditionally attributed to Seng-chao but seems to be a forgery, it is said:

> Suppose there is a man who, in a treasure house of golden utensils, sees the golden utensils, but pays no attention to their shapes and features. Or, even if he does pay attention to their shapes and features, he still recognizes that they are all gold. He is not confused by their varying appearances, and therefore is able to rid himself of their [superficial] distinctions. He always sees that their underlying substance is gold, and does not suffer any illusion. This is an illustration of what a sage is.[880]

This saying may not come from Seng-chao, but its metaphor has been constantly used by later Buddhists. The reality of the Buddha- nature is itself the phenomenal world, just as the golden utensils are themselves the gold. There is no other reality outside the phenomenal world, just as there is no other gold besides the golden utensils. Some people, in their Ignorance, see only the phenomenal world, but not the reality of the Buddha-nature. Other people, in their Enlightenment, see the Buddha-nature, but this Buddha-nature is still the phenomenal world. What these two kinds of people see is the same, but what one

876 Quoted in the *Nieh-pan-ching Chi-Chien* or *Collected Commentaries* to the *Parinirvana Sutra, Chuan* 1.

877 Quoted in Seng-chao's *Wei-mou-ching Chu* or *Commentary to the Vimalakirti Sutra, Chuan* 7.

878 *Id., Chuan* 9.

879 *Ibid.*

880 "The Treasure House,' Ch. 3.

person sees in his Enlightenment has a significance quite different from what the other person sees in his Ignorance. This is the meaning of a common saying of Chinese Buddhism: When ignorant, one is a common man; when enlightened, one is a sage."

Another theory of *Tao*-sheng is that even the *icchantika* (i.e., the being who opposes Buddhism) is capable of achieving Buddhahood. This is the logical conclusion of the assertion that every sentient being has the Buddha-nature. But it was in direct contradiction to the *Parinirvana Sutra,* as known at that time, and consequently *Tao*-sheng, because he uttered it, was banished for some time from the capital, Nanking. Many years later, however, when the complete text of the *Parinirvana Sutra* was translated, *Tao*-sheng's theory was found to be confirmed by one of its passages. His biographer, Hui-chiao (died 554), wrote:

> Because his interpretation of the *icchantika* came to be established by Scriptural evidence, his theories of Sudden Enlightenment and that a good deed entails no retribution, also came to be highly honored by the Buddhists of the time.[881]

Hui-chiao also reports another saying of *Tao*-sheng:

> The symbol serves to express an idea, and is to be discarded once the idea has been understood. Words serve to explain thought, and ought to be silenced once the thoughts have been absorbed.... It is only those who can grasp the fish and discard the fishing net that are qualified to seek the truth?[882]

This figure of speech refers to a saying in the Chuang-tzu which says: "The fishing net serves to catch fish. Let us take the fish and forget the net. The snare serves to catch rabbits. Let us take the rabbit and forget the snare."[883] Chinese philosophical tradition makes use of a term called the "net of words." According to this tradition, the best statement is one that does not "fall into the net of words."

We have seen that in Chi-tsang's theory of the three levels of double truth, when one reaches the third level one simply has nothing to say. On that level there is no danger of falling into the net of words. When *Tao*-sheng speaks of the Buddha-nature, he almost falls into this net, because by speaking of it as the Mind, he gives people the impression that the limitations of definition can be imposed on in. In this respect he is influenced by the *Parinirvana Sutra,* which emphasizes the Buddha-nature, and so he approaches the *Hsing tsung* or School of Universal Mind.

Thus, as we shall see in the next chapter, by the time of Tao-sheng, the theoretical background for Chanism had been prepared. The Chan Masters themselves, however, were needed to put the theories described in the present chapter into high relief. In what has been told here we can also find the germ of the Neo-Confucianism of several centuries later. The theory of *Tao*-sheng that every man can become a Buddha reminds us of the theory of Mencius that every

881 *Kao-seng Chuan* or *Biographies of Eminent Buddhist Monks, Chuan* 7.

882 *Ibid.*

883 *Chuang-tzu,* Ch. 26.

man can become a Yao or Shun (two traditional sage-kings).[884] Mencius also stated that by fully developing our mind, we come to know our nature; and by fully development of our nature, we come to know Heaven.[885] But what he called mind and nature are both psychological and not metaphysical. By giving them a metaphysical interpretation along the line suggested by *Tao*-sheng's theory, one arrives at Neo-Confucianism.

The idea of the Universal Mind is a contribution of India to Chinese philosophy. Before the introduction of Buddhism, there was in Chinese philosophy only the mind, but not the Mind. The *Tao* of the *Tao*ists is the "mystery of mysteries," as Lao Tzu put it, yet it is not Mind. After the period dealt with in this chapter, there is, in Chinese philosophy, not only mind, but also Mind.

884 *Mencius*, VIb, 2.
885 *Id.*, VIIa, 1.

XXII CHANISM: THE PHILOSOPHY OF SILENCE

The Chinese term *Chan* (Japanese reading: *Zen*) or *Chan-na* is a phonetic rendering of the Sanskrit *Dhyana,* which is usually translated in English as Meditation. The traditional account of the origin of the Chan or Zen school is that the Buddha, in addition to his Scriptures, possessed an esoteric teaching that was transmitted independently of written texts. This teaching he transmitted personally to one of his disciples, who in turn transmitted it to his own disciple. In this way, it was handed down until it reached Bodhidharma, who is supposed to have been the twenty-eighth Patriarch in India, and who came to China sometime between 520 and 526, where he became the first Tsu (Patriarch, literally, Ancestor) of the Chan school in China.

Traditional Account of the Origin of Chanism

There, Bodhidharma transmitted the esoteric teaching to Hui-ko (486-593) who was China's second Patriarch. The teaching was thus perpetuated until a major split in the school occurred, caused by the two chief disciples of the fifth Patriarch, Hung-*jen* (605-675).One of them, Shen-hsiu (died 7061 became the founder of the Northern school; the other, Hui-neng (638-713), founded the Southern school. The Southern school soon surpassed the Northern one in popularity, so that Hui-neng came to be recognized as the sixth Patriarch, the true successor of Hung-*jen*. All the later influential groups in Chanism took their rise from the disciples of Hui-neng.[886]

How far we can depend on the earlier part of this traditional account is much questioned, for it is not supported by any documents dated earlier than the eleventh century. It is not our purpose in this chapter to make a scholarly examination of this problem. Suffice it to say that no scholar today takes the tradition very seriously. Indeed, as we have already seen in the last chapter, the theoretical background for Chanism had already been created in China by such men as Seng-chao and *Tao*-sheng. Given this background, the rise of Chanism would seem to have been almost inevitable, without looking to the almost legendary Bodhidharma as its founder.

The split in the Chan school caused by Shen-hsiu and Hui-neng is, however, a historical fact. The difference between these founders of the Northern and Southern schools represents the earlier difference between the *Hsing tsung* (Universal Mind school) and *Kung tsung* (Empty school) that was described in the last chapter. This can be seen in Hui-neng's own autobiography. From this work we learn that Hui-neng was a native of the present Guangdong Province and became a student of Buddhism under Hung-*jen*. The account continues

886 For the traditional account, see Yang Yi (974-1020), *Chuan Teng Lei* or *Record of the Transmission of the Light, Chuan* 1.

that one day Hung-*jen*, realizing that his time was nearly over, summoned his disciples together and told them that a successor must now be appointed; this successor would be the disciple who could write the best poem summarizing the teaching of Chanism.

Shen-hsiu then wrote a poem which read:

The body is like unto the Bodhi-tree,
And the mind to a mirror bright;
Carefully we cleanse them hour by hour
Lest dust should fall upon them.

To refute this idea, Hui-neng then wrote the following poem:

Originally there was no Bodhi-tree,
Nor was there any mirror,
Since originally there new??? nothing,
Whereon can the dust fall?

It is said that Hung-*jen* approved Hui-neng's poem and appointed him as his successor, the sixth Patriarch.[887]

Shen-hsiu's poem emphasized the Universal Mind or Buddha Nature spoken of by *Tao*-sheng, while Hui-neng's emphasized the *Wu* (Non-being) of Seng-chao. There are two phrases that often occur in Chanism. One is, "The very mind is Buddha"; the other, "not-mind, and not-Buddha." Shen-hsiu's poem is the expression of the first phrase, and Hui-neng's of the second.

The First Principle Is Inexpressible

In later times the Chan school in its major development followed the line set by Hui-neng. In it the combination already begun between the Empty school and Taoism reached its climax.

What the Empty school called higher sense truth on the third level, the Chanists called the First Principle. As we have seen in the last chapter, on this third level one simply cannot say anything. Hence the First Principle is by its very nature inexpressible. The Chan Master Wen-yi (died 958) was once asked: "What is the First Principle?" To which he answered: "If I were to tell you, it would become the second principle."[888]

It was the principle of the Chan Masters to teach their disciples only through personal contact. For the benefit of those who did not have opportunity for such contact, however, written records were made of the sayings of the Masters, which were known as *yu lu* (recorded conversations). This was a practice that was later taken over by the Neo Confucianists. In these records, we often find that when a student ventured to ask some question about the fundamental principles of Buddhism, he would often be given a beating by his Chan Master, or some quite irrelevant answer. He might, for example, be told that the price of a certain vegetable was then three cents. These answers seem very paradoxical to those who are not familiar with the purpose of Chanism. But this purpose is simply

887 See the *Liu-tsu Tandung* or *Sutra Spoken by the Sixth Patriarch, Chuan.* t.

888 *Wen-yi Chan-shih Yu-lu* or *Sayings of the Chan Master Wenyi.*

to let the student know that what he asks about is not answerable. Once he understands that, he understands a great deal.

The First Principle is inexpressible, because what is called the *Wu* is not something about which anything can be said. By calling it "Mind" or any other name, one is at once giving it a definition and thus imposing on it a limitation. As the Chanists and *Tao*ists both say, one thereby falls into the "net of words." Ma-tsu or the Patriarch Ma (died 788), a disciple of the disciple of Hui-neng, was once asked: "Why do you say that the very mind is Buddha?"

Ma-tsu answered: "I simply want to stop the crying of children." "Suppose they do stop crying?" asked the questioner. "Then not-mind, not-Buddha," was the answer.[889]

Another student asked Ma-tsu: "What kind of man is he who is not linked to *all* things?" The Master answered: "Wait until in one gulp you can drink up all the water in the West River, then I will tell you."[890] Such an act is obviously impossible and by suggesting It Ma-tsu meant to indicate to the student that he would not answer his question. His question, in fact, was really not answerable, because he who is not linked to *all* things is one who transcends *all* things. This being so, how can you ask what kind of man he is?

There were Chan Masters who used silence to express the idea of *Wu* or the First Principle. It is said, for example, that when Hui-chung (died 775) was to debate with another monk, he simply mounted his chair and remained silent. The other monk then said" Please propose your thesis so I can argue." Hui-chung replied: "I have already proposed my thesis." The monk asked: "What is it?" Hui-chung said: "I know it is beyond your understanding," and with this left his chair.[891] The thesis Hui-chung proposed was that of silence. Since the First Principle or *Wu* is not something about which anything can be said, the best way to expound it is to remain silent.

From this point of view no Scriptures or Sutras have any real connection with the First Principle. Hence the Chan Master Yi-hsuan (died 866), founder of a group in Chanism known as the Liu-chi school, said:

> If you want to have the right understanding, you must not be deceived by others, you should kill everything that you meet internally or externally. If you meet Buddha, kill Buddha. If you meet the Patriarchs, kill the Patriarchs.... Then you can gain your emancipation.[892]

Method of Cultivation

The knowledge of the First Principle is knowledge that is non-knowledge; hence the method of cultivation is also cultivation that is non-cultivation. It is said that Ma-tsu, before he became a disciple of Huai-jang (died 744 lived on the Heng Mountain (in present Hunan Province). There he occupied a solitary hut in which, all alone, he practiced meditation. One day Huai-jang began to grind some bricks

889 Yi-tsang (of the Sung Dynasty), *Kutsun-hsu Yu-tu* or *Recorded Sayings of Ancient Worthies*, Chuan 1.

890 *Ibid.*

891 *Record of the Transmission of the Light, Chuan* 5.

892 *Recorded Savings of Ancient Worthies, Chuan* 4.

in front of the hut. When Ma-tsu saw it, he asked Huai-jang what he was doing. He replied that he was planning to make a mirror. Ma-tsu said "How can grinding bricks make a mirror?" Huai-jang said "If grinding bricks cannot make a mirror, how can meditation make a Buddha?" By this saying Ma-tsu was enlightened and thereupon became Huai-jang's Disciple.[893]

Thus according to Chanism, the best method of cultivation for achieving Buddhahood is not to practice any cultivation. To cultivate oneself in this way is to exercise deliberate effort, which is *yu-wei* (having action). This *yu-wei* will, to be sure, produce some good effect, but it will not be everlasting. The Chan Master Hsi-yun (died 847), known as the Master of Huang-po, said:

> Supposing that through innumerable lives a man has practiced the six *paramitas* [methods of gaining salvation], done good and attained the Buddha Wisdom, this will still not last forever. The reason lies in causation. When the force of the cause is exhausted, he reverts to the impermanent.[894]

Again he said:

> All deeds are essentially impermanent. All forces have their final day. They are like a dart discharged through the air; when its strength is exhausted, it turns and falls to the ground. They are all connected with the Wheel of Birth and Death. To practice cultivation through them is to misunderstand the Buddha's idea and waste labor.[895]

And yet again:

> If you do not understand *wu hsin* [absence of a purposeful mind], then you are attached to objects, and suffer from obstructions.... Actually there is no such thing as Bodhi [Wisdom]. That the Buddha talked about it was simply as a means to educate men, just as yellow leaves may be taken as gold coins in order to stop the crying of children....The only thing to be done is to rid yourself of your old Karma, as opportunity offers, and not to create new Karma from which will flow new calamities.[896]

Thus the best method of spiritual cultivation is to do one's tasks without deliberate effort or purposeful mind. This is exactly what the *Tao*ists called *wu-wei* (non-action) and wu-hsin (no-mind). It is what Hui-yuan's theory signifies, as well as, probably, the statement of *Tao*-sheng that "a good deed does not entail retribution." This method of cultivation does not aim at doing things in order to obtain resulting good effects, no matter how good these effects may be in themselves. Rather it aims at doing things in such a way as to entail no effects at all. When all one's actions entail no effect, then after the effects of previously accumulated *Karma* have exhausted themselves, one will gain emancipation from the Wheel of Birth and Death and attain *Nirvana*.

To do things without deliberate effort and purposeful mind is to do things naturally and to live naturally. Yi-hsuan said:

---

893 *Id., Chuan* 1.

894 *Id., Chuan* 3.

895 *Ibid.*

896 *Ibid.*

> To achieve Buddhahood there is no place for deliberate effort. The only method is to carry on one's ordinary and uneventful tasks: relieve one's bowels, pass water, wear one's clothes, eat one's meals, and when tired, lie down. The simple fellow will laugh at you, but the wise will understand.[897]

The reason why those who try to achieve Buddhahood so often fail to follow this course is because they lack self-confidence.

Yi-hsuan said:

> Nowadays people who engage in spiritual cultivation fail to achieve their ends. Their fault is not having faith in themselves.... Do you wish to know who are the Patriarchs and Buddha? All of you who are before me are the Patriarchs and Buddha.[898]

Thus the way to practice spiritual cultivation is to have adequate confidence in one's self and discard everything else. All one should do is to pursue the ordinary tasks of one's everyday life, and nothing more. This is what the Chan Masters call cultivation through non-cultivation.

Here a question arises: Granted that this be so, then what is the difference between the man who engages in cultivation of this kind and the man who engages in no cultivation at all? If the latter does precisely what the former does, he too should achieve *Nirvana*, and so there should come a time when there will be no Wheel of Birth and Death at all.

To this question it may be answered that although to wear clothes and eat meals are in themselves common and simple matters, it is still not easy to do them with a completely non- purposeful mind and thus without any attachment. A person likes fine clothes, for example, but dislikes bad ones, and he feels pleased when others admire his clothes. These are all the attachments that result from wearing clothes. What the Chan Masters emphasized is that spiritual cultivation does not require special acts, such as the ceremonies and prayers of institutionalized religion. One should simply try to be without a purposeful mind or any attachments in one's daily life; then cultivation results from the mere carrying on of the common and simple affairs of daily life. In the beginning one will need to exert effort in order to be without effort, and to exercise a purposeful mind in order not to have such a mind, just as, in order to forget, one at first needs to remember that one should forget. Later, however, the time comes when one must discard the effort to be without effort, and the mind that purposefully tries to have no purpose, just as one finally forgets to remember that one has to forget.

Thus cultivation through non-cultivation is itself a kind of cultivation, just as knowledge that is not knowledge is nevertheless still a form of knowledge. Such knowledge differs from original ignorance, and cultivation through non-cultivation likewise differs from original naturalness. For original ignorance and naturalness are gifts of nature, whereas knowledge that is not knowledge and cultivation through non-cultivation are both products of the spirit.

---

897 *Id, Chuan* 4 .

898 *Ibid.*

Sudden Enlightenment

The practice of cultivation, no matter for how long, is in itself only a sort of preparatory work. For Buddhahood to be achieved, this cultivation must be climaxed by a Sudden Enlightenment, such as was described in the last chapter as comparable to the leaping over of a precipice. Only after this leaping has taken place can Buddhahood be achieved.

Such Enlightenment is often referred to by the Chan Masters as the "vision of the *Tao*." Pu-yuan, known as the Master of Nan- chuan (died 830), told his disciple:

> The *Tao* is not classifiable as either knowledge or non-knowledge. Knowledge is illusory consciousness and non-knowledge is blind unconsciousness. If you really comprehend the indubitable *Tao*, it is like a wide expanse of emptiness, so how can distinctions be forced in it between right and wrong?[899]

Comprehension of the *Tao* is the same as being one with it. Its wide expanse of emptiness is not a void; it is simply a state in which all distinctions are gone.

This state is described by the Chan Masters as one in which "knowledge and truth become undifferentiable, objects and spirit form a single unity, and there ceases to be a distinction between the experiencer and the experienced.[900] "A man who drinks water knows by himself whether it is cold or warm." This last expression first appeared in the *Sutra Spoken by the Sixth Patriarch* (Hui-neng), but it was later widely quoted by the other Chan Masters, meaning that only he who experiences the non-distinction of the experiencer and the experienced really knows what it is.

In this state the experiencer has discarded knowledge in the ordinary sense, because this kind of knowledge postulates a distinction between the knower and the known. Nevertheless, he is not without knowledge, because his state differs from that of blind unconsciousness, as Nan-chuan calls it. This is what is called the knowledge that is not knowledge.

When the student has reached the verge of Sudden Enlightenment that is the time when the Master can help him the most. When one is about to make the leap, a certain assistance, no matter how small, is a great help. The Chan Masters at this stage used to practice what they called the method of "stick or yell" to help the leap to Enlightenment. Chan literature reports many incidents in which a Master, having asked his student to consider some problem, suddenly gave him several blows with a stick or yelled at him. If these acts were done at the right moment, the result would be a Sudden Enlightenment for the student. The explanation would seem to be that the physical act, thus performed, shocks the student into that psychological awareness of enlightenment for which he has long been preparing.

To describe Sudden Enlightenment, the Chan Masters use the metaphor of "the bottom of a tub falling out." When this happens, all its contents are

---

899 *Id.*, *Chuan* 13.

900 *Id.*, *Chuan* 32.

suddenly gone. In the same way, when one is suddenly enlightened, he finds all his problems suddenly solved. They are solved not in the sense that he gains some positive solution for them, but in the sense that all the problems have ceased any longer to be problems. That is why the *Tao* is called "the indubitable *Tao*."

The Attainment of Non-attainment

The attainment of Sudden Enlightenment does not entail the attainment of anything further. The Chan Master Ching-yuan, known as the Master of Shu-chou (died 1120), said:

> If you now comprehend it, where is that which you did not comprehend before? What you were deluded about before is what you are now enlightened about, and what you are now enlightened about is what you were deluded about before.[901]

As we have seen in the last chapter, the real is the phenomenal, according to Seng-chao and *Tao*-sheng. In Chanism there is the common expression that "the mountain is the mountain, the river is the river." In one's state of delusion, one sees the mountain as the mountain and the river as the river. But after Enlightenment one still sees the mountain as the mountain and the river as the river.

The Chan Masters also use another common expression "Riding an ass to search for the ass." By this they mean a search for reality outside of the phenomenal, in other words, to search for *Nirvana* outside of the Wheel of Birth and Death, Shu-chou said:

There are only two diseases; one is riding an ass to search for the ass; the other is riding an ass and being unwilling to dismount. You say that riding as ass to search for the ass is silly and that he who does it should be punished. This is a very serious disease. But I tell you, do not search for the ass at all. The intelligent man, understanding my meaning, stops to search for the ass, and thus the deluded state of his mind ceases to exist.

But if, having found the ass, one is unwilling to dismount, this disease is most difficult to cure. I say to you, do not ride the ass at all. You yourself are the ass. Everything is the ass. Why do you ride on it? If you ride, you cannot cure your disease. But if you do not ride, the universe is as a great expanse open to your view. With these two diseases expelled, nothing remains to affect your mind. This is spiritual cultivation. You need do nothing more.[902]

If one insists that after attaining Enlightenment one will still attain something else, this is to ride an ass and be unwilling to dismount.

Huang-po said "[If there be Enlightenment], speech or silence, activity or inactivity, and every sight and sound, all pertain to Buddha. Where should you go to find the Buddha? Do not place a head on top of a head or a mouth beside a mouth."[903] If there be Enlightenment, everything pertains to Buddha and everywhere there is Buddha. It is said that one Chan monk went into a temple

901 *Id., Chuan* 32.

902 *Ibid.*

903 *Id., Chuan* 3.

and spat on the statue of the Buddha. When he was criticized, he said: "Please show me a place where there is no Buddha."[904]

Thus the Chan sage lives just as everyone else lives, and does what everyone else does. In passing from delusion to Enlightenment, he has left his mortal humanity behind and has entered sagehood. But after that he still has to leave sagehood behind and to enter once more into mortal humanity. This is described by the Chan Masters as "rising yet another step over the top of the hundred-foot bamboo." The top of the bamboo symbolizes the climax of the achievement of Enlightenment. "Rising yet another step" means that after Enlightenment has come, the sage still has other things to do. What he has to do, however, is no more than the ordinary things of daily life. As Nan-chuan said: "After coming to understand the other side, you come back and live on this side."[905]

Although the sage continues living on this side, his understanding of the other side is not in vain. Although what he does is just what everyone else does, yet it has a different significance to him. As Hui-hai, known as the Master of Pai-chang (died 814), said: "That which before Enlightenment is called lustful anger, is after Enlightenment called the Buddha Wisdom. The man is no different from what he was before; it is only that what he does is different."[906] It would seem that there must be some textual error in this last sentence. What Pai-chang apparently intended to say was: "What the man does is no different from what he did before; it is only that the man himself is not the same as he was."

The man is not the same, because although what he does is what everyone else does, he has no attachment to anything. This is the meaning of the common Chan saying: "To eat all day and yet not swallow a single grain; to wear clothes all day and yet not touch a single thread."[907]

There is yet another common saying: "In carrying water and chopping firewood therein lies the wonderful *Tao*."[908] One may ask: If this is so, does not the wonderful *Tao* also lie in serving one's family and the state? If we were to draw the logical conclusion from the Chan doctrines that have been analyzed above, we should be forced to answer yes. The Chan Masters themselves, however, did not give this logical answer. It was reserved for the Neo-Confucianists, who are the subject of our next several chapters, to do so.

---

904 *Record of the Transmission of the Light*, *Chuan* 27.

905 *Recorded Sayings of Ancient Worthies*, *Chuan* 12.

906 *Id.*, *Chuan* 1.

907 *Id.*, *Chuan* 3 and 16.

908 *Record of the Transmission of the Light*, *Chuan* 8.

XXIII NEO-CONFUCIANISM: THE COSMOLOGISTS

In 589, after centuries of division, China was again unified by the Sui Dynasty (590617). The Sui, however, soon gave way to the powerful and highly centralized dynasty of Tang (618-906). Both culturally and politically the Tang was a golden age in China, which equaled and in some ways surpassed that of Han.

The examination system for the selection of officials, in which the Confucian Classics held a pre-eminent position, was reestablished in 622. In 628 Emperor Tai-tsung (627-649) ordered that a Confucian temple be established in the Imperial University, and in 630 he again ordered scholars to prepare an official edition of the Confucian Classics. As part of this work, standard commentaries on the Classics were selected from among the numerous commentaries that had been written before that time, and official sub commentaries were written to elucidate these standard commentaries. The resulting Classical texts, with their official commentaries and sub-commentaries, were then commanded by the Emperor to be taught in the Imperial University. In this way Confucianism was reaffirmed as the official teaching of the state.

But Confucianism had by this time already lost the vitality which it had once manifested in the form of such men as Mencius, Hsun Tzu, and Tung Chung-shu. The original texts were there, and their commentaries and sub commentaries were even more numerous than before, yet they failed to meet the spiritual interest and needs of the age. After the revival of Taoism and the introduction of Buddhism, people had become more interested in metaphysical problems and in what I call super-moral values, or as they were then phrased, the problems of the nature and Destiny (of man). As we have seen in Chapters IV, VII, and XV, discussions on such problems are not lacking in such Confucian works as the *Analects of Confucius*, the *Mencius*, the *Doctrine of the Mean*, and especially the *Book of Changes*. These, however, needed a genuinely new interpretation and elucidation in order to meet the problems of the new age, and this type of interpretation was as yet lacking despite the efforts of the Emperor's scholars.

Han Yu and Li Ao

It was not until the latter part of the Tang Dynasty that there arose two men, Han Yu (768-824) and *Li* Ao (died c. 844), who really tried to reinterpret such works as the *Ta Hsueh* or *Great Learning* and *Chung Yung* or *Doctrine of the Mean*, in such a way as would answer the problems of their time. In his essay titled "Yuan *Tao*" or "On the Origin and Nature of the Truth," Han Yu wrote:

> What I call the *Tao* is not what has hitherto been called the *Tao* by the *Tao*ists and the Buddhists. *Yao* [a traditional sage-king of antiquity] transmitted the *Tao* to Shun [another traditional sage-king supposed to be the successor of Yao]. Shun transmitted it to Yu [successor of Shun and founder of the Hsia Dynasty]. Yu transmitted it to [Kings] Wen and Wu

and the Duke of Chou [the three founders of the Chou Dynasty]. Wen and Wu and the Duke of Chou transmitted it to Confucius, and Confucius transmitted it to Mencius. After Mencius, it was no longer transmitted. Hsun [Tzu] and *Yang* [Hsiung] selected from it, but without reaching the essential portion; they discussed it, but without sufficient clarity.[909]

And *Li* Ao, in an essay titled "On the Restoration of the Nature," writes very similarly:

> The ancient Sages transmitted this teaching to Yen Tzu [i.e., Yen Hui, the favored disciple of Confucius] Tzu-ssu, the grandson of Confucius, received the teaching of his grandfather and composed the *Doctrine of the Mean* in forty-seven sections which he transmitted to Mencius....Alas, though writings dealing with the nature and Destiny are still preserved, none of the scholars understand them, and therefore they all plunge into Taoism and Buddhism. Ignorant people say that the followers of the Master [i.e., of Confucius] are incapable of investigating the theories on the nature and Destiny, and everybody believes them. When someone asked me about this, I transmitted to him what I knew.... My hope is that this long obstructed and abandoned Truth may be transmitted in the world.[910]

The theory of the transmission of the Truth from Yao and Shun downward, though already roughly suggested by Mencius[911], was evidently reinspired in Han Yu and *Li* An by the Chan theory that the esoteric teaching of the Buddha had been transmitted through a line of Patriarchs to Hung-jen and Hui-neng. At a later time one of the Cheng brothers (see Chapter XIV) even stated unequivocally that the *Chung Yung* or *Doctrine of the Mean* was the esoteric teaching of Confucius. (Quoted by Chu Hsi in his introduction to his *Commentary* on the *Chung Yung*) It was widely believed that the transmission of the Truth had become interrupted after Mencius. *Li* Ao, however, apparently felt that he himself possessed a certain understanding of it, and that through his teaching he could thus act as a continuator of Mencius. To do this became the ambition of all Neo-Confucianists after *Li* Ao's time. All of them accepted Han Yu's theory of the orthodox line of transmission of the *Tao* or Truth, and maintained that they were themselves links in that transmission. Their claim is not without justification, because, as we shall see in this and the following chapters, Neo-Confucianism is indeed the continuation of the idealistic wing of ancient Confucianism, and especially of the mystic tendency of Mencius. That is the reason why these men have been known as the *Tao hsueh chia* and their philosophy as the *Tao hsueh*, i.e., the Study of the *Tao* or Truth. The term Neo-Confucianism is a newly coined western equivalent for *Tao hsueh*.

There are three lines of thought that can be traced as the main sources of Neo-Confucianism. The first, of course, is Confucianism itself. The second is Buddhism, together with Taoism via the medium of Chanism, for of all the schools of Buddhism, Chanism was the most influential at the time of the

909 *Chang Hsien-sheng Chi*, or *Collected Works of Han Yu*, *Chuan* 11.

910 *Li Wen-kung Chi* or *Collected Works of Li Ao*, *Chuan* 2

911 *Mencius* VIIb, 38.

formation of Neo-Confucianism. To the Neo-Confucianists, Chanism and Buddhism are synonymous terms, and, as stated in the last chapter, in one sense Neo-Confucianism may be said to be the logical development of Chanism. Finally, the third is the *Tao*ist religion, of which the cosmological views of the *Yin-Yang* School formed an important element. The cosmology of the Neo-Confucianists is chiefly connected with this line of thought.

These three lines of thought were heterogeneous and even in many respects contradictory. Hence it took time for philosophers to make a unity out of them, especially since this unity was not simply eclecticism, but a genuine system forming a homogeneous whole. Therefore although the beginning of Neo-Confucianism may be traced back to Han Yu and *Li* Ao, its system of thought did not become clearly formed until the eleventh century. This was the time when the Sung Dynasty (960-1279), which reunited China after a period of confusion following the collapse of the Tang, was at the height of its splendor and prosperity. The earliest of the Neo-Confucianists were chiefly interested in cosmology.

Cosmology of Chou Tun-yi

The first cosmological philosopher is Chou Tun-yi, better known as the Master of Lien-hsi (1017-73). He was a native of Tao-chou in the present Hunan Province, and in his late years lived on the famous mountain Lushan, the same place where Hui-Yuan and *Tao*-sheng had taught Buddhism, as described in Chapter XXI. Long before his time, some of the religious *Tao*ists had prepared a number of mystic diagrams as graphic portrayals of the esoteric principles by which they believed a properly initiated individual could attain immortality. Chou Tun-yi is said to have come into possession of one of these diagrams, which he thereupon reinterpreted and modified into a diagram of his own designed to illustrate the process of cosmic evolution. Or rather, he studied and developed the ideas found in certain passages in the "Appendices" of the Book of Changes, and used the *Tao*ist diagram by way of illustration. His resulting diagram is called the *Tai-chi Tu* or *Diagram of the Supreme Ultimate*, and his interpretation of it is called the *Tai-chi Tu Shuo* or *Explanation of the Diagram of the Supreme Ultimate*. The *Shuo* or *Explanation* can be read quite intelligibly without referring to the diagram itself.

The text of the Explanation reads as follows:

> The Ultimateless [*Wu Chi*]! And yet the Supreme Ultimate [*Tai Chi*]! The Supreme Ultimate through Movement produces the *Yang*. This Movement, having reached its limit, is followed by Quiescence, and by this Quiescence, it produces the *Yin*. When Quiescence has reached its limit, there is a return to Movement. Thus Movement and Quiescence, in alternation, become each the source of the other. The distinction between the *Yin* and *Yang* is determined and the Two Forms [i.e., the *Yin* and *Yang*] stand revealed.

By the transformations of the *Yang* and the union therewith of the Yin, Water, Fire, Wood, Metal and Soil are produced. These Five Ethers [chi, i.e., Elements] become diffused in harmonious order, and the four seasons proceed in their course.

The Five Elements are the one *Yin* and Yang; the *Yin* and *Yang* are the one Supreme Ultimate; and the Supreme Ultimate is fundamentally the Ultimateless. The Five Elements come into being, each having its own particular nature.

The true substance of the Ultimateless and the essence of the Two [Forms] and Five [Elements] unite in mysterious union, so that consolidation ensues. The principle of *Chien* [the trigram symbolizing the *Yang*] becomes the male element, and the principle of *Kun* [the trigram symbolizing the *Yin*] becomes the female element. The Two Ethers [the *Yin* and *Yang*] by their interaction operate to produce all things, and these in their turn produce and reproduce, so that transformation and change continue without end.

It is man alone, however, who receives these in their highest excellence and hence is the most intelligent [of all beings]. His bodily form thereupon is produced and his spirit develops intelligence and consciousness. The five principles of his nature [the five constant virtues corresponding to the Five Elements] react [to external phenomena], so that the distinction between good and evil emerges and the myriad phenomena of conduct appear. The sage regulates himself by means of the mean, correctness, human-heartedness, and righteousness, and takes Quiescence as the essential. [Chou Tun-yi himself comments on this, "Having no desire, he is therefore in the state of Quiescence."] Thus he establishes himself as the highest standard for mankind....[912]

In the *Book of Changes*, "Appendix III," it is said "In the *Yi* there is the Supreme Ultimate, which produces the Two Forms." Chou Tun-yi's *Explanations* is a development of the idea of this passage. Brief though it is, it provides the basic outline for the cosmology of Chu Hsi (1130-1200) one of the greatest, if not the greatest, of the Neo-Confucianists, about whom I shall have more to say in Chapter XXV.

Method of Spiritual Cultivation

The ultimate purpose of Buddhism is to teach men how to achieve Buddhahood — a problem that was one of the most vital to the people of that time. Likewise, the ultimate purpose of Neo-Confucianism is to teach men how to achieve Confucian Sagehood.

The difference between the Buddha of Buddhism and the Sage of Neo-Confucianism is that while the Buddha must promote his spiritual cultivation outside of society and the human world, the Sage must do so within these human bonds. The most important development in Chinese Buddhism was its attempt to depreciate the other-worldliness of original Buddhism. This attempt came close to success when the Chan Masters stated that "in carrying water and chopping firewood, therein lies the wonderful *Tao*." But, as I said in the last chapter, they did not push this idea to its logical conclusion by saying that in serving one's family and the state therein also lies wonderful *Tao*. The reason, of course, is that, once they had said this, their teaching would have ceased to be Buddhism.

For the Neo-Confucianists, too, how to achieve Sagehood is one of the main

---

912 *Chou Lien-hsi Chi or Collected Works of Chou Tun-yi, Chuan* 1.

problems, and Chou Tun-yi's answer is that one should "be quiescent," which he further defines as a state of *wu-wei* or "having no desires." In his second major treatise, the Tung Shu or *General Principles of the "Book of Changes,"* we find that by *wu-yu* he means much the same as the *wu-wei* (having no effort) and *wu-hsin* (having no mind) of Taoism and Chanism. The fact that he uses *wu-yu*, however, instead of these other two terms, shows how he attempts to move away from the other-worldliness of Buddhism. So far as the terms are concerned, the *wu* in *wu*-yu is not so all-inclusive as that in *wu hsin*.

In the *Tung Shu* Chou Tun-yi writes:

> *Wu-yu* results in vacuity when in quiescence, and straightforwardness when in movement. Vacuity in quiescence leads to enlightenment, and enlightenment leads to comprehension. [Likewise] straightforwardness in movement leads to impartiality, and impartiality leads to universality. One is almost [a sage when one has] such enlightenment, comprehension, impartiality, and universality.[913]

The word *yu* used by the Neo-Confucianists always means selfish desire or simply selfishness. Sometimes they prefix it by the word *ssu* (selfish), in order to make their meaning clearer. Chou Tun-yi's idea in this passage may be illustrated by a passage from the *Mencius*, often quoted by the Neo-Confucianists:

> If today men suddenly see a child about to fall into a well, they will without exception experience a feeling of alarm and distress. This will not be as a way whereby to gain the favor of the child's parents, nor whereby they may seek the praise of their neighbors and friends, nor are they so because they dislike the reputation [of being unvirtuous][914]

According to the Neo-Confucianists, what Mencius here describes is the natural and spontaneous response of any man when placed in such a situation. Man is by nature fundamentally good. Therefore his innate state is one in which he has no selfish desires in his mind, or as Chou expresses it, one of "vacuity in quiescence." As applied to conduct, it will lead to an immediate impulse to try to save the child, and this sort of intuitive conduct is what Chou calls "straightforwardness in movement, If, however, the man does not act on his first impulse, but pauses instead to think the matter over, he may then consider that the child in distress is a son of his enemy, and therefore he should not save it, or that it is the son of his friend and therefore he should save it. In either case, he is motivated by secondary selfish thoughts and thereby loses both his original state of vacuity in quiescence and the corollary state of straightforwardness in movement.

When the mind lacks all selfish desires it becomes, according to the Neo-Confucianists, like a brilliant mirror, which is always ready to reflect objectively any object that comes before it. The brilliancy of the mirror is compared with the mind's "enlightenment," and its readiness to reflect with the mind's "comprehension." When the mind lacks any selfish desires, its natural response to external stimuli results in actions that are straightforward. Being

913 *Collected Works*, Chuan 5.

914 *Mencius*, IIa. 6.

straightforward, they are impartial, and being impartial, they are carried out without discrimination. Such is their nature of universality.

This is Chou Tun-yi's method of achieving Sagehood, and consists, like that of the Chan monks, of living naturally and acting naturally.

Cosmology of Shao Yung

Another cosmological philosopher to be mentioned in this chapter is Shao Yung, known as the Master of Pai-chuan (1011-77).He was a native of the present Henan Province. Though in a way somewhat different from that of Chou Tun-yi, he too developed his cosmological theory from the Book of Changes, and, like Chou, made use of diagrams to illustrate his theory.

In Chapter XVIII we have seen that the Han Dynasty saw the appearance of a number of uei shu or apocrypha, which were supposed to complement the original Six Classics. In the Yi Wei, or Apocryphal Treatise on the "Book of Changes," the theory is developed of the "influence" of each of the sixty-four hexagrams upon a certain period of the year. According to this theory, each of the twelve months is under the jurisdiction of several of the hexagrams, one of which plays a leading role in the affairs of that month and is hence known as its "sovereign hexagram." These sovereign hexagrams are Fu, Lin, Tai, Ta Chuang , Chueh , Chien, Kou, Tun, pi, kuan, po, and Kun,

The reason for their importance is that they graphically represent the waxing and waning of the *Yang* and *Yin* principles throughout the year.

In these hexagrams, as we have seen in Chapter XII, the unbroken lines represent the Yang, which is associated with heat, while the broken lines represent the *Yin*, which is associated with cold. The hexagram Fu , with five broken lines above and one unbroken line below, is the "sovereign hexagram" of that month in which the *Yin* (cold) has reached its apogee and the *Yang* (heat)then begins to reappear. That is the eleventh month of the traditional Chinese calendar, the month in which the winter solstice occurs. The hexagram Chien, with its six unbroken lines, is the "sovereign hexagram" of the fourth month, in which the *Yang* is at its apogee. The hexagram Kun, with five unbroken lines above and one broken line below, is the "sovereign hexagram" of the fifth month, in which the summer solstice is followed by the rebirth of the *Yin*. And the hexagram Kun, with its six broken lines, is the "sovereign hexagram" of the tenth month, in which the *Yin* is at its apogee, just before the rebirth of the *Yang* which follows the winter solstice. The other hexagrams indicate the intermediate stages in the waxing and waning of the *Yin* and *Yang*.

The twelve hexagrams in toto constitute a cycle. After the influence of the *Yin* has reached its apogee, that of the *Yang* appears at the very bottom of the following hexagram. Rising upward, it becomes steadily greater month by month and hexagram by hexagram, until it reaches its apogee. Then the *Yin* again appears at the bottom of the following hexagram, and grows in its turn until it too reigns supreme. It is followed in turn by the reborn Yang, and thus the cycle of the year and of the hexagrams begins again. Such is the inevitable course of nature.

It is to be noticed that Shao Yung's theory of the universe gives further illumination to the theory of the twelve sovereign hexagrams. As in the case of Chou Tun-yi, he deduces his system from a statement in "Appendix III" of the *Book of Changes* which reads: "In the *Yi* there is the Supreme Ultimate. The Supreme Ultimate produces the Two Forms. The Two Forms produce the Four Emblems, and the Four Emblems produce the eight trigrams." To illustrate this process, Shao Yung made a diagram as follows:

The first or lower tier of this diagram shows the Two Forms, which, in Shao Yung's system, are not the *Yin* and *Yang* but Movement and Quiescence. The second tier, looked at in conjunction with the first, shows the Four Emblems. For instance, by combining the unbroken line beneath *Yang* in the middle tier,

Greater Greater Lesser Lesser Lesser Lesser Greater
Greater Softness Hardness Softness Hardness *Yin* *Yang*
Yin *Yang* Softness Hardness *Yin* Yang
Quiescence Movement

with the unbroken line beneath Movement below, we obtain two unbroken lines which are the emblem of the Yang. That is to say, the *Yang* is not, for Shao Yung, represented by a single unbroken line, but by two unbroken lines . Likewise, by combining the broken line beneath *Yin* in the central tier with the unbroken line beneath Movement below, we obtain one broken line above and one unbroken line below, which are the emblem of *Yin*. That is to say, the emblem of the *Yin* is not but .

In the same way, the third or highest tier looked at in conjunction with both the central and lower tier, represents the eight trigrams. For instance, by combining the unbroken line beneath Greater *Yang* above with the unbroken line beneath *Yang* in the middle and the unbroken line beneath Movement below, we obtain a combination of three unbroken lines, which is the trigram for Chien. Likewise, by combining the broken line beneath

Greater *Yin* above with the unbroken line beneath *Yang* in the middle and the unbroken line beneath Movement below, we obtain the combination of one broken line above and two unbroken lines below, which is the trigram for Tui. And still again, by combining the unbroken line beneath Lesser *Yang* above with the broken line beneath *Yin* in the middle and the unbroken line beneath Movement below, we obtain the trigram for Li. By following the same process through the other combinations, we obtain the entire eight trigrams in the following sequence:

Chien, Tui, Li, Chen, Sun,
Kan, Ken, and Kun.

Each of these trigrams represents a certain principle or influence.

The materialization of these principles results in Heaven, Earth, and all things of the universe. As Shao Yung says:

Heaven is produced from Movement and Earth from Quiescence.

The alternating interplay of Movement and Quiescence gives utmost development to the course of Heaven and Earth. At the first appearance of Movement, the *Yang* is produced, and this Movement having reached its apogee, the *Yin* is then produced. The alternating interplay of the *Yang* and *Yin* gives utmost development to the functioning aspect of Heaven. With the first appearance of Quiescence, Softness is produced, and this Quiescence having reached its apogee, Hardness is then produced. The alternating interplay of Hardness and Softness gives utmost development to the functioning aspect of Earth.[915]

The terms Hardness and Softness are, like the others, borrowed by Shan Yung from "Appendix III" of the Book of Changes, which says:

"The Way of Heaven is established with the *Yin* and *Yang*. The Way of Earth is established with Softness and Hardness. The Way of Man is established with human-heartedness and righteousness."

Shao Yung writes further:

The Greater *Yang* Constitutes the sun, the Greater *Yin* the moon, the Lesser *Yang* the stars, the Lesser *Yin* the zodiacal spaces. The interplay of the sun, moon, stars, and zodiacal spaces gives utmost development to the substance of Heaven. The Greater Softness constitutes water, the Greater Hardness fire, the Lesser Softness soil, and the Lesser Hardness stone. The interplay of water, fire, soil, and stone gives utmost development to the substance of Earth.[916]

This is Shao Yung's theory of the origin of the universe, deduced strictly from his diagram. In this diagram, the Supreme Ultimate itself is not actually shown, but it is understood as being symbolized by the empty space beneath the first tier of the diagram. Shao Yung writes:

The Supreme Ultimate is a Unity which does not move. It produces a Duality, and this Duality is spirituality.... Spirituality produces numbers, the numbers produce emblems, and the emblems produce implements [i.e., individual things].[917]

These numbers and emblems are illustrated in the diagram.

Law of the Evolution of Things

By adding a fourth, fifth, and sixth tier to the above diagram, and following the same procedure of combination that was used there, we arrive at a diagram in which all the sixty-four hexagrams (derived from combination of the eight primary trigrams) are shown. If this diagram is then cut into two equal halves, each of which is bent into a half circle, and if the two half circles are then joined together, we have another of Shao's diagrams, known as "the circular diagram of the sixty-four hexagrams."

Upon examining this diagram (here, for the sake of simplicity, reduced from sixty-four to the twelve "sovereign hexagrams"), we see that these twelve appear in it in their proper sequence as follows (looking from the center, and progressing clockwise from above.)

915 Kuan-wu Pien or "*Observation of Things*," Inner Chapter, in the *Huang-chi Ching-shih* or *Cosmological Chronology*, Ch. 11a.

916 *Ibid.*

917 *Id.*, Ch. 12h.

This sequence is automatically arrived at by what is called "the method of doubling," because, as we have seen, the number of emblems in each tier in the diagram is always double that of the tier immediately below, so that combination of all six tiers results in the sixty-four hexagrams at the top. This simple progression makes the diagram appear as both something natural and at the same time mysterious. As a result, it was hailed by most of the Neo-Confucianists as one of the greatest discoveries of Shao Yung, in which could be found the universal law governing the evolution of all things, and the key to the mystery of the universe.

This law not only applies to the alternation of the seasons throughout the year, but also to the alternation of day and night every twenty-four hours. According to Shao Yung and the other Neo-Confucianists, the *Yin* can be interpreted as merely the negation of the Yang. Hence, if the *Yang* is the constructive force of the universe, the *Yin* is its destructive principle. Interpreting the *Yin* and *Yang* in this sense, the law represented by the diagram indicates the way in which all things of the universe go through phases of construction and destruction. Thus, the first or lowest line of the hexagrams Fu shows the beginning of the phase of construction, and in hexagram Chien we find the completion of this phase. The first line of the hexagram Kou shows the beginning of the phase of destruction, and in hexagram Kun this phase is completed. In this way the diagram graphically illustrates the universal law that everything involves its own negation, a principle that was stressed both by Lao Tzu and the "Appendices" of the *Book of Changes*.

The world as a whole is no exception to this universal law. Thus Shao Yung maintains that with the first line of the hexagram Fu, the world comes into existence. With the hexagram Tai, the individual things that belong to it begin to be produced. Mankind then appears, and with the hexagram *Chien* the golden age of civilization is reached. There follows a process of continuous decay, until with the hexagram *Po* all individual things disintegrate, and with the hexagram *Kun* the whole world ceases to be. Thereupon another world begins with the first line of the recurring hexagram Fu, and the whole process is repeated. Each world which is thus created and destroyed has a duration of 129,600 years.

Shao Yung's major work is the *Huang-chi Ching-shih*, which is an elaborate chronological diagram of our existing world. According to its chronology, the golden age of our world has already passed away. It was the age of Yao, the traditional philosopher king of China who reputedly ruled in the twenty-fourth century B.C. We today are now in an age corresponding to the hexagram Po, the time of the beginning of decline of all things. As we have seen in Chapter XIV, most Chinese philosophers have considered the process of history to be one of continuous degeneration, in which everything of the present falls short of the ideal past. Shan Yung's theory gives this view a metaphysical justification.

The theory that everything involves its own negation sounds Hegelian. But according to Hegel, when a thing is negated, a new thing commences on a higher level, whereas according to Lao Tzu and the "Appendices" of the *Book of*

Changes, when a thing is negated, the new thing simply repeats the old. This is a philosophy characteristic of an agrarian people, as I pointed out in Chapter II.

Cosmology of Chang Tsai

The third cosmological philosopher to be mentioned in this chapter is Chang Tsai, known as the Master of Heng-chu (1020-77). He was a native of the present Shaanxi Province. He too, though from yet another point of view, developed a cosmological theory based on the "Appendices" of the *Book of Changes*. In this he especially emphasized the idea of Chi, a concept which became more and more important in the cosmological and metaphysical theories of the later Neo-Confucianists. The word chi literally means gas or ether. In Neo-Confucianism its meaning is sometimes more abstract and sometimes more concrete, according to the different systems of the particular philosophers. When its meaning is more abstract, it approaches the concept of matter, as found in the philosophy of Plato and Aristotle, in contrast to the Platonic Idea or the Aristotelian form. In this sense, it means the primary undifferentiated material out of which all individual things are formed. When, however, its meaning is concrete, it means the physical matter that makes up all existing individual things. It is in this concrete sense that Chang Tsai speaks of *Chi*.

Chang Tsai, like his predecessors, bases his cosmological theory on the passage in "Appendix III" of the *Book of Changes* that state: "In the *Yi* there is the Supreme Ultimate which produces the Two Forms [i.e., the *Yin* and *Yang*]." For him, however, the Supreme Ultimate is nothing other than the Chi. In his main work, the *Cheng Meng or Correct Discipline for Beginners*, he writes:

> The Great Harmony is known as the *Tao* [by which he here means the Supreme Ultimate]. Because in it there are interacting qualities of floating and sinking, rising and falling, movement and quiescence, therefore there appear in it the beginnings of the emanating forces which agitate one another, overcome or are overcome by one another and contract or expand, one with regard to the other.[918]

The Great Harmony is a name for the *Chi* in its entirety, which Chang Tsai also describes as "wandering air."[919] The qualities of floating, rising, and movement are those of the *Yang*, while those of sinking, falling, and quiescence are those of the *Yin*. The Chi, when influenced by the *Yang* qualities, floats and rises, while when influenced by the *Yin* qualities, it sinks and falls. As a result the *Chi* is constantly either condensing or dispersing. Its condensation results in the formation of concrete things; its dispersion results in the dissolution of these same things.

In the *Cheng Meng*, Chang Tsai writes:

> When the *Chi* condenses, its visibility becomes apparent so that there are then the shapes [of individual things]. When it disperses, its visibility is no longer apparent and there are no shapes. At the time of its condensation,

918 *Chang-tzu Chuan-shu* or *Collected Works of the Master Chang*, *Chuan* 2.
919 *Ibid*.

can one say otherwise than that this is but temporary? But at the time of its dispersing, can one hastily say that it is then non-existent?[920]

Thus Chang Tsai tries to get away from the *Tao*ist and Buddhist idea of *Wu* (Non-being). He says: "If one knows the Void is the Chi, one knows that there is no *Wu*." The Void is not really an absolute vacuum; it is simply the *Chi* in its state of dispersion in which it is no longer visible.

One particularly famous passage of the Cheng Meng has become known as the *Hsi Ming* or "Western Inscription," because it was separately inscribed on the western wall of Chang Tsai's study. In this passage Chang maintains that since all things in the universe are constituted of one and the same *Chi*, therefore men and all other things are but part of one great body. We should serve *Chien* and *Kun* (by which Chang means Heaven and Earth) as we do our own parents, and regard all men as we do our brothers. We should extend the virtue of filial piety and practice it through service to the universal parents. Yet, no extraordinary acts are needed for this service. Every moral activity, if one can understand it, is an activity that serves the universal parents. If, for instance, one loves other men simply because they are members of the same society as one's own, then one is doing his social duty and is serving society. But if one loves them not merely because they are members of the same society, but also because they are children of the universal parents, then by loving them one not only serves society, but at the same time serves the parents of the universe as a whole. The passage concludes with the saying: "In life I follow and serve [the universal parents], and when death comes, I rest."[921]

This essay has been greatly admired by later Neo-Confucianists, because it clearly distinguished the Confucian attitude towards life from that of Buddhism and of *Tao*ist philosophy and religion.

Chang Tsai writes elsewhere:

> The Great Void [i.e., the Great Harmony, the *Tao*] cannot but consist of *Chi*; this *Chi* cannot but condense to form all things; and these things cannot but become dispersed so as to form [once more] the Great Void. The perpetuation of these movements in a cycle is inevitable and thus spontaneous.[922]

The sage is one who fully understands this course. Therefore, he neither tries to be outside it, as do the Buddhists, who seek to break the chain of causation and thus bring life to an end; nor does he try to prolong his life, as do the religious *Tao*ists, who seek to nurture their body and thus remain as long as possible within the human sphere. The sage, because he understands the nature of the universe, therefore knows that "life entails no gain nor death any loss."[923] Hence he simply tries to live a normal life. In life he does what his duty as a member of society and as a member of the universe requires him to do, and when death comes, he "rests."

He does what every man should do, but because of his understanding, what he does acquires new significance. The Neo-Confucianists developed a point of

920 *Ibid.*
921 *Ibid.*
922 *Id., Chuan* 2.
923 *Ibid.*

view from which all the moral activities valued by the Confucianists acquire a further value that is super-moral. They all have in them that quality that the Chanists called the wonderful *Tao*. It is in this sense that Neo-Confucianism is actually a further development of Chanism.

XXIV NEO-CONFUCIANISM: THE BEGINNING OF THE TWO SCHOOLS

Neo-Confucianism came to be divided into two main schools, which, by happy coincidence, were initiated by two brothers, known as the two Cheng Masters. Cheng Yi (1033-1108), the younger brother, initiated a school which was completed by Chu Hsi (1130-1200) and was known as the Cheng-Chu school or *Li* hsueh (School of Laws or Principles). Cheng Hao (1032-1085), the elder brother, initiated another school which was continued by Lu Chiu-yuan (1139-1193) and completed by Wang Shou-*jen* (1473-1529 and was known as the Lu-Wang school or *Hsin hsueh* (School of Mind). The full significance of the difference between the two schools was not recognized at the time of the two Cheng Masters themselves, but Chu Hsi and Lu Chiu-yuan began a great controversy which has been carried on until the present day.

As we shall see in the following chapters, the main issue between the two groups was really one of fundamental philosophical importance. In terms of Western philosophy, it was one as to whether the laws of nature are or are not legislated by the mind or Mind. That has been the issue between Platonic realism and Kantian idealism, and may be said to be the issue in metaphysics. If it were solved, there would not be much other controversy left. In this chapter I am not going to discuss this issue in detail, but only to suggest its beginnings in the history of Chinese philosophy.

Chang Hao's Idea of Jen

The Cheng brothers were natives of the present Henan Province. The elder of them, Cheng Hao, was known as Master Ming-tao, and the younger, Cheng Yi, as the Master of Yi-chuan. Their father was a friend of Chou Tun-yi and the cousin of Chang Tsai.

Hence in their youth the Cheng brothers received some teaching from Chou Tun-yi, and later they constantly held discussions with Chang Tsai. Furthermore, they lived not far from Shao Yung, with whom they often met. The close contact between these five philosophers was certainly a very happy incident in the history of Chinese philosophy.

Cheng Hao greatly admired Chang Tsai's *Hsi Ming* or "Western Inscription," because its central theme of the oneness of all things is also the main idea in his philosophy. According to him, oneness with all things is the main characteristic of the virtue of *jen* (human-heartedness). He says:

> The learner needs first to comprehend *jen*. The man of *jen* is undifferentiably one with all things. Righteousness, propriety, wisdom, and good faith, all these are *jen*. Get to comprehend this truth and cultivate it with sincerity and attentiveness, that is all that is required....The *Tao* has nothing that stands in contrast to it; even the word great is inadequate to express it. The function of Heaven and Earth is our function. Mencius said that all things

are complete within us. We must reflect and realize that this is really so. Then it is a source of immense joy. If we reflect and do not realize that it is really so, then there are still two things [the self and not-self] that stand in contrast with each other. Even if we try to unite the self and not-self, we still do not form a unity, and so how can there then be joy? In the "Correcting of the Ignorant" [another name for Chang Tsai's *Hsi Ming*] there is a perfect statement of this unity. If we cultivate ourselves with this idea, there is nothing further required to be done. We must do something, and never stop and never forget, yet never help to grow, doing it without the slightest effort. This is the way of spiritual cultivation.[924]

In Chapter VII I have fully discussed the statement of Mencius referred to by Cheng Hao in the above quotation. One must do something, but "never help-to grow"; this is Mencius' method for cultivating the Great Morale, a method which was greatly admired by the Neo-Confucianists. According to Cheng Hao, one must first understand the principle that one is originally one with all things.

Then all one needs to do is to keep this in mind and act in accordance with it sincerely and attentively. Through the accumulation of such practices, one will really come to feel that one is one with all things. The statement that one must act in accordance with this principle sincerely and attentively means that there is something one must do. There must, however, be no artificial striving to achieve the unity. In this sense, one must be "without the slightest effort."

The difference between Cheng Hao and Mencius is that the former gives to *jen* a much more metaphysical interpretation than does the latter. "Appendix III" of the *Book of Changes* contains the statement: "The supreme virtue of Heaven and Earth is *sheng*." The word *sheng* here may mean simply production or to produce; it may also mean life or to give birth to life. In Chapter XV I translated *sheng* as to produce, because that seems to be the meaning that best harmonizes with the ideas of the "Appendices." But according to Cheng Hao and other Neo-Confucianists, *sheng* really means life or to give birth to life. According to them there is a tendency towards life in all things, and this tendency constitutes the *jen* of Heaven and Earth.

It so happens that the expression "not-*jen*" is a technical term for paralysis in Chinese medicine. Cheng Hao says:

> The doctor describes the paralysis of a man's, arms or legs as not-*jen*; this is a very good description [of the disease] The man of *jen* takes Heaven and Earth as being one with himself. To him there is nothing that is not himself. Having recognized them as himself, what cannot he do for them? If there is not such relationship with the self, it follows that there is no connection between the self and others. If the hand or foot are no-*jen*, it means that the *chi* [vital force] is not circulating freely and the parts (of the body] are not connected with each other.[925]

924 *Erh-Cheng Yi-shu* or *literary Remains of the Two Chengs, Chuan* 24.

925 *Id., Chuan* 2a.

Thus, according to Cheng Hao, metaphysically there is an inner connection between all things. What Mencius called the "feeling of commiseration" or the "unbearing mind" is simply an expression of this connection between ourselves and other things. It often happens, however, that our "unbearing mind" is obscured by selfishness, or, to use the Neo-Confucian term, by selfish desires or simply desires. Hence the original unity is lost. What is necessary is simply to remember that originally there is a oneness between oneself and all things, and to act accordingly with sincerity and attentiveness. In this way the original unity will be restored in due course. Such is the general idea of the philosophy of Cheng Hao, which Lu Chiu-yuan and Wang Shou-*jen* later developed in detail.

Origin of the Cheng-Chu Idea of Li

In Chapter VIII we have seen that already in early times Kung-sun Lung made clear the distinction between universals and things. He insisted that whiteness is whiteness even though nothing is in itself white in the world. It would seem that he had some idea of the Platonic distinction of the two worlds, the eternal and the temporal, the intelligible and the visible. This idea was not developed by later philosophers, however, and the philosophy of the School of Names did not become a main current in Chinese thought. On the contrary, this thought moved in another direction, and it took more than one thousand years for Chinese philosophers to turn their attention once more to the problem of eternal ideas. The two main thinkers to do so are Cheng Yi and Chu Hsi.

The philosophy of Cheng Yi and Chu Hsi, however, is not a continuation of the School of Names. They paid no attention to Kungsun Lung or to the *ming-li* (principles based on the analysis of names) discussed by the Neo-Taoists whom we have treated in Chapter XIX. They developed their idea of *Li* (abstract Principles or Laws) directly from the "Appendices" of the *Book of Changes*. I have pointed out in Chapter XV that a distinction exists between the *Tao* of Taoism and the tao of the "Appendices." The *Tao* of Taoism is the unitary first "that" from which all things in the universe come to be. The tao of the "Appendices," on the contrary, are multiple, and are the principles which govern each separate category of things in the universe. It is from this concept that Cheng Yi and Chu Hsi derived the idea of Li.

The immediate stimulus for Cheng Yi and Chu Hsi, however, seems to be the thought of Chang Tsai and Shao Yung. In the last chapter we have seen that Chang Tsai explained the appearance and disappearance of concrete particulars in terms of the condensation and dispersion of the *Chi*. The condensation of the *Chi* results in the formation and appearance of things. But this theory fails to explain the reason for the different *categories* of things. Granted that a flower and a leaf are both condensations of the *Chi*, we are still at a loss as to why a flower is a flower and a leaf a leaf. It is here that Cheng Yi's and Chu Hsi's idea of *Li* comes in.

According to them, the universe as we see it is a result not only of the *Chi* but also of the *Li*. Different categories of things exist, because the condensation of the *Chi* takes place in different ways in accordance with different *Li*. A flower is a flower, because it is the condensation of the *Chi* taking place in accordance with the *Li* of the flower; and a leaf is a leaf, because it is the condensation of the *Chi* taking place in accordance with the *Li* of the leaf.

Shao Yung's diagrams also helped to suggest the idea of *Li*.

According to Shao, what the diagrams represent is the law that governs the transformations of individual things. This law is antecedent not only to the diagrams, but also to the existence of individual things. Shao maintained that before the trigrams were first drawn by their discoverer, the *Book of Changes* already ideally existed. One of the Cheng Masters says:

> [In one of his poems], Yao-fu f i.e., Shao Yung) writes: "Before the drawing [of the trigrams by Fu Hsi, a traditional sage supposed to have lived in the twenty-ninth century B.C.], there was already the *Book of Changes*" ... This idea has never been said before.[926]

This theory is the same as that of the new realists, who maintain that there is a Mathematics before there is mathematics.

Cheng Yi's Concept of Li

The combination of the philosophy of Chang Tsai and Shao Yung suggests the distinction between what the Greek philosophers called the form and the matter of things. This distinction Cheng Yi and Chu Hsi made very clear. For them, just as for Plato and Aristotle, all things in the world, if they are to exist at all, must be the embodiment of some principle in some material. If a certain thing exists, there must be for it a certain principle. If there be a certain principle, however, there may or may not exist a corresponding thing. The principle is what they call *Li*, and the material is what they call *Chi*. The latter, for Chu Hsi, is much more abstract than is the *Chi* in Chang Tsai's system.

Cheng Yi also distinguishes between what is "within shapes" and what is "above shapes." The origin of these two terms is traceable to "Appendix III" of the *Book of Changes* "What is above shapes is called the *Tao*; what is within shapes is called the implements." In the system of Cheng Yi and Chu Hsi, this distinction corresponds to that between the abstract and concrete in Western philosophy. The *Li* are the *Tao* which is "above shapes," or, as we would say, abstract; while the "implements," by which Cheng Yi and Chu Hsi mean particular things, are "within shapes," or, as we would say, concrete.

According to Cheng Yi, the *Li* are eternal, and can neither be added to nor reduced. As he says: "Existence or non-existence, addition or reduction, cannot be postulated about *Li*. All *Li* are complete in themselves; in them there can never be deficiency."[927]

Again he says:

> All the *Li* are pervasively present. We cannot say that the tao of kingship was more when Yao [a traditional sage-king] exemplified it as a king, nor can we say that the tao of sonship was more when Shun [the successor of

926 *Literary Remains of the Two Chengs, Chuan* 2a.

927 *Ibid.*

Yao, known for his filial piety] exemplified it as a son. These [the *Li*] remain what they are.[928]

Cheng Yi also describes the world "above shapes" as "void, with nothing in it, yet filled with all."[929] It is void because in it there are no concrete things; yet it is filled with all the *Li*. All the *Li* are there eternally, no matter whether or not instances of them occur in the actual world, nor does it matter whether we human beings know of them or not.

Cheng Yi's method of spiritual cultivation is expressed in his famous statement: "In cultivation one needs attentiveness; in the advancement of learning, one needs the extension of knowledge."[930]

The word "attentiveness" is a translation of the Chinese word *Ching*, which may also be translated as seriousness or earnestness. We have seen that Cheng Hao also said that the "learner" must first understand that all things are originally one, and then cultivate this understanding with sincerity and attentiveness. Attentiveness is the key word used by Neo-Confucianists after this time to describe their method of spiritual cultivation. It replaces the word used by Chou Tun-yi for this process, which was a different word also pronounced *Ching* but meaning quiescence. The replacement of "quiescence" by "attentiveness" in the methodology of spiritual cultivation marks further the departure of Neo-Confucianism from Chanism.

As pointed out in Chapter XXII, effort is needed for the process of cultivation. Even if one's ultimate aim is to be effortless, it requires an initial effort to attain the effortless state. This, however, the Chanists do not state, nor is it expressed by Chou Tun-yi's quiescence. Use of the word attentiveness, however, brings this idea of effort into the foreground.

In cultivation one must be attentive, but attentive to what? This is a controversial question between the two schools of Neo-Confucianism, which I will return to in the next two chapters.

Method of Dealing with the Emotions

In Chapter XX I said that Wang Pi maintained the theory that the sage "has emotions but is without ensnarement." It is also said in the *Chuang-tzu*:

> The mind of the perfect man is like a mirror. It does not move with things, nor does it anticipate them. It responds to things, but does not retain them. Therefore the perfect man is able to deal successfully with things but is not affected by them.[931]

Wang Pi's theory of the emotions seems to be an extension of this statement of Chuang Tzu.

The Neo-Confucian method of dealing with the emotions follows the same line as Wang Pi's. Its essential is the disconnecting of the emotions from the self. Cheng Hao says:

---

928 *Ibid.*

929 *Ibid.*

930 *Id.*, *Chuan* 18.

931 *Chuang-tzu*, Ch. 7.

> The normality of Heaven and Earth is that their mind is in all things, yet of themselves they have no mind. The normality of the sage is that his emotion follows the nature of things, yet of himself he has no emotion. Therefore, for the superior man nothing is better than being impersonal and impartial, and responding to things spontaneously as they come. The general trouble with man is that he is selfish and rationalistic. Being selfish, he cannot take action as a spontaneous response. Being rationalistic, he cannot take intuition as his natural guide. When the sage is pleased, it is because the thing is there which is rightly the object of pleasure. When the sage is angry, it is because the thing is there which is rightly the object of anger. Therefore the pleasure and anger of the sage are not connected with his mind, but with things.[932]

This is a part of Cheng Hao's "Letter on the Calmness of the Nature," which was written to Chang Tsai. The impersonalness, impartiality, and action with spontaneity and without self-rationalization, of which Cheng Hao speaks, are the same as the vacuity and straightforwardness spoken of by Chou Tun-yi. The same illustration from Mencius that was used in connection with Chou Tun-yi can be applied here.

> According to Cheng Hao's view, it is natural that even the sage should sometimes experience pleasure or anger. But since his mind has an impersonal, objective, and impartial attitude, when these feelings come, they are simply objective phenomena in the universe, and are not especially connected with his self. When he is pleased or angry, it is simply the external things, deserving of either pleasure or anger that produce corresponding feelings in his mind. His mind is like a mirror on which anything may be reflected. As a result of this attitude, when the object has gone, the emotion it produced goes with it. In this way the sage, though he has emotions, is without ensnarement. Let us return to the illustration mentioned earlier. Suppose a man sees a child about to fall into a well. If he follows his natural impulse, he will immediately rush forward to save the child. His success will certainly give him pleasure and his failure will equally certainly cause him sorrow.

But since his action is impersonal and impartial, once the affair is finished, his emotion is also gone. Thus he has emotions, but is without ensnarement.

Another illustration commonly used by the Neo-Confucianists is that of Yen Hui, the favorite disciple of Confucius, of whom the latter said: "Hui did not transfer his anger."[933] When a man is angry, he often abuses other people and destroys things that apparently have nothing to do with his emotion at all. This is called "transferring anger." He transfers his anger from something that is the object of his anger to something that is not. The Neo-Confucianists took this statement of Confucius very seriously, and considered this quality of Yen Hui as the most significant in the great Confucian disciple, whom they considered next to Confucius himself in spiritual perfection. Thus Cheng Yi comments:

932 *Ming-tao Wen-chi* or *Collected Writings of Cheng Hao, Chuan* 3.

933 *Analects*, V1, 2

> We must understand why it is that Yen Hui did not transfer his anger. In a bright mirror, a beautiful object produces a beautiful reflection, while an ugly object produces an ugly one. But the mirror itself has no likes or dislikes. There are some people who, being offended in their home, discharge their anger in the street. But the anger of the sage operates only in accordance with the nature of things; it is never he himself who possesses the anger. The superior man is the master of things; the small man is their slave.[934]

Thus according to the Neo-Confucianists, the reason why Yen Hui did not transfer his anger is because his emotion was not connected with the self. A thing might act to produce some emotion in his mind, just as an object may appear in a mirror, but his self was not connected with the emotion. Therefore there was nothing to be transferred to other objects. He responded to the thing that produced the emotion in his mind, but he himself was not ensnared by it. He was considered to be a happy man, and for that, was greatly admired by the Neo-Confucianists.

The Search for Happiness

In Chapter XX I have said that Neo-Confucianism attempted to find happiness in *ming-chiao* (morals, institutions). The search for happiness, indeed, is one of the professed aims of the Neo-Confucianists. Cheng Hao says, for example: "When we studied under Chou [Tun-yi], he always asked us to find out wherein lay the happiness of Kung [Confucius] and Yen [Hui], and what they found enjoyable."[935] There are, in fact, many passages in the *Analects* recording the happiness of Confucius and his disciple. Those commonly quoted by the Neo-Confucianists include the following:

Confucius said: "With coarse rice to eat, with only water to drink, and my bended arm for a pillow, I am happy in the midst of these things. Riches and honor acquired by means that I know to be wrong are to me as a floating cloud."[936]

About Yen Hui, Confucius said:

> Incomparable indeed was Hui. A handful of rice to eat, a gourdful of water to drink, and living in a mean street these, others would have found unbearably depressing, but for Hui's happiness they made no difference at all. Incomparable indeed was Hui.[937]

Another passage says that once when Confucius was sitting with several of his disciples, he asked each of them to express his desires. One replied that he would like to be minister of war in a certain state, another to be minister of finance, and still another to be master of ceremonies. But the fourth, Tseng Tien, paid no attention to what others were saying, but continued to strum his lute. When the others had finished, Confucius asked him to speak. He replied"[My desire would be], in the last month of spring, with the dress of the season all complete, along with five or six young men, and six or seven boys, to go to wash in the river Yi,

934 *Literary Remains of the Two Chengs, Chuan* 18.

935 *Id., Chuan* 2a.

936 *Analects*, VII, 15.

937 *Id.*, VI, 9.

enjoy the breezes among the rain altars, and return home singing." Whereupon Confucius said: "I am with Tien."[938]

Commenting on the first two passages, Cheng Yi says that there is nothing to be enjoyed in eating coarse rice and drinking water *per se*. What the passages mean is simply that Confucius and Yen Hui remained happy, despite the fact that they had only this meager fare. This comment is correct in itself, but the question remains what it was that did constitute their happiness.

A certain man once asked Cheng Yi: "Why is it that the happiness of Yen Hui remained unaffected [by external hardships]?" Cheng Yi answered: "[Do you know] what it was that Yen Hui enjoyed?" The man replied "He enjoyed the *Tao*." To which, Cheng Yi said "If Yen Hui enjoyed the *Tao*, he was not Yen Hui."[939] This statement is very much like that of the Chan Masters, which is why Chu Hsi, editor of the *Literary Remains of the Two Chengs*, did not include it there but placed it instead into the subsidiary work known as the *External Collection*. Nevertheless, the saying contains some truth. The happiness of the sage is a natural outcome of his state of mind, described by Chou Tun-yi as "vacuous in quiescence and straightforward in movement," and by Cheng Hao as "impersonal, impartial, and responding to things spontaneously." He does not enjoy the *Tao*; he simply enjoys what he himself is.

This view of the Neo-Confucianists can be seen by their interpretation of the third passage from the *Analects* quoted above. Chu Hsi's comment on this passage reads:

> The learning of Tseng Tien would seem to have attained to the complete elimination of selfish desires, and to the Heavenly Laws in their pervasiveness, which are to be found everywhere without the slightest deficiency. This is why, both in activity and at rest, he was so simple and at ease. Speaking about his intention, he simply based himself on his existing station [in society and the universe] and enjoyed the ordinary state of affairs. He did not have the slightest idea of living according to [the views of] others, but lived according to himself. His mind was so vast that it lay in a single stream with Heaven and Earth, in which all things enjoy themselves. This mysterious sense is behind his words and can be dimly seen [by us]. The other three disciples only paid attention to the lesser branches of affairs, so that they could bear no comparison with the mood of Tseng Tien. That is why the Master [Confucius] deeply approved of him.[940]

In Chapter XX I have said that the essential quality of *feng liu* is to have a mind that transcends the distinctions of things and lives in accord with itself, rather than with others. According to Chu Hsi's interpretation, Tseng Tien was precisely a person of this kind. He was happy, because he was *feng liu*. In this statement of Chu Hsi we also see the romantic element in Neo-Confucianism. The Neo-Confucianists, as I have said, tried to seek happiness in *ming chiao*, but at the same time, according to them, *ming Chiao* is not the opposite of *tzu*

938 *Id*, XI, 25.

939 *Erh-Cheng Wai-shu* or *External Collection of Sayings of the Two Chengs*, *Chuan* 7.

940 *Lun-yu Chi-chu* or *Collected Comments on the "Analects,"* *Chuan* 6.

jan (nature, natural), but rather its development. This, the Neo-Confucianists maintained, was the main thesis of Confucius and Mencius.

Did the Neo-Confucianists themselves succeed in carrying out this idea? They did, and their success can be seen in the following translation of two poems, one by Shao Yung and the other by Cheng Hao. Shao Yung was a very happy man and was referred to by Cheng Hao as a *feng liu* hero. He named his house the *An Lo Wo* or Happy Nest, and called himself the Master of Happiness. His poem, titled "Song on Happiness," reads:

The name of the Master of Happiness is not known.
For thirty Wars he has lived on the bank of the Lo River.
His feelings are those of the wind and moon;
His spirit is on the river and lake.
(To him there is no distinction)
Between low position and high rank,
Between poverty and riches.
He does not more?? with things nor anticipate them.
He has no restraints and no taboos.
He is poor but has no sorrow,
He drinks, but never to intoxication.
He gathers the springtime of the world into his mind.
He has a small pond on Ouch??? to read poems,
He has a small window under which to sleep;
He has a small carriage with which to divert his mind,
He has a great pen with which to enjoy his will
He sometimes wears a sun hat;
He sometimes wears a sleeveless shirt; He sometimes sits in the forests;
He sometimes walks on the river bank.
He enjoys seeing good men;
He enjoys hearing about good conduct;
He enjoys speaking good tuords????,
He enjoys carrying out a good will.
He does not flatter the Chan Masters;
He does not praise the man of occult arts.
He does not leave his home,
Yet he is one with Heaven and Earth.
He cannot be conquered by a great army;
He cannot be induced by a great salary.
Thus he has been a happy man,
For sixty-five years.[941]

Cheng Hao's poem, titled "Autumn Days," reads:

In these late wars there is nothing that comes
That is not easy and simple;
Each morning through my window shines the sun,

941 *Yi-chuan Chi fang Chi, Chuan* 14.

As I awake.
All creatures run their course in true content,
As I calmly observe.
The pleasure of each season through the year,
I enjoy with others.
Beyond Heaven and Earth and all that has shape,
The Tao is there.
The winds and clouds about me shift and change,
My thought is there.
By riches and high estate, I am not to be polluted;
Neither poverty nor low rank can affect my happiness.
A man like this is a hero indeed![942]

Men such as these are heroes in the sense that they cannot be conquered. Yet they are not such in the ordinary sense. They are what is known as the *feng liu* hero.

Among the Neo-Confucianists there were some who criticized Shao Yung to the effect that he made too much display of his happiness. But no such criticism is ever made about Cheng Hao. In any case we find here a combination of Chinese romanticism (*feng liu*) and classicism (*ming chiao*) at its best.

942 *Collected Writings of Cheng Hao, Chuan* 1.

XXV NEO-CONFUCIANISM: THE SCHOOL OF PLATONIC IDEAS

Only twenty-two years after the death of Cheng Yi (1033-1108), Chu Hsi (1130-1200) was born in the present Fujian Province. The political change that took place during these twenty years was tremendous. The Sung Dynasty, although culturally outstanding, was militarily never as strong as the Han and Tang dynasties, and was under constant threat from outside tribes in the north and northwest. Its greatest catastrophe came when it lost its capital, the present city of Kaifeng, to the Jurchen, a Tungusic tribe from the northeast, and was compelled to reestablish itself south of the Yangtze River in 1127. This event marked the division of the Sung Dynasty into two lesser parts: the Northern Sung (960-1126) and the Southern Sung (1127-1279).

Position of Chu Hsi in Chinese History

Chu Hsi, better known simply as Chu Tzu or the Master Chu, was a philosopher of subtle argument, clear thinking, wide knowledge and voluminous literary output. His Recorded Sayings alone amount to 140 chuan or books. With him, the philosophic system of the Cheng-Chu school, also known as the *Li hsueh* or School of *Li*, reached its culmination. Though the supremacy of this school was several times to be disputed, notably by the Lu-Wang school and by certain scholars of the Ching Dynasty, it remained the most influential single system of philosophy until the introduction of Western philosophy in China in recent decades.

In Chapter XVII I have said that the dynastic governments of China ensured the supremacy of their official ideology through the examination system. Persons who took the state examinations were required to write essays based on the official versions and commentaries of the Confucian Classics. In Chapter XXIII I also said that one of the major acts of Emperor Tai-tsung of the Tang Dynasty was to determine the official version and "correct meaning" of the Classics. During the Sung Dynasty, the great statesman and reformer, Wang An-shih (1021-1086), prepared "new interpretations" to some of these Classics, and in 1075 Emperor Shen-tsung ordered that Wang's interpretations should be made official. This order, however, was soon cancelled when the political rivals of Wang An-shih gained control of the government.

It is to be remembered that the Neo-Confucianists considered *Analects of Confucius*, the *Mencius*, the Chung Yung or *Doctrine of the Mean*, and the *Ta Hsueh* or *Great Learning*, as the most important texts, which they grouped together, giving them the collective title of the *Four Books*. For these Chu Hsi wrote a *Commentary*, which he considered to be the most important of his writings. It is said that even on the day before his death, he was still working on a revision of this *Commentary*. He also wrote *Commentaries* on the Book of Changes and the Shih Ching or *Book of Odes*. In 1313 Emperor Jen-tsung of the Yuan, the Mongol dynasty that succeeded the Sung, ordered that the *Four Books* should be the main texts used in the state examinations, and that their official interpretation should follow Chu Hsi's commentaries. The same governmental endorsement was given to Chu Hsi's commentaries on the other Classics; persons hoping for success in the examinations had to interpret these works in accordance with Chu's commentaries. This practice was continued throughout the Ming and Ching dynasties, until the abolition of the state examination system in 1905, when the government tried to introduce a modern educational system.

As pointed out in Chapter XVIII, one of the main reasons why Confucianism gained supremacy in the Han Dynasty was its success in combining speculative thought with scholarship. In Chu Hsi himself these two aspects of Confucianism are outstandingly exemplified. His wide knowledge and learning made him a notable scholar, and his deep insight and clear thinking made him a philosopher of the first rank. It is no accident that he has been the dominant figure in Chinese thought during the last several centuries.

Li or Principle

In the last chapter we have examined Cheng Yi's theory of *Li*, i.e., Principles or Laws. By Chu Hsi this theory was made still clearer. He says "What are *hsing shang* or above shapes, so that they lack shapes or even shadows, are Li. What are *hsing hsia* or within shapes, so that they have shapes and body, are things."[943] A thing is a concrete instance of its Li. Unless there be such-and-such a Li, there cannot be such-and-such a thing. Chu Hsi says: "When a certain affair is done, that shows there is a certain Li."[944]

For everything, whether it be natural or artificial, there is its Li.

In the *Recorded Sayings*, one passage reads:

> (Question :) "How can dried and withered things also possess the nature?" (Answer :) "They all possess *Li* from the first moment of their existence. Therefore it is said: In the universe there is not a single thing that is without its nature." Walking on the steps, the Master [Chu Hsi]continued "For the bricks of these steps there is the *Li* of bricks."And sitting down, he said "For the bamboo chair, there is the *Li* of the bamboo chair. You may say that dried and withered things have no life or vitality, yet among them, too, there are none that do not have Li."[945]

Another passage reads "(Question) 'Do things without feeling also possess Li?' (Answer :) 'Most certainly they possess M???. For example, a ship can go only on water, while a cart can go only on land."[946] And still another passage reads: (Question :) "Is there *Li* in dried and withered things?" (Answer :) "As soon as a thing exists, the *Li* is inherent in it. Even in the case of a writing brush—though it is not produced by nature but by man, who takes the long and soft hairs of the

943 *Chu-tzu Yu-lei* or *Classified Recorded Sayings of the Master Chu, Chuan* 95.

944 *Id, Chuan* 101.

945 *Classified Recorded Sayings of the Master Chu, Chuan* 4.

946 *Ibid.*

hare to make it—as soon as that brush exists, *Li* is inherent in it."[947] The *Li* that is inherent in the writing brush is the nature of that brush. The same is true of all other kinds of things in the universe each kind has its own Li, so that whenever the members of a certain kind of thing exist, the *Li* of that kind is inherent in them and constitutes their nature. It is this *Li* that makes them what they are. Thus, according to the Cheng-Chu school, not all categories of objects possess mind, i.e., are sentient; nevertheless, all of them do possess their own particular nature, i.e., Li.

For this reason, there are the *Li* for things already before the concrete things themselves exist. In a letter answering Liu Shu-wen, Chu Hsi writes: "There are *Li*, even if there are no things. In that case there are only such-and-such *Li*, but not such-and-such things."[948] For instance, even prior to the human invention of ships and carts, the *Li* of ships and carts was already present. What is called the invention of ships and carts, therefore, is nothing more than the discovery by mankind of the *Li* of ships and carts, and the construction of these objects accordingly. All *Li* are present even before the formation of the physical universe. In the Recorded Sayings one passage reads: "(Question :) 'Before heaven and earth had yet come into existence, were all the things of later times already there?' (Answer :) 'Only the *Li* were there.'"[949] The *Li* are always there; that is to say, they are eternal.

Tai Chi or the Supreme Ultimate

For every kind of thing there is the *Li*, which makes it what it ought to be. The *Li* is the chi of that thing, i.e., it is its ultimate standard. (The word chi originally was a name for the ridge pole at the peak of the roof of a building. As used in Neo-Confucianism, it means the highest ideal prototype of things.) For the universe as a whole, there must also be an ultimate standard, which is supreme and all embracing. It embraces the multitude of *Li* for all things and is the highest summation of all of them. Therefore it is called the Supreme Ultimate or Tai Chi. As Chu Hsi says "Everything has an ultimate, which is the ultimate Li. That which unites and embraces the *Li* of heaven, earth, and all things is the Supreme Ultimate."[950]

He also says:

> The Supreme Ultimate is simply what is highest of all, beyond which nothing can be. It is the most high, most mystical, and most abstruse, surpassing everything. Lest anyone should imagine that the Supreme Ultimate has bodily form, Lien-hsi [i.e., Chou Tun-yi] has said of it: "The Ultimateless, and yet also the Supreme Ultimate." That is, it is in the realm of no things that there is to be found the highest Li.[951]

From these statements we see that the position of the Supreme Ultimate in

947 *Ibid.*
948 *Chu Wen kung Wen-chi* or *Collected Literary Writings of Chu Hsi, Chuan* 46.
949 *Classified Recorded Sayings of the Master Chu, Chuan* 1.
950 *Id., Chuan* 94.
951 *Chu-tzu Chuan-shu* or *Complete Works of the Master Chu, Chuan* 49.

Chu Hsi's system corresponds to the Idea of the Good or to God in the systems of Plato and Aristotle respectively.

There is one point in Chu Hsi's system, however, that makes his Supreme Ultimate more mystical than Plato's Idea of the Good or Aristotle's God. This is the fact that, according to Chu Hsi, the Supreme Ultimate is not only the summation of the *Li* of the universe as a whole, but is at the same time immanent in the individual examples of each category of things. Every particular thing has inherent in it the *Li* of its particular category of things, but at the same time the Supreme Ultimate in its entirety is inherent in it too. Chu Hsi says: "With regard to heaven and earth in general, the Supreme Ultimate is in heaven and earth. And with regard to the myriad things in particular, the Supreme Ultimate is in every one of them too."[952]

But if this is so, does not the Supreme Ultimate lose its unity?

Chu Hsi's answer is no. In the *Recorded Sayings* he says:

> There is but one Supreme Ultimate, which is received by the individuals of all things. This one Supreme Ultimate is received by each individual in its entirety and undivided. It is like the moon shining in the heavens, of which, though it is reflected in rivers and lakes and thus is everywhere visible, we would not therefore say that it is divided.[953] We know that in Plato's philosophy there is a difficulty in explaining the relation between the intellectual and sensible worlds, and between the one and the many. Chu Hsi, too, has this difficulty, which he meets with an illustration which is really a metaphor of constant use in Buddhism. The question as to how the *Li* of a whole class of things is related to the individual things within that class, and as to whether this relationship may also involve a division of the *Li*, is not raised. If it were, I think Chu Hsi would meet it with the same illustration.

Chi or Matter

If there were nothing but *Li*, there could be nothing more than a world that is "above shapes." Our own concrete physical world, however, is made possible by the presence of *Chi* upon which is imposed the pattern of the *Li*. Chu Hsi says:

In the universe there are *Li* and Chi. The *Li* is the *Tao* that pertains to "what is above shapes," and is the source from which all things arc produced The *Chi* is the material [literally, instrument] that pertains to "what is within shapes," and is the means whereby things are produced. Hence men or things, at the moment of their production, must receive this *Li* in order that they may have a nature of their own. They must receive this *Chi* in order that they may have their bodily form.[954]

Again he says:

> It seems to me that the *Chi* depends upon the *Li* for its operation. Thus when there is an agglomeration of Chi, the *Li* is also present within it. It is so, because the *Chi* has the capacity to condense and thus form things;

952 *Recorded Sayings, Chuan* 94.

953 *Ibid.*

954 Reply to Huang Tao-fu," *Collected Literary Writings, Chuan* 58.

> but the *Li* lacks volition or plan, and has no creative power.... The *Li* constitutes only a pure, empty, and vast world, without shapes or traces, and so incapable of producing anything. But the *Chi* has the capacity to undergo fermentation and condensation, and thus bring things into existence. And yet, whenever the *Chi* exists, the *Li* is present within it.[955]

Here we see how Chu Hsi says what Chang Tsai should have said but did not. Any individual thing is a condensation of Chi, but it is not only an individual thing; it is at the same time a member of some category of objects. As such, it is not merely a condensation of the Chi, but is a condensation that takes place in accordance with the *Li* for that category of objects as a whole. That is why, whenever there is a condensation of the Chi, *Li* must always necessarily be present within it.

The question as to the relative priority of *Li* and *Chi* is one much discussed by Chu Hsi and his disciples. On one occasion he says:

> Before the instances of it exist, there is the *Li*. For example, before there exist any sovereign and subject, there is the *Li* of the relationship between sovereign and subject. Before there exist any father and son, there is the *Li* of the relationship between father and son.[956]

That there is a *Li* prior to the instances of it in our physical universe, is certainly clear from Chu Hsi's statement. But is *Li* in general also prior to *Chi* in general? Chu Hsi says:

> *Li* is never separable from Chi. Nevertheless, *Li* pertains to "what is above shapes," whereas *Chi* pertains to "what is within shapes." Hence if we speak of "what is above shapes" and "what is within shapes," how can there not be priority and posteriority?[957]

Elsewhere there is a passage: (Question :) "When there is Li, there is then Chi. It seems that we cannot say that either one is prior to the other." (Answer:) "In reality, *Li* is prior. We cannot say, however, that there is *Li* today and *Chi* tomorrow. Yet there must be apriority of the one to the other."[958] From these passages we can see that what Chu Hsi has in mind is that as a matter of fact "there is no *Li* without *Chi* and no *Chi* without *Li*."[959] There is no time when there is no Chi. And since *Li* is eternal, it is absurd to speak about it as having a beginning. Hence the question as to whether it is *Li* or *Chi* that comes into being first is really nonsensical. Nevertheless, to speak about the beginning of *Chi* is only a factual absurdity, while to speak about the beginning of *Li* is a logical one. In this sense it is not incorrect, as between *Li* and Chi, to say that there is priority and posteriority.

Another question is this As between *Li* and Chi, which is it that Plato and Aristotle would have called the "First Mover"? *Li* cannot be so, because it "lacks volition or plan, and has no creative power." But though *Li* itself does not move, yet in the "pure, empty, and wide world" of *Li* there are the *Li* of movement and the *Li* of quiescence. The *Li* of movement does not itself move, nor does the *Li* of

---

955 *Recorded Sayings, Chuan* 1.

956 *Id., Chuan* 95.

957 *Id., Chuan* 1.

958 *Complete Works, Chuan* 49.

959 *Recorded Sayings, Chuan* 1.

quiescence itself rest, but as soon as the *Chi* "receives" them, the latter begins to move or rest. The *Chi* that moves is called Yang; the *Chi* that rests is called *Yin*. Thus, according to Chu Hsi, the dualistic elements that are the fundamentals of the universe in Chinese cosmology is produced. He says:

Whereas the *Yang* is in movement and the *Yin* in quiescence, the Supreme Ultimate is neither in movement nor in quiescence. But there are the *Li* of movement and of quiescence. These *Li* are invisible, and become manifest to us only when there are the movement of *Yang* and the quiescence of *Yin*. The *Li* rests upon the *Yin* and *Yang* just as a man rides on a horse.[960]

Thus the Supreme Ultimate, like God in the philosophy of Aristotle, is not moved, yet at the same time is the mover of all.

The interaction of *Yin* and *Yang* results in the production of the Five Elements, and from these the physical universe as we know it is produced. In his cosmological theory, Chu Hsi endorses most of the theories of Chou Tun-yi and Shao Yung.

Nature and Mind

From the above we see that, according to Chu Hsi, when an individual thing comes into existence, a certain *Li* is inherent in it, which makes it what it is and constitutes its nature. And a man, like other things, is a concrete particular produced in the concrete world Hence what we call human nature is simply the *Li* of humanity that is inherent in the individual. The saying of Cheng Yi that "the nature is *Li* is endorsed and commented on by Chu Hsi in many places." The *Li* here spoken of is not *Li* in its universal form; it is simply the *Li* that is inherent in the individual. This explains the rather paradoxical saying of Cheng Hao: "When something is said about the natures it is then already not the nature." By this he simply means that it is then the individualized *Li*, and not *Li* in its universal form.

A man, in order to have concrete existence, must be the embodiment of Chi. The *Li* for all men is the same, and it is the *Chi* that makes them different. Chu Hsi says:

> Whenever there is Li, then there is Chi. Whenever there is *Chi* there must be Li. Those who receive a *Chi* that is clear, are the sages in whom the nature is like a pearl lying in clear cold water. But those who receive a *Chi* that is turbid, are the foolish and degenerate in whom the nature is like a pearl lying in muddy water.[961]

Thus any individual, besides what he receives from Li, also has what he receives from Chi, and this is what Chu Hsi calls the physical endowment.

Such is Chu Hsi's theory of the origin of evil. As pointed out by Plato long ago, every individual, in order to have concreteness, must be an embodiment of matter, by which, consequently, he is implicated, so that he necessarily falls short of the ideal. A concrete circle, for example, can only be relatively and not absolutely round. That is the irony of the concrete world, in which man is no exception. Chu Hsi says:

Everything depends on its physical endowment. Li, on the other hand, is

960 *Complete Works, Chuan* 49.

961 *Recorded Sayings, Chuan* 4.

nothing but good, for since it is Li, how can it be evil? What is an evil lie in the physical endowment? Mencius' doctrine asserts absolutely that the nature is good. In this he apparently takes account only of the nature *per se* but not of the *Chi*, and thus in this respect his statement is incomplete. The Cheng School, however, supplements this with the doctrine of the physical nature, and so in it we get a complete and all-round view of the problem.[962]

The term "physical nature" here means the nature as it is found actually inherent in the physical endowment of an individual. As thus found, it always strives for the ideal, as Plato would say, but always falls short of it and cannot attain it. *Li* in its originally universal form, however, Chu Hsi calls "the nature of Heaven and Earth," by way of distinction. This distinction was already made by Chang Tsai and is followed by Cheng Yi and Chu Hsi. According to them, the use of this distinction completely solves the old controversy as to whether human nature is good or bad.

In Chu Hsi's system, nature is different from mind. In the *Recorded Sayings*, one passage reads: "(Question :) 'Is the mental faculty in man the mind or the nature?' (Answer :) 'The mental faculty is the mind but not the nature. The nature is nothing but *Li*.'"[963] Another passage reads:

(Question:) "With regard to consciousness is it the mental faculty of the mind that is thus conscious, or is it the action of the *Chi*?' (Answer :)"It is not wholly *Chi*. There is first the *Li* of consciousness; but by itself it cannot exercise consciousness. There can be consciousness only when the *Chi* has agglomerated to form physical shapes, and the *Li* has united with the *Chi*. The case is similar to that of the flame of this candle. It is because the latter receives this rich fat that we have so much light."[964]

Thus the mind, just as all other individual things, is the embodiment of *Li* with *Chi*. The distinction between mind and nature is that mind is concrete and nature is abstract. Mind can have activities, such as thinking and feeling, but nature cannot. But whenever such an activity takes place in our mind, we can deduce that there is a corresponding *Li* in our nature. Chu Hsi says:

In discussing the nature, it is important first of all to know what kind of entity the nature is. Master Cheng put it well when he said: "Nature is *Li*" Now if we regard it as *Li*, then surely it is without shapes and features. It is nothing but principle. In man the principles of human-kindness???, righteousness, propriety, and wisdom belong to the nature. They are principles only. It is because of them that we are capable of having commiseration, that we can be ashamed of wrongdoing, that we can be courteous, and that we can distinguish between what is right and wrong. Take as an illustration the nature of drugs: some have cooling and some heating properties. But in the drugs themselves you cannot see the shapes of these properties. It is only by the result that follows upon taking the drug that we know what its property is, and this constitutes its nature.[965]

962 *Complete Works, Chuan* 43.
963 *Recorded Sayings, Chuan* 5.
964 *Ibid.*
965 *Complete Works, Chuan* 42.

In Chapter VII we have seen how Mencius maintained that in human nature there are four constant virtues which manifest themselves as the "four beginnings." In the above quotation Chu Hsi gives a metaphysical justification to this theory of Mencius, which is primarily psychological. According to Chu, the four constant virtues pertain to *Li* and belong to the nature, while the four beginnings are the operations of the mind. We cannot know the abstract except through the concrete. We cannot know our nature except through our mind. As we shall see in the next chapter, the Lu-Wang school maintained that the mind is the nature. This is one of the main issues between the two schools.

Political Philosophy

If every kind of thing in this world has its own *Li*, then for the state, as an organization having concrete existence, there must also be the *Li* of statehood or government. If the state is organized and governed in accordance with this *Li*, it will be stable and prosperous; if not, it will become disorganized and fall into disorder.

According to Chu Hsi, this *Li* is the principle of government as taught and practiced by the former sage-kings. But it is not something subjective. It is eternally there, no matter whether or not it is taught or practiced. Regarding this point, Chu had some warm debates with his friend Chen Liang (1143-1194), who held a different point of view. Arguing with him, he wrote:

> During a period of fifteen hundred years, the *Tao* the principle of government, [as handed down by Yao and Shun two traditional sage-kings] ... and Confucius, has never been put into practice for even a single day in the world. But beyond human intervention, it is eternally there. It is simply what it is, and is eternal and immortal. It cannot perish, even though men have done violence to it during the last fifteen hundred years.[966]

"*The Tao*," he said again, "does not cease to be. What ceases to be is man's practice of it."[967]

As a matter of fact, not only have the sage-kings governed their states in accordance with the *Tao*, but all persons who have achieved something in politics must, to a certain degree, have followed the same *Tao*, even though sometimes unconsciously or incompletely. Chu Hsi writes:

> I always think that this *Li* [principle of government] is one and the same both in times past and present. Those who follow it, succeed; those who violate it, fail. Not only did the sages of antiquity practice it, but even among the heroes of modern times, none can have any achievement without following this *Li*. Herein, however, is a difference. The ancient sages, being cultivated in the wisest way in what is fundamental, could hold the golden mean, and therefore what they did was all entirely good from the beginning to the end. The so-called heroes of modern times, however, have never undergone such cultivation, and have only moved in the world of selfish desires. Those of them who were talented have succeeded in coming into a seeming agreement [with the *Li*] , each making

966 "Reply to Chen Liang," *Collected Literary Writings*, *Chuan* 36.
967 *Ibid.*

accomplishment to the extent that he followed this *Li.* There is one aspect in which all the so-called heroes are the same; that is, what they do can never be completely in accordance with the Li, and therefore is not perfectly good.[968]

To illustrate Chu Hsi's theory, let us take as an example the building of a house. A house must be built in accordance with the principles of architecture. These principles eternally remain, even if in the physical world itself no house is actually built. A great architect is a man who fully understands these principles and makes his plans in accordance with them. For example, the house he builds must be strong and durable. Not only great architects, however, but all who want to build a house, most follow the same principles, if their houses are to be built at all. Such non-professional architects, however, may simply follow these principles through intuition or practical experience, without understanding or even knowing about them. As a result, the houses they build cannot completely accord with the principles of architecture and therefore cannot be of the best. Such is the difference between the government of the sage-kings and that of the lesser so-called heroes.

As we have seen in Chapter VII, Mencius maintained that there are two kinds of government that of the *wang* or king and that of the *pa* or military lord. Chu Hsi's argument with Chen Liang is a continuation of the same controversy. Chu Hsi and other Neo-Confucianists maintain that all governments from the Han and Tang dynasties downward have been those of *pa,* because their rulers have all governed in their own interests and not in the interests of the people. Here again, therefore, Chu Hsi follows Mencius, but, as before, gives a metaphysical justification to the latter's theory, which is primarily political.

Method of Spiritual Cultivation

The Platonic idea that we cannot have a perfect state "until the philosopher becomes king or the king philosopher," is shared by most Chinese thinkers. In the *Republic,* Plato dwells at great length upon the education of the philosopher who is to become king. And Chu Hsi too, as we have seen, says that the sage-kings of antiquity were cultivated in the wisest way in what is fundamental. What is this method of cultivation? Chu Hsi has already told us that in every man, and indeed in everything, there is the Supreme Ultimate in its entirety. Since the Supreme Ultimate is the totality of the *Li* of all things, hence those *Li* are all within us, but, because of our physical endowment, they are not properly manifested. The Supreme Ultimate that is within us is like a pearl in turbid water. What we have to do is to make this pearl become visible. The method for so doing is, for Chu Hsi, the same as that taught by Cheng Yi, which, as we have seen in the last chapter, is twofold "The extension of knowledge through the investigation of things, "and "the attentiveness of the mind."

This method has its basis in the Ta Hsueh or *Great Learning,* which was considered by the Neo-Confucianists as "the beginner's door for entering the life of virtue." As we have seen in Chapter XVI, the method of self-cultivation as taught by the *Great Learning* begins with the "extension of knowledge" and "investigation

968 *Ibid.*

of things." According to the Cheng-Chu school, the purpose of the "investigation of things" is to extend our knowledge of the eternal *Li*. Why does not this method start with the investigation of *Li* instead of things? Chu Hsi says:

> The *Great Learning* speaks of the investigation of things but not of the investigation of *Li*. The reason is that to investigate *Li* is like clutching at emptiness in which there is nothing to catch hold. When it simply speaks of "the investigation of things," it means that we should seek "what is above shapes" through "what is within shapes."[969]

In other words, *Li* are abstract and things are concrete. We investigate the abstract through the concrete. What we as a result come to see lies both within the eternal world and within our own nature. The more we know *Li*, the more our nature, ordinarily concealed by our physical endowment, becomes visible to us.

As Chu Hsi says:

> There is no human intelligence [utterly] lacking knowledge, and no single thing in the world without D???. But because the investigation of *Li* is not exhaustive, this knowledge is in some ways not complete. This is why the first instruction of the Great Learning is that the student must, for all the separate things in the world, by means of the *Li* which he already understands, proceed further to gain exhaustive knowledge of those [with which he is not yet familiar], thus striving to extend his knowledge] to the farthest point. When one has exerted oneself for a long time, finally one morning a complete understanding will open before one. Thereupon there will be a thorough comprehension of all the multitude of things, external or internal, fine or coarse, and every exercise of the mind will be marked by complete enlightenment.[970]

Here we have again the theory of Sudden Enlightenment.

This seems to be enough in itself, so why should it be supplemented by the "attentiveness of the mind?" The answer is that without such attentiveness, the investigation of things is likely to be simply a kind of intellectual exercise and thus will not lead to the desired goal of Sudden Enlightenment. In investigating things we must keep in mind that what we are doing is to make visible our nature, to cleanse the pearl so that it can shine forth. In order to be enlightened, we must always think about Enlightenment.

This is the function of the attentiveness of mind.

Chu Hsi's method of spiritual cultivation is very like that of Plato. His theory that in our nature there are the *Li* of all things, is very like Plato's theory of a previous knowledge. According to Plato, "We acquire knowledge before birth of all the essences."[971] Because there is this previous knowledge, therefore he who "has learned to see the beautiful in due course and succession," can" suddenly perceive a nature of wondrous beauty."[972] This, too, is a form of Sudden Enlightenment.

969 *Complete Works, Chuan* 46

970 *Commentary on the "Great Learning"* Ch. 5.

971 *Plaedo*, 75.

972 *Symposium* 211.

XXVI NEO-CONFUCIANISM: THE SCHOOL OF UNIVERSAL MIND

As we have seen in Chapter XXIV, the Lu-Wang school, also known as the Hsin hsueh or Mind school, was initiated by Cheng Hao and completed by Lu Chiu-yuan and Wang Shou-*jen*. Lu Chiu-yuan (1139-1193), popularly known as the Master of Hsiang-shan, was a native of the present Kiangsi Province. He and Chu Hsi were friends, despite their widely divergent philosophic views. Their verbal and written debates on major philosophical problems evoked great interest in their day.

Lu Chiu-yuan's Conception of the Mind

Both Lu Chiu-yuan and Wang Shou-jen are said to have become convinced of the truth of their ideas as a result of experiencing Sudden Enlightenment. One day, it is said, Lu was reading an ancient book in which he came upon the two words *yu* and *chou*. An expositor remarked: "What comprises the four points of the compass together with what is above and below: this is called *yu*. What comprises past, present, and future: this is called *chou*." Thereupon Lu Chiu-yuan experienced an instantaneous enlightenment and said: "All affairs within the universe come within the scope of my duty; the scope of my duty includes all affairs within the universe."[973] And on another occasion he said: "The universe is my mind; my mind is the universe."[974]

Whereas Chu Hsi endorses Cheng Yi's saying that "the nature is *Li*," Lu Chiu-yuan replies that "the mind is *Li*."[975] The two sayings differ only by one word, yet in them lies the fundamental division between the two schools. As we have seen in the last chapter, the mind, in Chu Hsi's system, is conceived of as the concrete embodiment of *Li* as found in Chi; hence it is not the same as the abstract *Li* itself. Chu Hsi, consequently, can only say that the nature is Li, but not that the mind is Li. But in Lu Chiu-yuan's system, on the contrary, the mind itself is the nature, and he considers the presumed distinction between nature and mind as nothing more than a verbal one. Regarding such verbal distinctions, he says:

> Scholars of today devote most of their time to the explanation of words. For instance, such words as feeling, nature, mind, and ability all mean one and the same thing. It is only accidental that a single entity is denoted by different terms.[976]

Yet as we have seen in the last chapter, Chu Hsi's distinction between nature and mind is certainly far from a verbal one, for from his point of view, there actually exists such a distinction in reality. This reality as seen by him, however, is not the same as that seen by Lu Chiu-yuan. For the former, reality consists

973 *Lu Hsiang-shan Chuan-chi* or *Collected Works of Lu Hsiangshan*, *Chuan* 33.

974 *Id.*, *Chuan* 36.

975 *Collected Works*, *Chuan* 12.

976 *Collected Works*, *Chuan* 35.

of two worlds, the one abstract, the other concrete. For the latter, however, it consists of only one world, which is the mind or Mind.

But the sayings of Lu Chiu-yuan give us only a sketchy indication of what the world system of the Mind school is. For a more complete exposition, we must turn to the sayings and writings of Wang Shou-*jen*.

Wang Shou-Jen's Conception of the Universe

Wang Shou-jen (1472-1528) was a native of the present Zhejiang Province, and is generally known as the Master of Yang-ming. He was not only an outstanding philosopher, but was also notable as a practical statesman of high capacity and moral integrity. In his early years he was an ardent follower of the Cheng-Chu school; and, determined to carry out Chu Hsi's teaching, once started to investigate the principle or *Li* of bamboo. He concentrated his mind upon the bamboo day and night for seven consecutive days, yet failed to discover anything. Finally he was forced to give up the attempt in great despair. Afterwards, however, while living amid primitive surroundings in the mountains of southwest China, to which he had been temporarily exiled because of political intrigue at court, enlightenment came to him suddenly one night. As a result, he gained a new understanding of the central idea of the Great Learning, and from this viewpoint reinterpreted this work. In this way he completed and systematized the teaching of the Mind school.

In the *Chuan Hsi Lu* or *Record of Instructions*, which is a selection of Wang Shou-*jen*'s recorded sayings made by one of his disciples, one passage reads:

> While the Master was taking recreation at Nan-chen, one of our friends, pointing at the flowers and trees on a cliff, said: "You say there is nothing under heaven that is external to the mind. What relation, then, do these high mountain flowers and trees, which blossom and drop off themselves, have to my mind?" The Master replied, "When you do not see these flowers, they and your mind both become quiescent. When you see them, their color at once becomes clear. From this fact you know that these flowers are not external to your mind."[977]

Another passage reads:

> The Master asked "According to you, what is the mind of Heaven and Earth?" The disciple answered "I have often heard that man is the mind of Heaven and Earth." "And what is it in man that is called his mind?" "It is simply the spirituality or consciousness." "From this we know that in Heaven and Earth there is one spirituality or consciousness. But because of his bodily form, man has separated himself from the whole, my spirituality or consciousness is the ruler of Heaven and Earth, spirits and things.... If Heaven, Earth, spirits, and things are separated from my spirituality or consciousness, they cease to be. And if my spirituality or consciousness is separated from them, it ceases to be also. Thus they are all actually one body, so how can they be separated?"[978]

---

977 *Record of Instructions*, Pt. 3.

978 *Id.*, Pt, 3.

From these sayings we gain an idea of Wang Shou-jen's conception of the universe. In this conception, the universe is a spiritual whole, in which there is only one world, the concrete actual world that we ourselves experience. Thus there is no place for that otherworld of abstract Li, which Chu Hsi so much emphasized.

Wang Shou-*jen* also maintains that mind is *Li*: "Mind is *Li*. How can there be affairs and *Li* outside the mind?[979] Again:

> The substance of the mind is the nature and the nature is Li.
>
> Therefore, since there is the mind of filial love, hence there is the *Li* of filial piety. If there were no such a mind, there would be no such a *Li*. And since there is the mind of loyalty to the sovereign, hence there is the *Li* of loyalty. If there were no such a mind, there would be no such a *Li*. How can *Li* be outside our mind?[980]

From these sayings we can see still more clearly the difference between Chu Hsi and Wang Shou-*jen* and between the two schools they represent. According to Chu Hsi's system, we can only say that since there is the *Li* of filial piety, therefore there is the mind of loving one's parents; and since there is the *Li* of loyalty, therefore there is the mind of loyalty to one's sovereign. We cannot, however, say the converse. But what Wang Shou-*jen* said is precisely this converse. According to Chu Hsi's system, all the *Li* are eternally there, no matter whether there is mind or not. But according to

Wang Shou-*jen*'s system, if there is no mind, there will be no *Li*.

Thus the mind is the legislator of the universe and is that by which the *Li* are legislated.

"The Illustrious Virtue"

With this conception of the universe, Wang Shou-*jen* gives a metaphysical justification to the *Great Learning*. As we have seen in Chapter XVI, this work speaks of what are later called the "three major cords" and eight "minor wires." The three "cords" are "to manifest the illustrious virtue, love people, and rest in the highest good." Wang Shou-*jen* defines great learning as the learning of the great man. Regarding the "manifestation of the illustrious virtue," he writes:

> The great man is an all-pervading unity, which is one with Heaven, Earth, and all things. He considers the world as one family, and the Middle Kingdom as one man. Those who emphasize the distinction of bodily forms and thus make cleavage between the self and others are the small men. The reason that the great man is able to be one with Heaven, Earth, and all things, is not that he is thus for some purpose, but because the human-heartedness of his mind is naturally so. The mind of the small man is exactly the same, only he himself makes it small. When the small man sees a child about to fall into a well, he will certainly experience a feeling of alarm and distress. This shows that in his love he is one with the child. And when he hears the pitiful cry or sees the frightened appearance

979 *Record of Instructions*, Pt. 1.

980 *Id.*, Pt. 2.

of a bird or beast, he will certainly find it unbearable to witness them. This shows that in his love he is one with birds and beasts.... From all this it may be seen that the original unity lies in the small man [as well as the great man]. Even the small man has his heavenly nature, the light of which cannot be obscured.

Therefore it is called the illustrious virtue.... Thus when there is no obscuring caused by selfish desires, even the small man has the love for the whole, just as does the great man. But when there is this obscuring, even the mind of the great man is divided and hampered, just as is the small man. The learning of the great man serves simply to clear away the obscuring and thus to manifest the illustrious virtue, so as thus to restore the original unity of Heaven, Earth, and all things. It is not possible to add anything to this original state.[981]

Regarding the second of the "three cords" in the Great Learning, that of "loving people," Wang Shou-jen writes:

To manifest the illustrious virtue is to establish the nature of the unity of Heaven, Earth, and all things; to love people is to exercise the function of that unity. Therefore the manifestation of the illustrious virtue consists in loving people, and to love people is to manifest the illustrious virtue. If I love my own father, the fathers of some other men, and the fathers of all men, my love will be truly extended with my love of these fathers.... Beginning with all these human relationships, and reaching to mountains, rivers, spirits and gods, birds and beasts, grasses and trees, all should be loved in order to extend our love. In this way there is nothing that is not manifested in our illustrious virtue; and then we are really one with Heaven, Earth and all things.[982]

Regarding the third "cord," that of "resting in the highest good," he writes:

The highest good is the highest standard for the manifesting of the illustrious virtue and loving people. Our original nature is purely good. What cannot be obscured in it is the manifestation of the highest good and of the nature of the illustrious virtue, and is also what I call intuitive knowledge. When things come to it, right is right, wrong is wrong, important is important, and inferior is inferior. It responds to things and changes with circumstances, yet it always attains the natural mean. This is the highest standard for the actions of man and of things, to which nothing can be added, and from which nothing can be reduced.

If there is any addition or reduction, that is selfishness and a petty kind of rationalization, and is not the highest good.[983]

Intuitive Knowledge

Thus the three "main cords" are reduced to a single "cord," that of the manifestation of the illustrious virtue, which is simply the original nature of our

981 *Ta Hsueh Wen* or *Questions on the Great learning* in the *Wang Wen-cheng kung Chuan-shu* or *Complete Works of Wang Shou-jen, Chuan* 26.

982 *Ibid.*

983 *Ibid.*

mind. All of us, whether good or bad, fundamentally have the same mind, which can never be wholly obscured by our selfishness, and always manifests itself in our immediate intuitive reaction to things. A case in point is the feeling of alarm which we all automatically experience upon suddenly seeing a child about to fall into a well. In our first reaction to things, we know naturally and spontaneously that the right is right and the wrong is wrong. This knowing is the manifestation of our original nature, and for it Wang uses the term "intuitive knowledge" (literally, "good knowledge"). All we need to do is simply to follow the dictates of this knowledge and go unhesitatingly forward. For if we try to find excuses for not immediately following these dictates, we are then adding something to, or reducing something from, the intuitive knowledge, and are thus losing the highest good. The act of looking for excuses is a rationalization which is due to selfishness. As we have seen in Chapters XXIII and XXIV, Chou Tun-yi and Cheng Hao expressed the same theory, but Wang Shou-jen here gives it a more metaphysical basis.

It is said that when *Yang* Chien (died 1226) first met Lu Chiu-yuan, he asked the latter what our original mind is. It may be noted in passing that this term, "original mind," was originally a Chanist one, but it also came to be used by the Neo-Confucianists of the Lu-Wang school. Answering the question, Lu Chiu-yuan recited the passage in the *Mencius* about the "four beginnings." Yang Chien said that he had read this passage since boyhood, but still did not know of what the original mind consists. He was then an official, and during the conversation was called upon to attend to some official business, in the course of which he had to pass a verdict on a certain lawsuit. When the business was concluded, he turned to Lu Chiu-yuan again with the same question. Lu then said: "Just now in announcing your verdict, the right you knew to be right, and the wrong you knew to be wrong. That is your original mind." Yang said: "Is there anything else?" To which Lu in a very loud voice answered: "What else do you want?" Thereupon *Yang* was suddenly enlightened and thus became the disciple of Lu.[984]

Another story says that a follower of Wang Shou-jen once caught a thief in his house at night, whereupon he gave him a lecture about intuitive knowledge. The thief laughed and asked: "Tell me, please, where is my intuitive knowledge?" At that time the weather was hot, so the thief's captor invited him first to take off his jacket, then his shirt, and then continued: "It is still too hot. Why not take off your trousers too?" At this the thief hesitated and replied "That does not seem to be quite right." Thereupon his captor shouted at him: "There is your intuitive knowledge!"

The story does not say whether the thief gained enlightenment as a result of this conversation, but it and the preceding story certainly are typical of the Chan technique of initiating a student to Enlightenment. They show that every man possesses that intuitive knowledge which is the manifestation of his original mind, and through which he immediately knows that right is right and wrong is wrong. Everyone, in his original nature, is a sage. That is why the followers

984 *Tzu-hu Yi-shu* or *Literary Remains of Yang Chien*, *Chuan* 18.

of Wang Shou-*jen* were in the habit of saying that "the streets are full of sages."

What they meant by this is that every man is potentially a sage.

He can become an actual sage if he but follow the dictates of his intuitive knowledge and act accordingly. What he needs to do, in other words, is to carry his intuitive knowledge into practice, or, in Wang Shou-*jen*'s terminology, to extend his intuitive knowledge. Thus the "extension of intuitive knowledge" became the key term in Wang's philosophy, and in his later years he mentioned only these words.

"The Rectification of Affairs"

It will be remembered that the *Great Learning* also speaks of "eight minor wires," which are the eight steps to be followed in the spiritual cultivation of the self. The first two of them are the "extension of knowledge" and "investigation of things." According to Wang Shou-jen, the extension of knowledge means the extension of the intuitive knowledge. Cultivation of the self is nothing more than the following of one's intuitive knowledge and putting it into practice.

The Chinese term for the "investigation of things" is *ko wu*, and it is Cheng Yi and Chu Hsi who interpret it as having this meaning. According to Wang Shou-*jen*, however, ko means to rectify and *wu* means affairs. *Ko wu*, therefore, does not mean "investigation of things," but "rectification of affairs." The intuitive knowledge, he maintains, cannot be extended through the techniques of contemplation and meditation taught by the Buddhists. It must be extended through our daily experience in dealing with ordinary affairs.

Thus he says:

> The activity of the mind is called yi [will, thought], and the objects towards which yi is directed are called *wu* [things, affairs]. For instance, when the object of one's yi is the serving of one's parents, then this serving of one's parents is the *wu*. And when the object of one's yi is the serving of the sovereign, then this serving of the sovereign is the *wu*.[985]

The *wu* may be right or wrong, but as soon as this can be determined, our intuitive knowledge will immediately know it.

When our intuitive knowledge knows a thing to be right, we must sincerely do it, and when our intuitive knowledge knows it to be wrong, we must sincerely stop doing it. In this manner we rectify our affairs and at the same time extend our intuitive knowledge. There is no other means of extending our intuitive knowledge except through the rectification of our affairs. That is why the *Great Learning* says: "The extension of knowledge consists in the rectification of affairs."

The next two steps of the "eight wires" are "sincerity of thought [yi] and rectification of the mind." According to Wang Shou-jen, sincerity of thought is nothing more than the rectification of affairs and the extension of intuitive knowledge, both being carried out with the utmost sincerity. When we try to find excuses for not following the dictates of our intuitive knowledge, we are insincere

985 *Record of Instructions*, Pt. 1.

in thought, and this insincerity is the same as what Cheng Hao and Wang Shou-jen call selfishness and rationalization. When our thought is sincere, our mind is rectified; the rectification of the mind is no other than sincerity in thought.

The next four steps of the "eight wires" are the cultivation of the self, regulation of the family, setting in order of the state and bringing of peace to the world. According to Wang Shou-jen, the cultivation of the self is the same as the extension of the intuitive knowledge. For how can we cultivate ourselves without extending our intuitive knowledge? And in cultivating ourselves what should we do besides extending our intuitive knowledge? In extending our intuitive knowledge, we must love people, and in loving people, how can we do otherwise than regulate our family, and contribute our best to creating order in our state, and bringing peace to the world? Thus all the "eight wires" may after all be reduced to a single "wire," which is the extension of the intuitive knowledge.

What is the intuitive knowledge? It is simply the inner light of our mind, the original unity of the universe, or, as the *Great Learning* calls it, the illustrious virtue. Hence the extension of the intuitive knowledge is nothing else than the manifestation of the illustrious virtue. Thus all the ideas of the *Great Learning* are reduced to the one idea expressed in the key words, the extension of the intuitive knowledge.

To quote Wang Shou-jen again:

> The mind of man is Heaven. There is nothing that is not included in the mind of man. All of us are this single Heaven, but because of the obscurings caused by selfishness, the original state of Heaven is not made manifest. Every time we extend our intuitive knowledge, we clear away the obscurings, and when all of them are cleared away, our original nature is restored, and we again become part of this Heaven. The intuitive knowledge of the part is the intuitive knowledge of the whole. The intuitive knowledge of the whole is the intuitive knowledge of the part. Everything is the single whole.[986]

Attentiveness of the Mind

Thus Wang Shou-jen's system follows the same lines as those of
Chou Tun-yi, Cheng Han and Lu Chiu-yuan, but he expresses it in more systematic and precise terms. The fact that the "cords" and "wires" of the *Great Learning* fit so well into his system brings both conviction to himself and authority to others.

The system and its method of spiritual cultivation are simple and direct -- qualities which themselves give it a powerful appeal. What we need is first of all the understanding that each and every one of us possesses the original mind, which is one with the universe. This understanding is referred to by Lu Chiu-yuan as "first establishing the most important," a phrase he borrows from Mencius. On one occasion he said:

> Recently there have been people who have criticized me by saying that apart from the single statement in which I lay emphasis upon first establishing

986 *Ibid.*

the most important, I have no other tricks to offer. When I heard this, I exclaimed: "Quite so!"[987]

In Chapter XXIV it was pointed out that, according to the Neo-Confucianists, spiritual cultivation requires that one should be attentive; but attentive to what? According to the Lu-Wang school, one must "first establish the most important," and then be attentive to it. And it is the criticism of this school that the Cheng-Chu school, without "first establishing the most important," starts immediately and haphazardly with the task of investigating things. Under these conditions, even attentiveness of mind cannot lead to any results in spiritual cultivation. This procedure is compared by the Lu-Wang school to starting a fire for cooking, without having any rice in the pot.

To this, however, the Cheng-Chu school would reply that unless one begins with the investigation of things, how can anything be definitely established? If one excludes this investigation of things, the only way left of "establishing the most important" is through instantaneous Enlightenment. And this the Cheng-Chu school regarded as more Chanist than Confucianist.

In Chapter XXIV, we have seen that Cheng Hao also says that the student must first understand *jen* (human-heartedness), which is the unity of all things, and then cultivate it with sincerity and attentiveness. Nothing else requires to be done. We merely need have confidence in ourselves and go straight forward. Lu Chiu- yuan remarks in similar strain: "Be courageous, be zealous, break open the net, burn the thorns in your path, and wash away the mire." When so doing, even the authority of Confucius need no longer necessarily be respected. As Lu states again: "If in learning one gains a comprehension of what is fundamental, then the Six Classics become but one's footnotes." In this respect we see clearly that the Lu-Wang school is a continuation of Chanism.

Criticism of Buddhism

Yet both the Lu-Wang and Cheng-Chu schools strongly criticize Buddhism. In this criticism, the difference between the two is again revealed. Thus Chu Hsi says:

> When the Buddhists speak of "emptiness," this does not mean that they are [entirely] incorrect. But they must know that in this emptiness there are the D??. For if we are merely to say that we are "empty," without understanding that there are still the real *Li*, what is the use [of such a doctrine]? The *case* is like that of a pool of clear water, the cold clearness of which extends to the very bottom. When it is first seen, it will appear to have no water in it at all, and a person will then say that this pool is only "empty." If this person does not put in his hand to feel whether there is coldness or warmth, he will not know that there is water within. And such, precisely, is the view of the Buddhists.[988]

Again he says: "The Confucianists consider *Li* as without birth and indestructible. The Buddhists consider spirituality and consciousness as without

987 *Collected Works, Chuan* 34.

988 *Recorded Sayings, Chuan* 126.

birth and indestructible."[989] According to Chu Hsi, the Buddhists are not without justification in saying that the concrete world is empty, because things in the concrete world do change and are impermanent. But there are also the *Li*, which are eternal and not subject to change. In this sense, then, the universe is not empty. The Buddhists do not know that the *Li* are real, because they are abstract, just as some men do not see the water in the pool, because it is colorless.

Wang Shou-jen also criticizes Buddhism, but from quite a different point of view:

> When the *Tao*ists [i.e., the religious *Tao*ists] speak of *hsu* [vacuity, unrealness], can the Confucian sage add to it a hair of shih [actualness, realness]? And when the Buddhists speak of *wu* [non-being, non-existence], can the Confucian sage add to it a hair of *yu* [being, existence]? But when the *Tao*ists speak of *hsu*, their motive is to preserve life, whereas when the Buddhists speak of *wu*, their motive is to escape the suffering of life and death. When they add these ideas to the original nature of the mind, their original meaning of hsu and *wu* is somewhat lost, and thereby the original nature of the mind is not freed from obstruction. The Confucian sage simply restores the original condition of the intuitive knowledge and adds to it no idea whatsoever.... Heaven, Earth, and all things all lie within the function and activity of our intuitive knowledge. How, then, can there be anything outside it to hinder or obstruct it?[990]

Again he says:

> The claim of the Buddhists that they have no attachment to phenomena shows that they do have attachment to them. And the fact that we Confucianists do not claim detachment to phenomena, shows that we do not have attachment to them.... The Buddhists are afraid of the troubles involved in human relationships, and therefore escape from them. They are forced to escape because they are already attached to them. But we Confucianists are different. There being the relationship between father and son, we respond to it with love. There being the relationship between sovereign and subject, we respond to it with righteousness. And there being the relationship between husband and wife, we respond to it with mutual respect. We have no attachment to phenomena.[991]

If we follow this argument, we can say that the Neo-Confucianists more consistently adhere to the fundamental ideas of Taoism and Buddhism than do the *Tao*ists and Buddhists themselves. They are more *Tao*istic than the *Tao*ists, and more Buddhistic than the Buddhists.

989 *Ibid.*
990 *Record of Instructions*, Pt. 3.
991 *Ibid.*

XXVII THE INTRODUCTION OF WESTERN PHILOSOPHY

Every system of philosophy is likely to be misunderstood and misused, and so it was with the two schools of Neo-Confucianism. According to Chu Hsi, one must in principle start with the investigation of things in order to understand the eternal *Li* or Laws, but this principle Chu Hsi himself did not strictly carry out. In the record of his sayings, we see that he did make certain observations on natural and social phenomena, but most of his time was devoted to the study of, and comment on, the Classics. He not only believed that there are eternal *Li*, but also that the utterances of the ancient sages are these eternal *Li*. So in his system there is an element of authoritarianism and conservatism, which became more and more apparent as the tradition of the Cheng-Chu school went on. And the fact that this school became the official state teaching did much to increase this tendency.

Reaction Against Neo-Confucianism

The Lu-Wang school is a revolution against this conservatism, and in the time of Wang Shou-jen, the revolutionary movement was at its highest. In a very simple way, it appealed directly to the intuitive knowledge of every man, which is the inner light of his "original mind." Though never recognized by the government, as was the Cheng-Chu school, the Lu-Wang school became as influential as the former.

But, the philosophy of Wang Shou-jen was also misunderstood and misused. According to Wang, what the intuitive knowledge immediately knows is the ethical aspect of our will or thought. It can only tell us what we ought to do, but not how to do it. It lacks what Americans would now call "know-how." In order to know how to do what we ought to do in certain situations, Wang said that we have to study practical methods of action in relation to the existing state of affairs. Later on, however, his followers seemed to come to the belief that the intuitive knowledge can itself tell us everything, including the "know-how." This is absurd, and the followers of the Lu-Wang school have certainly suffered the con-sequences of this absurdity.

At the end of the last chapter we have seen that Wang Shou-jen used the Chan method of argument to criticize Buddhism. This is precisely the sort of argument that is most likely to be misused. A satiric story tells us that when a scholar once paid a visit to a certain Buddhist temple, he was treated with only scant respect by the monk in charge. While he was there, however, the temple was also visited by a prominent official, to whom the monk showed the greatest respect. After the official had gone, the scholar asked the monk the reason for this difference. The monk answered: "To respect is not to respect, and not to respect is to respect." The scholar immediately gave him a hearty blow on the face. The monk protested angrily: "Why do you beat me?" To which the scholar replied: "To beat is not to beat, and not to beat is to beat." This story became current after the time of Wang Shou-jen, and no doubt was intended to criticize him and the Chanists.

The Ming Dynasty (1368-1643), under which Wang Shou-jen lived and had his influence, was a native Chinese dynasty which replaced the Yuan or Mongol Dynasty (1281-1367). In due course it in turn was overthrown as a result of internal revolts coupled with invasion from the outside, and was replaced by the Ching Dynasty (1644-1911), under which, for the second time in Chinese history, all of China was ruled by an alien group, this time the Manchus. The Manchus, however, were far more sympathetic to Chinese culture than the Mongols had been, and the first two-thirds of their dynasty was, on the whole, a period of internal peace and prosperity for China, during which, in certain respects, Chinese culture made important advances, though in other respects it was a period of growing cultural and social conservatism. Officially, the Cheng-Chu school was even more firmly entrenched than before. Unofficially, however, the Ching Dynasty witnessed an important reaction against both this school and the Lu-Wang school. The leaders of this reaction accused both schools of having, under the influence of Chanism and Taoism, misinterpreted the ideas of Confucius, and of thus having lost the practical aspect of original Confucianism. One of the attackers said: "Chus Hsi was a *Tao*ist monk, and Lu Chiu-yuan was a Buddhist monk." This accusation, in a sense, is not entirely unjustified, as we have seen in the last two chapters.

From the point of view of philosophy, however, it is entirely irrelevant. As was pointed out in Chapter XXIII, Neo-Confucianism is a synthesis of Confucianism, Buddhism, and philosophical Taoism (through Chanism), and religious Taoism. From the point of view of the history of Chinese philosophy, such a synthesis represents a development, and therefore is a virtue rather than a vice.

In the Ching Dynasty, however, when the orthodox position of Confucianism was stronger than ever before, to assert that Neo-Confucianism was not the same as pure Confucianism was equal to asserting that Neo-Confucianism was false and wrong. According to its opponents, indeed, the harmful effects of Neo-Confucianism were even greater than those of Buddhism and Taoism, because its seeming agreement with original Confucianism could more easily deceive people and so lead them astray.

For this reason the scholars of the Ching Dynasty started a "back-to-the-Han" movement, meaning by this a return to the commentaries that the scholars of the Han Dynasty had written on the early Classics. They believed that because these Han scholars lived nearer in time to Confucius and before the introduction of Buddhism into China, their interpretations of the Classics must therefore be purer and closer to the genuine ideas of Confucius. Consequently, they studied numerous writings of the Han scholars which the Neo-Confucianists had discarded, and termed this study the *Han hsueh* or learning of the Han Dynasty. It was so called in contrast to that of the Neo-Confucianists, which they termed the *Sung hsueh* or learning of the Sung Dynasty, because the major schools of

Neo-Confucianism had flourished in this dynasty. Through the eighteenth century until the beginning of the present century, the controversy between the Ching adherents of the *Han hsueh* and *Sung hsueh* has been one of the greatest in the history of Chinese thought. From our present point of view, it was really one as between the philosophical and scholarly interpretation of the ancient texts. The scholarly interpretation emphasized what it believed was their actual meaning; the philosophical interpretation emphasized what it believed they ought to have meant.

Because of the emphasis of the *Han hsueh* scholars on the scholarly interpretation of ancient texts, they made marked developments in such fields as textual criticism, higher criticism, and philology. Indeed, their historical, philological, and other studies became the greatest single cultural achievement of the Ching Dynasty.

Philosophically, the contribution of the *Han hsueh* scholars was less important, but culturally, they did much to open the minds of their time to the wider reaches, of Chinese literary achievement. During the Ming Dynasty, most educated people, under the influence of Neo-Confucianism, a knowledge of which was required for success in the state examinations, devoted their whole attention to the "Four Books" (*the Analects of Confucius, Mencius, Great Learning, and Doctrine of the Mean*). As a result, they knew but little about other literature. Once, the Ching scholars became interested in the scholarly reevaluation of the ancient texts, however, they could not confine themselves simply to the Confucian Classics. These, to be sure, engaged their first attention, but when the work in this field had been done, they began to study all the other ancient texts of the schools other than orthodox Confucianism, including such writings as the *Mo-tzu, Hsun-tzu* and *Han fei-tzu,* which had long been neglected. They worked to correct the many corruptions that had crept into the texts, and to explain the ancient usage of words and phrases. It is owing to their labors that these texts are today so much more readable than they were, for example, in the Ming Dynasty. Their work did much to help the revival of interest in the philosophical study of these philosophers that has taken place in recent decades under the stimulus of the introduction of Western philosophy. This is a topic to which we shall now turn.

Movement for a Confucian Religion

It is not necessary to examine here precisely the manner in which the Chinese first came in contact with Western culture.

Suffice it to say that already towards the end of the Ming Dynasty, i.e., in the latter part of the sixteenth century and early part of the seventeenth, many Chinese scholars became impressed by the mathematics and astronomy that were introduced to China at that time by Jesuit missionary-scholars. If Europeans call China and surrounding areas the Far East, the Chinese in, the period of early Sino-European contacts referred to Europe as the Far West or *Tai Hsi*. In earlier centuries they had spoken of India as "the West"; hence they could only refer to countries to the west of India as the "Far West." This term has now been discarded, but it was in common usage as late as the end of the last century.

In Chapter XVI I said that the distinction which the Chinese have traditionally made between themselves and foreigners or "barbarians" has been more cultural than racial. Their sense of nationalism has been more developed in regard to culture than to politics. Being the inheritors of an ancient civilization, and one geographically far removed from any other of comparable importance, it has been difficult for them to conceive how any other people could be cultured and yet live in a manner different from themselves. Hence whenever they have come into contact with an alien culture, they have been inclined to despise and resist it -- not so much as something alien, but simply because they have thought it to be inferior or wrong. As we have seen in Chapter XVIII, the introduction of Buddhism stimulated the foundation of religious Taoism, which came as a sort of nationalistic reaction to the alien faith. In the same way, the introduction of Western culture, in which Christian missionaries played a leading part, created a very similar reaction.

In the sixteenth and seventeenth centuries, as just noted, the missionary scholars impressed the Chinese not so much by their religion as by their attainments in mathematics and astronomy. But later, especially during the nineteenth century, with the growing military, industrial, and commercial predominance of Europe, and the coincident decline of China's political strength under the Manchus, the impetus of Christianity became increasingly felt by the Chinese. After several major controversies had broken out in the nineteenth century between missionaries and Chinese, a movement for a native Confucian religion to counteract the growing impact of the West was started at the very end of that century by the famous statesman and reformer, Kang Yu-wei (1858-1927). This event was no mere accident -- even from the point of view of the inner development of Chinese thought -- because the scholars of the *Han hsueh* had already paved the way.

In chapters seventeen and eighteen, we saw that the Han Dynasty was dominated by two schools of Confucianism: one the Old Text and the other the New Text school. With the revival during the Ching Dynasty of the study of the works of the Han scholars, the old controversy between these two schools was also revived. We have also seen that the New Text school, headed by Tung Chung-shu, believed Confucius to have been the founder of an ideal new dynasty, and later even went so far as to consider him as a supernatural being having a mission to perform on this earth, a veritable god among men. Kang Yu-wei was a leader of the Ching adherents of the New Text school in the *Han hsueh*, and found in this school plenty of material for establishing Confucianism as an organized religion in the proper sense of the word.

In studying Tung Chung-shu, we have already read Tung's fantastic theory about Confucius. The theory of Kang Yu-wei is even more so. As we have seen, in the *Chun Chiu* or *Spring and Autumn Annals*, or rather in the theory of its Han commentators, as well as in the *Li Chi* or *Book of Rites*, there is the concept that the world passes through three ages or stages of progress. Kang Yu-wei now revived this theory, interpreting it to mean that the age of Confucius had been the first age of decay and disorder. In our own times, he maintained, the growing communications between East and West, and the political and social reforms in Europe and America, show that men are progressing from the stage of disorder to the second higher stage, that of approaching peace. And this in turn will be followed by the unity of the whole world, which will be the realization of the last stage of human progress, that of great peace. Writing in 1902, he said: "Confucius knew all these things beforehand."[992]

Kang Yu-wei was the leader of the notable political reforms of 1898, which, however, lasted only a few months, and were followed by his own flight abroad, the execution of several of his followers, and renewed political reaction on the part of the Man-chu government. In his opinion, what he was advocating was not the adoption of the new civilization of the West, but rather the realization of the ancient and genuine teachings of Confucius. He wrote many commentaries on the Confucian Classics and read his new ideas into them. Besides these, he also in 1884 wrote a book titled the *Ta Tung Shu* or *Book of the Great Unity*, in which he gave a concrete picture of the utopia that will be realized in the third stage of human progress, according to the Confucian scheme.

Although this book is so bold and revolutionary that it will startle even most utopian writers, Kang Yu-wei himself was far from being a utopian. He insisted that his program could not be put into practice except in the highest and last stage of human civilization. For his immediate practical political program he insisted on merely instituting a constitutional monarchy. Thus throughout this life he was hated first by the conservatives because he was too radical, and later by the radicals because he was too conservative. But the twentieth century is not one of religion, and together with, or in addition to, the introduction of Christianity into China, there also came modern science, which is the opposite of religion. Thus the influence of Christianity *per se* has been limited in China, and the movement for a Confucian religion suffered an early death. Nevertheless, with the overthrow of the Ching Dynasty and its replacement by the Republic in 1912, there was a demand by Kang Yu-wei's followers, when the first Constitution of the Republic was drafted in 1915, that it proposed that the Republic adopt Confucianism as the state religion. A vigorous controversy developed over this point, until a compromise was reached, the Constitution asserting that the Chinese Republic would adopt Confucianism, not as a state religion, but as the fundamental principle for ethical discipline. This Constitution was never put into practice, and no more has since been heard about Confucianism as a religion in the sense intended by Kang Yu-wei.

It is to be noted that up to 1898, Kang Yu-wei and his comrades knew very little, if anything, about Western philosophy. His friend Tan Ssu-tung (1865-1898), who died a martyr's death when the political reform movement failed, was a much more subtle thinker than Kang himself. He wrote a book titled *Jen Hsueh*

992 *Lun-yu Chu* or *Commentary to the "Analects," Chuan* 2.

or *Science of Jen* (human-heartedness), which introduces into Neo-Confucianism some ideas taken from modern chemistry and physics. In the beginning of his work, he lists certain books to be read before one study his *Science of Jen*. In that list, among books on Western thought, he mentions only the *New Testament* and "some treatises on mathematics, physics, chemistry, and sociology." It is plain that men of his time knew very little about Western philosophy, and that their knowledge of Western culture, in addition to machines and warships, was confined primarily to science and Christianity.

Introduction of Western Thought

The greatest authority on Western thought at the beginning of the present century was Yen Fu (1853-1920). In his yearly years he was sent to England by the government to study naval science, and while there read some of the works on the humanities current at the time. After returning to China, he translated into Chinese the following works: Thomas Huxley, *Evolution and Ethics*, Adam Smith, *An Enquiry into the Nature and Causes of the Wealth of Nations*, Herbert Spencer, *The Study of Sociology*, John Stuart Mill, *On Liberty*, and half of his *A System of Logic*; E. Jenks, *A History of Politics*, Montesquieu, *Esprit des Lois*, and an adapted translation of Jevons, *Lessons in Logic*. Yen Fu began to translate these works after the first Sino-Japanese war of 1894-95. After that he became very famous and his translations were widely read.

There are three reasons to account for this popularity. The first is that China's defeat in the Sino-Japanese war, following a series of earlier humiliations at the hands of the West, shook the confidence of the Chinese people in the, superiority of their own ancient civilization, and therefore gave them a desire to know something about Western thought. Before that time they fancied that Westerners were only superior in science, machines, guns, and warships, but had nothing spiritual to offer. The second reason is that Yen Fu wrote comments on many passages of his translations, in which he compared certain ideas of his author with ideas in Chinese philosophy, in order to give a better understanding to his readers. This practice is something like the *ko yi* or interpretation by analogy, which was mentioned in Chapter XX in connection with the translation of Buddhist texts. And the third reason is that in Yen Fu's translations, the modern English of Spencer, Mill, and others was converted into Chinese of the most classical style. In reading these authors in his translation, one has the same impression as that of reading such ancient Chinese works as the *Mo-tzu* or *Hsun-tzu*. Because of their traditional respect for literary accomplishment, the Chinese of Yen Fu's time still had the superstition that any thought that can be expressed in the classical style is *ipso facto* as valuable as are the Chinese classical works themselves.

But the list of his translations shows that Yen Fu introduced very little Western philosophy. Among them, the ones really concerned with the subject are Jevons' *Lessons in Logic* and *Mill's System of Logic*, of which the former was an abridged summary, and the latter was left unfinished. Yen Fu recommended Spencer as the greatest Western philosopher of all time, thus showing that his knowledge of Western philosophy was rather limited.

There was another scholar of Yen Fu's time who in this respect had a better understanding and deeper insight, but who did not become known to the public until after he gave up the study of philosophy. He was Wang Kuo-wei (1877-1927 a scholar renowned as one of the greatest historians, archaeologists, and literary writers of recent times. Before he was thirty, he had already studied Schopenhauer and Kant, in this respect differing from Yen Fu, who studied almost none but English thinkers. But after he turned thirty, Wang Kuo-wei gave up the study of philosophy, for a reason mentioned in one of his writings titled, "A Self-Account at the Age of Thirty." In this he says:

I have been tired of philosophy for a considerable time, among philosophical theories, it is a general rule that those that can be loved cannot be believed, and those that can be believed cannot be loved. I know truth, and yet I love absurd yet great metaphysics, sublime ethics, and pure aesthetics. These are what I love most. Yet in searching for what is believable, I am inclined to believe in the positivistic theory of truth, the hedonistic theory of ethics, and the empiricist theory of aesthetics. I know these are believable, but I cannot love them, and I feel the other theories are lovable, but I cannot believe in them. This is the great vexation that I have experienced during the past two or three years. Recently my interest has gradually transferred itself from philosophy to literature, because I wish to find in the latter direct consolation.[993]

He says again that such men as Spencer in England and Wundt in Germany are but second-rate philosophers, their philosophies being but a syncretism of science or of earlier systems. Other philosophers known to him at that time were only historians of philosophy. He said that he himself could become a competent historian of philosophy, if he continued to study it. "But," said he, "I cannot be a pure philosopher, and yet I do not like to be a historian of philosophy. This is another reason why I am tired of philosophy!"[994]

I have quoted Wang Kuo-wei at length, because judging from these quotations, I think he had some insight into Western philosophy. He knew, as a Chinese expression says, "what is sweet and what is bitter in it." But on the whole, at the beginning of the 20th century, there were very few Chinese who knew anything about Western philosophy. When I myself was an undergraduate student in Shanghai, we had a course on elementary logic, but there was no one in Shanghai at the time capable of teaching such a course.

At last a teacher was found who asked us to buy a copy of Jevons' *Lessons in Logic* and to use it as a textbook. He asked us to read it in the way a teacher of English expects his pupils to go through an English reader. When we came to the lesson on judgment, he called on me to spell the word "judgment," in order to make sure that I would not insert an "e" between the "g" and "m"!

Before long we were at the mercy of another teacher who conscientiously tried

993 *Chung-an Wen-chi* or *Collected Literary Writings of Wang Kuo-wei, Second Collection.*
994 *Ibid.*

to make the course a real one on logic. There are many exercises at the end of Jevons' book which this teacher did not ask us to do, but I nonetheless prepared them on my own account. It so happened that there was one exercise that was beyond my understanding, which I requested the teacher to expound after class. After discussing it with me for half an hour without being able to solve it, he finally said: "Let me think it over and I shall do it for you the next time I come." He never came again, and for this I felt rather sorry, for I had no desire to embarrass him.

The University of Peking was then the only national university in China which was supposed to have three departments of philosophy: Chinese, Western, and Indian. But as the University was then constituted, there was only the one department of Chinese philosophy. In 1915 it was stated that a department of Western philosophy would be established, since a professor had been engaged who had studied philosophy in Germany and presumably could teach courses in that subject. I accordingly went to Peking in that year and was admitted as an undergraduate, but to my disappointment the professor who was to have taught us had just died, and I had therefore to study in the department of Chinese philosophy.

In this department we had professors who were scholars representing the Old Text, New Text, Cheng-Chu, and Lu-Wang schools. One of them, a follower of the Lu-Wang school, taught us a course on the history of Chinese philosophy, a two-year course meeting four hours a week. He began with the traditional sage-kings, Yao and Shun, and by the end of the first semester had gone only as far as the Duke of Chou-that is to say, about five centuries before Confucius. We asked him how long, if he continued at this rate, it would take to finish the course. "Well," he replied, "in the study of philosophy there is no such thing as finishing or not finishing. If you want this course to be finished, I can finish it in one word; if you do not want it to be finished, it can never be finished."

Introduction of Western Philosophy

John Dewey and Bertrand Russell were invited in 1919-20 to lecture at the University of Peking and other places. They were the first Western philosophers to come to China, and from them the Chinese for the first time received an authentic account of Western philosophy. But what they lectured about was mostly their own philosophy. This gave their hearers the impression that the traditional philosophical systems had all been superseded and discarded. With but little knowledge of the history of Western philosophy, the great majority of the audience failed to see the significance of their theories. One cannot understand a philosophy unless one at the same time understands the earlier traditions which it either approves or refutes. So these two philosophers, though well received by many, were understood by few. Their visit to China, nevertheless, opened new intellectual horizons for most of the students at that time. In this respect, their stay had great cultural and educational value.

In Chapter XXI I have said that there is a distinction between Chinese

Buddhism and Buddhism in China, and that the contribution of Buddhism to Chinese philosophy is the idea of Universal Mind. In the introduction of Western philosophy there have been similar cases. Following the visit of Dewey and Russell, for example, there have been many other philosophical systems that, at one time or another, have become popular in China. So far, however, almost all of them have simply represented Western philosophy in China. None has yet become an integral part of the development of the Chinese mind, as did Chan Buddhism.

So far as I can see, the permanent contribution of Western philosophy to Chinese philosophy is the method of logical analysis. In Chapter XXI I have said that Buddhism and Taoism both use the negative method. The analytic method is just the opposite of this, and hence maybe called the positive method. The negative method attempts to eliminate distinctions and to tell what its object is not, whereas the positive method attempts to make distinction and tell what its object is. It is not very important for the Chinese that the negative method of Buddhism was introduced, because they had it already in Taoism, though Buddhism did serve to reinforce it. The introduction of the positive method, however, is really a matter of the greatest importance. It gives the Chinese a new way of thinking and a change in their whole mentality. But as we shall see in the next chapter, it will not replace the other method; it will merely supplement it.

It is the method, not the ready-made conclusions of Western philosophy that is important. A Chinese story relates that once a man met an immortal who asked him what he wanted. The man said that he wanted gold. The immortal touched several pieces of stone with his finger and they immediately turned to gold. The immortal asked the man to take them but he refused. "What else do you want?" the immortal asked. "I want your finger," the man replied. The analytic method is the finger of the Western philosophers, and the Chinese want the finger.

That is the reason why among the different branches of philosophical study in the West, the first to attract the attention of the Chinese was logic. Even before Yen Fu's translation of J. S. Mill's *System of Logic*, Li Chih-tsao (died 1630) had already translated with the Jesuit Fathers a medieval textbook on Aristotelian logic. His translation was titled *Ming-li Tan* or *An Investigation of Ming-li*. We have seen in Chapter XIX that *ming-li* means the analysis of principles through the analysis of names. Yen Fu translated logic as *ming hsueh* or the Science of Names. As we have seen in Chapter VIII, the essence of the philosophy of the School of Names as represented by Kungsun Lung is precisely the analysis of principles through the analysis of names. But in that chapter I also pointed out that this philosophy is not exactly the same as logic. There is a similarity, however, and when the Chinese first heard something about Western logic, they immediately noticed the similarity, and so connected it with their own School of Names.

Up to recent times the most fruitful result of the introduction of Western philosophy has been the revival of the study of Chinese philosophy, including Buddhism. There is nothing paradoxical in this statement. When one encounters new ideas that are unfamiliar, it is only natural that one should turn to familiar ones for illustration, comparison,' and mutual confirmation. And when one turns to these ideas, armed with the analytic method, it is only natural that one should make an analysis of them. We have already seen at the beginning of this chapter that for the study of the ancient schools of thought other than Confucianist, the scholars of the *Han hsueh* paved the way. Their interpretation of the ancient texts was primarily textual and philological, rather than philosophical. But that is exactly what is needed before one applies the analytic method to analyze the philosophical ideas of the various ancient Chinese schools of thought.

Because logic was the first aspect of Western philosophy that attracted the attention of the Chinese, it is natural that among the ancient Chinese schools, the School of Names was also the first to receive detailed study in recent years. Dr. Hu Shih's book, *The Development of the Logical Method in Ancient China,* since its first publication in 1922 has been one of the important contributions to this study. Scholars like Liang Chi-chao (1873-1930) have also contributed much to the study of the School of Names and of the other schools.

The interpretation and analysis of the old ideas through use of the analytic method characterized the spirit of the age up to the outbreak of the Sino-Japanese war in 1937. Even Christian missionaries could not escape from the influence of this spirit. This may be why many missionaries in China have translated Chinese philosophical works and written books on Chinese philosophy in Western languages, whereas few have translated Western philosophical works and written books on Western philosophy in Chinese. Thus in the philosophical field they seem to have conducted what might be called a reverse form of missionary work. It is possible to have reverse missionary work, just as it is possible to have reverse lend-lease.

XXVIII CHINESE PHILOSOPHY IN THE MODERN WORLD

After all that has been said about the evolution and development of Chinese philosophy, readers may be inclined to ask such questions as: What is contemporary Chinese philosophy like, especially that of the war period? What will Chinese philosophy contribute to the future philosophy of the world? As a matter of fact, I have often been asked these questions, and have been somewhat embarrassed by them, because it is difficult to explain what a certain philosophy is to someone who is unfamiliar with the traditions that it either represents or opposes. However, now that the reader has gained some acquaintance with the traditions of Chinese philosophy, I am going to try to answer these questions by continuing the story of the last chapter.

The Philosopher and the Historian of Philosophy

In so doing, I propose to confine myself to my own story, not at all because I think this is the only story worth telling, but because it is the story I know best and it can, perhaps, serve as a sort of illustration. This, I think, is better than merely giving a list of names and "isms," without any fuller exposition of any of them, a procedure which results in no kind of picture at all. By simply saying that a philosopher is a certain "ist," and nothing more, one usually creates misunderstanding instead of understanding.

My own larger *History of Chinese Philosophy*, the second and last volume of which was published in 1934, three years before the outbreak of the Sino-Japanese war, and the first volume of which was translated into English by Dr. Bodde and published in China in 1937, three months after the war began, is an expression of that spirit of the age mentioned by me at the end of the last chapter. In that work I utilized the results of the studies of the *Han hsueh* scholars on the texts of the ancient philosophers, and at the same time applied the analytic method to clarify the ideas of these philosophers. From the point of view of the historian, the use of this method has its limits, because the ideas of the ancient philosophers, in their original form, may not be as clear as in the presentation of their modern expositor. The function of a history of philosophy is to tell us what the words of the philosophers of the past actually meant to these men themselves, and not what we think they ought to mean. In my *History* I have tried my best to keep my use of the analytic method within its proper limits.

From the point of view of the pure philosopher, however, to clarify the ideas of the philosophers of the past, and push their theories to their logical conclusions in order to show their validity or absurdity, is certainly more interesting and important than merely to find out what they themselves thought about these ideas and theories. In so doing there is a process of development from the old to the new, and this development is another phase of the spirit of the age mentioned above. Such a work, however, is no longer the scholarly one of an historian, but the creative one of a philosopher. I share the feeling of Wang Kuo-wei, that is to say, I do not like to be simply an historian of philosophy. Therefore after I had finished the writing of my *History*, I immediately prepared for new work, but at this juncture the war broke out in the summer of 1937.

Philosophical Production in Wartime

Before the war, the philosophy departments of the University of Peking, from which I graduated, and of Tsing Hua University, where I am now teaching, were considered to be the strongest in China Each of them has had its own tradition and emphasis. Those of the University of Peking have been towards historical studies and scholarship, with an idealistic philosophical trend, which, in terms of Western philosophy, is Kantian and Hegelian, and, in terms of Chinese philosophy, is Lu-Wang. The tradition and emphasis of Tsing Hua, on the contrary, have been towards the use of logical analysis for the study of philosophical problems, with a realistic philosophical trend, which, in terms of Western philosophy, is Platonic in the sense that the philosophy of neo-realism is Platonic, and in terms of Chinese philosophy, is Cheng-Chu.

These two universities are both situated in Beijing and on the outbreak of the war they both moved to the southwest, where they combined with a third, the Nankai University of Tientsin, to form the Southwest Associated University throughout the entire war period. Together, their two Philosophy Departments formed a rare and wonderful combination, comprising nine professors representing all the important schools both of Chinese and Western philosophy. At first, the Associated University as a whole was situated in Changsha in Hunan Province, but our Philosophy Department, together with the other Departments of the humanities, was separately located in Hengshan, known as the South Holy Mountain.

We stayed there only about four months before moving again to Kunming, farther southwest, in the spring of 1938. These few months, however, were spiritually very stimulating. We were then in a national crisis which was the greatest in our history, and we were in the same place where Huai-jang had tried to grind a brick into a mirror, as mentioned in Chapter XXII, and where Chus Hsi had also once lived. We were sufferers of the same fate met by the Southern Sung Dynasty, that of being driven southward by a foreign army. Yet we lived in a wonderful society of philosophers, writers, and scholars, all in one building. It was this combination of the historical moment, the geographical location, and the human gathering, that made the occasion so exceptionally stimulating and inspiring.

During these few months, myself and my colleagues, ProfessorsTang Yung-tung and Y. L. Chin, finished books on which we had been working. Tang's book is the first part of his *History of Chinese Buddhism*. Chin's book is titled *On the Tao*, and mine the *Hsin Li-hsueh* or *New Li-hsueh*. Chin and myself have many ideas in common, but my work is a development of the Cheng-Chu school, as the title indicates, while his is the result of an independent study of metaphysical problems. Later in Kunming I wrote a series of other books: the *Hsin Shih-lun*, also titled *China's Road to Freedom*; the *Hsin Yuan jen* or *New Treatise on the Nature of Man*; the *Han Yuan-tao*, also titled *The Spirit of Chinese Philosophy*, which has been translated from the manuscript by Mr. E.R. Hughes of Oxford University and is published in London; and the *Hsin Chih-yen* or *New Treatise on the Methodology of Metaphysics*. (All these, in their original Chinese editions, have been published by the Commercial Press, Shanghai.) In the following, I shall try to summarize some of their results, as an illustration of one trend in contemporary Chinese philosophy, and in so doing we may perhaps get a partial glimpse of what Chinese philosophy can contribute to future philosophy.

Philosophical, or rather metaphysical, reasoning starts with the experience that something exists. This something may be a sensation, an emotion, or anything else. From the statement: "Something exists," I have in my *Hsin Li-hsueh* deduced all the metaphysical ideas or concepts not only of the Cheng-Chu school but also of the *Tao*ists. They are all considered in such a way that they are simply the logical implications of the statement that something exists. It is not difficult to see how the ideas of *Li* and *Chi* are deducible from this statement, and other ideas are also treated in the same way. For instance, the idea of Movement is treated by me not as a cosmological idea for some actual initial movement of the world, but as a metaphysical idea implied in the idea of existence itself. To exist is an activity, a movement. If we think about the world in its static aspect, we will say with the *Tao*ists that before anything comes into being there must first be the being of Being. And if we think about the world in its dynamic aspect, we will say with the Confucianists that before anything comes to exist, there must first be Movement, which is simply another way of speaking of the activity of existing. In what I call men's pictorial form of thinking, which is really imagination, men imagine Being or Movement as God, the Father of all things. In imaginative thought of this kind, one has religion or cosmology, but not philosophy or metaphysics. Following the same line of argument, I have been able in my *Hsin Li-hsueh* to deduce all the metaphysical ideas of Chinese philosophy and to integrate them into a clear and systematic whole. The book was favorably received, because in it critics seemed to feel that the structure of Chinese philosophy was more clearly stated than hitherto.

In the Cheng-Chu school, as we have seen in the last chapter, there is a certain element of authoritarianism and conservatism, but this is avoided in my *Hsin Li-hsueh*. In my opinion, metaphysics can know only that there are the *Li*, but not the content of each *Li*. It is the business of science to find out the content of the individual *Li*, using the scientific and pragmatic method. The *Li* in themselves are absolute and eternal, but as they are known to us, that is, in the laws and theories of science, they are relative and changeable.

The realization of the *Li* requires a material basis. The various types of society are the realization of the various *Li* of social structure, and the material basis each *Li* requires for its realization is the economic foundation of a given type of society. In the sphere of history, therefore, I believe in an economic interpretation, and in my book, *China's Road to Freedom,* I apply this interpretation to Chinese civilization and history, as I also have in Chapter II of the present book.

I think Wang Kuo-wei's trouble in philosophy has been due to his failure to realize that each branch of knowledge has its own sphere of application. One does not need to believe in any theory of metaphysics, if that theory, does not make much assertion about matters of fact. If it does make such assertions, however, it is bad metaphysics, which is the same as bad science. This does not mean that a good metaphysical theory is unbelievable, but only that it is so evident that one does not need to say that he believes in it, just as one need not say that one believes in mathematics. The difference between metaphysics and mathematics and logic is that in the latter two one does not need to start with the statement that something exists, which is an assertion about matters of fact, and is the only one that metaphysics need make.

The Nature of Philosophy

The method I use in the *Hsin Li-hsueh* is wholly analytic. After writing that book, however, I began to realize the importance of the negative method which has been mentioned in Chapter XXI.

At present, if someone were to ask me for a definition of philosophy, I would reply paradoxically that philosophy, especially metaphysics, is that branch of knowledge which, in its development, will ultimately become the knowledge that is not knowledge. If this be so, then the negative method needs to be used. Philosophy, especially metaphysics, is useless for the increase of our knowledge regarding matters of fact, but is indispensable for the elevation of our mind. These few points are not merely my own opinion, but, as we have previously seen, represent certain aspects of the Chinese philosophical tradition. It is these aspects that I think can contribute something to future world philosophy. In the following I shall try to develop them a little further.

Philosophy, as well as other branches of knowledge, must start with experience. But philosophy, especially metaphysics, differs from these other branches in that its development will lead it ultimately to that "something" which transcends experience. In this "something" there is that which cannot logically be sensed, but can only be thought. For instance, one can sense a square table, but cannot sense squareness. This is not because one's sense organ is insufficiently developed, but because squareness is a *Li,* which logically can only be thought but not sensed.

In the "something" there is also that which not only cannot be sensed, but strictly speaking, cannot even be thought. In Chapter II said that philosophy is systematic reflective thinking on life. Because of its reflective nature, it ultimately has to think on "something" that logically cannot be the object of thought. For instance, the universe, because it is the totality of all that is, cannot logically be the object of thought. As we have seen in Chapter XIX, the Chinese word *Tien* or Heaven is sometimes used in this sense of totality, as when Kuo Hsiang says: "Heaven is the name of all things." Since the universe is the totality of all that is, therefore when one thinks about it, one is thinking reflectively, because the thinking and the thinker must also be included in the totality. But when one thinks about that totality, the totality that lies in one's thought does not include the thought itself. For it is the object of the thought and so stands in contrast to it. Hence the totality that one is thinking about is not actually the totality of all that is. Yet one must first think about totality in order to realize that it is unthinkable. One needs thought in order to be conscious of the unthinkable, just as sometimes one needs a sound in order to be conscious of silence. One must think about the unthinkable, yet as soon as one tries to do so, it immediately slips away. This is the most fascinating and also most troublesome aspect of philosophy.

What logically cannot be sensed transcends experience; what can neither be sensed nor thought of transcends intellect. Concerning what transcends experience and intellect, one cannot say very much. Hence philosophy, or at least metaphysics, must be simple in its nature. Otherwise it again becomes simply bad science. And with its simple ideas, it suffices for its function.

The Spheres of Living

What is the function of philosophy? In Chapter I I suggested that, according to Chinese philosophical tradition, its function is not the increase of positive knowledge of matters of fact, but the elevation of the mind. Here it would seem well to explain more clearly what I mean by this statement.

In my book, *The New Treatise on the Nature of Man*, I have observed that man differs from other animals in that when he does something, he understands what he is doing, and is conscious that he is doing it. It is this understanding and self-consciousness that give significance for him to what he is doing. The various significances that thus attach to his various acts, in their totality, constitute what I call his sphere of living. Different men may do the same things, but according to their different degrees of understanding and self-consciousness, these things may have varying significance to them. Every individual has his own sphere of living, which is not quite the same as that of any other individual. Yet in spite of these individual differences, we can classify the various spheres of living into four general grades. Beginning with the lowest, they are: the innocent sphere, the utilitarian sphere, the moral sphere, and the transcendent sphere.

A man may simply do what his instinct or the custom of his society leads him to do. Like children and primitive people, he does what he does without being self-conscious or greatly understanding what he is doing. Thus what he does has little significance, if any, for him. His sphere of living is what I call the innocent sphere.

Or man may be aware of himself, and be doing everything for himself. That does not mean that he is necessarily an immoral man. He may do something, the consequences of which are beneficial to others, but his motivation for so doing is self-benefit. Thus everything he does has the significance of utility for himself. His sphere of living is what I call the utilitarian sphere.

Yet again a man may come to understand that a society exists, of which he is a member. This society constitutes a whole and he is a part of that whole. Having this understanding, he does everything for the benefit of the society, or as the Confucianists say, he does everything "for the sake of righteousness, and not for the sake of personal profit." He is the truly moral man and what he does is moral action in the strict sense of the word. Everything he does has a moral significance. Hence his sphere of living is what I call the moral sphere.

And finally, a man may come to understand that over and above society as a whole, there is the great whole which is the universe. He is not only a member of society, but at the same time a member of the universe. He is a citizen of the social organization, but at the same time a citizen of Heaven, as Mencius says. Having this understanding, he does everything for the benefit of the universe. He understands the significance of what he does and is self-conscious of the fact that he is doing what he does. This understanding and self-consciousness constitute for him a higher sphere of living which I call the transcendent sphere.

Of the four spheres of living, the innocent and the utilitarian are the products of man as he is, while the moral and the transcendent are those of man as he ought to be. The former two are the gifts of nature, while the latter two are the creations of the spirit. The innocent sphere is the lowest, the utilitarian comes next, then, the moral, and finally the transcendent. They are so because the innocent sphere requires almost no understanding and self-consciousness, whereas the utilitarian and the moral require more, and the transcendent requires most. The moral sphere is that of moral values, and the transcendent is that of super-moral values.

According to the tradition of Chinese philosophy, the function of philosophy is to help man to achieve the two higher spheres of living, and especially the highest. The transcendent sphere may also be called the sphere of philosophy, because it cannot be achieved unless through philosophy one gains some understanding of the universe. But the moral sphere, too, is a product of philosophy. Moral actions are not simply actions that accord with the moral rule, nor is moral man one who simply cultivates certain moral habits. He must act and live with an understanding of the moral principles involved, and it is the business of philosophy to give him this understanding.

To live in the moral sphere of living is to be a *hsien* or morally perfect man, and to live in the transcendent sphere is to be a *sheng* or sage. Philosophy teaches the way of how to be a sage. As I pointed out in Chapter I, to be a sage is to reach the highest perfection of man as man. This is the noble function of philosophy.

In the *Republic*, Plato said that the philosopher must be elevated from the "cave" of the sensory world to the world of intellect. If the philosopher is in the world of intellect, he is also in the transcendent sphere of living. Yet the highest achievement of the man living in this sphere is the identification of himself with the universe, and in this identification, he also transcends the intellect.

Previous chapters have already shown us that Chinese philosophy has always tended to stress that the sage need do nothing extraordinary in order to be a sage. He cannot perform miracles, nor need he try to do so. He does nothing more than most people do, but, having high understanding, what he does has a different significance to him. In other words, he does what he does in a state of enlightenment, while other people do what they do in a state of ignorance. As the Chan monks say: "Understanding -- this one word is the source of all mysteries." It is the significance which results from this understanding that constitutes his highest sphere of living.

Thus the Chinese sage is both of this world and the other world, and Chinese philosophy is both this-worldly and other-worldly. With the scientific advancement of the future, I believe that religion with its dogmas and superstitions will give way to science; man's craving for the world beyond, however, will be met by the philosophy of the future -- a philosophy which is therefore likely to be both this-worldly and other-worldly. In this respect Chinese philosophy may have something to contribute.

The Methodology of Metaphysics

In my work, *A New Treatise on the Methodology of Metaphysics,* I maintain that there are two methods, the positive and the negative. The essence of the positive method is to talk about the object of metaphysics which is the subject of its inquiry; the essence of the negative method is not to talk about it. By so doing, the negative method reveals certain aspects of the nature of that something, namely those aspects that are not susceptible to positive description and analysis.

In Chapter II I have indicated my agreement with Professor Northrop that philosophy in the West started with what he calls the concept by postulation, whereas Chinese philosophy started with what he calls concept by intuition. As a result, Western philosophy has naturally been dominated by the positive method, and Chinese philosophy by the negative one. This is especially true of Taoism, which started and ended with the undifferentiable whole. In the *Lao-tzu* and *Chuang-tzu,* one does not learn what the *Tao* actually is, but only what it is not. But if one knows what it is not, one does get some idea of what it is.

This negative method of Taoism was reinforced by Buddhism, as we have seen. The combination of Taoism and Buddhism resulted in Chanism, which I should like to call a philosophy of silence. If one understands and realizes the meaning and significance of silence, one gains something of the object of metaphysics.

In the West, Kant may be said to have used the negative method of metaphysics. In his *Critique of Pure Reason,* he found the unknowable, the noumenon. To Kant and other Western philosophers, because the unknowable is unknowable, one can therefore say nothing about it, and so it is better to abandon metaphysics entirely and stop at epistemology. But to those who are accustomed to the negative method, it is taken for granted that, since the unknowable is unknowable, we should say nothing about it. The business of metaphysics is not to say something about the unknowable, but only to say something about the fact that the unknowable is unknowable. When one knows that the unknowable is unknowable, one does know, after all, something about it. On this point, Kant did a great deal.

The great metaphysical systems of all philosophy, whether negative or positive in their methodology, have crowned themselves with mysticism. The negative method is essentially that of mysticism. But even in the cases of Plato, Aristotle, and Spinoza, who used the positive method at its best, the climaxes of their systems are all of a mystical nature. When the philosopher in the Republic beholds and identifies himself with the Idea of the Good, or the philosopher in the *Metaphysics* with God "thinking on thinking" or the philosopher in the *Ethics* finds himself "seeing things from the point of view of eternity" and enjoying the "intellectual love of God," what can they do but be silent? Is their state not better described by such phrases as "not one," "not many," not not-one," not not-many"?

Thus the two methods do not contradict but rather complement one another. A perfect metaphysical system should start with the positive method and end with the negative one. If it does not end with the negative method, it fails to reach the final climax of philosophy. But if it does not start with the positive method, it lacks the clear thinking that is essential for philosophy. Mysticism is not the opposite of clear thinking, nor is it below it. Rather, it is beyond it. It is not anti-rational; it is super-rational.

In the history of Chinese philosophy, the positive method was never fully developed; in fact, it was much neglected. Therefore, Chinese philosophy has lacked clear thinking, which is one of the reasons why it is marked by simplicity. Lacking clear thinking, its simplicity has been quite naive. Its simplicity as such is commendable, but its naiveté must be removed through the exercise of clear thinking. Clear thinking is not the end of philosophy, but it is the indispensable discipline that every philosopher needs. Certainly it is what Chinese philosophers need. On the other hand, the history of Western philosophy has not seen a full development of the negative method It is the combination of the two that will produce the philosophy of the future.

A Chan story describes how a certain teacher used to stick out his thumb when he was asked to explain the Buddhist *Tao*. On such occasions, he would simply remain silent, but would display his thumb. Noticing this, his boy attendant began to imitate him. One day the teacher saw him in this act, and quick as lightning chopped off the boy's thumb. The boy ran away crying. The teacher called him to come back, and just as the boy turned his head, the teacher again stuck out his own thumb. Thereupon the boy received Sudden Enlightenment.

Whether this story is true or not, it suggests the truth that before the negative method is used, the philosopher or student of philosophy must pass through the positive method, and before the simplicity of philosophy is reached, he must pass through its complexity.

One must speak very much before one keeps silent.

BOOK THREE:

ESSAYS AND SPEECHES

WHY CHINA HAS NO SCIENCE–AN INTERPRETATION OF THE HISTORY AND CONSEQUENCES OF CHINESE PHILOSOPHY[995]

In one of his articles published in *The New Republic*, Professor Dewey said:

> It may be questioned whether the most enlightening thing he (the visitor) can do for others who are interested in China is not to share with them his discovery that China can be known only in terms of itself, and older European history. Yet one must repeat that China is changing rapidly; and that it is as foolish to go on thinking of it in terms of old dynastic China as it is to interpret it by pigeon-holing its facts in Western conceptions. China is another world politically and economically speaking, a large and persistent world, and a world bound no one knows just where.[996]

It is truly a discovery. If we compare Chinese history with the history of Europe of a few centuries ago, say before the Renaissance, we find that, although they are of different kinds, they are nevertheless on the same level. But now China is still old while the Western countries are already new. What keeps China back? It is a natural question.

What keeps China back is that she has no science. The effect of this fact is not only plain in the material side, but also in the spiritual side, of the present condition of Chinese life. China produced her philosophy at the same time with, or a little before, the height of Athenian culture. Why did she not produce science at the same time with, or even before, the beginning of modern Europe? This paper is an attempt to answer this question in terms of China herself.

It is beyond question that geography, climate, and economic conditions are very important factors in making history, but we must bear in mind that they are conditions that make history possible, not that make history actual. They are the indispensable settings of a drama, but not its cause. The cause that makes history actual is the will to live and the desire for happiness. But what is happiness? People are far from agreeing in their answers to this question. It is due to this fact that we have many different systems of philosophy, many different standards of value, and consequently many different types of history. At the end of this paper I shall venture to draw the conclusion that China has no science, because according to her own standard of value she does not need any. But before we come to this conclusion, we have first to see what the older Chinese standard of value is. In doing so, a general survey of the history of Chinese philosophy is indispensable.

---

995 In publishing this paper I take the opportunity to thank many members of the faculty of the Philosophy Department of Columbia University for encouragement and help. By science I mean the systematic knowledge of natural phenomena and of the relations between them. Thus it is the short term for Natural Science.

996 *The New Republic*, Vol. XXV, 1920, New York, p. 188. Vol. XXXII-No. 3.

I

At the end of the Chou Dynasty, the emperors lost their power to control the feudal princes who began to regard themselves as independent, and the land was subjected to warfare. It was an age of political confusion indeed, but of great intellectual initiative. It was equivalent to the Athenian period of mental vigor in Europe.

Before attacking the different types of Chinese ideals, for the sake of convenience I shall introduce two words which seem to me to indicate respectively two general tendencies of Chinese philosophy. They are "nature" and "art," or, to translate more exactly, "nature" and "human." To illustrate this I cite from the *Chuang-tzu* a passage: "What is nature? What is human? That ox and horse have four feet is nature; to halter the head of a horse or to pierce the nose of an ox is human."[997]

Thus "nature" means something natural; "human" means something artificial. The one is made by nature, the other by man. At the end of the Chou Dynasty there were two tendencies representing these two extremes and a third representing a mean between the two. The one said that nature is perfect in itself and that men are self-sufficient and need no help from outside; the other said that nature is not perfect in itself and that men are not self-sufficient and need something outside in order to be better; the third made a compromise. These three main types of ideas did not appear one after the other, but rather arose simultaneously, and expressed at one time the different aspects of human nature and experience. Now, according to the History of the Han Dynasty, at the end of the Chou Dynasty there were nine branches of thought Confucianism, Taoism, Mohism, the *Yin-Yang* school, the legalist school, the School of Names, the School of Diplomatists, the School of Agrarians, and the School of Eclectics. But among them the most influential at that time were Confucianism, Taoism, and Mohism.

In almost every book written at the end of the Chou Dynasty, we are informed that these three were struggling for existence. To illustrate this I cite from the polemic speeches of Mencius, a great defender of Confucianism at that time:

> Philosopher emperors cease to arise; the princes of states give rein to their lusts; and the scholars indulge in irrational discussions. The words of Yang Chu and Mo Ti fill the world. The discourse of the people has adopted the views either of *Yang* or of Mo. Yang's doctrine is each one for himself; then there will be no king. Mo's doctrine is: love all equally; then there will be no father to have neither king nor father is to be beasts.... If the doctrines of *Yang* and Mo are not stopped and the doctrine of sages not set forth, then the perverse speaking will delude the people, and stop the path of benevolence and righteousness. When benevolence and righteousness are stopped, beasts will be led onto devour men and men will themselves devour one another. I am alarmed by these things and

997 From the chapter entitled 'The Autumn Floods." Compare with H. A. Giles' translation in his book, *Chuang Tzu, Mystic, Moralist, and Social Reformer*. London, 1889, p. 211.

address myself to the defense of the doctrines of the former sages, and to oppose Yang and Mo....[998]

Now Mo Ti was the founder of Mohism, and Yang Chu was the disciple of the founder of Taoism, Lao Tzu. This passage seems to me to be a vivid picture of the state of war existing between these three powers. They were not only struggling for existence, but each one of them had the ambition to conquer the whole empire.

To illustrate their doctrines a little more in detail I choose Lao Tzu (570 B.C.?-480 B.C.?), Yang Chu (440 B.C.?-360 B.C.?), and Chuang Tzu (350 B.C.?-275 B.C.?) to represent Taoism; Mo Tzu (Mo Ti, 500 B.C.?-425 B.C.?) to represent Mohism; and Confucius (551 B.C.-479 B.C.) and Mencius (372 B.C: 289 B.C.) to represent Confucianism. Referring to the three tendencies which I just mentioned, Taoism stands for nature, Mohism for art, and Confucianism for the means. It seems to me that in every aspect of their doctrines, Taoism and Mohism were always at the two extremes and Confucianism in the middle. For instance, with regard to their ethical theories, Mencius agrees in arranging them in a scheme as I do. He said:

> The doctrine of the philosopher *Yang* was, each one for himself.
>
> Though he might benefit the whole world by plucking out a single hair, he would not do it. The doctrine of the philosopher Mo was: to love all equally. If by rubbing smooth his whole body from the crown to the heel he could benefit the world, he would do it. Mo held a mean between them. By holding it without leaving room for the changeableness of circumstances, he resembled them in maintaining his one point to the exclusion of others.[999]

It goes without saying that to hold the means while leaving room for the changeableness of circumstances is the only right way of action. It is exactly the teaching of Confucianism. I shall make it clearer a little later.

II

The teaching of Taoism can be summarized in one phrase: "returning to nature." The omnipotent *Tao* gives everything its own nature, in which it finds its own satisfaction. For instance:

> In the northern ocean there is a fish, called the Leviathan, many thousand li[1000] in size. This Leviathan changes into a bird, called the Rukh, whose back is many li in breadth. With a mighty effort it rises and its wings obscure the sky like clouds. At the equinox, this bird prepares to start for the southern ocean, the Celestial Lake. And in the "Record of Marvels" we read that when the Rukh flies southwards, the water is smitten for a space of three thousand li around, while the bird itself mounts upon a typhoon to a height of ninety thousand li for a flight of six months' duration.... A cicada laughed, and said to a dove: "Now when I fly with my might, it is as much as

998 James Legge's translation, with some modification. See the *Chinese Classics*, second ed., London, 1895, Vol. II, pp. 282-83.

999 James Legge's translation, with some modification. See the *Chinese Classics*, Vol. II, pp. 464-465.

1000 One *li* is about one-third of an English mile.

I can do to get from tree to tree. And sometimes I do not reach, but fall to the ground midway. What, then, can be the use of going up ninety thousand if in order to start for the South?"[1001]

This passage is cited from a chapter entitled "The Happy Excursion" from Chuang Tzu's work. It shows clearly that both the great Rukh and the small cicada are perfectly satisfied, each with his own excursion. They continue to be so as long as they live in accordance with their nature without imitating artificially each other. So everything is perfect in its natural condition. Art simply disturbs nature and produces pain. For, as Chuang Tzu said:

> A duck's legs, though short, cannot be lengthened without pain to the duck, and a crane's legs, though long, cannot be shortened without misery to the crane, so that which is long in nature cannot be cut off, nor that which is short be lengthened. All sorrows are thus avoided.[1002]

Yang Chu's egoism, therefore, is not selfish in the ordinary sense of that word. He was simply teaching that every man should live as his nature wishes to live; but he need not impose upon others what he thinks to be good. So he said:

> If the ancient by injuring a single hair could have rendered a service to the world, he would not have done it; and had the world been offered to a single person, he would not have accepted it. If nobody would damage even a hair, and nobody would have the world for profit, the world would be in a perfect state.[1003]

Another passage from Chuang Tzu:

> "Tell me," said Lao Tzu, "in what consist charity and duty to one's neighbor?" "They consist," answered Confucius, "in a capacity for rejoicing in all things; in universal love, without the element of self. These are the characteristics of charity and duty to one's neighbor." "What stuff!" cried Lao Tzu, "does not universal love contradict itself? Is not your elimination of self a positive manifestation of self? There is the universe, its regularity is unceasing; there is the sun and the moon, their brightness is unceasing; there are the stars, their groupings never change; there are birds and beasts, they flock together without varying; there are trees and shrubs, they grow upwards without exception. Be like these; follow *Tao*; and you will be perfect. Why, then, these struggles for charity and duty to one's neighbor, as though beating a drum in search of a fugitive? Alas! Sir, you have brought much confusion into the mind of man."[1004]

Thus the *Tao*ists see only the good aspects of what is called the state of nature. Every kind of human virtue and social regulation is to them against nature. As Lao Tzu said:

> Cast off your holiness, rid yourself of sagacity, and the people will benefit a hundredfold. Discard benevolence and abolish righteousness, and the people will return to filial piety and paternal love. Renounce your scheming

1001 H. A. Giles' translation, See his *Chuang-tzu*, etc., pp. 1-2.

1002 From the chapter entitled "The Joined Toes." See Giles' *Chuang-tzu*, etc., p 101.

1003 From the chapter, "Yang Chu," in the work of Lich Tzu.

1004 From the chapter entitled "The Way of Nature." See Giles' *Chuang tzu*, etc., p.167.

and abandon gain, and the thieves and robbers will disappear. These three precepts mean that outward show is insufficient, and therefore they bid us be true to our proper nature to show simplicity, to embrace plain dealing, to reduce selfishness, to moderate desire.[1005]

The government, if the *Tao*ists need any, must be extreme *laissez faire*.

As restrictions and prohibitions are multiplied in the country, the people grow poorer and poorer. When the people are subjected to overmuch government, the land is thrown into confusion. When people are skilled in many cunning arts, strange are the objects of luxury that appear. The greater the number of laws and enactments, the more thieves and robbers there will be.[1006]

Government should imitate nature: "The *Tao* in its regular course does nothing and so there is nothing which it does not do."[1007] This is because the *Tao* lets everything work for itself in its own way:

> Therefore the sage said "So long as I do nothing, the people will work out their own reformation, So long as I love calm, the people will be right themselves. So long as I am free from meddling, the people will grow rich. So long as I am free from desire, the people will come naturally back to simplicity."[1008]

So what man ought to do is to accord with his nature and be content with his destiny. To illustrate this passive nature of Taoism I cite from Chuang Tzu:

> Tzu Lai fell ill.... Tzu *Li* went to see him. Leaning against the door, he asked the dying man: "Great indeed is the Creator! What will He now make you to become? Where will He take you to? Will He make you the liver of a rat? Or an arm of an insect?" Tzu Lai answered "Where a parent tells a son to go, East, West, South, or North, he simply follows the command. The *Yin* and *Yang* (the two forces of nature) are more to a man than his parents are. If they hasten my death and I do not quietly submit to them, I shall be obstinate and rebellious, but they are not mistaken. The great mass of nature makes me to be moved with the body, to be busy with life, to be at ease with old age, and to be at rest with death. Therefore what has made my life a good makes also my death a good."[1009]

Knowledge is of no use and can do only harm: "Our life is limited, but knowledge is not limited. With what is limited to pursue what is not limited is a perilous thing."[1010] What we need and ought to know and to get is the *Tao*, but it is in us. It is like the God of the pantheistic philosophy. So what we ought to do is to know and to control ourselves: "He who knows others is clever, but he who knows himself is enlightened. He who overcomes others is strong, but he who overcomes himself is mightier still."[1011]

Besides, we have to use an altogether different method to know and to get the

1005 Lionel Giles: *The Sayings of Lao Tzu*, p. 44.
1006 Lionel Giles: *The Sayings of Lao Tzu*, p. 38.
1007 James Legge: *The Texts of Taoism* (in the *Sacred Books of the East Series*) London, 1891, Pt I, p. 70.
1008 *Id*, p 38.
1009 From the chapter on "The Great Master," James Legge's *Texts of Taoism*, Pt. 1, p.249.
1010 From the chapter on "Nourishing the Essence of Life." *Id*., p. 198.
1011 Lionel Giles: *The Sayings of Lao Tzu*, p. 44.

Tao. Lao Tzu said:

> He who devotes himself to knowledge seeks from day to day to increase. He who devotes himself to the *Tao* seeks from day to day to diminish. He diminishes and again diminishes till he arrives at doing nothing. Having arrived at the point of doing nothing, there is nothing which he does not do.[1012]

As the *Tao* is already in us, it can be known not by adding something artificially to it, but by taking away what has been artificially added to it before. That is what Lao Tzu meant by "diminish." So the arguments of those who were simply interested in intellectual exercise were to the *Tao*ists of little value. Thus in Chuang Tzu's book one passage reads:

> To wear out one's intellect in trying to argue without knowing the fact that the arguments are the same is called "three in the morning." "What is three in the morning?" asked Tzu Yu. "A keeper of monkeys," replied Tzu Chi, "said once to his monkeys with regard to their chestnuts, that each was to have three in the morning and four in the night. But to this the monkeys were very angry, so the keeper said that they might have four in the morning and three in the night, with which arrangement they were all well pleased."[1013]

Thus Taoism stood for nature as against art.

III

The fundamental idea of Mohism is utility. The sanction of virtue is not that it is natural, but that it is useful. In the book bearing Mo Tzu's name one passage reads: "Righteousness is what is beneficial to us. Benefit is that which we are glad to have."[1014] Thus Mo Tzu's position in ethics was essentially that of utilitarianism. He was also a pragmatist and an empiricist. He said:

> For argument there must be a standard. If we argue without a standard, it is just like fixing morning and night on a moving circle we cannot know clearly whether it is right or wrong, useful or harmful. For testing an argument there are three standards. What are these three standards? They are to trace it, to examine it, and to use it. Where trace it? Trace it in the authority of the ancient philosopher kings. Where examine it? Examine it in the facts which the common people see and hear. Where use it? Put it into practice and see whether it is useful for the benefit of the country and the people. These are the three standards for argument.[1015]

Among these three standards, the third seems to be the most important. So Mo Tzu taught the doctrine of universal love, because it seemed to him to be the most "useful for the benefit of the country and the people." To let him speak for himself, I select from the chapters entitled "Universal Lover":

> The business of the benevolent man must be to strive to promote what is

1012 James Legge: *The Texts of Taoism*, Pt. 1, p. 90.

1013 From the chapter on "The *I*dentity of Contraries," H. A Giles: *Chuang-tzu*, etc., p. 20.

1014 From the first of the two chapters on "Definitions."

1015 From the first of the three chapters on the "Absurdity of Predestination"

> advantageous to the world and to take away what is injurious to it. At the present time, what are to be accounted the most injurious things to the world? They are such as the attacking of small states by the great ones; the inroad on small families by the great ones; the plunder of the weak by the strong; the oppression of the few by the many... Let us ask whence all these injurious things arise. Is it from loving others or advantaging others? It must be replied "No"; and it must likewise be said "They arise clearly from hating others and doing violence to others." Do those who hate and do violence to others hold the principle of loving all, or that of making distinctions between man and man? It must be replied, "They make distinctions." So then it is the principle of making distinctions between man and man, which gives rise to all that is most injurious to the world. On this account we conclude that that principle is wrong.... There is a principle of loving all which is able to change that which makes distinctions.... If the princes were as much for the state of others as for their own, which one among them would raise the forces of his state to attack that of another? He is for that as much as for his own.... So then it is the principle of universal, mutual love, which gives rise to all that is most beneficial to the world. On this account we conclude that that principle is right... Others may say, "It is good, but it is extremely hard to be carried into practice." But how can it be good, and yet incapable of being put into practice? ... I apprehend there is no one under heaven, man or woman, however stupid, though he condemns the principle of universal love, but would at such a time (the most dangerous time), make one who held it the subject of his trust.... I apprehend there is no one under heaven, however stupid, man or woman, though he condemns the principle of universal love, but would at such a time (the most dangerous time), prefer to be under the sovereign who holds it.[1016]

This shows that the doctrine of universal love is not only advantageous to others, but to those as well who act according to this principle. In the book that bears Mo Tzu's name three chapters are devoted to describing the disadvantages of war. War is not only injurious to the conquered, but to the conqueror as well. Even occasionally some of the states may make profit at the expense of others, it still cannot be justified. He compared this to medicine.

There is medicine; if ten thousand people use it and only four or five are benefited, it is surely not a good medicine. Mo Tzu stood for the greatest happiness of the greatest number.

He also, unlike the *Tao*ist, knew the imperfection of human nature. Mankind is too shortsighted to see its own interests. Men cannot be convinced that loving others is advantageous to themselves and selfishness can do only harm. So, Mo Tzu, again unlike the *Tao*ist, saw the need of authorities to regulate human action. He taught that there is a personal God. Men should love each other, not only because so doing is advantageous, but also because it is the will of God. Even belief

1016 Up to the present time there is no English translation of the book bearing Mo Tzu's name. But these three chapters on universal love were translated by James Legge in the introduction to the work of Mencius. See the *Chinese Classics*, Vol. II, pp. 108-111.

in the existence of spirits and ghosts as the invisible watchers over men's conduct is upheld as a valuable aid in maintaining morality.

The function and authority of the state are likewise emphasized by Mo Tzu as aids to a right life:

> In ancient times, when mankind just began to enter the world and had no political association, everyone had his own righteousness. If there was one man, there was one righteousness; if two, two righteousnesses; if ten, ten righteousnesses; the more men, the more righteousnesses. Everyone considered his own righteousness as right and others' as wrong. Therefore, people were against each other.... The world was in disorder and people were like birds and beasts. They knew that the reason that the world was in disorder was that there was no right leader; therefore, they elected a wise and able man to be their emperor.... Then the emperor ordered the people, saying: "If you hear what is good and what is not good, tell all of them to your superior. Your superior considers as right, all of you must consider as right; what your superior considers as wrong, all of you must consider as wrong."[1017]

This is altogether different from the *Tao*istic conception of the state. Besides this, Mo Tzu also emphasized the importance of education. In the book that bears his name, one chapter is entitled: "What Is Dyed," in which one passage reads:

> Master Mo Tzu saw one dyeing silk. He sighed and said "Dyed in blue, the silk becomes blue; dyed in yellow, the silk becomes yellow. What it enters changes; it changes its color accordingly by entering five times. It is turned into five colors. Therefore it is necessary to take care of the dyeing."[1018]

Following this he cited a long list of facts to show how some men became good by associating with good men, and others bad by associating with bad men. Human nature seems to him to be a *tabula rasa* and its color depends entirely on how one dyes it.

This again is very different from the *Tao*istic conception of human nature.

In contrast with Taoism Mo Tzu denied predestination. Reward and punishment either by God or by the state are the results of men's voluntary action. If the will is not free, men will not be responsible for their bad doing, and will not be encouraged to do well. They will think, as Mo Tzu said:

> "He who is punished is predestined to be punished but not because he is bad. He who is rewarded is predestined to be rewarded but not because he is good. Therefore if they become princes, they will not be righteous; if they become ministers, they will not be loyal...[1019]

Thus Mo Tzu worked out many devices for making people good. His ideal is to have the greatest number of population, with the necessary external goods, living together peacefully and loving each other. Mo Tzu said:

> When a philosopher governs a country, the wealth of that country can be

1017 From the first of the three chapters on "The Preference of Uniformity."

1018 From the chapter on "What Is Dyed."

1019 From the first of the three chapters on "The Absurdity of Predestination."

> doubled; when he governs the world, the wealth of the world can be doubled. It is doubled not at the expense of others, but by utilizing the country and by cutting off useless expenditures.... What is it that is not easy to be doubled? It is the population only that is not easy to be doubled. But there is a way to double it. The ancient philosopher kings had a law saying "When the boy is twenty years old, he must have a home; when the girl is fifteen years old, she must have her man ..."[1020]

This is Mo Tzu's ideal of progress. Progress is possible not by struggle and competition, but by universal love and mutual help.

To this I must add that the ideal of Mo Tzu is not a Platonic one. Mo Tzu was too realistic to be content to put his pattern in heaven. He was ready to fight against anything that seemed to him to be incompatible with the increase of wealth and population. He taught economy of expenditure because, as he said: "Philosopher kings do not do those things which increase the expenditure but not the profit of the people."[1021] He was also against music and fine art, because they have nothing to do with the fact that: "People have three troubles: those who are hungry but have no food; those who are cold but have no clothes; and those who are tired but cannot rest."[1022] He was also against the Confucianist teaching of the luxurious way of burying the dead and the three years' mourning on occasion of the death of parents. Because people ought not to spend their time, energy, and wealth in this way; in doing so, "The country must become poor; the population must become small; and politics must become corrupted."[1023] These steps probably represent the decisive attitude of Mohism to oppose nature. Indeed if one sees things wholly from the point of view of intellect, music and fine art are really of no use at all. If we know that death is a natural process, what is the use of mourning? Hsun Tzu said "Mo Tzu was blinded by utility, and did not know refinement."[1024] This criticism is quite justified.

Anyway, Mo Tzu was certainly a philosopher who taught men to find happiness in the external world. He did not think, as the Taoists did, that men are most happy in the state of nature, and that what men need and should do is to return to nature, instead of turning away from it. He knew, in contrast with *Tao*ists, that men in nature are imperfect, foolish, and weak; that, in order to be perfect, strong, and wise, they need the help of the state, of virtue, and of a personified God. So in his philosophy there was a strong sense of progress and of the future. In the book bearing his name one passage reads:

> Peng Ching Sheng Tzu said "The past can be known, but not the future." Mo Tzu said "Suppose that your parents are at a place one hundred li from here, and meet some trouble; they ask you to go to them within one day; if you can do so, they will be alive; if not, they will die. Now there is a good car with a good horse, and a bad horse with a car with square wheels. I ask you to choose

1020 From the first of the three chapters on "The Economy of Expenditure."

1021 *Id.*, Ch 2.

1022 From the chapter on "Against Music."

1023 From the chapter on "The Economy of Burying."

1024 From the chapter on "The Elimination of Blindness" in the work of Hsun Tzu.

between them. Which one will you take?" "I take the good car with the good horse in order that I may be able to arrive earlier" was the answer. Mo Tzu said "Then why do you say that you cannot know the future?"[1025]

This is indeed a good illustration of utilizing the past to control the future. The spirit is scientific. In the book bearing Mo Tzu's name there were several chapters devoted to what we now call logic or definitions. They must be the product of Mo Tzu's followers, if not of the master himself. They contain many definitions which are sometimes interesting and scientific. For instance:

> Space is that that covers different places. Duration is that that covers different times. Cause is that after getting which a thing can be. Circle is that one middle has the same length to all sides. Energy is that by which a form arises.[1026]

There are many others like these, which seem to be germs of science. Indeed Mo Tzu was famous also for making machines to defend the city wall, to which several chapters in the book bearing his name are devoted.

This is all I wish to say to support my statement that Mohism stood for art as over against nature. Now let us turn to the third system, Confucianism.

IV

Confucianism, as I said before, is a mean between the two extreme standpoints of nature and art. But at the time immediately after Confucius, there were two types of Confucianism. The one, represented by Mencius, stood nearer to the extreme of nature; the other, represented by Hsun Tzu, stood nearer to that of art. The teaching of Confucius himself was nearer to the extreme of nature.

So afterwards Mencius was, and is, considered as the true and legal heir of Confucianism. Here I follow tradition in choosing Confucius and Mencius to represent Confucianism, but shall discuss Hsun Tzu in another place and shall consider him as another philosopher in Chinese history who attempted to develop the art line of Chinese thought.

Confucius, as Mencius said, was a "sage of time."

When it was proper to go away quickly, he did so; when it was proper to delay, he did so; when it was proper to keep retirement, he did so; when it was proper to go into office, he did so; this was Confucius.[1027]

So Confucius emphasized discrimination of situations. It is not a first question whether I should love a person in such and such a way or not; the first question is who that person is. Mencius said:

> In regard to the inferior creatures, the superior man is kind to them, but not loving. In regard to people generally, he is friendly to them, but not affectionate. He is affectionate to his relatives, and friendly to people generally. He is friendly to people generally, and kind to creatures.[1028]

He said again in another place:

1025 From the chapter "Lu Wen."

1026 All are selected from the first of the two chapters on "Definitions."

1027 James Legge: *Chinese Classics*, Vol. II, p. 371.

1028 *Id.*, p. 476.

Here is a man, and a stranger bends his bow to shoot him. I will advise him not to do so, but speaking calmly and smilingly, for no other reason but that he is not related to me. But if my brother be bending his bow to shoot the man, I will advise him not to do so, weeping and crying the while, for no other reason but that he is related to me.[1029]

Thus was developed the doctrine of loving with a difference of degree, as over against that of universal love on the one hand and that of each for himself on the other. We ought to love with difference of degree, because it is human nature. Thus one passage in the work of Mencius reads:

Yi Tzu said, "According to the principle of the learned, we find that the ancients acted towards the people as if they were watching over an infant. What does this expression mean? To me it seems that we are to love all without difference of degree; but in practice we begin with our parents." Hsu Tzu reported this to Mencius. Mencius said: "Does Yi Tzu really think that a man's affection for the child of his brother is merely like his affection for that of his neighbor? ... Heaven gives birth to creatures in such a way that they have one root, and Yi Tzu makes them to have two roots."[1030]

Human nature, according to the teaching of Confucianism, is essentially good. This seems to have been a tradition even before the time of Confucius. Because human nature is originally good, so the sanction of virtue is its being admirable and desirable. Thus Mencius said:

Men's mouths agree in having the same relishes; their ears agree in enjoying the same sound; their eyes agree in recognizing the same beauty; shall their minds alone be without that which they similarly approve? It is, I say, reason and righteousness. The sages only apprehended before us what our mind also approves. Therefore reason and righteousness are agreeable to our mind, just as good food is agreeable to our mouth.[1031]

In another place he said: "What is desirable is what is called good,"[1032] But, although human nature is originally good, it is not to be inferred that men are born perfect. They cannot be perfect until their innate reason is completely developed, and their lower desires are wholly taken away. Thus Mencius said:

The feeling of commiseration is the beginning of benevolence; the feeling of shame and dislike is the beginning of righteousness; the feeling of modesty and complaisance is the beginning of propriety; the feeling of approving and disapproving is the beginning of wisdom.... Since all men have these four feelings in themselves, let them know how to give them their development and their completion, and the issue will be like that of fire which has begun to burn, or that of a spring which has begun to find vent. If they have their complete development, they will suffice to love and to protect all within the

1029 *Id.*, p. 427.

1030 *Id.*, pp. 258-259.

1031 *Id.*, pp. 406-407.

1032 *Id.*, p. 490.

four seas. If they be denied their development, they will not suffice for a man to serve his parents.[1033]

And to develop reason on the one hand is to diminish the lower desires on the other: "To nourish the mind there is nothing better than to make the desires few."[1034] So in order to develop men's natural faculties, they need some positive organization. The simple *Tao*istic way of returning to nature is not sufficient here. Therefore the state is indispensable: "In the *Book of History* it is said 'Heaven having produced the people in the lower earth, appointed for them rulers and teachers."[1035] But teachers and rulers are not to be separated. Most of the Chinese political ideals are the same as Plato's. King must be philosopher; philosopher must be king. This is especially emphasized in the Confucianist's conception of the state. The chief duty of the state is first to maintain a certain amount of wealth to enable people to live, and then to teach them. Thus one passage in the Confucian *Analects* reads:

> When the Master went to the state of Wei, Yen Yu acted as the driver of his carriage. The Master observed "How numerous are the people!" Yu said "Since they are thus numerous, what shall be done for them?" "Enrich them," was the answer. "And when they have been enriched, what more shall be done?" The Master said "Teach them."[1036]

Moreover in a state, teaching is more important than enriching. In the Confucian *Analects* another passage reads:

> The Duke King of *Chi* asked Confucius about government. Confucius replied: "The prince is prince, the minister is minister, the father is father, and the son is son." "Good," said the duke, "If, indeed, the prince is not prince, the minister not minister, the father not father, and the son not son, although there is food, can we enjoy it?"[1037]

As for the individual, external things are determined by destiny. Therefore in the Confucian Analects we read "Death and life have their determined appointment; riches and honors depend on Heaven."[1038] And Mencius said:

> When we get by our seeking and lose by our neglecting; in this case seeking is of use to getting, and the thing sought for is something which is in ourselves. When our seeking is conducted properly, but the getting is only as destiny determines, in this case our seeking is of no use to getting, and the thing sought for is that which is without us."[1039]

Therefore, what man should do is to seek what is in himself. The fact that he is not able to control what is outside him does not make him imperfect; he is given by Heaven the godly reason within him, in which he can find truth and be happy. So Mencius said:

> He who has exhausted all his mind, knows his nature. Knowing his nature,

1033 *Id*, pp. 203-204.
1034 *Id*, p. 497.
1035 *Id*., P. 156.
1036 *Id*., pp. 266-267.
1037 *Id*, P. 256.
1038 *Id*., p. 253.
1039 *Id*., Vol. I, p. 450.

> he knows Heaven. To preserve one's mind and nourish one's nature, is the way to serve Heaven. When neither a premature death nor a long life makes any difference, but he waits in the cultivation of his character for whatever comes; this is the way in which he establishes his Heaven-ordained being.[1040]

In another place he said "All things are already in us. Turn our attention to ourselves and find there this truth; there is no greater delight than that."[1041] In this point Confucianism is much nearer Taoism than Mohism. Happiness and truth are in our mind. It is in our own mind, not in the external world, that we can seek for happiness and truth. We are self-sufficient, if only we develop our innate power. To learn is to cultivate our character according to our rational nature, not to make intellectual exercise or simply to remember mechanically what the books said.

We have now completed our general survey of the three original types of Chinese ideals. We have seen that in the theory of existence, the power that governs the universe, to Taoism is the omnipotent *Tao* or Nature, to Mohism is a personified God, and to Confucianism is the Heavenly Reason. In the theory of the state, Taoism needed a "laissez faire" government, if any; Mohism needed the state to regulate the different individual opinions, and Confucianism needed it to develop men's moral faculties. In the theory of life, Taoism said that human nature is perfect in itself and that everyone should only live in accordance with one's own nature; Mohism said that human nature is not perfect in itself, and that one should love all equally in order to make possible the prosperity of all; Confucianism said that although human nature is good, one needs efforts to "develop," to "nourish," and to "complete" it, and that although one should love others, the difference of natural relation should be considered. In the theory of education, Taoism taught a return to nature, Mohism taught control of the environment, and Confucianism taught the way of self-realization. These seem to me to have justified my statement that in the history of Chinese thought Taoism stood for nature, Mohism for art and Confucianism for the mean. We have seen that they struggled bitterly for existence. The result of that great war was the complete failure of poor Mohism, which soon disappeared once and for all.

The cause of the failure of Mohism were unknown; but, I think the chief cause must have been the defect of the system itself. To illustrate this I cite from Chuang Tzu a passage:

> Mo Tzu composed the treatise "Against Music" and the subject of another was called "Economy in Expenditure." He would have no singing in life, and no wearing of mourning on the occasion of death. He inculcated universal love and a common participation in all advantages, and condemned fighting.... The teaching of such lessons cannot be regarded as a proof of his love for men; his practicing them in his own case would certainly show that he did not love himself. But this has not been sufficient to overthrow the doctrine of Mo Tzu. Notwithstanding, men will sing, and he condemns

1040 *Id.*, Vol. I, pp. 448-449, with some modification.
1041 *Id.*, Vol. II, pp. 450-451.

singing; men will wail, and he condemns wailing; men will express their joy, and he condemns such expression. Is this truly according to men's nature? Through life toil, and at death niggardliness, causing men sorrow and melancholy and difficult to be carried into practice, I fear it cannot be regarded as the way of sages. Contrary to the minds of men, men will not endure it. Though Mo Tzu himself might be able to endure it, how is the aversion of the world to it to be overcome?[1042]

Truly the aversion of the world to Mohism had not been overcome, and people turned their back from it after the disappearance of the enthusiastic, great personality of Mo Tzu himself.

But, as already noted, there was another man at that time, who, although different from Mo Tzu, tried to develop the art line of Chinese ideal. He was Hsun Tzu (298 B.C.?-238 B.C.?), who considered himself as the true successor of Confucianism. He taught that human nature is absolutely bad and that to make it good is the duty of ruler and teacher. He condemned Chuang Tzu as: "One who was blinded by nature and did not know humans."[1043] According to his own ideal, he would conquer nature instead of returning to it: "It is better to treat nature as a thing and regulate it than to consider it very great and always think of it. It is better to control nature and use it than to follow and admire it."[1044] This is nearly the same as the Baconian conception of power. But, unfortunately his pupils did not develop his thought along this line. They carried out their master's political philosophy and carried it too far. In the third century B.C., Shi Huang Ti, or the "First Emperor," of the Chin

Dynasty, unified again warring states into one, and Li Szu, the disciple of Hsun Tzu, became the Premier. He helped the Emperor in every respect to unify the empire and carried the authority of the government to an extreme. Having abolished the existing feudalism and thus absolutely unified the empire politically, he took a step further to unify the people's thought. He burned books, killed scholars, and ordered the people to come to the state or government professors to learn things. Thus the emperor became an extreme tyrant and the people rebelled. Hsun Tzu's teaching, together with the Chin Dynasty, disappeared soon and forever.

V

After the Chin Dynasty the "art" motive of Chinese thought almost never reappeared. Soon came Buddhism, which again is a "nature" philosophy of the extreme type. The Chinese mind oscillated among Taoism, Confucianism, and Buddhism for a long time. It was not until the tenth century A.D. that a new group of men of genius succeeded in combining these three, Taoism, Confucianism, and Buddhism, into one, and instilling the new teaching into the Chinese national mind, which has persisted to the present day.

1042 From the chapter "The World." James Legge Tears of Taoism, Pt. II, pp. 218-219.

1043 From the chapter on "The Elimination of Blindness" in the work of Hsun Tzu.

1044 From the chapter of "On Nature" in the work of Suen. Tse.

Because this new teaching started in the Sung Dynasty, it is known as the "Learning of Sung." These philosophers themselves claimed that their teaching was the genuine Confucianism. But it must be a new Confucianism, if it is Confucianism at all. Most of its representatives were at first believers in Taoism and Buddhism, and afterwards came back to Confucianism. Then they picked from the *Li Chi* (*Book of Rites*) as their textbooks two chapters, to which few scholars had paid any attention before that time. Truly it was their merit to call attention to these two chapters, "The Great Learning" and "The Doctrine of the Mean," which embodied Confucianism in a very systematic way. I cannot refrain from citing from "The Great Learning" certain passages, which were regarded till very recent time by the Chinese people as the sole aim of life. The passages are:

> The doctrine of "The Great Learning" is: to enlighten the enlightened virtue, to make people love each other, and to stop at the supreme good.... The ancients who wish to enlighten the enlightened virtue in the world first ordered well their own states. Wishing to order well their own states, they first regulated their own families. Wishing to regulate their own families, they first cultivated their own characters. Wishing to cultivate their own characters, they first rectified their minds. Wishing to rectify their minds, they first sought to be sincere in their wishes. Wishing to be sincere in their wishes, they first extended their wisdom. Such extension of wisdom lay in the investigation of things.[1045]

This in a few words gave an admirable exposition of the Confucianist aim and art of life. The philosophers of Neo-Confucianism picked out these passages and unconsciously read Taoism and Buddhism into them. They differed from the original Confucianism in that they set up what they called the "heavenly reason" as over against "human desire," conceptions which were really suggested by the ideas of "Norm" and "Ignorance" in Buddhism, and were never spoken of very much before this period. According to the genuine Confucianism, as we have seen, although human nature is good, the good is only a germ or a "beginning," to use the term of Mencius, and much effort is needed to "nourish," to "develop," and to "complete" it. Now according to Neo-Confucianism, the heavenly reason, though covered by human desires, is as perfect as ever, and men need only to remove these desires, and the true mind, like a diamond, will shine itself. This is very like what Lao Tzu called "to diminish." Yet Neo-Confucianism differed from Taoism and Buddhism radically and attacked them seriously. It held that in order to "diminish" human desire and to recover the heavenly reason, it is not necessary for one to be in a state of complete negation of life. What is necessary is to live according to reason, and it is only in life that the reason can be fully realized.

Now these philosophers set out to investigate the "things" of the above quotation, and faced immediately the question: What are these things? This gave rise to two types of Neo-Confucianism. The one said that the "things" are all external things and affairs. It is impossible to investigate all of them at once, and no one carried this interpretation into practice, not even the interpreter,

1045 James Legge: *Chinese Classics*, Vol. I, pp.356-358, with modification.

Chu He, himself. The other said that "things" refer to phenomena in our mind. This interpretation was more successfully carried out. There were many subtle and convincing arguments from both sides, and all of them made some great contributions to the theory and what may be called the art of life.

This period of the history of Chinese philosophy was almost perfectly analogous to that of the development of modern science in European history, in that its productions became more and more technical, and had an empirical basis and an applied side. The only, but important, difference was that in Europe the technique developed was for knowing and controlling matter, while in China that developed was for knowing and controlling mind. To the later technique India has also made a great contribution. But while the Indian technique can be practiced only in the negation of life, the Chinese technique can be practiced only within life. Arts differ according to the difference of ideals.

But these controversies are not important for the present purpose. What concern us here are the ideals that direct the Chinese mind, not the methods of realizing them. We may, therefore, say that so far as the ideal or aim is concerned all types of Neo-Confucianism are the same: the ideal is to diminish the human desire in order to recover the heavenly reason, and that is all.

VI

Such is the Chinese idea of good. In the history of mankind

Medieval Europe under Christianity tried to find good and happiness in Heaven, while Greece tried, and Modern Europe is trying to find them on earth. St. Augustine wished to realize his "City of God," Francis Bacon his "Kingdom of Man." But China, ever since the disappearance of the "nature" line of her national thought, has devoted all her spiritual energy to another line, that is, to find good and happiness directly in the human mind. In other words, Medieval Europe under Christianity tried to know God and prayed for his help; Greece tried, and Modern Europe is trying to know nature and to conquer, to control it; but China tried to know what is within ourselves, and to find there perpetual peace.

What is the use of science? The two fathers of modern European philosophy gave two answers. Descartes said that it is for certainty; Bacon said that it is for power. Let us first follow Descartes and consider science as for certainty. We see at once that if one is dealing with one's own mind, there is at first no need of certainty. Bergson says in *Mind Energy* that Europe discovered the scientific method, because modern European science started from matter. It is from the science of matter that Europe gets the habit of precision, of exactness, of the anxiety for proof, and of distinguishing between what is simply possible and what is certain.

Therefore science, had it been applied in the first instance to the things of mind, would have probably remained uncertain and vague, however far it may have advanced; it would, perhaps, never have distinguished between what is simply plausible and what must be definitely accepted.[1046]

So China has not discovered the scientific method, because Chinese thought

1046 H. Bergson: *Mind Energy*, translated by H. W. Carr; New York, 1920, p. 102.

started from mind, and from one's own mind. Is it necessary for me when I am hungry to prove to myself with roundabout, abstract, scientific method that I am desiring food?

Besides, Chinese philosophers considered philosophy as something most serious. It is not for intellectual information, it is for doing. Chu Hsi, the philosopher of Neo-Confucianism, said that the sages would not tell what virtue was like; they simply asked you to practice it; as they would not tell how sugar was sweet, they simply asked you to taste it. In this sense we may say that Chinese philosophers loved the certainty of perception, not that of conception, and therefore, they would not, and did not translate their concrete vision into the form of science. In one word China has no science, because of all philosophies the Chinese philosophy is the most human and the most practical. While the philosophers of the West are proud of their clear thinking and scientific knowledge, the Chinese philosopher would say with Marcus Aurelius:

> Thanks, too, that in spite of my ardor for philosophy, I did not fall into the hands of a professor, or sit poring over essays or syllogisms, or become engrossed in scientific speculations.[1047]

Nothing is more disheartening than the weary round of spying anything, probing (as Pindar says) "the depth of the earth," guessing and prying at the secrets of our neighbors' souls, instead of realizing that it is enough to keep solely to the god within, and to serve him with all honesty...[1048]

But, although in comparison with the West, China is short of clear thinking, in compensation she has more rational happiness.

Bertrand Russell said in the Nation (London) that the Chinese people seem to be rational hedonists, differing from Europeans through the fact that they prefer enjoyment to power.[1049] It is because of the fact that the Chinese ideal prefers enjoyment to power that China has no need of science, even though science, according to Bacon, is for power. The Chinese philosophers, as I said just now, had no need of scientific certainty, because it was themselves that they wished to know; so in the same way they had no need of the power of science, because it was themselves that they wished to conquer. To them the content of wisdom is not intellectual knowledge and its function is not to increase external goods. To Taoism, external goods seem to be something that can only bring confusion to man's mind. To Confucianism, while they are not so bad as Taoism supposes, they are by no means the essentials of human welfare. Then what is the use of science?

It seems to me that if the Chinese people had followed Mo Tzu identifying good with useful, or Hsun Tzu so as to try to control nature instead of admiring it, it is very likely that China would have produced science at a somewhat early time. Of course this is only a speculation. But this speculation is justified by the fact that in the books of Mo Tzu and Hsun Tzu we do find the germs of science.

Unfortunately or fortunately this "art" line of Chinese thought was conquered by its opponents. What is the use of science, if intellectual certainty and the

1047 Marcus Aurelius Antoninus *To Himself* translated by G. H. Rendall; London, 1910, I, 17, p. 9.

1048 *Id.*, II, 13, p. 15.

1049 Vol. XXVIII (1921) p. 505.

power to conquer the external world are not included in the idea of good?

One question may be raised: Why could Europe turn its attention from heaven to earth, whereas China at the same time could not turn from the internal to the external? To this I answer: No matter whether the people of Europe tried to find good and happiness in heaven or in earth, their philosophies all belong to what I called the line of "art." Before the establishment of Christianity, Stoicism, which seems to me to be the "nature" line of European thought, taught man to serve his god within. But then came Christianity, which taught man to serve his God without. Man was no longer a self-sufficient being, but a sinner. Accordingly the European mind occupied itself in proving the existence of God. Philosophers proved it with the Aristotelian logic and by the study of natural phenomena. Philosophy and science, according to most philosophers of scholasticism, even Roger Bacon, were needed to explain the contents of the Scripture. Modern Europe has continued this spirit of knowing and proving the outside, only changing God for "Nature," creation for mechanism—that is all. There is a continuation of history, but no clear demarcation between medieval and modern Europe. Both try to know the outside world. They first try to know it, and after getting acquainted with it, they try to conquer it. So they are bound to have science both for certainty and for power. They are bound to have science, because they all suppose that human nature is imperfect in itself. Men are weak, foolish, and helpless. In order to be perfect, strong, and wise, they need something that is to be added artificially. They need knowledge and power. They need society, state, law, and virtue. Besides they need the help of a personified God. But how about what I called the "nature" line of thought? If everything good is already in us for all eternity, what use to search for happiness in the external world? Will that not be like what the Buddhist said about a beggar asking for food with a golden bowl? What is the use of scientific certainly and power?

To speak of things in abstract and general terms is always dangerous. But here I cannot refrain from saying that the West is extension, the East is in tension; and that the West emphasizes what we have, the East emphasizes what we are. The question as to how to reconcile these two so that humanity may be happy both in body and in mind is at present difficult to answer. Anyway, the Chinese conception of life may be mistaken, but the Chinese experience cannot be a failure. If mankind shall afterwards become wiser and wiser, and think that they need peace and happiness in their mind, they may turn their attention to, and gain something from, the Chinese wisdom. If they shall not think so, the mind energy of the Chinese people of four thousand years will yet not have been spent in vain. The failure itself may warn our children to stop searching for something in the barren land of human mind. This is one of China's contributions to mankind.

THE CONFUCIANIST THEORY OF MOURNING, SACRIFICIAL AND WEDDING RITES

Confucius said that he was a transmitter but not an originator.[1050] He thought that in his teaching there was nothing new. It is true that Confucius taught much to uphold the traditions of his time. His time was one when, with the decay of feudalism, the traditional institutions and ideas were falling to pieces. Confucius tried his best to uphold them. But in doing this, he gave them new interpretations and read into them new ideas. He was not simply transmitting; in transmitting he originated something new.

This spirit of originating in transmitting was carried on by the later Confucianists. For instance, the mourning, sacrificial and wedding rites as mentioned in the *Yi Li* were not the inventions of the Confucianists. They were the current practice of the time; they were not without superstition and mythology. But in upholding or transmitting these rites, the Confucianists gave them new interpretations and read into them new ideas. These interpretations and ideas we find in the *Works of Hsun Tzu* and the *Li Chi*. The meaning and significance of them we are going at present to discuss.

(I)

Our mind has two aspects, the intellectual and the emotional.

When our beloved ones die, through our intellect, we know that the dead is dead and that there is no rational ground for our believing in the immortality of soul. If we act solely under the direction of our intellect, we need no mourning rite. In the *Mo-tzu* one passage reads:

> Kung Mung Tzu said: "The three years' mourning is an expression of our infantile feeling, which is the endless longing for the parents." Master Mo Tzu said "The child has no other knowledge besides the longing for parents. Therefore when the parents are absent, it continues to cry. The cause of this fact is its extreme ignorance. The Confucianists are not even wiser than a child."[1051]

From the point of view of intellect, the whole mourning rite is meaningless, a sort of childish nonsense. The cause of its existence is man's "extreme ignorance."

But since our mind has also its emotional aspect, when our beloved ones die, we *hope* that the dead might live again, and that there might be a soul that continues to exist in the other world. If we thus give way to our fancy, we can take superstition as truth, and deny the judgment of our intellect. Religions in the world are thus produced.

Thus there is a difference between what we *know* and what we *hope*. Knowledge is important, but we cannot live with knowledge only. We need emotional

1050 *Analects of Confucius*, Book VII.
1051 Chap. XLVIII.

satisfaction as well. In determining our attitude towards the dead we have to take both into consideration.

According to the Confucianists, the mourning and sacrificial rites, as they upheld them, did take both into consideration. As we said, these rites were not without superstition and mythology. Rev. Henry Dore's work "Researches into Chinese Superstitions" had several chapters dealing with mourning, sacrificial and wedding rites. These rites as described in Rev. Dore's work were not exactly the same as that prescribed in the *Yi Li*. In both of them superstitions certainly there were. They were religious in a certain sense. But so far as the rites prescribed in the *Yi Li* were concerned, with the interpretations of the Confucianists, superstition and mythology were purged the religious element in them was transformed into poetry; they were no longer religious, but simply poetic.

The Confucianist Theory of Rites

Religion and poetry are both the expression of the fancy of man. They both mingle imagination with reality. The difference between them is that religion takes what itself says as true, while poetry takes what itself says as false. What poetry presents is not reality, and it knows that it is not. Therefore, it deceives itself yet without being deceived. It is very unscientific, yet it does not contradict science. In poetry we get emotional satisfaction without obstructing the progress of intellect.

According to the Confucianists, in the mourning and sacrificial rites, people are deceiving themselves without being deceived. As one passage in the *Li Chi* reads:

Confucius said, "In dealing with the dead, if we treat them as if they were really dead, that would mean a want of affection, and should not be done; or, if we treat them as if they were really alive, that would mean a want of wisdom, and should not be done. On this account the vessels of bamboo (used in connection with the burial of the dead) are not fit for actual use.... They are called vessels to the eye of fancy; that is, the dead are thus treated as if they were spiritual intelligences."[1052]

Another passage reads:

> Confucius said: "He who made the vessels (used in connection with the burial of the dead) which are so only in imagination, knew the principles underlying the mourning rites. They were complete in all appearance, and yet could not be used."[1053]

If we treat the dead as really dead, as we know, we show a want of affection. If we treat the dead as really alive, as we *hope*, we show a want of wisdom. The middle way it is to treat the dead as if they were living. We prepare for them vessels which are "complete in all appearance, but could not be used." We prepare vessels for them, because we *hope* the dead might still be able to use them.

Yet the vessels are not made for use, because we *know* that the dead can no longer use anything. The Confucianist theory of mourning and sacrificial rites emphasizes the emotional satisfaction that these rites can give to man, because,

1052 Legge's translation, in the *Sacred Bows of the East* series, Vol. XXVII, P. 148.
1053 *Id.*, pp. 172-173.

as we know, the dead are gone forever and there is nothing which can be said concerning their objective existence. Thus one passage in the *Li Chi* reads:

> The rite of mourning is the expression of man's extreme grief and sorrow. It also regulates man's grief and sorrow and adjusts him to the unfortunate circumstances. In this rite the superior man is mindful of those to whom he owes his being.... In the mourning and sacrificial rites, one who practices them simply completes his own devotion. How can he know whether there are spirits that will accept his offerings? He is guided only by his pure and reverent heart.[1054]

In mourning and sacrificial rites, people simply want to complete their own devotion. They treat the dead as if they were living. They deceive themselves without being deceived. To the details of the mourning rite these different chapters in the *Li Chi* also give interpretations. But it is beyond our present scope to discuss them.

In Hsun Tzu's *Treatise on Rites*, the meaning and significance of mourning rite were also fully discussed. Hsun Tzu said:

> Rite is careful about the treatment of man's life and death. Life is the beginning of man; death is his end. If the beginning and the end of man are both well treated, human conduct is complete. The superior man, therefore, is serious at the beginning and cautious at the end. He is careful from the beginning to the end. This is the way of the superior man, the way of morality. If we render adequate service to our parents when they are living but not when they are dead, that means that we respect our parents when they have knowledge, but neglect them when they have not. One's death means that one is gone forever. That is the last chance for a minister to serve his sovereign, and a son his parents....The mourning rite is to decorate the dead by the living, to send off the dead as if they were still living, to render the same service to the dead as that to the living, a service uniform from beginning to the end.... Therefore the function of the mourning rite is nothing but to make clear the meaning of life and death, to send off the dead with sorrow and respect and thus to complete the end of a man....[1055]

Seeing mourning rite from this light, the Confucianists considered it as having a psychological basis. Thus one passage in the *Li Chi* reads:

> It does not come down from heaven; it does not come forth from the earth. It is simply the expression of human feelings."[1056]

(II)

According to the Confucianists, the sacrificial rite is also the expression of human feeling. One passage in the *Li Chi* reads:

> Of all the methods for governing men, rite is the most urgent. Of the five kinds of rite, the sacrificial is the most important. Sacrifice is not a thing

1054 *Id*, pp. 167-169, with modifications.

1055 *Hsun-tzu*, Chap, 19.

1056 Legge's translation, in the *Sacred Books of the East series*, Vol. XXVIII, P. 379.

coming to a man from without; it issues from within and has its birth in his heart. When the heart is deeply moved, it expresses itself in the rites. This idea of sacrifice, only the man of virtue knows completely. The sacrifice of such men has it's blessing -- not indeed what the world calls blessing. Blessing here means perfection, which means the complete discharge of all duties.... Hence in the sacrifice of such a man he brings into exercise all sincerity and good faith, with loyalty and reverence.... He offers his sacrifice, without seeking for anything beyond. Such is the heart and mind of a filial son.[1057]

In his *Treatise on Rites*, Hsun Tzu also said:

> The sacrificial rite is the expression of man's affectionate longing. It represents the height of piety and faithfulness, of love and respect. It represents also the completion of propriety and refinement. Its meaning cannot be understood except by the sages. The sages understand its meaning. The superior men enjoy its practice. It becomes the routine of the officer. It becomes the custom of the people. The superior men consider it as the activity of man, while the ordinary people consider it as something to do with the spirit.... It is to render the same service to the dead as that to the living, to render the same service to the lost as that to the existing. What it serves has neither a shape nor even a shadow, yet it is the completion of refinement.[1058]

Because we are longing for and revering the dead, we have to express our longing and reverence. The rite of sacrifice gives such an expression. "What it serves has neither a shape nor even a shadow, yet it is the completion of refinement." So it is poetic and not religious.

Besides the sacrifice offered to our ancestors, there are other kinds of sacrifice. These the Confucianists interpreted from the same point of view. In Hsun Tzu's Treatise on Nature, one passage reads:

> "Why is it that it rains when people offer sacrifice for rain?" HsunTzu said "There is one special reason for that. It is the same as it rains without praying for it. When there is eclipse of the sun or the moon, we make demonstrations to save them. When the rain is deficient, we pray for it. When there are important affairs, we divine before we reach any decision. We do these not because from them we can get what we want. They are simply a sort of decorum. The superior men consider these practices as a sort of decorum, while the ordinary people consider them as having supernatural force. One would be happy if one considers them as a sort of decorum; one would be not, if one considers them as having supernatural force."[1059]

We pray for rain, because we want to express our feeling of anxiety. We divine before we make any important decisions, because we want to show our extreme prudence. That is all. If we take prayer as really being able to move the gods or divination as really being able to foretell, we are superstitious and will take the natural results of superstition.

1057 *Id.*, p. 236.

1058 *Hsun-tzu*, Chap. 19.

1059 *Id*, Chap. 17.

In sacrifice there is also an expression of our gratitude to those to whom we "owe our being." In his *Treatise on Rites*, Hsun Tzu said:

> There are three origins that rites take into consideration. Heaven and earth are the origin of life. Our ancestors are the origin of our group. Our sovereign and our teachers are the origin of peace. If there were no heaven and earth, whence comes life? If our ancestors did not exist, whence comes our group? If there were no sovereign and no teachers, whence comes peace? If there were not these three origins, there would be no man living in peace. Therefore, in the rites we serve heaven above and earth below; we respect our ancestors and revere our sovereign and teachers. These are the three origins that rites take into consideration.[1060]

From this idea we offer sacrifice to anything to which we owe something. In these sacrifices, "the highest sentiments of benevolence and righteousness were expressed," as said in one passage in the *Li Chi*.[1061] From the same idea we also offer sacrifices to the benefactors of society. One passage in the *Li Chi* reads:

> According to the institutes of the sage-kings about sacrifice, sacrifice should be offered to him who had given laws to the people; to him who had labored to death in the discharge of his duties; to him who had strengthened the state by his laborious toil; to him who had boldly and successfully met great calamities; and to him who had warded off great evils.[1062]

We owe something to the heroes and benefactors of our society, and therefore we should worship and offer sacrifice to them. What Auguste Comte called the "Religion of Humanity" seems to have this idea. In Chinese society every craft has its own god that is assumed to be the inventor or the symbol or the representative of the inventors of this craft. In these kinds of worship as they are, there are not without superstition and mythology. But according to the Confucianist theory, in them there are only poetry and ethics. If they are to be called religion, they are the "Religion of Humanity."

According to the Confucianists, the practice of mourning and sacrificial rites is also a sort of education to the people. As Tseng Tzu, a disciple of Confucius, said:

Let there be a careful attention to perform the mourning rites to parents, and let there be followed when long gone with the rites of sacrifice -- then the virtue of the people will resume its proper excellence.[1063]

If we can treat the dead with much love and respect, we cannot treat the living with less. In a society if there is only mutual love, but no mutual hatred, the society will certainly be in peace.

(III)

Such is the Confucianist theory of mourning and sacrificial rites. There is another point, which is the implication of the above theory, though about it the Confucianists made no clear statement. From the above discussion, we know

1060 *Id*, Chap. 19.

1061 Legge's translation, in the *Sacred Books of the East series*, Vol. XXVII, p. 43Z

1062 *Id*., Vol. XXVIII, pp. 207-208.

1063 *The Analects of Confucius*, Book I.

that the Confucianists, at least a part of them, did not think that after our death we have souls still existing. But no matter whether we have souls or not, that death is not necessarily an end of life is evident. Our children and grandchildren are part of our body that continues to exist after our death. In this sense, so far as our posterity continues to exist, we are so far immortal. This is true to all living beings, and is simply a truism. This kind of immortality can be called biological immortality.

Besides this there is another consideration. If one once lived, that there has been one man living in a certain time at a certain place is an established fact in the universe -- which nobody can change. Even God does not seem to be able to change the past, if there is God. In this sense everyone who has been once born into the world is immortal. An ordinary contemporary of Confucius was just as immortal as Confucius. The difference between them is simply that Confucius is known while his poor contemporary is not. The case is the same as that we now all exist, but among us some are great men and some are insignificant people; the former are well known while the latter are not. But even if there is one who is not known by anybody, we cannot on this account deny his existence. In this sense, therefore, everyone who has once lived cannot but be immortal. But this kind of immortality is different from the biological one, and can be called ideal immortality.

But ideal immortality as such is not considered as valuable by most people. Most people are not satisfied with the fact that they have lived, but only with that that people know they have lived. They must have something in order to be known by later generations. But the something of such kind cannot be achieved by everyone. The majority of mankind consists of ordinary people that simply cannot have such achievements. They can only make themselves known to their own families. With the emphasis of mourning and sacrificial rites, every man lives in the memory of his descendants and will thus be ideally immortal, if only he is competent in his biological function to produce children. This is the implication of the Confucianistic theory of mourning and sacrificial rites.

This implication can be seen also in the Confucianist theory of wedding rites. The Confucianist conception of marriage is biological. According to the Confucianists, the importance of marriage consists in its biological function. Thus one passage in the *Li Chi* reads:

> The wedding rite is intended to unite the relationship of two families, with a view to secure retrospectively the services in the ancestral temple, and prospectively the continuance of the family line.[1064]

Another passage reads: "There is no congratulation on marriage, because it indicates that one generation will succeed another."[1065] The biological function of marriage is the production of children. We marry and thus produce new ego to replace the old. From the point of view of biology, the purpose of the union of the two sexes is the production of the young. The pleasure and affection

1064 Legge's translation, in the *Sacred Books of the East series*, Vol. XXVIII, p. 428.

1065 *Id.*, Vol. XXVII, p. 442.

accompanied with the union are a sort of psychological by-product and thus of no importance. The Confucianist conception of marriage is biological, therefore, the Confucianists did not consider love as an essential factor in marriage. Marriage is not to be congratulated, because from this point of view, marriage is as pathetic as digging graves; the very fact proves that we are mortals after all.

We are mortals, but we are afraid of death and longing for immortality. Religion teaches the immortality of soul and thus tries to remove our fear and to satisfy our longing. But this teaching cannot be proved on rational ground. The Confucianists, at least apart of them, did not teach the immortality of soul, but emphasized the way through which we can have biological and ideal immortality. Most country people in China, in their old age, when their sons have married and their grandsons have come, when they think there is no danger for the continuance of the life of their ancestors and of themselves, will wait for death with every satisfaction, and never care whether they have souls or not, or whether their souls are immortal or not. Their spirit is really Confucianist.

THE PLACE OF CONFUCIUS IN CHINESE HISTORY

Historically, Confucius was primarily a *teacher*. But soon after his death, in the fourth and the third century B.C., gradually he was considered the *Teacher*. In the second century B.C. he was considered as more than the Teacher. According to many Confucianists of that time, Confucius was actually appointed by Heaven to start a new dynasty to succeed that of Chou. Ideally, though without a crown he was a King; ideally though without a government, he ruled the empire. How he did it, the *Spring and Autumn Annals* could tell. In the first century B.C. he was considered as more than a King. According to many people of that time, Confucius was a god among men. He knew that after him there would be the Han Dynasty, so he prepared everything for this new dynasty to come. In the *Spring and Autumn Annals* he set forth a political ideal complete enough for the Han Dynasty to realize. That was the climax of Confucius' glory, and at that time Confucianism could be genuinely called a religion.

But that time did not last very long. Confucianists of the more rationalistic type soon got the upper hand. After the first century A.D., Confucius was again considered as *the Teacher*. Only at the end of the nineteenth century, a little over three decades ago, the theory that Confucius was actually appointed by Heaven to be a King revived for some time. But soon after, he was considered less than that, and even less than *the Teacher*. At present we say that historically he was primarily a *teacher*.

The theories that Confucius was actually appointed by Heaven to be a King and that he was a god among men are obviously without foundation. They are simply the exaggerated form of the theory that Confucius was *the Teacher*. No student of history at present will take the trouble to consider whether they are true or false. But the theory that Confucius was the Teacher was actually held by most people through almost twenty centuries. Were these people utterly wrong, if historically Confucius was primarily a teacher? In one respect, yes; in another, no. In the following, we will consider in what respect they were wrong, and in what respect they were right.

Those who held that Confucius was ideally a King insisted that he was the author of all the six classics. Those who held that Confucius was a god among men were of the same opinion. Those who held that Confucius was the *Teacher* took a view more moderate. They said that Confucius was the author of the *Spring and Autumn Annals*, the commentator of the *Book of Changes*, and the editor of the rest. Although there was a difference of opinion among these Confucianists, they all attached the importance of Confucius to his connection with the six classics. According to them, it was his contribution to the classics that made Confucius what he was.

But as a matter of fact, Confucius was neither the author, nor the commentator, nor even the editor of any of the six classics. In the *Analects of Confucius*, the disciples of Confucius reported his sayings and even the details of his mode of living. But nothing is said therein regarding his authorship, or commentatorship, or even editorship. In one respect, Confucius was a conservative. He upheld traditions. In ceremony and music, he tried to rectify any deviation from the traditional practice or standard. These his disciples told us in the *Analects*. But judging from their reports, Confucius had neither the deed, nor even the idea, of writing something to teach all generations to come. More than one century later, after the death of Confucius, Mencius began to make the report that Confucius was the author of the *Spring and Autumn Annals*, and the report that Confucius was the commentator of the *Book of Changes* came out still later. It is incredible that Mencius and those later than Mencius could know more about Confucius than his contemporaries did.

Thus in the light of modern scholarship, Confucius should be deprived of almost all the important works that tradition attributed to him. The *Analects* alone is left for him, but that is not of his own writing. In the *Analects*, we can see him as a man interested in political and social affairs, and in knowledge in general, "tireless in practicing virtue, tireless in teaching others,"[1066] as he said of himself. In the *Analects* we can also learn his thought. But in comparison with the later thinkers, his thought was simple and undeveloped. Thus in this respect those who held that Confucius was *the Teacher* were obviously wrong.

But it is not without reason for most people to think that Confucius did have close relation with the six classics. Although he was neither the author, nor the commentator, nor even the editor of any of the classics, he did teach his disciples with them. To teach with the classics, Confucius was not the first man. The Kuo Yu tells us that in the sixth century B.C. King Chuang of Chu made Hsi Wei the tutor of his heir apparent. Having received this appointment, Hsi Wei asked Shen Shu Shih for advice; the latter suggested for him the subjects to be taught including several of the six classics.[1067] In the *Tso Chuan* and *Kuo Yu*, we see that gentlemen of that time, in their conversations, often quoted the *Book of Poetry* and the *Book of History*. They practiced ceremony in their intercourse and applied the *Book of Changes* in their divination. This shows that in that time at least one part of the education of the aristocrats was to learn these classics. But though Confucius was not the first man to teach with the classics, he was the first man to teach *any man* with them. This point we will explain later.

At present let us point out that in his method and aim of teaching, Confucius was different from the other Masters that came after him. The other Masters, Mo Tzu or Chuang Tzu, for instance, all were exponents of their own thought. But Confucius was primarily an educator. He wanted his disciples to be "round men" useful to state and society, but not as followers of a certain school. So he taught his disciples different branches of knowledge, and took the different classics as the subjects of his teaching. He thought that his function was to interpret the classics to his disciples. Therefore he said that he was a transmitter but not an originator.[1068]

1066 "Shu Erh," Analects.

1067 "Chu Yu," Discussions of the States (Kuo Yu)

1068 "Shu Erh," *Analects*.

After Confucius the Confucianists followed his example and continued to teach the classics. At the same time most of the other Masters all gave up this sort of old stuff and taught only their own new ideas. Under this contrast, it seemed that the classics belonged only to the Confucian school, but as a matter of fact, they were really the common property of that time.

Thus Confucius was primarily a teacher of classics. As we just said, to teach with the classics Confucius was not the first man, but he was the first to teach *any man* with the classics. In this respect, Confucius was no longer a conservative. In this respect his work was revolutionary. In the following we want to make clear four points:

(1) In China Confucius was the first man to popularize learning, the first professional educationist. He was the founder, or at least one of the founders, of the class of scholars, which afterwards became the leading class of the four classes (the scholars, the farmers, the craftsmen, and the merchants).

(2) Confucius was the beginner, or at least one of the beginners, who tried to rationalize traditional institutions and ideas.

(3) Confucius was much like the Greek sophists.

(4) Confucius' place and influence in Chinese history was much like that of Socrates in Western history.

In the above we have seen that in the *Kuo Yu* an indication is given of how the Prince of Chu was to be educated. But in that time, not everybody could be educated in that way. In the Chou Dynasty, the political and social organization was an aristocracy. Power and learning were concentrated in the hands of aristocrats.

Common people were their slaves or serfs. They worked for the aristocrats, their masters, in time of peace, and fought for them in time of war. They had no chance either for power or for learning.

Besides, as there were no printed books, the diffusion of learning was much limited. The State of Lu was the state of Grand Duke Chou, the brother of King Wu, the founder of the Chou civilization. So among the different states, Lu was often considered as the center of learning. Han Hsun Tzu, the Prime Minister of the State of Tsin, had no chance to see the *Book of Changes* and the *Spring and Autumn Annals* until he went to Lu on diplomatic service.[1069] *Chi Cha*, brother of the Prince of the State of Wu, was also for the first time to listen to the songs and the music of the different states when he was in Lu.[1070] So it was difficult even for an aristocrat to complete an education, if he was not fortunate enough.

Confucius was a native of Lu and his family was of aristocratic origin. He was in a position fortunate enough to learn everything that man could learn at that time. Then he popularized what he learned. He taught anyone who wanted to learn, no matter what sort of person one was.[1071] He said himself that he would

1069 The Second Year of Duke Chao," *Tso Chuan*.

1070 "The Twenty-ninth Year of Duke Hsiang," *Tso Chuan*.

1071 "Wei Lin Kung," *Analects*.

teach anybody who paid him something for tuition.[1072] Thus he let the door open; everyone could come in to learn what one formerly had never the chance to learn. What an emancipation!

Followed by his disciples, Confucius travelled through the different states. Wherever he went, he discussed political and social problems with the authorities. His living was supported by his disciples and the princes. Thus he was not only a teacher; he was also a politician. In this respect, his action was again revolutionary. Formerly, to govern was the profession of the aristocrats. Only the aristocrats, who actually governed, had anything to do with politics. The common people were either farmers, or craftsmen, or merchants. With politics they had nothing to do. As Confucius said: "When the world was in good order, the common people would not talk about politics."[1073] There were no such men who were not aristocrats, but always talked about politics, who were common people, but were neither farmer, nor craftsman, nor merchant. But Confucius began to be such a man. In his later years, he took teaching disciples and discussing political problems as his profession. He would not do other work. He condemned his disciples who wished to do other work. Thus one of his disciples, Fan Chin, wished to learn the arts of husbandry and gardening; upon this Confucius said: "A small man is Fan Chih!"[1074] Tzu Kung, another disciple of Confucius, was a businessman. Speaking of him, Confucius said: "Tzu does not acquiesce in the appointments of Heaven, but tries to increase his goods."[1075] Therefore, one of the hermits at that time condemned Confucius as "having four limbs unaccustomed to toil and being unable to distinguish the five kinds of grain."[1076] The *Tao*ists also condemned him. In one chapter of the *Chuang-tzu*, it was reported that Robber Chih called Confucius the man "who consumes where he does not sow and wears clothes he does not weave." And in his quarrel with Confucius, the Robber said: "You are the biggest thief I know of, and if the world calls me Robber Chih, it most certainly ought to call you Robber Chiu."[1077] These were the possible criticisms of that time against Confucius.

At the time of Mencius, there were other Masters, who, besides expounding their new ideas, had other professions to make their living. Thus speaking of Hsu Hsing, Mencius said: "His disciples, amounting to several tens, all wore clothes of haircloth, and made sandals of hemp and wove mats for a living."[1078] Speaking of Chen Chung Tzu, Kuang Chang, one the disciples of Mencius, said: "He himself weaves sandals of hemp, and his wife twists hempen threads to barter food."[1079] These Masters were living in accordance with ancient custom. But Mencius was a true follower of Confucius. His mode of living was questioned even by his own disciples. Thus Peng Keng asked Mencius, saying:

1072 Shu Erh," *Analects*.

1073 "Chi Shih," *Analects*.

1074 "Tzu Lu," *Analects*.

1075 "Hsien Chin," *Analects*.

1076 "Wei Tzu," *Analects*.

1077 Robber Chih," *Chuang-tzu*.

1078 "Teng Wen Kung Section I," *Mencius*.

1079 "Teng Wen Kung, Section II," *Mencius*.

"Is it not extravagant to go from one prince to another and live upon them, followed by several tens of carriage, and attended by several hundred men?" After Confucius, most Confucianists and others lived in this way. And soon the class of scholars emerged. Those who belonged to this class could do only two things: be a politician or a school teacher. This remained substantially unchanged until the present time. At present, Chinese college graduates, no matter what they specialize in, can do no more than these two things, and they are not expected by their old-type family to do anything more.

We said above that Confucius was a conservative, He upheld traditional institutions and ideas. Therefore in teaching his disciples he emphasized ancient learning. In this respect, he was a transmitter. But in transmitting the traditional institutions and ideas, he gave them new interpretations and read into them new meanings. Thus speaking of the institution of three years' mourning in case of the death of one's parents, Confucius said, "The child cannot leave the arms of its parents, until it is three years old. The three years' mourning, therefore, is universally observed throughout the world."[1080] Because the son needs the parents at least in the first three years of his life, so upon the death of his parents, he mourns for the same length of time to express his gratitude. That was the theoretical justification that Confucius gave to that institution. In teaching the classics, Confucius often gave them new interpretations also. Thus in speaking of the *Book of Poetry*, Confucius said "In the *Book of Poetry* there are three hundred poems. But the essence of them can be expressed in one sentence: 'Have no depraved ideas.'"[1081] In this respect 'Confucius was not a transmitter only. In transmitting, he originated something new. To the above quotations, we see that his interpretations were rather crude and certainly brief. But this spirit of originating in transmitting was carried on by the later Confucianists. The commentaries to, and the interpretations of, the texts of the classics accumulated as the texts were handed down from one generation to another. A great part of what were called later the thirteen classics were the commentaries to the original texts. It is this part that has influenced later generations the most. Thus there is reason to say that Confucius was the author of all the classics, if by this we mean that Confucius was the man who started the whole Confucianist movement along this line.

Confucius was much like the Greek sophists. They broke the ancient custom and formally took those who wanted to be educated to be their disciples. A new human relation, the relation between teacher and disciple, was thus established. The sophists collected tuition fees to make their living. This the conservatives of that time condemned as selling knowledge. Confucius also expected his disciples to pay something for tuition, though not necessarily in the form of money. We say therefore that in China Confucius was the first professional educationist.

There is another point in which Confucius was much like the sophists. The sophists were all very learned, and versed in different branches of knowledge.

1080 "Yang Huo," *Analects*.

1081 "Wei Cheng," *Analects*.

So they could teach any subject that their disciples might wish to learn. Confucius was also famous for his extensive knowledge. Therefore, one of his contemporaries said:

"Great is the Master Kung! His learning is extensive, and thus cannot be called by one name."[1082] Another said: May we not say that the Master is a sage? How various are his skills!"[1083] This no doubt was one of the reasons that Confucius could gather around him many disciples.

Confucius was much like Socrates. In fact Socrates was also a sophist. The difference between them was that Socrates did not collect tuition fees from his disciples; he did not sell knowledge. He had no interest in ontological and cosmological problems. He believed in the existence of the gods, and in this respect he was a conservative. Confucius also had interest only in human affairs. He also believed in the existence of an intelligent Heaven, so far as we can see in the *Analects*. Socrates thought that he was appointed by a divine order to awake the Greeks. Confucius had the same consciousness. When he was in trouble at the place of Kuang, he said: "If Heaven had wished to let civilization perish, the future generations will be without it. If Heaven does not wish to let civilization perish, what can the people of Kuang do to me?"[1084] One of his contemporaries also said: "The world has long been without order; Heaven is going to use the Master as a bell with its wooden tongue."[1085] Socrates searched for definition with the method of induction, as Aristotle said, and made the definition of virtues as the standard of human conduct. Confucius, influenced by the *Spring and Autumn Annals*, also taught the doctrine of the rectification of names. He wanted all the individual fathers in the society to behave according to the name, the definition, of father, and all the individual sons according to that of son. He thought that if this could be done, the world would be in peace.[1086] Socrates, in educating his disciples, emphasized their moral character. In educating his disciples, Confucius also valued their virtue much more than their ability of conducting public affairs. Thus, speaking of the ability of his disciples, Confucius said "In a kingdom of one thousand chariots, Yu is able to manage the military levies, but I do not know whether he is perfectly virtuous. In a city of one thousand families, or a house of one hundred chariots, Chiu is able to be a governor, but I do not know whether he is perfectly virtuous. With his sash girt and standing in the court, Chih is able to converse with the visitors and guests, but I do not know whether he is perfectly virtuous."[1087] How difficult and how desirable it is to be perfectly virtuous!

Socrates himself wrote nothing, but later many sayings were put in his mouth. Confucius also wrote nothing, but later many writings were attributed to him. After the death of Socrates, his spirit and teaching were substantiated

---

1082 "Tzu Han," *Analects*.
1083 *Ibid*.
1084 *Ibid*.
1085 "Pa Yi," *Analects*.
1086 "Yen Yuan," *Analects*.
1087 "Kung Yeh Chang" *Analects*.

and developed by Plato and Aristotle, and thus became the fountain of the main current of Western thought. In the same way, the spirit and the teaching of Confucius were substantiated and developed by Mencius and Hsun Tzu, and thus became the fountain of the main current of Chinese thought. Thus Confucius was a Chinese Socrates. He was more than a Chinese Socrates, because he was also the first man who popularized learning, and because he was also the founder, or at least one of the founders, of the scholar class.

Therefore, in Chinese history though historically Confucius was primarily *a teacher,* yet it is not without reason to consider him as *the Teacher.*

PHILOSOPHY IN CONTEMPORARY CHINA[1088]

Since the emphasis of the present Congress, as we are informed by the Organizing Committee, is on "the criticism of the prevailing philosophic ideas in relation to the needs of life," and "the analysis of the influence of philosophy upon public affairs," in the brief report I will not touch the technical philosophical problems that are discussed in the academic circle, such as the constitution of the universe, or the validity of knowledge. I will confine myself to what I consider to be the intellectual expression of the spirit of the time in China, which is the indication, if not the guidance, of where China is moving.

China is now at a present that is not the natural growth of her past, but something forced upon her against her will. In the completely new situation that she has to face, she has been much bewildered. In order to make the situation more intelligible and to adapt to it more intelligently, she has to sometimes interpret the present in terms of the past and sometimes the past in terms of the present. In other words, she has to connect the new civilization that she has to face with the old that she already has, and to make them not alien but intelligible to each other. Besides interpretation, there is also criticism. In interpreting the new civilization in terms of the old, or the old in terms of the new, she cannot help but to criticize sometimes the new in the light of the old, and sometimes the old in the light of the new. Thus the interpretation and criticism of civilizations is the natural product in China of the meeting of the West and the East and is what has interested the Chinese mind and has constituted the main current of Chinese thought during the last fifty years.

It may be noticed that the interpretation and criticism of the civilizations new and old, within the last fifty years, differ in different periods according to the degree of the knowledge or of the ignorance of the time regarding the new civilization that comes from outside. Generally speaking there have been three periods.

The first period is marked with the ill-fated political reformation with the leadership of Kang Yu-wei under the Emperor Kuang Hsu in 1898. Kang Yu-wei was a scholar of one of the Confucianist schools, known as the Kung *Yang* School. According to this school, Confucius was a teacher with divine personality. He devised a scheme that would cover all stages of human progress. There are mainly three stages. The first is the stage of disorder; the second, the stage of progressive peace; and the third, the stage of great peace. In the stage of disorder, everyone is for one's own country. In the stage of progressive peace, all the civilized countries are united in one. In the stage of great peace, all men are civilized and humanity is united in one harmonious whole. Confucius knew beforehand all these that are to come. He devised accordingly three systems of social organization. According to Kang Yu-wei, the communication between the East and the West and the political and social reformations in Europe and America show that men are progressing from the stage of disorder to the higher

1088 Read before the Eighth International Philosophy Congress, Prague, 1934.

stage, the stage of progressive peace. Most, if not all, of the political and social institutions of the West are already implied in the teaching of Confucius. Kang Yu-wei was the leader of the New Movement at his time. But in his opinion, what he was doing was not the adoption of the new civilization of the West, but rather the realization of the old teaching of Confucius. He wrote many commentaries to the Confucian classics, reading into them his new ideas. Besides these he also wrote a book entitled *The Book on the Great Unity,* in which he gave a concrete picture of the utopia that will become a fact in the third stage of human progress according to the Confucianist scheme. Although the nature of this book is so bold and revolutionary that it will startle even most of the utopian writers, but Kang Yu-wei himself was not a utopian. He insisted that the program he set forth in his book cannot be put into practice except in the highest stage of human civilization, the last stage of human progress. In his practical political program he insisted to have a constitutional monarchy.

One of the colleagues of Kang Yu-wei in the New Movement of that time was Tan Ssu-tung, who was a more philosophical thinker. He wrote a book entitled On Benevolence in which he also taught the Confucianist teaching of the three stages of human progress.

According to him, although Confucius set forth the general scheme of the three stages, most of the teaching of Confucius was for the stage of disorder. It is the reason why Confucius was often misunderstood as the champion of traditional institutions and conventional morality. The Christian teaching of universal love and the equality of men before God is quite near the Confucian teaching for the stage of progressive peace. The teaching that is near the Confucian teaching for the last stage of human progress is Buddhism which goes beyond all human distinctions and conventional morality.

The main spirit of this time is that the leaders were not antagonistic to the new civilization that came from the West, nor did they lack appreciation of its value. But they appreciated its value only in so far as it fits in the imaginary Confucian scheme. They interpreted the new in terms of, and criticized it in the light of, the old. It is to be noticed that the philosophical justification of the Revolution of 1911 with the result of the establishment of the Republic was mainly taken from Chinese philosophy. The saying of Mencius that "the people is first important, the country the second, the sovereign unimportant" was much quoted and interpreted. The teachings of the European revolutionary writers such as Rousseau also played their role, but people often thought that they are right because they agree with Mencius.

The second period is marked with the New Culture Movement which reached its climax in 1919. In this period the spirit of the time is the criticism of the old in the light of the new. Chen Tu-hsiu and Hu Shih were the leaders of the criticism. The latter philosopher wrote *An Outline of the History of Chinese Philosophy,* of which only the first part was published. It is in fact rather a criticism of Chinese philosophy than a history of it. The two most influential schools of Chinese philosophy, Confucianism and Taoism, were much criticized and questioned from a utilitarian and pragmatic point of view. He is for individual liberty and development and therefore he found that Confucianism is wrong in the teaching of the subordination of the individual to his sovereign and his father, to his state and his family. He is for the spirit of struggle and conquering nature and therefore he found that Taoism is wrong in the teaching of enjoying nature. In reading his book one cannot but feel that in his opinion the whole Chinese civilization is entirely on the wrong track.

In reaction there was a defender of the old civilization. Soon after the publication of Hu Shih's History, another philosopher, Liang Sou-ming, published another book entitled *The Civilizations of the East and the West and Their Philosophies*. In this book Liang Sou-ming maintained that every civilization represents a way of living. There are mainly three ways of living the way aiming at the satisfaction of desires; that at the limitation of desires, and that at the negation of desires. If we choose the first way of living, we have the European civilization; if the second, the Chinese civilization; if the third, the Indian civilization. These three civilizations should represent three stages of human progress. Men should at first try their best to know and to conquer nature. After having secured sufficient ground for their place in nature, they should limit their desires and know how to be content. But there are certain inner contradictions in life that cannot be settled within life. Therefore the last resort of humanity is the way of negating desires, negating life. The Chinese and the Indians are wrong not in the fact that they produced civilizations that seem to be useless. Their civilizations are of the first order and in them there is something that humanity is bound to adopt. The Chinese and the Indians are wrong in the fact that they adopted the second and the third ways of living without living through the first. They are on the right track but at the wrong time. Thus the defender of the East also thought there must be something wrong in it. His book therefore is also an expression of the spirit of his time.

The third period is marked with the Nationalist Movement of 1926 with the result of the establishment of the present National Government. This movement was originally undertaken with the combined force of the Nationalists and the Communists. Sun Yat-sen, the leader of the Revolution of 1911 and of this movement, held the communistic society as the highest social ideal. But he was not a communist in that he was against the theory of class struggle and the dictatorship of the proletariat. He thought that the ideal society should be the product of love, not that of hatred. The Nationalists and the Communists soon split, and the latter is being suppressed. With this movement the attitude of the Chinese towards the new civilization of the West takes a new turn. The new civilization of the West as represented in its political and economic organizations, once considered as the very perfection of human institutions, is now to be considered as but one stage of human progress. History is not closed; it is in the making. And what is now considered as the final goal that history is achieving, the peace of the world and the unity of man, looks more congenial to the old East than to the modern West. In fact, if we take the Marxian theory of human progress without its materialistic explanation of it, we see that between it and the teaching of the Kung Yang School as represented by Kang Yu-wei there is some similarity.

Indeed Tan Ssu-tung, in his book *On Benevolence,* knowing nothing about either Hegel or Marx, also pointed out what the Marxists may call the dialectical nature of human progress. He pointed out that there is some similarity between the future ideal society and the original primitive ones. But when we attained to the ideal, we are not returning to the primitive, we advanced.

Is the spirit of this third period the same as that of the first? No, while the intellectual leaders of the first period were interested primarily in interpreting the new in terms of the old, we are now also interested in interpreting the old in terms of the new. While the intellectual leaders of the second period were interested in pointing out the difference between the East and the West, we are now interested in seeing what is common to them. We hold that if there is any difference between the East and the West, it is the product of different circumstances. In different circumstances men have different responses. If we see the response with the circumstances that produce it, we may probably say with Hegel that what is actual is also reasonable. Thus we are not interested now in criticizing one civilization in the light of the other, as the intellectual leaders of the first and the second periods did, but in illustrating the one with the other so that they may both be better understood. We are now interested in the mutual interpretation of the East and the West rather than their mutual criticism. They are seen to be the illustrations of the same tendency of human progress and the expressions of the same principle of human nature. Thus the East and the West are not only connected, they are united.

The same spirit is also seen in the work in technical philosophy.

The Chinese and European philosophical ideas are compared and studied not with any intention of judging which is necessarily right and which is necessarily wrong, but simply with the interest of finding what the one is in terms of the other. It is expected that before long we will see that the European philosophical ideas will be supplemented with the Chinese intuition and experience, and the Chinese philosophical ideas will be clarified by the European logic and clear thinking.

This is what I consider to be the characteristics of the spirit of time in the three periods within the last fifty years in Chinese history. If we are to apply the Hegelian dialectic, we may say that the first period is the thesis, the second the antithesis, and the third the synthesis.

THE ORIGIN OF JU AND MO

Among the philosophic schools of ancient China, the *Ju* (the Confucianist School) and the *Mo* (the Mohist School) were the most influential. They were not only philosophic schools in the technical sense, but also leading forces of political and social movements. They were to a certain extent the makers of Chinese history. But the makers of history were also made by history. They were the product of the social circumstances of time, not simply the creation of the genius of their leaders. Their leaders, such as Confucius and Mo Tzu, certainly had their role to play, but there must be something already there to serve as the basis for their thought and action. From nothing, nothing could be created. In the following we shall attempt to show the social origin of the *Ju* and the *Mo*, to find out, so far as we can, the social circumstances that were responsible for the production of the two schools.

In order to simplify our discussion, let us start from something that we shall take for granted. In our present knowledge of ancient Chinese history, there is something, about the validity of which one will raise no question, if one follows closely the recent development in the study of Chinese history. Let us take for granted that in the Chou Dynasty, the social and political organization of the time was essentially an aristocracy. The aristocrats were the political and economic lords of the common people, and also the possessors of knowledge and culture. They maintained different sorts of specialists who served as the officials of their governments. Both the aristocrats and the specialists held their positions hereditarily. Generation after generation the aristocrats governed and the specialists assisted them to govern.

For reasons which we shall not discuss here, the ancient aristocracy broke down at the middle part of the Chou Dynasty. The state of confusion in the later part of the Chou Dynasty as described by the Chinese historians was simply the symptom of the breakdown. With this breakdown, there were the aristocrats, who, having lost their position and fortune, could no longer afford to maintain their specialists. The specialists who were former officials maintained by the aristocrats, now lost their occupations and scattered among the common people. As Confucius remarked:

> The grand music-master, Che, went to Tse. The master of the band at the second meal (of the Prince), Kan, went to Chu. The band-master at the third meal, Liao, went to Tsai. The band-master at the fourth meal, Kueh, went to Chin. The drum-master, Fang-shu withdrew to the neighborhood of the Yellow River. The master of the hand-drum, W u, withdrew to the neighborhood of the River Han. The assistant music-master, Yang, and the master of musical stones, Hsiang, went to the neighborhood of the sea.[1089]

This remark served as an example of the scattering of the specialists. This state of affairs was indicated by sayings of the ancient historians such as: "The

1089 *Analects of Confucius*, Bk. XVIII, Chap. IX, Sec. 1-5.

officials lost their occupations," and "The culture was lost, but one can find it in the country."

The aristocrats could not maintain the specialists, but they still needed them. They needed them for the education of their young and on such occasions as the performing of ceremonies. There was still demand for the service of the specialists. They, therefore, continued to practice their old professions. But at former times they were officials maintained by the aristocrats, now they had to work for their living from time to time as professionals in liberal professions. There were also the aristocrats or their descendants, who, having lost their former position, also made their living by selling what they had received in their early education. They thus also practiced a sort of liberal profession and ranked themselves on the same level with the other wandering specialists. Confucius himself was an example of such descendants of former aristocrats.

These wandering specialists may be divided into two groups: the literary and the chivalrous. The one consists of the professionals of ceremony and music, the specialists for peace, the other of that of fighting, the specialists for war. The *Ju* were of the former group. Thus "Duke Ling of Wei asked Confucius about tactics; Confucius replied 'I have heard all about sacrificial ceremonies, but about military matters I learned nothing.' "[1090] He was one of the *Ju*, and therefore was a specialist for peace, not for war.

Among the *Ju* group, there were some who were not satisfied with the practice of their profession, but had the further ambition of setting the world in order. They gave their ceremony and music rational basis and thought they could be the instruments for changing the world. From these men sprang the *Ju* school. The *Ju* as a school of philosophy was originated from the Ju as a profession, but the former was not the same as the latter. We do not know who were among the first of the *Ju* as a profession, but it is certain that Confucius was the first who found the Ju as a school of philosophy. It is natural that at later times Confucius became The teacher, when the *Ju* philosophy became the orthodox teaching of the state.

Thus from the literary group of the professional specialists the *Ju* as a school of philosophy was originated. No more proof need be cited to support this theory, since about it there is no longer any serious dispute. In the following I shall attempt to show that, in the same way, from the chivalrous group of the professional specialists, the Mo or the Mohist school originated.

How do we know that the Mohist school originated from the chivalrous group of the professional specialists, the professional fighters? Or indeed how do we know that in ancient China there was such a group at all? There is much evidence. We learn from the *Huai Nan Tzu* (*Book of Prince Huai Nan*) that "Mo Tzu, the founder of the Mohist school, had one hundred and eighty men at his service, all ready to go to fire or water at his command."[1091] From this we can see that the group led by Mo Tzu was well known for its fighting spirit. In the *Mo-tzu* one passage reads:

1090 *Id.*, Bk. XX, Chap. I, Sec. 1.

1091 *Huai Nan Tzu*, Chap. XX.

Kung Shu-pan had completed the construction of Cloud-ladders for the state of Chu and was going to attack the state of Sung with them. Mo Tzu heard of it and set out from Chi. He walked ten days and ten nights and arrived at *Ying*, the capital of the Chu state.... Then he told the King of Chu, saying "My disciples numbering three hundred are already armed with my implements of defense waiting on the city wall of Sung for your invasion."[1092]

In the same book another passage reads:

There was a man in Lu who sent his son to Mo Tzu for tutoring. The son perished in a battle. The father blamed Mo Tzu for it. Mo Tzu said "You wanted to have your son trained. Now he had completed his training and died in a battle. And you become sore. This is like trying to sell your grain, and yet becoming sore when it is sold."[1093]

These passages show clearly that Mo Tzu and his disciples participated in inter-state wars, and his disciples were trained for such participation.

In the same book we also have evidence to show that Mo Tzu's advice to the princes was sometimes made from a military point of view. Thus Mo Tzu said:

There are seven causes of worry to a state and they are: (1) When the outer and inner city walls are not defensible; (2) When the enemy state is approaching and one's neighbors do not come to rescue; ... (5) When the Prince is over-confident of his own wisdom and holds no consultation, when he feels he is secure and makes no preparations for attack, and when he does not know that he must be watchful while neighbors are planning against him.... With these seven causes present in the maintenance of a state, the state will perish, and in the defense of a city, the city will be reduced to ruin by the approaching enemy.[1094]

It is to be noticed that among the seven causes, three are military ones. In the same book another passage reads:

Mo Tzu said to Kung Liang Huan Tzu: "We find in your house hundreds of decorated vehicles, hundreds of horses fed on grain, and hundreds of women clothed with finery and embroidery. If the expenditures for the decoration of the vehicles, for food to the horses, and for the embroidered clothes are used to maintain soldiers, there should be more than a thousand. At the time of emergency, several hundred of them can be stationed at the van and several hundred in the rear. To do this or to let the several hundred women hold the van and the rear, which is more secure? I should think to keep woman is not so secure as to maintain soldiers."[1095]

This shows that Mo Tzu encouraged the princes or feudal lords to make military preparations.

Here we see the difference between Mo Tzu and Confucius.

Confucius "learned nothing about military matters," but, judging from what we have cited above, Mo Tzu was a military expert. In the Mo-tzu, there are twenty

1092 *Mo-tzu*, Chap. L; cf. *The Works of Mo Tzu*, tr. by Y. P. Mei, pp. 257-258.
1093 *Mo-tzu*, Chap. XLIX, cf. Mei, op or. p. 248.
1094 *Mo-tzu*, Chap. V, cf. Mei, op cil. pp. 17-18.
1095 *Mo-tzu*, Chap. XLVII, cf. Mei, op, cil. p. 227.

chapters devoted to the discussion of defensive warfare, though some of them have now been lost. These were what the Mohists specialized in, just as ceremony and music were what the *Ju* specialized in.

Though the *Ju* and the *Mo* were different, they both were professional specialists, seeking employment to make their living. As Mencius said:

> When Confucius was not employed by some ruler for three months, he looked disappointed and unhappy. When he passed over the border of a state, he was sure to carry with him the proper gift of introduction.[1096] He said again: "Among the ancients, when one was three months without being employed by some ruler, he was condoled with."[1097]

He said again: "The loss of his place to an officer is like the loss of his state to a prince."[1098] This shows how the *Ju* were anxious to seek employment. The Mohists were also seeking employment. In the *Lu-shih Chun-chiu* a story was told about one of the later leaders of the Mohists, Meng Shen. Meng Shen was entrusted by a feudal lord *Yang* Chen-chun to guard his fief, and was told not to surrender it without the proper identification from the lord. Then *Yang* Chen-chun was involved in a court intrigue and fled to another country. The King of Chu confiscated the fief. Meng Shen said: "I was entrusted by the Lord with the fief and was ordered not to surrender without the proper identification. Now the King's men came to take over the fief without the proper identification from the Lord, and it is beyond my power to stop them. I have no other choice but to die." One of his disciples Hsu Jueh tried to stop him by saying to Meng Shen: "You should die, if your death would be useful to *Yang* Chen-chun. Now it has no use to *Yang* Chen-chun at all, but with your death the teaching of the Mohists would certainly suffer interruption. Therefore you should not die." To this Meng Shen said "My relation to *Yang* Chen-chun is that between friends if not that between a teacher and his disciple; it is that between a Lord and his subordinate if not that between friends. If I should not die for him, then afterwards, those who want to have a rigorous teacher would not seek for him among the Mohists; those who want to have a faithful friend would not seek for him among the Mohists; and those who want to have a loyal subordinate would not seek for him among the Mohists. For me, therefore, to die is to realize the teaching of the Mohists and to expand their influence." He died for his faith, and the disciples who died with the master numbered eighty-three.[1099] This shows that the Mohists were very strict in keeping their word. They were careful not to give a bad impression to people, because, if so they would be considered as unreliable and the future Mohists would find difficulty seeking employment.

Thus it became a traditional morality that when one was entrusted by others to perform a service, one must try one's best to fulfill his trust. Even death will not compel him to do otherwise. "A man would die for him who appreciates

1096 *Mencius*, BK, III Pt. II, Chap. III, Sec. 1.

1097 *Ibid.*

1098 *Id.*, Sec. 3.

1099 "*Shang Tai*," Su-shih Chun-chiu.

his excellence; a woman would adorn for him who admires her beauty"—as an ancient dictum goes.

The *Ju* also put emphasis on this morality. Thus, Tseng Tzu, one of the disciples of Confucius, said:

> He is a superior man who can be entrusted with the charge of a young orphan prince, and can be commissioned with authority over a state of one hundred li, and whom no emergency however great can compel him to yield his stand. He is a superior man indeed.[1100]

The *Tso Chuan* gave a detailed report of the death of Tzu Lu, another disciple of Confucius. Tzu Lu was the "family minister" of Kung Kwei, the minister of the Wei state. When Kung Kwei was kidnapped by a deposed successor to the throne in order to effect a restoration, Tzu Lu rushed to rescue. He was going to enter the city, when he met Tzu Kau, another disciple of Confucius, who was about to leave it and said to him: "The gate is shut." "But I wish to try to go there," replied Tzu Lu. "It was not your doing," said Tzu Kau, "you need not share in this misfortune." "I have eaten his pay," rejoined the other, "and I will not try to escape from his difficulties." Tzu Lu entered the city and went to the tower where the prince and Kung Kwei were detained. He tried to burn the tower in order to force the prince to release Kung Kwei. The prince then sent down two men to resist Tzu Lu, whom they struck with their spears, cutting also the strings of his cap."The superior man," said he, "does not let his cap fall to the ground when he dies," He tied his strings again and died. When Confucius heard of the disorder in Wei, he said: "Chai (Tzu Kau) will come back, but Yu (Tzu Lu) will die there."[1101] Thus Tzu Lu died with the same spirit as Meng Shen, the Mohist leader.

But on this point, the *Ju* seemed not to be as strict as the Mo.

Thus Mencius said: "Sometimes it is proper to sacrifice one's life; sometimes it is not. To sacrifice when it is not proper, is contrary to bravery."[1102] The Confucianists emphasized the doctrine of "Golden Mean," which teaches that the right thing must be done in the right place at the right time; there is no fixed rule for the changing circumstances. Therefore in the above example, Tzu Kau and Tzu Lu took different actions, and Confucius seemed to approve both of them.

Although the *Mo* originated from the chivalrous group of the professional specialist, they in many respects differed from them, The differences between the Mo and the ordinary chivalry amount to three points.

The first point is that the Mohists participated only in wars which conformed to their principle. Mo Tzu taught the condemnation of offensive wars, so the Mohists took part only in wars that were defensive. They only fought for the weak. As we have seen in the Mo-tzu, Mo Tzu fought for Sung, but not for Chu. In the *Mo-tzu* only the implements and the strategy for defensive war were discussed.

The second point is that Mo Tzu also taught the principle of government. In this respect Mo Tzu was influenced by Confucius Therefore it is said

1100 *Analects*, Bk. VIII, Chap. VI.

1101 "The Fifteenth Year of Duke Ai," Tso, Chuan, cf. Legge's translation, *The Chinese classics*, vol. V, ft. II, p. 843.

1102 *Mencius*, Bk. IV, Pt. II, Chap. XXIII.

in the *Huai Nan Tzu* that "Mo Tzu learned from the *Ju* and received the teaching of Confucius."[1103]

The third point is that Mo Tzu systematized and rationalized the morality which the ordinary chivalry maintained and practiced. He also attempted to universalize it as the common standard of action for all people. This point we shall discuss presently.

As we have said in the above, both the literary and the chivalrous groups of the professional specialists were the members of society who lost their occupations in the breakdown of the ancient aristocracy. Afterwards the recruits of the former group came usually from the upper and middle classes of the society, while that of the latter group usually from the lower class. A greater part of the teaching of Confucius and Mencius was concerned with the maintaining of the traditional ceremonies and institutions. They thus took a point of view nearer to that of the upper class. But, Mo Tzu's teaching was different. In the Mo-tzu, one passage reads:

> Mo Tzu travelled south to Chu to interview the King of that state.
> The King refused to see him with the excuse of his being old, and let Mu Ho receive him. Mo Tzu talked to Mu Ho, and the latter was greatly pleased. He said to Mo Tzu, "Your ideas are certainly good. But our King is the great king of the world. I am afraid that he will refuse to consider them because they are that of the humble men."[1104]

This shows that the teaching of Mo Tzu was nearer to the point of view of the lower class.

The most famous teaching of Mo Tzu is the teaching of universal love. The essence of this teaching is the morality of mutual help.

As Mo Tzu said:

> When we set up universal love as the moral standard, those who can hear and see will hear and see for one another, those who can work will work for one another, and those who have knowledge will mutually teach one another. Thus the old who have neither wife nor children will have the support and supply to spend their old age with, and the young who have neither father and mother will have the care and admonition to grow up in.[1105]

This teaching seemed to originate from the morality that "friends have everything in common" as maintained and practiced by the chivalrous group. The group led by Mo Tzu certainly maintained and practiced this morality. In the Mo-tzu one passage reads:

> Mo Tzu had recommended his disciple Keng Chu Tzu to Chu. Some other disciples of Mo Tzu visited him. They were not generally entertained. The disciples returned and reported to Mo Tzu, saying: "It is of no use to us for Keng Chu Tzu to be in Chu. When we visited him, we were not well entertained." Mo Tzu said: "You cannot tell as yet." Soon after, Keng Chu Tzu sent Mo Tzu some money, saying, "Your disciple sends you this money

1103 *Huai Nan Tzu*, Chap. X.

1104 Mo-tzu, Chap. XLVII, cf *The Works of Mo Tzu*, translated by Y. P. Mel, p. 223.

1105 Mo-tzu, Chap. XVI, cf. Mei, op. cit. p. 89.

which he hopes you will use." Thereupon Mo Tzu said "So, indeed we cannot tell."[1106]

This shows that in the group led by Mo Tzu "friends had everything in common." The Confucianists emphasized family relations.

From their point of view, therefore, when Mo Tzu's teaching prevails, "there will be no place for the peculiar affection due to the father."[1107]

Another important teaching of Mo Tzu is the "agreement with the superior," which is his political philosophy. Mo Tzu thought that in the primitive world, when there was neither ruler nor government, the world was in great disorder. "People knew that disorder was due to the fact that there was no ruler. They therefore chose the virtuous in the world and crowned him the emperor. Feeling the insufficiency of his capacity, the emperor chose the virtuous in the world and installed them as the ministers.... When the rulers were installed, the emperor issued a mandate to all the people, saying "Upon hearing good or evil one shall report it to the superior. What the superior should think to be right, all shall think to be right. What the superior think to be wrong all shall think to be wrong."[1108] This morality of absolute obedience to the superior seemed also to be originated from the morality maintained tamed and practiced by the chivalrous group. The group led by Mo Tzu certainly maintained and practiced this morality. According to the *Lu-shih Chun-chin*, the son of Fu Kuan, who was one of the later leaders of the Mohists, killed a man. Seeing that Fu Kuan had this only son, the King pardoned the offender. But Fu Kuan explained to the King that according to the rules of the Mohists, his son must be executed. "Though you have ordered your officers not to execute my son, I will execute him according to the rule of the Mohists." He did what he said.[1109] This shows how rigid was the discipline of the Mohists. In the political philosophy of the Confucianists, the relation between the prince and the subjects is analogous to that between father and son. So in the political philosophy of the Confucianists, affection is more emphasized than severe discipline.

The saying of Mo Tzu that the people "chose the virtuous in the world and crowned him emperor" has been interpreted by some writers as the expression of Mo Tzu's democratic idea in politics. Other writers were skeptical in regard to this interpretation, because, they thought, the democratic idea that the government was originated by popular election could not be originated in an environment in which there was nothing to suggest this idea. But if we know that the Mohists originated from the chivalrous group, we can see there was something to suggest this idea. We know that the Mohists group had a leader who was the dictator of the group. The leader could appoint his successor, but the first leader such as Mo Tzu himself might be elected by the members of the group.

This practice is well known in the chivalrous groups of later times. The belief of the existence of a personal God, and that of ghosts and spirits who can reward the good and punish the bad, is the belief of the lower class of society. In Mo

1106 Mo-tzu, Chap. XLVI, cf. Mei, op. cit. p. 214.

1107 *Mencius*, Bk. III, Pt. II, Chap. IX, Sec. 9.

1108 *Mo-tzu*, Chap. XI, cf. Mei, op. cit. p. 56.

1109 "Chu Hsi," *Lu-shih Chu-chiu*,

Tzu's time, because of the fact that the society as a whole was changing, the old beliefs also became shaken. According to Mo Tzu the disorder of the time was due to the shaking of the old beliefs, he therefore tried to restore them, just as the Confucianists thought that the disorder of the time was due to the breakdown of the old institutions, and tried to restore them. In the Mo-tzu there are chapters on the "will of God" and on "the existence of ghosts." Both the Mohists and the Confucianists did not realize that the breakdown of the old beliefs and the old institutions were the results of social change, but not its cause. In this respect both the Mohists and the Confucianists were conservatives.

Mo Tzu's teaching of simplicity in funeral ceremonies and brevity in the mourning period also came from the point of view of the lower class of society. The old institutions of elaborate funeral and extended period of mourning as supported by the Confucianists needed change especially from the point of view of the lower class. The proletarians naturally are poor and have to work day by day for their living. They cannot do as the rich who have money for elaborate funerals and leisure for extended periods of mourning. From this point of view Mo Tzu taught the simplicity of funeral and the short period of mourning to replace the old institutions.

From the same point of view Mo Tzu condemned music and luxury. Here the Mohists were again in opposition to the Confucianists, who thought that ceremonies, and to a certain extent luxury, are needed to make the distinction between the higher and the lower, between the superior man and the small man.

The Mohists were also specialists in manufacturing the implements for war, though only for defensive war. We have seen that Mo Tzu, in defending Sung against the invasion of Chu, sent his disciples to Sung with his implements of defense. The same story tells us that in going to Chu to persuade the King not to invade Sung, Mo Tzu called upon Kung Shu Pan, the engineer who made the Cloud-ladders for attacking Sung. "Mo Tzu untied his belt," as the story goes, "and laid out a city with it, and used a small stick for a weapon. Kung Shu-pan set out nine different machines for attack. Mo Tzu repulsed him nine times. Kung Shu-pan was at end with his machines of attack, while Mo Tzu was far from being exhausted in contrivances of defense."[1110] For manufacturing machines or implements, the Mohists had to know something about physics and mathematics. They did have some knowledge in these respects as we see in the *Mo-tzu*.

From what is said above we see the reasons why Confucianists and the Mohists differed and always stood in opposition. In ancient times, Mo Tzu had a reputation and influence equal to that of Confucius, because they both represented schools, each of which had its own social background, and each was a living social force. We may also similarly explain the fact that since the Han Dynasty. Confucianism was upheld while Mohists were suppressed. The reason is that the ruling class needed a philosophy that stands for the higher class of society. But, though Mohism was suppressed, the chivalrous groups continue to exist, which we can find even today, if only we can have a real contact with the lower part of our society.

1110 *Mo-tzu*, Chap. L. cf. Mei, op. cit. P. 259.

THE PHILOSOPHY AT THE BASIS OF TRADITIONAL CHINESE SOCIETY

Traditional Chinese society originated long before the Christian era, and continued to exist, without fundamental change, until the latter part of the last century. It began to break down with what is usually called the invasion of the East by the West but which was really an invasion of medieval by modern society. The basic factor in modern society is its industrialized economy. The use of machines revolutionized the preindustrial economy which might be agrarian like that of China or commercial like that of Greece and England. The old economy had to give way to the new, as did the old social structure. It is astonishing to see how profound is man's ignorance of history and even of contemporary affairs. The social structure of European life has changed and is undergoing changes that may be called industrial, political and social revolutions. But when the same thing happens in Asia, Occidentals are prone to call it the invasion of the East by the West.

Modern industrialism is destroying the traditional Chinese family system and thereby the traditional Chinese society. People leave their land to work in the factories, together with other people who are neither their brothers nor their cousins. Formerly they were attached to the land but now they are more mobile. Formerly they cultivated their lands collectively with their fathers and brothers, so that there were no products they could claim as their own. Now they have their own income in the form of wages received in the factory. Formerly they usually lived with their parents and perhaps grandparents, but now they live by themselves or with their wives and children. Ideologically, this is known in China as the "emancipation of the individual from the family."

With this change of social structure, it is natural that filial piety, which was the ideological basis of the traditional society, should receive the most severe attacks. That is exactly what has happened in China. The attacks reached a climax during the earlier period of the Republic which was established in 1912 when the abolition of *chung* or loyalty to the sovereign as a moral principle took place. As we shall see, in traditional Chinese society, *chung* and *hsiao*, or filial piety, were parallel moral principles. *Hsiao*, once considered the foundation of all moral good, is now regarded by some critics as the source of all social evil. In one popular book of the Taoist religion it is said "Among all the evils, adultery is the first: among all the virtues, filial piety is the first." In the earlier period of the Republic one writer paraphrased this statement by saying that among all the evils filial piety is the first, although he did not go so far as to say that among virtues adultery is the first.

During recent years there have been fewer attacks on filial piety and the traditional family system. This fact does not mean that they have recovered much of their lost influence but rather indicates that they have almost completely lost their traditional position in Chinese society. They are dead tigers, to use a Chinese expression, and attacking dead tigers is no evidence of courage. I remember quite clearly that during my youth I often heard people arguing over the advantage or disadvantage of the traditional family system. But now it ceases to be a question of argument. People realize that they simply cannot keep it, even if they want to.

The attacks on the traditional family system have been mostly polemic in character; as a consequence some of the criticisms have failed to do justice to it. For instance, among the many criticisms a major one is that, in the traditional family system, an individual completely loses his individuality. His duties and responsibilities for the family are so many that it seems he can be only the son and grandson of his parents and ancestors, but never himself.

In answer to this criticism it may be said that an individual, in so far as he is a member of a society, must assume some responsibility for the society. The assumption of responsibility is not the same as the abolition of one's personality. Moreover, it is questionable whether an individual's burden of responsibility towards his family and society in the traditional Chinese scheme is really greater than that of an individual in the modern industrial order.

A society under the industrial system is organized on a basis broader than blood relationship. In this system the individual has less responsibility for the family but more for society as a whole. In modern industrialism the individual has less obligation to obey his parents but more of a duty to obey his government. He is less bound to support his brothers and cousins but is under greater pressure to give, in the form of income tax and community chest, to support the needy in society at large.

In modern industrialized society the family is just one of many institutions. But in traditional China the family, in the wider sense, was actually a society. In traditional China the duties and responsibilities of an individual towards his greater family were really those of an individual towards his family in the modern sense, plus those towards his state or society. It is due to this combination that the duties and responsibilities of an individual towards his family looked heavy.

So far as the traditional Chinese social philosophy is concerned, the emphasis is upon the individual. It is the individual who is a father or a son, a husband or a wife. It is by becoming a father or a son, a husband or wife, that an individual enlists himself as a member of society, and it is by this enlistment that man differentiates himself from the beasts. In serving his father and sovereign a man is not giving up his personality. On the contrary, it is only in these services that his personality has its fullest development. Another point to be noted is that, according to traditional social theory, although a family in the wider sense may become indefinitely large, the responsibility of the individual towards it is not without a definite limit. Within the limit there are also degrees of greater and lesser responsibility. These are expressed by what is known as the "mourning system." According to it, a man, at the death of his parents, must wear mourning dress for three years (actually twenty-five months); this is called mourning of the first degree. At the death of his grandparents he is to wear mourning dress for one year; this is called mourning of the second degree. Theoretically a man would not wear mourning dress at the death of his great-great-great-grandparents even though they lived long enough to see their great-great-great-grandchildren. This indicates that a man's duty as a son of a family has a limit, which includes only his parents, his grandparents, his great-grandparents, and his great-great-grandparents.

A man, at the death of his son, is to wear mourning dress for one year, and for shorter periods at the death of his grandson, great-grandson, and great-great-grandson. He would not wear any mourning dress at the death of his great-great-great-grandson even if he lived long enough to see his death. This indicates that his responsibility as a father of a family has a limit, which includes only his son, grandson, great-grandson, and great-great-grandson,

At the death of his brother a man is to wear mourning dress for one year, and for shorter periods at the death of the son of his father's brother, the grandson of his grandfather's brother, the great-grandson of his great-grandfather's brother, and the great- great-grandson of his great-great-grandfather's brother. This indicates that his responsibility as a brother of a family has a limit, which includes not more than the descendants of his great-great-grandfather.

Thus, according to traditional social theory each individual is a center from which relationships radiate in four directions: upward being his relationship with his father and ancestors, downward being that with his sons and descendants, to the right and left being that with his brothers and cousins. In James Legge's translation of the *Li* Chi,[1111] or Book of Rites, there are several tables illustrating this point. Within the radius there are different degrees of greater and lesser affections and responsibilities. Persons outside the limit of the radius are considered by the person at the center as "affection ended" and are to be treated by him on the basis of the relationship of friends.

Thus, according to traditional social theory every individual is the center of a social circle which is constituted of various social relationships. He is a person and is to be treated as a person.

Whatever may be the merit or demerit of traditional Chinese society and its family system, it is quite wrong to say that there was no place for the personality of the individual.

I mention these arguments only to show that, although traditional Chinese society is radically different from a modern one, it is not so irrational as some of its critics may suppose. In saying this I have no intention of supporting it as a working social system in present-day China. In order to live in the modern world in a position worthy of her past China must be industrialized. When there is industrialization, there is no place for the traditional family system and the traditional social structure. But this does not mean that we should not try to have a sympathetic understanding of them and their underlying ideas.

I shall try to give a brief account of these ideas as expounded in the classics and accepted by most of the educated people in traditional China.

1111 *Sacred Books of the East*, F. Max Müller, ed. (Oxford, The Clarendon Press XXVII, 209.

THE IDEA OF HSIAO OR FILIAL PIETY

The central philosophical idea at the basis of traditional Chinese society was that of filial piety. "Filial piety" is the common translation of the Chinese word *hsiao*, which in Chinese traditional literature has a very comprehensive meaning. In the book *Hsiao Ching*, or the Classics of *Filial Piety*, translated by Ivan Chen under the title, The Book of *Filial Piety*,[1112] it is said that there is a "perfect virtue and essential principle, with which the ancient kings made the world peaceful, and the people in harmony with one another."

This perfect virtue is *hsiao*, and this essential principle is also *hsiao*, which was considered as "the foundation of all virtues, and the fountain of human culture."

In the *Li Chi* one passage reads:

> The body is that which has been transmitted to us by our parents. Dare anyone allow himself to be irreverent in the employment of their legacy? If a man in his own house and privacy, be not grave, he is not filial. If in serving his sovereign, he be not loyal, he is not filial. If in discharging the duties of office, he be not serious, he is not filial. If with friends he be not sincere, he is not filial. If on the field of battle he be not brave, he is not filial. If he fails in these five things, the evil (of disgrace) will reflect on his parents. Dare he but be serious?

The fundamental lesson for all is filial piety.... True love is the love of this; true propriety is the doing of this; true righteousness is the rightness of this; true sincerity is being sincere in this; true strength is being strong in this. Music springs from conformity to this; punishments come from violation of this.... Set up filial piety, and it will fill the space from heaven to earth. Spread it out, and it will extend over all the ground to the four seas. Hand it down to future ages, and it will be forever observed. Push it on to the eastern sea, the western sea, the southern sea, and the northern sea, and it will be everywhere the law of men, and their obedience to it will be uniform.[1113]

This passage was attributed to Tseng Tzu, one of the great disciples of Confucius. The *Hsiao Ching* also consists of a dialogue between Tseng Tzu and Confucius, so it too was attributed to Tseng Tzu or some of his disciples. It is not our purpose to inquire into the authenticity of these works. It suffices here to say that during the third century B.C. the theory that filial piety is the foundation of all the virtues of man had already prevailed. In Book XIV of the *Lu-shih Chun-chiu*, which is a work of that century and a product of the eclectic school, it is said: "If there is one principle by holding which one can possess all the virtues and avoid all the evils, and have a following of the whole world, it is filial piety." All the social and moral philosophers of later times agreed with this statement. Even the emperors of the following dynasties in Chinese history used to say proudly with the *Hsiao Ching*: "Our dynasty rules the world with the principle of filial piety."[1114]

1112 *Hsiao Ching*, translated by Ivan Chen (London, J. Murray, 1908).

1113 *Sacred Books of the East*, XXVIII, 226-227.

1114 *Hsiao Ching*, Chap. VII, Chap. VIII.

Such is the very comprehensive implication of the word *hsiao*, which the simple English phrase "filial piety" can hardly suggest. To those who are not familiar with its Chinese equivalent, filial piety may mean simply taking care of one's parents. But as the *Li Chi* says: "To prepare fragrant flesh and grain which one has cooked, tasting and then presenting before one's parents, is not filial piety; it is only nourishing them."[1115] This is no doubt an overstatement, but from the above quotations we can see that taking care of one's parents is certainly only a very small part of the comprehensive implication of the word *hsiao*.

One would not be surprised to find that the virtue of *hsiao* was so much emphasized in the traditional Chinese social philosophy if one realized that traditional Chinese society is founded on a family system and that *hsiao* is the virtue that holds the family together.

THE BACKGROUND OF THE TRADITIONAL CHINESE SOCIAL SYSTEM

It must be remembered that China is a continental country. To the ancient Chinese their land was the world. Since it happened that the Chinese people found themselves in a continental country, they had to make their living by agriculture before the industrialization of their economy by science and technology. Even today that portion of the Chinese population which is engaged in farming is estimated to be 75 to 80 percent. In an agrarian country land is the primary source of wealth. In the minds of the people in traditional Chinese society land was the symbol of permanence and safety. One could not be considered well established in society unless one had possession of some land.

Farmers have to live on their land, which is immovable. Unless one has special talent or is especially fortunate, one has to live where one's father or grandfather lived and where one's children will continue to live. That is to say, the family in the wider sense must live together for economic reasons. So people in traditional Chinese society, when they possessed some land, meant to live there permanently. For them their land was not only their one home during their lifetime but also that of their children and grandchildren, in whom they saw the continuation of their lives and works.

In the *Li Chi* it is said that when Chao Wu, a minister of the state of Chin in the sixth century B.C., completed the construction of his residence, the officers of the state went to the housewarming. One of the officers said "How elegant it is, how lofty! How elegant and splendid. Here will you have your songs! Here will you xxxxxx your wailings! Here will you gather together your great family!" Then Chao Wu replied: "If I can have my songs here, and my wailings, and gather together my family (it will be quite enough) I will then only seek to live peacefully to follow my ancestors in their graves." Commenting on this story the *Li Chi* says: "A superior man will say (of the two gentlemen), that the one was skilful in the expression of his praise and the other in his prayer."[1116]

1115 *Sacred Books of the East*, XXVIII, 226-227.

1116 *Sacred Books of the East*, P. 196.

Such praise and prayer expressed the aspiration of agrarian people who built their houses on their land and wished to live there permanently. The praise and prayer are both well said because they are very human. They did not pretend that there would be only happiness and no sorrow. They did not express belief in life after death. They only expressed the desire of the owner of the house and land that he might remain there whether happy or sad, whether alive or dead. The sentiment is that of attachment to the land, and the praise and prayer well expressed this sentiment.

Agrarian people are attached to the land both physically and sentimentally. Their family trees are really like the trees that have their roots deep in the earth and spread their branches in different directions. The family in the wider sense must live together because they cannot separate. Since they must live together, there must be some moral principle to serve as a sort of unwritten constitutional law of the group, and the principle is that of filial piety.

THE TRADITIONAL CHINESE FAMILY SYSTEM

Filial piety is the organizing principle of a society based on a family system. Such a society is the product of an agrarian economy, which is in turn conditioned by geography. There have been other continental countries and agrarian societies besides China. But it happened that traditional Chinese society, because of its long history, had become such a society in the most developed form. The traditional Chinese family system was no doubt one of the most complex and well organized in the world. The complexity of the system can be seen in the different terms for various family relationships. Thus, in the *Erh Ya*, the oldest dictionary of the Chinese language, dating from before the Christian era, there are more than one hundred terms for various family relations, most of which have no equivalent in the English language. When Mr. A says in English that Mr. B is his uncle, to the Chinese it is a very ambiguous statement. Is Mr. B the brother of Mr. A's mother, or the husband of his mother's sister? Or is Mr. B the brother of Mr. A's father? And, if that is the case, the elder or the younger brother? In the Chinese language there is a term for each of these relationships. When Mr. A says in Chinese that Mr. B is his so-and-so, one knows exactly what the relation is between them. There is no Chinese word for "uncle" as such.

The family system was the social system of preindustrial China.

The family was the foundation of the social structure. The state was an organization which might be called "united families." In the United States of America there are different states, each with its own constitution and tradition, and over and above these states there is the Federal Government taking care of matters concerning all the states. Traditional Chinese society might be called politically the "United Families of Asia." In that union there were different families, each with its own traditions, and among these families there was one taking care of matters that concerned all the families. This was the royal family of the reigning dynasty, the head of which was called the Son of Heaven. Was this family also over and above the other families? In one sense, yes; in another, no. This is a very interesting point which I will discuss later.

Traditional Chinese society was organized with what were known as the five social relationships. They were those between sovereign and subject, father and son, husband and wife, elder and younger brothers, and friend and friend. Each relationship was governed by a moral principle. As Mencius said:

> Father and son should love each other. Sovereign and subject should be just to each other. Husband and wife should distinguish their respective spheres. Elder and younger brothers should have a sense of precedence. Between friends there should be good faith.[1117]

1117 Mencius, III a, 4.

These relationships and the moral principles governing them were considered as the "common way of the world,"[1118] which should be followed by all men.

Later, Tung Chung-shu (c. 179-c. 104 B.C.), a great Confucianist philosopher of the Han Dynasty, selected out of the five relationships those between sovereign and subject, father and son, and husband and wife as the more important and called them the three *kang* cardinal principles. The literal meaning of *kang* is a major cord in a net, to which all the other strings are attached. Thus the sovereign is the *kang* of his subjects, that is, he is their master. Likewise, the father is the master of the son and the husband is that of the wife.

Besides the three *kang* there were the five *chang*, which were upheld by all the Confucianists. *Chang* means a norm or constant, and the five *chang* were the five virtues of Confucianism, namely, *jen* (human-heartedness), *yi* (righteousness), *li* (propriety, rituals, rules of proper conduct), *chih* (wisdom), and *hsin* (good faith). The five *chang* were the virtues of an individual, and the three kang were the organizing principles of society. The compound word *kang-chang* meant, in olden times, morality or moral law in general.

All the acts of an individual were regulated, in olden times, by these social relationships. Each term of the relationships, according to Confucianism, is a *ming* or name which represents a moral principle. Every individual must have some name in terms of the relationships, and it is his duty to behave according to the moral principle represented by that name. For instance, if an individual is a son in relation to his father, he must behave according to the moral principle represented by the name son; in other words, he must behave according to what a son ought to do. If he later becomes a father in relation to his son, he must behave according to the moral principle represented by the name father, which is what a father ought to do. This whole theory was known in olden times as the *ming-chiao*, or instruction based on names.

Of these five social relationships, three are family relationships. The remaining two, the relationships between sovereign and subjects and between friends, though not family relationships, can be conceived in terms of family. The relationship between sovereign and subject can be conceived in terms either of that between father and son or of that between husband and wife. The relationship between friends can be conceived in terms of that between brothers. Such, indeed, was the way in which they were usually conceived.

That is why *hsiao* or filial piety was considered the foundation of all virtues. The whole structure of social relationships can be conceived as a family matter, and *hsiao* is essentially loyalty to family.

THE IDEA OF CHUNG OR LOYALTY TO THE SOVEREIGN

The relationship between sovereign and subject can be conceived in terms either of that between father and son or of that between husband and wife. That is why I say that in ancient times the royal family of the ruling dynasty was considered in one respect as a family over and above the other ones but in another

1118 Chunk Yung, XX, 8.

respect as theoretically only one of the many families. It was quite common to consider the Son of Heaven as the Father of the people. It was a common saying that "the serving of the sovereign by the subject was analogous to the serving of the parents by the son." In the *Book of Filial Piety* it is said:

From the way in which one serves one's father, one learns how to serve one's mother. The love towards them is the same. From the way in which one serves one's father, one learns how to serve one's sovereign. The respect shown to them is the same. To one's mother, one shows love, to one's father both love and respect.[1119]

In these sayings the relationship between sovereign and subject is conceived in terms of that between father and son. If this relationship is considered in this way, then the royal family of the ruling dynasty must be considered as a super family over and above all other families.

But it was also very common for the relationship between sovereign and subject to be conceived in terms of that between husband and wife. One of the similarities between the two relationships is that the tie between sovereign and subject, like that between husband and wife, is, as the Chinese philosophers said, a "social or moral" one, not a "natural" one. That is to say, the tie is not one of blood. That is why, as it is said in the above quotation, one shows one's father both respect and love but to one's sovereign only respect, which is also, according to the Chinese philosophers, what husband and wife should show to each other.

> One does not have a chance to choose one's father, That is something determined by fate. But one can choose one's sovereign, just as a girl, before her marriage, can have a choice as to who should be her husband. It was a common saying that "the wise bird chooses the right tree to build its nest; the wise minister chooses the right sovereign to offer his service." It is true that traditionally all the people of the Chinese Empire were theoretically the subjects of the emperor. But it is also true that traditionally the common people had not the same obligation of allegiance towards the emperor as those who entered the official ranks of the government. It was to the officials that the relationship between sovereign and subject was especially relevant. So even in the time of unification when there was only one sovereign, one still could choose whether to join the official ranks or not, just as a girl might choose to remain single, even though there was only one man whom she could marry. In Chinese history, if a scholar chose to remain outside the official ranks, he was a man, as a traditional saying puts it, "whom the Son of Heaven could not take as his minister, nor the princes take as their friend." He was a great free man, without any obligation to the emperor except the paying of taxes.

Traditionally the analogy between the relationship of sovereign and subject and that of husband and wife was carried further in the common saying that, "a good minister will not serve two sovereigns, nor a good wife, two husbands." Before a man decided whether to join the official rank or not, he was quite free to make the choice, but once it was made the choice was final and irrevocable. In

1119 *Hsiao Ching*, Chap. V.

the same way, traditionally, a girl before getting married was free to choose her husband, but after marriage her choice was made once and for all.

Traditionally, a marriage was a transference of a girl from the family of her parents to that of her husband. Before marriage she was the daughter of her parents; after it she became the wife of her husband. With this transformation she had new duties and obligations, and above all she had to be absolutely faithful to her husband. This faithfulness is called then or chieh and was considered the most important virtue for a wife.

Traditionally, when a man joined the official ranks, he was in a sense "married" to the sovereign. He transferred himself from his own family to the royal family, which in this sense was but one of the many families. Before this transference he was the son of his parents, but after it he became the minister of the sovereign. With this transformation he had new duties and new obligations, and above all he had to be absolutely loyal to the sovereign. This loyalty was called *chung* and was considered the most important virtue of a minister.

When a man "married" himself to the royal family, he should devote himself completely to his new duties and obligations, just as, after marriage, a woman should devote herself completely to the management of the household of her husband. Such a change in a man's status was called in olden times the "transformation of filial piety into loyalty to the sovereign."

In traditional Chinese society *chung* and *hsiao* were considered the two major moral values in social relations. A loyal minister and a filial son both commanded universal respect, But this does not mean that *hsiao* is not the basic moral principle underlying traditional Chinese society. In the transformation mentioned above a filial son does not cease to be a filial son. On the contrary, in his new circumstances, this is the only way in which he can continue to be a filial son. As shown in the above quotations, a son becomes truly filial by being loyal to the sovereign, if that is his duty. So in traditional Chinese society *chung* or loyalty to the sovereign was considered an extension of haiao or filial piety, but *hsiao* could not be considered an extension of chung.

THE CONFLICT BETWEEN CHUNG AND HSIAO

This fact can be illustrated with certain historical moral situations. In history there were moral situations in which the conflict between *chung* and *hsiao*, that is, between one's duty as a son and that as a minister, became so great that it was a grave moral question which of them should receive the first consideration. The classic case in Chinese history is that of Chao Pao of the second century A.D. He was the governor of a frontier province in present Manchuria and was attacked by an invading force of a certain tribe. The invading army happened to get hold of his mother who was on her way to join him. They then told Chao Pao to surrender or they would slaughter his mother. For Chao Pao there was a real moral dilemma. He made the decision and said, "Before, I was my mother's son, but today I am a minister of my sovereign. I cannot do otherwise." He fought the enemy and defeated them with the sacrifice of the life of his mother. After the war was over Chao Pao said "My mother died because of me, I cannot live after her death." He died of grief at his mother's grave.

There are many historic discussions of the moral implications of Chao Pao's conduct. The History of the Later Han Dynasty regarded him as an extremist who took only one aspect of the situation into account. But what Chao Pao should have done if he had considered all the aspects, the History of the Later Han Dynasty did not say. Several hundred years later a great philosopher of the Neo-Confucianist school, Cheng Yi (1033-1108), made the suggestion that Chao Pao might have resigned his post as the governor of the province and transferred his military power to a deputy. In that case the enemy might not have killed his mother because there would not have been any point in it. Even if the enemy still had done it, Chao Pao would have been less responsible for her death. Anyway he should have made some attempt, even if unsuccessful, to save his mother.

Cheng Yi's reasoning had the support of the authority of Mencius. According to the book of Mencius, he was once asked "When Shun (a traditional sage emperor) was the emperor, and Kao Yao (a traditional very just judge) was the chief justice, suppose Ku Sou (Shun's father) committed the crime of homicide, what would Shun have done?" To this question Mencius answered "Shun would have stolen his father from the jail, and run away with him. He then would have hidden himself with his father in a corner at the sea shore, and gladly lived with him through his whole life, and have entirely forgotten the empire."[1120] This imaginary situation is similar to that in which Chao Pao actually found himself. In both cases there is a conflict of a very serious nature between one's duty as a functionary of the state and one's duty as a son. There is a moral dilemma for which Mencius and Cheng Yi suggested similar solutions.

I have mentioned this extreme case in order to show the moral temper of traditional Chinese society. The point is that, normally, if one chose to join the official rank, one had "to transform filial piety into loyalty to the sovereign"; but that when these two virtues seriously conflicted it was the duty of the son as a son that should receive first consideration. This is further evidence that the family system was the foundation of traditional Chinese society and filial piety the basis of all its moral principles.

THE CONTINUATION OF THE FAMILY

According to traditional Chinese social theory, of the five social relationships that between father and son is the first in importance but that between husband and wife is the first in origin. In the *Book Of Changes* it is said:

> Following the existence of Heaven and Earth there is the existence of all things. Following the existence of all things, there is the distinction of male and female. Following this distinction, there is the relationship between father and son. Following this, there is the relationship between sovereign and subjects.[1121]

1120 *Mencius*, VIIa, 35.

1121 *Book of Changes*, Appendix VI.

Before the establishment of the relationship between husband and wife, "people only knew that there were mothers, but not that there were fathers." In this situation men were the same as the beasts. The establishment of the relationship between husband and wife was the first step in the development of the distinction whereby men distinguish themselves from the beasts, Hsun Tzu, one of the great Confucianists in the third century B.C., said:

> Man is not truly man in the fact that he, uniquely, has two feet and no hair (over his body but rather in the fact that he makes social distinctions. Birds and beasts have parents and offspring, but not the affection between father and son. They are either male or female, but do not have the proper distinction between male and female. Hence in the way of humanity, there must be distinctions. No distinctions are greater than those of society.[1122]

In other words, that there are males and females and their offspring in the animal world is a fact of nature, but that there are the relationships between husband and wife and between father and son is a fact of social organization. It is this that distinguishes men from other animals.

In traditional Chinese society the establishment of the relationship between husband and wife was considered the first step towards social organization. In the Book of Poetry, one of the ancient classics, it happens that the first ode is a love song.

According to the traditional moral interpretation, this is so because the relationship between husband and wife is the "first of the social relationships."

The marriage of man and woman becoming husband and wife is the beginning of the family. Once there is the family, the marriage of its younger members is needed to continue its existence. In the continuance of one's family one enjoys an immortality that is both biological and ideal. In this continuance one has both the remembrance of the past and the hope of the future.

An individual must die, but death is not necessarily the absolute end of his life. If he has descendants, they are actually portions of his body that are perpetuated. So he who has descendants does not actually die. He enjoys a biological immortality which is possible for all living creatures. This is a fact of nature, but it is only with the social organization of the family system that this fact is brought into bold relief.

With the social organization of the family system, one who has descendants enjoys not only a biological immortality through their bodies but also an ideal immortality through their works and their memories. In their works one's own work is continued, and in their memories one continues to be known in the world. Thus in the family system one is kept both from physical extinction and spiritual oblivion.

Traditionally, marriage was considered in this light. It is said in the *Li Chi* that the purpose of marriage is "to secure the service of the ancestral temple for the past, and to secure the continuance of the family for the future."[1123] Marriage

---

1122 *Hsun-tzu*, Chap. V.

1123 *Sacred Books of the East*, p. 428

provides a means for the transference of the life of the ancestors in the past to the children in the future. Traditionally, it was a great duty of a son to become a father. If he failed to do this, not only would his own life face extinction, but what is more important, the life of his ancestors, carried on by him, would also be terminated. So Mencius said:

> "There are three things (meaning many things) that are unfilial, and to have no posterity is the greatest of them."[1124]

In traditional Chinese society, to have a son or sons was the greatest blessing of human life and to have none the greatest curse. The proverb says: "If only one has a son, he should be satisfied with everything." "To play with the grandchildren" was considered the greatest happiness that an old man could have. In traditional Chinese society, when a man had sons and grandsons, he could look on them as extensions of his own life. Hence in his old age he could regard his existence and that of his ancestors as already having been entrusted to others and so could await death calmly, without further care as to whether his soul after death would continue to exist or not. Why should he be anxious about an immortality that was extremely doubtful when he already had one that was assured?

ANCESTOR WORSHIP

Here we see the essential meaning of the practice of ancestor worship. In traditional Chinese society, the function of this practice was both social and spiritual. Socially it served as a means for achieving the solidarity of the family. Since the traditional Chinese family was a very complex organization, its solidarity depended upon some symbol of unity, and the ancestors of the family were the natural symbol.

In traditional China, in places where the family system was carried out in strict accordance with the ideal pattern, the people of the same surname living in one place used to have a clan temple. The temple had its own land and income, which were considered the common property of the clan. The income of the temple was to be used for preparing sacrifices to the ancestors, for helping the widows, orphans, and needy of the clan to live, and also for offering scholarships to the promising youth of the clan to study or take state examinations in the capital. Thus the temple functioned actually as a social work center for the clan.

In the practice of ancestor worship, according to the theory of the Chinese philosophers, the dead are called back by the living descendants, not as ghosts coming from a supernatural world, but as forms cherished in the minds of the descendants. This is the spiritual or emotional, personal side of the practice, as it comforts the individual and strengthens his morale, in addition to fostering the solidarity of society. In the chapter entitled "The Meaning of Sacrifice," the *Li Chi* says:

> During the days of vigil (in preparation of the sacrifice), the one who is going to offer the sacrifice thinks of his departed, how and where they sat, how they smiled and spoke, what were their aims and views, what they delighted

1124 *Mencius*, IV, p. 428.

> in, and what things they desired and enjoyed,... On the day of sacrifice, when he enters the apartment (of the temple), he will seem to see (the deceased) in the place (where their spirit-tablets are) After he has moved about (and performed his ceremonies) and is leaving at the door, he will seem to be arrested by hearing the sound of their movements, and will sigh as he seems to hear the sound of their sighing.
>
> Thus the filial piety taught by the ancient kings required that the eyes of the son should not forget the looks (of his parents) nor his ears their voices; and that he should retain the memory of their aims, likings, and wishes. As he gave full play to his love, they seemed to live again; and to his reverence, they seemed to stand out before him. So seeming to live and standing out, so unforgotten by him, how could sacrifices be without the accompaniment of reverence?[1125]

Thus in the practice of ancestor worship the departed, no matter whether they are good or bad, great or insignificant, become familiar once more in the living world. They are not in the world of oblivion but in the living memory of those who are actually the perpetuation of their own flesh and blood. He who practices the worship has the feeling that he will be known to his descendants in the same way also. In such circumstances, he feels that his life is one of the links in a series of an indefinite number of lives, and this fact is at once the insignificance and the significance of his living.

So, in theory there is nothing superstitious in the practice of ancestor worship as conceived by the Chinese philosophers. The fundamental idea of this practice, as they conceived it, is quite scientific. Westerners used to call the practice "religion." I do not wish to argue about terms, especially about such an ambiguous term as religion. But I wish to point out that, if this practice can be called religion, it is one without dogma or supernaturalism. It takes life and death as biological facts. Yet the psychological effect is that a man is "saved" from the momentariness of his life and gains a genuine feeling of a life beyond. Through ancestor worship a man can have salvation without a God or divine savior.

1125 Sacred Books of the East, p. 211.

A GENERAL STATEMENT ON NEO-CONFUCIANISM[1126]

Mr. Chairman, Ladies and Gentlemen:

I am very happy to be here to participate in the International Conference on Chu Hsi. Besides what I shall learn from other scholars coming from many countries, I will also have a chance to renew my memory of thirty-five years ago, when I had the privilege of being a visiting professor here in this university. During the Christmas vacation, together with a friend and his family I engaged a yacht to travel to the other islands. Everywhere I was impressed by the beauty of the land and the hospitality of the people. The conference now gives me a chance to see these old places and to meet old friends.

I take this opportunity to express my congratulations on the seventy-fifth anniversary of the University of Hawaii. The islands of Hawaii are midway between the West and the Far East. Taking advantage of this geographical location, this university considers herself a suitable meeting place for cultural exchange and inter-flow between the East and the West. The university has done much work in that respect. This conference is a work of this kind. Under the sponsorship of the University of Hawaii and the American Council of Learned Societies, the conference will be successful in promotion of cultural exchange between the East and the West in general and the study of Chu Hsi in particular.

Chu Hsi was a leader of what is known in the West as Neo-Confucianism. In the following I shall try to make a general statement of what I take to be the essence of Neo-Confucianism. Neo-Confucianism may be called "the learning of man." It deals with such topics as man's place and role in the universe, the relation between man and nature, and the relations between man and man, human nature and human happiness. Its aim is to achieve unity of opposites in the life of man, and to show how to accomplish this.

Generally speaking, there are two sets of fundamental opposites, hence, two fundamental contradictions. They are fundamental because they are common to everything in the universe.

In the universe, everything, big or small, is an individual, human beings included. Being an individual, it must be an individual of some kind. It must have some qualities. Nothing is without some kind of quality. The individual is a particular; its quality is the universal inherent in it. So, in everything there is the contradiction of universality and particularity. This is one kind of contradiction. Being an individual, it must consider itself as the subject, and the others as objects. This is another kind of contradiction, the contradiction of subjectivity and objectivity.

These two kinds of contradiction are the consequence of the same fact that an individual is an individual. This fact is common to everything. What is peculiar in man is that he is conscious of it. In this respect, the outstanding representative is

1126 A speech at an international conference on Chu Hsi, held in Hawaii in July1982.

the philosopher; the learning of man is the philosophy of the philosophers.

In philosophy, there are three ways to approach the above-mentioned fact, the ontological, the epistemological and ethical.

In the West, Plato was the representative of the ontological approach. Inspired by the suggestion of mathematics, he introduced his theory of Ideas. Geometry defines the circularity of the circles, only to find that among concrete circles, no one circle is exactly in accordance with the definition. That is to say, among concrete circles, no one is perfectly circular. The definition is not merely words of geometry, nor merely the thought of the mathematician. The definition of circularity expresses the objective standard of criticism and action. With this standard people could say this or that circle is more or less circular, pointing out its defects and imperfections. With this standard people could strive to correct its defects and imperfections. Plato pointed out that the standard is the Idea, the original of circularity, the concrete circles are mere imitations, mere copies of circularity. An imitation can never be exactly the same as the original.

Plato made clear the contradiction of universality and particularity, only to show that the contradiction is much sharper and more acute than what is understood by people.

In consequence, in human life, he considered what is due to particularity such as sensuous desires as such, are by nature base and evil. Reason is by nature superior and higher than the sensuous, just as slave masters were by nature superior and higher than the slaves. The order of nature is that the higher should control and oppress the lower.

Kant started with the opposites of subjectivity and objectivity. According to him, the subject could know the object only through its own subjective forms and categories. What is known through subjective forms and categories is only the phenomena, not the noumena. Even with regard to man's own spiritual world, what is known to him is also only a phenomenon, because that is also through his subjective forms and categories. Kant made clear the contradiction between subjectivity and objectivity only to show that the contradiction is much sharper and more acute than what is understood by the common people.

According to Kant there is something like a flashlight through which man could have a glimpse of the <??noumena.??> The flashlight is the moral conduct of man. According to Kant, the moral conduct is moral because it represents a universal law. Through the universal law, which man legislates for himself, he could have a glance of the noumena, God, immortality and freedom. By logical inference it would mean that, through accumulation of moral conduct man could have a complete knowledge of noumena or a whole experience of it. Kant did not make this inference, but still regarded the noumena as the "other side." What men could know and experience is "this side." The "other side" is beyond the reach of man.

The Neo-Confucianists, came with the ethical approach. They did not altogether neglect the ontological approach. Without the ontological approach, the contradiction between universality and particularity could not be made clear. In fact, Chu Hsi himself was one of the great ontologists in the history of Chinese philosophy. But the Neo-Confucianists did not stop with the ontological approach. They did not stop with the analysis of the opposites of universality and particularity, but tried to achieve a unity between the two. The way to achieve this is the accumulation of moral conduct.

According to the Neo-Confucianists the universal is inherent in the particular. The particular is not merely the imperfect imitation of the universal, but rather the realization of the universal. The realization may be imperfect, but without the particular, the universal could not exist at all. On this point, the different schools of Neo-Confucianism were not in agreement. Even Chu Hsi himself was inconsistent in his sayings. But I think it should be the correct conclusion for Neo-Confucianism.

For the Neo-Confucianists the nature of man is that by which man is distinguished from other kinds of animal. It is the universal of man inherent in man as a particular. The nature of man is not equivalent to the instinct of man. The nature of man is a logical concept, not a biological concept. It includes the biological instincts but not as these instincts. It is in this sense that Neo-Confucianism insisted that human nature is good. It could not be otherwise.

Even sensuous desires as such are not by nature base and evil as Plato thought. These desires derived from the body. The body is the material foundation of human existence. According to Neo-Confucianism what is bad and evil is the selfishness associated with sensuous desires, not these desires themselves. The standard for judging a conduct moral or immoral is whether the conduct is "for private" or for public." If it is "for private," it is immoral or non-moral; if it is "for public," it is moral. Moral conduct means that the selfishness of man is reduced. The accumulation of moral conduct means the accumulation of this diminution of selfishness. When the accumulation of the diminutions reaches a certain point, selfishness is completely overcome, and a unity of particularity and universality comes as a result. This point is what Chu Hsi called the "thorough understanding" (豁然贯通) or Chanism called "sudden enlightenment" (顿悟) "With the thorough understanding... the complete nature and the great function of the mind are illuminated," (一旦豁然贯通，吾心全体大用无不明矣), as Chu Hsi said. When the selfishness is overcome, the sensuous desire is not abolished altogether, what is abolished is the selfishness associated with it. With this unity, there comes also the unity of subjectivity and objectivity.

The Neo-Confucianists considered benevolence as the first of four fundamental virtues, or even including all four. Benevolence means love for others. The man who loves others is called the "benevolent man." According to Neo-Confucianism the spiritual world of the "benevolent man" merges into a whole with the universe. He considers all men as his brothers and everything as his companion. The Chinese word "benevolence" and the word "humanity" have the same sound. In the classics, the two words mutually defined each other. The "learning of man" may be defined as the "learning of benevolence."

According to Neo-Confucianism, when this kind of unity is achieved, there comes supreme happiness. It is a kind of happiness different in quality from sensuous pleasures. It is an enjoyment of emancipation and freedom from the boundaries and limitations of particularity and subjectivity. It is an emancipation not in the political sense, but an emancipation from the finite to the infinite, from time to eternity. What Kant said about the three important matters in the world of noumena; God, immortality and freedom, is something like it.

Plato offered a parable. It tells of a man who, imprisoned in a cave for life, began to see the brilliance of the sun and the beauty of the world immediately after he had escaped from the cave. His view broadened, he experienced a joy which he had never experienced before. Plato used this parable to illustrate the mind of the man who has gained the insight of the world of Ideas. What the Neo Confucianists called "supreme happiness" is something like this.

This may be called intellectual happiness, because it is the result of the activity of the intellect. It differs in quality from sensuous pleasures resulting from the satisfaction of the sense organs. In order to achieve this, one does not have to do anything special, to leave society or abandon one's family. There is no need of worship and prayer. One just accumulates moral conduct in daily life and always keeps in mind the need to fight against selfishness. That is all. In this way, the "this side" becomes the same as the "other side," the "other side" resides in "this side." This is the contribution of Neo-Confucianism to the development of the human intellect and the advancement of human happiness.

A moral conduct, as a particular, is unavoidably associated with the existing social institutions and involved in the social regulations of the time. The Neo-Confucianists lived in the feudal society of China what they considered as moral was naturally associated with and involved in the feudal institutions and regulations. This is also a contradiction of universality and particularity. The concrete moral conduct is the particular, the character of being "for public' is the universal. The universal is inherent in the particular. In the feudal society of China, the ruling class honored Neo-Confucianism as the ruling philosophy, in the time of anti-feudalism, Neo-Confucianism is denounced as reactionary. Both are not without reason, both are the consequences of the dialectical development of history. What I am saying here is confined to the philosophical aspect of Neo-Confucianism.

As time is limited I did not quote much from the sayings of the Neo-Confucianists to illustrate my points. Instead I talked about Plato and Kant, which is not irrelevant. This shows that the East and the West, although divided by oceans, face the same problems in life, which are reflected in philosophy.

Thank You.

SPEECH OF RESPONSE DELIVERED AT THE CONVOCATION OF SEPTEMBER 10, 1982, AT COLUMBIA UNIVERSITY

President Sovern, Professor de Bary, Ladies and Gentlemen

I am very happy and grateful for the honor my Alma Mater bestows on me. I enrolled in the graduate school of Columbia in the spring of 1920, and passed the final examination for the Ph.D. in the summer of 1923. Because my dissertation had not yet been published, I did not participate in the commencement exercises of 1923. The degree was formally conferred in 1924 after I had already returned to China, so that I missed receiving the diploma in person. Today, however, my Alma Mater gives me the opportunity to make up what I missed in 1923 and 1924.

Now, nearly six decades later, I have come back to Columbia at last. I do so with many emotions. The University, I find, has grown tremendously. I also find the campus has remained much the same, but the people are different now. My professors Dewey, Woodbridge, and Montague are all gone, but my memories of them, of their teachings, and help remain vivid for me.

When I was a student here, I applied for a scholarship. For this I asked Professor Dewey to write a letter of recommendation. He immediately wrote a long letter, the last sentence of which read: "Mr. Fung is a student of real scholarly caliber." I did not get the scholarship, but this sentence gave me encouragement and confidence. If Professor Dewey were alive today, he might be glad to see that the student is not wholly unworthy of his commendation.

Sixty years is a long time to make a journey, a journey full of hopes and disappointments, successes and failures, being understood and being misunderstood, being even applauded at times and being often blamed. To many people, especially to those abroad, I seem to be a bit of a puzzle. Let me take this opportunity to say something about the nature of my journey, and perhaps to clarify what may be puzzling.

I live in a period of conflict and contradiction between different cultures. My problem is how to understand the nature of this conflict and contradiction, how to deal with it, and how to adjust myself within this conflict and contradiction.

I first came to America at the end of what is known as the May Fourth Movement, which was a climax to the conflict and contradiction of different cultures at that time. I came with these problems and I began to deal with them seriously. In so doing, my thought developed in three stages. In the first stage, I interpreted the difference of cultures in terms of geographical areas, that is to say, the difference of cultures is the difference between the East and the West. In the second stage, I interpreted the difference of cultures in terms of historical epochs, that is to say, the difference of cultures is the difference between the ancient and the modern. In the third stage, I interpreted the difference of cultures in terms of social development, that is to say, the difference of cultures is the difference between types of society.

In 1922, I presented a paper to the Conference of the Philosophy Department entitled "Why China Has No Science." Later it was published in the *International Journal of Ethics*. In this paper, I maintained that the difference between cultures is the difference between the East and the West. This in fact was the prevailing opinion at that time. However, as I further studied the history of philosophy, I found this prevailing opinion to be incorrect. I discovered that what is considered to be the philosophy of the East has existed in the history of philosophy of the West as well, and vice versa. I discovered that mankind has the same essential nature, with the same problems of life. This view then became the thesis of my dissertation. I selected examples both from the history of Chinese philosophy and from European philosophy to illustrate my point. This thesis and illustrations constituted my dissertation, which was published in 1924 under the title, *A Comparative Study of Life Ideals*.

Though this book denied the then current interpretation of the conflict and contradiction between different cultures, it did not provide a new interpretation in its place. Such a new interpretation, however, appeared implicitly in my later work, *A History of Chinese Philosophy*, a more scholarly work, perhaps. Thanks to Professor Derk Bodde's translation, it could enjoy a wide circulation. The book did not follow the traditional way of dividing history into three epochs: the ancient, the medieval, and the modern. Instead, I divided the history of Chinese philosophy into two periods: the period of the philosophers and the period of classical learning, which correspond to the ancient and medieval periods in the history of Western philosophy. The book asserted that, strictly speaking, there had been no modern philosophy in China, but as soon as China would become modernized there would be a modern Chinese philosophy. This assertion implicitly suggests that what is called the difference between the cultures of the East and the West is, in fact, the difference between the medieval and the modern.

But what are the contents of these words medieval and modern?

Later on I began to realize that the difference between the medieval and the modern is, in fact, a difference between types of society. In the Western countries, the transformation from one type of society into another took place one step earlier than in the Eastern countries. The key to the transformation has been the industrial revolution. Before the industrial revolution, the family was the basic unit of production. After the revolution, because of the introduction of machinery production became enlarged in scope, that is, it was performed by large groups of people, not by separate families. In the forties, I wrote six books, one of them entitled China's Way to Freedom, in which I proposed that this way consists of modernization and that the main content of modernization is an industrial revolution.

In the forties, I became dissatisfied with being a historian and became a philosopher. A historian of philosophy tells what others think about certain philosophical problems; a philosopher tells what he himself thinks about certain philosophical problems. In my *History of Chinese Philosophy*, I said that modern Chinese philosophy is in the making, and in the forties I tried to be one of the makers of this modern Chinese philosophy. I began to think that the interpretation of the conflict and contradiction between cultures either in terms of geographical area or of historical epoch is not as satisfactory as in terms of types of society. This is because the former two interpretations do not point out the way of adjustment, whereas the latter interpretation does point out the way, namely, the industrial revolution.

Then came the revolution in China, and with it the philosophy of Marxism. The overwhelming majority of the Chinese people, including the intellectuals, supported the Revolution and accepted Marxism. They believe that it was the Revolution that had stopped the imperialist invasion, overthrown the oppression of the militarists and landlords, saved China from a semi-feudalistic and semi-colonialistic status, and regained China's independence and freedom. They believe Marxism to be true.

Some say this is a pragmatic attitude towards truth. The Chinese people do not accept this accusation. For my part, I am not a complete pragmatist, although John Dewey was my professor. I do not think pragmatism discloses the nature of truth, but I do think pragmatism provides a method of discovering truth. The nature of truth is a subjective idea coinciding with objective facts. But human beings are human after all. How do they know which idea coincides with objective facts? The test is by practice and experiment. This is an open secret. This method is used by all people in their daily lives. Professor Dewey's How We Think gives plenty of examples to illustrate this point. After all, the Chinese people, including intellectuals, have only used the method of common sense.

Be that as it may, the prestige of the Chinese Communist Party was very high in the fifties, not only politically but, what is more important, also morally. The intellectuals, encouraged by the victory of the Revolution, made efforts to help build a new socialist society. My own effort was to revise my book A History of Chinese Philosophy. Only the first two volumes of the revised edition of this early work were published, before I found the revision unsatisfactory to myself. I set out to revise the revision, but before it went to press, I found that this newly revised edition needed to be done over again. This time, I began to rewrite from the very beginning. Thirty years have passed, and between rewriting and revising, the complete edition has yet to be put into print. The delay, though due in part, I must say, to circumstances beyond my control, has also been caused by the many points on which I hesitated to make a final decision. I have vacillated between the right and the left. The source of my hesitation and vacillation is really question of how to adjust to conflict and contradiction between different cultures. This question manifested itself in the further questions of how to inherit the spiritual heritage of the past. In the early fifties, I raised this question, the discussion of which was rather warm for a time.

The simplest way to make the adjustment is simply to declare that the philosophy of the part was all for the sake of the exploiting classes. Thus, there is nothing worthy to be inherited. The present should disregard the past, and consider it nonexistent. The present should start from zero and build everything anew. This view is obviously an oversimplification in theory and an impossibility in practice. That the past existed is an objective fact, which no subjective view can deny. People holding this view do not understand that the present is a continuation and development of the past. The higher type of society supersedes the lower just as a steamship supersedes a rowboat. The steamship replaces the row- boat but it is built and operated on the same general principles that apply to all ships, including those rowboats. The experience and the experiment of the rowboat are the basis of the steamship. In this sense the steamship is the development of the rowboat and this is the real meaning of the word "development." The process of the development is a dialectical movement. To use Hegelian terms, there are affirmation, negation, and negation of negation. In other words, there are thesis, antithesis, and synthesis. Such synthesis embraces all of the best in the thesis and antithesis. In this sense, the present should embrace all the best of the past. This is the natural way of adjustment of different cultures. The adjustment should be a process of what Hegel called Aufheben. This is indeed a very complex process, the exact opposite of over simplification. This is what I understand now as the meaning of the development of history. With this understanding, I have no more hesitation and vacillation in the revision of my work *A History of Chinese Philosophy*.

Throughout Chinese history, after a great dynasty had unified the country and established a strong central government and after people of different nationalities were living together harmoniously, there usually appeared a new and very comprehensive philosophy. Such a philosophy, with its interpretations of nature, society, and man, reflected the unity of the country and, at the same time, served as a theoretical foundation for the structure of the society of the time and its spiritual content. Confucianism and Neo-Confucianism were such philosophies, and China today needs such a comprehensive philosophy to embrace all aspects of the new civilization and to be her guide.

Generally speaking, we in China today have Marxism and Mao Tse-tung Thought. Marxism will become Chinese Marxism, Mao Tse-tung Thought will further develop. To some, the term Chinese Marxism seems curious indeed. But actually a Chinese Marxism already exists, and that is Mao Tse-tung Thought. Mao Tse-tung Thought is defined as the unity of the universal principles of Marxism with the practice of the Chinese Revolution. Being thus united with the practice of the Chinese Revolution, it is Chinese Marxism, not simply Marxism in China. In the early stages of the Revolution, the unity was well carried out. The theories by which the proletariat led the peasants in military insurrection and by which the village besieged the city are examples of this unity, and also of Chinese Marxism. Strategies based on these theories led the Revolution to victory. In later stages, however, when the unity was not so well carried out and it was then further distorted by the intrigues of the "Gang of Four," there appeared the extreme leftist policy known as the "Cultural Revolution," the results of which are well known.

Marxism has three sources, one of which is classical German philosophy.

Will the coming comprehensive philosophy for modern China need Chinese classical philosophy as one of its sources? I think it will. We should pave the way by preparing the materials for this coming comprehensive philosophy. I do not mean by this to collect passages from the writings of classical philosophers and compile them into sourcebooks. A system of philosophy is not a patchwork. Philosophy is a living thing. You can patch together ready-made parts to produce a machine but not a living thing, even such a living thing as a tiny insect or a blade of grass. You can only furnish nourishment to the living thing and let it absorb the nourishment itself. Under present circumstances, I feel I have a new task with the revised edition of my book A History of Chinese Philosophy. It should not only be a narration of the story of the past but also a nourishment for the philosophy of the future.

When the new comprehensive system of philosophy comes, the conflict and contradiction between cultures will be resolved, so far as China is concerned. Of course, there will be new contradictions, but that is another question.

To this end, previous efforts for the adjustment of different cultures are simply a beginning. Our present effort may not be the beginning of the end, but it may be the end of the beginning.

I always recall one line that appears in the Book of Poetry of the Confucian classics. It reads, "Although Chou is an old nation, it has a new mission." At the present time, China is an ancient nation which has a new mission, and that mission is modernization. My effort is to preserve the identity and individuality of the ancient nation, yet, at the same time, to promote the fulfillment of the new mission. Sometimes I emphasize the one, sometimes the other.

People on the right applaud my effort to preserve the identity and individuality of the ancient nation, but blame my effort to promote the fulfillment of the new mission. People on the left appreciate my efforts to promote the fulfillment of the new mission, but blame my effort to preserve the identity and individuality of the ancient nation. I understand their reasons and accept the applause as well as the blame. Applause and blame may cancel each other out. I shall go on according to my own judgment.

This is what I have done and this is what I hope to do.

Returning to this convocation, I am fully aware that the honor my University confers on me is not simply a personal honor. It is a token of the appreciation of the American scholarly world for the scholarship of the Chinese nation. It is a token of the continuing development of the traditional friendly relations between the Chinese and the American peoples. This development is certainly the common desire of the Chinese people.

I thank you.